Dictionary of Literary Biography

Documentary Series

Yearbooks

Concise Series

British Novelists
Since 1960
Second Series

Dictionary of Literary Biography® • Volume One Hundred Ninety-Four

British Novelists Since 1960
Second Series

Edited by
Merritt Moseley
University of North Carolina at Asheville

A Bruccoli Clark Layman Book
Gale Research
Detroit, Washington, D.C., London

Printed in the United States of America

The paper used in this publication meets the minimum requirements
of American National Standard for Information Sciences–Permanence
Paper for Printed Library Materials, ANSI Z39.48-1984. ∞ ™

Library of Congress Cataloging-in-Publication Data

British novelists since 1960. Second series / edited by Merritt Moseley.
   p. cm.–(Dictionary of literary biography; v. 194)
"A Bruccoli Clark Layman book."
Includes bibliographical references and index.
ISBN 0-7876-1849-7 (alk. paper)
1. English fiction–20th century–Bio-bibliography–Dictionaries. 2. Novelists, English–20th century–Biography–Dictionaries. 3. English fiction–20th century–Dictionaries.
I. Moseley, Merritt, 1949– . II. Series.
PR881.B732 1998
823'.91409'03–dc21   98-7839
[b]   CIP

10 9 8 7 6 5 4 3 2 1

Contents

Plan of the Series

. . . Almost the most prodigious asset of a country, and perhaps its most precious possession, is its native literary product — when that product is fine and noble and enduring.

Mark Twain*

The advisory board, the editors, and the publisher of the *Dictionary of Literary Biography* are joined in endorsing Mark Twain's declaration. The literature of a nation provides an inexhaustible resource of permanent worth. We intend to make literature and its creators better understood and more accessible to students and the reading public, while satisfying the standards of teachers and scholars.

To meet these requirements, *literary biography* has been construed in terms of the author's achievement. The most important thing about a writer is his writing. Accordingly, the entries in *DLB* are career biographies, tracing the development of the author's canon and the evolution of his reputation.

The purpose of *DLB* is not only to provide reliable information in a convenient format but also to place the figures in the larger perspective of literary history and to offer appraisals of their accomplishments by qualified scholars.

The publication plan for *DLB* resulted from two years of preparation. The project was proposed to Bruccoli Clark by Frederick C. Ruffner, president of the Gale Research Company, in November 1975. After specimen entries were prepared and typeset, an advisory board was formed to refine the entry format and develop the series rationale. In meetings held during 1976, the publisher, series editors, and advisory board approved the scheme for a comprehensive biographical dictionary of persons who contributed to North American literature. Editorial work on the first volume began in January 1977, and it was published in 1978. In order to make *DLB* more than a reference tool and to compile volumes that individually have claim to status as literary history, it was decided to organize volumes by topic, period, or genre. Each of these freestanding volumes provides a biographical-bibliographical guide and overview for a particular area of literature. We are convinced that this organization—as opposed to a single alphabet method—constitutes a valuable innovation in the presentation of reference material. The volume plan necessarily requires many decisions for the placement and treatment of authors who might properly be included in two or three volumes. In some instances a major figure will be included in separate volumes, but with different entries emphasizing the aspect of his career appropriate to each volume. Ernest Hemingway, for example, is represented in *American Writers in Paris, 1920–1939* by an entry focusing on his expatriate apprenticeship; he is also in *American Novelists, 1910–1945* with an entry surveying his entire career, as well as in *American Short-Story Writers, 1910–1945, Second Series* with an entry concentrating on his short stories. Each volume includes a cumulative index of the subject authors and articles. Comprehensive indexes to the entire series are planned.

Since 1981 the series has been further augmented by the *DLB Yearbooks,* which update published entries and add new entries to keep the *DLB* current with contemporary activity. There have also been *DLB Documentary Series* volumes which provide biographical and critical source materials for figures whose work is judged to have particular interest for students. One of these companion volumes is entirely devoted to Tennessee Williams.

We define literature as the *intellectual commerce of a nation:* not merely as belles lettres but as that ample and complex process by which ideas are generated, shaped, and transmitted. *DLB* entries are not limited to "creative writers" but extend to other figures who in their time and in their way influenced the mind of a people. Thus the series encompasses historians, journalists, publishers, book collectors, and screenwriters. By this means readers of *DLB* may be aided to perceive literature not as cult scripture in the keeping of intellectual high priests but firmly positioned at the center of a nation's life.

From an unpublished section of Mark Twain's autobiography, copyright by the Mark Twain Company

DLB includes the major writers appropriate to each volume and those standing in the ranks behind them. Scholarly and critical counsel has been sought in deciding which minor figures to include and how full their entries should be. Wherever possible, useful references are made to figures who do not warrant separate entries.

Each *DLB* volume has an expert volume editor responsible for planning the volume, selecting the figures for inclusion, and assigning the entries. Volume editors are also responsible for preparing, where appropriate, appendices surveying the major periodicals and literary and intellectual movements for their volumes, as well as lists of further readings. Work on the series as a whole is coordinated at the Bruccoli Clark Layman editorial center in Columbia, South Carolina, where the editorial staff is responsible for accuracy and utility of the published volumes.

One feature that distinguishes *DLB* is the illustration policy—its concern with the iconography of literature. Just as an author is influenced by his sur-roundings, so is the reader's understanding of the author enhanced by a knowledge of his environment. Therefore *DLB* volumes include not only drawings, paintings, and photographs of authors, often depicting them at various stages in their careers, but also illustrations of their families and places where they lived. Title pages are regularly reproduced in facsimile along with dust jackets for modern authors. The dust jackets are a special feature of *DLB* because they often document better than anything else the way in which an author's work was perceived in its own time. Specimens of the writers' manuscripts and letters are included when feasible.

Samuel Johnson rightly decreed that "The chief glory of every people arises from its authors." The purpose of the *Dictionary of Literary Biography* is to compile literary history in the surest way available to us—by accurate and comprehensive treatment of the lives and work of those who contributed to it.

The *DLB* Advisory Board

Introduction

The British novel since 1960 is a large, diverse, and robust category of literature, and it continues to become ever more so. Clamorous voices are often raised in opposition to this view. The novel, some declare, is in critical condition. In his article "Facing the New" in *New Writing* (1992), edited by Malcolm Bradbury and Judy Cooke, Valentine Cunningham sums up some of their accusations:

> The allegations about the "crisis" in Our Novel Now are awfully familiar. It's too bourgeois. It's too English. It's certainly no longer new enough. It's stifling to death on old-fashioned technique, allegiance to Jane Austen, or Classic Realism, or Humanism, and the like. On the other hand, it's claimed Our Novel is also being killed off by sordid and ill-advised experimenters. There's been nothing good after—and because of—*Ulysses* or *Finnegans Wake* and their heirs and assigns.

Despite such perennial "Death of the Novel" laments (or, sometimes, celebrations) that appear in journals of opinion—additional causes of death include lack of financial support for the arts, too much financial support for the arts, the rise of new media, the conglomeration of the publishing world, illiteracy, television, or some other force—no really plausible signs of death are visible. Novels of high quality continue to appear. Brilliant men and women decide to spend their lives writing novels instead of doing something else. The numbers alone are illustrative of this rude health: Richard Todd estimates in his *Consuming Fictions: The Booker Prize and Fiction in Britain Today* (1996) that "Somewhere between 4,500 and 7,000 new Booker-eligible fiction titles appeared annually in Britain during the 1980s alone, the total rising throughout the decade from the lower figure to the higher." He points out that the total number of such titles in some years has been the same as in the United States, with its much larger population.

The concept of "Booker eligibility" is a useful one for considering the diversity and richness of the British novel since 1960. The Booker Prize, first awarded in 1969, goes to a novel published in Britain and written in English by a citizen of the United Kingdom, the British Commonwealth of Nations, the Republic of Ireland, Pakistan, Bangladesh, or South Africa. (It has been observed that nearly any author who writes in English is eligible for the Booker Prize except an American.) That authors from such vastly different countries and cultures are all "British" is a proposition that is easy to ridicule, and many of the authors themselves would reject it; but that their *novels* are British—through being published in Britain in the English language or through historic colonial connections of the authors' countries with Britain—is less controversial. The criteria for inclusion in *DLB 194: British Novelists Since 1960, Second Series* and the series that will follow it are similar to those for eligibility for the Booker Prize: novelists who have made their careers in the British Isles are included, whatever their country of birth, with two exceptions: American novelists, even if they live in Britain (Paul Theroux, for example), and Canadian novelists, even though they are eligible for the Booker, are excluded.

The history of serious British fiction since 1960 may be divided into two eras, with the line of demarcation falling around 1980. As evidence of this division one might consult the table of Booker Prize shortlists from 1969 through 1996 that follows this introduction. (The shortlist is the announced list of finalists from which the winner is drawn.) The table confirms that the short-listed novelists in the early years of the Booker tended to be English, Scottish, Welsh, or Irish; those from the dominions came from the white portions of the Commonwealth—Canada, Australia, and the white minorities of Rhodesia and South Africa. V. S. Naipaul, born in Trinidad of Indian ancestry and short-listed in 1971 for *In a Free State,* is the solitary exception. The shortlist for 1991 shows a striking contrast: the winner, Ben Okri, is a Nigerian; the list also includes Rohinton Mistry, born in India and a resident of Canada; Timothy Mo, born in Hong Kong; William Trevor and Roddy Doyle, both Irish; and a single Englishman, Martin Amis. By this time some observers were starting to murmur that things had gone too far, that perhaps the Booker selectors were biased against the English. The 1994 list would have confirmed their fears: the winner, James Kelman, and one other writer are Scottish, and Kelman is a highly politicized—that is, anti-English—Scot; they were joined on the list by a Sri Lankan and a Tanzanian. Even the two English writers on the 1994 list have a "minority" flavor: Alan Hollinghurst writes openly gay fiction, and his novel was about a homosexual affair; Jill Paton Walsh's *Knowledge of Angels* had been rejected by English publishers and had been self-published.

Another way of interpreting these results is as a tribute to the fecundity, diversity, and breadth of what may still be called the "British" novel. The inclusion of Sri Lankan authors—the 1992 cowinner, Michael Ondaatje, and Romesh Gunesekera, who appears on the 1994 list—along with major novelists from the Indian subcontinent, most notably Salman Rushdie and, most recently, Arundhati Roy, and Antipodeans such as Thomas Keneally (Australian), Peter Carey (Australian), and Keri Hulme (New Zealander)—strengthens the argument that the modern British novel is of international importance.

Looking again at the 1991 shortlist, one sees that the winner was thirty-two years old and that three others had been born since 1949; William Trevor, born in 1928, is the only "senior citizen" listed. Moreover, these young authors did not all have long publishing records: Mistry was nominated for his first novel, Roddy Doyle for his second. Earlier lists look more conservative. The nominees in 1970, for example, averaged almost fifty years in age, and—with the exception of Terence Wheeler, who was nominated for his first novel—all had well-established careers (especially Elizabeth Bowen, whose first novel had been published forty-two years earlier). Twenty years later the seventy-eight-year-old Sybille Bedford was nominated; the Booker Prize had not, therefore, become exclusively a young person's award. On the other hand, experimental novels were nominated as early as the late 1960s and early 1970s and in 1972 one of them, John Berger's *G,* even won the award. Nevertheless, there is a perceptible trend in the direction of younger and less-established authors and a more multicultural shortlist.

The most celebrated novelists of the 1960s continued to be writers such as Kingsley Amis, Anthony Burgess, William Golding, Graham Greene, Doris Lessing, and Iris Murdoch. Amis, Burgess, Golding, and Murdoch began publishing novels in the 1950s and were well established by the turn of the decade; moreover, their age and their experience of World War II align them with an older generation than the one that came of age in the 1960s. And one should not forget that Aldous Huxley (born in 1894), Evelyn Waugh (born in 1903), and Anthony Powell (born in 1905), whose first novels were published in 1921, 1928, and 1931, respectively, were still active in the 1960s. (Powell is still publishing books in the late 1990s.) Such considerations dictate considerable caution in characterizing

literary periods, particularly under the assumption that a change in decades brings a change in writing. As Allen Massie observes in *The Novel Today: A Critical Guide to the British Novel 1970–1989* (1990), "the novel has always been a loose and capacious term; for every discernible trend it has been possible to find contemporary counter-currents."

It is something of a commonplace now to observe that the political and cultural upheavals, sexual liberation, "youth rebellion," and other phenomena that are generally identified with "the Sixties" mostly took place in the 1970s. The same is true in fiction. In *The British Novel since the Thirties: An Introduction* (1986) Randall Stevenson sums up some of the changes that occurred during the period:

> In the sixties, especially towards the end of the decade, and in the early seventies, "angry-provincial-neorealist" writing was gradually replaced by a more wide-ranging, sophisticated fiction, whose promise extends to the present day. Recent novels have sometimes integrated particularly fruitfully moral awareness partly engendered by the war and technical resourcefulness partly learned from modernism. In some ways, the English novel in the past two decades has probably come closer than at any previous stage of the century to combining the various strengths of conventional and of innovative fiction which have been available at least since 1930.

Stevenson's distinction of conventional from innovative fiction raises the question of experimentation and tradition. The controversy between supporters of the traditional novel, on the one hand, and those of experimental, modernist, or postmodernist fiction, on the other, has been hard fought on both sides. One side argues that modernism was an anomaly, a cul-de-sac down which the novel briefly turned before returning to the main road; critics such as Kingsley Amis and Philip Larkin, for whom *experimentation* was another term for "oddity" and "incomprehensibility," and novelists such as Amis, Anita Brookner, Barbara Pym, and C. P. Snow may be said to represent the more traditional view. A survey of some of the traditionalist principles and practices (in the cases of Amis and Snow) may be found in Rubin Rabinovitz's tellingly named *The Reaction Against Experiment in the English Novel, 1950–1960* (1967). James Gindin, in his *Postwar British Fiction: New Accents and Attitudes* (1962), directs attention to the traditional features of the fiction written by his selected authors: "In addition to their formal conservatism and their attempts to revive older novelistic traditions, their insistence on man's limitations, their comic perspective, and their partial or hesitant commitment are all reminiscent of characteristics we tend to apply to eighteenth-century writers." These features did not vanish in the early 1960s, as Amis's 1986 Booker Prize indicates.

Opposed to the traditionalists are those who argue, through both prescription and practice, for a more daring British novel: Kelman, Rushdie, John Berger, and Kingsley Amis's son, the novelist Martin Amis. The two Amises illustrate in one family the dichotomy in the modern British novel. The 1992 Booker shortlist illustrates it, too, in the judges' decision to split the prize between Ondaatje's poetic *The English Patient* and Barry Unsworth's more traditional historical novel, *Sacred Hunger.* The 1984 shortlist illustrates it, as well: the winner, Brookner's *Hotel du Lac,* is a lapidary, beautifully crafted novel of the sort that could almost have been written in 1920 or 1870. Alongside it on the list are Julian Barnes's breakthrough novel, *Flaubert's Parrot,* which challenges the definition of what a novel is, and David Lodge's *Small World,* an "academic romance" with the self-consciousness, reflexivity, playfulness, and overt proclamation of its own fictiveness that characterize the postmodern novel.

Lodge, a distinguished critic of the novel, as well as a practitioner, has frequently addressed this apparent dichotomy. In "O Ye Laurels" in *The New York Review of Books* (8 August 1996) he surveys the scene and comments:

> In contemporary British fiction fabulation (represented variously by writers like Rushdie, [Jeanette] Winterson, Okri, [Lawrence] Norfolk, Jim Crace) flourishes alongside realism which fully earns the epithet "dirty." There has been a spate of novels by young writers (including women writers) in Britain recently dealing with contemporary society in a way designed to *épater les bourgeois,* full of obscenity, scatology, violence, sexual perversion, alcoholism and drug addiction, black humor, and opaque slang. Much of this fiction is crudely sensational and clumsily constructed, but it has a raw and reckless energy that is a sign of life.

In his *The Novelist at the Crossroads and Other Essays on Fiction and Criticism* (1971) Lodge comments on the "two types of modern fiction": the highly fictional (including metafiction) and the highly empirical (the realistic novel, with the "nonfiction novel" as a limiting case). He returns to this analysis in *The Modes of Modern Writing: Metaphor, Metonymy, and the Typology of Modern Literature* (1977), in which he aligns the two basic modes of modern writing (the paths that diverge at "the crossroads") with two figures of speech: metaphor—modernism, fictional narrative, poetry; and metonymy—traditionalism, empirical narrative, prose. (Bradbury likewise speaks, in his *No, Not Bloomsbury* [1988], of "the steady oscillation between realistic and abstract impulses which seem to me to have dominated aesthetically since the war.") Lodge is unwilling to validate one term of the dichotomy over the other; he stands at the crossroads and declines to choose. His own novels sometimes seem to alternate between the experimental and the traditional (for instance, *Ginger, You're Barmy* [1962], a realistic novel about military service, was followed by *The British Museum Is Falling Down* [1965], a playful set of pastiches), or to combine them in one text, just as he proclaims his literary indebtedness almost equally to James Joyce and to Kingsley Amis.

The conflict, or mixture, of experimental and traditional motives and practices in the novel of the past thirty-eight years is not unique to Britain. Those who wish to castigate British writers for timidity and narrow aspirations often use the American novel as a scourge. D. J. Taylor (whose own novel, *English Settlement* [1996], is about English culture viewed from an American perspective) claims in his *A Vain Conceit: British Fiction in the 1980s* (1989) that "Any sort of comparison with America is, inevitably, mutually injurious. In the 1970s, while the English novel (with a few exceptions) confined itself to sniffish studies of adultery and coy self-examination, its American cousin flew off out of the window." "Flying off out the window" is not a desirable aim for all writers, but elsewhere in his book Taylor makes it clear that in his estimation (and he would not be alone) American writers are risk-takers while the English writer plays it safe.

In general, it is probably true that the English novel is less given to modernist avant-gardism than the American, or, as Bradbury suggests in his *The Modern British Novel* (1993), "even in British metafiction the gravitational tug of liberal realism frequently remains." One might remember that the High Modernist novel in English, in its classic phase, is largely an American, or American and Irish, phenomenon, with the exception of the works of Virginia Woolf. The English novelist seems more prone to compromise, to pursue the "English settlement." Stevenson speaks to this impulse of inclusion, or integration, when he describes recent novels' combining "moral awareness partly engendered by the war"—clearly a traditional concern, firmly anchored in the past—and "technical resourcefulness partly learned from modernism" and when he explains that "postmodernism is not at its strongest in England, where modernist initiatives seem more often accommodated within traditional forms rather than genuinely extended." Integration, accommodation, compromise, or, at least, collaboration may be marked in many of the most striking British novels openly gay fiction, and his novel was about a homosexual affair; Jill Paton Walsh's *Knowledge of Angels* had been rejected by English publishers and had been self-published.

Another way of interpreting these results is as a tribute to the fecundity, diversity, and breadth of what may still be called the "British" novel. The inclusion of Sri Lankan authors—the 1992 cowinner, Michael Ondaatje, and Romesh Gunesekera, who appears on the 1994 list—along with major novelists from the Indian subcontinent, most notably Salman Rushdie and, most recently, Arundhati Roy, and Antipodeans such as Thomas Keneally (Australian), Peter Carey (Australian), and Keri Hulme (New Zealander)—strengthens the argument that the modern British novel is of international importance.

Looking again at the 1991 shortlist, one sees that the winner was thirty-two years old and that three others had been born since 1949; William Trevor, born in 1928, is the only "senior citizen" listed. Moreover, these young authors did not all have long publishing records: Mistry was nominated for his first novel, Roddy Doyle for his second. Earlier lists look more conservative. The nominees in 1970, for example, averaged almost fifty years in age, and—with the exception of Terence Wheeler, who was nominated for his first novel—all had well-established careers (especially Elizabeth Bowen, whose first novel had been published forty-two years earlier). Twenty years later the seventy-eight-year-old Sybille Bedford was nominated; the Booker Prize had not, therefore, become exclusively a young person's award. On the other hand, experimental novels were nominated as early as the late 1960s and early 1970s and in 1972 one of them, John Berger's *G*, even won the award. Nevertheless, there is a perceptible trend in the direction of younger and less-established authors and a more multicultural shortlist.

The most celebrated novelists of the 1960s continued to be writers such as Kingsley Amis, Anthony Burgess, William Golding, Graham Greene, Doris Lessing, and Iris Murdoch. Amis, Burgess, Golding, and Murdoch began publishing novels in the 1950s and were well established by the turn of the decade; moreover, their age and their experience of World War II align them with an older generation than the one that came of age in the 1960s. And one should not forget that Aldous Huxley (born in 1894), Evelyn Waugh (born in 1903), and Anthony Powell (born in 1905), whose first novels were published in 1921, 1928, and 1931, respectively, were still active in the 1960s. (Powell is still publishing books in the late 1990s.) Such considerations dictate considerable caution in characterizing literary periods, particularly under the assumption that a change in decades brings a change in writing. As Allen Massie observes in *The Novel Today: A Critical Guide to the British Novel 1970–1989* (1990), "the novel has always been a loose and capacious term; for every discernible trend it has been possible to find contemporary counter-currents."

It is something of a commonplace now to observe that the political and cultural upheavals, sexual liberation, "youth rebellion," and other phenomena that are generally identified with "the Sixties" mostly took place in the 1970s. The same is true in fiction. In *The British Novel since the Thirties: An Introduction* (1986) Randall Stevenson sums up some of the changes that occurred during the period:

> In the sixties, especially towards the end of the decade, and in the early seventies, "angry-provincial-neorealist" writing was gradually replaced by a more wide-ranging, sophisticated fiction, whose promise extends to the present day. Recent novels have sometimes integrated particularly fruitfully moral awareness partly engendered by the war and technical resourcefulness partly learned from modernism. In some ways, the English novel in the past two decades has probably come closer than at any previous stage of the century to combining the various strengths of conventional and of innovative fiction which have been available at least since 1930.

Stevenson's distinction of conventional from innovative fiction raises the question of experimentation and tradition. The controversy between supporters of the traditional novel, on the one hand, and those of experimental, modernist, or postmodernist fiction, on the other, has been hard fought on both sides. One side argues that modernism was an anomaly, a cul-de-sac down which the novel briefly turned before returning to the main road; critics such as Kingsley Amis and Philip Larkin, for whom *experimentation* was another term for "oddity" and "incomprehensibility," and novelists such as Amis, Anita Brookner, Barbara Pym, and C. P. Snow may be said to represent the more traditional view. A survey of some of the traditionalist principles and practices (in the cases of Amis and Snow) may be found in Rubin Rabinovitz's tellingly named *The Reaction Against Experiment in the English Novel, 1950–1960* (1967). James Gindin, in his *Postwar British Fiction: New Accents and Attitudes* (1962), directs attention to the traditional features of the fiction written by his selected authors: "In addition to their formal conservatism and their attempts to revive older novelistic traditions, their insistence on man's limitations, their comic perspective, and their partial or hesitant commitment are all reminiscent of characteristics we tend to apply to eighteenth-century writ-

Introduction

The British novel since 1960 is a large, diverse, and robust category of literature, and it continues to become ever more so. Clamorous voices are often raised in opposition to this view. The novel, some declare, is in critical condition. In his article "Facing the New" in *New Writing* (1992), edited by Malcolm Bradbury and Judy Cooke, Valentine Cunningham sums up some of their accusations:

> The allegations about the "crisis" in Our Novel Now are awfully familiar. It's too bourgeois. It's too English. It's certainly no longer new enough. It's stifling to death on old-fashioned technique, allegiance to Jane Austen, or Classic Realism, or Humanism, and the like. On the other hand, it's claimed Our Novel is also being killed off by sordid and ill-advised experimenters. There's been nothing good after—and because of—*Ulysses* or *Finnegans Wake* and their heirs and assigns.

Despite such perennial "Death of the Novel" laments (or, sometimes, celebrations) that appear in journals of opinion—additional causes of death include lack of financial support for the arts, too much financial support for the arts, the rise of new media, the conglomeration of the publishing world, illiteracy, television, or some other force—no really plausible signs of death are visible. Novels of high quality continue to appear. Brilliant men and women decide to spend their lives writing novels instead of doing something else. The numbers alone are illustrative of this rude health: Richard Todd estimates in his *Consuming Fictions: The Booker Prize and Fiction in Britain Today* (1996) that "Somewhere between 4,500 and 7,000 new Booker-eligible fiction titles appeared annually in Britain during the 1980s alone, the total rising throughout the decade from the lower figure to the higher." He points out that the total number of such titles in some years has been the same as in the United States, with its much larger population.

The concept of "Booker eligibility" is a useful one for considering the diversity and richness of the British novel since 1960. The Booker Prize, first awarded in 1969, goes to a novel published in Britain and written in English by a citizen of the United Kingdom, the British Commonwealth of Nations, the Republic of Ireland, Pakistan, Bangladesh, or South Africa. (It has been observed that nearly any author who writes in English is eligible for the Booker Prize except an American.) That authors from such vastly different countries and cultures are all "British" is a proposition that is easy to ridicule, and many of the authors themselves would reject it; but that their *novels* are British—through being published in Britain in the English language or through historic colonial connections of the authors' countries with Britain—is less controversial. The criteria for inclusion in *DLB 194: British Novelists Since 1960, Second Series* and the series that will follow it are similar to those for eligibility for the Booker Prize: novelists who have made their careers in the British Isles are included, whatever their country of birth, with two exceptions: American novelists, even if they live in Britain (Paul Theroux, for example), and Canadian novelists, even though they are eligible for the Booker, are excluded.

The history of serious British fiction since 1960 may be divided into two eras, with the line of demarcation falling around 1980. As evidence of this division one might consult the table of Booker Prize shortlists from 1969 through 1996 that follows this introduction. (The shortlist is the announced list of finalists from which the winner is drawn.) The table confirms that the short-listed novelists in the early years of the Booker tended to be English, Scottish, Welsh, or Irish; those from the dominions came from the white portions of the Commonwealth—Canada, Australia, and the white minorities of Rhodesia and South Africa. V. S. Naipaul, born in Trinidad of Indian ancestry and short-listed in 1971 for *In a Free State,* is the solitary exception. The shortlist for 1991 shows a striking contrast: the winner, Ben Okri, is a Nigerian; the list also includes Rohinton Mistry, born in India and a resident of Canada; Timothy Mo, born in Hong Kong; William Trevor and Roddy Doyle, both Irish; and a single Englishman, Martin Amis. By this time some observers were starting to murmur that things had gone too far, that perhaps the Booker selectors were biased against the English. The 1994 list would have confirmed their fears: the winner, James Kelman, and one other writer are Scottish, and Kelman is a highly politicized—that is, anti-English—Scot; they were joined on the list by a Sri Lankan and a Tanzanian. Even the two English writers on the 1994 list have a "minority" flavor: Alan Hollinghurst writes fantasy and extremity, seemed all that would serve to encompass the disordered psychic and social landscape of an age where actuality leaked into the world of the thriller, self leaked into social disorder, and the moral wholeness of the times was set in doubt. Both displayed a new attitude growing in fiction, as writers crossed its known frontiers and broke its limits, attempting to link the social aspects of British fiction with the underground psychic and sexual realms where the sense of contemporary crisis was most strongly felt.

Bradbury is one observer who doubts that the British novel is "in crisis." He suggests, however, that it responds to a felt crisis in the culture that may be traced to intellectual developments arising in France and the United States as well as to political developments, including economic distress and–not to be underestimated after the election of Thatcher in 1979 and Ronald Reagan in 1980–anxiety about the nuclear threat. McEwan's oratorio *Or Shall We Die?* (1983) and Amis's short-story collection *Einstein's Monsters* (1987) were both prompted by worry over a nuclear apocalypse.

A shift has taken place, then, but a shift to what? How can the contemporary state of British fiction best be summed up? In one sense this is an impossible project. If some eight thousand new novels are published each year in Britain, no one person can read even a majority of them; and if they demonstrate the thrilling but bewildering pluralism that has come more and more to characterize the British novel, how are they to be categorized? It is possible to indicate some trends, particularly those detected by knowledgeable British observers, including both novelists and critics. Lodge observes in his article "The Novelist Today: Still at the Crossroads" in *New Writing,* edited by Bradbury and Cooke, that

> contemporary writing, whatever particular style or mode it follows, whether realist or nonrealist, whether fabulation or metafiction or non-fiction novel [these are the paths canvassed by Lodge in *The Novelist at the Crossroads*], or a combination of all of these, is likely to be reader-friendly. The contemporary writer is interested in communicating.

Peter Kemp, in his article "British Fiction of the 1980s" in the same volume, calls attention to a different trait: "Probably the most striking feature of British fiction of the 1980s is how much of it is set neither in Britain nor the 1980s." He demonstrates the multiplicity of exotic or multicultural novels and the perhaps surprising strength of the historical novel. Commentators on the Booker Prize are often at pains to explain why the novel of contemporary life in Britain is so poorly represented in the nominations; just since 1990, authors of winners such as

Byatt's *Possession,* set in the mid-Victorian period; Ondaatje's *The English Patient,* set during World War II, and its cowinner, Unsworth's *Sacred Hunger,* set in the eighteenth century; and Pat Barker's *The Ghost Road* (1995), set during World War I, have found the past more compelling or, perhaps, just more interesting than the present. During the same years the Booker shortlist has included Martin Amis's *Time's Arrow* (1991), about the Holocaust; McEwan's *Black Dogs* and Michele Roberts's *Daughters of the House* (both 1992), set during World War II and its immediate aftermath; Abdulrazak Gurnah's *Paradise* (1994), set in colonial Africa; Walsh's *Knowledge of Angels,* set in the early Renaissance; Unsworth's *Morality Play* (1995), set during the Middle Ages; Margaret Atwood's *Alias Grace* (1996), set in nineteenth-century Canada; and Beryl Bainbridge's *Every Man for Himself* (1996), about the sinking of the *Titanic* in 1912. Whether this propensity to re-envision the past represents a reaction against the "crisis" of the present, whatever that crisis may entail; or a turn away from an England in which, in William Leith's dismissive phrase, "nothing ever happens," there is no doubt that the historical novel is very much alive. It may be problematized or ironized, as in Amis's *Time's Arrow* or Barnes's *A History of the World in 10 1/2 Chapters* (1989), or used to comment on the present, as in Byatt's recent works.

In *The Modern British Novel* Bradbury asks: what is the condition of the British novel at the end of century? After tallying the common complaints against it–it is too conventional, weak in historical sensibility, lacking in experimental vigor–he concludes by affirming its strength. One measure of that strength is its success:

> Novels are probably more widely read than they ever were before, and the generic categories multiply constantly. The most visible sign of the state of the novel is its sheer plurality. This is the age of the busy bookstore, and the novel as a highly commercialized commodity.

Commercial success is only one measure of health, and a partial one at best. But the British novel, in part by its energetic expansion into new territories and new techniques and in part through the incorporation of new novelists and new themes, continues to excite, satirize, amuse, scandalize, inform, and judge in ways that only the novel can.

–Merritt Moseley

Acknowledgments

This book was produced by Bruccoli Clark Layman, Inc. Karen L. Rood is senior editor for the *Dictionary of Literary Biography* series. Philip B. Dematteis was the in-house editor. He was assisted by Tracy Simmons Bitonti and Jan Peter van Rosevelt.

Administrative support was provided by Ann M. Cheschi and Brenda A. Gillie.

Bookkeeper is Joyce Fowler.

Copyediting supervisor is Samuel W. Bruce. The copyediting staff includes Phyllis A. Avant, Patricia Coate, Christine Copeland, and Thom Harman. Freelance copyeditors are Charles Brower, Leslie Haynsworth, Rebecca Mayo, and Jennie Williamson.

Editorial associate is Jeff Miller.

Layout and graphics staff includes Janet E. Hill and Mark J. McEwan.

Office manager is Kathy Lawler Merlette.

Photography editors are Margaret Meriwether and Paul Talbot. Photographic copy work was performed by Joseph M. Bruccoli.

Production manager is Philip B. Dematteis.

Systems manager is Marie L. Parker.

Typesetting supervisor is Kathleen M. Flanagan. The typesetting staff includes Pamela D. Norton and Patricia Flanagan Salisbury. Freelance typesetters include Deidre Murphy and Delores Plastow.

Walter W. Ross, Steven Gross, and Ronald Aikman did library research. They were assisted by the following librarians at the Thomas Cooper Library of the University of South Carolina: Linda Holderfield and the interlibrary-loan staff; reference-department head Virginia Weathers; reference librarians Marilee Birchfield, Stefanie Buck, Stefanie DuBose, Rebecca Feind, Karen Joseph, Donna Lehman, Charlene Loope, Anthony McKissick, Jean Rhyne, and Kwamine Simpson; circulation-department head Caroline Taylor; and acquisitions-searching supervisor David Haggard.

Booker Prize Shortlists, 1969–1996

For each year except 1992, the winner of the Booker Prize is listed first. In 1992 there were two co-winners; they are listed first and second.

Title	Author	Year of Birth	Nationality	First Published Work
1969				
Something to Answer For	P. H. Newby	1918	English	1945
Figures in a Landscape	Barry England	1932	English	1968
The Impossible Object	Nicholas Mosley	1923	English	1951
The Nice and the Good	Iris Murdoch	1919	English	1953
The Public Image	Muriel Spark	1918	Scottish	1957
From Scenes Like These	G. M. Williams	1934	Scottish	1965
1970				
The Elected Member	Bernice Rubens	1928	Welsh	1960
John Brown's Body	A. L. Barker	1918	English	1947
Eva Trout	Elizabeth Bowen	1899	Irish	1928
Bruno's Dream	Iris Murdoch	1919	English	1953
Mrs. Eckdork in O'Neill's Hotel	William Trevor	1928	Irish	1958
The Conjunction	Terence Wheeler	1936	English(?)	1970
1971				
In a Free State	V. S. Naipaul	1932	Trinidadian	1957
The Big Chapel	Thomas Kilroy	1934	Irish	1969
Briefing for a Descent into Hell	Doris Lessing	1919	Rhodesian	1950
St. Urban's Horseman	Mordecai Richler	1931	Canadian	1954
Goshawk Squadron	Derek Robinson	1932	English	1971
Mrs. Palfrey at the Clairmont	Elizabeth Taylor	1912	English	1945
1972				
G	John Berger	1926	English	1958
Bird of Night	Susan Hill	1942	English	1961
The Chant of Jimmie Blacksmith	Thomas Keneally	1935	Australian	1964
Pasmore	David Storey	1935	English	1960
1973				
The Siege of Krishnapur	J. G. Farrell	1935	English	1963
The Dressmaker	Beryl Bainbridge	1933	English	1967
The Green Equinox	Elizabeth Mavor	1927	Scottish	1959
The Black Prince	Iris Murdoch	1919	English	1953
1974				
The Conservationist	Nadine Gordimer	1923	South African	1953
Holiday	Stanley Middleton	1919	English	1958
Ending Up	Kingsley Amis	1920	English	1953
The Bottle Factory	Beryl Bainbridge	1934	English	1967
In Their Wisdom	C. P. Snow	1905	English	1932

1975

Heat and Dust	Ruth Prawer Jhabvala	1927	Polish/English	1955
Gossip from the Forest	Thomas Keneally	1935	Australian	1964

1976

Saville	David Storey	1933	English	1960
An Instant in the Wind	Andre Brink	1935	South African	1960
Rising	R. C. Hutchinson	1907	English	1930
The Doctor's Wife	Brian Moore	1926	Canadian	1951
King Fisher Lives	Julian Rathbone	1935	English	1967
The Children of Dynmouth	William Trevor	1928	Irish	1958

1977

Staying On	Paul Scott	1920	English	1941
Peter Smart's Confessions	Paul Bailey	1937	English	1967
Great Granny Webster	Caroline Blackwood	1931	Irish	1973
Shadows on Our Skin	Jennifer Johnston	1930	Irish	1972
The Road to Lichfield	Penelope Lively	1933	English	1970
Quartet in Autumn	Barbara Pym	1913	English	1950

1978

The Sea, The Sea	Iris Murdoch	1919	English	1953
Jake's Thing	Kingsley Amis	1920	English	1953
Rumours of Rain	Andre Brink	1935	South African	1960
The Bookshop	Penelope Fitzgerald	1916	English	1975
God on the Rocks	Jane Gardam	1928	English	1971
A Five-Year Sentence	Bernice Rubens	1928	Welsh	1960

1979

Offshore	Penelope Fitzgerald	1916	English	1977
Confederates	Thomas Keneally	1935	Australian	1964
A Bend in the River	V. S. Naipaul	1932	Trinidadian	1957
Joseph	Julian Rathbone	1935	English	1967
Praxis	Fay Weldon	1931	English	1967

1980

Rites of Passage	William Golding	1911	English	1954
A Month in the Country	J. L. Carr	1912	English	1964
Earthly Powers	Anthony Burgess	1917	English	1956
Clear Light of Day	Anita Desai	1937	Indian	1963
The Beggar Maid	Alice Munro	1931	Canadian	1968
No Country for Young Men	Julia O'Faalain	1932	Irish	1970
Pascali's Island	Barry Unsworth	1930	English	1966

1981

Midnight's Children	Salman Rushdie	1947	Indian	1975
The Sirian Experiments	Doris Lessing	1919	Rhodesian	1950
The Comfort of Strangers	Ian McEwan	1948	English	1975
Good Behaviour	Molly Keane	1904	Irish	1928
Rhine Journey	Anne Schlee	1934	English	1971
Loitering with Intent	Muriel Spark	1918	Scottish	1957
The White Hotel	D. M. Thomas	1935	English	1979

1982

Schindler's Ark	Thomas Keneally	1935	Australian	1964

Silence among the Weapons	John Arden	1930	English	1955
An Ice-Cream War	William Boyd	1952	English	1981
Sour Sweet	Timothy Mo	1950	Hong Kong	1978
Constance or Solitary Practices	Lawrence Durrell	1912	Irish	1935
The 27th Kingdom	Alice Thomas Ellis	1932	English	1977
1983				
Life and Times of Michael K.	J. M. Coetzee	1940	South African	1974
Rates of Exchange	Malcolm Bradbury	1932	English	1959
Flying to Nowhere	John Fuller	1937	English	1961
The Illusionist	Anita Mason	1942	English	1981
Shame	Salman Rushdie	1947	Indian	1975
Waterland	Graham Swift	1949	English	1980
1984				
Hotel du Lac	Anita Brookner	1928	English	1981
Empire of the Sun	J. G. Ballard	1930	English	1962
Flaubert's Parrot	Julian Barnes	1946	English	1980
In Custody	Anita Desai	1937	Indian	1963
According to Mark	Penelope Lively	1933	English	1970
Small World	David Lodge	1935	English	1960
1985				
The Bone People	Keri Hulme	1947	New Zealander	1984
Illywhacker	Peter Carey	1943	Australian	1981
The Battle of Pollock's Crossing	J. L. Carr	1912	English	1964
The Good Terrorist	Doris Lessing	1919	Rhodesian	1950
Last Letters from Hav	Jan Morris	1926	Welsh	1956
The Good Apprentice	Iris Murdoch	1919	English	1953
1986				
The Old Devils	Kingsley Amis	1920	English	1953
The Handmaid's Tale	Margaret Atwood	1939	Canadian	1969
Gabriel's Lament	Paul Bailey	1937	English	1967
What's Bred in the Bone	Robertson Davies	1913	Canadian	1951
An Artist of the Floating World	Kazuo Ishiguro	1954	Japanese/English	1982
AnInsular Possession	Timothy Mo	1950	Hong Kong	1978
1987				
Moon Tiger	Penelope Lively	1933	English	1970
Anthills of the Savannah	Chinua Achebe	1930	Nigerian	1958
Chatterton	Peter Ackroyd	1949	English	1982
The Colour of Blood	Brian Moore	1926	Canadian	1951
The Book and the Brotherhood	Iris Murdoch	1919	English	1953
1988				
Oscar and Lucinda	Peter Carey	1943	Australian	1981
Utz	Bruce Chatwin	1940	English	1977
The Beginning of Spring	Penelope Fitzgerald	1916	English	1977
Nice Work	David Lodge	1935	English	1960
The Satanic Verses	Salman Rushdie	1947	Indian	1975
The Lost Father	Marina Warner	1946	English	1972
1989				
The Remains of the Day	Kazuo Ishiguro	1954	Japanese/English	1982

Cat's Eye	Margaret Atwood	1939	Canadian	1969
The Book of Evidence	John Banville	1945	Irish	1970
Jigsaw	Sybille Bedford	1911	English	1956
A Disaffection	James Kelman	1946	Scottish	1984
Restoration	Rose Tremain	1943	English	1976
1990				
Possession	A. S. Byatt	1936	English	1964
An Awfully Big Adventure	Beryl Bainbridge	1934	English	1967
The Gate of Angels	Penelope Fitzgerald	1916	English	1977
Amongst Women	John McGahern	1934	English(?)	1962
Lies of Silence	Brian Moore	1926	Canadian	1951
Solomon Gursky Was Here	Mordecai Richler	1931	Canadian	1954
1991				
The Famished Road	Ben Okri	1959	Nigerian	1980
Time's Arrow	Martin Amis	1949	English	1973
The Van	Roddy Doyle	1958	Irish	1988
Such a Long Journey	Rohinton Mistry	1952	Indian	1991
The Redundancy of Courage	Timothy Mo	1950	Hong Kong	1978
Reading Turgenev	William Trevor	1928	Irish	1958
1992				
The English Patient	Michael Ondaatje	1943	Sri Lankan	1976
Sacred Hunger	Barry Unsworth	1930	English	1966
Serenity House	Christopher Hope	1944	South African	1974
The Butcher Boy	Patrick McCabe	1955	Irish	1986
Black Dogs	Ian McEwan	1948	English	1975
Daughters of the House	Michele Roberts	1949	English	1978
1993				
Paddy Clarke, Ha-Ha-Ha	Roddy Doyle	1958	Irish	1988
Under the Frog	Tibor Fischer	1959	English	1992
Scar Tissue	Michael Ignatieff	1947	Canadian	1978
Remembering Babylon	David Malouf	1934	Australian	1975
Crossing the River	Caryl Phillips	1958	West Indian	1981
The Stone Diaries	Carol Shields	1935	American/Canadian	1976
1994				
How Late It Was, How Late	James Kelman	1946	Scottish	1984
Beside The Ocean of Time	George MacKay Brown	1921	Scottish	1969
Reef	Romesh Gunesekera	?	Sri Lankan	1992
Paradise	Abdulrazak Gurnah	1948	Tanzania	1987
The Folding Star	Alan Hollinghurst	1954	English	1984
Knowledge of Angels	Jill Paton Walsh	1937	English	1972
1995				
The Ghost Road	Pat Barker	1943	English	1982
In Every Face I Meet	Justin Cartwright	1933	South African	1977
The Moor's Last Sigh	Salman Rushdie	1947	Indian	1975
Morality Play	Barry Unsworth	1930	English	1966
The Riders	Tim Winton	1960	Australian	1982
1996				
Last Orders	Graham Swift	1949	English	1980

Reading in the Dark	Seamus Deane	1940	Irish	1996
The Orchard on Fire	Shena McKay	1944	Scottish	1964
Alias Grace	Margaret Atwood	1939	Canadian	1969
Every Man for Himself	Beryl Bainbridge	1933	English	1967
A Fine Balance	Rohinton Mistry	1952	Indian	1991

1997

The God of Small Things	Arundhati Roy	1960	Indian	1997
Grace Notes	Bernard MacLaverty	1942	Northern Irish	1979
Quarantine	Jim Crace	1946	English	1986
The Underground Man	Mick Jackson	1960	English	1997
Europa	Tim Parks	1954	English	1985
The Essence of the Thing	Madeleine St. John	1942	Australian	1993

British Novelists Since 1960
Second Series

Dictionary of Literary Biography

Gilbert Adair
(29 December 1944 –)

Dan Friedman
Yale University

BOOKS: *Hollywood's Vietnam: From* The Green Berets *to* Apocalypse Now (London & New York: Proteus, 1981; revised and enlarged edition, London: Heinemann, 1989);

Alice through the Needle's Eye (London: Macmillan, 1984; New York: Dutton, 1984); republished as *Alice through the Needle's Eye: A Third Adventure for Lewis Carroll's Alice* (London: Picador, 1985);

A Night at the Pictures: Ten Decades of British Film, by Adair and Nick Roddick (London: Columbus Books in association with British Film Year, 1985);

Myths & Memories (London: Fontana, 1986);

Peter Pan and the Only Children (London: Macmillan, 1987; New York: Dutton, 1988);

The Holy Innocents: A Romance (London: Heinemann, 1988; New York: Dutton, 1989);

Love and Death on Long Island (London: Heinemann, 1990; New York: Grove, 1998);

The Rape of the Cock (Caen: Editions du Dam, 1991);

The Death of the Author (London: Heinemann, 1992);

The Postmodernist Always Rings Twice: Reflections on Culture in the 90s (London: Fourth Estate, 1992);

Flickers: An Illustrated Celebration of 100 Years of Cinema (London & Boston: Faber & Faber, 1995);

The Key of the Tower: A Novel (London: Secker & Warburg, 1997);

Surfing the Zeitgeist (London & Boston: Faber & Faber, 1997).

TRANSLATIONS: Michel Ciment, *Kubrick* (London: Collins, 1983; New York: Holt, Rinehart & Winston, 1983);

Ciment, *John Boorman* (London & Boston: Faber & Faber, 1986);

Gilbert Adair

François Truffaut, *Letters,* edited by Gilles Jacob and Claude de Givray, translated and edited by Adair (London & Boston: Faber & Faber, 1989); republished as *Correspondence 1945–1984* (New York: Noonday Press/Farrar Straus Giroux, 1990);

Georges Perec, *A Void* (London: Harvill, 1994; New York: HarperCollins, 1994);

Marie-Jeanne l'Heritier de Villandon, "The Subtle Princess," in *Wonder Tales,* edited by Marina Warner (London: Chatto & Windus, 1994; New York: Farrar, Straus & Giroux, 1996), pp. 65–97.

MOTION PICTURE: *Le Territoire,* screenplay by Adair and Raúl Ruiz, 1981.

Gilbert Adair is probably best known for his writing in several national magazines and newspapers (including *The Guardian, The Telegraph,* and *Esquire*), especially the weekly "Scrutiny" column he wrote for the *The Sunday Times* between 1992 and 1996. His most widely acclaimed achievement is his brilliant, highly inventive translation of Georges Perec's lipogrammatic novel *La Disparition* (1969)–the novel with no *es*–as *A Void* (1994). His reputation as a writer of original fiction rests mainly on four short novels written since 1988. The same contemporary culture that he observed acidly in the lines of "Scrutiny" provides the backdrop and the motivation for his compulsive characters. The single protagonists of these novels follow their obsessions to their inexorable conclusions, however absurd or pathetic. Adair wrote too indulgently for some early reviewers' tastes because he insisted on taking his characters through to a bitter and often unsympathetic end. His novels have met with increasing appreciation, with Terry Eagleton suggesting in the *Times Literary Supplement* (21 August 1992) that *The Death of the Author* (1992) is "a first-class postmodernist novel [that] might have bordered on perfection."

Adair was born in Edinburgh on 29 December 1944. He broke with his parents at an early age and declines to speak of his childhood and education. During his youth he developed the Francophilia that has remained a dominant feature of his life. He learned French in school, and as soon as a small inheritance enabled him to do so, he left England for France. He was teaching English in Paris in 1968 when the student revolts that form the background of his first novel, *The Holy Innocents: A Romance* (1988), broke out. Adair lived in Paris for a decade, publishing poems in French and English but earning his living as an English teacher. Realizing that he would have to return to an Anglophone country if his career were to progress satisfactorily, he moved to England in 1979. Since then he has divided his time between London and Paris.

The cinema recurs as a subject and as a motif throughout Adair's early work. He coauthored with the director, Raúl Ruiz, the motion picture *Le Territoire* (released in English as *The Territory*), which was produced in France in 1981. (Wim Wenders appro-

priated its entire cast and crew the following year to make *The State of Things*.) Much of his criticism and journalism has been about motion pictures, including his first book, *Hollywood's Vietnam: From* The Green Berets *to* Apocalypse Now (1981); *A Night at the Pictures: Ten Decades of British Film* (1985), coauthored with Nick Roddick; and *Flickers: An Illustrated Celebration of 100 Years of Cinema* (1995). He also translated Michel Ciment's books on the directors Stanley Kubrick (1983) and John Boorman (1986) and the correspondence of the French director François Truffaut (1989). He also wrote sequels to two children's classics: *Alice through the Needle's Eye* (1984) and *Peter Pan and the Only Children* (1987). His *Myths & Memories* (1986) was initially inspired by Roland Barthes's *Mythologies* (1957; translated, 1972) and its application of mythological analysis to everyday life. The impetus to add a second part to the work came when a friend introduced him to the work of Perec by giving him a copy of *Je me souviens* (I Remember, 1978). These books demonstrate the extent to which Adair is receptive not only to the subject matter of other writers but also to their styles; this trait is shared by his novels.

Although Adair witnessed the events of 1968 that form its historical context, he did not begin writing *The Holy Innocents* until 1987. The title acknowledges the debt that this novel owes to Jean Cocteau's *Les Enfants terribles* (1929; translated as *Enfants Terribles,* 1930), but the book is more than a pastiche. Cocteau's prose and the actions of the "enfants" are frighteningly detached; the intrusions of the events into the lives of the characters in *The Holy Innocents* do not allow the same blithe disregard of the outside world that Cocteau's characters display. From the ironic title to the epilogue's cinematic replay of the opening, the reader of *The Holy Innocents* is constantly made complicit in the protagonists' failed attempts at detachment.

The title characters of *The Holy Innocents* are three movie lovers who are thrown together by the closure of the Cinémathèque Française in the spring of 1968. Forced to create their own amusement, the twins, Guillaume and Danielle, adopt Matthew, a young American, into their claustrophobically intense and incestuous relationship. Their initial reaction to the closing of the Cinémathèque–the screen that "screens them from the world"–is to retreat further into their own self-contained lives of sexual experimentation. The three parts that comprise the novel follow the Innocents' oscillation from the "real" world of Paris to the self-absorbed adolescent world of their homes in Paris and Normandy. The central section was too childishly "pornographic" for Mansel Stimpson in the *Times Literary Supplement*

Dust jacket for the 1997 work that Adair claims will be his last novel

(9 September 1988), and it is true that the prose is occasionally awkward, especially in its choice of image and its depiction of sex. In his first novel Adair is exploring his style, just as his Holy Innocents awkwardly, and not entirely successfully, learn about themselves and those closest to them.

The narrator of Adair's second novel, *Love and Death on Long Island* (1990), is the aging novelist Giles—his surname is never given. The cloistered, routine existence Giles has lived since the death of his wife is shattered by a chance viewing of the movie *Hotpants College II*. The writer becomes infatuated with the teenage star of the movie, Ronnie Bostock, and is thrust into a modern world of profanity, videotapes, and teen and gay pornographic magazines. His obsession irrevocably changes his life; he leaves his home in the London suburb of Hampstead and travels to the imaginary town of Chesterfield on Long Island to pursue the object of his desires, who ultimately rejects him.

Critics praised the novel but accused Adair of being insufficiently sympathetic to his characters and of leaving the reader with a cruel "farce" rather than a "tragicomedy." This criticism overlooks the subtle treatment of narration in the novel, which is written in the clear but pompous prose style of the narrator. The first word of the novel is "I"—an ironic opening for a fictional novelist who had not used the first-person singular pronoun in any of his four famous novels.

In 1997 a motion-picture adaptation of *Love and Death on Long Island,* coproduced by Canadian and British companies, premiered at the Cannes Film Festival and won the Pierrot Award for best first film; in the movie Giles is given the surname De'Ath.

Adair's third and best-received novel, *The Death of the Author,* takes place in a present-day New Harbor, a thinly disguised New Haven, Connecticut; the title is taken from Barthes's famous 1968 essay. The protagonist, Léopold Sfax, is a literature professor modeled on Paul de Man. Like de Man, who, with Jacques Derrida, devised the approach to literary criticism known as deconstruction, Sfax is responsible for developing an approach called "The Theory." Also like de Man, Sfax has a hidden background as a collaborationist writer during the Nazi occupation of France. Sfax is investigating the circumstances of his own life and death (he is killed in the course of the novel but continues to relate its narrative), prompted by, and in competition with, Astrid, a graduate student who is researching his biography. The story is told as a detective novel, but the reader can never really trust Sfax's narrative. As with *Love and Death on Long Island,* the narrator is a writer, and the novel is wryly self-conscious of its own status as fiction. The style is a highly accomplished "satire of literary-critical pretension," as Anthony Quinton put it in the London *Evening Standard* (24 August 1992), that never falls into parody or banality.

Theories and theorists both real and imagined are scattered through the text, and Sfax's engagement with them allows Adair to bring to bear his concerns about the conceptual problems underlying Modernist and Postmodernist thought. When Adair went to New Haven to do some research for the novel some years after de Man's death in 1983, he was horrified to find books developing sophisticated theoretical apologies for de Man's collaborationist articles. *The Death of the Author* is an amusing account of a murder investigation, but it raises a serious question: who will take responsibility for writing once what Barthes called "the death of the author" allows writers to avoid responsibility for their own writing?

The most remarkable achievement of Adair's career so far, and the one that has received universal critical approval, has been his translation of Perec's *La Disparition*. Adair, with his love of contemporary French writing and his childlike delight in word games, would seem peculiarly well suited to undertake such a work, but he turned down the opportunity when it was first presented to him. After twice refusing the commission, he finally accepted the task in 1990 on the condition that no deadline be set for its completion. Four years later the publisher's persistence was vindicated by a vibrant English translation. Perec's three-hundred-page original is based on the deliberate exclusion of any word containing the letter *E,* and Adair's translation remains true to the formula. While it is relatively faithful to the plot and tone of Perec's text, Adair's imaginative rendering of it as *A Void* is a highly original contribution to English novel writing. The strategies employed to avoid the use of a single *E* are completely different in English from those used in French.

The Key of the Tower (1997) is an attempt to write a novel entirely driven by plot, a Hitchcockian thriller in book form. The intrigue is based on a series of outrageous coincidences that occur during the vacation in France of the convalescent British protagonist. Having lost faith in contemporary culture, Adair intends this work to be his last novel; his interests have turned to nineteenth-century mathematical thought.

Although he may be destined to be remembered as the man who brought *La Disparition* into English, Gilbert Adair's achievements as a novelist in his own right are considerable. His stylistic accuracy and self-conscious plotting have been too Gallic for the tastes of English reviewers, but as the writers he uses as his starting points—Barthes, Perec, and de Man—have been absorbed into wider culture, he is becoming increasingly appreciated for his translation of their ideas not only into English but also into fiction.

Martin Amis

(25 August 1949 -   )

David Thomson
University of British Columbia

See also the Amis entry in *DLB 14: British Novelists Since 1960.*

BOOKS: *The Rachel Papers* (London: Cape, 1973; New York: Knopf, 1974);

Dead Babies (London: Cape, 1974; New York: Knopf, 1976); republished as *Dark Secrets* (St. Albans: Panther, 1977);

My Oxford, by Amis and others, edited by Ann Thwaite (London: Robson, 1977; revised, 1986);

Success (London: Cape, 1978; New York: Harmony, 1987);

Other People: A Mystery Story (London: Cape, 1981; New York: Viking, 1981);

Invasion of the Space Invaders (London: Hutchinson, 1982; Millbrae, Cal.: Celestial Arts, 1982);

Money: A Suicide Note (London: Cape, 1984; New York: Viking, 1985);

The Moronic Inferno: And Other Visits to America (London: Cape, 1986; New York: Viking, 1987);

Einstein's Monsters (London: Cape, 1987; New York: Harmony, 1987);

London Fields (London: Cape, 1989; New York: Harmony, 1989);

Time's Arrow; or, The Nature of the Offense (London: Cape, 1991; New York: Harmony, 1991);

Visiting Mrs. Nabokov and Other Excursions (London: Cape, 1993; New York: Harmony, 1993);

Two Stories (London: Moorhouse & Sørensen, 1994)—comprises "Denton's Death" and "Let Me Count the Times";

The Information (London: Flamingo/HarperCollins, 1995; New York: Harmony, 1995);

Night Train (London: Cape, 1997; New York: Harmony, 1998).

MOTION PICTURE: *Saturn 3,* screenplay by Amis, ITC Films, 1980.

OTHER: "The Sublime and the Ridiculous: Nabokov's Black Farces," in *Vladimir Nabokov, His Life, His Work, His World: A Tribute,* edited by

Martin Amis (photograph © 1997 by Ovina Fonseca)

Peter Quennell (New York: Morrow, 1980), pp. 73–86.

SELECTED PERIODICAL PUBLICATIONS– UNCOLLECTED:

FICTION

"Career Move," *New Yorker* (29 June 1992): 30–38;

"Straight Fiction," *Esquire* (December 1995): 138–148;

"State of England," *New Yorker* (24 June–1 July 1996): 92–107.

NONFICTION

"Lolita Reconsidered," *Atlantic Monthly* (September 1992): 109–120;

"Don Juan in Hull," *New Yorker* (12 July 1993): 74–82;

"Travolta's Second Act," *New Yorker* (20-27 February 1995): 212–218;

"Buy My Book, Please," *New Yorker* (26 June–3 July 1995): 96–99;

"Jane's World," *New Yorker* (8 January 1996): 31–35.

It must be among Martin Amis's greatest fears that when his obituary is published in *The Times* of London it will begin, "The son of noted novelist Kingsley Amis. . . ." To follow in the shadow of such a literary institution would seem a daunting prospect for any writer, but Amis *fils* has done an admirable job of finding his own limelight. If the father, as the most eloquent of the Angry Young Men, was the voice of his generation, then the son has staked out a claim to be considered, if not the most highly regarded, certainly the most widely imitated novelist of his generation. Dubbed "the rock star of English literature" by the London *Daily Telegraph* (24 May 1996), Martin Amis has never shied away from the issue of his own literary importance, admitting in a 1996 interview with Eleanor Wachtel to "writerly envies and ridiculous flashes of megalomania and all the rest." Fittingly, his 1995 novel, *The Information,* is about the competing egos of two writers; it is, he told Susan Morrison in a 1990 *Rolling Stone* interview, "a literary-envy novel." His first novel was published while Amis was twenty-four; he has written eight others since then, along with a screenplay for a science-fantasy film, short stories for magazines such as *The Atlantic Monthly* and *The New Yorker,* and a steady stream of reviews, interviews, and articles for periodicals that include *The Observer* (London), *The Sunday Times, Esquire,* and many others. Five of his short stories were collected as *Einstein's Monsters* in 1987, and two collections of his journalism have appeared. This impressive body of work is infused with an original and inventive literary style that marries an eye for astute observation with a wicked satirical tongue. In twenty-five years of writing Amis has combined commercial success with critical acclaim. In Britain he has achieved a level of celebrity—and notoriety—second only to that of Salman Rushdie.

Martin Louis Amis was born in Oxford on 25 August 1949, the second son of Kingsley and Hilary Bardwell Amis. His early childhood was uneventful although his parents' frequent moves resulted in his changing schools frequently. When he was ten, he spent a year in Princeton, New Jersey, while his father taught at the university, and he spent a further year in Spain with his mother following her divorce from Kingsley Amis in 1961. In all, he attended thirteen schools; he was expelled from one of them—a grammar school in Battersea—because he took an extended absence to act in Alexander Mackendrick's motion picture *A High Wind in Jamaica* (1965). He preferred comic books to serious fiction for most of his adolescence; it was Elizabeth Jane Howard Amis, his father's second wife, who got him interested in reading and academic achievement.

After a period of intensive cramming Amis passed his university entrance examinations and was admitted to Exeter College, Oxford. He graduated in 1971 with a formal First in English and became a book reviewer for *The Observer.* Soon he was also working as an editorial assistant for the *Times Literary Supplement,* and in 1973 he was hired to review books for *The New Statesman.*

The work that signaled Amis's arrival on the British literary scene takes the form of a memoir by the precocious Charles Highway. *The Rachel Papers* (1973) is literally a coming-of-age novel: the narrative is shaped by the clock counting down the hours to Charles's twentieth birthday, and the book's twelve chapters correspond to precise moments in a single evening. Ostensibly a record of Charles's sexual conquest of Rachel Noyes, the novel is a scathing and hilarious glimpse into the mind of a nineteen-year-old boy.

Charles lives in Oxford with his father, who is a successful writer, and his distant, distracted mother. The atmosphere in the home is tense because of Charles's father's indiscreet affairs, of which his mother pretends to be ignorant; therefore, to prepare for his university entrance examinations Charles goes to London to stay with his sister and her husband. He meets Rachel at a party; his first attempts to attract her attention fail miserably, but he finally lures her to Oxford for a family function. Charles's quest to sleep with Rachel is the primary focus of his narrative, but along the way he sketches his family background, provides updates on his preparations for the entrance examinations, and describes, with unsettling candor, the social pursuits of a late-adolescent at the end of the 1960s. As he and Rachel overcome a succession of hurdles placed between them by friends and family, it seems that Amis has set his first novel firmly within the generic conventions of romantic comedy. In this respect *The Rachel Papers* recalls his father's first novel, *Lucky Jim* (1954), but the younger Amis is far more willing to deviate, and deviate much further, from the boundaries of literary propriety than his father had been. With its descriptions of masturbation and other sex acts rendered in pornographic detail, *The Rachel Papers* is clearly a document from the permissive side of the sexual revolution. "Nasty things are funny," writes Charles Highway, and *The Rachel Papers* is thoroughly darkly comic. Charles's vanity and unrelenting self-absorption also undermine the conventions of romantic comedy. In addition to the usual self-consciousness of teenagers, Charles is possessed by a peculiarly literary self-awareness: not only does he write "Don't I ever do anything else but take soulful walks down the Bayswater Road, I thought, as I walked soulfully down the Bayswater Road" but he also spends a lengthy paragraph analyzing that thought, with references to the critics Northrop Frye and Angus Wilson. A narrator who is so visibly aware of literary traditions and conventions cannot be taken at face value, and, indeed, he admits early on that his pursuit of Rachel has less to do with love than with his desire to satisfy the conventional requirements of adolescence: "There were several teenage things still to be done: get a job. . . ; have a first love, or at least sleep with an Older Woman; write a few more callow, brittle poems." His decision to break up with Rachel is, similarly, motivated by the idea that on turning twenty it is appropriate to leave childhood and its attachments behind. Thus, the novel ends without the anticipated union and with Charles still incapable of expressing any genuine thoughts or emotions without a protective veneer of ironic detachment and literary pretense.

The only character to get close to jeopardizing Charles's ironic distance from events is Dr. Charles Knowd, an Oxford tutor who interviews him after he has passed his entrance examinations. Knowd derides Charles's showy erudition and confronts him with the contradictory and derivative quality of his critical essays. He urges Charles to "stop reading critics. . . . Just read the poems and work out whether you like them, and why." Characteristically Charles responds to this challenge to his pretensions by opting for his second-choice college, thereby avoiding further confrontations with Dr. Knowd.

The Rachel Papers was greeted with considerable enthusiasm by reviewers, mainly for its comic insights and wildly inventive prose style. It won the Somerset Maugham Award of the National Book League as the best first novel of the year, as Kingsley Amis's *Lucky Jim* had in 1954. In 1974 Amis became fiction and poetry editor for the *Times Literary Supplement.*

Dead Babies (1974) is in many ways a continuation of the comic excesses of *The Rachel Papers,* but in Amis's second novel the satire is sharper, and there is no expression of sympathy or forgiveness for its characters, a handful of twenty-somethings engaged in a weekend-long party in the English countryside. As *The Rachel Papers* uses and abuses the conventions of the comic novel, *Dead Babies* initially emulates a peculiarly British form, the country-house novel. At

an indeterminate time in the near future ten people, including three Americans, gather for a three-day weekend at Appleseed Rectory. The hosts, the Honourable Quentin Villiers and his beautiful wife, Celia, seem to be the image of sophisticated gentry, yet they join their friends in activities that rapidly degenerate into deviant sex as well as drug and alcohol abuse. As each character is profiled in turn by the narrator, he or she is systematically stripped of any redeeming features. Giles Coldstream, for example, is a wealthy and ineffectual alcoholic with a paralyzing phobia about his teeth. Diana Parry takes part in the general depravity to punish her negligent parents. Diana's boyfriend, Andy Adorno, is a child of the 1960s whose mother abandoned him within weeks of his birth; he is full of aggression and sexual energy although he no longer has much interest in sex. Keith Whitehead is included in the group as a kind of grotesque pet. Amis uses all his verbal ingenuity and talent for exaggeration to render "little Keith" as physically loathsome as possible; Keith's physical shortcomings function as a material embodiment of the moral deformations and shortcomings of the others.

Amis is merciless in his depiction of a permissive society taken to extremes. He counterpoints the amoral thoughts and actions of the Appleseed residents with a detached, omniscient narrator who interjects comments that reinforce the connection between their depravity and the moral laxity of contemporary society. Almost every form of perversity is explored in the novel, including sodomy, rape, and a mock crucifixion. As the "Appleseeders" go about their experiments with drugs and sex, each becomes the victim of a tasteless joke perpetrated by a mysterious figure who calls himself "Johnny" and whose identity is a source of speculation among the group. As the weekend winds down, Giles attempts to commit suicide and is rushed to the hospital. The novel reaches an apocalyptic conclusion with the emergence of Johnny's true identity.

There is little conventional plot development in *Dead Babies*. Instead, an interchangeable series of episodes is presented, each featuring drugs or alcohol and the worst aspects of human nature. The ferocity of Amis's satire, the relentless presentation of characters at their most callous and corrupt, never builds to any intelligible rationale. Amis dismissed the work in *The New York Times* (21 October 1981) as "showing off," and it is true that he demonstrates in it a remarkable talent for powerful and arresting metaphors. The force of the language in *Dead Babies* is undeniable, but because it is directed at making the characters as unpleasant and unsympathetic as possible, the purpose of all of this verbal energy re-

MARTIN AMIS

TIME'S ARROW

Dust jacket for Amis's novel in which time runs backward

mains unclear. The novel's offensive title was changed to *Dark Secrets* for the paperback edition (1977).

Amis left the *Times Literary Supplement* in 1977 to become literary editor of *The New Statesman*. His next novel, *Success* (1978), is set in London and is the story of the changing fortunes of Terry Service and his foster brother, Gregory Riding. Each chapter consists of a section narrated by Terry followed by one narrated by Gregory, giving their quite different perspectives on the events. Terry reveals that he was adopted into the Riding family at nine years of age after having witnessed his younger sister's murder at the hands of their abusive father. Terry is well aware of his clichéd status as an "orphan of underprivilege," and his insecurity touches every aspect of his life. He is miserable in his work, yet he is terrified of losing his job as the company prepares for unionization. Obsessed with sex, he is physically incapable of intercourse or even masturbation. He tries to ingratiate himself but is treated with hostility and contempt by all. Gregory seems to be the antithesis of Terry: he has an elegant appearance, a

fashionable job in an art gallery, a dynamic social life, and plenty of money. His rhetorical style is ornate and comically pompous, recalling the worst of Charles Highway in *The Rachel Papers* but without any of the latter's moments of self-mockery.

The novel is a study in shifting fortunes: Terry's lot in life improves incrementally, and the tone of Gregory's reportage wavers as he watches with incredulity Terry's rise while, at the same time, his own position is rocked by family problems. Eventually Gregory confesses to the reader that most of his claims to sexual, social, and financial success are fabrications. All of the aspects of his personality that he had previously held up for admiration are shown to be outright lies or substantial exaggerations, examples of ostentatious verbal style making up for threadbare reality.

As Gregory's world falls apart, Terry gains in confidence and strength. The negative consequences of his improved self-esteem are eventually confirmed in an incident in which he viciously assaults a decrepit tramp with whom he had repeatedly traded insults and mockery.

Success is a disturbing book. The veneer of a cautionary moral tale fades away quickly, and what remains is an elaborate literary experiment in shifting perspective and narrative deception. Gregory's preening narcissism owes a clear debt to Vladimir Nabokov's *Lolita* (1955) and its classic egotist Humbert Humbert; but unlike Humbert's, Gregory's self-regard collapses to allow a glimpse at the unstable, pathetic figure behind the mask of rhetoric. Terry is an important precursor to Amis's stock figure of the articulate, self-loathing "yob," and his material advancement is clearly shown to be at the expense of his (admittedly erratic) sense of human decency. By the novel's conclusion Terry's character is highly unsympathetic—in fact, he and Gregory are equally contemptible, confirming Amis's preference for the artistry of narrative form at the expense of reader satisfaction.

In 1980 Amis resigned from *The New Statesman* to devote all his time to writing. His fourth novel, *Other People: A Mystery Story* (1981), is in a quite different mode from his earlier work. James Diedrick considers it "one of Amis's most important novels" for its ambitious attempt to make "the familiar hauntingly strange"; Evan Hunter, writing in the 26 July 1981 *New York Times Book Review,* was less impressed, complaining of the novel's "obscurity" and of the "sophomorically philosophical" tone of "this short, bitter book."

In *Other People* the emphasis is on literary style, not narrative clarity. Amis's technique in the novel, in which quotidian events and objects are presented from a radically alienated perspective, has been compared to Craig Raine's poem "A Martian Sends a Postcard Home," though Amis has pointed out that he had been at work on *Other People* for a year before Raine's poem was published. Amis, like Raine, invents a situation that allows him to describe quite ordinary scenes through fresh eyes. The main character's amnesia gives her an innocence akin to an alien perspective that Amis exploits for surprising and comic effects.

The protagonist awakes in a hospital bed to a world utterly unfamiliar to her; she has no idea who she is or why she is in the hospital. Shortly after returning to consciousness she is discharged onto the street with only her clothes and a tattered bag containing a few possessions. She takes the name "Mary Lamb" after overhearing a nursery rhyme and is soon wandering through an unfamiliar city inhabited by a violent, aimless underclass and a bored and idle upper class. Many of the people she encounters seem to recognize in her a strong resemblance to a young woman named Amy Hide, who has disappeared. A police officer, John Dark, is particularly interested in the resemblance, and it becomes clear that he is keeping Mary under surveillance. Through him she learns about Amy's background and personality, eventually regaining familiarity with her surroundings and recapturing some memories. The novel's conclusion is deliberately ambiguous. The story is told by a third-person narrator who at times directly addresses the reader. Although the novel only hints that the narrator is Dark, Amis confirmed the identification in a 1985 interview with John Haffenden in which he called Dark "the narrator and the murderous demon-lover" of Mary Lamb/Amy Hide.

The plot of *Other People* is deliberately vague and unsettling. The novel proceeds without concern for probability or realism. Characters are introduced and abandoned; peripheral figures are thinly drawn and are often scarcely more than stereotypes. Amis's intent is less to explore characters than to explore the narrative possibilities of his tale. In the interview with Haffenden, Amis said that "the novel is the girl's death, and her death is a sort of witty parody of her life." Interruptions by the narrator are constant reminders that Mary inhabits a fictional world. The ambiguous, possibly circular conclusion also points to the literary, rather than the realistic, quality of the novel. The title alludes to Jean-Paul Sartre's play *Huis clos* (1945; translated as *In Camera*, 1946, and as *No Exit*, 1947), in which one of the characters remarks, "Hell is . . . other people." Amis attempts to build a novel from this pessimistic observation; but however one chooses to interpret the

work and its shadowy conclusion, the strength of *Other People* lies in the imaginative re-creation of an amnesiac's encounter with the world.

In 1984 Amis married Antonia Phillips, an American teacher of philosophy. By then he was in the paradoxical situation of having a reputation as a major literary talent without having published a major novel; and as often as he was praised for his verbal artistry and vigorous use of language, he found himself criticized for echoing earlier writers. The spirit of Nabokov presides over Amis's early work; as a consequence, it shares the concerns of that master stylist, for whom literature was a self-referential system unrelated to the social world. It is in this Nabokovian spirit that Amis defended *Other People* in the interview with Haffenden: insisting that the work is formally consistent, he admitted that it is not realistic—"Realism is a footling consideration." The acceptance of this trade-off suggests that the formal niceties of structure, not the strictures of mimesis, preoccupy Amis in his early fiction. As a result, the elevation of formal concerns over narrative plausibility is as great in *Dead Babies* and *Success* as it is in Nabokov's *Lolita* or *Ada* (1969). Perhaps the novels before *Money: A Suicide Note* (1984) should be seen as well-crafted apprenticeship pieces, whereas *Money* is the result of a writer finally comfortable with and in command of his own voice. When Michiko Kakutani, in *The New York Times* (20 August 1981), described *Other People* as a novel written by someone "who has clearly been reading a lot of Nabokov and [Jorge Luis] Borges," she identified a weakness in Amis's writing that disappears with *Money*. The early novels are brilliant and funny—particularly if the reader agrees with Charles Highway that "the nastier a thing is, the funnier it gets"—but they seem slim and insubstantial beside the bulk of *Money*. Perhaps this is because the main character, John Self, is so resolutely unliterary that Amis is able to escape his preoccupation with literary form. In an interview with Janet Ungless for *Newsday* (9 May 1995) Amis said,

> when I was thirty-something I'd written four novels that were all 225 pages long and well made, balanced, a lot of form, decor. I kept thinking this is what the English novel wants. A part of me must have said—and I only realize this in retrospect—I just want out of here a bit. I'm just going to see it my way and not worry too much about the form. It's all to do with shedding constraints. It's just a determination to tell the truth and f–k it if it's upsetting, or embarrassing, or in bad taste.

A tour de force of comic energy, *Money* is an exhausting book that runs at full throttle for nearly four hundred pages. It is exhausting because the narrator, John Self, cannot stop. He cannot stop drinking; he cannot stop smoking; he cannot stop saying things that he knows he will regret; and most of all, he cannot stop moving–flying, driving, walking, running–long enough to reflect on what his actions might mean. As a representative figure of the 1980s variety of conspicuous consumption, Self is a perfect emblem of the worst tendencies of materialism: in a rare moment of insight he comments that he is "addicted to the twentieth century."

Money traces Self's hyperkinetic and degenerate downward spiral. A director of exploitative television commercials for junk food and other disposable consumer products, he attracts the attention of Hollywood with a thirty-minute short subject, *Dean Street*. On a flight from Los Angeles he gets into a conversation with a patrician American, Fielding Goodney, and soon finds himself in a partnership with Goodney to make a feature-length movie titled "Good Money" (later retitled "Bad Money"). Setting up the picture requires Self to fly back and forth between London and New York. In the latter city he is drawn to the bars, pornography shops, and strip clubs of Forty-second Street. On his first trip to New York he meets with Martina Twain, a cultured and intelligent woman who embodies precisely the qualities that Self lacks. On this trip he also receives an anonymous telephone call from a man who is obsessed with the wrongs Self has committed in his life. Each trip to New York will involve both of these figures, one representing an avenue of redemption for Self, the other forcing him to confront his least attractive characteristics.

In London, Self's relationship with his girlfriend, Selina Street, is founded on jealousy, lust, and money rather than love, but Self treats this as unremarkable. His family life is similarly mercenary: Self recounts the day his father presented him with a bill for his childhood. In London he meets Doris Arthur, a writer hired by Goodney to write the screenplay for "Bad Money," and another writer, "Martin Amis," who will become a pivotal figure in the novel.

Back in New York, between drinking binges and visits to Third Avenue massage parlors Self meets with the actors Goodney has lined up for the movie. Amis's satirical eye cannot resist the targets afforded by movie stars, and the four leads for Self's picture are rendered in great detail: Caduta Massi is a fading European beauty, childless and obsessed with children; Butch Beausoleil is blonde and beautiful, stupid and vain; Spunk Davis is a muscular caricature of good health who is drawn to the latest fads; Lorne Guyland is a matinee idol long past his prime, a supreme egomaniac whose delusions of

sexual vigor are belied by his advanced state of physical decrepitude. The caricatures are as broad as any Amis has attempted, yet they seem entirely in place in Self's exaggerated, hyperkinetic narrative. Eventually Arthur delivers a script, but it is a cruel parody of the story Self had envisioned, replacing the hero with a wicked caricature of Self and turning the other characters into pathetic figures. Self is furious, but the principal actors are even more irate. Self flees to London with a flurry of legal threats trailing in his wake. Amis's depiction of moviemaking American-style was based on his experiences during the shooting of *Saturn 3* (1980), a science-fiction movie for which he wrote the screenplay. His script was subjected to so many rewrites that he refers to it as his screenwriting "debit," rather than debut, and he admits that Kirk Douglas, the male star of *Saturn 3,* provided much of the inspiration for the character of Lorne Guyland.

In London, Self contracts with "Martin Amis" to revise the script along the lines of his original concept. With the revised script Self returns to New York and begins rehearsals for the movie. A brief period of happiness and productivity is brought to a halt when Self discovers to his horror that the mysterious phone caller is his partner, Goodney. The movie project is rapidly revealed to be a complicated swindle, and Self is again forced to flee to London. The novel closes with Self, after an unsuccessful suicide attempt, reflecting on his new position: he is without influence, unemployed, bankrupt, and threatened with legal action from the United States.

Money is savage, funny, and brilliant because of the way Self's voice captures the spirit of a decade of greed and excess. Especially in the light of Martina's virtuous example, Self's helplessness in the face of his basest desires makes him a truly sympathetic character. Self is dimly aware of how badly he behaves, but he is incapable of resisting the cheap pleasures of life in the 1980s. The novel earned praise on both sides of the Atlantic and reached a far wider audience than any of Amis's previous works. In *The Washington Post* (24 March 1985) Jonathan Yardley called it "a big, brave book"; in *The New York Times* (15 March 1985) John Gross said it was "a highly original and often dazzling piece of work"; and in *The London Review of Books* (20 September 1984) Ian Hamilton labeled it "one of the key books of the decade." Choosing a wider canvas evidently suited Amis; the looser form allowed for greater comic action, and the theme of materialism running amok brought his satirical eye into sharp focus. The novelist Will Self, who interviewed Amis for the British edition of *Esquire* in 1995, wrote that while Amis's first four novels were "cruel but essentially

Dust jacket for Amis's novel about the rivalry between two writers

local satirical dissections of the English class system," with *Money* he "seemed to go global."

In 1987 Amis published *Einstein's Monsters,* a short-story collection introduced by "Thinkability," an essay on nuclear weapons. The collection demonstrates Amis's interest in social and political issues, especially a newfound concern for the environment and the threat of nuclear war. "Bujak and the Strong Force, or, God's Dice" integrates social commentary with fiction. Bujak fought with the Polish resistance in World War II; Samson, the narrator, lost both sets of grandparents at Auschwitz; Samson's Japanese wife is a survivor of the bombing of Nagasaki. The story uses the metaphors of retaliation and unilateral disarmament to explore Bujak's moral crisis following a grisly attack on his family. Thus a short story about a personal tragedy is tied to the central horrors of the twentieth century. "Insight at Flame Lake" is told through two sets of diary entries: one set is written by Dan, a young schizophrenic; the other is by Dan's uncle, a nuclear scientist. The uncle's entries possess a forced cheerfulness that suggests he is out of his depth in dealing with Dan's condition while Dan's entries become increasingly deluded after he secretly stops taking his medication. In "The Time Disease" a future world

of environmental decay and social polarization serves as the backdrop for a satire on the mania for longevity as the characters try to avoid any excitement or extreme emotions: a life of scrupulous banality and minimal enjoyment is seen as the only way to avoid succumbing to the "time disease." "The Little Puppy That Could" is a fable based on the Greek myth of Andromeda, updated for a postapocalyptic landscape. A hallmark of the future, as Amis imagines it, is the inversion of common-sense notions—an inversion he blames on nuclear weapons. The survivors of a nuclear holocaust try to cope with a mutated, monstrous animal by offering it human sacrifices until a puppy destroys the monster in a heroic act of self-sacrifice. The narrator of "The Immortals" is an undying being who has lived on Earth since shortly after it was formed. He has watched the destructive tendencies of humanity with growing alarm, and with the arrival of nuclear weapons he gives up hope and attempts to die by traveling to the center of Tokyo in time for an atomic attack. He survives the blast and winds up in a remote New Zealand village in which the inhabitants suffer from the delusion that they are immortal. The narrator also has a delusion: that he is not immortal at all but only "a second-rate New Zealand schoolmaster who . . . is now painfully and noisily dying of solar radiation along with everybody else."

Most critics were unhappy with the overly simplistic politics and strident tone of *Einstein's Monsters:* "Amis the author is at war with Amis the nuclear theoretician," said David Lipsky in the *National Review* (20 November 1987). Amis notes in "Thinkability" that his sudden interest in the fate of the Earth was a response to the birth of his first child, Louis, in 1985; a second son, Jacob, was born in the year of the book's publication.

The concerns that surface in *Einstein's Monsters* reappear in Amis's next novel, *London Fields* (1989), which is set in 1999 and filled with millennial angst and apocalyptic portents. The work's depiction of a society in steep decline and an environment ravaged by pollution recalls the pessimistic social commentary of *Money,* but the crisis is rendered more acute by the specter of nuclear war. The triple threat of nuclear annihilation, political crisis, and environmental collapse is, however, only a backdrop to a perverse story of love and murder. The narrator, Samson Young, is a failed American author who is suffering from a twenty-year case of writer's block. He has come to London in the grip of a mysterious illness, hoping to write a final book before he dies. The chapters of *London Fields* alternate between excerpts from Samson's novel in progress and passages from the notebooks he keeps in preparation for the novel. By making Samson an omniscient narrator in his novel but a participant in the events recorded in the notebooks, Amis continues the metafictional playing with novelistic conventions he began in *Money.* The rationale for this narrative sleight of hand is Samson's insistence that he is incapable of making anything up; the events take place before his eyes, and he merely records them.

In a pub called The Black Cross thirty-four-year-old Nicola Six encounters two men, one of whom, she thinks, will be her murderer; the murder will not occur, however, until she sets in motion an elaborate plot to drive him to kill her. Nicola believes that she has the ability to foresee her own death, and the plot of *London Fields* revolves around her efforts to fulfill this vision before her next birthday. She is a self-conscious stereotype of the femme fatale, beautiful and ruthless in her ability to manipulate men. The recruits she meets in The Black Cross are the confidence man Keith Talent and the wealthy, upper-class Guy Clinch. Keith is a less intelligent and less self-aware version of John Self in *Money* although he is just as fixated as Self on money, sex, and alcohol. His one true passion is darts, and some of the novel's richest scenes come from the descriptions of the pubs where his matches are held. With hardly any effort on Nicola's part, Keith becomes her accomplice: the slightest hint of a sexual reward is enough to assure his cooperation.

Guy is at the other end of the class spectrum from Keith, but his wealth and education fail to provide him with any real satisfaction. His wife, Hope, treats him with weary contempt, and his infant son, Marmaduke, takes every opportunity to cause him physical pain. "He wanted for nothing and lacked everything," the narrator of Samson's novel observes. Guy is, thus, susceptible to Nicola's beauty and air of mystery and is willing to help when she asks for money to locate a fictitious child of a friend. Nicola plays the two men off against each other, promising money and sex to Keith and appealing to Guy's clichéd ideals of chivalry and romance to the point where he is willing to sacrifice his marriage for her.

On the night of Keith's big darts tournament Nicola brings about the downfall of her two stooges at the precise moment of her death. Samson is in attendance, horrified but unable to prevent Nicola's plan from reaching fruition. Adding to the symbolic weight of the event, it is Guy Fawkes Day, and there is a solar eclipse. Although the personal catastrophes occur on cue, Amis backs down from the threatened planetary apocalypse.

London Fields is Amis's most ambitious project to date, both in length and in complexity. At times the apocalyptic symbolism threatens to overwhelm the novel, but for the most part the work is Amis at his satirical best. Keith's schemes and Marmaduke's monstrous personality result in inspired comic passages while the contrast between Keith's humble quarters and Guy's mansion is almost Dickensian. Most critics were impressed by the novel's scope and by Amis's characteristically energetic prose. The book was a best-seller in Britain and in North America, and Amis's status as the "rock star of English literature" was confirmed when he was dubbed a "hot writer" and interviewed by Morrison for *Rolling Stone.*

Amis earned still more critical respect with *Time's Arrow; or, The Nature of the Offense* (1991). The novel was short-listed for the prestigious Booker Prize; while it did not win, its inclusion was important to Amis, whose previous two novels had been strong contenders for nomination but had been passed over. (The exclusion of *Money* from the Booker Prize shortlist in 1984 had resulted in an especially violent exchange of opinion in the pages of Britain's newspapers and literary supplements, highlighting both Amis's high profile in the media and the sharp polarity in critical opinion of his work.) *Time's Arrow* is a departure from *Money* and

London Fields and recalls the literary experimentation of Amis's earlier novels. The narrative rests on the conceit that the universe is running in reverse, growing younger with each passing day. The novel does not abandon the social issues that entered Amis's fiction with *Einstein's Monsters,* as the subject of *Time's Arrow* is, ultimately, the moral imponderability of the Holocaust.

The nameless narrator wakes up in a hospital and finds that his consciousness inhabits the body of a man named Tod Friendly, who is oblivious to the narrator's presence. With painstaking attention to detail and a sharp eye for the absurd, Amis exploits the discrepancy between the narrator's observations and the reader's expectations. Although it is essentially a one-joke performance, Amis's inventiveness keeps the narrative device from seeming strained. It helps, too, that Amis wisely chose to make the book quite short, and the brevity leads to a narrative economy that would seem quite alien to readers familiar with *Money* or *London Fields*. Reduced to the status of helpless observer, the narrator is an astute but innocent passenger on a journey backward through the century. The narrator records Tod's painful old age, his retirement, his years as a doctor in upstate New York, his increasingly (that is, decreasingly) frequent affairs with women, and his move to New York City, where he is an orderly in a busy, rundown hospital. Years pass, and in due time Tod boards a ship and sails to Spain, where he spends several months living a nervous, hunted existence in the countryside. His name and his language have changed: he is now called Odilo Unverdorben, and he speaks fluent German. He travels across a war-torn landscape to Germany, where he participates first in the systematic extermination of the Jews at Auschwitz, then in a series of actions against Jews and Gypsies in Poland, and then in the eradication of mentally deficient or deformed children in Germany. He marries, enters medical school, moves home, suffers through World War I, and gradually shrinks away to nothing in the arms of his mother.

While reversing time's arrow creates a stylistic challenge that allows Amis to exploit his gifts for arresting images and clever turns of phrase, it also causes the inversion of the moral order of the world: doctors open wounds, thugs replace teeth with a single punch, and the crematoriums of Auschwitz become the birthplace for a race of people. Many reviewers were troubled by Amis's idiosyncratic "revisionism," wondering if the Holocaust is a suitable subject for literary experimentation. In his defense Amis argued in a 1996 interview with Wachtel that reading *Time's Arrow* requires one to confront the true horror of the Holocaust: "The reader's in the position of rewriting . . . everything that happens to him from his own historical knowledge. . . . the reader has to become a kind of soul or conscience and has to do the moral reordering from his chair." As the reader is forced to reverse Odilo's actions to figure out what is being described, he or she is forced to participate imaginatively in the horror of the Holocaust. The easy comedy of the early part of the book gives way to a discomfort that is intensified by the narrator's inability to comprehend the events around him.

Amis had taken time out from another project to write *Time's Arrow,* and it took him four years to complete what he had called in the *Rolling Stone* interview "a light novel about literary envy." At 375 pages, however, *The Information* (1995) could hardly be classed as a light read. It is a savage and satirical look at London's literary world, featuring two novelists whose friendship disintegrates when one of them becomes a huge success.

After a leaked report revealed that he was seeking an advance of £500,000 for the novel, Amis became the target of speculation and commentary in the British tabloids. That the negotiations were taken over by an American literary agent, Andrew Wylie, only increased the interest of the newspapers. By the end of 1994 Amis had split with his longtime literary agent Pat Kavanagh and had left Jonathan Cape, the publisher of his previous novels, for Flamingo/HarperCollins. Parting with Kavanagh meant parting with the novelist Julian Barnes, Kavanagh's husband and one of Amis's closest friends. Expensive dental work to correct a congenital problem with his teeth also became headline material as Amis the media figure eclipsed Amis the literary novelist. Also during this period Amis was in the process of separating from his wife. Adding to his personal troubles were stories in the tabloids revealing the existence of an illegitimate daughter he had fathered in 1975 and a police report concluding that his cousin Lucy Partington had been among the serial killer Fred West's victims in 1973 (*The Information* is dedicated to Lucy's memory). The death of his father in October 1995 was the last and most difficult blow in a traumatic twelve months; many commentators have noted that, in addition to the personal loss, his father's death deprived Amis of one of the central literary figures against whom he has defined himself. In sum, the period represents an intense, highly public midlife crisis, and Amis was among the first to note that *The Information,* the novel at the center of his *annus horribilis,* features a wickedly funny account of the main character's midlife crisis.

Like *Success, The Information* is a study in contrasts. The novelists Richard Tull and Gwyn Barry, close friends since their Oxford days, are turning forty as the novel opens. Gwyn is about to release a sequel to his best-selling novel *Amelior;* Richard, whose previous four books were unsuccessful, has almost finished his fifth, "Untitled." Richard is convinced that *Amelior* and its sequel are rubbish and views the popularity of the former, and the likely success of the latter, as a cosmic joke directed at him. He resolves to dedicate his energies to making Gwyn's life as unpleasant as possible. All of Richard's plots backfire, with consequences that grow progressively more serious.

Unaware of his friend's activities, Gwyn secures an assignment for Richard to write a profile of him for a respected magazine. He is about to embark on a publicity tour of the United States, and he invites Richard to accompany him. Richard learns just prior to their departure that a New York publisher has accepted "Untitled," and the journey through the United States becomes a study in the contrasting experiences of the successful and the unsuccessful writers. Richard's tour is humiliating; he fails to sell a single book while Gwyn is treated royally and sells out the auditorium every time he gives a reading. After they return to Britain, Richard's plans for revenge grow more urgent and more violent: he arranges with a young hoodlum to have Gywn beaten up. At the same time, his profile of Gwyn grows into a lengthy and detailed character assassination.

As is usual in an Amis novel, much happens away from the main action. Richard's moods and failings are put into the context of a massive midlife crisis, which, for Amis, is caused by knowledge of one's mortality. Much is made of Richard's deteriorating, middle-aged physique, and "the information" of the title includes the dawning certainty that death is inevitable. There are many references to astronomy as the events in Richard's life are measured against a universal scale. The astronomical asides are provided by a shadowy first-person narrator who eventually emerges as Amis himself. The two writers follow their assigned trajectories for the entire course of the novel: Richard fails to dent Gwyn's smug success while Gwyn is rewarded with "the Profundity Requital," a prestigious literary award that bears a suspicious resemblance to the Booker Prize that Amis has found so elusive.

Although *The Information* never approached the success it would have needed to earn back the advance Amis received, the publicity surrounding the negotiations made him, as Mark Lawson put it in *The Guardian* (18 December 1996), "newsworthy in a way no other serious English literary novelist has

managed without the inconvenience of being sentenced to death by an Islamic regime." Amis was interviewed and profiled in many newspapers and magazines, including *Vanity Fair* and the British editions of *Vogue* and *Esquire.* The full scale of the controversy generated by *The Information* is best conveyed by Jonathan Wilson in his article "A Very English Story" (1995). It seems unlikely that anything Amis does in the future will receive the media attention paid to *The Information.*

In addition to fiction Amis has written scores of book reviews; he also regularly has articles published in newspapers and magazines. A brief account of the video-game craze, *Invasion of the Space Invaders,* appeared in 1982. A collection of articles about America was released in 1986; the title, *The Moronic Inferno: And Other Visits to America,* is borrowed from Saul Bellow, who is the subject of the first essay in the book (a compilation of Amis's reviews of two of Bellow's novels) and the last (an interview with Bellow). Also included are pieces written between 1977 and 1985, including a profile of Hugh Hefner, an interview with Norman Mailer combined with a review of Mailer's work, an interview with Gloria Steinem, and a typically observant and pitilessly funny article on Jerry Falwell and the evangelical right. Taken individually, the pieces are insightful and amusing but fairly inconsequential. Collected, they take on an added importance; in them the larger concerns of Amis's fiction appear in embryo. They are like the field notes of a dedicated researcher, and it comes as no surprise to find a passage from one of Amis's Bellow articles recycled verbatim to be spoken by one of the characters in *The Information. Visiting Mrs. Nabokov and Other Excursions* (1993) comprises a dozen literary profiles, a half-dozen celebrity pieces, and another dozen or so articles on such subjects as chess, nuclear weapons, the Frankfurt Book Fair, and snooker. The earliest of the articles dates to 1977; most are from the late 1980s and early 1990s, and they indirectly document the stages in Amis's rise to the status of a celebrity in his own right. His enhanced notoriety is rendered most clearly in a 1992 piece on Madonna, who refused his request to interview her because he was "too famous." Instead Amis reviews her just-released book *Sex* and reflects on the nature of celebrity in a media-saturated, postmodern age. His accounts of playing snooker with Barnes and of his poker night with three other noted writers are windows into the life of a literary celebrity.

A strong autobiographical streak runs through all of Amis's work, fiction and nonfiction. In his novels his characters' concerns have evolved to reflect Amis's changing preoccupations: the late-adolescent cravings of Charles Highway give way to the workaday anxieties of Terry Service; the irresponsible bachelorhood of John Self is replaced by the child-centered worlds of characters in *London Fields* and *The Information*. There are, however, several constants in Amis's fictional universe. He has returned obsessively to the motif of the double—Mary Lamb and Amy Hide, Martin and Martina, Marmaduke and Kim, Keith and Guy, Terry and Gregory, Richard and Gwyn. In the interview with Wachtel, Amis said that his interest in doubles comes from the period of his life when he lived in the shadow of his older brother, Philip (to whom *Success* is dedicated). He recalled that when he was growing up, small differences were perceived as huge disparities; this perception continues to form the foundation of his comic vision. In Amis's fiction conflicting impulses, such as altruism and spite or self-confidence and self-doubt, are magnified and projected into narratives in which they come into conflict, leading to situations that are both comically absurd and unsettlingly familiar to readers in whom such impulses exist in uneasy tension.

Throughout his career Amis has cultivated a morbid fascination with aging and with bodily betrayal. Even the young characters in *The Rachel Papers* and *Dead Babies* are tormented by fears of physical decline; as Adam Mars-Jones points out in the *Times Literary Supplement* (24 March 1995), "a writer who in his twenties considers the body a site of embarrassment and humiliation will have much to write about in his forties." An unholy trinity of thinning hair, bad teeth, and sexual impotence haunts Amis's novels, but it is always treated in an ironic manner in which distress over the effects of aging acts as a punishment for personal vanity. More serious is the trope of decay as applied to the world his characters inhabit—a situation that occurs most powerfully in *London Fields,* where the personal traumas of aging that Samson Young records are intertwined with meditations on the declining state of the planet and the entropic drift of the universe. In *The Information* Richard Tull bears the full force of Amis's distaste for middle age. His features show the effects of years of smoking and drinking, and he is rendered impotent in his sex life as well as in his art. Richard proposes a "history of increasing humiliation" that extends the trope of decline to literature, which at first told stories of gods, then of kings and heroes, then of the gentry, then of the middle class, "then it was about *you*. . . . Then it was about *them:* lowlife, Villains." Literature as a subject is never far from view in Amis's work. It is a prominent feature of every novel, and the majority of his journalism centers on writers and their works. The reverence he

pays to words is evident in the energy he imparts to the metaphors, invented slang, and rhythms that make up his dialogue. He is clearly aware of his tradition, and he signals this awareness to careful readers through a liberal use of allusions and references to and quotations from works by canonical figures from William Shakespeare to Charles Dickens to Rushdie. His first character, Charles Highway, is a self-conscious narrator, and every novel since, with the exception of *Time's Arrow,* has featured a narrator fully aware of the manipulative power of storytelling. Samson Young's ironic refrain "Boy, am I a reliable narrator" suggests the doubleness with which Amis practices and reveals the illusions of fiction.

The weaknesses of Amis's novels—excessively structured plots and an overreliance on caricature are easily tolerated in exchange for the pleasures provided by their comic excesses and energetic wordplay. Mars-Jones's comment about *The Information*—that it is enjoyable "for the ride, if not the view"—could be applied to Amis's work as a whole, suggesting that his chief virtue as a novelist is his inventive and wickedly comic language and that reveling in his prose is more satisfying than examining the often overwrought and excessively bleak scenery that the prose presents, especially in the early novels. The strides Amis has made since *Other People* cannot be overestimated: he "went global," in Will Self's phrase, and his writing benefited from the exercise.

For some years Amis has worked in an apartment that he uses as an office in Westbourne Park, London. He lives with Isabel Fonseca, an American writer, in Regent's Park, a fashionable area of London; their daughter, Fernanda, was born in 1996. In December 1996 he signed a four-book contract with his old publisher, Jonathan Cape, with one book rumored to be his account of the events surrounding the publication of *The Information*. He maintains an uneasy relationship with the rest of Britain's literary community: his novels, shocking in their willingness to deal with disturbing subjects, stood for years in blatant opposition to the decorous mainstream of contemporary British literature. Once cast as a noisy iconoclast, however, Amis is now increasingly viewed as a spokesman for the literary establishment. The enfant terrible label that has dogged him since the early 1970s has become something of an embarrassment. As he told Morrison in the *Rolling Stone* interview, "It slightly alarms me when people call me 'the bad boy of English fiction.' I'm not a boy. I don't mind the 'bad' really. It's the 'boy' that is embarrassing."

In the words of Auberon Waugh, another famous son of a famous novelist, in the *Sunday Telegraph* (23 June 1996):

> Martin Amis is the only superstar in the English literary firmament. Others may make more money, others may seem cleverer in what they write, but he is the only literary novelist with a mass, adulatory following like an up-market pop star. Others may be tempted to feel jealous of him, but he is also their only guarantee that there is a pot of gold at the end of the rainbow, that the literary novel can still bring fame, wealth and beautiful women.

Amis's place in literary history is secure on the strength of *Money* and *London Fields* alone, but his new contract with Cape will give him the opportunity to continue to shock and delight readers and critics into the next millennium.

Interviews:

John Haffenden, "Martin Amis," in *Novelists in Interview,* edited by Haffenden (London: Methuen, 1985), pp. 1–24;

Charles Michener, "Britain's Brat of Letters," *Esquire,* 107 (January 1987): 108–111;

Patrick McGrath, "Interview with Martin Amis," *Bomb* (Winter 1987): 26–29;

Susan Morrison, "The Wit and the Fury of Martin Amis," *Rolling Stone,* no. 578 (17 May 1990): 95–102;

Christopher Bigsby, "Martin Amis," in *New Writing,* edited by Malcolm Bradbury and Judy Cooke (London: Minerva, 1992), pp. 169–184;

Will Self, "Something Amiss in Amis Country," *Esquire: British Edition* (April 1995): 70–76;

Michael Shnayerson, "Famous Amis," *Vanity Fair,* 58 (May 1995): 132–140, 160–162;

Eleanor Wachtel, "Interview," *Malahat Review,* no. 114 (Spring 1996): 43–58;

Nicci Gerrard, "The Year of Living Desperately," *W* (Spring/Summer 1996): 2–9.

References:

James Diedrick, *Understanding Martin Amis* (Columbia: University of South Carolina Press, 1995);

Laura L. Doan, "'Sexy Greedy *Is* the Late Eighties': Power Systems in Amis's *Money* and Churchill's *Serious Money,*" *Minnesota Review,* 34–35 (Spring/Summer 1990): 69–80;

Adam Mars-Jones, *Venus Envy* (London: Chatto & Windus, 1990);

David Moyle, "Beyond the Black Hole: The Emergence of Science Fiction in the Recent Work of Martin Amis," *Extrapolation,* 36, no. 4 (1995): 305–313;

Richard Todd, "The Intrusive Author in British Postmodern Fiction: The Case of Alisdair Gray and Martin Amis," in *Exploring Postmodernism,* edited by Matei Calinescu and Douwe Fokkema (Amsterdam & Philadelphia: Benjamins, 1987), pp. 123–137;

Jonathan Wilson, "A Very English Story," *New Yorker,* 71 (6 March 1995): 96–106.

Iain Banks
(16 February 1954 –   )

Tim Middleton
University College of Ripon & York, St. John

BOOKS: *The Wasp Factory* (London: Macmillan, 1984; Boston: Houghton Mifflin, 1984);

Walking on Glass (London: Macmillan, 1985; Boston: Houghton Mifflin, 1986);

The Bridge (London: Macmillan, 1986; New York: St. Martin's Press, 1986);

Consider Phlebas, as Iain M. Banks (London: Macmillan, 1987; New York: St. Martin's Press, 1987);

Espedair Street (London: Macmillan, 1987; New York: St. Martin's Press, 1987);

The Player of Games, as Iain M. Banks (London: Macmillan, 1988; New York: St. Martin's Press, 1989);

Canal Dreams (London: Macmillan, 1989; Garden City, N.Y.: Doubleday, 1991);

The State of the Art, as Iain M. Banks (Willimantic, Conn.: M. V. Ziesing, 1989; London: Orbit, 1991);

The Use of Weapons, as Iain M. Banks (London: Macdonald, 1990; New York: Bantam, 1992);

The Crow Road (New York: Scribners, 1992; London: Abacus, 1992);

Against a Dark Background, as Iain M. Banks (London: Orbit, 1993; New York: Bantam, 1993);

Complicity (London: Little, Brown, 1993; New York: Talese/Doubleday, 1995);

Feersum Endjinn, as Iain M. Banks (London: Orbit, 1994; New York: Bantam, 1995);

Whit; or, Isis amongst the Unsaved (London: Little, Brown, 1995; New York: Bantam, 1997);

Excession, as Iain M. Banks (London: Orbit, 1996; New York: Bantam, 1997);

A Song of Stone (London: Abacus, 1997; New York: Villard, 1998).

Iain Banks's fiction captures the complexities of subjectivity and locale. At its best his writing offers insights into the tensions of masculine identity in a competitive consumerist culture. His prose can be vibrant, flexible, and stylish. It can catch idiosyncrasies without turning them into stereotypes, evoke complexity through nuances rather than omniscient

Iain Banks (photograph © 1984 by Jerry Bauer)

intervention, and create narratives that are both technically sophisticated and compelling to read. Banks is an author whose works are both critically acclaimed and popular in the marketplace. In 1993 he was listed by *Granta* magazine as one of the twenty "Best Young British Novelists," and his fiction regularly appears in the best-seller lists. In recent years Banks has begun to receive attention from academic critics, and increasingly his works are on reading lists at many universities.

Iain Menzies Banks was born on 16 February 1954 in the Scottish town of Dunfermline and until the age of nine lived in the village of North Queensferry in a house with views of the Forth Rail Bridge, a structure which features in *The Bridge* (1986). His father worked in the Admiralty, and his mother was at one time a professional ice-skater. Although Banks was an only child his parents came from large Scots families, and he has numerous relatives. In 1963 the family moved to the west-coast town of Gourock, and in 1972 Banks went to Stirling University, where he studied English literature, philosophy, and psychology. During the vacations he worked as a hospital porter, estate worker, pier porter, road worker, dustman, and gardener; the experiences gleaned from four years of what he later called "wee daft jobs and travelling" doubtless inform his ability to capture the traits and idiosyncrasies of a diverse range of people. One of these jobs, as a technician for British Steel at their Nigg Bay site near Inverness in northeast Scotland, provided him with the landscape that features in *The Wasp Factory* (1984). Another job, for IBM in Greenock, may account for his knowledge of early computer systems, which forms a part of *The Crow Road* (1992). In 1980 he traveled south to England in search of employment and worked as a clerk in a London law firm; something of these years appears in the convincing evocation of North London in *Walking on Glass* (1985).

While *The Wasp Factory,* which burst on the literary scene in 1984 to considerable acclaim and much outrage, is Banks's first published novel, it is worth noting that Banks had in fact been writing since the mid 1970s. As Thom Nairn notes, *The Wasp Factory* is actually "the seventh [novel] he had written but the first he had revised." Many of his early fictions were developed from outlines written in this period; a version of *The Player of Games* (1988), for example, was written before *The Wasp Factory* and came close to being accepted for publication in 1979.

Banks moved back to Scotland in 1988 and now lives in North Queensferry. In March of 1997 he was awarded an honorary D.Litt. by the University of St. Andrews.

The Wasp Factory is an antibildungsroman detailing the childhood and adolescence of Frank Cauldhame, who lives on an island in the Moray Firth. Frank's story is told through his first-person narration and sequences of recollection in which it is revealed that he has killed two cousins and his younger brother. The novel is also a thriller concerning the escape and impending return to the island of Frank's half brother, Eric, from a secure mental institution. The novel ends with Eric's destructive homecoming and the revelation that Frank is in fact Frances—that his father's hatred of women has led him to disguise the fact that he has a daughter. On an initial reading one is faced with a gleefully anarchic book about a dysfunctional childhood told with immense conviction. The denouement forces a second reading that brings out several ironies and ultimately calls into question the veracity of Frank/Frances's narration.

The novel incorporates several themes and stylistic quirks that recur in Banks's later works. Through the linked stories of Frank and Eric, Banks examines the relationship between normalcy and obsessive madness. The Cauldhame brothers are the first of many examples of Banks's interest in the deviant double, that venerable theme of Scottish fiction. In this text the theme is overlaid with a sibling rivalry plot that appears again in later works. *The Wasp Factory* offers a tour de force of characterization that focuses on the ways in which the individual is constructed by a cultural milieu, an issue to which Banks's fiction returns time and again. The mixing and subversion in the novel of literary genres and modes such as the bildungsroman, family saga, Gothic thriller, and murder mystery are part of what has become Banks's characteristic eclecticism. Much of the anarchic energy of Banks's writing seems to derive from a desire to push back the boundaries of what is acceptable in fiction: in addition to the lavish descriptions of Frank's violence and Eric's madness-inducing encounter with a maggot-infested dead baby, the book also contains accounts of defecation and vomiting.

The Wasp Factory has a strong absurdist comic dimension that should stop readers from taking its horrors too seriously. But the tendency among commentators is to gloss over the comic aspects of the novel, suggesting that the book has been widely misread. There is nothing to indicate that readers should believe Frank's versions of events; indeed all the evidence suggests that the Cauldhames are, at best, unstable and prone to obsessive behavior or, at worst, fundamentally unbalanced and pathological liars. The novel provides much evidence of how adept Frank is at disguising his part in the murders of his relatives. Readers may begin to wonder whether Frank is trying to seem more deranged than he actually is and whether the "murders" are all wish fulfillment: the children may die, but Frank's assumption that he has caused their deaths could be just one more example of his desire to control his environment.

This hypothesis is given further support by the fact that Banks has Frank provide a wealth of detail about each murder, detail that paradoxically helps undermine the credibility of Frank's account. For example, the killing of Blyth involves an adder, a snake notoriously sensitive to noise, and yet the

PRAISE FOR IAIN BANKS

'His technical facility with language now matches his instinct for story-telling, and the combination makes him one of the best British novelists'
Guardian

'[Banks] may be a classic story-spinner, purveyor of the proverbial Good Read: but in among all the contrasts, the genre-hopping and the fun, there's a small, serious common purpose to his work'
Scotsman

'The most imaginative British novelist of his generation ... An exceptional talent'
The Times

'A Nineties' Robert Louis Stevenson at ease with fashion and faxes but still writing breathless adventure stories that never ignore the injustices and moral conundrums of the real world'
Independent on Sunday

'Currents of dark wit swirl through Banks' writing, enriching its buoyancy ... and like Graham Greene, he can readily open the reader's senses to the "foreign-ness" of places'
Scotland on Sunday

WHIT   IAIN BANKS

IAIN BANKS
WHIT

Dust jacket for Banks's novel about a woman caught up in a religious cult

reader is supposed to believe that Frank has not disturbed it, despite making machine-gun noises "for ages" in the enclosed space of a disused gun emplacement before he notices its presence. The reader is also expected to take seriously the attack of a rabbit, an episode clearly modeled on the absurd rabbit attack scene in the movie *Monty Python and the Holy Grail* (1975). Finally, Frank's narrative is a retrospective one, yet he manages to keep control of the secret behind his narration; in other words the whole novel is based on an elaborate hoax since Frances narrates as Frank and so disguises the truth about her identity.

Most reviewers focused on the violence in the novel, and only recently, as Banks's work has been given more considered treatment, have accurate appraisals appeared. Richard Todd argues that Banks uses excess in the novel to explore the ways in which fiction can "impose sense on senselessness," while Nairn argues that it is a story about Scottish masculinity.

The problems of narrative indeterminacy are also to the fore in Banks's second novel, *Walking on Glass*. As Ronald Binns has argued, the novel owes much to Mervyn Peake's Gormenghast novels (1946–1959) both in its mood and in some of its locations. The book opens with the story of art student Graham Park, who is studying at a college in North London in the early 1980s. Park is friendly with the flamboyantly gay Richard Slater and hope-

lessly in love with Slater's friend Sara Ffitch. Uninterested in Park's attentions, Sara is unhappily married and having an affair with a man called Stock. The story develops into a tale of deceptions designed to disguise an incestuous relationship: Slater is bisexual and Sara is his sister and lover, while Stock is simply a fiction designed by the lovers to mislead the private detectives employed by Sara's husband. In this story Banks is again concerned with siblings and also with the tensions of being normal versus pursuing potentially destructive desires.

The second narrative thread in *Walking on Glass* is the tale of Steven Grout, a paranoid young man who believes that he has been a warrior in "the ultimate war, the final confrontation between Good and Evil," but because of an unspecified act of betrayal he has been "ejected from the real battle ground to languish here, in this cesspit they called a 'life.'" Grout's story allows Banks some fun at the expense of the British social-security system and connects with the Slater narrative when Grout is knocked down by the motorbike that Slater rides while pretending to be Stock. Following the accident, Grout ends up in a psychiatric hospital that has many points of similarity with the milieu featured in the third strand of the narrative. This strand is the story of a woman called Ajayi and a man called Quiss, two warriors from a battle zone who have been aged and sent to a crumbling castle as punishment for some unspecified transgression.

There they must play several games whose rules they have to discover by trial and error. When each game has been completed they are given another chance to answer a riddle: "What happens when an unstoppable force meets an immovable object?" If they answer the riddle correctly, they will escape the castle. This riddle appears on a matchbox in Grout's hospital, a place that still houses some patients from the time of World War I. Ajayi and Quiss's world does connect with Earth, as Quiss discovers by using a kind of virtual-reality machine through which it is possible to enter the minds of people on the planet; at one point Quiss witnesses the accident that leads to Grout's hospitalization.

The novel is obsessively intra- and intertextual in its narrative organization, generating a compelling complexity. The castle Quiss and Ajayi inhabit is made of books, and at the end of the final section in which they appear Ajayi begins reading a book that has the same beginning as *Walking on Glass*. This device and all the other points of connection between the three stories give the book a high degree of cohesiveness. The novel also parades a wide range of literary connections, including Douglas Adams's *The Hitchhiker's Guide to the Galaxy* (1979), Franz Kafka, Jorge Luis Borges, and Samuel Beckett. In the manipulation of Park there are echoes of the work of John Fowles, notably *The Magus* (1965).

The novel is unusual in Banks's canon for its use of third-person narration throughout the text; the narrative is focalized through the main characters, and this focalization promotes sympathy for their predicaments—Park's unrequited love, Grout's paranoia, and Ajayi and Quiss's entrapment—while also maintaining a level of uncertainty as to the characters' motivations. Characterization is effective if rather schematic (the tripartite narrative does not really lend itself to sustained character development), and with Sara, Banks attempts to portray the sexy, strong-willed, and ultimately destructive femme fatale, a type that he develops in many of his later fictions.

Most critical commentators (and Banks himself) view *The Bridge* (1986) as his most technically accomplished work. The novel is structurally similar to *Walking on Glass* in that its narrative yokes together a carefully evoked real-world setting and a Kafkaesque dystopia, in this case one set on a gigantic version of the Forth Rail Bridge. The story of the rise of a working-class Glaswegian, Lennox, to commercial success in Edinburgh during the 1970s and 1980s is interlaced with the story of the life of Leonard Orr on the bridge. Orr's story is dreamed by Lennox as he lies in a coma following an accident on the Forth Road Bridge. As in much of Banks's work,

the linking of fantasy with reality in the novel suggests a version of Scottish identity which seems close to what the critic G. Gregory Smith called "Caledonian antisyzygy" in his *Scottish Literature: Character and Influence* (1919). Smith argues that Scottish literature frequently juxtaposes genres and moods that appear to be totally opposed. This idea, popularized by Hugh MacDiarmid and still influential in critical assessments of Scottish writing today, has many resonances in Banks's work.

Lennox's journey from the dystopia of his unconscious as Orr back to consciousness as Lennox in an equally dystopian Edinburgh of the 1980s puts him in the roles of psychiatric patient, lover, prisoner, and storyteller. Interspersed with Orr's experiences on the bridge are several other narratives; most of these are faked dreams that Orr makes up for his analyst, but others, notably one that concerns the adventures of a Scottish barbarian out of a swords-and-sorcery novel, are Orr's "real" dreams. These sequences operate as further clues to understanding Lennox, and when set in the context of the rise-to-riches story of Lennox's real-world life, the story of Lennox's failure to change can be viewed as a critique of masculinity. His coma dreams allow him to revisit aspects of his "real" life, but when he awakens he plans to remain broadly the same. Given Lennox's intractability there is little that is positive about the ending of the novel, but this is Banks's point. That Lennox is not going to change is part of what the novel identifies as the problem of how contemporary culture constructs masculinity.

Other critics have argued that Lennox's narrative is essentially a romance and that the closure provided in the novel offers the consoling fiction of resolution and wholeness which for much of the text has been called into question. This argument is undermined by Banks's elaborate use of intertextuality in the novel as a means of making relative the authority of all its discourses. From the contents page, with its use of geological, rhetorical, medical, and musical terms, through the persistent use of diverse systems of signification—ranging from movies to politics to pop music—*The Bridge* insists that meaning is to be found outside the text. The rounded closure of the novel (rounded by Banks's standards at least) is thus deliberately undercut by that section being entitled "Coda," which in music refers to a short section added after the natural ending of a composition to create an artificial sense of closure. This kind of playfulness is evident throughout the text and underscores the way in which reality is constructed by and mediated through competing discourses.

The burgeoning field of Iain Banks criticism has generally adopted Banks's own enthusiasm for the novel. Reviewers and interviewers also routinely point to it as central to Banks's status as a serious, technically adroit, and intellectually challenging writer. Though *The Bridge* is the best of the early Banks, it has yet to escape from an at times too self-consciously deliberate use of intertextuality to evoke the postmodern condition. In *The Crow Road* and *Complicity* (1993) Banks's narrative technique is just as accomplished as it is in *The Bridge*, but in the later novels the textual strategies are employed without obvious knowingness.

Walking on Glass and *The Bridge* cemented Banks's reputation as a writer working at the cutting edge of British fiction in the 1980s. *Espedair Street* (1987) was something of a step backward in terms of narrative complexity. The novel tells the story of Daniel Weir, a retired rock musician who lives in a churchlike building in a district of Glasgow. Weir lives under the assumed name of James Hay (a jokey reworking of the Scots greeting "Hey Jimmy"), and the action of the novel largely consists of sequences of Weir's retrospective narration detailing the rise and fall of his band Frozen Gold and charting his various unsuccessful relationships. As in *The Bridge* the story is that of a working-class boy who makes it only to discover that in doing so he has become cut off from the community which socialized him. In the end Weir deals with his isolation by giving away all his wealth and heading north in search of his childhood sweetheart. While the happy ending of *The Bridge* was carefully set up as faked, the ending of *Espedair Street* accepts the sentimental myth that returning home fixes everything. The ending is harmlessly anodyne but as such blunts anything which Banks might wish to say through Weir's story about how desire, identity, and socialization are related. In terms of Banks's development as a writer the novel is most notable for his extensive use of retrospective narrative interspersed with Weir's contemporary experiences. By this stage in his career this technique has become central to Banks's writing.

Between the publication of *Espedair Street* and *The Crow Road* in 1992 Banks published three science-fiction works and the thriller *Canal Dreams* (1989). The science-fiction novels produced in this period—*The Player of Games*, *The State of the Art* (1989), and *The Use of Weapons* (1990)—are all readily linked in both thematic and technical terms to the best of Banks's non-science-fiction work, whereas *Canal Dreams* is generally accepted as his least successful mainstream work.

The central character of *Canal Dreams* is a Japanese cellist, Hisako Onada, whose fear of flying means that she has to travel by sea to undertake a European concert tour. En route, the ship she is on gets caught up in a political crisis in Panama, and for some weeks she is trapped on the canal. The political situation deteriorates, and the ship is taken over by what appear at first to be revolutionaries but are in fact CIA-backed counterrevolutionaries. The action becomes increasingly frenetic as the gunmen annihilate the crew and then gang-rape Onada. Her martial arts training allows her to escape from captivity and to wreak revenge on her captors.

While Onada's upbringing and life in Japan are carefully evoked through flashbacks and her capacity for violence is prefigured in several violent dreams, her transformation into a female Rambo strains credulity. The novel veers between a potentially subtle analysis of the impact of American capitalist corruption on Japanese society and a crude account of American dealings with Latin American countries. In its exploration of Onada the novel tries to raise issues about the psychological impact of the nuclear bombing of Hiroshima and Nagasaki, but the death by fire that Onada deals out in the end is a weak retribution.

In *The Crow Road* Banks returns to form with a complex, multilayered novel that tackles profound issues about nationhood, community, and identity. The novel tells many stories, most notably Prentice McHoan's attempts to piece together the events of his long-lost (actually dead) Uncle Rory's life from the scrappy evidence of Rory's work-in-progress, "The Crow Road." Prentice tells his own story while the remainder of the novel offers a third-person narrative detailing the related stories of the McHoans, the Urvills, and the Watts. The book links the story of these families and the history of the imaginary Scottish west-coast town of Gallanach with the history of Europe from 1948 to the fall of the Berlin Wall in 1989. The novel has its share of Banksian black humor, most notably the opening chapter, in which Prentice's grandmother's pacemaker explodes during her cremation. *The Crow Road* is not just a family saga but also a contemporary bildungsroman about the maturation of Prentice McHoan and a murder mystery about what happened to his Uncle Rory; part of its strength arises from its mixing of genres.

The novel is further evidence of Banks's ability to handle a multilayered narrative to open up the parameters of the male psyche. Prentice McHoan is Banks's most complete male character outside his science fiction: in part his credibility stems from the way Banks has saturated Prentice's narrative with references to the youth culture of the 1980s. Prentice's obsessive and unrequited love for Verity

Walker is well evoked, as are scenes of pub talk and the dubious joys of student flat life. The main character is not the only center of interest—a clear advance over Banks's earlier works. Some of the strongest characters in the novel can be seen as reworkings of types presented in earlier fictions—Ashley Watt combines elements of Andrea Crammond from *The Bridge,* and the feisty sexual and social independence of Sma in *The Use of Weapons.* Fergus is a darker version of Lennox in *The Bridge* while the wandering Rory has elements of the Daniel Weir character in *Espedair Street*—not least of which is his involvement with a divorcée with a daughter—and also embodies another of Banks's critical takes on the mind-set of the late 1960s and early 1970s.

Banks's major achievement in *The Crow Road* is the evocation of place; the creation of the imagined small town of Gallanach (a simplified version of the west-coast town of Oban moved a few miles south) is marvelously done. Banks takes a real landscape with particular historical significance for Scottish identity and builds on it, often with ironic results. Banks's use of the Scottish landscape and of Scottish culture has tended to be ignored. David Daiches's authoritative *New Companion to Scottish Culture* (1993) in its one reference to Banks suggests that Scottish subjects do not "loom large" in his work. *The Crow Road* clearly illustrates the misreading inherent in such remarks; the book can literally be used as a guide to the region of Argyll between the village of Lochgair and the fishing port of Crinan, but this landscape is far more than a mere backdrop. Of particular significance is the placing of Fergus Urvill's castle close to the Dark Age fort of Dalraida, the site where the Scots as a race first arrived from Ireland in A.D. 503 under the leadership of one Fergus mac Erc. Banks's Fergus—in a jokey revisionism—is revealed to be a self-centered thug who hides his true identity behind a veneer of respectability and conspicuous consumption: he is one of Banks's more memorable Tory villains.

Through its carefully evoked setting *The Crow Road* explores identities rooted in a specifically Scottish community that has depth and historical coherence. In this the novel can be seen as part of that wider trend in Scottish culture in the 1980s and 1990s described by Cairns Craig as the "struggle to reconstruct a mythic identity that is particular to Scotland," a struggle shaped by the political intention "to redeem us from the banality of a universal economism that would make us indistinguishable from everyone who lives in a modern industrial state."

Of course the reality of Gallanach is ultimately an effect of narration, and in this novel of storytell-ers readers must be cautious about accepting any narrative as a means of giving access to the truth. Both Kenneth's fictions and Rory's work-in-progress are concerned with "the Subjectivity of Truth," and this idea links their writing with Prentice's adolescent search for Truth (for example, his turn to religion to explain such things as the cruelly early death of Ashley's artist brother, Darren) and his quest for the truth about Rory's disappearance. The idea that truth is subjective—a product of the discourses which shape our beliefs and values—also connects with Kenneth's atheism, with Hamish McHoan's weird version of Christianity, and with Lewis's comedy of recognition. The novel strongly evokes a millennial sense of the failure of any single narrative to capture truth. The complex narration of *The Crow Road,* and in particular the playful relationship between the novel and Rory's work-in-progress, means that even as readers become immersed in the plot they are forced to see the ways in which the novel's events are fictions: narratives which present only partial truths.

The underlying complexity of *The Crow Road* has not been generally acknowledged. The book tackles "big" philosophical issues about attitudes toward death, the role of religion in a postmodern culture, and the pressures of living in a rapidly changing world. But many reviewers appear to see only the popular writing.

After the gentle profundity of *The Crow Road,* Banks's twelfth novel, *Complicity,* marks a turn back to the murderousness seen in works such as *Canal Dreams* and *The Wasp Factory.* The novel's central character is Cameron Colley, a sleazy Edinburgh journalist whose first-person narrative is interspersed with sequences of second-person narration which graphically describe the murders of establishment and business leaders, some of whom Colley is investigating. The killer is eventually revealed to be Colley's friend Andy Gould, a former soldier and onetime yuppie entrepreneur with a grudge against the establishment. As was the case with *Canal Dreams* and *The Crow Road,* Banks uses the thriller format to explore the relationship between self and society, and specifically (and far more explicitly than with Lennox in *The Bridge*) Gould's story is a vehicle for a savage critique of the mind-set engendered by Thatcherite Britain.

The sequence of murders graphically described in the novel's second-person narration makes for a bleak view of a society bereft of moral values. The grotesque violence in the novel should not be read as a sign of artistic failure but rather as evidence of a deliberate attempt to reveal a culture's deepest anxieties. In the double life of Gould the theme of identity as fabrication is again to the fore, and *Complicity* can be read as a critique of the kind of masculinity promoted by 1980s culture. The novel clearly seeks to open up issues of masculinity and violence by juxtaposing the materialist individualism of 1980s commercialism—Gould's Gadget Shop business—and the obsessive egocentrism of his serial killing. The novel also plays off Colley's journalistic persona as a hard-drinking, Tory-hating, coke-snorting, computer-gaming, good-time boy with his paralysis in the face of real violence experienced in his brief stint as a foreign correspondent during the Gulf War and as the victim of Andy's machinations.

The novel was generally regarded as a return to the shock tactics of *The Wasp Factory,* and for some its politics were too overbearing. In one of the few academic commentaries to be published to date Richard Todd praises *Complicity* for giving "the by now conventional idea of postmodernist self-reflexiveness an original twist by suggesting that the real complicity is between those who connive at society's ills not simply by allowing them to happen, but by reading about them in—and writing about them for—the media."

After the excellence of his writing in the early 1990s, Banks's more recent fiction has been disappointing. Banks's mainstream novel, *Whit; or, Isis amongst the Unsaved* (1995), is enjoyable but lacks both the intellectual depth of some of his earlier work and the cultural breadth of later fictions such as *The Crow Road.*

Whit depicts the experiences of Isis Whit, a resourceful young woman with the kind of independence found in the women of Banks's science fiction (but without their sexual appetites). Isis is the retrospective narrator of the novel, and her narration mixes recollections of her childhood with discussion of the founding and development of the Luskentyrian sect to which she belongs. The main action of the novel concerns Isis's search for her cousin Morag and the (ultimately interrelated) discovery that the religious cult in which she has spent her entire life is founded on lies and fabrications.

Cousin Morag is caught up with just one of the many lies that Isis decodes but is also a key to the kind of solution Isis needs to find in order to deal with the male dominance of the cult and its use of her as "the Beloved" who will be the focus of its Leap Year fertility festival. Morag is supposed to be a musician, earning respect for the cult in the wider world, but Isis's investigations reveal that she is a pornographic-movie star famed for fellatio. Morag is intended to serve as a contrast to Isis—both are women whose sex is a commodity controlled by men—and the novel is ultimately concerned with how women deal with the power relations of patriarchy. Morag is set up as someone who is subverting those relations for her own ends (she plans to retire from the sex industry and set up her own business), while Isis's investigations give her the knowledge that allows her to take over the cult and (the implication is) run it in a slightly less hypocritical way. Aside from the two younger women there are many other strong female characters: Isis's grandmother, Zhobelia, is shown to have been the true visionary whose experiences provided the cult's founder, Salvador, with its theology; her Aunt Yolanda, an aging but hard-living Texas party girl, is a match for all who cross her path. Finally, there is Isis's best friend, Sophi Woodbean, to whom Isis turns for comfort in the crisis occasioned by her brother's treachery and her grandfather's supposedly divinely approved plan to commit incest with her. There are moments in the text where it is implied that the virginal Isis may have lesbian tendencies, but these hints are never expanded: as the narration is focalized through Isis the reader might be tempted to ask what she has to hide, but in this case she is not an unreliable narrator, just an innocent one.

The technophile Banks creates a splendidly technophobic cult, and much of the novel's humor stems from Isis's encounters with modernity in the course of her quest. Banks also has fun creating the cult's hybrid cuisine—a mixture of Scottish and Asian foods such as "Haggis Pakora" and "skink aloo, porridge tarka, shell pie aloo gobi . . . chips peas pulao." Central to the novel is the comic deflation of religious excess: The Luskentyrian sect is revealed as little more than a means for its founder (Isis's grandfather) to live a relatively easy life as a bigamist. As in *The Crow Road* one generation discovers the hidden secrets of another, but this novel lacks the profundity of the earlier work. The comic deflation of religious excess is enjoyable but an easy target, and the politics in the novel are ultimately confused. Morag's involvement in the sex industry is handled in a rather "laddish" way: it is never clear whether she is meant as someone to be pitied or to be seen as slyly subversive.

The strengths of the novel lie in its plotting—the gradual revelation that all is not right with the sect and that its version of its history is faked all come through Isis, and thus there is the interesting spectacle of a believer being brought to unbelief by her own investigations. The novel also makes use of real Scottish landscapes—notably the sect's latter-day headquarters at a farm on the banks of the River Forth some miles northwest of the town of Stirling and its initial home in the village of Luskentyre on the west coast of the Isle of Harris in the

Outer Hebrides—and also draws upon real and imagined locations from England. In depicting Isis's journey down the River Forth to Edinburgh, Banks has reworked a journey which he made in the summer of 1994.

In many ways the novel can be ranked alongside *Canal Dreams* or *Espedair Street* as an accomplished, enjoyable, but ultimately undemanding work. That Banks's two mainstream attempts to write a novel with a credible woman character at their center have been only partial successes does not mean that he cannot create coherent and believable women. One only has to look at his science fiction to see that this is far from true. What it does suggest is that in order to be credible within the real-world setting of his mainstream texts his women characters have to be placed under constraints of realism that do not apply in his science-fiction texts.

A Song of Stone (1997), Banks's most recent novel, does little to suggest a return to the form of the early 1990s. The novel is set in a dystopian future in which Britain has descended into postwar anarchy. The central characters, an aristocratic couple named Abel and Morgan, flee their castle stronghold as a band of mercenaries approaches, only to be captured and brought back. Their captors are led by a charismatic woman known simply by her title of lieutenant. The aristocrats share a dark secret: they are incestuous lovers. During their captivity they experience powerlessness and are brutally treated. The novel is narrated in the first person by Abel in a rich, often overblown prose that contrasts markedly with the brutality of the lieutenant and her mercenary band. Although there are dramatic elements, including a raid on a nearby farm, most of the action is psychological; as the narrative unfolds, the secrets of the castle and its inhabitants are gradually revealed. The novel ends with much violence; the brutal killing of the lieutenant recalls some of the excesses of Banks's first novel.

A Song of Stone was poorly received, with many commentators suggesting that it was little more than an overdeveloped short story. Most reviewers missed the ways Banks carefully uses the classical four elements—earth (in this case, stone), air, fire, and water—as motifs within this tale of decadence and degeneracy. In yoking together an elaborately literary narration and a carefully wrought system of imagery within a thriller framework, Banks again insisted on offering a hybrid fiction that left many reviewers puzzled.

Banks has recently signed a new four-book deal with his publishers and has collaborated with Gary Lloyd in the production of an abridged CD version of *The Bridge* with musical accompaniments for Codex Records. After the success of the 1996 BBC television adaptation of *The Crow Road* there are plans for movie versions of *Complicity* and *The Player of Games*. A movie version of *The Wasp Factory* is also rumored to be under consideration. Iain Banks's work is covered by a reliable, though unofficial, web site called *Culture Shock* which contains a wealth of interviews and related Banks material.

Interviews:

James Robertson, "Bridging Styles: A Conversation with Iain Banks," *Radical Scotland,* 42 (December 1989/January 1990): 26–27;

Stan Nicholls, "Cultural Difference," *Interzone,* 86 (August 1994): 22–23;

Oliver Morton, "A Cultured Man," *Wired* (June 1996): 46–48.

References:

Lucie Armitt, "Drifting in and out of the Unconscious: Lessing's *Briefing* and Banks's *The Bridge,*" in *Theorising the Fantastic* (London: Arnold, 1996), pp. 89–118;

Ronald Binns, "Castles, Books and Bridges: Mervyn Peake and Iain Banks," *Peake Studies,* 2, no. 1 (1990): 5–12;

Cairns Craig, *Out of History: Narrative Paradigms in Scottish & British Culture* (Edinburgh: Polygon, 1996);

David Daiches, *New Companion to Scottish Culture* (Edinburgh: Polygon, 1993);

Tim Middleton, "Constructing the Contemporary Self: The Works of Iain Banks," in *Contemporary Writing & National Identity,* edited by Tracey Hill and William Hughes (Bath: Sulis Press, 1995), pp. 18–28;

Thom Nairn, "Iain Banks & the Fiction Factory," in *The Scottish Novel Since the Seventies,* edited by Gavin Wallace and Randall Stevenson (Edinburgh: Edinburgh University Press, 1993), pp. 127–135;

Richard Todd, *Consuming Fictions* (London: Bloomsbury, 1996), pp. 131–163.

Julian Barnes
(19 January 1946 –   )

Merritt Moseley
University of North Carolina at Asheville

See also the Barnes entry in *DLB Yearbook: 1993.*

BOOKS: *Metroland* (London: Cape, 1980; New York: St. Martin's Press, 1980);

Duffy, as Dan Kavanagh (London: Cape, 1980; New York: Pantheon, 1986);

Fiddle City, as Kavanagh (London: Cape, 1981; New York: Pantheon, 1986);

Before She Met Me (London: Cape, 1982; New York: McGraw-Hill, 1986);

Flaubert's Parrot (London: Cape, 1984; New York: Knopf, 1985);

Putting the Boot In, as Kavanagh (London: Cape, 1985);

Staring at the Sun (London: Cape, 1986; New York: Knopf, 1987);

Going to the Dogs, as Kavanagh (London: Viking, 1987; New York: Pantheon, 1987);

A History of the World in 10 1/2 Chapters (London: Cape, 1989; New York: Knopf, 1989);

Talking It Over (London: Cape, 1991; New York: Knopf, 1991);

Bodlivo Svinche, translated by Dmitrina Kondeva (Sofia, Bulgaria: Izd-vo Obsidian, 1992); original English version published as *The Porcupine* (London: Cape, 1992; New York: Knopf, 1992);

Letters from London: 1990–1995 (London: Picador, 1995); republished as *Letters from London* (New York: Vintage, 1995);

Cross Channel (London: Cape, 1996; New York: Knopf, 1996).

TRANSLATION: Volker Kriegel, *The Truth about Dogs* (London: Bloomsbury, 1988).

Julian Barnes is one of the most celebrated and most variously rewarding of Britain's younger writers—that is, those who were born in the late 1940s and began publishing in the late 1970s or the 1980s, a group that also includes Martin Amis and Ian McEwan. The author of seven novels under his own name—*Flaubert's Parrot* (1984) and *A History of the*

Julian Barnes (photograph by Jillian Edelstein)

World in 10 1/2 Chapters (1989) are probably the ones best known in the United States—he has also published four exceptional detective novels under the pseudonym "Dan Kavanagh" and a book of short stories. Furthermore, he is a busy and knowledgeable journalist. From 1990 to 1995 he was the London correspondent for *The New Yorker,* contributing the "Letter from London" column every few months on topics such as the royal family and the quirkier side of British politics. These pieces, which were published in book form in 1995, demonstrate his skill as an interpreter of British culture to a foreign audience; in his other writings he has often been an interpreter of, or guide to, France for his own countrymen.

Barnes's fiction has been acclaimed by readers as different as Carlos Fuentes and Philip Larkin; reviewers and interviewers sum him up with praise such as Mark Lawson's claim that he "writes like the teacher of your dreams: jokey, metaphorical across both popular and unpopular culture, epigrammatic." On the other hand, he has been subjected to a persistent argument that the books he calls novels are really collections of short stories or essays or some other nonfiction genre and are only "marketed" as novels. Although he is regularly called "erudite" and "philosophical," he is also witty and humane; as David Coward explains in the *Times Literary Supplement* (5 October 1984), "The modern British novel finds it easy to be clever and comic. Barnes also manages that much harder thing: he succeeds in communicating genuine emotion without affectation or embarrassment." Barnes's work has stimulated considerable critical discussion over its allegedly post-modern traits, including questions about whether it is dangerously relativistic or nihilistic. That his novels have never won the Booker Prize, the most prestigious award for British fiction—although *Flaubert's Parrot* was one of the six finalists for the prize in 1984—has baffled some observers. His *Metroland* (1980) won the William Somerset Maugham Prize, which is given for an outstanding first book; he has won other English literary awards, and *Flaubert's Parrot* was honored in France with the Prix Medicis. Barnes has also been named an Officer de l'Ordre des Arts et des Lettres.

Partly because of comparisons with his slightly younger contemporary Amis, a famously precocious author, Barnes sees himself as a late starter: he was thirty-four when *Metroland* was published. It was, however, the product of a long gestation period, and he published another book—his first Dan Kavanagh detective thriller, *Duffy* (1980)—that same year. Since then his output has been impressive in quantity as well as quality.

Julian Patrick Barnes was born in Leicester, an industrial city in England's East Midlands, on 19 January 1946; his parents, Albert Leonard and Kaye Scoltock Barnes, were teachers of French. The family moved to the London suburb of Northwood when Barnes was quite young; he attended the City of London School on a scholarship, commuting on the Metropolitan Line of the London Underground—an experience that helped to produce *Metroland*. He studied languages at Magdalen College, Oxford, teaching in France in 1966–1967 and receiving a B.A. with honors in 1968. He took a job as editorial assistant at the *Oxford English Dictionary*. As a man working mostly with women, he explained in a 1989 interview with Amanda Smith, he was assigned most of the "rude words and sports words."

In 1972 he moved to London, where he studied law and passed his final bar exams. He also be-

came involved in journalism, reviewing novels and then serving as assistant literary editor and television critic of *The New Statesman,* contributing editor of the *New Review* (where he published under the name "Edward Pygge"), deputy literary editor of the *Sunday Times,* and television critic for *The Observer* (London). During this period he also wrote a restaurant column for the *Tatler* under the pseudonym "Basil Seal," named for one of Evelyn Waugh's characters. He left *The Observer* in 1986 to become a full-time writer, but he wrote the "Letter from London" column for *The New Yorker* for five years and still reviews and comments regularly for such journals as the *Times Literary Supplement* and the *New York Review of Books.* Since 1979 he has been married to Pat Kavanagh, a prominent literary agent. His pseudonym Dan Kavanagh seems to be a tribute to his wife, to whom many of his novels are dedicated.

Mira Stout has called Barnes "the chameleon of British letters" because each of his "mainstream" novels is distinctive. This is less true of the detective novels: as Dan Kavanagh he seems able to satisfy any need he may feel for predictability, formula, and generic continuity, while as Julian Barnes he is careful not to repeat himself. In the interview with Amanda Smith he speaks contemptuously of some reviewers' expectation that after *Flaubert's Parrot,* his first great success, he would repeat himself by writing "Victor Hugo's Dachshund."

Barnes's first novel took him eight years to write. The deceptively calm *Metroland,* like many first novels, is a story of adolescence and coming-of-age; but a mark of the work's maturity is that it shows coming-of-age as involving a coming to terms with lowered expectations. *Metroland* demonstrates certain features that will be constants in Barnes's fiction: wit, familiarity with French culture, shapeliness and high finish, and a delicate concern with love and jealousy.

In the first part of this three-part novel, "Metroland (1963)," the teenage Christopher Lloyd, who lives in one of the London suburbs served by the Metropolitan Underground line, and his friend Toni are disdainful of school, sports, and, especially, the English middle-class culture represented by their parents. The values they treasure are art, sexual liberation (which is entirely theoretical to them as yet), and France. They spend much of their time in art museums making fun of the bourgeois families they see there. They wish to affront the smooth mediocrity of their times, but their rebellion is mostly verbal and quite funny. Barnes presents Christopher as a young man who is sufficiently unusual to be interesting while sufficiently typical to be a representative of the intelligent, urban adolescent filled

ONE : Prelude

There is no rule against carrying binoculars in the National Gallery.

On this particular Wednesday afternoon in the summer of 1963, Toni had the notebook and I had the glasses. It had been quite a *uncharacteristically* productive visit. There was the grey-haired lady smiling, and then frowning, *with a few disapproving clucks* at the Arnolfini Wedding. There was the girl so transfixed by the Crivelli altarpiece that I could put down the binoculars *we just stood on either side of her &* and we could both observe, from separate sides *and record noted* ~~down to~~ the subtlest parting of the lips *and* the slightest tautening of the skin across the cheekbones. ~~And then~~ There had *was* ~~been~~ the man in the city suit, *chalk stripe* hair parted precisely on the right-hand side, who had kept turning away from, and then back towards, a small Monet landscape. He puffed his cheeks, (he) jiggled his money in his trouser pocket, (he) leant back slightly and opened *on his heels* his eyes wider.

Then we came to one of our favourite rooms, and one of our ~~favourite~~ pictures – *most protective* Van Dyck's equestrian portrait of Charles I. There was a middle-aged lady in a red mackintosh *just* sitting down on a seat in front of it. *she was* gazing up as if it were an altar-piece. Toni and I walked quietly to the padded bench at the other end of the room, pretending to take in a jocund Franz Hals, and then, as he ~~sat backwards~~ *shielded me* sat backwards, I moved slightly forward and focussed the glasses on her. We were far enough away for me to whisper notes to Toni without fear ~~of being overheard~~ of it being taken for more than ~~the traditional~~ *normal* background murmur of admiration and assent.

There was no one else around, and the woman was quite ~~relaxed in front of~~ *at ease with* the portrait. Her eyes hosed it swiftly up and down, then settled, ~~moving~~ *& began to* more slowly from one part to another. At times, her head would cock sideways and her neck thrust forward; her nostrils seemed to widen, as if she sniffed some new connection in the painting; her hands moved slightly on her thighs in little twitches. Gradually, a sort of *religious* peace appeared to come over her, as I noted in a whisper to Toni. I focussed on her hands again: now they were clasped together, like an altar boy's. The gesture seemed entirely appropriate, and I commented on it. Then I tilted the binoculars back (on) to her face; she had closed her eyes, as if ~~she was~~ recreating to herself the ~~beauty~~ beauty of what was still in front of her. I kept the glasses on her for a full two minutes, while Toni waited for my next comment.

~~either~~ beyond visible pleasure, or she was
She was asleep.

You could read it one of two ways: either

First page of the typescript for a late draft of Barnes's novel Metroland *(Collection of Julian Barnes)* with longing and dissatisfaction. Part 2, "Paris (1968)," finds Christopher in the French capital during the May 1968 student rebellion—of which, ironically, he is completely unaware. He has come to France ostensibly to write a thesis but really to satisfy his youthful fascination with French culture and to take advantage of the opportunities for sexual liberation he associates with Paris. He does achieve a sexual initiation with a French girl, Annick, who eventually leaves him because of his dishonesty about his attraction to an English girl whom he later marries. As for art, Christopher does some desultory writing; it is, predictably, derivative—in this case, of Charles-Pierre Baudelaire. In the third part, "Metroland II (1977)," Christopher is back in metropolitan London. He has settled down into marriage, gone into business, and forgotten about the artistic life. His bourgeois existence is complicated by arguments with Toni, who is not nearly as assimilated to middle-class "adulthood," and by stresses in his mainly happy marriage.

Metroland is a short, unexciting, but highly accomplished study of becoming adult—with all that that implies about narrowing horizons, settling down, and accepting one's ordinariness. Although it is possible to argue, as Paul Bailey did in an unsympathetic review in the *Times Literary Supplement* (28 March 1980), that *Metroland* is a "prig's progress" and that it is about "settling for suburbia," Christopher is no prig. Barnes allows the reader to choose between Christopher's realistic accommodation to normal life and Toni's embodiment of the artist as untameable wild man.

Barnes's first Dan Kavanagh novel, *Duffy,* published the same year as *Metroland,* is a tense thriller set in London's sleazy Soho district; the title character is a bisexual private detective who is no longer with the police because he was blackmailed by crooked cops. Barnes went on to write three more Duffy novels: *Fiddle City* (1981), *Putting the Boot In* (1985), and *Going to the Dogs* (1987). Not only are these louche, violent, thoroughly plotted thrillers published under the Kavanagh pseudonym quite different from the mainstream novels published under his real name, but he also writes them in a different place (in the country; he writes the mainstream novels of his home in the city) and on a different typewriter. There has been considerable speculation about the reason for this split career; perhaps the conventional plot-making that some critics miss in *Metroland* or *Flaubert's Parrot* is held over for the Duffy books. The first two Duffy novels appeared in the United States in 1986 as paperbacks in the Pantheon International Crime series; *Putting the Boot In* has not yet received an American publication.

Nick Duffy is a complicated man, rather tormented in his bisexuality. He loves a woman, Carol, but is currently impotent with her as a result of trauma, while he is perfectly capable of performing in his casual affairs with men. As the series moves through the 1980s the rise of AIDS is reflected in Duffy's fear of the disease and in his less promiscuous behavior. All of the books are firmly anchored in what feels like reality. While the central crime in each book tends to be theft or fraud rather than murder, Barnes imbues the novels with a mood of menace. There is, to be sure, plenty of overt violence in the series: Duffy is beaten up, motorists are run off the road, women are tied up and slashed, thugs throw paraffin (kerosene) heaters into shops. Sometimes the criminals commit imaginative sorts of violence against animals, such as cooking a cat in an oven; such incidents are perhaps more troubling to the animal-loving British readership than are acts directed against people.

In the tradition of hard-boiled American detectives, Duffy is no paragon of respect for the law, partly because he was driven from the force by dishonest policemen and still has dealings with "bent coppers" and partly because he pursues moral rather than legal justice. In *Fiddle City* the narrator explains this ethos:

> Duffy's moral outlook had always been pragmatic. Three years in the force had made it more so, and it wasn't going to change now. He wasn't idealistic about the law, or about how it was implemented. He didn't mind a bit of give-and-take, a bit of blind-eye, a bit of you-naughty-boy-on-yer-bike and forget it. He didn't think the ends justified the means—except that sometimes, just occasionally, they did. He didn't believe all crimes were equal; some he couldn't get worked up about. But always, at the back, there were absolutes. Murder was one, of course, everyone agreed on that. Bent coppers was one; but then, Duffy had a little private experience of that, and could be expected to feel strongly. Rape was one; Duffy was disgusted how some coppers thought it was little more than a mild duffing up with a bit of pleasure thrown in. And heroin was one as well.

In the first three Duffy books the detective does not so much "solve" crimes—he usually already knows who the malefactor is—as restore some sort of moral balance. In *Duffy,* for instance, in pursuing the question of who slashed Mrs. McKechnie he enters the slimy world of the Soho sex industry, with his client turning out to be a pornography merchant and his opponent a Maltese Mr. Big. The action includes a harrowing assault on Duffy in a massage parlor. At the end Duffy exacts a sort of rough justice, aware that the police—especially those in his old

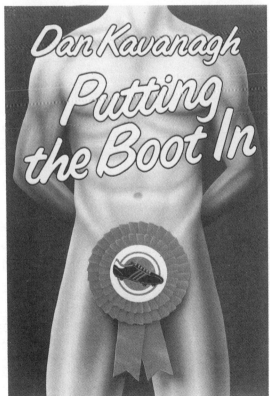

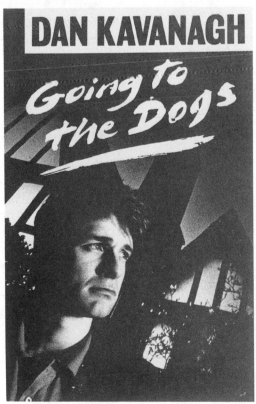

Dust jackets for Barnes's four novels about the bisexual private detective Nick Duffy

beat, Soho, who are shown as particularly corrupt—are not likely to achieve justice of any kind.

The next installment in the Duffy series is set at Heathrow Airport, called "Fiddle City" because of the enormous opportunities it provides for crime (*fiddle* is British slang for cheating or graft). The novel's beginning is reminiscent of that of *Duffy,* which opens with the laconic sentence "The day they cut Mrs. McKechnie, not much else happened in West Byfleet." *Fiddle City* begins, "The day they crashed McKay, not much else happened on the M4 [highway]." Duffy takes over the investigation McKay had been conducting; through a series of developments, including a one-night stand with a man he meets in a bar, he goes underground at a shipping concern. Most of the menace to Duffy in this book comes from his coworkers and supervisors at the warehouse. He solves the mystery of who ran McKay off the road (McKay did not die but was seriously injured) and the much bigger one that involves a major heroin-smuggling ring. The solution brings him great satisfaction, both because he is able to gain revenge against the sadist who ripped the stud out of his ear with a pair of pliers and because his friend Lesley died as a result of heroin abuse. He reflects, "At one end of the chain there were dead babies in Thailand"—a reference to an account he has been given of women hollowing out dead babies to carry heroin across borders; "at the other end there were Lesleys fixing themselves to death."

Almost all of Barnes's novels, whatever their main themes may be, are partly about love and jealousy. A relatively understated, tender, but penetrating treatment of infidelity and jealousy appears in the last section of *Metroland,* but Barnes's next mainstream novel, *Before She Met Me* (1982), displays the strongest, grimmest, and most menacing kind of jealousy. Graham Hendrick, a dull university lecturer, is married to Ann, a former actress for whom he left his first wife, Barbara. Still bitter, Barbara urges their daughter, Alice, to ask Graham to take her to see a certain movie; as he soon realizes, the point is for him to see Ann, in a minor role, "committing adultery" with an actor in the picture. Although Ann has been totally faithful to Graham since their marriage, he becomes obsessed with her sex life before they met. He neglects his work to travel all over London to see all of her movies again and again, studying the actors with whom she had love scenes and worrying about whether she had slept with any of them in real life (she had); he goes to the other movies of the actors with whom Ann had worked; he cross-examines her and makes exhaustive mental notes. Clearly he has become unbalanced. For consolation and advice he consults Jack,

a novelist friend; unbeknownst to him, Jack is another of Ann's former lovers. The novel ends extremely violently.

Before She Met Me is gripping, disturbing, and moving. It is comparable to the macabre, unsettling novels Barnes's contemporaries Amis and McEwan were writing—for instance, Amis's *Dead Babies* (1974) and McEwan's *The Cement Garden* (1978), which deals with oedipal and incest themes. In the interview with Smith, Barnes calls *Before She Met Me*

> a rather nasty book about unpleasant sexual feelings, jealousies and obsessions. It was meant to have had a rather sour and hard-driving edge to it. I think it's my funniest book, though the humor is rather bleak and in bad taste usually.

The novel certainly is funny, and its black humor survives even its growing horror. It is this book, perhaps more than any other, that has led critics to oversimplify Barnes as a writer obsessed with obsession, but Graham Hendrick is obsessed in a way that none of Barnes's other characters is. Barnes's recurrent subjects of infidelity (in this case, wholly imaginary) and jealousy occur here in their starkest form. He will go on to revisit and refine these themes.

In a 1987 interview with Patrick McGrath, Barnes emphasizes the novel's social commentary:

> In a way it's a sort of anti-'60s book. It's against the idea that somehow the 60s sorted sex out, that everyone was all fucked up beforehand. Queen Victoria was still in charge—and then along came the Beatles, suddenly everyone started sleeping with everyone else, and that cured the lot. That's a rough plan of English sexual history, as seen by many people. And I just wanted to say, it's not like that; that what is constant is the human heart and human passions. And the change in who does what with whom—that's a superficial change.

Obviously it is not a superficial change for Graham Hendrick or for some of Barnes's other troubled and cuckolded men; but this affirmation is important to keep in mind in considering Barnes's central novelistic concerns.

In 1984 Barnes published his "breakthrough" novel, *Flaubert's Parrot.* He says that he feels "enormous affection" for it "because it's the book that launched me." Experimental in both form and content, *Flaubert's Parrot* presents itself as a nonfiction book about Gustave Flaubert written by a widowed English doctor, Geoffrey Braithwaite. Braithwaite's book grows out of the discovery that there is more than one stuffed parrot in Normandy that is identified as the bird Flaubert borrowed while he was writing "Un Coeur Simple" (1877; translated as "A

Simple Heart," 1923) and develops into a subtle, witty speculation on the relationship between life and art, the knowability of the human personality, the nature of fame, and many other topics. There are also a sly but increasing emphasis on Braithwaite's autobiography and, as usual with Barnes, serious discussions of the nature and meaning of married love. The book is eclectic in form: it includes alternative chronologies of Flaubert's life, a dictionary of received ideas about the author, an examination paper on Flaubert by Braithwaite, and an account of Flaubert as it might have been written by his mistress, Louise Colet. It is an erudite and playful work; in Coward's words, it is "an extraordinarily artful mix of literary tomfoolery and high seriousness."

It is also the first of Barnes's novels to be thought of as some sort of "case," or even as a "problem." For some critics it was distinguished from Barnes's earlier works by its postmodernism—a tendency that was welcomed or rejected, depending on the critic's point of view. John Bayley disapproved of the "modish"—that is, slippery postmodern or poststructuralist—notions that he believed the novel espoused:

> The conscious implication of *Flaubert's Parrot* is that since one cannot know everything about the past, one cannot know anything; but its actual effect—and its success—is to suggest something different: that the relative confirms the idea of truth instead of dissipating it, that the difficulty of finding out how things were does not disprove those things but authenticates them. It may be that few things happened as they are supposed to, and many things did not happen at all, but why should this be a reason for abandoning traditional conceptions of history, of art, of human character?

James B. Scott, on the other hand, approved of the postmodern skepticism about truth and knowability he, like Bayley, saw in the novel:

> reality and truth are the illusions produced when systems of discourse (especially artistic discourse) impinge on human consciousness. In practice, this has led postmodern novelists to strive to undermine hermeneutic responses to art by foregrounding the discourse that informs their artifact, thereby implying that not only is the final "meaning" of a work of art forever unknowable, but also any orthodox truth is actually a discourse-generated fluke.

Bayley's theory is probably closer to what Barnes is trying to suggest in the novel: that is, he is not endorsing the idea that all truths are contingent, discourse-generated, and unreliable.

Dust jacket for Barnes's "breakthrough" novel, about the necessity and significance of literature

Some reviewers and literary journalists suspected *Flaubert's Parrot* of not being a novel at all. One line of argument was summed up by David Sexton in the *Sunday Telegraph* (11 June 1989): "Barnes writes books which look like novels and get shelved as novels but which, when you open them up, are something else altogether. *Flaubert's Parrot* was for the most part a set of studies of Flaubert and his parrot." A burlesque by Eric Metaxas, titled "That Post-Modernism," pretended to describe "Flaubert's Panda," by "Boolean Jarnes," as "part biography, part literary criticism, part fire hydrant, and part decayed wolf's pelt—in short, the post-modernist novel at its best." Defending his claim that the book is, indeed, a novel, Barnes is quoted by Sexton as invoking the more experimental Continental novelists and showing that his work fits the definition of the genre: "It's an extended piece of prose, largely fictional, which is planned and executed as a whole piece."

Dust jacket for Barnes's experimental novel in which the Ark is a recurring theme

Questions of the knowability of truth are important in Barnes's later novels *A History of the World in 10 1/2 Chapters* and *Talking It Over* (1991), and *A History of the World in 10 1/2 Chapters* was subjected to even sharper challenge on the grounds that it was not a proper novel. So *Flaubert's Parrot* helped to create the critical atmosphere in which Barnes's novels would be received, not least by making him a celebrated novelist whose works henceforth would receive a great deal of attention—not all of it admiring.

Barnes's next book was another Dan Kavanagh Duffy mystery, *Putting the Boot In,* set in the world of minor-league professional soccer. Like his first two detective books, it shows a command of the conventions of the genre and the kind of authority that comes from getting the details right. The soccer scenes are quite well done; this authenticity may, in fact, explain why the book has never been published in the United States, where the sport does not have a large following. Duffy, previously a moderately promiscuous bisexual, is so ter-

rified of AIDS that he is now celibate (though he and Carol share a bed).

The first, third, and fifth parts of the novel, titled "Warm-Up, "Half-Time," and "Extra Time," respectively, are an amusing account of a soccer match played by the Western Sunday Reliables, for whom Duffy keeps goal. Geoff Bell is a member of the team and uses his electronics skills to eavesdrop on the other team's plans. Framed by the match is a story of small-town corruption and mayhem centering around a lower-division soccer club, the Athletic, whose run of bad luck turns out to be part of a scheme to ruin the club and make its property available for development. Although Duffy uncovers the conspiracy, nobody is arrested or even discomfited; and the novel ends without even the rough balance between the forces of right and wrong that was restored in the first two Duffy books.

The next novel published under Barnes's real name was *Staring at the Sun* (1986), an understated study of a woman named Jean Serjeant from her childhood during World War II to the 2020s. The main character, while she is quietly strong, enduring, and even heroic, is an "ordinary," "private" woman. The events of her life are not particularly exciting; the high points are a game of golf, a visit to the Grand Canyon, some other tourism, and an airplane flight that gives rise to the central image of the novel: by diving his plane dramatically at dawn, the pilot can see the sun come up twice. This phenomenon is described as an "ordinary miracle," and Jean Serjeant's life is meant to be the same sort of miracle. Barnes wants to reveal the heroism that exists within the ordinary; in the interview with McGrath he pointed out that people "tend to think of courage as a male virtue, as something that happens in war . . . but there are 85,000 other sorts of courage." In this book Barnes, who was reared without religion and has never been a churchgoer, delves into ultimate questions about death, an afterlife, and God; in a 1989 interview with Kate Saunders he described the contents of *Staring at the Sun* as "DIY [do it yourself] theology."

Although it received many positive reviews, *Staring at the Sun* disappointed some readers; after the tour de force of *Flaubert's Parrot* they found it tame, even a bit dull. Barnes clearly has been nettled by this reaction. In a 1991 interview with Andrew Billen he said: "As soon as you say you were disappointed, I get deeply protective about the novel. I say: Carlos Fuentes [who reviewed it in *The New York Times*] liked it—so sod you. This is the writer's response. It's like criticising your fourth child."

In 1987 Barnes published what he has claimed is his last Duffy book, *Going to the Dogs;* in a 1991 interview he told Mark Lawson that a "recyclable hero" had proved to be "more tiresome than he expected," and this Duffy novel is weaker than its predecessors. The title refers both to greyhound racing, which plays a minor role in the book, and rich people's pets, one of which comes to a violent end in the novel. Duffy is called in to solve a crime for an old acquaintance, a not entirely honest but successful man whose wealth has permitted him to live the country life and make friends with snobs and pretentious idlers. In this novel Duffy's class consciousness comes strongly to the fore. There is also some self-referential humor as Duffy, flirting with a beautiful socialite, derides the restaurant column in the *Tatler* written by "Basil Berk." In fact, the restaurant columnist for the *Tatler* at the time, writing as "Basil Seal," was Barnes himself.

In 1989 came the novel that, in ambition, complexity, and experimental quality, seemed to be the real successor to *Flaubert's Parrot. A History of the World in 10 1/2 Chapters* is really a history of the world: the first chapter is about Noah's ark, the last about heaven. In between are chapters on a medieval church prosecution of termites, an American astronaut's quest for the remnants of the ark, the making of a movie in a South American jungle, and Théodore Géricault's painting *The Raft of the Medusa* (1819). The chapters are as variable in form as in content, including art criticism, letters, a journal, the records of a trial, and a dream.

Like *Flaubert's Parrot, A History of the World in 10 1/2 Chapters* challenges conventional definitions of the novel. It lacks a unified plot, developing characters, consistent fictionality, and consistent verisimilitude. In the interview with Lawson, Barnes responded to critics who say that he is really an essayist who disguises his essays as fiction for commercial reasons: "My line now is I'm a novelist and if I say it's a novel, it is. . . . And it's not terribly interesting to me, casting people out of the realm of fiction."

One of the characters in *A History of the World in 10 1/2 Chapters* announces that "Everything *is* connected, even the parts we don't like, especially the parts we don't like." Although she may be delusional, her comment is true, at least, of the novel in which she appears. Its parts are connected by a network of motifs, the most obvious one being voyages of salvation by water: Noah and his ark recur in most of the chapters. Another striking motif is woodworms; a slightly less important one is reindeer.

Like most of Barnes's books, this one is philosophically rich. There is meditation on the meaning of human life, on religion and the afterlife, on the nature of history—is there History, or are there only

Dust jacket for Barnes's novel about a romantic triangle

various "histories"?—and, most prominently, on love. The "half chapter" is about love, and its message is that in a universe where history is an unreliable set of stories of disasters, salvation is to be found in love: "We must believe in it, or we're lost." Perhaps the voice that speaks these words is, like the other voices in the book, wrong; perhaps this chapter is ironic. But such does not seem to be the case. Love is set against history and connected with truth. As in *Flaubert's Parrot,* the possibility of truth is contested in this novel: is there a truth, or are there merely competing truths? The first chapter—the unorthodox story of Noah's ark as told by a stowaway woodworm—seems to suggest that there are only alternate versions. And yet the claim that people tell the truth when they are in love implies that some truth exists for them to tell, and it justifies Joyce Carol Oates's description of Barnes as a "quintessential humanist, of the pre-post-modernist species."

Barnes's next book, *Talking It Over,* returns to the territory of *Metroland:* it is a study of love, sex, and marriage set in contemporary London. The rather dull but worthy Stuart feels, and is treated as, inferior to his witty and flashy friend Oliver. Soon after Stuart marries Gillian, Oliver decides that he loves Gillian and dedicates his life to making her fall in love with him; eventually he succeeds. *Talking It Over* is a story of how love works and how jealousy feels. The two men and the woman are artfully distinguished, particularly stylistically: Stuart writes dully; Oliver has a clever, allusive style, to which Barnes has added some of his own favorite turns of phrase. Each of the three addresses the reader much more directly than is common in novels, pleading with the reader, asking questions about the other characters, suggesting ways to test the truth of the story, asking for belief and even assistance; each has his or her own version of the story, none of which is completely reliable. One minor character, a discarded girlfriend of Stuart's, provides a unique perspective on the plot—she is highly dubious of Gillian's motives, for instance—but is "thrown out" of the novel through the combined efforts of Stuart and Oliver and despite an appeal to the author. *Talking It Over* is both moving and funny.

The Porcupine (1992) is set in a fictional country clearly based on Bulgaria; it was first published in that country and in Bulgarian. An overthrown dictator, Stoyo Petkanov, justifies himself, resists the attempts of his accusers (many of whom were formerly his supporters) to change the rules by which Stalinist societies measure successful government, and tweaks his prosecutor, the anguished former communist Peter Solinsky.

Although Petkanov is a monster, he is given arguments that are by no means easy to dismiss; in their disputes he often seems to get the better of Solinsky. As Solinsky's obsession with convicting Petkanov—on charges other than the ones of which he is really guilty—grows, his own self-doubts strengthening his determination, his wife loses her respect for him and leaves. Solinsky gives himself to evil means for a good end; were Petkanov's crimes any different? The apparent convergence of Solinsky and Petkanov raises questions about the moral superiority of the reformed system over the communist regime.

Letters from London: 1990–1995 (1995) is a collection of Barnes's columns from *The New Yorker*. There are essays on garden mazes, on the financial problems of Lloyd's of London, on Harrods, and on literary topics, including former prime minister Margaret Thatcher's memoirs. Barnes, a Labour Party supporter, is at his best when writing about politics. His account of himself campaigning with Glenda Jackson for Parliament is engaging, but his language becomes richest in satire: he describes

Thatcher at Prime Minister's Question Time, standing "rather stiffly at the dispatch box, with swept-back hair, firm features, and an increasingly generous embonpoint thrusting at her tailored suit of Tory blue or emerald green; there, butting into the spray and storm of Her Majesty's Loyal Opposition, she resembles the figurehead on the prow of some antique sailing ship, emblematic as much as decorative." For one who is often characterized as a postmodernist mandarin playing intellectual games, he is solidly in touch with the real world, and he always finds something unusual to report (for example, changing fashions in pictures on currency) or a new approach to a familiar topic (such as Thatcher or her successor as prime minister, John Major) and a witty way of expressing it.

As a prepublication announcement in *Granta* (Spring 1994) put it, Barnes's *Cross Channel* (1996) is "a collection of short stories occasioned by historical meetings between the English and the French." Three of the stories were originally published in *The New Yorker,* another in *Granta;* the others appear for the first time in the book. Themes include the wars of religion, the nature of the artist, the trickery of memory, and sexual infidelity. In "Interference" an aging English artist living in France thinks about the problem of belonging:

> He was an artist, did she not see? He was not an exile, since that implied a country to which he could, or would, return. Nor was he an immigrant, since that implied a desire to be accepted, to submit yourself to the land of adoption. But you did not leave one country, with its social forms and rules and pettinesses, in order to burden yourself with the parallel forms and rules and pettinesses of another country. No, he was an artist. He therefore lived alone with his art, in silence and in freedom.

In "Experiment" the narrator recounts some sexual experiments among the Surrealists, with whom his English uncle Freddy became involved in 1928. The story is full of delightful wordplay—Freddy may have said "je suis, sire, rallyiste," meaning that he was in town for a motor rally, and been misunderstood as declaring himself to be a Surrealist—and deepening levels of complexity as the narrator discovers truths Freddy could not have known.

In a 1996 interview with Carl Swanson for the on-line magazine *Salon,* Barnes claimed that he is "the one middle-class English writer who loves France but doesn't have a house there." He spends much time there, however, and is sometimes accused by English friends of being too French. He explained to Swanson:

I think everybody needs another country. . . . You need another country on which to project, perhaps, your romanticism and idealism. I think this is a good idea, but I don't think it happens to most people. Most people think mostly about their own country, and idealize their own country, and I think that's dangerous. I think one's own country should be scrupulously and skeptically examined [as in *Letters from London,* perhaps]. And you should allow your idealism and romanticism to be projected onto something else.

It is a telling comment, both about Barnes's attitude toward France and about his combination of skepticism with romanticism and idealism.

Lawson, trying to encapsulate Barnes's style, offers the phrase "alternative versions." It is an apt characterization of a writer whose characters Stuart and Oliver in *Talking It Over* present alternative versions of how Oliver ended up with Stuart's wife; who depicted, in the same year, the ironic domesticity of *Metroland* and the desperate and squalid vice of *Duffy;* and who offers with each new book a different approach, even a new and distinctive voice. There are constants in his fiction: high craft, verbal brilliance, a determination to deal in ideas without giving way to didacticism, frequent experimentation in subject or form or both; but another constant is variation itself. His career illustrates his adherence to his maxim that a novel should be *novel;* "what is constant," as he told McGrath, "is the human heart and human passions."

Interviews:

Patrick McGrath, "Julian Barnes," *Bomb,* 21 (Fall 1987): 20–23;

Kate Saunders, "From Flaubert's Parrot to Noah's Woodworm," *Sunday Times,* 18 June 1989, p. G9;

Amanda Smith, "Julian Barnes," *Publishers Weekly,* 236 (3 November 1989): 73–74;

Andrew Billen, "Two Aspects of a Writer," *Observer Colour Magazine,* 7 July 1991, pp. 25–27;

Mark Lawson, "A Short History of Julian Barnes," *Independent Magazine,* 13 July 1991, pp. 34–36;

Mira Stout, "Chameleon Novelist," *New York Times Magazine,* 22 November 1992, pp. 29, 68–72, 80;

Carl Swanson, "Old Fartery and Literary Dish," *Salon* [on-line magazine](13 May 1996).

References:

Martin Amis, "Snooker with Julian Barnes," in his *Visiting Mrs. Nabokov and Other Excursions* (New York: Harmony, 1993), pp. 154–158;

John Bayley, *The Order of Battle at Trafalgar and Other Essays* (New York: Weidenfeld & Nicolson, 1987);

David Leon Higdon, "'Unconfessed Confessions': The Narrators of Graham Swift and Julian Barnes," in *The British and Irish Novel Since 1960,* edited by James Acheson (New York: St. Martin's Press, 1991), pp. 174–191;

Ann Hulbert, "The Meaning of Meaning," *New Republic,* 196 (11 May 1987): 37–39;

Michiko Kakutani, "Britain's Writers Embrace the Offbeat," *New York Times,* 5 July 1990, pp. C11, C15;

Paul Levy, "British Author, French Flair," *Wall Street Journal,* 11 December 1992, p. A10;

Eric Metaxas, "That Post-Modernism," *Atlantic Monthly,* 259 (January 1987): 36–37;

Mark I. Millington and Alison S. Sinclair, "The Honourable Cuckold: Models of Masculine Defence," *Comparative Literature Studies,* 29 (1992): 1–19;

Joyce Carol Oates, "But Noah Was Not a Nice Man," *New York Times Book Review,* 1 October 1989, pp. 12–13;

Salman Rushdie, *Imaginary Homelands: Essays and Criticism 1981–1991* (London: Granta, 1991);

Gregory Salyer, "One Good Story Leads to Another: Julian Barnes' *A History of the World in 10 1/2 Chapters,*" *Journal of Literature and Theology,* 5 (June 1991): 220–232;

James B. Scott, "Parrot as Paradigms: Infinite Deferral of Meaning in 'Flaubert's Parrot,'" *Ariel: A Review of International English Literature,* 21 (July 1990): 57–68;

David Sexton, "Still Parroting on about God," *Sunday Telegraph,* 11 June 1989;

Richard Todd, "Domestic Performance: Julian Barnes and the Love Triangle," in his *Consuming Fictions: The Booker Prize and Fiction in Britain Today* (London: Bloomsbury, 1996), pp. 260–280.

Anita Brookner
(16 July 1928 –   )

Kate Fullbrook
University of the West of England

See also the Brookner entry in *DLB Yearbook: 1987.*

BOOKS: *J. A. Dominique Ingres,* The Masters, no. 16 (Paulton: Purnell, 1965);

Jacques-Louis David, The Masters, no. 91(Paulton: Purnell, 1967);

Watteau (London: Hamlyn, 1968);

The Genius of the Future: Studies in French Art Criticism: Diderot, Stendhal, Baudelaire, Zola, The Brothers Goncourt, Huysmans (London & New York: Phaidon, 1971; Ithaca, N.Y.: Cornell University Press, 1988;

Greuze: The Rise and Fall of an Eighteenth-Century Phenomenon (London: Elek, 1972; Greenwich, Conn. & New York: Graphic Society, 1974);

Jacques-Louis David, A Personal Interpretation: Lecture on Aspects of Art (London: Oxford University Press, 1974);

Jacques-Louis David (London: Chatto & Windus, 1980; New York: Harper & Row, 1980);

A Start in Life (London: Cape, 1981); republished as *The Debut* (New York: Linden, 1981);

Providence (London: Cape, 1982; New York: Pantheon, 1984);

Look at Me (London: Cape, 1983; New York: Pantheon, 1983);

Hotel du Lac (London: Cape, 1984; New York: Pantheon, 1984);

Family and Friends (London: Cape, 1985; New York: Pantheon, 1985);

A Misalliance (London: Cape, 1986); republished as *The Misalliance* (New York: Pantheon, 1986);

A Friend from England (London: Cape, 1987; New York: Pantheon, 1987);

Latecomers (London: Cape, 1988; New York: Pantheon, 1988);

Lewis Percy (London: Cape, 1989; New York: Pantheon, 1989);

Brief Lives (London: Cape, 1990; New York: Random House, 1990);

A Closed Eye (London: Cape, 1991; New York: Random House, 1991);

Anita Brookner (photograph © Jerry Bauer)

Fraud (London: Cape, 1992; New York: Random House, 1992);

A Family Romance (London: Cape, 1993); republished as *Dolly* (New York: Random House, 1993);

A Private View (London: Cape, 1994; New York: Random House, 1994);

Incidents in the Rue Laugier (London: Cape, 1995; New York: Random House, 1996);

Altered States (London: Cape, 1996; New York: Random House, 1996);

Soundings (London: Harvill, 1997);

Visitors (London: Cape, 1997; New York: Random House, 1998);

Falling Slowly (London: Viking, forthcoming, 1998; New York: Random House, forthcoming, 1999).

OTHER: George Waldemar, *Utrillo*, translated by Brookner (London: Oldbourne Press, 1960);

Jean-Paul Crespelle, *The Fauves*, translated by Brookner (London: Oldbourne Press, 1962);

Maximilien Gauthier, *Gauguin*, translated by Brookner (London: Oldbourne Press, 1962);

Margaret Kennedy, *The Constant Nymph*, introduction by Brookner (London: Virago, 1983; Garden City, N.Y.: Dial, 1984);

Kennedy, *Troy Chimneys*, introduction by Brookner (London: Virago, 1985; New York: Penguin, 1985);

Edith Templeton, *The Island of Desire*, introduction by Brookner (London: Hogarth Press, 1985);

Templeton, *Summer in the Country*, introduction by Brookner (London: Hogarth Press, 1985);

Templeton, *Living on Yesterday*, introduction by Brookner (London: Hogarth Press, 1986);

Edith Wharton, *The House of Mirth*, introduction by Brookner (New York: Macmillan, 1987);

Wharton, *The Stories of Edith Wharton: Selected and Introduced by Anita Brookner*, 2 volumes (London & New York: Simon & Schuster, 1988–1989);

Wharton, *The Custom of the Country*, introduction by Brookner (New York: Penguin, 1990);

Wharton, *The Reef*, introduction by Brookner (New York: Penguin, 1995).

SELECTED PERIODICAL PUBLICATIONS–
UNCOLLECTED: "A Stooge of the Spycatcher," *Spectator* (25 July 1987): 13–14;

"Prize-Winning Novels from France," *Spectator* (10 December 1988): 39–40;

"Rosamund Lehmann," *Spectator* (17 March 1990): 19–20;

"Prize-Winning French Novels," *Spectator* (5 January 1991): 27–28.

With the appearance of her first novel in 1981 Anita Brookner immediately secured a reputation as one of the finest stylists among contemporary writers of fiction in Britain. After a late start as a novelist Brookner has proved a prolific source of the morally engaged novel of consciousness and of exquisite sensibility. Since her fourth novel, *Hotel du Lac* (1984), won the prestigious Booker McConnell Prize for fiction, her work has consistently attracted attention from British and American readers. Equally admired and criticized for her attention to the themes of stoicism, loneliness, and melancholy which beset her contemporary, genteel characters, Brookner's voice is instantly recognizable as the most recent distinguished contributor to a tradition of British women's writing that runs from Jane Austen through Elizabeth Bowen, Rosamond Lehmann, Elizabeth Taylor, and Barbara Pym.

Brookner was the only child of middle-class, socialist, nonreligious Jewish parents. She was born and grew up in Herne Hill, a well-heeled suburb in south London. Her birth date is 16 July 1928, although when she started to write she deducted ten years from her age until a friend pointed out the discrepancy in *The Times* (London). Brookner wrote back to *The Times* (London), saying "I am 47, and have been for ten years." Brookner's maternal grandfather was a Polish immigrant who founded a tobacco factory in London. Her mother, Maude Schiska, was a professional singer who gave up her career to marry Brookner's father, Newson Bruckner. He had come from Poland to England when he was sixteen and, after fighting in the British army in World War I, worked in the Schiskas' factory. Maude changed the family name to Brookner to deflect British anti-German feeling: Brookner's father's first name was a replacement for his original Polish name, which his new family found unpronounceable. Brookner remembers her childhood as both crowded and lonely. Living in a suburban villa with her grandmother, parents, bachelor uncle, and many servants, she remembers her parents as silent and unhappy. In the 1930s and during World War II the household was also filled with Jewish refugees. The tragic situation of Jews in Europe permeated Brookner's childhood and adolescence.

From the first Brookner showed great academic promise. After attending a local primary school and James Allen's Girls' School in Dulwich, she studied history as an undergraduate at King's College, London, and then completed a doctorate in art history at the distinguished Courtauld Institute of Art in London, where its director, the magisterial art historian and spy, Anthony Blunt, both encouraged her as her teacher and used her as an unknowing stooge in his covert operations (a fact of which Brookner was not aware until the publication of Peter Wright's book *Spycatcher* in 1987). After studying the art of Jean-Baptiste Greuze in Paris on a French government scholarship (against her parents' wishes), Brookner was launched on her first distinguished career as an art historian. Her first job was at the University of Reading, where she lectured from 1959 to 1964. She then returned to the Courtauld, where she was promoted to reader in 1977. She taught there for the rest of her career, retiring in

Dust jacket for the U.S. edition of Brookner's novel about a lonely librarian

1988. From 1967 to 1968 Brookner served as the first female Slade Professor at the University of Cambridge. She is a Fellow of New Hall, Cambridge, has received honorary doctorates from the University of Loughborough in Britain and Smith College in the United States, and was made a C.B.E. (Commander of the British Empire) in 1990. As an art historian Brookner's area of specialization is late-eighteenth-century and early-nineteenth-century French art, and her books on the subject are not only respected but composed with the kind of narrative drive that in retrospect merges seamlessly with her talent as a novelist.

Brookner spent a good part of the 1960s caring for her dying parents. She never married; she has no religious affiliations. In an interview with Olga Kenyon published in 1989, Brookner summed up her life and the mental state that turned her toward fiction at the age of fifty-three. "Mine was a dreary Victorian story: I nursed my parents till they died. I write out of a sense of powerlessness and injustice, because I felt invisible and passive. Life is so badly plotted. The novel speaks about states of mind which forced me to do something about those states of mind."

In her interview with Kenyon, Brookner chose Henry James and Charles Dickens as the two novelists who warred for supremacy in her mind, and she also called Marcel Proust "very precious to me." James and the French novelists, she explained, satisfied the taste for "*scrutiny*"; "if you want *indignation*, then it's Dickens." Brookner's work both borrows from and differs from that of the writers she admires. Like Dickens (and despite the limitations of her range), she is a chronicler of London life. Like James, she is an intense moralist, examining the dilemmas of the upper class. Like Proust, she has a deep interest in psychological obsession and the failure of desire. Brookner has a compelling interest in the individual and the family, in romance, and in the ways that art structures expectations. She also writes in a thoughtful and sometimes combative dialogue using the cruder versions of feminism of her day, with the topic of the life of the solitary, independent, intelligent woman one of the hallmarks of her fiction.

Although she has given just a handful of interviews, Brookner has always spoken in illuminating ways about her writing. In 1994 Brookner told Blake Morrison that she wrote her first novel, *A Start in Life*, in three months. Morrison suggested that in her "miniature moral universe" there are "two inflexible rules": first, that "virtue is not rewarded," and second, that "love doesn't do people any good." Brookner agreed with the first proposition and disagreed with the second. And, she argued, if some of her fiction has been written in response to the depression from which she has sometimes suffered, even that experience has been turned to good use. What Morrison calls Brookner's "inwardness," along with her characteristic themes of "love, marriage, work, age, solitude, loyalty and innocence; the inevitability of failure; what we owe to others and what we owe to ourselves," all combine to make her an intelligent and quietly thoughtful novelist in a period where the raucous and the outrageous tend to grab the limelight.

Brookner wrote *A Start in Life* during her summer vacation. "It was most undramatic," she told Amanda Smith in 1985. "Nothing seemed to be happening and I could have got very sorry for myself and miserable . . . and I'd always got such nourishment from fiction. I wondered—it just occurred to me to see whether I could do it. I didn't think I could. I just wrote a page, the first page, and nobody seemed to think it was wrong . . . So I wrote another page, and another, and at the end of the summer I had a story. That's all I wanted to do—tell a story." The influential editor, Liz Calder, accepted the novel for Jonathan Cape. Even taking into account the fact that Brookner was a successful and much-published writer of art history before she turned to fiction, *A Start in Life* marks an exceptionally accomplished performance as a first novel. It is a highly literary text shadowed by Leo Tolstoy, Gustave Flaubert, Dickens, Molière, James, Stendhal, Jean-Jacques Rousseau, W. H. Auden, and, especially, Honoré de Balzac. The central character, Dr. Ruth Weiss, the author of a book on Balzac's women, moves through the world of academic training into a successful career and a disappointing personal life. Looking back at the age of forty on her life "ruined by literature," Ruth is the first of Brookner's intelligent, successful, but lonely female protagonists. *A Start in Life* (which borrows its title from *Un Début dans la vie* [1844], a minor novel by Balzac) weaves together autobiographical elements with the general outline of Balzac's *Eugénie Grandet* (1834) to produce a story of a woman contending with the demands of elderly parents, the treachery of a couple who promised friendship but practiced exploitation, and a brief marriage made out of daughterly duty to a man she did not love. As Ruth tries to escape Eugénie's fate of unselfish loneliness, her own wishes are overruled by the rapacious relatives and acquaintances who surround her.

Kitty Maule, the heroine of Brookner's second novel, *Providence* (1982), is another academic with a blighted life. Still drawing heavily on her own life for details of her plots (all Brookner's novels are autobiographical to some extent), Brookner makes elegant, intelligent, and deeply literary Kitty the daughter of a French mother raised by immigrant grandparents in Dulwich who never feels quite at home in the England of her birth. A specialist in Romanticism (like Brookner herself), Kitty's "Frenchness" sets her apart culturally and emotionally from those around her. As in *A Start in Life* a French novel—here Benjamin Constant's *Adolphe* (1816), which Kitty is teaching—provides an ironic analogue with the central character's experiences. Another of Brookner's key topics, food, enters this novel with the death of Kitty's mother at dinner, and Kitty's subsequent association of trauma with eating. Kitty's French fastidiousness in clothes and manners also sets her apart from the dowdy academics who surround her, and the discretion and cultivated passivity that accord with the rest of her character simply underscore her real and painful loneliness. In her attempt to secure a lover (a rather dull but very English professor of medieval history named

Maurice) so she can "begin her life," she is repeatedly disappointed. And although Kitty gives her first public lecture with professional success, at the subsequent party Maurice reveals his relationship with one of her students. Kitty, for whom Maurice was less a man and more an imaginary reconciliation with both life and with England, is bereft and confused, feeling she has been playing the wrong game with the wrong "information." As demure as a nineteenth-century governess, Kitty is a compendium of womanly stereotypes—some operative, some repressed, but all designed to lead her to false behavior and permanent, if civilized, isolation.

The appearance of Brookner's third novel, *Look at Me* (1983), confirmed her ability to produce an exquisitely wrought novel annually. As Robert E. Hosmer Jr. remarks, "Brookner's first three novels bear such striking resemblances to one another that they can be considered together as delicate variations on a single theme: the plight of a painfully sensitive, lonely woman on the cusp of middle age, who, despite keen intelligence and considerable learning never does quite 'get things right.'" Brookner's early heroines are "victimized," says Hosmer, not so much by their "romantic idealism" as by a failure to assert themselves aggressively enough to secure what they desire. This description is apt for Frances Hinton, the first-person narrator of *Look at Me,* whose life, like the tropes of madness and melancholy dominating the novel itself (underscored by the novel's repeated references to Francisco José de Goya), is bathed in sadness. Frances, who has lived with her mother until she died, and who now lives in her deceased parents' flat with an ancient family servant, works in the reference library of a medical research institute in London, and counts herself an observer of the lives of the happy. She comforts herself, after her days filled with filing images of madness, by writing about her observations. Picked up by Nick and Alix, a lively couple who pair her with their shy friend, James (who lives with his mother), Frances rejoices in the prospect of her sad and passively decorous life changing into one with real human connection. The rapacious Alix, however, who likes to play with people and their emotions for her own pleasure, has other plans. Frances ends by withdrawing, hurt, from James, who takes up with a more voluptuous woman. Locked into her loneliness, balked of love, once again invisible to others, Frances ends the novel intending to write a novel about her experiences.

With the award of the Booker Prize for *Hotel du Lac,* Brookner received accolades that assured her of a place among the ranks of the best contempo-

Denholm Elliott and Anna Massey, as Edith, in a scene from the 1985 BBC/Arts & Entertainment Network adaptation of Hotel du Lac *(courtesy of Arts & Entertainment Network)*

rary writers of British fiction. The novel, dedicated to Lehmann, pulled together all the strengths of Brookner's characteristic concerns in an updated Jamesian performance of great skill. *Hotel du Lac* is one of the finest novels of the intersection of consciousness and manners produced by a British writer in the second half of the twentieth century, and many critics and readers regard it as Brookner's best novel to date. The outline of the novel is classic Brookner. The heroine, Edith Hope, an English writer of popular romantic fiction who publishes under the pseudonym of Vanessa Wilde and who looks like Virginia Woolf, has retired to a Swiss lakeside resort to work on her latest novel ("Beneath the Visiting Moon") and to absent herself for a month from her married lover, David. In the deadly quiet and all-encompassing gray of the out-of-season hotel, Edith feels overwhelmed by absence. The hotel seems designed for the variety of cast-off women whom she observes and among whom Edith is not quite willing to number herself. The precise reason for Edith's Swiss exile is revealed late in the novel: she had left her fiancé—the kindly, dull Geoffrey—standing at the registry office on the morning of their wedding rather than marry a man she did not really love. Embarrassed by her rash behavior and by her refusal to settle for a second-best life of tame propriety, Edith's friend has packed her off to Switzerland until the scandal dies

down. With the man she loves most passionately being married and unavailable, Edith comes close to marrying a sympathetic stranger at the Swiss hotel but abandons this prospect when she discovers his sexual connection with another woman. She will, after all, commit herself to David and live an unmarried half-life with a man whom she does, at least, love.

Hotel du Lac is the most stylistically adventurous of Brookner's early novels and is structured around sophisticated debates about contemporary morality signaled by its references to Friedrich Nietzsche and the ethics of love. A philosophical novel that includes questions about feminism and the feminine, as well as interesting material on the impact of popular notions of romance and on the devastation caused by conventions of polite behavior, *Hotel du Lac* brought Brookner a significantly greater readership. The novel, however, also crystallized criticism of Brookner's writing now that she was seen as an important enough writer to attack. For example, Adam Mars-Jones, writing in *The New York Review of Books,* stresses the "masochism" of Brookner's view of romance and comments that "*Hotel du Lac* works so hard at the limpness of its heroine that it has a perversely bracing effect." The novel, in his view, "is divided between narcissism and self-mortification, between wallowing and astringency."

Such strictures, however, along with those of pretentiousness and parochialism, did Brookner no harm in terms of sales. After winning the Booker Prize in a particularly controversial year *Hotel du Lac* attracted many additional reviews and a great deal of publicity. In an article "Up for the Cup" in *The Bookseller* in 1985, Rupert Lancaster, the publicity director at Brookner's British publisher, Jonathan Cape, described the impact the award had on the sales of Brookner's fiction. Where her first three well-reviewed novels had been building from a base of roughly 2,000 to sales of 3,000, the initial print run of 4,000 copies of *Hotel du Lac* soon proved inadequate. With excellent publicity and reviews the first printing of the novel sold out two weeks after its publication on 6 September 1984, and a reprint of 4,500 was ordered. The shortlist for the Booker appeared on 18 September, and cumulative sales figures had climbed to 5,745 by 12 October. Winning the prize on 18 October meant that Cape went into overdrive to produce more copies. The novel sold 51,021 copies by the week of 25 January 1985. Brookner also received an award of £15,000 that accompanied the prize. By April 1985 Cape had sold another 19,000 copies. These figures do not include sales in the United States, where Pantheon, then

Brookner's American publisher, found that it had a best-seller on its hands. As Lancaster remarked, its success was phenomenal.

Brookner, herself, was a phenomenon, albeit a quiet one. From this time onward the annual publication of one of her novels automatically attracted reviews, commentary, and interviews. The latter Brookner handled with great courtesy and conviction. For example, talking to an American interviewer about the imminent publication of her fifth novel, *Family and Friends,* in 1985, Brookner stressed the seriousness of fiction. Invoking her admiration for Dickens and James, Brookner commented on the importance of fiction as "the great repository of the moral sense." She noted the centrality of her interest in behavior: "form and style and standards of behavior are going to save us all. Once we abandon any kind of obligation to behave well or to present ourselves in a good light, then I think it's the jungle." She agreed that she was especially concerned with the "inner lives" of women and that she loathed a particular kind of successful woman. She was, she said, more interested in the reasons why women fail, and that this conflict between "the moral sense and the desire to win" is everyone's concern. Brookner, furthermore, insisted on the small-scale nature of her interests (she emphatically disavowed any pretentiousness), and on her recurring analysis of two kinds of love—the settled love akin to friendship and the terrifying love called "romantic," with all its dangers—as one of her key subjects. Noting, too, her interest in the topic of humiliation and failure, she said that in England her books were criticized for being depressing. She attributed this to her "semi-outsider" position in England and her affinity with French life, especially that of Paris, where family background seems to count for less than the value of the individual. Brookner says that she finds the English obsession with class distasteful and adds that although she has thought of leaving England, where she is does not much matter because she sees herself as a "recluse" for whom place is relatively unimportant. Aside from her affection for wandering through cities, hers is an indoor life. Winning the Booker Prize made her "sleepy," with all the additional letters to write and interviews to give in addition to carrying on with her work as a lecturer. She noted that she seemed "to have been slightly knocked out by it," although it had also "been great fun." Her new novel was "an accident":

Somebody showed me a wedding photograph in which my grandmother was standing rather regally . . . it was such a potent image that I took off from there, literally from the photograph. I wrote the story of my family, my mother, her sisters, her brothers. Of course, I made it up as I went along. But it helped having known them.

She found "the amount of affection that came through" the process of writing "liberating" and a way of healing her mental rift with her family, with whom she had always felt at odds. *Family and Friends,* she added, was written in three months, "dependent on nudges from the unconscious." She approaches each new novel worried that it will not happen. "If it didn't happen again," she closed the interview by saying, "I should feel absolutely incapacitated."

Brookner need not have worried. *Family and Friends* marked a broadening of her historical range and an increase in her power in handling a wider range of characters. With an epigraph from Johann Wolfgang von Goethe's *The Sorrows of Young Werther* (1774), the novel charts the progress of a German-Jewish immigrant family in England from early in the twentieth century to the present. The Dorn family forms a complex human network with the children of the widowed Sofka dividing into two groups. The "good" children, Alfred and Mimi, continue the family traditions with sober and often disappointed devotion, while the wild charmers, Frederick and Betty, pursue exciting if somewhat ludicrous adventures. Managing multiple shifts of perspectives, Brookner sweeps through the possibilities of modern life in this novel, one of her most expansive, while never losing the sensitivies that characterize her earlier fiction. The family photographs (especially those of weddings) that punctuate the novel provide convincing images for tracing the family's history, which matches so tellingly with the history of its times.

In 1986 the BBC and the Arts and Entertainment network collaborated on a television version of *Hotel du Lac,* and Brookner began reviewing fiction extensively for *The Spectator.* Her novel *A Misalliance,* published in that year, focuses on a lonely woman, Blanche Vernon, who has been divorced by Bertie, her husband of twenty years, who has taken up with a woman twenty years his junior. Blanche is baffled by this all-too-familiar plight and meditates on the difference between two images of women: that of the wife and that of the woman who lives for pleasure; the difference between the Christian and the pagan worldviews symbolized for her by Titian's painting *Bacchus and Ariadne* (1520–1523) in London's National Gallery. To assuage her loneliness Blanche involves herself with the lively Sally Beamish and Sally's three-year-old stepdaughter, Elinor, a mute child whose life is clearly as stoic as

From the reviews of
A PRIVATE VIEW

'She is our Henry James, conveying emotional nuances
by what is left unsaid, observing the shaming secrets we
dare not admit even to ourselves.'
Philip Howard, *The Times*

'This is classic Brookner territory... The ordinary is
transformed into the beguiling, and there is a tumult of
unused feeling to be discovered.'
Helen Dunmore, *Observer*

'A beautiful book... Its Augustan shape, feeling for
words, economy of style and deliberate understatement
make most of its contemporaries seem inchoate,
uncouth and adolescent.'
Gillian Avery, *Evening Standard*

'As a novelist Anita Brookner is both infinitely various
and adorably unique.'
John Bayley, *Spectator*

ISBN 0-224-04124-X

ANITA BROOKNER

Incidents in the
RUE LAUGIER

Incidents in the
RUE LAUGIER

Dust jacket for Brookner's novel about an unhappy marriage

Blanche's own. Blanche, Sally, and Elinor make up a strange threesome, with the older woman and the child numbing themselves into seriousness and mildness while Sally, the nymph, simply cavorts her way through life. In the end Sally decamps for Cornwall with the now-speaking Elinor, while Bertie returns to Blanche, who sees her time with Sally and Elinor as her own misalliance.

In September 1985, just before the publication of *Family and Friends,* while she was working on *A Misalliance* (her fiction at this point was all written during her summer holidays), Brookner told Simon Banner in an interview in *The Guardian* that she wanted to go back to writing art history. Admitting to feeling disloyal to the Courtauld, she said (as she would do frequently thereafter) that this novel might be her last. Writing about an eccentric such as Blanche made her depressed, she noted. Brookner's associating depression with writing fiction, and noting the recurrence of mild depression in her own life, are altogether characteristic. Yet Brookner's attraction to fiction continues to prove exceedingly robust, and her work as an accomplished stylist was as evident in *A Misalliance* as in her earlier work.

Brookner's next novel was *A Friend from England* (1987), another novel concentrating on a lonely, solitary heroine. The narrator of the novel, Rachel Kennedy, is a one-third partner in a bookshop. Oscar Livingstone, who was her deceased father's accountant, wins the football pools and retires, a millionaire, to live with his wife, Dorrie, and grown daughter, Heather, in Wimbledon. Oscar and Dorrie are wistful and innocent, and Rachel is drawn to their melancholy gentleness. She battens on them as a substitute for what she misses in her life. Although Rachel is only thirty-two and Heather is twenty-seven, Rachel frets maternally about Heather's upcoming marriage to Michael Sandberg (who is spotted by Rachel in a bar wearing women's makeup). The marriage does, indeed, turn out to be a disaster. Heather leaves Michael and goes to Venice to live with her Italian lover, Marco, whom she now intends to marry. When Rachel pursues Heather in a nightmarish trip to Venice, Heather reveals her dismal opinion of Rachel's life without husband or children. And while Heather does return home briefly for her mother's funeral, she returns to Marco as soon as she can, leaving Rachel, a typical Brookner character, to confront the emptiness of her life as an independent woman. In a classically Brooknerian move, the novel is provided with a famous work of art as its analogue. In this case the work is a painting, Giorgione's *The Tempest* (circa 1505), with its configuration of a woman suckling her child, a knight, a storm, a village, and a broken column. It is a painting that arrests Rachel's attention during her self-imposed mission in Venice and represents a vision of life that she cannot quite comprehend but that seems to be embodied in Heather.

In her most revealing interview to date, with Shusha Guppy for *The Paris Review* in 1987, Brookner spoke about the significance of *A Friend from England.* "It is a very old fashioned moral tale . . . about an extremely emancipated young woman . . . who is drawn into a family of blameless innocence whom she feels called upon to protect, but by whose innocence she finds herself finally vanquished. She can't measure up to it." The interview turned to the subject of her most important precursors. Along with her enthusiasm for James and Dickens, she cited Edith Wharton, Émile Zola, Balzac, Stendhal, Flaubert, George Eliot, Proust, and the great Russians as being particularly important to her. Among her favorite women writers she named Lehmann, Taylor, Storm Jameson, and Jean Rhys (though she sees Rhys as limited by her "pathology"). She also mentioned her admiration for Edith Templeton, Mavis Gallant, and Edith de Born and her enthusiasm for Philip Roth and Peter Ackroyd. For herself, she said that writing had become her link with life: "Now I write because I enjoy it. Writing has freed me from the despair of living. I feel well when I am writing." At the end of the interview, she looked forward to her imminent retirement from the Courtauld after twenty-five years with pleasure at the happiness her career as a teacher had given her and said that she would no longer even try to write art history. (Brookner is remembered as an exceptionally good teacher who was not only a spectacular lecturer but extremely kind to her students). In the interview with Guppy she said goodbye to her academic career and underlined her commitment to writing fiction, speaking of her slow work on her next novel.

The novel in question was Brookner's eighth, *Latecomers,* published in 1988. The central figures are two Jewish men in their sixties, Thomas Hartmann and his friend and partner, Thomas Fibich, both of whom escaped as children from Hitler's Germany to England, while their families were exterminated. The two lifelong friends, though sharing a terrible background of exile and estrangement, are quite different. Hartmann is hearty and expansive, happy with the relative success he has made of his life, while Fibich is worried, depressed, haunted by his German past the memory of which he has blocked. While subplots deal with Hartmann's and Fibich's wives and children, the most memorable part of the novel concerns Fibich, who returns to Berlin to confront his terrors, from which he is temporarily freed. Though his panic returns, he is able to leave his son a book of memories that grows out of a peace he has never before felt. The novel as a whole contemplates the horrors of twentieth-century European history, yet ends with several different kinds of affirmation.

In *Lewis Percy* (1989) Brookner continued her concentration on male heroes with a portrait of two decades in the life of a young man who is an innocent and an idealist. Beginning in 1959 the novel follows the eponymous hero through the 1960s and 1970s as he, the adored only son of a devoted mother, becomes first a student of literature in Paris, writing about heroism in the nineteenth-century novel, and then a librarian unhappy with both his job and his rashly made marriage. His wife, Tissy, whom he had innocently selected as a substitute housekeeper after his mother's death, leaves him when she becomes pregnant, and although Lewis loves their baby daughter, his wife, emboldened by feminism, will not return to him. When Lewis finally publishes his book on heroism he realizes that he has shown none in his private life. He quits his job and moves to Paris with his new lover, having discovered that women do not exist solely as mothers and do not give love simply in exchange for politeness. In this flawed comedy, which suffers from a certain degree of staginess, Lewis Percy, suburban man, becomes an altogether more intriguing figure: a man who has learned that innocence—even his own—must be sacrificed.

In 1990 not only was Brookner's next novel, *Brief Lives,* published, but so was the first full-length academic study of her writing. Twayne, in Boston, published Lynn Veach Sadler's *Anita Brookner* in its English Authors Series. In 1989 Patrica Waugh had devoted a section of her book, *Feminine Fictions,* to what was then a new kind of discussion of Brookner, locating her in a complex relationship to postmodernism and to the feminism from which she had always publicly distanced herself while writing in illuminating ways about issues that deeply concern feminist readers.

Like *Family and Friends, Brief Lives,* which concerns itself with the suffering of privileged women, uses descriptions of photographs as catalysts for the narrative. The novel opens with the narrator, Fay Langdon, a widow who had been a singer in her youth, commenting on the death at nearly eighty of Julia Morton, an elegant, selfish woman who had had a successful stage career and a sexually rapacious private life. Because Fay's husband, Owen, had been a junior partner in Julia's husband Charlie's legal firm, the two women had been linked for life, even though Fay has no affection for Julia. After an initial passion, Owen had been a distant husband, yet Fay, who has left her professional career (her special song was "Arcady") for marriage, is lost when he dies in a car crash on the Riviera. After moving into a bright and sunny flat Fay has a passionate affair with Charlie, who also dies. Facing

Dust jacket for Brookner's novel about a middle-aged lawyer's disappointments in love

her old age, Fay is lonely but is reconciled to a life that is now free from longing.

If Brookner's first heroines seemed prematurely middle-aged, the widows who tend to populate her novels of the 1990s are all concerned not only with growing old but with aging as the signpost of pleasures missed, chances not taken, dangers not risked. In *A Closed Eye,* published in 1991, Harriet Lytton, a rich widow of fifty-four, opens the book with a letter inviting Lizzie Peckham to join her in Switzerland. Lizzie is the daughter of Harriet's deceased friend, Tessa, and Tessa's husband, Jack, a man to whom Harriet had been passionately attracted. Harriet's own marriage, to Freddie, a man old enough to be her father, had made for a dull life, which Harriet spent in a state of innocent sadness. Harriet had adored her own daughter, Imogen, whom Freddie did not want. But the girl, who had been a charming baby, turned impassive as she grew up. She dies in an automobile accident while still a young woman. The grieving Harriet, left alone in the world, her life "an empty room," is comforted by Lizzie, who tells her the polite, petty lies she needs to hear to reconcile herself to the paucity of her experience. In the novel Brookner invokes Dickens, James, and Charlotte Brontë, who provide apt touchstones for this highly characteristic story of innocence and lifelong loneliness.

These are Brookner's key themes, and they are put to new uses in her 1992 novel, *Fraud,* a text

in which no one is quite what he or she seems. Miss Anna Durrant, a kindly but marginal woman of fifty, has been missing for four months. Her tidy, exquisite Kensington flat is found empty by the police, who have been notified of her absence by her doctor, Lawrence Halliday. Having lived with her vibrant mother until the mother's death the previous year, Anna has had a gentle, protected, but dull life in which she dreams of a marriage of an old-fashioned kind that no longer exists. While her mother had wanted a man for Anna, Anna wants only to preserve her own innocence. Anna has wanted to marry Halliday, who has made a disastrous marriage, realizing too late that Anna was, after all, the right partner for him. But Anna has new plans. She goes to Paris and announces her determination to stop being a fraud. She intends to go into business designing clothes. Punctuated by images of longing for the sun associated with Joseph Turner's paintings, and caught in the dilemma figured in Titian's painting of sacred and profane love, this is one Brookner novel that ends by embracing life rather than with a melancholy acceptance of it.

Jane Manning, in *A Family Romance* (1993), published in the United States as *Dolly,* is another of Brookner's bookish heroines. A successful author of children's books by the end of the novel, Jane narrates the story of her eccentric family. Her now-deceased, childlike parents were both raised by powerful mothers who treated them as possessions.

Jane's mother, Henrietta, was seen as a distasteful encumbrance by a mother who scarcely looked at her, while Jane's Uncle Hugo, adored by her mother, was subject to obsessive possessiveness. Paul, Jane's father, had a forceful mother whose interests were limited to dogs, religion, and general heartiness. The narrative focuses on Dolly, Hugo's widow, a vibrant but penniless Parisian of German-Jewish stock who is inherited as a charity case by successive generations of the Manning family.

Dolly is one of Brookner's most intriguing attempts at creating a flamboyant, life-loving figure who makes her way as a parasite battening onto the well-to-do but pallid characters who accept responsibility for her, even when her extravagant demands on them are beyond reason. Dolly herself is the product of the displacements created by recent European history: a maddening but irresistible creature formed by war, exile, and abandonment, yet retaining a lust for living at a high and expensive pitch. If she is exasperating and shameless she is also a marvel of tenacity, clinging to her creed of charm, singing and dancing even when the chips are down. As a figure of the dependent woman she also provides a foil for the inward, intellectual, and independent Jane, who recounts her selfish aunt's story and who assumes final responsibility for her.

A Private View, published in 1994, is one of Brookner's best treatments of a characteristic constellation of moral topics: stoicism, freedom and its uses, pity, desire, and, inevitably, melancholy. As in *Fraud* the lure of the sun as the sign of the life force features strongly as a central metaphor in the text. This is also, as are *Fraud* and *A Closed Eye,* a book centrally concerned with the process of grieving. At the start of the novel George Bland, sixty-five, retired, is in Nice, mourning his lifelong friend, Michael Putnam, who has died three weeks earlier. George has not been to Nice for forty years and is unaccustomed to leisure. The friends, both of whom rose to some success after impoverished beginnings, and neither of whom ever married, had planned to make this trip together. On George's return to London a young woman inserts herself into his life, claiming to have been allowed to stay in an absent neighbor's flat. The young woman, Katy Gibb, plays with identities, dressing herself as a hippie, then as a schoolgirl, then as a sophisticate. While art and literature are important comforts for George, Katy, a New Age creature who is just back from America, treats herself as a continuously transformable work of art. The artists whose works serve as analogues for the George's state of mind and his dreams include Peter Paul Rubens, Tintoretto, and Odilon Redon, but the central figurative experience is George's visit to a Walter Sickert exhibition that crys-

tallizes his imagination. Overlooking Katy's trendy interest in color therapy, personal growth, and other tacky but fashionable forms of psychotherapy, George, in a Proustian mode, dreams of possessing Katy and committing scarcely imagined follies with her. In the end, finding Katy is only after his money, George dispatches her back to the United States and asks his old lover Louise if she will go on a cruise with him. In this novel Brookner satirizes current therapeutic fashions as crass and vulgar. The novel touches on her repeated themes of the fantasy of happy families and on the Nietzschean dimensions of modern morality as a struggle for power.

In *Incidents in the Rue Laugier* (1995) Brookner returns to the subjects of mothers and daughters, of unsuccessful rebellion, and of the inequities of desire. Beginning in the late 1950s, the plot revolves around the life of Maud Gonthier, who lives in Dijon and who wants to escape to Paris rather than accept her mother Nadine's plans for a safe marriage. The deceptively decorous Maud is swept off her feet by an exciting young Englishman, David Tyler, who seduces and then abandons her, destroying her innocence but giving her the gift of having experienced real passion. When she finds herself pregnant, Edward Harrison, Tyler's friend, marries Maud and takes her back with him to lead a comfortable life in England. Maud miscarries, but her mother puts her in a position where she must continue with this marriage of convenience. While Maud is grateful and always polite to Edward, she does not love him, and she spends the rest of her life outwardly calm but regretting her lack of affection for her husband and obsessively recalling the passion she had felt for Tyler when young. The story is told by Maffy, Maud and Edward's daughter, who pieces together her tale from a few words written in a notebook that she looks at some years after her mother's death. Maffy's remarks provide a frame in the first and final chapters, positioning the tale as the product of her imagination, constructed to give reality to the unknown private lives of her parents, whose secrets she never penetrated. As an excursus on the imagined origins of the family and the calculus of love that underpins it, this is one of Brookner's most successful productions.

Brookner's sixteenth novel in sixteen years, *Altered States,* published in 1996, is narrated by fifty-five-year-old Alan Sherwood, a fastidious but passive solicitor. Sherwood becomes suddenly inflamed, however, on encountering his redhaired relative Sarah, and becomes sexually entangled with her. When the affair becomes a source of misery Sherwood takes up with Angela, who both attracts and repels him. In a further twist of disappointment, Angela dies after she has a stillborn child. The selfish Alan is left to mourn his lack of fulfillment. Disappointment dominates the novel, the key themes of which are the classic ones of sorrow and regret.

Despite her success in two highly public careers, Brookner's has been a quiet, fastidious life. She is not part of the social scene of literary London, and she told Valerie Grove in a 1995 interview in *The Times* (London) that she did not want biographers and would not write an autobiography. "I have," she said, "no private papers. I shall leave no trace." For many years she has lived in the same small apartment in Chelsea in London, and her needs are simple: no word processor, answering machine, microwave, cellular telephone, or car. Brookner's characteristic wry modesty was in evidence at the end of the interview when she summed up her writing: "Mine are not great works. They are middle-brow, middle-class novels. But I enjoy writing them, you see. So I don't mind." Despite this polite self-deprecation, the verdict on Brookner's work is likely to be higher, and the longevity of her reputation much more secure, than the author herself is ever apt to suggest.

Interviews:

Simon Banner, "Too Good to Be True," *Guardian,* 4 September 1985, p. 22;

Amanda Smith, "Anita Brookner," *Publishers Weekly,* 228 (6 September 1985): 57–68;

John Haffenden, "Anita Brookner," in *Novelists in Interview,* edited by Haffenden (London & New York: Methuen, 1985), pp. 57–75;

Shusha Guppy, "The Art of Fiction XCVIII: Anita Brookner," *Paris Review,* 104 (Fall 1987): 147–169;

"Novelist with a Double Life," *Observer* (London), 7 August 1988, p. 13;

Olga Kenyon, "Anita Brookner," in *Women Writers Talk: Interviews with 10 Women Writers,* edited by Kenyon (Oxford: Lennard, 1989), pp. 7–24;

Blake Morrison, "A Game of Solitaire," *Independent on Sunday,* 19 June 1994, pp. 12–14;

Valerie Grove, "Hell Would Be Quiz Night at the Bull in Ambridge," *Times* (London), 16 June 1995, p. 14.

References:

Gisèle Marie Baxter, "Clothes, Men and Books: Cultural Experiences and Identity in the Early Novels of Anita Brookner," *English,* 42 (Summer 1993): 125–139;

Deborah Bowen, "Preserving Appearances: Photography and the Postmodern Realism of Anita Brookner," *Mosaic,* 28 (June 1995): 123–148;

Anne Fisher-Wirth, "Hunger Art: The Novels of Anita Brookner," *Twentieth Century Literature,* 41 (Spring 1995): 1–15;

David Galef, "You Aren't What You Eat," *Journal of Popular Culture,* 28 (Winter 1994): 1–7;

Jan Zita Grover, "Small Expectations," *Women's Review of Books,* 11 (July 1994): 38–40;

Robert E. Hosmer Jr., "Paradigm and Passage: The Fiction of Anita Brookner," in *Contemporary British Women Writers,* edited by Hosmer (London: Macmillan, 1993), pp. 26–54;

Olga Kenyon, "Anita Brookner," in *Women Novelists Today: A Survey of English Writing in the Seventies and Eighties* (Brighton: Harvester, 1988), pp. 144–165;

Rupert Lancaster, "Up for the Cup," *Bookseller* (13 April 1985): 1604–1605;

Brent MacLaine, "Photofiction as Family Album: David Galloway, Paul Theroux, and Anita Brookner," *Mosaic,* 24 (Spring 1994): 131–149;

Adam Mars-Jones, "Women Beware Women," *New York Times Review of Books,* 31 January 1985, pp. 17–19;

Lynn Veach Sadler, *Anita Brookner* (Boston: Twayne, 1990);

Mary Anne Schofield, "Spinster's Fare: Rites of Passage in Anita Brookner's Fiction," in *Cooking by the Book: Food in Literature and Culture,* edited by Schofield (Bowling Green, Ohio: Bowling Green State University Popular Press, 1989), pp. 61–77;

John Skinner, *The Fictions of Anita Brookner: Illusions of Romance* (London: Macmillan, 1992);

Margaret Diane Stetz, "Anita Brookner: Woman Writer as Reluctant Feminist," in *Writing the Woman Artist: Essays on Poetics, Politics, and Portraiture,* edited by Suzanne W. Jones (Philadelphia: University of Pennsylvania Press, 1991), pp. 96–112;

Patricia Waugh, *Feminine Fictions: Revisiting the Postmodern* (London & New York: Routledge, 1989), pp. 126–127, 139–151.

Anthony Burgess

(25 February 1917 – 25 November 1993)

Geoffrey Aggeler
University of Utah

See also the Burgess entry in *DLB 14: British Novelists Since 1960.*

BOOKS: *Time for a Tiger* (London: Heinemann, 1956);

The Enemy in the Blanket (London: Heinemann, 1958);

English Literature: A Survey for Students, as John Burgess Wilson (London: Longmans Green, 1958);

Beds in the East (London: Heinemann, 1959);

The Doctor Is Sick (London: Heinemann, 1960; New York: Norton, 1966);

The Right to an Answer (London: Heinemann, 1960; New York: Norton, 1962);

One Hand Clapping, as Joseph Kell (London: Peter Davis, 1961); as Anthony Burgess (New York: Knopf, 1972);

Devil of a State (London: Heinemann, 1961; New York: Norton, 1962);

The Worm and the Ring (London: Heinemann, 1961);

A Clockwork Orange (London: Heinemann, 1962; New York: Norton, 1963);

The Wanting Seed (London: Heinemann, 1962; New York: Norton, 1963);

Inside Mr. Enderby, as Joseph Kell (London: Heinemann, 1963); enlarged as *Enderby,* as Anthony Burgess (New York: Norton, 1968);

Honey for the Bears (London: Heinemann, 1963; New York: Norton, 1964);

The Eve of St. Venus (London: Sidgwick & Jackson, 1964; New York: Norton, 1970);

Language Made Plain, as John Burgess Wilson (London: English Universities Press, 1964); as Anthony Burgess (New York: Crowell, 1965);

Malayan Trilogy, as John Burgess Wilson (London: Heinemann, 1964)—comprises *Time for a Tiger, The Enemy in the Blanket,* and *Beds in the East;* republished as *The Long Day Wanes: A Malayan Trilogy,* as Anthony Burgess (New York: Norton, 1965);

Anthony Burgess (photograph © Jerry Bauer)

Nothing Like the Sun: A Story of Shakespeare's Love Life (London: Heinemann, 1964; New York: Norton, 1964);

Here Comes Everybody: An Introduction to James Joyce for the Ordinary Reader (London: Faber & Faber, 1965); republished as *Re Joyce* (New York: Norton, 1965); revised edition, with original title (Feltham, U.K.: Hamlyn, 1982);

A Vision of Battlements (London: Sidgwick & Jackson, 1965; New York: Norton, 1966);

Tremor of Intent (London: Heinemann, 1966; New York: Norton, 1966);

Coaching Days of England (London: Elek/Greenwich, Conn.: New York Graphic Society, 1966);

The Age of the Grand Tour, by Burgess and Francis Haskell (London: Elek, 1967; New York: Crown, 1967);

The Novel Now: A Student's Guide to Contemporary Fiction (London: Faber & Faber, 1967; New York: Norton, 1967);

Enderby Outside (London: Heinemann, 1968);

Urgent Copy: Literary Studies (London: Cape, 1968; New York: Norton, 1969);

Shakespeare (London: Cape, 1970; New York: Knopf, 1970);

MF (London: Cape, 1971; New York: Knopf, 1971);

Joysprick: An Introduction to the Language of James Joyce (London: Deutsch, 1973; New York: Harcourt Brace Jovanovich, 1975);

Napoleon Symphony (London: Cape, 1974; New York: Knopf, 1974);

The Clockwork Testament, or, Enderby's End (London: Hart-Davis, MacGibbon, 1974; New York: Knopf, 1975);

Moses: A Narrative (New York: Stonehill, 1976; London: Dempsey & Squires, 1976);

New York, by Burgess and the editors of Time-Life Books (Amsterdam: Time-Life International, 1976);

A Long Trip to Teatime (London: Dempsey & Squires, 1976; New York: Stonehill, 1978);

Beard's Roman Women (New York: McGraw-Hill, 1976);

ABBA ABBA (London: Faber & Faber, 1977; Boston: Little, Brown, 1977);

Ernest Hemingway & His World (New York: Scribners, 1978; London: Thames & Hudson, 1978);

1985 (London: Hutchinson, 1978; Boston: Little, Brown, 1978);

Man of Nazareth (New York: McGraw-Hill, 1979);

Earthly Powers (New York: Simon & Schuster, 1980; London: Hutchinson, 1980);

On Going to Bed (London: Deutsch, 1982; New York: Abbeville Press, 1982);

The End of the World News: An Entertainment (London: Hutchinson, 1982; New York: McGraw-Hill, 1983);

This Man and Music (London: Hutchinson, 1982; New York: McGraw-Hill, 1983);

Enderby's Dark Lady, or, No End to Enderby (London: Hutchinson, 1984; New York: McGraw-Hill, 1984);

Ninety-Nine Novels: The Best in English since 1939: A Personal Choice (London: Allison & Busby, 1984; New York: Summit, 1984);

Flame into Being: The Life and Work of D. H. Lawrence (London: Heinemann, 1985; New York: Arbor House, 1985);

The Kingdom of the Wicked (London: Hutchinson, 1985);

Blooms of Dublin: A Musical Play Based on James Joyce's Ulysses (London: Hutchinson, 1986);

Homage to QWERT YUIOP: Essays (London: Hutchinson, 1986); republished as *But Do Blondes Prefer Gentlemen?: Homage to Qwert Yuiop, and Other Writings* (New York: McGraw-Hill, 1986);

Little Wilson and Big God: Being the First Part of the Confessions of Anthony Burgess (New York: Weidenfled & Nicolson, 1986; London: Heinemann, 1987);

The Pianoplayers (London: Hutchinson, 1986; New York: Arbor House, 1986);

A Clockwork Orange: A Play with Music Based on His Novella of the Same Name (London: Hutchinson, 1987);

They Wrote in English (London: Hutchinson, 1988);

Any Old Iron (New York: Random House, 1989; London: Hutchinson, 1989);

The Devil's Mode: Stories (London: Hutchinson, 1989);

You've Had Your Time: The Second Part of the Confessions (London: Heinemann, 1990; New York: Weidenfeld, 1991);

Mozart and the Wolf Gang (London: Hutchinson, 1991); republished as *On Mozart: A Paean for Wolfgang* (New York: Ticknor & Fields, 1991);

A Mouthful of Air: Language and Languages, Especially English (London: Hutchinson, 1992);

A Dead Man in Deptford (London: Hutchinson, 1993; New York: Carroll & Graf, 1995);

Byrne: A Novel (London: Hutchinson, 1995; New York: Carroll & Graf, 1997).

TRANSLATIONS: Michel de Saint-Pierre, *The New Aristocrats,* translated by Burgess and Llewela Burgess (London: Gollancz, 1962);

Jean Pelegri, *The Olive Trees of Justice,* translated by Burgess and Lynn Wilson (London: Sidgwick & Jackson, 1962);

Jean Servin, *The Man Who Robbed Poor Boxes* (London: Gollancz, 1965);

Edmond Rostand, *Cyrano de Bergerac* (New York: Knopf, 1971);

Sophocles, *Oedipus the King* (Minneapolis: University of Minnesota Press, 1972).

OTHER: James Joyce, *A Shorter "Finnergans Wake,"* edited by Burgess (London: Faber & Faber, 1966).

Widely regarded as one of the foremost contemporary fiction writers in English, Anthony Burgess began his long and prolific literary career while living in Malaya during the late 1950s. In 1949 he had written a fictional account of his wartime experiences in Gibraltar, but this work did not appear until 1965 as *A Vision of Battlements*. He started writing fiction during his Malayan years "as a sort of gentlemanly hobby, because I knew there wasn't any money in it." At the time he was an education officer with the British Colonial Service, and the fiction he was writing included realistic portrayals of actual events and personalities. Since it was regarded as indiscreet for one in his position to have such fiction published under his own name, he adopted the nom de plume "Anthony Burgess," which consists of his confirmation name and his mother's maiden name. His full name, which he seldom uses, is John Anthony Burgess Wilson.

Abundantly reflected in Burgess's fiction is his Roman Catholic background, which was part of an ancient regional and family heritage. He came from an old Lancashire family whose Catholic heritage reaches back through centuries. Like other Catholic families, his forebears suffered severely for their faith during the penal days of the Reformation, and one of Burgess's ancestors, also named John Wilson, was martyred during the reign of Elizabeth I. Moreover, being Catholic, the family lost what land it possessed. Its later history parallels that of other steadfastly Roman Catholic Lancashire families. During the civil war it "hid its quota of undistinguished Royalist leaders in Lancashire cloughs, and supported the Pretenders after 1688." Burgess renounced Catholicism at about age sixteen, but the renunciation gave him little joy. Although intellectually he was convinced that he could be a freethinker, emotionally he was keenly aware of hell and damnation, and to some extent he remained so.

His most persistent youthful ambition was to become a composer, and when he entered the University of Manchester, he wanted to study music. However, lacking the science background required by the music department, he had to take English language and literature instead. His personal tutor, whom he admired, was Dr. L. C. Knights, author of *Drama and Society in the Age of Jonson* (1937), coeditor of *Scrutiny,* and one of the leading exponents of New Criticism. Through Knights, Burgess met critic F. R. Leavis and came under his influence as well as that of I. A. Richards. He was struck by their method, which enabled one to assess a novel critically by close analysis and explication of the text.

Dust jacket for Burgess's satiric dystopian novel in which government scientists "cure" a teenage sociopath of his propensity to violence by robbing him of his free will

Burgess managed to get through the required courses at Manchester without much effort, but he tended to neglect subjects other than English. The energy he failed to spend on course work he poured into editing the university magazine, *The Serpent,* and into the dramatic society. Unlike many of his contemporaries, who were involved in some form of political activity, he had no interest in politics. The university's socialist society had no more appeal for him than its fascist society, and he maintained, as he has maintained since about age fourteen, a stance neither radical nor conservative nor anything but "just vaguely cynical." This point of view manifests itself in his fictional conflicts between "Pelagians" and "Augustinians."

While at Manchester he met a Welsh girl, Llewela Isherwood Jones, a distant cousin of Christopher Isherwood. Four years younger than Burgess, she was an economics honors student at the university. They were married in 1942, and the marriage lasted until her death in 1968 after many years of severe illness.

In October 1940 after taking his degree Burgess joined the British army and was assigned to the Royal Army Medical Corps. He was then sent to join a small entertainment group as a pianist and arranger. The group, all of whose members except Burgess had been professional entertainers, gave concerts at camps and lonely batteries, relieving the boredom of soldiers who were sick of the "phoney war." Then in 1943, having been transferred to the Army Education Corps, he was sent to Gibraltar, where he remained until 1946. The story of Richard Ennis in *A Vision of Battlements* is, he said, "pretty close to my own story." Like Ennis, Burgess lectured to the troops and taught them useful skills, such as map reading and foreign languages. Unlike Ennis, however, he was involved with army intelligence in cipher work. It was a frustrating, dreary time for him. He composed a good deal of music, including a symphony and a concerto, but not much literature.

Burgess's first year on Gibraltar was made especially miserable by the news that his wife was hospitalized in London with severe injuries. She had been assaulted on the street by American GIs, deserters bent on robbery, who had beaten her and caused her to abort the child she was carrying. In time Burgess overcame the consuming rage he had felt initially against all American soldiers, but his horror of the action itself, senseless male violence against a defenseless woman, remained undiminished. Clearly this horror was the inspiration for the most shocking scene in *A Clockwork Orange* (1962), the brutal assault on the writer and his wife, as well as the woman-beating incidents in *The Right to an Answer* (1960).

After his discharge from the army in 1946 Burgess's career oscillated between music and teaching. For a time he was a pianist with a little-known jazz combo in London and did arrangements for Eddie Calvert, "the Man with the Golden Trumpet." Then he became a civilian instructor at an army college of education, a lecturer in an emergency training college for potential teachers, and finally a senior master in a grammar school in Banbury, Oxfordshire, where he remained for four years.

The situation of grammar school teachers was, as he says, "ghastly beyond belief in those days." Negotiations were going on for a new salary scale, but nothing came of them, and Burgess's salary was so wretched that he found it "increasingly impossible to live." His dismal situation was essentially the same as that of Christopher Howarth in *The Worm and the Ring* (1961). Discouraged and desperate, he kept applying for jobs to better himself. Then one night in a drunken stupor he "quite unconsciously"

scrawled out an application for a teaching post in Malaya. He was subsequently offered a post on the staff of a public school for Malays in Kuala Kangsar, Malaya, which he accepted with little hesitation.

Burgess found Malaya a fascinating, indeed fantastic, cultural and linguistic melange, and he was eager to record what he saw. As a musician his first impulse was to orchestrate it, and he actually composed a symphony in which the different ethnic groups reveal themselves in snatches and strains. But the symphony was not well received, and he sought another medium. The resultant oeuvre, published together as the *Malayan Trilogy* in 1964, may be likened to a symphony or a giant canvas upon which Burgess has painted portraits representing most of the generic types he knew. He introduces Malays, Tamils, Sikhs, and Eurasians as well as a collection of largely maladapted British colonials. The vocabulary of the novel is enriched by the addition of many words and expressions in Malay, Urdu, Arabic, Tamil, and Chinese. A glossary is included in the back of the book, but, as he does in *A Clockwork Orange,* Burgess weaves the strange vocabulary into the context so the meaning is readily apparent.

The trilogy—*Time for a Tiger* (1956), *The Enemy in the Blanket* (1958), and *Beds in the East* (1959)—is unified by Malaya and by the presence of Victor Crabbe, a young British schoolmaster who has come to the Far East in search of a new life. *Time for a Tiger* concerns the hilarious trials and adventures of one of Crabbe's most remarkable acquaintances, a gigantic colonial police lieutenant named Nabby Adams, for whom "Tiger" beer is a raison d'etre, hence the title of the novel. It received mixed reviews in England. Peter Quennell in *The Daily Mail* (27 September 1956) found it "remarkably entertaining" while the critic for the *Times Literary Supplement* (9 November 1956) thought it had "too much drifting, drinking and droning, although Mr. Burgess is at his best in the drinking scenes."

In *The Enemy in the Blanket* Burgess dealt somewhat more seriously than he had in his first novel with the problems of adjustment to a darker civilization. One of the protagonists, Rupert Hardman, an albinistic lawyer, becomes, albeit reluctantly, absorbed into the Islamic culture of Malaya. His case reveals how Islam might lose its enchantment for an Englishman—as it once did for Burgess himself, who had actually considered becoming a Muslim. Meanwhile Crabbe loses his wife to a Malayan but contents himself with the hope of being a spokesman for sound Western values as Malaya moves toward independence. Just how little effect such well-meaning efforts are going to have is suggested by the disqui-

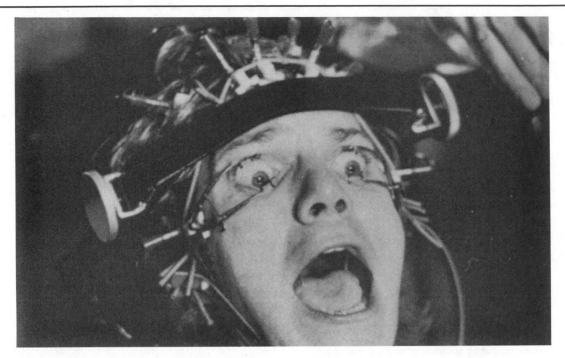

*Alex, played by Malcolm McDowell, undergoing behavior-modification therapy in a scene from Stanley Kubrick's
1971 movie version of* A Clockwork Orange *(Warner Brothers)*

eting glimpses of the future provided by scenes depicting representatives of the various dominant races—Tamils, Sikhs, Malays, Chinese—who despise each other and are united only in their hatred of the common enemy, the British. *The Enemy in the Blanket* was well received by reviewers, one of whom remarked that "there's more meat here than in half a dozen novels."

Encouraged by the critical reception of his first two novels and by his publisher, Burgess completed the trilogy with *Beds in the East*. This novel begins with a description of a Malay family arising for one of the last days of British rule and concludes with a description of a lovely Tamil girl wiping away a tear for Victor Crabbe, who has drowned miserably in a river upcountry. Most of the novel is concerned with native Malayans, members of groups Burgess introduced briefly in the first two books; and as anticipated, the only change accompanying the "dawn of freedom" is an intensifying of interracial hostilities. The book is unquestionably pessimistic, and one reviewer objected that there was "too little sympathy" in it. Other critics appreciated its "brilliant comedy" and accomplished writing.

Although Burgess might have become a major novelist without going to Malaya and writing the trilogy, the importance of this experience in his development as a novelist was in many ways analogous to the importance of *Endymion* (1818) in John Keats's development as a poet. His success in capturing so much of the cultural variety of Malaya in an extended piece of fiction seems to have been a tremendous impetus for him toward writing other fiction dealing with other worlds he either knew or imagined. He also had the encouragement of perceptive critics.

Burgess enjoyed his teaching in Malaya in spite of a tendency to clash with administrative superiors. After a quarrel with one headmaster he was assigned to the east coast of Malaya as a senior lecturer in a teacher-training college. Then in 1957 Malaya gained its independence, and the future of British expatriates grew doubtful. Shortly thereafter the Malayan government generously provided each erstwhile colonial with a sum of money and then deported him. Burgess soon found another teaching post in Brunei, Borneo. Despite the favorable reception of his Malayan books, he viewed himself not primarily as a novelist but as a professional teacher who simply wrote novels "as a kind of hobby."

In Borneo, as in Malaya, Burgess refused to join the British colonials in their isolation from the native community. His perfect command of Malay and genuine interest in the people enabled him to mix freely with them, and at the expense of antagonizing his fellow colonial officers he won their trust and respect. This relationship led to an invitation to lead the people's Freedom party, which he refused. Even so, rumors about his loyalty began to circulate within the British community, and he was stuck with the appellation "bolshy." The antagonism of his fellows and superiors was further augmented by an incident during a garden party in honor of Prince Philip, who was in Brunei on an official visit. As the prince wandered dutifully from group to group, he inquired casually about local conditions: "Everything all right?" All the dazzled colonials replied appropriately that indeed everything was as it should be—all, that is, except Burgess's fiery Welsh wife, who was rumored to be British socialist Aneurin Bevan's sister. She replied bluntly and insultingly that "things bloody well weren't all right," and that, moreover, the British were largely to blame.

After this episode Burgess's days in Brunei would probably have been few even without the physical breakdown that finally sent him back to England. Not long after the garden party Burgess was giving his students a lecture on phonetics when he, like Edwin Spindrift in *The Doctor Is Sick* (1960), suddenly collapsed on the floor of the classroom. He later suspected that it was "a willed collapse out of sheer boredom and frustration." Whatever the cause, with incredible dispatch he was loaded aboard an airliner for England, where doctors at the National Hospital for Nervous Diseases diagnosed his ailment as a brain tumor. The neatness with which he was thereby eliminated as a source of official embarrassment in Borneo led him to guess that his hasty removal had as much to do with his general intransigence and the garden-party incident as with his collapse on the classroom floor.

The political situation in Borneo was now among the least of his worries. The existence of the brain tumor had been determined primarily on the basis of a spinal tap, which revealed an excess of protein in the spinal fluid. Other excruciating tests followed. Initially the doctors considered removing the tumor, and Burgess was apprehensive lest "they hit my talent instead of my tumor," but they then decided that removal was impossible. Burgess was told he would probably be dead within the year, but that if he managed to live through the year, he could infer that the prognosis had been excessively pessimistic and that he would survive. His situation was extremely dismal—he had no pension, was unable to get a job, and saw no way of providing for his prospective widow. Fortunately, they had been able to bring a bit of money with them from the Far East. His wife, having graduated in economics from the University of Manchester, was knowledgeable in money matters, and she shrewdly invested on the stock exchange the £1,000 they had taken out of Malaya. The stock exchange was a free organization in those days; she could buy and sell on margins, and in a few years she had doubled, then quadru-

pled, the original sum. The initial sum enabled them to live through the year, from 1959 into 1960, that Burgess had been told would be his last.

Instead of moping about in self-pitying depression he began writing novels, chiefly to secure posthumous royalties. Surprisingly, he felt more exhilarated than depressed, and his "last year on earth" was one the most productive he has ever known. Five of his novels were written during this period—*The Doctor Is Sick* (1960), *One Hand Clapping* (1961), *The Worm and the Ring* (1961), *The Wanting Seed* (1962), and *Inside Mr. Enderby* (1963). These books include some of his best work, and they were not the only things he wrote. (In the following discussion, Burgess's works will be considered in roughly the order in which they were composed. However, where it is illuminating to consider together novels that are closely related thematically, the discussion will not adhere to this order.) Thus he launched himself as a professional novelist under less than favorable and quite accidental circumstances. But as he said in a lecture at Simon Fraser University in Vancouver, British Columbia, on 5 March 1969, "most writers who actually do become novelists do so by accident. If a man deliberately sets out to become a novelist, he usually winds up as a critic, which is, I think, something less."

His productivity astonished the critics and, paradoxically, alarmed his publisher, Heinemann. The fecundity of writers such as Charles Dickens, Anthony Trollope, and Henry James had long been forgotten in England, where it was generally thought that writers of quality followed the example of E. M. Forster and produced a canon of perhaps four or five books over a period of eighty to ninety years. Fecundity, Burgess found, was looked upon as a kind of literary disease. His publisher suggested that he conceal the malady by taking another pseudonym, so *One Hand Clapping* and *Inside Mr. Enderby* were published under the name Joseph Kell.

Burgess intended *Inside Mr. Enderby* to be a "kind of trumpet blast on behalf of the besieged poet of today—the man who tries to write his poetry not on the campus, but in the smallest room in the house," the lavatory, where he can have some privacy. His hero, Mr. F. X. Enderby, is a shy, harmless, flatulent little poet whose misadventures reveal the condition of poetry and the poet in the 1960s. The novel was destined to have several sequels. Burgess followed it in 1968 with *Enderby Outside,* and the two books were published together the same year in America as a single novel titled *Enderby*. A third Enderby novel, *The Clockwork Testament, or, En-*

derby's End, appeared in 1974, and still another one, *Enderby's Dark Lady, or, No End to Enderby,* in 1984.

The first Enderby novel was well received by the critics. The reviewer in *The Sunday Times* (26 September 1960) called it "a brilliantly fly piece of work" and remarked that "Mr. Kell's narrative crackles with witticisms." The critic for *The Spectator* termed the book "a little masterpiece," and it also received high praise in the *Times Literary Supplement* and *The Listener.* Neither *Inside Mr. Enderby* nor *One Hand Clapping* sold well, however, mainly because no one had ever heard of Joseph Kell. *One Hand Clapping* is a clever tour de force, a parable of life in modern England narrated by the twenty-three-year-old wife of a used-car salesman. Although it is not one of Burgess's best books, not on a level with *Inside Mr. Enderby,* it was republished profitably under the name Anthony Burgess in 1972. A comical result of the Kell business was that Burgess was asked to review one of his own novels; the editor who sent him the book did not know that he was Joseph Kell. Appreciating what he took to be the editor's sense of humor, Burgess wrote the review—and was never again asked to write for that journal.

Another significant novel Burgess produced during his "terminal year," *The Doctor Is Sick,* was based to some extent on his experiences in Borneo and as a patient at the National Hospital for Nervous Diseases. The protagonist, a thirty-eight-year-old philologist named Edwin Spindrift, collapses on the floor of a classroom in the Far East, is flown back to England, and is told that he must undergo brain surgery. He promptly escapes into the night clad like a concentration camp inmate in striped pajamas and undergoes a series of ordeals in the seamier districts of London. Once outside the "safe" confines of the hospital, Spindrift goes in search of love, or more precisely, the meaning of love. This is one of the many respects in which his experience parallels the quest of Leopold Bloom in Joyce's *Ulysses* (1922). Like some of Burgess's other novels, *The Doctor Is Sick* parallels Joyce's masterpiece and may be regarded as one of his own treatments of Joyce's major themes.

As the novels came out, his health improved steadily, and he began to take on various nonfiction writing chores as well. For a time he was both music critic for *Queen*—a British magazine read in the United States—and drama critic for *The Spectator.* One of the trials of this dual role was being dogged by spies assigned "to see whether I really saw an opera and a play on the same night." He also wrote television scripts, including one on Percy Bysshe Shelley and Lord Byron in Switzerland and another on James Joyce. Other projects included a play writ-

Frank De Wolfe, Anne Bancroft, James Mason, and Robert Powell in a scene from the 1977 television production Jesus of Nazareth, *for which Burgess wrote the script*

ten at the request of the Phoenix Theatre, London; another one for the BBC; and still another for Independent TV. In addition he was becoming more and more in demand as a book reviewer, and his average yearly output in reviews alone was estimated by one reporter at 150,000 words. But Burgess was primarily a writer of fiction, and most of his boundless energy during the early 1960s went into the writing of novels. He also wrote some short fiction and, although he found the short story a constricting form, contributed several stories to *The Hudson Review, Argosy, Rutgers Review,* and other journals. He also contributed verse to various periodicals, including *The Transatlantic Review, Arts and Letters,* and *The New York Times;* the latter commissioned him to write a poem on the landing of Apollo 11.

Burgess never, however, remained rooted to his writer's chair. Always restless, he traveled a great deal, and so far as his fiction is concerned one of his most productive trips was a visit to Leningrad in 1961. His purpose in going "was to experience life in Leningrad without benefit of Intourist–i.e., as one of the crowd." Before the trip he spent about six weeks reviving his Russian, acquired during the war; his use of the language enabled him to gain a great deal from the experience. One of his first discoveries in Russia was that it was possible to enter the country without a passport. One simply left the ship long after everyone else, after the immigration officials had gone off duty. If one were really willing to live dangerously, one could also reap a tidy profit selling smuggled Western goods. One could smuggle a man out of the country by securing a deluxe cabin with a bathroom in which he could be hidden. Burgess actually did some of these things himself or heard about others who had succeeded in doing them. On top of all this he found that one could get to know the secret police on a friendly basis. Late one evening these stock villains of Western spy thrillers were kind enough to take a drunken Burgess home in one of their cars. This and other experiences finally led him to conclude that "the Russian soul is all right; it's the state that's wrong."

One of the fruits of this hair-raising "research" was *Honey for the Bears* (1963), a hilarious entertainment in which an unconsciously homosexual ("gomosexual") antiques dealer goes to Russia to sell smuggled dresses and in the process loses his wife to a lesbian. Another product was *A Clockwork Orange,* a seriously philosophical picaresque tale narrated by a demonic young hoodlum who could be either Russian or English or both. Burgess and his wife encountered some of his prototypes late one evening outside a Leningrad restaurant. As they were finishing their meal, they were startled to hear loud hammering at the door. Having been filled with the usual Western propaganda, they immediately had the terrifying thought that the hammerers were after them as the capitalist enemy. In fact these hardfisted young toughs, called "stilyagi," were after different prey. When the Burgesses wanted to leave the restaurant, the stilyagi courteously stepped aside, allowed them to pass, and then resumed their hammering. Burgess was struck by the Nabokovian quality of the incident, the way in which their conduct reflected the "chess mind": "Even lawless violence must follow rules and ritual." He was also struck by their resemblance to the English teddy boys of the 1950s whom they were copying, and he went home with an even sturdier conviction that "Russians are human." (When he described this incident during the lecture at Simon Fraser University, he accidentally said "Humans are Russian," but he would not correct the slip, considering it ben trovato.)

In the same year he went to Russia his novels *Devil of a State* and *The Worm and the Ring* appeared and were fairly well received critically. The entire edition of the latter book was, however, withdrawn and turned into pulp because of a purely coincidental resemblance of events and characters to actual incidents and persons, and his publisher was obliged to pay £100 to the aggrieved parties in an out-of-court settlement.

Devil of a State was a Book Society choice when it first appeared, but like so many of Burgess's novels it had a mixed critical response. A *New Statesman* reviewer observed that its comic devices would have been more effective "if Mr. Burgess hadn't been Scooped long ago." He and others had noted that the book seems to echo Evelyn Waugh's early satires, *Black Mischief* (1932) and *Scoop* (1938). Indeed, the African setting and the sardonic detachment with which Burgess presents the chaos of life in a newly emergent state are liable to give a reader of the Waugh satires a sense of déjà vu. Certainly Burgess had acknowledged a general indebtedness to Waugh, as well as to Joyce, Laurence Sterne, and Vladimir Nabokov. But the book is essentially Burgess's own vision of life in such a state, and he quite likely saw the same sorts of things in the Far East that Waugh saw in Africa. "Dunia," the imaginary caliphate in *Devil of a State,* is, Burgess said, "a kind of fantasticated Zanzibar," but one senses that the real setting may be Borneo.

The protagonist of the novel, Lydgate, like backward-looking Crabbe in the *Malayan Trilogy,* progresses toward a terrible reckoning with his past; his progress, like Crabbe's, is set against the chaotic progress of a former British colony toward independence. But while it is possible to become involved with Crabbe and the Malaya he loves, in *Devil of a State* Burgess does not permit involvement with Lydgate and Dunia. He compels instead sardonic detachment from the horribly comic spectacle of irresponsibility and its fruits both on the individual and the state level. The book is both farce and parable. Like the satire of Jonathan Swift, it points in many directions and sustains its irony throughout.

The Worm and the Ring was based upon Burgess's experiences as a grammar school teacher in Banbury, Oxfordshire. It is a kind of mock epic, or more exactly, a mock opera, a burlesque of Richard Wagner's *Der Ring des Nibelungen* (1869–1876). Wagner's allegorical tale of a struggle for power between Nibelung dwarfs, giants, and gods is translated into a struggle for the control of a grammar school in a little English borough. The protagonist, Christopher Howarth, an ineffectual Siegfried, is a thirty-nine-year-old assistant master who teaches German and leads an ungratifying existence. For one thing, his relationship with his wife is tense, partly because of their poverty but mainly because of her submission to the rules of the Catholic Church. The wretchedness of Howarth's poverty, the stupid tyranny of mindless Catholic orthodoxy, and the philistinism of the English borough are all presented with angry force.

But Burgess's anger does not cause him to present any of his criticisms simplistically. If the society is drifting toward philistinism, it is not entirely due to the strength or cunning of the philistine "giants." The liberal humanism of the headmaster, his unshakable faith in human goodness, gives him excuses to shirk responsibility and ignore the demands of the community for stability. Burgess's balanced critical treatment of the extreme of rule based on liberal idealism versus the extreme of cynical autocracy agrees with his other novels. As in his dystopian books, *The Wanting Seed* and *A Clockwork Orange,* Burgess exposes the inadequacies and dangers of both as governing philosophies. Reviewing the novel, one critic praised the treatment of Howarth's private life and the terrible dilemma of his son, who must reconcile his love of God and the Catholic Church with love for his father. The reviewer also remarked that Burgess "has a gift for near-caricature which makes the damp grey atmosphere of his Midland town almost bearable."

A year after these two novels were published in England, another novel, *The Right to an Answer,* was published in America, and Burgess's reputation across the Atlantic began to grow. Like *The Worm and the Ring,* this novel focuses on the decadence of modern England. The narrator-protagonist, Mr. J. W. Denham, is a plump, balding, middle-aged businessman who takes what he can get out of life in pleasure and novel experiences. After living in the Far East he feels alienated, but he is troubled more by the spectacle of "irresponsibility" and "instability" in "hideous, TV-haunted England." What he has seen of life in the East and the West has given him a Hobbesian view of human affairs. He values stability more than freedom and is convinced that "you definitely can't have both."

The brief glimpses of dreary or sordid suburban life in a "rather large smug Midland city" are a prelude to the entrance of Mr. Raj, a Ceylonese gentleman who provides yet another vantage point of Far Eastern experience. He has come to England to carry out research for a thesis on "Popular Conceptions of Racial Differentiation." He tries to bridge some gaps between East and West by attempting to have an affair with a woman who has been involved in the game of wife-swapping, and the results are tragic.

The range of subjects treated in *The Right to an Answer*—from culture clashes to love and moral responsibility—is considerable, yet the relevance of each subject to the others is evident. The nature of

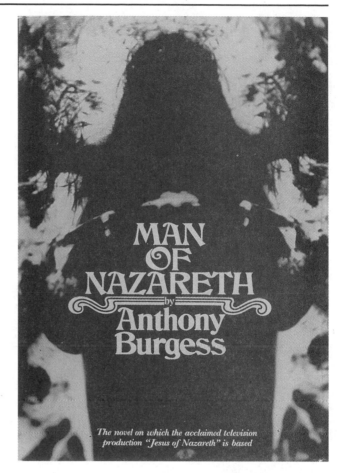

Dust jacket for Burgess's novelization of Jesus of Nazareth. *The description on the jacket reverses the order in which the two works were written.*

the subjects themselves may have been one reason why British reviewers were not enthusiastic when the novel first appeared in Britain in 1960. It received a rather tepid review in the *Times Literary Supplement* from a critic who wondered "whether the experiences recounted add up to anything of much importance." Critics in America had no such doubts and praised the book as "a nicely controlled examination of some human predicaments," "a book made out of the author's own head and not from other Zeitgeist books."

As time passed and Burgess's "terminal year" receded, he became less worried about his own health but more about his wife's. She had never fully recovered from the injuries she received in 1943, and the years in the Far East had been hard on her. She died in 1968 of portal cirrhosis brought on partly by alcoholism but mainly by years of vitamin deprivation in Malaya and Borneo. Although there was little Burgess could do to ease the pain of her last years, he was still burdened with a strong residue of guilt about her death, and this conflict may be reflected in one of his novels, *Beard's Roman Women* (1976).

Some months after his first wife's death he married a lovely, dark-haired Italian contessa, Liliana Macellari, whom he had known for several years. She is a philologist and translator whose works include Italian translations of Thomas Pynchon's *V* (1963) and Lawrence Durrell's *Alexandria Quartet* (1962). Burgess found the latter project "hard to forgive," not because of the quality of her translation but because he considered the original hardly worth translating, especially into Italian, which he knew and revered.

With their son, Andrea, the Burgesses moved to Malta in 1969, where they lived, between lecture tours and a teaching stint in North Carolina, for nearly two years. They soon found that the island had little to recommend it besides its Mediterranean climate. The repressive rule exercised by a church-dominated government made life exceedingly dreary if not intolerable. Yet during his brief, unhappy residence on the island Burgess managed to produce two books: a biography of Shakespeare and the novel *MF* (1971), which is set in the United States and a tyrannically ruled Caribbean island called "Castita." The striking resemblance this supposedly chaste little island bears to Malta appears to be more than coincidental.

In 1971 Burgess and his wife purchased a flat in Rome (the flat that appears in *Beard's Roman Women*) and acquired a house in the nearby lakeside town of Bracciano (the house that appears in the conclusion of *MF*). Between tours and visits abroad they lived alternately in the two residences until 1976. Although they found the atmosphere in Rome a good deal more civilized and bearable than that of Malta, after five years they felt compelled to move again. Italy, Burgess believed, was on the verge of civil war. There was a state of general chaos, prices were rising intolerably, and shortages were becoming more than irksome. In addition there was the omnipresent danger of his son Andrea's being kidnapped, since Italians tended to believe that all foreigners, especially foreign writers, are rich and capable of paying high ransoms. To escape these nuisances and threats, Burgess moved his family to Monaco.

Although Burgess had been a professional writer for many years, he still did a considerable amount of teaching. He taught widely in the British Commonwealth and Europe as well as in the United States, where he held several visiting appointments at universities, including Princeton and the City University of New York. He was fairly impressed by the quality of American students "from a human point of view," noting:

> They're good and sincere, aspirant and very different from their parents. They do question everything. But it worries me that they lack basic equipment. They haven't read very widely. I don't mind their cutting themselves off from the 1930s or '40s, but I do object to their cutting themselves off from the Roman and Hebraic civilizations which made our own. It means that if one is giving a lecture on Shakespeare or Marlowe, one cannot take it for granted that they know who Niobe was, or Ulysses, or Ajax. And this is undoubtedly going to get worse in America; may indeed lead to the entire cutting off of America from the whole current of culture which gave it birth. A man like Benjamin Franklin, a great American, may become an unintelligible figure to modern Americans. This is very frightening.

He objected as well to the utilitarian view of literature held by many American students—their insistence that it is to be valued primarily in terms of the "messages" it conveys and their concomitant tendency to regard a purely aesthetic aim as irrelevant, sinful, or reactionary.

Though he enjoyed university teaching, he did not see himself as an intellectual ("If I am one, I'm fighting against it all the time"). He did not want to become too much a part of the rarified, cerebral campus atmosphere in which the enwombed academic thrives. His attitudes stemmed largely from his view of the nature of literature and indeed of reality itself. To some extent he agreed with the Shakespeare/Burgess composite hero of *Nothing Like the Sun: A Story of Shakespeare's Love Life* (1964) that literature is "an epiphenomenon of the action of the flesh":

> I don't think it's an intellectual thing. It's not made out of concepts; it's made out of percepts. People often think you're being trivial or superficial if you think it's important to describe a bottle of sauce or beer as neatly, as cleverly, as evocatively as you can. It's really more important to do that than to express an idea or concept. I believe the world of physical things is the only world that really exists, and the world of concepts is a world of trickery, for the most part. Concepts only come to life when they're expressed in things you can see, taste, feel, touch, and the like. One of the reasons I have a sneaking regard for the Catholic Church is that it turns everything into tangible percepts. There's no mystical communion with God as there is in Hinduism or Buddhism. Instead you get God in the form of a meal, which is right, which is good.

With regard to religion, Burgess maintained a "renegade Catholic" stance that was oddly conservative in some respects. He despised liberal Catholicism, which seemed to have become another religion in the process of gaining acceptance in the modern world. The ecumenical movement repelled him, as did the liturgical changes and the use of the vernacular:

> when I say that I am a Catholic now, I mean solely that I have a Catholic background, that my emotions, my responses are Catholic, and that my intellectual convictions, such as they are, are very meager compared with the fundamental emotional convictions. Certainly, when I write, I tend to write from a Catholic point of view—either from the point of view of a believing Catholic, or a renegade Catholic, which is I think James Joyce's position. Reading *Ulysses,* you are aware of this conflict within a man who knows the Church thoroughly and yet has totally rejected it with a blasphemous kind of vigor.

To an extent Burgess subscribed to the Manichaean heresy, although he agreed with the Church that it should be condemned as heresy. He shared the Manichaean belief that there is a perpetual conflict between two forces that dominates the affairs of the universe, and whether the forces can be accurately labeled "good" and "evil" is by no means certain. They might as reasonably be designated by terms such as "right" and "left," or "x" and "y," or even "hot" and "cold." All that is certain is that the opposed forces exist, that they are in conflict, and that earthly turmoils are relatively trivial affairs which merely figure the great cosmic clash. Burgess believed that the man who is aware of this conflict yet deliberately and cynically refuses to involve himself in it is a contemptible self-server.

The novels Burgess produced during his "terminal year" exhibit themes that he was to develop again and again—the role and situation of the artist vis-à-vis an impinging world, love and decay in the West, the quest for a darker culture, and his view of history as a perpetual oscillation or "waltz" between "Pelagian" and "Augustinian" phases.

The Pelagian-Augustinian theme is the central focus of *The Wanting Seed* (1962), Burgess's first Orwellian proleptic nightmare. The novel presents a horrifying, though richly comic, picture of life in a future world freed of the scourge of war but overpopulated beyond Thomas Malthus's most fearful imaginings. As the novel opens, it is apparent that a suffocatingly crowded England is applying what Malthus would call checks through "vice" and "improper arts." Homosexuality, castration, abortion, and infanticide are much encouraged by a desperate government. The leaders share Malthus's belief that the educated classes can be persuaded rationally while the proletariat cannot. Hence, while the state makes little attempt to sway the "proles," it seeks to

Dust jacket for the U.S. edition of Burgess's novel about Sigmund Freud, Leon Trotsky, and the destruction of the world

influence the more "responsible" classes by education, propaganda, and social pressure. Everywhere posters blare "It's Sapiens to be Homo." A "Homosex Institute" offers both day and evening classes. People are able to improve their social and economic positions only if they can maintain a reputation either of "blameless sexlessness" or nonfertile sexuality. The protagonist, Tristram Foxe, misses a deserved promotion because, as a superior tells him, "A kind of aura of fertility surrounds you, Brother Foxe." Among other things, Tristram has fathered a child, and while each family is legally allowed one birth, "the best people just don't. Just don't."

But even if the "best people" can accept these inverted standards, the gods cannot. (The term "gods" is used advisedly since Burgess's Manichaenism is clearly evidenced in the novel.) Blights and animal diseases reduce the food supply severely. Malthus's checks through "misery" come into play in the form of famine and bloodshed. Starvation causes a total abandonment of the restraints imposed by the perverted society. People are murdered and devoured by anthropophagic "dining clubs." Frequently these cannibal feasts are followed by heterosexual orgies "in the ruddy light of the fat-spitting fires."

In a fairly short time order is restored by a hastily created army, and it becomes apparent that the experience of cannibalism has suggested to government leaders new methods of population control. Implementation of these methods requires a re-creation of war as it had been fought long before, during the twentieth century. The objectives of the war and the character of the enemy are top secret matters, but an uninformed civilian population cheers on an equally uninformed soldiery, and only the government and civilian contractors know that the heroes are bound for a Valhalla where they will be processed for consumption. Although few people are aware of the real nature of this "warfare," there is a widely held assumption that canning makes cannibalism a relatively civilized affair. As one soldier tells Tristram Foxe, "It makes all the difference if you get it out of a tin."

The cyclical theory of history Burgess illustrates in this novel is one he had partially formulated in *A Vision of Battlements*. In that novel an American officer describes how the Pelagian denial of original sin had spawned "the two big modern heresies—material progress as a sacred goal; the State as God Almighty." The former has produced "Americanism" and the latter, "the Socialist process." In all government history is seen to be an oscillation between Pelagian and Augustinian phases. When a government is functioning in its Pelagian phase, or "Pelphase," it is socialistic and committed to a Wellsian liberal belief in man and his ability to achieve perfection through his own efforts. Inevitably man fails to fulfill the liberal expectation, and the ensuing disappointment causes a chaotic "Interphase," during which terrorist police strive to maintain order by force and brutality. Finally the government, appalled by its own excesses, lessens the brutality but continues to enforce its will on the citizenry on the assumption that man is an inherently sinful creature from whom no good may be expected. This pessimistic phase is appropriately named for the saint whose preoccupation with the problems of evil led him, like Burgess, into Manichaenism. During "Gusphase" there is a capitalist economy but little real freedom for the individual. What Burgess appears to be suggesting is that a godless society which accepts Augustine's view of unregenerate human nature is apt to be a fascist dictatorship.

In 1962 what was to become Burgess's most widely read novel, *A Clockwork Orange,* was published. (Even before Stanley Kubrick filmed it in 1971, it was his most popular novel, a fact that did not greatly please Burgess, who valued some of his other works more.) Like *The Wanting Seed, A Clockwork Orange* is a proleptic nightmare with antiutopian implications. Although it can be read as an answer to and a rejection of the main ideas of psychologist B. F. Skinner, Burgess was less directly influenced by Skinner's ideas in particular than by accounts he had read of behaviorist methods of reforming criminals that were being used in American prisons with the avowed purpose of limiting the subjects' freedom of choice to what society called "goodness." This effort struck Burgess as "most sinful," and his novel is, among other things, an attempt to clarify the issues involved in the use of such methods.

The setting of *A Clockwork Orange* is a city somewhere in either Western Europe or North America where a civilization has evolved out of a fusion of the dominant cultures east and west of the Iron Curtain. This cultural merger seems partly the result of successful cooperative efforts in the conquest of space, efforts that have promoted a preoccupation with outer space and a concomitant indifference to exclusively terrestrial affairs, such as the maintenance of law and order in the cities. A reader is apt to assume that Burgess was thinking of the United States when he envisioned this situation of the future. In fact, he was more influenced by what he had seen during his visit to Leningrad in 1961. At that time Russia was leading in the space race, and the gangs of young thugs called stilyagi were becoming a serious nuisance in Russian cities. At the same time, London police were having their troubles with the teddy boys. Having seen both the stilyagi and the teddy boys in action, Burgess was moved by a renewed sense of the oneness of humanity, and the murderous teenaged hooligans who are the main characters in *A Clockwork Orange* are composite creations. Alex, the fifteen-year-old narrator-protagonist, could be either an Alexander or an Alexei. The names of his three comrades, Dim, Pete, and Georgie, are similarly ambiguous, suggesting both Russian and English given names.

A reader may miss these and other hints completely, but what he cannot overlook is the effect of the cultural fusion on the teenage underworld patois in which the story is narrated. The language, Burgess's invention, is called *nadsat,* which is a transliteration of a Russian suffix equivalent to the English suffix -*teen,* as in *fifteen.* Most, but by no means all, of the words nadsat comprises are Russian, and Burgess has altered some of them in ways that one might reasonably expect them to be altered in the mouths of English-speaking teenagers. For instance, the word *horrorshow* is a favorite adjective of nadsat speakers meaning everything from "good" to "splendid." The word sounds like a clever invention by an observer of teenagers who is aware of their fondness for films such as *I Was a Teen-Age Werewolf* and *Frankenstein Meets the Wolf Man.* Actually, it is an imagined development from *kharashó,* a Russian adjective meaning "good" or "well."

Many of the non-Russian words in nadsat are derived from British slang. For example, a member of the city's finest, the ineffectual safeguards of law and order, is referred to as a *rozz,* a word derived from the English slang term *rozzer,* meaning "policeman." The American edition of the novel has a glossary, prepared without Burgess's consultation, which is not entirely accurate either in its translation of nadsat words or in the information it gives concerning their origins. Actually, after a few pages of the novel, a reader of even moderate sensitivity should not need a glossary and will do well to refrain from consulting this one; the translations, even when they are accurate, may substitute terms which lack the rich onomatopoeic suggestiveness of Burgess's language.

The novel is more than a linguistic tour de force. It is also one of the most devastating pieces of multipronged social satire in recent fiction, and, like *The Wanting Seed,* it passes the test of "relevance." Alex is one of the most appallingly vicious creations in recent fiction. Although his name suggests his composite Russian-English identity, it is ambiguous in other ways as well. The fusion of the negative prefix *a* with the word *lex* suggests simultaneously an absence of law and a lack of words. The idea of lawlessness is readily apparent in Alex's behavior, but the idea of wordlessness is subtler and harder to grasp, for Alex seems to have a great many words at his command, whether he happens to be snarling at his "droogs" in nadsat or respectfully addressing his elders in Russianless English. He is articulate but wordless in that he apprehends life directly, without the mediation of words. Unlike the characters who seek to control him and the rest of the society, he makes no attempt to explain or justify his actions through abstract ideals or goals such as liberty or stability. Nor does he attempt to define any role for himself within a large social process. Instead he simply experiences life directly, sensuously, and while he is free, joyously.

Indeed, his guiltless joy in violence of every kind—from the destruction or theft of objects to practically every form of sexual and nonsexual assault—suggests, however incongruously, innocence to the reader. Alex also has a fine ear for European classical music, especially Ludwig van Beethoven and Wolfgang Amadeus Mozart, and although such widely differing tastes within one savage youngster might seem incongruous, they are in fact complementary. Knowing his own passions, Alex is highly amused by an article he reads in which some would-be reformer argues that "Modern Youth" might become more "civilized" if "A Lively Appreciation Of The Arts," especially music and poetry, were encouraged.

The first third of the novel is taken up with Alex's joyful satiation of all his appetites; and as rape and murder follow assault, robbery, and vandalism, the spectacle of pleasure in violence overwhelms. While it might be argued that psychopathic delight could not be experienced by a sane person, there is no implication in the novel that Alex is anything but sane—sane and free to choose what delights him. Since his choices are invariably destructive or harmful, it appears that the right of society to deprive him of his freedom, if not his life, can hardly be disputed. What the novel does dispute is the right of society to make Alex less than a human being by depriving him of the ability to choose a harmful course of action.

Partly as a result of his own vicious activities and partly as a result of struggles between Pelagian and Augustinian factions in government, Alex is destined to experience life as a well-conditioned "good citizen." (Although the labels "Pelagian" and "Augustinian" are not used, it is not difficult to recognize these factions by their policies.) The Pelagian-controlled government that is in power as the novel opens is responsible by its laxness for the widespread crime that occurs. When Alex is finally caught while attempting to escape from a burglary involving a fatal assault on an old woman, it is mainly because his gang has betrayed him and facilitated the capture. He is sentenced to fourteen years in prison, and while there he will feel the effects of a major change in government policy.

The failure of liberal methods of government generates the usual "DISAPPOINTMENT" and the concomitant yearning for Augustinian alternatives. Realizing that the terrorized electorate cares little about "the tradition of liberty" and is actually willing to "sell liberty for a quieter life," the government seeks to impose order by the most efficient means available. Unlike the Augustinian-controlled government in *The Wanting Seed,* this body does not resort to mass murder. Instead it relies upon the genius of modern behavioral technology, specifically the branch of it that aims at the total control of human will. When Alex brings attention to himself by murdering a fellow inmate, he is selected as a "trailblazer" to be "transformed out of all recognition."

The purpose of Alex's transformation is to eliminate his capacity to choose socially deleterious courses of action. Psychological engineers force upon him what Skinner might call "the inclination to behave." Strapped in a chair, he is forced to watch films of incredible brutality, some of them contrived and others actual documentaries of Japanese and Nazi atrocities during World War II. In the past, violence has given him only the most pleasurable sensations; now he is suddenly overcome by the most unbearable nausea and headaches. After suffering several of these agonizing sessions, he finds that the nausea has been induced not by the films but by injections given beforehand. Thus his body is being taught to associate the sight or even the thought of violence with unpleasant sensations. His responses and, as it were, his moral progress are measured by electronic devices wired to his body. Quite by accident, his body is conditioned to associate not only violence but also his beloved classical music with nausea. The last movement of Beethoven's Fifth Symphony (1807) accompanies a documentary on the Nazis, and the connection of the two with bodily misery is firmly fixed.

Having gratified his rehabilitation engineers with proof that he is a "true Christian," Alex is free to enter society again—if not as a useful citizen, at least as a harmless one—as living proof that the government is doing something to remedy social ills and therefore merits reelection. He is not only harmless but helpless as well. Shortly after his release he is the victim of a ludicrous, vengeful beating by one of his most helpless former victims, an old man assisted by some of his ancient cronies. Unable to endure even the violent feeling needed to fight his way clear, he is rescued by three policemen. The fact that one of his rescuers is a former member of his own gang and another a former leader of a rival gang suggests that the society is experiencing a transitional "Interphase" as it progresses into its Augustinian phase. These young thugs, like the "greyboys" in *The Wanting Seed,* have been recruited into the police force apparently on the theory that their criminal desires can be expressed usefully in the maintenance of order on the streets. Again it is tempting to suppose that Burgess was influenced by conditions in some American cities where, as he remarked in an unpublished interview with Geoffrey Aggeler on 10 September 1972, the police seem to represent little more than "a kind of alternative criminal body."

Having been beaten by his rescuers, Alex drags himself to a little cottage that was the scene of the most savage atrocity he and his droogs had carried out before his imprisonment. One of his victims, a writer named F. Alexander, still lives there. The writer's political and philosophical ideals incline toward Pelagian liberalism, and he has remained, in spite of his experience as a victim of human depravity, committed to the belief that man is "a creature of growth and capable of sweetness." Because of this view he remains unalterably opposed to the use of "debilitating and willsapping techniques of conditioning" in criminal reform. To some extent he is an autobiographical creation. Like Burgess, he has written a book titled *A Clockwork Orange* with the purpose of illuminating the dangers of allowing such methods. The fact that he has had the sincerity of his beliefs about criminal reform tested by the personal experience of senseless criminal brutality is something else he shares with Burgess, whose first wife had been assaulted. But here the resemblance ends. Although Burgess believes man is capable of sweetness and should not be turned into a piece of clockwork, he is no Pelagian, and his book, unlike F. Alexander's, is no lyrical effusion of revolutionary idealism.

Although F. Alexander and his associates seem motivated by the loftiest of liberal ideas, they are incapable of seeing Alex as anything but a propaganda device. To them Alex is not an unfortunate human being to be assisted but "a martyr to the cause of Liberty" who can serve "the Future and our Cause." When F. Alexander begins to suspect that Alex is one of the attackers who invaded his home, he and his associates decide that Alex will be more effective as a dead "witness" against the government than as a living one. Utilizing the responses implanted in him by the government psychologists, they attempt to drive him to suicide, and they nearly succeed. Thus Burgess effectively underlines what Pelagian idealism shares with Augustinian cynicism. The Pelagian preoccupation with the tradition of liberty and the dignity of man, like the Augustinian preoccupation with stability, will make any sacrifice for "the Good of Man" worthwhile, including the destruction of Man himself.

The government receives ample amounts of embarrassing publicity concerning Alex's attempted suicide but somehow survives. One day Alex awakens to find himself fully as vicious as before his treatment. More psychological engineers, using "deep hypnopaedia or some such slovo," have restored his moral nature, his "self," and his concomitant appetites for Beethoven and throat cutting. In this depraved condition he cannot further embarrass the Augustinian government.

At this point the American edition of *A Clockwork Orange* ends, and Stanley Kubrick, following the American edition, ends his film. In its earlier British editions, however, the novel has one additional chapter that makes a considerable difference in how one may interpret it. This chapter, like the chapters that begin the three main parts of the novel, opens with the question, "What's it going to be then, eh?" The reader has been led to believe that, aside from imprisonment or hanging, the two conditions presented are the only possible alternatives for Alex. The omitted chapter, however, reveals yet another alternative; Alex is shown becoming weary of violence. Having met one of his old comrades who has married and settled down, he realizes that this is what he wants for himself. He wants to marry and have a son, whom he will try to teach to avoid his own mistakes, though he knows he will not succeed.

Burgess's American publisher insisted on omitting this chapter so that the book would end "on a tough and violent note," and Burgess agreed that the omission was in some ways an improvement. The missing chapter in effect suggests that individuals are capable of growing and learning through suffering and error. It suggests further that suffering, fallen human beings, not behavioral technology or the revolutionary schemes of idealists, bring "goodness" into the world.

Between 1962 and the end of 1980 Burgess produced fifteen novels. Some of these, such as *The Eve of St. Venus* (1964), *The Clockwork Testament, Beard's Roman Women,* and *ABBA ABBA* (1977), are rather slight books. The most significant are *Nothing Like the Sun, Tremor of Intent* (1966), *Enderby Outside, MF, Napoleon Symphony* (1974), and *Earthly Powers* (1980).

One of Burgess's most remarkable achievements in the novel is *Nothing Like the Sun,* a book that, unfortunately, did not receive its due from critics at the time of its appearance in the year of the Shakespeare quadricentennial. Its setting is a classroom somewhere in Malaya or Borneo; the narrator, as Burgess states in a prologue, is "Mr. Burgess," who has just been "given the sack" by his headmaster, and it is time to bid his students farewell. His farewell speech, a last lecture, will be primarily for the benefit of those "who complained that Shakespeare had nothing to give to the East." It is a long discourse, but he is well fortified with a potent Chinese rice spirit called *samsu,* a parting gift from his students. The samsu and his considerable knowledge of Shakespeare enable him to transport himself and his class back into sixteenth-century England. In a sense, however, he also brings Shakespeare for-

Dust jacket for the U.S. edition of Burgess's novel about a piano player's daughter who becomes headmistress of a sex school for wealthy gentlemen

ward into the twentieth century through identification with himself. As his lecture progresses, accompanied by much samsu swigging, the identification becomes stronger and stronger until finally, in the epilogue, readers are able to hear the voice of a Shakespeare-Burgess composite hero.

The lecture begins with a vision of an adolescent Master Shakespeare at home in Stratford. As a youth he dreams of a "goddess," a dark golden lady who is his muse, his ideal of beauty, and his forbidden fruit. He finds her literally embodied in various dark-complexioned country maidens, and occasionally she inspires verse. Next comes "WS the married man," who has been trapped into marriage with a fair-complexioned lady, Anne Hathaway. Burgess's characterization of her reveals how she might have served as a model for Regan in *King Lear* (1605 or 1606), Lady Ann in *Richard III* (circa 1591–1592), and Gertrude in *Hamlet* (circa 1600–1601).

A position as a Latin tutor enables WS to escape for a time from Anne and the glove-making trade, and this experience gives birth to Shakespearean comedy in *The Comedy of Errors* (circa 1592–1594), which is based on a Latin play, Plautus's *Menaechmi*. A careless bit of pederasty ends his teaching career, but the play enables WS to join a touring company of players with a completed script in hand. Soon he is with Philip Henslowe's company, and several events occur that are destined to influence his art. Perhaps the most momentous is his meeting with Harry Wriothesley, third Earl of Southampton, who is to become "Mr. W. H." of the sonnets. Like the poet himself, Harry is sexually ambiguous; and when he seems to favor other effeminate young lords and a rival poet named Chapman, WS is wracked by jealousy.

As he rises to prominence as both playwright and poet, WS is drawn on by occasional glimpses of his goddess. No longer an unsophisticated country boy, he does not see her embodied in every dark-haired wench, but when he catches a glimpse of Fatimah, more commonly known as Lucy Negro, a brown-gold girl from the East Indies, the old yearning to know his goddess fully in the flesh overwhelms him again. His conquest of this dark lady is a long and arduous process, but he finally succeeds and finds himself in a state of desperate sexual bondage.

His deliverance from this enchantment is painful and disillusioning. His two "angels" (as he describes them in Sonnet 144) meet each other, and, knowing the lady's courtly ambitions and Wriothesley's voluptuous nature, he must before long "guess one angel in another's hell." Eventually he is reconciled with Wriothesley, but then his refusal to join the young man in supporting the Essex revolt causes another break, which is permanent. Eventually he is also reconciled with the dark lady, whose relationship with Wriothesley has been terminated by a pregnancy for which WS is probably responsible. The golden son she bears is to be raised as a gentleman and sent to her homeland in the Far East, and the poet is exhilarated by the thought that "his blood would, after all, flow to the East." Unfortunately, she also bears within her "hell" the fatal spirochete, a gift of Wriothesley, which will have a profound influence on the development of Shakespeare's art.

With the poet's discovery that he is syphilitic, Mr. Burgess is near the end of both his lecture and the samsu. In the "Epilogue" the voice of the poet merges completely with that of the writer-lecturer, and although the latter is not himself syphilitic, he describes how the disease molded "his" art even as it ravaged his body. Burgess has observed that students of serious literature may owe as much to the

spirochete as they do to the tubercle bacillus. Tuberculosis and syphilis would seem to be the most "creative" diseases, and it is significant that Keats, who had "an especially good hand," had both, Mr. Burgess says. The list of syphilitic poets is long, including such widely differing talents as Charles-Pierre Baudelaire and Edward Lear, and to this list Burgess would add the greatest name of all. His reasons are based chiefly upon close study of the poet's later works and his own experience, while he was serving with the Royal Army Medical Corps, of seeing genius flower in individuals suffering the last stages of the disease.

This is not to suggest that Burgess simply used his imagination in lieu of doing his homework. His knowledge of the late Tudor period and its well-documented events was considerable, and by his deft use of allusion and descriptive detail, as well as his imitation of Elizabethan idiom, he gives us an extremely convincing picture of the vigor, violence, filth, and color of Elizabethan town and country life.

In 1966 Burgess, having already experimented successfully with a wide variety of subgenres of the novel—mock epic, historical romance, picaresque, proleptic satire—turned his hand to a type that seems to be, by its very nature and purpose, fatally constricting to a writer with Burgess's philosophical and artistic concerns. *Tremor of Intent* is a spy thriller, and upon the well-worn framework of Ian Fleming's James Bond formula Burgess has fleshed out and molded a tale of intrigue that must fire the senses of even the most Bond-weary aficionado of the spy thriller. The typical Bond feats of appetite are duplicated and surpassed, sometimes to a ridiculous extent. The protagonist, Denis Hillier, has bedroom adventures that make Bond's conquests seem as crude and unfulfilling as an adolescent's evening affair with an issue of *Playboy*. His gastronomic awareness is such that Bond is by comparison an epicurean tyro. In addition Hillier possesses a mind that is good for something besides devising booby traps and playing games with supervillains.

Hillier is one of Burgess's Augustinians, a believer in original sin and a pessimist about human nature, and the novel focuses on the course of his spiritual progress as he tries to carry out a final mission for Her Majesty's Secret Service. He must sneak into Russia in disguise and kidnap a British scientist who has defected to Russia. The scientist, Dr. Edwin Roper, is an old friend.

In the course of attempting the kidnap he encounters an obese supervillain by the name of Theodorescu, who exemplifies the state of self-serving "neutrality" that Burgess regarded as the most contemptible and evil moral attitude a human being can assume. He agreed with Dante that such human beings are unworthy of the dignity of damnation. His protagonist, Hillier, discovers that the world is full of such "neutrals," and his mission for his government, which is dominated by bureaucratic neutrals, becomes a search for a way to make a meaningful commitment of himself against evil in the modern world. He is assisted in his spiritual progress by two women who represent stages in a Dantesque progress through hell into heaven. One of them, an Indian woman named Miss Devi, is herself a "hell," in the Elizabethan sense of a locus of sexual excitement. The other, a young girl named Clara, becomes for him a Beatrice figure. Eventually Hillier finds his way back into the Catholic Church, which he had left as a youth because of its puritanical view of the flesh. Only the church can satisfy his craving for commitment in the great conflict between the forces of "God and Notgod" that dominates the universe. Like other Burgess protagonists, he has become a Manichee.

Burgess accomplished something amazing in *Tremor of Intent*. He presents violence and a variety of sensual experience with an evocative linguistic verve that must dazzle even the most jaded sensibility. At the same time, he makes some provocative eschatological statements and conjectures. This in itself is amazing because the spy thriller by its very nature tends to avoid eschatology. In the hands of a less competent novelist any involved religious or philosophical questions would be a fatally distracting burden, but *Tremor of Intent* is such a brilliantly integrated package that somehow readers pass easily from an irresistible, corrupting, and vicarious involvement in gastronomy, fornication, and bloodshed to involved questions of ethics and eschatology and back again.

In several of his novels, notably *The Wanting Seed, The Eve of St. Venus, The Worm and the Ring,* and the Enderby novels, Burgess builds deliberately upon mythic frames and, like his master Joyce, even reveals some mythopoeic tendencies. Many of Burgess's characters are ironically modified archetypes who undergo archetypical experiences or ironic parodies of such experience. However, none of these novels fits wholly within a mythic frame, presumably because Burgess found archetypes too confining for his purposes. In his novel *MF,* however, he found a framework large enough to accommodate his total artistic design. He fused incest myths—Algonquin Indian and Greek—and gave them new meaning as a devastating satiric indictment of contemporary Western cultural values that goes well beyond the criticisms leveled in the Enderby novels.

The title of the novel, *MF,* derives in part from the initials of the narrator-protagonist, Miles Faber. It also stands for "male/female," a valid human classification that the book implicitly contrasts with various false taxonomies, and it has another reference to the all-encompassing theme of incest, especially when certain racial factors, bases of false taxonomies, are revealed in the conclusion. While the obscenity *motherfucker* has a wide range of usages in the North American black idiom, Burgess reveals that the range can be widened further to encompass all the maladies currently afflicting Western culture.

The novel consists mainly of Faber's recollections of youthful experiences. As a young man he had been gifted with an Oedipean skill as a riddle solver. This talent emphasizes his role as an archetypal MF, and it becomes more and more important as the mythic design of the novel unfolds. Like "that poor Greek kid" who had been crippled and left to die, he is propelled unwittingly but inexorably toward a solution to the riddle of his own origins and destiny. The gods have managed to place him under the influence of a professor who introduces him to the works of one Sib Legeru, a poet and painter who had lived, created, and died in almost total obscurity on the Caribbean island of Castita. The samples he has seen of Legeru's work lead Faber to hope that the main corpus will reveal the "freedom" he passionately yearns to see expressed in art—"beyond structure and cohesion . . . words and colors totally free because totally meaningless." To be vouchsafed this vision, he must make a pilgrimage to the island and seek out a museum where Legeru's works have been decently interred.

In the course of relating the story of this pilgrimage and the events that take place on the island of Castita, Faber reveals the connections between riddling and incest. In developing this theme Burgess was heavily influenced by Claude Lévi-Strauss's essay *The Scope of Anthropology* (1967), which discusses the parallels between American Indian myths involving incest and the story of Oedipus. Riddling and incest, Lévi-Strauss argues, have become associated in myth because they are both frustrations of natural expectation. Just as the answer to a riddle succeeds against all expectation in getting back to the question, so the parties in an incestuous union—mother and son, brother and sister, or whoever—are brought together despite any design that would keep them apart.

Burgess uses the Algonquin-Greek mythic framework to encompass much of Western culture and especially those branches that seemed to be flowering in North America during the late 1960s.

Clearly Burgess's American experiences, perhaps as much as his reading of Lévi-Strauss, had a great deal to do with generating his vision of incest. According to Miles Faber's grandfather (who may or may not be expressing Burgess's own point of view), incest "in its widest sense" signifies "the breakdown of order, the collapse of communication, the irresponsible cultivation of chaos." This same character, who has a Tiresian vision of the corruption of the world as a result of a long lifetime's immersion in it, observes that the totally free (because totally meaningless) "works of Sib Legeru exhibit the nastiest aspects of incest. . . . In them are combined an absence of meaning and a sniggering boyscout codishness. It is man's job to impose order on the universe, not to yearn for Chapter Zero of the Book of Genesis. . . . Art takes the raw material of the world about us and attempts to shape it into signification. Antiart takes that same material and seeks insignification."

For several reasons one may suspect that these are Burgess's sentiments. For one thing they echo sentiments expressed by the semiautobiographical Shakespeare (WS) in *Nothing Like the Sun*. In refusing to support Essex's revolt, WS explains that "the only self-evident duty is to that image of order we all carry in our brains," and this duty has a special meaning for the artist: "To emboss a stamp of order on time's flux is an impossibility I must try to make possible through my art, such as it is."

The focus of *MF* is actually much broader than art. The whole pattern of Western culture, as Burgess sees it, is incestuous. Race consciousness in particular, which has in no way diminished in recent years, is symptomatic of an incestuous pull. In Burgess's view "the time has come for the big miscegenation." He had ridiculed white racial consciousness in several of his earlier novels, including the *Malayan Trilogy* and *A Vision of Battlements*. In *MF* he focuses on what he regards as the equally absurd and incestuous black preoccupation with race. Some months before he began writing *MF* he observed in the interview with Aggeler "that it's about time the blacks got over this business of incest, of saying they're beautiful and they're black, they're going to conquer, they're going to prevail." In *MF* he attempts to jolt his readers out of their race consciousness by allowing them to finish the entire novel before he reveals a racial factor that most writers would feel compelled to clarify on their first page. And one of the "alembicated morals" he offers the reader is "that my race, or your race must start thinking in terms of the human totality and cease weaving its own fancied achievements or miseries into a banner. Black is beauty, yes, BUT ONLY WITH ANNA SEWELL PRODUCTS."

Burgess has invited the recognition of the incestuous pattern on the racial plane as it mirrors the incestuous yearning in art, or rather, antiart. The two are related in that they both reveal a colossal willed ignorance and laziness on the part of Western man. Just as it is a good deal easier to shirk the burdens of true art in the name of "freedom," so it is easier to allow oneself to be defined and confined by a racial identity so that the search for truths that concern "the human totality," truly a "man's job," can be put off. Both the "freedom" of the artist who incestuously allows his own masturbatory "codishness" to create for him and the "identity" of the black or white racial chauvinist are pernicious illusions that the artist, perhaps more than anyone else, is bound to expose.

Burgess's next important novel after *MF* was an attempt to fuse his two major interests, the novel and music. *Napoleon Symphony* presents the life of Napoleon Bonaparte, from his marriage to Josephine until his death, in the "shape" of Beethoven's *Eroica* symphony (1803). On the title page of his score Beethoven had written "Sinfonia grande intitolata Bonaparte" (Grand Symphony titled Bonaparte). Burgess deliberately matched the proportions of four "movements" within the novel to each of the four movements within the symphony. He began the project by playing the symphony on the phonograph and timing the movements. He then worked out a proportionate correspondence of pages to seconds of playing time. He worked with the score of the *Eroica* in front of him, making sections within his prose movements match sections within the *Eroica;* thus a passage of so many pages corresponds to a passage of so many bars. Beyond this, he sought to incorporate the actual dynamics of the symphony, the same moods and tempo. The project probably would not have astonished Beethoven, for as Burgess observed while he was in the process of writing *Napoleon Symphony:*

Beethoven himself was a more literary composer than many people imagine. He was a great reader of Plutarch's *Lives,* which of course always deal with two parallel lives. And he seems to have done something like this in the *Eroica,* though we have no external evidence to prove it. It has seemed to many musicologists that the first two movements of the *Eroica* deal with a sort of Napoleonic man. We see him in action, then we hear his funeral oration, and after that we get away from the modern leader and back to the mythical. The scherzo and the finale of the *Eroica* both seem to deal with Prometheus. In the last movement Beethoven puts all his cards on the table because it is a series of variations on a theme taken from his own ballet music about Prometheus and his creatures.

Burgess was left with the task of writing a set of variations on a Promethean theme. After his death on St. Helena, Burgess's Napoleon turns into a Promethean character in the last two "movements" of the novel, and there is a posthumous resurgence of the triumphant mood of the earlier movements, with Napoleon being crowned for having, despite all obstacles, at least partly fulfilled his dream of a united Europe.

Reading *Napoleon Symphony* is a pleasure despite the complexity of its form. Napoleon emerges as a human being in a way he has seldom been allowed to emerge in lengthy historical tomes or even other works of historical fiction. Like Coriolanus, he is simultaneously tragic and ridiculous, a grand comic creation demanding sympathy as well as laughter. He is seen from within engaged in spectacular rationalization and romantic self-delusion, and from without through the eyes of the lesser creatures who follow his fortunes–cynical political observers in Paris, wretched foot soldiers in Egypt and elsewhere, and his faithless empress. The disastrous effects of his Promethean efforts are in no way softened, but there is sympathy for the dreams inspiring the efforts.

Napoleon Symphony was followed by *The Clockwork Testament,* which outraged many New Yorkers, and two novellas, *Beard's Roman Women* and *ABBA ABBA.* The latter two works represent, Burgess says, "a sort of farewell-to-Rome phase." In *Beard's Roman Women* he drew upon his experiences as a scriptwriter and, as he did in *The Clockwork Testament,* put cinematic art in its proper place, well below literature in the hierarchy of artistic achievement. *ABBA ABBA* is primarily a collection of sonnets by the blasphemous dialect poet Giuseppe Giocchino Belli (1791–1863), which Burgess translated, maintaining the Petrarchan rhyme scheme, ABBA ABBA CDC CDC. The collection, comprising seventy-two of Belli's nearly three thousand poems, is introduced by a brief novella about Keats's death in Rome and his possible meeting there with Belli in 1820 or 1821. Another poetic exercise for Burgess, written at about the same time as *ABBA ABBA,* is a long original poem in free verse titled *Moses: A Narrative* (1976). As he explained in an unpublished letter to Aggeler of 3 September 1975, the poem was actually the "source" of the script for the television epic *Moses the Lawgiver,* starring Burt Lancaster, which in turn became a movie for theatrical release (titled *Moses,* 1975): "I was trying to get a rhythm and a dialogue style, and verse-writing helped." The *Moses* epic was part of what Burgess called his "TV tetralogy," which also includes specials on Shake-

Dust jacket for the U.S. edition of Burgess's novel about an historic sword

speare and Michelangelo and the widely acclaimed *Jesus of Nazareth.* This latter script became a novel, *Man of Nazareth* (1979), in which Jesus is portrayed as a man among men, married and widowed, a miracle worker fulfilling the scriptural prophecies but also living a fully human life. Like the original script, the novel is generally faithful to the Gospels, but there are some imaginative interpolations. Joseph's quiet acceptance of Mary's pregnancy is explained by his impotence. The wedding at Cana was Jesus' own, to a young woman who died several years later. Salome, driven by remorse over the death of John the Baptist, becomes a follower of Jesus. The book also includes useful information for the general reader regarding local customs, history, and Roman politics.

As a result of the highly favorable reception of these productions, he was asked to write scripts for several others, including a six-hour television epic on "Vinegar Joe" Stillwell, who hated the British; a Persian film on Cyrus the Great; and a disaster epic for Zanuck and Brown of Universal, "ultimate, really, since it's about the end of the world." Like *Jesus of Nazareth,* this script became a novel, *The End of the World News: An Entertainment* (1982).

The End of the World News is actually three stories in one: a fictionalized account of the dying Sigmund Freud being exiled from Vienna; a libretto for a musical about Leon Trotsky in New York in 1917; and the ultimate disaster that gives the entertainment its title. The inspiration for this work, he said in a BBC interview on 10 September 1985, was a photograph, "widely published in European picture magazines in the last year of President Carter's tenure . . . of himself and his lady viewing simultaneously three television programmes."

The same year that he produced this entertainment Burgess also published a witty little book, *On Going to Bed.* In it he included some history, some anecdotes, and an explanation of why he personally preferred to sleep on a mattress on the floor: "I am a great faller out of beds . . . A mattress also allows you to spread your possessions around the bed, within easy reach."

Burgess remained, however, primarily a novelist, and in December 1980 he published what many regard as his masterpiece, *Earthly Powers.* It is a long book, about the length of *Ulysses,* and it took Burgess nearly a decade to complete it. The original title was "The Affairs of Men." Then it became "The Prince of the Powers of the Air," and finally *Earthly Powers.* The second title was taken from Thomas Hobbes's description of Satan and his kingdom in Part IV of *Leviathan* (1651).

The protagonist, Don Carlo Campanatti, is modeled on the late Pope John XXIII, a pontiff whom Burgess did not admire. In the unpublished 1972 interview with Aggeler he referred to John as a "Pelagian heretic" and an "emissary of the devil" who caused the Church enormous damage by raising unrealistic hopes that there would be radical doctrinal changes to accommodate the pressures of twentieth-century life. His character Don Carlo is a Faustian figure who made a bargain with the devil in return for the earthly powers of the papacy.

Perception of Don Carlo is dependent upon another protagonist, Kenneth M. Toomey, an eighty-one-year-old homosexual novelist-playwright modeled deliberately on W. Somerset Maugham. The ubiquitous references to Maugham and the obvious parallels between Toomey's career and Maugham's make the identification virtually explicit. Toomey has throughout his long life acted in accord with his nature and his occupation as a writer. Where they have brought him is clearly revealed in what Burgess himself calls, in the first paragraph, the *"arresting opening"* of the novel: "It was the afternoon of my eighty-first birthday, and I was in bed with my catamite when Ali announced that the archbishop had come to see me." Especially suggestive in this first sentence is the word "catamite," evoking as it does an image of refined decadence and pagan luxury in a quasi-Olympian setting. Generally acknowledged "greatness" as a writer has eluded Toomey, but he has achieved a kind of Olympian eminence of fame and wealth and the freedom of fleshly indulgence that goes with wealth. The Ganymede (a Greek name from which the Latin word "catamite" derives), however, is no downy-chinned little Greek boy but a fat, sadistic drunkard named Geoffrey Enright, whom Toomey keeps and who may be modeled on one of Maugham's secretary-companions. Burgess demonstrates that the freedom of fleshly indulgence is also the bondage. Enright is only one in a line of lovers who have made Toomey pay for their favors with more than money. To escape the pain of loneliness he has had to repeatedly endure humiliation, spite, and treachery.

As with so many of Burgess's novels, the Pelagian versus Augustinian theme is central to *Earthly Powers.* He introduces it subtly in several places in the novel by means of a fragment from Catullus: "*Solitam . . . Minotauro . . . pro caris corpus.*" In other Burgess novels, notably *The Worm and the Ring* and *Inside Mr. Enderby,* the Minotaur is described as a Greek mythic analogue of original sin, and Theseus (who killed the monster) is analogous to the heretic Pelagius, who denied original sin and asserted that man was capable of achieving perfection without the aid of divine grace. Enderby is in the process of writing a long poem about Theseus and the Minotaur, the argument of which is "Without Original Sin there is no civilization."

Earthly Powers is mainly about the monsters that abide within the labyrinth of the human soul. That there are such monsters is something Toomey and Don Carlo both believe. For Toomey, one of Burgess's "Augustinians," the monsters are the forms of badness that are part of fallen human nature. His personal monster is his homosexual nature, which he has managed to overcome only once, through the experience of a nonphysical love for another man that in effect drove out all desire. The death of this man, which is the result of diabolical machinations, in effect deprives Toomey of a grace bearer, indeed the only source of grace in his life, leaving him prey to the monster of his own nature and the monstrous relationships his nature demands. For Don Carlo, on the other hand, the monsters within are all intruders who have come from the kingdom of darkness. Since man is God's creation, he is perfect. Evil is wholly from the devil, who taught man how to be evil and is still teaching him. God permits this because He will in no way abridge human freedom. Man is free to reverse the consequences of the fall: "the return to perfection is possible." These beliefs shape Carlo's theology and his career. Toomey emphasizes and reemphasizes their importance in his thinking. Initially they lead him into prominence in the field of exorcism, and Toomey sees him in action against devils in Malaya and the devils inhabiting Italian mobsters in Chicago. Wherever the devil is at work, it seems, he may expect to encounter Carlo.

While Carlo sees himself as Satan's enemy and a champion of mankind against the powers of darkness, it is suggested early in the novel that he is vulnerable to these same powers, and the reader must be attentive to these suggestions if he is to accept some of the later developments in the novel as plausible. The genuinely heretical nature of Carlo's beliefs in human perfectability is made clear in a treatise he writes which includes, among other things, a defense of Pelagius. Burgess effectively juxtaposes Carlo's and Toomey's views and explanations of various evils in the twentieth century, and he suggests that both views are to some extent partially correct, but both are also significantly limited. Toomey would attribute such triumphs of evil as Nazism wholly to innate human depravity while Carlo would credit them wholly to the devil. Burgess's depiction of events suggests, however, that there is an interaction, a cooperation between the demons that are a part of man's nature and the devil himself. Failure to recognize the existence of both may lead to dreadful consequences.

Earthly Powers has been generally praised by critics, and it was a Book-of-the-Month Club choice. Enormous in scope, encompassing much of twentieth-century social, literary, and political history, it inevitably has some flaws; parts of the book are wearisome, and the language is occasionally pedantic. These flaws are, however, minor and unavoidable in a work so large and ambitious. Overall it is a magnificent performance.

Another novel, *1985* (1978), was less well-received by critics than *Earthly Powers.* Originally conceived as an introduction to George Orwell, it begins with a 106-page dialogue-discussion of *1984* (1949) which suggests, among other things, that Orwell's vision of England in 1984 was shaped essentially by his vision of England in 1948. The remaining 166 pages present Burgess's own proleptic vision, one that differs markedly from those of *A Clockwork Orange* and *The Wanting Seed* as well as that of *1984.* One of Burgess's more sympathetic critics has argued convincingly that this latter section of

1985, Burgess's fiction, is intended as an ironic counterpoint to *1984,* one that presents a near future that is "harrowing but not horrific." The England of Burgess's *1985* has left behind any belief in moral absolutes and is populated almost entirely by small people who are moral neutrals. What makes it such a bad place is the all-pervasive dullness that is the end result of social impulses carried too far, thus leveling intelligence, taste, and knowledge.

A nonfiction work that should interest students of Burgess's fiction is *This Man and Music* (1982). Burgess still composed music, and in this book he takes the reader step-by-step through the writing of his *Symphony No. 3 in C* (1972). He goes on to discuss the relationship between music and life, the language of music, and music in literature, focusing mainly on the work of Gerard Manley Hopkins and Joyce. Then he concludes with an illuminating discussion of the musical motifs in *MF* and *Napoleon Symphony.* While several critics have discussed the relationship between the latter novel and the *Eroica,* the musical elements in *MF* have been generally overlooked.

Readers who were distressed by the death of the poet Enderby in *The Clockwork Testament* were "placated" ten years later by his reappearance in *Enderby's Dark Lady, or, No End to Enderby* (1984). The novel begins and ends with Elizabethan fantasy scenes involving Shakespeare and several of his fellow dramatists, but most of it focuses on Enderby. Very much alive, Enderby returns to America, hired by a theater company in Indiana to write the libretto for a musical about the life of Shakespeare. The Dark Lady in the cast, a "numinous" black singer named April Elgar, rescues him from artistic paralysis, and he himself plays Shakespeare in what turns out to be a disastrous production. He also masquerades as a preacher and delivers an improvised sermon to a black congregation in North Carolina. As in *Enderby,* the poet finds himself unable to enjoy his muse both sexually and artistically.

In a prefatory note Burgess explains how the inspiration for the Enderby novels came to him in Borneo in 1959 when, "delirious with sandfly fever, I opened the door of the bathroom in my bungalow and was not altogether surprised to see a middle-aged man seated on the toilet writing what appeared to be poetry. The febrile vision lasted less than a second, but the impossible personage stayed with me and demanded the writing of a novel about him." He left open the possibility of still another Enderby novel, saying that Enderby existed for him and "may probably go on existing."

Burgess's next novel, *The Kingdom of the Wicked* (1985), appeared the following year. An historical novel, it draws primarily from the classical historians, especially Tacitus, Suetonius, and Josephus, and the Acts of the Apostles. Like *Earthly Powers,* another study of Christianity and evil, it is enormous in scope, placing the apostles and the founding of Christianity within a context of events that includes the razing of the Temple, the conquest of Britain, the burning of Rome, and the destruction of Pompeii. Again, as in *Man of Nazareth,* there are imaginative interpolations, some of them highly comic, including an account of how the doctrine of the Trinity evolved in twenty seconds while the disciples were napping on Pentecost.

In 1986 Burgess published the first volume of his autobiography, *Little Wilson and Big God: Being the First Part of the Confessions of Anthony Burgess.* The second volume, *You've Had Your Time: The Second Part of the Confessions,* appeared in 1990. The first volume is an account of his first forty-two years, concluding with his being told that he had an inoperable cerebral tumor. He did not believe the prognosis, but, granting that it might be true, he was exhilarated by the prospect of "something I had never had before: a whole year to live." Having remarked to his wife that she would "need money" as a widow, he turned to his typewriter: "'I'd better start,' I said. And I did."

Everything that led up to this "start" is presented with startling frankness and apparently a total lack of self-concealment. He describes his adolescent struggles between his conscience and sex, in which the latter was generally victorious. Marriage to his first wife did not end these conflicts. She believed in free love and had a fondness for liquor, and he came to share these proclivities.

His wartime experiences in Gibraltar, which became *A Vision of Battlements,* and his years as a teacher in England and the Far East, which gave him material for the *Malayan Trilogy* and other early novels, are chronicled, providing material not available in any of the biographical sources to students of his fiction. Of interest to more general readers are the entertaining digressions upon various topics—Malayan expressions for a variety of sexual acts and recipes for old-fashioned Lancashire dishes, among others. He also describes the enormous impact of discovering new languages in the Far East: "The Malay Language, and later the Chinese, changed not just my attitude to communication in general but the whole shape of my mind."

Burgess's frankness in *Little Wilson and Big God,* especially with regard to his erotic adventures, offended some critics, who depicted him "as though I were a priapic monster or, at best, unforgivably indiscreet." The second volume, *You've Had Your Time,* is more restrained. It begins as Burgess returned from Borneo in 1959 and ends in 1982, with the centenary celebration of James Joyce.

The same year that *Little Wilson and Big God* appeared Burgess published *The Pianoplayers,* a novel based in part on his father's career as a pub and cinema pianist. The narrator, Ellen Henshaw, recalls how her father, a piano player in silent-movie houses, tried to cope financially with the arrival of the talkies. He attempts a thirty-day nonstop piano marathon, playing an incredible string of selections that ranges from Beethoven and George Frideric Handel to pop songs, along with improvised pieces. He is given two hour-long breaks at midnight and lunchtime but not allowed to leave the piano for any other purpose, even having to relieve himself through a rubber tube connected to a gasoline can. Well before he completes his marathon, the old man is totally exhausted and dies of cardiac failure. The remainder of this entertaining novel is Ellen's account of how she progressed from a teenage prostitute to headmistress of the London School of Love, where wealthy gentlemen are taught to play a woman's body like a musical instrument.

The Pianoplayers is not the first novel in which Burgess assumed the narrative voice of a lower-class Englishwoman. *One Hand Clapping* is narrated by a clever working-class girl, Janet Shirley; however, *The Pianoplayers* is a much better book, partly because the main characters are so much more alive and engaging but mainly because of Burgess's skillful use of Ellen's "Uneducated English" to achieve some delightfully outrageous comic effects throughout, and the brilliant integration of musical motifs.

In 1989 Burgess published two more books of fiction: *Any Old Iron,* a novel, and *The Devil's Mode,* a collection of stories. The latter work includes a novella about Attila the Hun and eight short stories. Attila is presented as the brutal conqueror every schoolchild meets in history books, but he also reveals a surprising anxiety about how he will be remembered by posterity. Especially notable among the stories are one dealing with an imagined meeting between Miguel de Cervantes and Shakespeare in Spain, a retelling of Richard Strauss's comic opera *Der Rosenkavalier* (libretto by Hugo von Hofmannsthal, 1911), and a new Sherlock Holmes tale pompously narrated by Dr. John Watson. In all of these pieces Burgess exhibits his characteristic fondness for literary and historical allusions and his knowledge of language and music. His erudition and tendency to be didactic are balanced by his playfulness and wit. Perhaps the best critical summation of this collection is that of John Melmoth in the *Times Literary Supplement* (15 December 1989):

"*The Devil's Mode* is chipper, extravagant, eclectic and logophiliac."

Any Old Iron is, like *The Kingdom of the Wicked* and *Earthly Powers,* epic in scope. Its title refers to a sword, thought to have belonged to Attila and subsequently to King Arthur, that prompts the main characters, members of a Welsh-Russian and Jewish-French family, to undertake various hazardous activities in connection with the major events of the twentieth century–the two world wars, the Russian Revolution, and the Spanish civil war, among others. There is a great deal of human suffering, but the tragic elements are skillfully blended with comedy to generate in the reader the same sort of complex response that one has watching Henrik Ibsen's *The Wild Duck* or Gloucester's attempted suicide in Shakespeare's *King Lear.* If one had to reduce *Any Old Iron* to a statement or theme, it would probably be that mankind must learn to love and forgive and overcome ethnic barriers if peace is to be achieved. This was the message of earlier Burgess novels, from the *Malayan Trilogy* to *MF,* but Burgess's presentation of it has lost neither freshness nor vitality.

During his last years Burgess and his wife lived in Monte Carlo and in Lugano, Switzerland. He loved to gamble, and when in Monte Carlo he visited the casinos nightly. He knew the royal family well and frequently strolled with Princess Grace, whose death, he suspected, involved foul play.

Wherever he was living, Burgess continued to work systematically from 10 A.M. to 5 P.M., drinking strong tea, chain-smoking small cigars, and producing a thousand words a day, using a word processor for his journalism and a typewriter for fiction. Even when his health began to fail and he had to return to England, he continued writing. Another novel, *A Dead Man in Deptford,* was completed and published in 1993, the year he died of cancer in London.

A Dead Man in Deptford focuses on the career and death of Christopher Marlowe, one of the most tantalizing unsolved mysteries in the history of English literature. Burgess had always been fascinated by Marlowe and had written his undergraduate thesis on him at Manchester. The fact that 1993 was the quatercentenary of Marlowe's assassination gave Burgess the impetus to produce the novel. While not on the same level with his novel about Shakespeare, *Nothing Like the Sun,* it is a considerable achievement and was critically well received. Burgess depicts the Elizabethan world he knew so well and follows Marlowe's progress from Cambridge into the secret service of Sir Francis Walsingham; his meteoric rise in the theater; and finally his miserable death in the tavern at Deptford.

Dust jacket for Burgess's final novel, much of which is written in verse

Burgess's skill and enjoyment of his craft are evident in his last work, left completed at his death and published in 1995. *Byrne: A Novel* is written primarily in ottava rima, and it chronicles the life of Michael Byrne–Irish composer, painter, and womanizer–and some of his offspring. Burgess's sparkling wit earned praise from critics when the book appeared in America in 1997; one writer for *Kirkus Reviews* (15 July 1997) called *Byrne* "a swan song like no other, and one of the most delightful books of the decade."

Burgess's stature as one of the major British novelists of the century was recognized by critics at least two decades before his last works appeared, and his later novels did not diminish his importance as a force in English fiction. It should also be noted that he produced a considerable body of criticism. He regularly contributed reviews of new novels and produced book-length studies of various writers intended to be helpful to and increase the critical appreciation of what he called "the average reader."

The earliest of these was a useful overview of British literature titled *English Literature: A Survey for Students* (1958). His other early critical works included several studies on the fiction of James Joyce. *Here Comes Everybody: An Introduction to James Joyce for the Ordinary Reader* (1965) focuses on *Dubliners* (1914), *Ulysses,* and *Finnegans Wake* (1939). *A Shorter "Finnegans Wake"* (1966) is an abridgement with linking commentaries designed to guide the reader through the complete novel, and *Joysprick* (1973) is an introduction to Joyce's language. *Shakespeare* (1970) is an entertaining biography full of fanciful conjecture and is useful to the beginning student. *Language Made Plain* (1964) is an introduction to linguistics that persuasively encourages readers to become involved in the matter of language and in languages other than their own. *Urgent Copy: Literary Studies* (1968), a collection of essays and reviews on various topics, mostly literary, includes an essay on Lévi-Strauss that is of considerable interest to readers of Burgess's *MF. The Novel Now: A Student's Guide to Contemporary Fiction* (1967) is a survey of the contemporary novel in various languages. Burgess intended to update it to include "more Americans" and did so partially in *Ninety-Nine Novels: The Best in English since 1939: A Personal Choice* (1984). *Ernest Hemingway & His World* (1978) is a critical biography, as is *Flame into Being: The Life and Work of D. H. Lawrence* (1985). Burgess was a perceptive, sympathetic critic of the works of other writers, and students of his fiction will find that he frequently illuminates his own work in the process of discussing the works of others.

Bibliographies:

Beverly R. David, "Anthony Burgess: A Checklist (1956–1971)," *Twentieth Century Literature,* 19 (July 1973): 181–188;

Carlton Holte, "Additions to 'Anthony Burgess: A Checklist (1956–1971),'" *Twentieth Century Literature,* 20 (January 1974): 44–52;

Paul Boytinck, *Anthony Burgess: An Enumerative Bibliography with Selected Annotations,* second edition, with foreword by Burgess (Norwood, Pa.: Norwood Editions, 1977);

Jeutonne Brewer, *Anthony Burgess: A Bibliography,* with foreword by Burgess (Metuchen, N.J. & London: Scarecrow Press, 1980);

Boytinck, *Anthony Burgess: An Annotated Bibliography and Reference Guide* (New York: Garland, 1985).

References:

Geoffrey Aggeler, *Anthony Burgess: The Artist as Novelist* (University: University of Alabama Press, 1979);

Aggeler, ed., *Critical Essays on Anthony Burgess* (Boston: G. K. Hall, 1986);

Harold Bloom, ed., *Anthony Burgess* (New York: Chelsea House, 1987);

Samuel Coale, *Anthony Burgess* (New York: Ungar, 1982);

A. A. DeVitis, *Anthony Burgess* (New York: Twayne, 1972);

Carol M. Dix, *Anthony Burgess* (London: Longman, 1971);

Martina Ghosh-Schellhorn, *Anthony Burgess: A Study in Character* (Frankfurt am Main & New York: Peter Lang, 1986);

Richard Mathews, *The Clockwork Universe of Anthony Burgess* (San Bernardino, Cal.: Borgo Press, 1978);

Modern Fiction Studies, special Burgess issue, 27 (Autumn 1981);

Robert K. Morris, *The Consolations of Ambiguity: An Essay on the Novels of Anthony Burgess* (Columbia: University of Missouri Press, 1971);

John J. Stinson, *Anthony Burgess Revisited* (Boston: Twayne, 1991).

Papers:

Most of Anthony Burgess's papers are collected at the Mills Memorial Library, McMaster University, Hamilton, Ontario.

Alan Burns

(29 December 1929 –   )

David W. Madden
California State University, Sacramento

See also the Burns entry in *DLB 14: British Novelists Since 1960.*

BOOKS: *Europe after the Rain* (London: Calder, 1965; New York: Day, 1970);

Celebrations (London: Calder & Boyars, 1967);

Babel (London: Calder & Boyars, 1969; New York: Day, 1970);

Buster (New York: Red Dust Books, 1972); first published in *New Writers,* volume 1 (London: Calder, 1961), pp. 63–140;

Dreamerika!: A Surrealist Fantasy (London: Calder & Boyars, 1972);

The Angry Brigade: A Documentary Novel (London: Allison & Busby, 1973);

The Day Daddy Died, with photo-collages by Ian Breakwell (London & New York: Allison & Busby, 1981);

Revolutions of the Night (London: Allison & Busby, 1986).

PLAY PRODUCTION: *Palach,* London, Open Space Theatre, 11 November 1970.

OTHER: *To Deprave and Corrupt: Technical Reports of the United States Commission on Obscenity and Pornography,* edited and abridged by Burns (London: Davis-Poynter, 1972);

Untitled chapter in *London Consequences,* edited by Margaret Drabble and B. S. Johnson (London: Greater London Arts Association, 1973);

Palach, in *Open Space Plays,* edited by Charles Marovitz (London: Penguin, 1974), pp. 191–252;

"Essay" and "Wonderland," in *Beyond the Words,* edited by Giles Gordon (London: Hutchinson, 1975), pp. 63–85;

The Imagination on Trial: British and American Writers Discuss Their Working Methods, edited by Burns and Charles Sugnet (London & New York: Allison & Busby, 1981);

"Writing by Chance," *Times Higher Education Supplement,* 29 January 1982, pp. 11–12.

Alan Burns

Alan Burns is one of the most challengingly innovative novelists in contemporary British fiction. Inspired by painters, he strives to create what René Magritte once described as the "magic of unforeseen affinities" by means of a collage, cut-up technique that he attributes to the fiction of William Burroughs. The result is a surreal assemblage of events, images, even syntactical arrangements that challenge the reader's comfortable assumptions about what a novel is or can be. Burns possesses a thoroughly original voice.

Burns was born in London on 29 December 1929 into the middle-class family of Harold and Anne Marks Burns and educated at the Merchant

Taylors' School. When he was thirteen his mother died, and his older brother died two years later; both deaths profoundly affected him both emotionally and artistically. Burns has described the impact of these separations: "The consuming nature of this experience showed itself not only in the disconnected form but also in the content of my 'work.'" The most obvious treatment of these experiences is in *Buster* (1972; originally published in *New Writers*, 1961); however, the theme of death pervades all his novels. From 1949 to 1951, Burns served in the Royal Army Education Corps, stationed at Salisbury Plain. After his discharge he traveled through Europe; he married Carol Lynn in 1954. He was called to the Bar in 1956 and practiced as a London barrister until 1959, when he spent a year as a postgraduate researcher in politics at the London School of Economics. For the next three years Burns was assistant legal manager for Beaverbrook Newspapers, "vetting [appraising] copy for libel and copyright."

While walking down Carey Street on his lunch hour one day he saw, in a jeweler's window, a photograph of a man and woman kissing, which reminded him of a photo of his mother and father on their honeymoon. Having previously felt stymied in his attempts to write, Burns describes the artistic significance of this moment: "I understood in literary terms, the value of the image because I saw that I didn't have to grapple, as it were in essay form, with the endless complexities and significances of the love and other feelings that existed between my mother and father, and what they meant to me. I could let it all go by the board, let it take care of itself; I could, in the time-honoured phrase, show, not tell. . . . I could tell this story in a series of photographs, which is to say, a series of images, and let the stories emerge and the ideas emerge from that series of fragments, and that's how I found myself able to write that first book, *Buster*."

Although quite different from the novels that follow it, *Buster* suggests some of the fictional concerns and techniques Burns employs in all his works. Central to his fictions is the technique of fragmentation, and although *Buster* is more conventional than any of his other novels, it too employs a limited form of fragmentation. Events in the work follow one another rapidly, and the temporal links between incidents are implied more than they are stated. The effect is one of an associative rather than a temporal pattern of organization.

The novel's protagonist, in fact, hints at the truncated method in Burns's later works when he attempts to write a story that concludes with the lines "Uniqueness demanded disjointedness. Irrelevance was the key." The hero goes on to define some of Burns's attitudes toward the nature and function of language when he thinks, "Words don't describe, they point, and poets hit the source in history, the shadow behind each word. . . . Words are abstract isolate ancient huge, flipping and floating in coloured balloons in fanlight air." The quality of disjointedness and the idea of the "shadow behind each word" play increasingly larger roles in the compositional techniques of later novels.

Buster chronicles the growth from childhood to maturity of Dan Graveson, apple of his father's eye and failure in the eyes of others. At an early age the boy loses his mother when she is blown apart by a bomb before his eyes, and soon after that his older brother dies in military service. Graveson then deliberately flunks out of school, is dismissed from the army for Communist sloganeering, initiates and abruptly quits a peace committee, fails his law exams twice, and is eventually evicted bodily from his apartment. The novel ends with Graveson returning to his father's home where he greedily consumes the meal left in the pantry for his parent.

The domestic theme featured in this autobiographical novel is shared by many of Burns's other novels. Beginning and ending with the line "They stood over him," *Buster* records the joys and suffocations that domestic life breeds. Continually feeling the pressure to succeed and please his father, Graveson inevitably fails at every undertaking, and the novel's epigraph, which is a collection of dictionary definitions of the title, describes Graveson's fate—"to fall or be thrown."

Buster also introduces readers to another significant feature of Burns's fiction: his keen eye for detail, often rendered in arresting descriptive and figurative language. Frequently he will interrupt or clarify the ambiguity or disjointedness of a scene with a vivid metaphor or image, as in the following passage in which the narrator describes the dead mother's body: "The foot had a slight unnatural twist at the ankle. She could not have bent her foot like that if she had been alive. The difference was small, an angle of ten degrees. But alive she could not have done it without breaking the bone, gouging one bone into the other, wrenching the muscle enough to make her scream with pain or come as near screaming as an ill middle-aged woman can, not a young clean scream, but a choke, a sob, a cough, a constriction in the throat caused by too much trying to escape at one time."

John Calder published *Buster* in 1961 in the first volume of the *New Writers* anthology series. Encouraged by the critical success of his novel, Burns ended his legal career and on a monthly £50 sub-

EUROPE
AFTER THE RAIN

EUROPE
AFTER
THE
RAIN

EUROPE
AFTER THE RAIN

'Europe After the Rain' by Max Ernst
(Courtesy Wadsworth Atheneum, Hertford, U.S.A.)

ALAN
BURNS

ALAN BURNS

JOHN CALDER (PUBLISHERS) LTD.,
18, BREWER ST., LONDON, W.1.

CALDER

Dust jacket for Burns's novel about a nightmarish future dominated by violence and chaos

sidy from Calder moved to Dorset, where he spent the next four years writing. During this period he and his wife adopted a son, Daniel Paul, and a daughter, Alshamsha. In 1965 Calder published his second novel, *Europe after the Rain*. Taking the title from a 1942 painting by Max Ernst, Burns creates a horrifying vision of lives and of a landscape devastated by war. He was inspired not only by Ernst's painting but also by transcripts of the Nuremberg trials and by an account of life in Poland after World War II. He set his novel in an indefinite future in which people and events lack logic and hope. Wandering throughout this waking nightmare, the unnamed narrator searches for an unnamed girl he may have loved at one time. The girl is being held prisoner by a battalion commander, who is later demoted to command a labor camp. She eventually murders him, escapes, and then wastes away. To say this much is to imply a greater cohesiveness than the plot actually offers.

Developing his fragmented style, Burns presents the reader with a phantasmagoric assortment of horrors and brutalities as anonymous characters struggle against one another to survive an intolerable life. Sentences are terse and clipped, employing almost no subordination or transitional devices.

Consequently, images and events take on an intensely isolated, disconnected relationship with each other, where linguistic austerity mirrors the austere conditions of the environment. Burns has explained that much of the fragmentation in the novel results from the semihypnotic state in which it was composed. Glazing his eyes over as he typed, Burns wrote "from the unconscious" by emphasizing only the strongest and most concrete words, usually nouns. It is a technique he has compared with that used by many landscape painters.

In *Europe after the Rain* the domestic theme reappears, but in a less evident way than in many of Burns's other works. Although the narrator is the focus of the novel, the reader knows less about his family than that of the nameless girl for whom he searches. Like the children in Burns's other works, she has been separated from her father (here by the leader of an opposing political faction), and her eventual reunion with him leads not to a new life but to a physical decline. Family is finally an ineffective alternative to the violence and chaos of this world and may perhaps even contribute to the widespread devastation.

As in *Buster,* the images of death in this second novel are compelling and abundant. Burns renders these events with detailed precision, in a thoroughly prosaic tone. The disturbing quality of a passage such as the following stems not only from its graphic nature but, more important, from the matter-of-fact manner in which the narrator relates such carnage: "Disturbed, she gave the cry, went up to the body and touched it, dragged it down as the others crowded round, clamoured for it, each one desperate for it. She wrenched off the leg, jabbed it, thick end first, into her mouth, tried hard to swallow it, could not get it down, the thicker part became less visible, there was nothing but the foot, she twisted off the protruding foot." Critical reaction to *Europe after the Rain* was mixed, as it would be toward many of Burns's later novels.

In 1967 Burns received an Arts Council Maintenance Grant and saw the publication of his third work. In a much more obvious way than *Europe after the Rain, Celebrations* explores the tensions and ambushes of family life, and, similar to the pattern in *Buster,* the work presents a family in which the woman is dead and one of the sons, Phillip, is killed when his brother Michael crushes him under a machine. Overseeing these two is the father, Williams, who as factory boss dominates his sons as both parent and employer. After Phillip's death, the father and Michael compete for the affections of Phillip's wife, Jacqueline, and for leadership of the company. Although she weds Michael, Jacqueline sleeps with and controls each man.

Once again the narrative technique is a disjointed one, as events crowd ridiculously and inexplicably in upon each other. Punctuating the details of the familial rivalry are descriptions of the various rituals that form the "celebrations" of the title. Beginning with Phillip's inquest and funeral, Burns catalogues Michael and Jacqueline's wedding, their advance in wealth and social stature, Williams's physical and professional decline, Michael's unexpected death, and Jacqueline's remarriage. The novel grows from "a mosaic of fragments" as Burns uses these celebrations to create absurdly comic and surreal sequences in, for instance, Williams's funeral march: "A procession of black castles slowly through the suburbs, patience of the dead face, his clothes taken from him, his feet buried in nettles, there was no significance. Black walnut, brick wall. Michael asked for a carton of coffee, it was water heated up. A brick wall advocated huge white letters hidden by coal. A seizure. Vegetable houses. A grubby bird, fancy-dress Spaniard, did not stay long. The living were talking." As in Surrealist paintings, striking and outlandishly dissimilar images are juxtaposed, producing new, comic, and startling effects.

Like the novel which preceded it, *Celebrations* frequently eschews rational logic for the logic of the dream. Thus the reader moves between different levels of time and of consciousness, discovering a pattern of thought and emotion beneath the sequence of the narrative's events. One of the best examples of this method is the description of Williams's death in a car accident, one that leaves details ambiguous but the result certain: "In the street there were few people, he had not begun, it was unfair, life had gone badly, he had begun and ended." Passages such as this remind the reader of Burns's preoccupation with the theme of death and the spare, abrupt manner with which he renders its horrors, inevitability, and finality. The novel enjoyed a favorable reception, with reviews by B. S. Johnson and Robert Nye being particularly perceptive.

In 1969 Burns received a second Arts Maintenance Grant as well as a £2,000 Writing Bursary from the Arts Council. During this period he and Johnson founded Writers Reading, a collective to "establish a circuit, organize bookings and publicity, create a recognized 'norm' for fees, [and] be generally a co-operative centre for otherwise isolated and scattered fictioneers." They produced a booklet with photos and biographies of twelve writers, among them Ann Quin, Alan Sillitoe, Barry Cole, Carol Burns, Stephen Themerson, and Eva Figes, and organized readings throughout the United Kingdom. Although the organization began to fade by 1972, it was only officially terminated following the deaths of Johnson and Quin in 1973.

In the same year that Writers Reading began, Calder published Burns's fourth novel, *Babel*. Inspired once more by a painting, in this case *The Tower of Babel* (1563) by Pieter Brueghel the Elder, Burns took his fragmented snapshot method as far as possible. His most experimental, surreal, and difficult work, *Babel* is composed of a series of isolated paragraphs that occasionally center on an identifiable character and that frequently lead to incidents or personages in later paragraphs. More often than not the effect is nonsensical because "I used the cut-up method to join the subject of one sentence to the object from another with the verb hovering uncertainly between." Thus Burns rejects the methods of traditional storytelling, and his novel is best viewed as a series of voices competing with one another for the reader's attention. Using the biblical image of the tower of conflicting languages and purposeless action, *Babel* details the chaos, dislocations, and disjunctions of modern life.

As it was in his earlier novels, Burns's prose style here is sparse, concise, and thoroughly compressed, while thematically the work expresses the writer's concern with the power of the state. Of the theme, Burns writes: "*Babel* described not the obvious apparatus of dictatorship but the hints nudges nods assents implications agreements and conspiracies, the network of manipulations that envelops the citizens and makes them unaware accomplicies [*sic*] in the theft of their liberty. In *Babel* the crude despots of the earlier books, camp commander, factory manager, death, are re-constituted in the subtle dominance of the amorphous State." The critics, however, either glibly dismissed or bitingly denounced *Babel* as a failure.

During the summer of the following year Burns gave a single lecture on censorship for the National County Libraries Summer School, and he was approached by producer Charles Marowitz to write a play. The result was *Palach,* which was performed at London's Open Space Theatre on 11 November 1970 and was published four years later. Employing four separate stages, speakers blaring various voices, and actors interrupting and speaking over one another's lines, the play concerns the self-immolation of the Czech student Jan Palach, who died on 16 January 1969 protesting the Soviet invasion and occupation of his country. The multiple stages and conflicting voices remind one once again of Burns's commitment to random methods of storytelling, and the play's theme reflects the author's continuing concern with the sacrifice of youth and the overwhelming power of the state.

For ten weeks in the summer of 1971 Burns was the first holder of the Henfield Fellowship (with a stipend of £600) at the University of East Anglia, Norwich, where he spent most of his time writing. Here he gave a pair of lectures ("Writing by Accident," which explored various aleatoric writing methods, and "The Novel of the Future"), held weekly writers' workshops, and helped found and edit a magazine of student creative writing.

In 1972 *Buster* was published by Red Dust Books of New York, marking both its first American and first separate publication. Burns also had two new works published in 1972: *To Deprave and Corrupt,* a study of pornography and censorship; and *Dreamerika!: A Surrealist Fantasy,* his fifth novel. Since he had gone as far as he felt he could with the fragmented technique in *Babel,* Burns attempted to give the reader of *Dreamerika!* specific points of reference for his collagelike images in the figures of the Kennedy clan. Using offset litho printing, the novel combines a fantastic vision of the family with cuttings from newspaper headlines that act as commentaries on and counterpoints to the fiction's activities. As Burns describes it, "I played hell with the documented facts, made crazy distortions of the alleged

truth, in order to get some humour out of it, and also to raise questions about the nature of documentary realism. Screwing up the story made some very undocumentary truths emerge."

Once again the themes of the power of the state and of the family fueled by rivalry and torn apart by death are immediately recognizable. In Burns's hands the Kennedys become the embodiments of the American dream in its most mercenary and exploitative form, with the reality of the dream suffusing all action and painting an emotional landscape of a culture gone awry.

Although roundly criticized as bitter and cruel, the work is an especially important one in Burns's career because it marks a turning point in his artistic development. While it uses the cut-up, collage effects of *Babel* and the surreal exaggerations of his earlier works, *Dreamerika!* also represents a recovery from the artistic dead end that *Babel* implied. By linking the fragmented method to a comprehensible narrative line, Burns was able to give this "surrealist fantasy," as he calls it, the cohesion that his earlier work lacked. The penultimate chapter, in which grandson Joe Kennedy dallies with communes and Marxism, foreshadows the lost revolutionaries who people Burns's next novel, *The Angry Brigade* (1973).

In 1973 Burns was again awarded an Arts Council Bursary and held the C. Day Lewis Writing Fellowship at Woodberry Down School in London. In the same year he and eleven other writers—among them Margaret Drabble, Johnson, Piers Paul Reid, Themerson, and John Brunner—published a "group novel," *London Consequences,* commissioned and published by the Greater London Arts Association. Meeting one evening in Drabble's house in Hampstead, the group assigned each contributor a separate chapter, and the entire project was completed in ten weeks.

Also in 1973 another novel, *The Angry Brigade,* was published. Here Burns again experiments with documentary realism in what is ostensibly a transcription of tape-recorded interviews with six London revolutionaries. Extending the method of *Dreamerika!,* he relies less on the subconscious for his material than on found pieces woven into a fictional framework. While in the preface the author contends that he met and interviewed six people, Burns admits in a letter to David W. Madden that the work is entirely fictional. He did, however, interview subjects,

mainly friends who agreed to talk with me about many matters unconnected with the book's content. I transcribed the tapes and then altered them to suit my purpose, the book's purpose. Thus I retained, I hope, the convincing rhythm of real speech and thus helped maintain the fiction of a journalistic *coup*—real interviews with real members of the Brigade. As an example, one of very many: I talked with and taped a friend who'd been on a series of visits to the dentist. She'd been scared and nervous about the visits. Also the dentist and his nurse had the habit of talking to each other, rather intimately, "over the patient's head." The resulting discomfort-tending-toward-paranoia characterised the story my friend told. I transcribed the tape and then changed, particularly the nouns, to make the story fit one of my character's recollection of attending meetings of a faction of the Brigade at which she had felt rather intimidated, a bit scared, and had the sense that the others were discussing rather dangerous topics "over her head."

Divided into six chapters, which are then broken into the language and recollections of the four men and two women, *The Angry Brigade* presents the ignorant, misguided, and selfish attempts of a group of young, disaffected street kids and pseudo-intellectuals who vainly try to make a "political statement." Such statements result in the occupation and defacement of the Ministry of Housing, an action that brings about the five-year imprisonment of one member; the bombing of a railway embankment, which blinds a child, leads to the arrest of one of the women, and prompts another member to flee to his native India; the bombing of the Post Office Tower, which kills a waitress; and an ambush on police, with uncertain casualties.

Employing his now characteristic political theme, Burns shows the conflict between the powers of the state and the personal sacrifice made by some of the youths. However, the seriousness of many of the revolutionaries' actions is undercut by their own internecine power struggles and forms of personal and gender inequity. Ultimately the novel reveals not only the state's deadly powers but also the ways in which victims and the exploited can easily turn into victimizers and exploiters. Burns, however, has admitted to a rather different intention for his work:

I wrote the novel in protest against, and with the intention of off-setting, the demonizing of the members of The Angry Brigade in the press and other media. However, the book was pretty widely reviewed, and generally seen as an attack on the "real" Brigade, satirizing them, depicting their petty squabbles, their male chauvinism, and so on. Those negatives were part of my intended subtle characterization of people I did not see as simple heroes and heroines, but with whom I had many sympathies.

Although it uses the collage technique once again, the book is scrupulously controlled and concise. Unlike the profusion of voices that confound the reader of *Babel,* the differing voices in *The Angry Brigade* establish varying points of view for the same incident and thus question assumptions about the nature of verifiable facts. Burns uses ambiguity to reinforce the tension and paranoia that animate these lives. And, like the children in his earlier novels, the youths in this novel, dispossessed of their biological families and frightened by their own confusion and isolation, strive to create a pathetic substitute family in their commune. Casually dismissed by many critics, *The Angry Brigade* is actually one of Burns's strongest works.

Feeling artistically exhausted and financially strapped, Burns accepted a position in 1975 as senior tutor in creative writing at the Western Australian Institute of Technology in South Bentley, Australia. He spent his time teaching fiction writing and also oversaw a student production of *Palach* that was performed at the National Australian Student Drama Festival in Sydney. In the same year Hutchinson published *Beyond the Words,* an anthology, edited by Giles Gordon, of works by eleven contemporary British novelists. Burns's contributions consist of a particularly revealing essay about his fictional methods and concerns and a short story, "Wonderland."

Prepared at first to remain permanently in Australia, he nevertheless returned to London the next year to accept an Arts Council Fellowship. There, attached to the City Literary Institute, Burns enjoyed a good deal of free time for writing and the generosity of a £4,000 stipend. In 1977 he returned to teaching, accepting a position in the English department at the University of Minnesota, where he remained until 1993. In 1978 he and his second wife, Jean, had a child, Katherine Anne. While on leave in England in 1981, Burns turned five years of note taking and writing into his seventh novel, *The Day Daddy Died.* Returning to the domestic theme, the novel presents a tough, working-class woman, Norah, who, despite repeated pregnancies and financial difficulties, perseveres. During the Depression her father loses his job and later dies, leaving a lonely, adolescent Norah to find a succession of lover-father surrogates. Despite her poverty she manages to raise five children, the eldest of whom commits suicide, but unlike Burns's other fictional families, which ultimately tear one another apart, this family bands together and eventually buys the woman her first house.

Interwoven with this narrative, which is delivered in a conversational, straightforward manner, is a second story of a girl who has a love affair with her father. This narrative strand is highly surreal, and the novel shifts back and forth between the two

151

SQUEALING   I think nuclear war is an issue on which you have to be strident, and if somebody says,'But you're squealing,' you say,'Yes, I'm squealing, it's my life that is at stake.'

STATE OF   We can now use chemicals to alter the state of mind,
MIND   reversing the maturing process, making a mind abnormal. I say abnormal, but it appears normal. Yet every single cell in the brain is changed.

STIMULATE   ... and digging, he catches the end of a ... are all his ... y revolver, and ... shot-gun is a ... that you are ... shot-gun made. ... kill ... lver might ... The ... someone's

STRAIGHT   Straight white road, trees either side, a man mending a wall.

STRIPES   Coloured stripes are sewn on his clothes for shame, red bands perpendicular on the back, red bands crossed, red bands with yellow circles, red bands with blue circles, blue bands, finally: horizontal yellow.

SURRENDER

Page from the typescript for Burns's work in progress, "An Imaginary Dictionary" (Collection of Alan Burns)

modes. Interspersed with both of these are photo-collages by Ian Breakwell, which form a parallel narrative of memories and imaginings that float through the book. Despite the generally cool response, a review in *The Times Literary Supplement* was especially favorable and insightful.

Several months later Allison and Busby published another book, *The Imagination on Trial*. Coedited with University of Minnesota colleague Charles Sugnet, this is a series of interviews of twelve contemporary British and American novelists, including Burns, Alan Sillitoe, John Gardner, John Hawkes, J. G. Ballard, Michael Moorcock, Eva Figes, Grace Paley, Ishmael Reed, Wilson Harris, Tom Mallin, and B. S. Johnson. The interviews focus on the ways each writer's ideas germinate and evolve into fictions.

Burns's next novel, *Revolutions of the Night* (1986), in many ways hearkens back to techniques and concerns of his earlier fictions. Once again a Max Ernst painting—this time Ernst's *Revolution by Night* (1923)—inspires the novel's title and strongly hints at still another exploration of the domestic and familial themes. Once more, dreams, the workings of the unconscious, and surreal effects are clearly manifested. In fact, the last chapter, which is highly surreal and confusing, is actually an exactingly precise description of Ernst's painting *Europe after the Rain*, suggesting a movement full circle in Burns's career. This passage also exemplifies a narrative technique used throughout the novel, where detailed descriptions of various paintings or sketches by Ernst suddenly invade and blend with the workings of plot. The effect is obviously startling and disorienting yet dramatic proof of Burns's renewed commitment to the vision that has informed his entire career.

The story involves the death of a mother, who is replaced by her husband's lover. The children, Hazel and Harry, are emotionally unhinged and fall into an incestuous relationship. Later Hazel turns her attention to a middle-aged capitalist named Bob, whom she jettisons from a hot-air balloon, while Harry takes up with a cocktail waitress named Louise. Eventually the siblings escape to the country for a brief pastoral interlude that is destroyed when invaders murder Hazel and threaten her brother.

In his description of Ernst's painting *Europe after the Rain,* Burns writes that "caught between two pillars was a youth, blindfolded and gagged," and this image of a young person trapped between intractable forces is a perfect metaphor for the situation in all of Burns's fictions. In each of his works the young are sacrificed by the selfishness

and obsessions of their elders, yet they continually struggle, like young Palach, for a freedom that is rarely achieved. Burns describes the connection between dreams, surrealism, and the yearning for freedom in this way: "we are free in our dreams. Not only free, but we are expressing those deep impulses that, if unleashed, are upsetting to the social order. And anything that expresses the essence of our free selves is itself subversive and dangerous to the hierarchy and the settled order. That's what my books are about, I hope, to share that, to push it."

In 1993 Burns returned to England, a return prompted by a definite sense of cultural unease, as he explains in a letter: "my connection with the States was never solid and uninterrupted. I also had very strong reservations about the US political setup. Great country to have a good job in, hell if not. On the buses I saw Dickensian poverty, faces and bodies mutilated by bad diet and living conditions. I was appalled by the desecration of that beautiful land. . . . I think, those unfamiliar accents got on my nerves . . . more the timbre than the accent maybe. . . . those years [were a] kind of exile that made me discover how English I felt, my delight at being here, the greens, the way folks are with each other—not to idealize, for the same lousy Tory lot [were] in power, [and I] think the English upper classes are even more obnoxious than your rotten gang, but there it is."

Currently Burns is at work on four separate nonfiction projects; "Art by Accident" is nearly completed. The book represents the culmination of and elaboration on his earlier essay on aleatoric art, where the creator, by design or chance, has allowed random forces to determine the result of the artistic process. The book is unique in its broad range of references and in its multidisciplinary approach; novelists, poets, painters, and composers are all represented, and the work demonstrates a spirit of mutual dependence and influence among these media.

A second work in progress is a biography of his close friend and colleague, Johnson. Burns attempts to capture the diversity of Johnson's personality, moods, and influences on others through a variety of sources, assembled in a fashion that has much in common with the fragmentational method he has used in his fiction. Another biography, provisionally titled "Gangster," examines the life of the British convict Frank Cook, who has spent most of his adult life incarcerated. At age thirty-eight Cook began sculpting in prison and showed such promise that a pair of his works have been exhibited at the Metropolitan Gallery in New

York. Burns's approach is in no way apologetic, à la Norman Mailer with Jack Henry Abbott; both convict and biographer are quick to reveal the scope of Cook's vicious past, but he is nevertheless humanized by the close inspection of his life and motives.

"Imaginary Dictionary," the fourth work in progress, is in the tradition of "alternative" dictionaries by such writers as Gustave Flaubert and Ambrose Beirce. It is by turns playful and profound but is always subversive: words become animated and assume unique characteristics independent of their traditional usages and the expectations of readers. Parts of the Johnson biography and the dictionary were published in *The Review of Contemporary Fiction* in the summer of 1997.

All of Burns's emphasis on fragmentation, the cut-up method, surreal intrusions, and wild juxtapositions may suggest rather formidable reading. After all, Burns has admitted that he wants "to shock readers into a new awareness" and that he seeks "to work more like a painter than a writer; place images side by side and let them say something uncertain and fluctuating. This work will not be literary and will not lead to discussion or redefinition, but simply exist—like a Magritte painting." Such remarks may give the impression of an utterly anarchic art, but this is not the case.

At the heart of these methods of fictional disorientation is Burns's resistance to traditional notions of the novel and his rejection of any idea of the genre as being an inflexible monolith of changeless features. "The great attraction of the novel," he has said, "lies in its search for form. The secret may lie in the word *novel* itself. If it's new, then it's novel." Thus the novel, in his view, is malleable and accommodating to the mutable nature of a writer's and audience's perceptions, and by insisting that it shares in the characteristics of painting, Burns reveals his adamant concern for hard, concrete prose, a prose that is nearly palpable and strongly visual. Scenes and chapters often have an almost independent relationship with their larger narrative, which is nowhere more obvious than in *Babel*.

Burns is also a writer of strong ideological convictions that, while deeply held, never prompt him to lapse into didactic preaching. His political beliefs and his aesthetic proclivities underscore a deeply humanist point of view. "It sounds pathetic—this avant-garde novelist wanting to change the world—but I do, I simply want to leave it a little bit better." Burns is a champion of individual freedom and consistently attempts to reveal those forces that would stunt or limit expressions of individuality. As he explains, "Like others, I have in a way been writing and rewriting the same basic book, again and again. All that material about the recurrent father figures, and the father–State, and the absent mother, and the young man dead." Such a characterization might imply simple repetition, yet what this description reveals is the consistency of his vision and his steadfast dedication to opposing the most destructive tendencies of human beings.

Interviews:

"The Disintegrating Novel," *Books and Bookmen,* 15 (15 September 1970): 6–7, 53;

Paddy Kitchen, "Surrealism and Sculpture in Words," *Times Educational Supplement,* 18 September 1970, p. 21;

Peter Firchow, "Alan Burns," in *The Writer's Place: Interviews on the Literary Situation in Contemporary Britain,* edited by Firchow (Minneapolis: University of Minnesota Press, 1974), pp. 50–62;

I. G. Leask, "The Value of the Image," *FallOut* (Spring/Summer 1980): 20–22;

Shawn Gillen, "Slash and Burns," *Minnesota Daily,* 11 November 1988, pp. 11–12;

"Alan Burns," *Minnesota* (July–August 1989): 22–24.

References:

John Hall, "Novels from the Unconscious," *Guardian,* 30 April 1970, pp. 9–10;

Review of Contemporary Fiction, special Burns section, edited by David W. Madden, 17 (Summer 1997): 108–214.

A. S. Byatt

(24 August 1936 –   )

P. B. Parris
University of North Carolina at Asheville

and

Caryn McTighe Musil
University of Maryland at College Park

See also the Byatt entry in *DLB 14: British Novelists Since 1960.*

BOOKS: *Shadow of a Sun* (London: Chatto & Windus, 1964; New York: Harcourt, Brace & World, 1964); republished as *The Shadow of the Sun* (San Diego: Harcourt, Brace, 1993);

Degrees of Freedom: The Novels of Iris Murdoch (London: Chatto & Windus, 1965; New York: Barnes & Noble, 1965);

The Game (London: Chatto & Windus, 1967; New York: Scribners, 1968);

Wordsworth and Coleridge in Their Time (London: Nelson, 1970; New York: Crane, Russak, 1973); republished as *Unruly Times: Wordsworth and Coleridge in Their Time* (London: Hogarth Press, 1989);

Iris Murdoch, Writers and Their Work Series (Harlow: Published for the British Council by the Longman Group, 1976);

The Virgin in the Garden (London: Chatto & Windus, 1978; New York: Knopf, 1979); republished in *The Virgin in the Garden and Still Life: An Omnibus* (London: Chatto & Windus, 1991);

Still Life (London: Chatto & Windus, 1985; New York: Scribners, 1985); republished in *The Virgin in the Garden and Still Life: An Omnibus*;

Sugar and Other Stories (London: Chatto & Windus, 1987; New York: Scribners, 1987);

Possession: A Romance (London: Chatto & Windus, 1990; New York: Random House, 1991);

Passions of the Mind: Selected Writings (London: Chatto & Windus, 1991; New York: Turtle Bay Books, 1992);

Angels and Insects (London: Chatto & Windus, 1992); republished as *Angels & Insects: Two Novellas* (New York: Random House, 1993);

A. S. Byatt (photograph © Peter Peitsch)

The Matisse Stories (London: Chatto & Windus, 1993; New York: Random House, 1995);

The Djinn in the Nightingale's Eye: Five Fairy Stories (London: Chatto & Windus, 1994; New York: Random House, 1997);

Imagining Characters: Six Conversations about Women Writers, by Byatt and Ignes Sôdré (London: Chatto & Windus, 1995; New York: Vintage, 1997);

Babel Tower (London: Chatto & Windus, 1996; New York: Random House, 1996);

Collected Stories (London: Chatto & Windus, 1998).

OTHER: "The Lyrical Structure of Tennyson's *Maud,*" in *The Major Victorian Poets: Reconsiderations,* edited by Isobel Armstrong (London: Routledge & Kegan Paul, 1969), pp. 69–92;

Elizabeth Bowen, *The House in Paris,* introduction by Byatt (London: Penguin, 1976; New York: Penguin, 1994);

George Eliot, *The Mill on the Floss,* edited, with an introduction, by Byatt (London: Penguin, 1979);

Grace Paley, *Enormous Changes at the Last Minute,* introduction by Byatt (London: Virago, 1979);

"People in Paper Houses: Attitudes to 'Realism' and 'Experiment' in English Postwar Fiction," in *The Contemporary English Novel,* edited by Malcolm Bradbury and David Palmer (London: Edward Arnold, 1979; New York: Holmes & Meier, 1979), pp. 19–41;

Willa Cather, *A Lost Lady,* introduction by Byatt (London: Virago, 1980);

Cather, *My Antonia,* introduction by Byatt (London: Virago, 1980);

Paley, *The Little Disturbances Man,* introduction by Byatt (London: Virago, 1980);

Cather, *My Mortal Enemy,* introduction by Byatt (London: Virago, 1982);

"Identity and the Writer," in *Identity Documents 6* (London: ICA, 1987), pp. 23–26;

Cather, *Death Comes to the Archbishop,* introduction by Byatt (London: Virago, 1989);

Cather, *The Song of the Lark,* introduction by Byatt (London: Virago, 1989);

Eliot, *Selected Essays, Poems and Other Writings,* edited by Byatt and Nicholas Warren, with an introduction by Byatt (London: Penguin, 1989);

Robert Browning, *Dramatic Monologues,* edited by Byatt (London: Folio Society, 1990);

"Envy," in *Deadly Sins,* edited by Thomas Pynchon (New York: Morrow, 1993), pp. 82–102;

Jane Austen, *The History of England: From the Reign of Henry the 4th to the Death of Charles the 1st,* introduction by Byatt (New York: Algonquin, 1993);

Kees Fens, *Finding the Place: Selected Essays on English Literature,* edited by W. Bronzwaer and H. Verdaasdonk, introduction by Byatt (Amsterdam: Rodopi, 1994);

Marie-Catherine D'Aulnoy, "The Great Green Worm," translated by Byatt, in *Wonder Tales: Six French Stories of Enchantment,* edited by Marina Warner (London: Chatto & Windus, 1994; New York: Farrar Straus Giroux, 1996);

New Writing 4, edited by Byatt and Alan Hollinghurst (London: Vintage, 1995):

"A Lamia in Cévennes," in *The Year's Best Fantasy and Horror: Ninth Annual Collection,* edited by Ellen Datlow and Terri Windling (New York: St. Martin's Press, 1996);

New Writing 6, edited by Byatt and Peter Porter (London: Vintage, 1997);

Oxford Book of English Short Stories, edited by Byatt (Oxford & New York: Oxford University Press, 1998).

SELECTED PERIODICAL PUBLICATIONS–UNCOLLECTED: "The Obsession with Amorphous Mankind," *Encounter,* 27 (September 1966): 63–69;

"Real People and Images," *Encounter,* 28 (February 1967): 71–78;

"Wallace Stevens: Criticism, Repetition, and Creativity," *American Studies,* 12, no. 3 (1978): 369–375;

"Insights Ad Nauseam," *Times Literary Supplement,* 14 November 1986, pp. 43–63;

"Obscenity and the Arts," *Times Literary Supplement,* 12–18 February 1988, p. 159;

"Writing and Feeling," *Times Literary Supplement,* 18–24 November 1988, p. 1278;

"After the Myth, the Real," *Times Literary Supplement,* 29 June–5 July 1990, pp. 683–684;

"The Hue and Cry of Love," *New York Times,* 11 February 1991, p. A19;

"Love's Rhyme Knows Reason," *New York Times,* 14 February 1992, pp. A19, A29;

"Reading, Writing, Studying: Some Questions about Changing Conditions for Writing and Readers," *Critical Quarterly,* 35 (Winter 1993): 3–7;

"A. S. Byatt on *Angels and Insects,*" *Architectural Digest,* 53 (April 1996): 100–108.

With the publication of her prizewinning fifth novel, *Possession: A Romance* (1990), A. S. Byatt expanded her audience from a previously small but dedicated one in Britain to a wide, enthusiastic readership on both sides of the Atlantic. A respected critic, reviewer, editor, and scholar as well as writer of fiction, Byatt has often been praised for her prodigious intellect, her erudition, and her talent for creating long, complex novels; in addition, she has demonstrated her ability to tell a good story.

Antonia Susan Drabble was born on 24 August 1936 in the sooty steel town of Sheffield, Yorkshire, the eldest of the four children of Kathleen Marie Bloor Drabble and John Frederick Drabble. Her father was a barrister and later a judge; her mother was a former elementary schoolteacher, neurotic and frustrated, angrily unhappy at being a full-time housewife. Both came from working-class families but had studied at Cambridge, and the household was one of books, book talk, and slamming doors. Byatt's passion for the Victorians, which shows itself in her later fiction, was instilled by her mother; asthmatic, often bedridden, she read a good deal as a child. Because her father and several aunts published novels, it is understandable that she wanted to grow up quickly and become a writer herself.

Antonia's younger sister, Margaret Drabble, also became a novelist, critic, and academic, which has led to a public sibling rivalry. Both attended Cambridge, have married twice, have won many literary and scholarly prizes, and have been awarded honors by the Queen. And both have written books on William Wordsworth and novels about literate Yorkshire families. Not surprisingly, a recurring theme in Byatt's novels is the struggle of the individual to discover and live out one's own identity.

Although she considers herself an agnostic, Antonia Drabble was educated from the age of thirteen at Mount School, a Quaker boarding school in the city of York. She was an exceptionally bright student, and it was there that she began her writing, devising a secret work space for herself in the school's boiler room, where she could sit and scribble by the light of the fire. Offered scholarships to Somerville College, Oxford, and Newnham College, Cambridge, she chose the latter and, in 1954, entered the challenging, exhilarating arena of ideas and personalities. Meanwhile she continued to fill her black notebooks with what would become her first novel, *Shadow of a Sun* (1964). In an introduction to a 1991 reprinting of the book, she says that it was written "in libraries and lectures, between essays and love affairs." She distinguished herself at Cambridge, receiving her B.A. degree with first-class honors in 1957. Following a year of postgraduate study at Bryn Mawr College in Pennsylvania on an English-Speaking Union Scholarship, she sailed back to England to work on a doctorate in seventeenth-century literature at Somerville College, Oxford.

Antonio Drabble was writing both her dissertation and her novel at the same time. Dame Helen Gardner, under whom she was studying, tried to discourage her fictional work, telling her that every young woman with a first-class degree in English fancies herself capable of writing a novel, though none are; "anything you write," Byatt recalls, "would fall so woefully short of the highest standards that it was better not to try." Gardner urged her to get on with her more serious research. Her anger at Gardner's slighting remarks led her to redouble her creative efforts.

Antonia Drabble married Ian Charles Rayner Byatt, an English economist, on 4 July 1959, and left Oxford without completing her degree because, as was the case at that time for women students who married, her scholarship grant was withdrawn. After moving to Durham they became parents of two children: Antonia, born in 1960, and Charles, born in 1961. In spite of the demands of housewifery and motherhood Byatt taught part-time and completed her first novel, *Shadow of a Sun*.

While it has much of the "toughness of thought" of Iris Murdoch and of Marcel Proust, Byatt says in the 1991 introduction that "the underlying shape of *The Shadow of the Sun* was dictated by Elizabeth Bowen and Rosamond Lehman." The novel tells the story of Anna Severall, a shy, aspiring young writer longing to shape her own life and work yet suffering from paralyzing self-doubt. Anna is the daughter of novelist Henry Severall, a monumental figure who "looked like a cross between God, Alfred Lord Tennyson, and Blake's Job." Standing in the shadow of this famous sun, Anna adopts two means of defending her fragile ego: she becomes passive and withdrawn, and, given the opportunity, she runs away. In a previous abortive attempt at escape she left her boarding school with the fantasy of beginning a writing life in York. Once installed in a dreary hotel room in that cold and desolate city, she felt trapped, "confronted by a blank wall and a dark window." She returned home, defeated.

Enter Oliver Channing, who has gained a reputation as a critic of Henry Severall's work. On an extended stay in the Severall house with his wife Margaret, Channing engages the interest of seventeen-year-old Anna, and the relationships among the four of them—Oliver and Margaret, Henry and Anna—shift and change. Anna's dependency moves from her preoccupied father to the more attentive Oliver while Margaret turns to Henry. Paradoxically, Oliver directs Anna to take control of her own life and then proceeds to make several important decisions for her, becoming as stifling to Anna's independence as Henry has been. She is caught between the two powerful men: her father, a creative visionary, a maker of art; and Oliver, a realist, a critic, a user of Henry's imaginative productions. Oliver tutors Anna so that she can go to Cambridge, but his motives are suspect. When he takes her sexually, it is an act of triumph over Henry in their rivalry for Anna's affection and admiration.

Again feeling trapped, Anna seeks release. It comes during a storm that reflects her inner turmoil; as thunder rolls and lightning flashes, she turns a drinking glass in her hand and feels "balanced and complete, between all this trapped, plotted light and the approaching storm" and thinks, "not knowing quite what she meant, 'I can do something with this. Oh, I can do something with this, that matters.'" Moments later she tells Oliver, "I shall suffocate in this house if I stay any longer," and she runs out into the rain. When he attempts to reassert his power over her, she feels only pity for him. Having detached herself from both father and lover, Anna is ready, at the end of part 1 of the novel, to create her own independent life.

Part 2 finds Anna at Cambridge, again under the domination of men. She retreats once more into passivity and self-doubt, giving herself over to a fellow student, the aristocratic Peter Hughes-Winterton. Oliver reappears, like the proverbial knight in shining armor, and rescues her, and Anna welcomes what seems to her to be a safe affair, which will allow her to postpone difficult decisions about her future.

As she considers leaving Cambridge to become the writer that she once imagined herself, she spots a green bottle floating in the River Cam, drifting along just as she has been. She gazes at the glass bottle. No lightning, no creative illumination comes as it had in the remembered rainstorm; the "the possible glory was gone." What she feels is nausea, a sign that she is pregnant. Peter offers to marry her and takes her to his family's home, but she does not want to be a wife or a mother. Faced again with the necessity of making serious choices, she reverts to earlier behavior and flees to York and longed-for independence. But Oliver intercedes, and she accepts passively that she will bear the child and continue under Oliver's control. Her biology has become her destiny. The novel ends with her sad resignation: "But it doesn't matter. I wouldn't have gone far I suspect."

Though not an autobiographical novel in the usual sense, *Shadow of a Sun* does, in many ways, embody Byatt's conflict between two strong intellectual influences during her own undergraduate years at Cambridge: D. H. Lawrence and the critic F. R. Leavis. Byatt writes in her 1991 introduction that "if the two had ever met they would have hated each other." One can readily picture Lawrence as Henry and Leavis as Oliver, with Byatt as Anna caught between the two.

A second autobiographical conflict in the novel is that faced by women in the 1950s, when Anna's story is set. Byatt notes that "the female belief in, or illusion of, the need to be 'in love' was the danger which most threatened my heroine." At the time women were encouraged, some would say required, to play passive and domestic roles despite their increasing educational and professional opportunities. Anna is trapped between two sets of conflicting expectations, as was Byatt herself. But creating the character of Anna and having her accept the domestic/maternal alternative at the end of the novel somehow freed Byatt to follow her own aspirations and become both a wife/mother and a novelist/critic. It was, however, not easy. In her 1991 introduction, Byatt recalls, "I sat rocking my son with one hand in a plastic chair on the table, and wrote with the other."

Moving from the creative to the analytical, Byatt next published *Degrees of Freedom* (1965), a critical study of Murdoch's novels. Murdoch's influence on Byatt's own fiction has been remarked on frequently by critics.

Byatt had begun drafting her second novel, *The Game* (1967), while doing postgraduate work at Bryn Mawr in 1957–1958; remarkably, she finished the initial draft between starting and completing *Shadow of a Sun*. *The Game* has at its center the antagonistic relationship between an unmarried, introverted Oxford professor, Cassandra Corbett, and Julia, her younger sister, who is an outgoing, successful novelist and television personality. The Corbett sisters have been seen by critics as shadows of Byatt and her own younger sister Margaret, and critical discussion has linked *The Game* to Drabble's 1963 novel, *A Summer Bird-Cage,* which also focuses on the rivalry of two sisters. Byatt's own explanation of *The Game* is that it is a technical exercise in the use of metaphor. It is that, certainly, and a piece of fine writing too, alive with imagery of jungles, snakes, Eden, good and evil, and the spiritual and the sensual, intertwining the modern and the medieval.

Cassandra and Julia share a fantasy life that makes it impossible for them to see one another clearly. The elder sister, named for Homer's unheeded sibyl, is a medieval scholar who lives a life of almost monastic self-denial, convinced that love is dangerous, that it consumes and destroys the lovers. Cassandra's self-containment is a defense against the destruction of her self, and behind her fortification of chains and locks and crosses she immerses herself in her writing and study, her life of the mind.

Julia, on the other hand, is the picture of worldly success; she is a literary and media star as well as a wife and mother. However, she suffers from deep insecurities, and her success is the consequence of her need for constant public affirmation. She also needs Cassandra's approval, but at the beginning of the novel, the sisters, now in their thirties, are estranged from one another. Only their father's terminal illness brings the hostile siblings together again.

The source of their alienation is recounted: as children they had shared an imaginary world in which they played the Game. Much like the Brontës, they created knights and ladies, castles and queens. Battles for control of their relationship were acted out symbolically through the Game, with Cassandra devising horrific scenarios and Julia contributing more pleasant ones. Finally, Julia, the budding writer, produced a short story that revealed to others their imaginary world, and Cassandra refused to go on with their fantasy play.

Another decisive conflict between the sisters involved a young man, Simon Moffitt, with whom Cassandra was in love before she went off to university. He became Julia's friend in her absence, and Cassandra felt betrayed, never forgiving either of them. It is the reappearance in London of Simon, now a herpetologist doing research in Africa, that ultimately destroys the sisters' temporary reconciliation brought on by their father's death.

Julia comes to Oxford to visit Cassandra, who feels menaced by her sister. Her defenses shattered, Cassandra leaves her medieval studies and takes up painting in the Botanic Gardens, a setting connected symbolically both with the biblical Eden and with the jungle where Simon has been doing his research. Subsequently Julia publishes a novel, *A Sense of Glory;* its central character is a woman based largely upon her sister who is faced with the appearance of a long-lost lover, a version of Cassandra's relationship with Simon. Having written the novel and altered the Cassandra character's personality to suit herself, Julia believes that she has freed herself from her sister's control.

When Simon comes to Oxford, and he and Cassandra are placed in the same circumstances as Julia imagined in her novel, Cassandra resolves to elude her sister's fictive control. She pulls back into her fortified self, locks her doors, and commits suicide. Julia is left with the knowledge that in creating a character who resembled her sister she had distanced herself further from the living person, and now that person is dead. She will have to live the rest of her life without the struggles with her sister, without an opposition that previously had given her own life form and purpose. Both Simon and Julia's husband, Thor, are gone by the end of the novel,

and she is forced back upon her own internal resources to make her meaning of herself, for herself, from the inside out.

After completing *The Game* Byatt, as she had done after her previous novel, produced a book of criticism: *Wordsworth and Coleridge in Their Time* (1970). This study of the early Romantic poets was republished nineteen years later under the title *Unruly Times;* it is a scholarly examination of the two poets and their personal and poetic connections, placed within their historical context, and it reflects Byatt's admiration for the originality of their visions.

Eleven more years would pass before Byatt's next novel. Her life was in turmoil. She and Ian Byatt divorced in 1969, and shortly thereafter she married Peter John Duffy, a London investment analyst. From this union Byatt bore two more children: Isabel, born in 1970, and Miranda, born in 1973. The death in 1972 of her son, Charles, devastated Byatt; the eleven-year-old was killed by a drunk driver. Overwhelmed by the loss, Byatt scrapped what she had drafted of her third novel and accepted a teaching post at University College, London.

In a 1991 interview with Mira Stout, Byatt said, "I think what saved me was the students. . . . They were so selfish, talking about their own concerns. They were in another world; I had to change gear." Along with her teaching she continued to review books for magazine and newspapers, write academic articles, and appear on radio and television programs. In 1976 she produced another book about Murdoch, this time for the British Council's Writers and Their Work Series. Byatt remained a professor of English and American literature at University College until 1983.

The Virgin in the Garden (1978) broke Byatt's long silence as a novelist. A denser, more ambitious novel than its predecessors, it makes greater intellectual demands upon the reader, repaying every effort. The novel is the first in a proposed quartet chronicling England in the 1950s and 1960s. The seeds of *The Virgin in the Garden* were sown in Byatt's postgraduate research into seventeenth-century literature at Oxford in 1959; the novel's central symbol is Queen Elizabeth I, who succeeded, Byatt believes, because she used her intellect and remained the Virgin Queen. Elizabeth saw the dangers of giving in to her heart and did not lose her head, literally or figuratively, as did her cousin, Mary, Queen of Scots. In *The Virgin in the Garden,* Byatt once again examines the risks of falling in love.

The novel's prologue is set in the National Portrait Gallery, evoking the look of the late 1960s with a kind of national portrait in miniature. Byatt describes a group of young people in sandals and floppy velvet, khaki jackets from Vietnam, antique military tunics with tarnished braid, and garments made from Indian bedspreads: "they imitate anything and everything out of an unmanageable combination of aesthetic curiosity, mocking destructiveness and affectionate nostalgia." In an interview with John F. Baker for the 20 May 1996 *Publishers Weekly* Byatt speaks of the spirit of that time as "a longing for freedom leading to excess and ultimately to cruelty."

Set against the backdrop of the 1950s and 1960s the quartet of novels follows the development of Frederica Potter, who, like all of Byatt's female protagonists, is intelligent and given to analysis and literary reflection. The principal action of *The Virgin in the Garden* takes place in Blesford, a small Yorkshire town preparing to celebrate the coronation of Queen Elizabeth II in 1953. A verse drama about Queen Elizabeth I, written by Alexander Wedderburn, a good-looking English professor, is about to be performed, and several of the townspeople are involved. When the story begins, Frederica, who is seventeen, has been selected for the lead in the drama; her older sister Stephanie, a Cambridge graduate, is teaching at the local girls' grammar school; and Marcus, their younger brother, silent and withdrawn, is haunted by strange visions. Bill Potter, their father, is overbearing; Winifred, their mother, ineffectual.

Although the novel's main character is Frederica, the three Potter siblings' lives are woven through the account of the production of the play. For all of them love brings pain. Marcus, because he is largely nonverbal, exists in a self-enclosed world, not caring to touch or be touched. When he is approached in a sexual manner by Lucas Simmonds, his biology teacher, Marcus is so frightened that Lucas, painfully ashamed at his own behavior, attempts suicide and is taken to a mental hospital. Marcus is drawn out of his self-isolation and attempts to comfort Lucas; overcome by the effort, he suffers a breakdown of his own and takes refuge in the home of his sister Stephanie and her husband, Daniel Orton. Stephanie's marriage to Daniel, a kindly, humanitarian clergyman, is followed by painful disappointments. Stephanie, like her mother, quietly accepts her domestic situation and, in the end, is pictured as a pregnant saint, a patient Virgin Mary.

Frederica's infatuation with the playwright Wedderburn is filled with the girl's adolescent pain. Her selection to play Elizabeth I opens for her a range of new experiences; the play is performed at Long Rowston, the Crowe estate, where she glimpses a grand world previously unknown to her. But when the play is over, the gates to that world close behind her: "It really was like being shut out of paradise." Nevertheless, Frederica pursues Alexander, arranging a rendezvous with him, but panics and fails to meet him because she is afraid he will find out that she is a virgin. Alexander leaves Blesford to enjoy the success his drama has gained him, and Frederica seeks solace in a less emotionally charged relationship. From this liaison she learns a valuable lesson: "You could sleep all night with a strange man . . . and be more self-contained than anywhere else." Like Anna in *Shadow of a Sun*, Frederica wants to have both an intellectual and a sexual life; but unlike Anna she discovers, for the moment, the means to have both. The prologue, set in 1968, has made clear that Frederica will grow into adulthood, enjoying "love, passion, sex, and those things" as well as "the life of the mind, ambition, solitude."

The Virgin in the Garden closes with the young Frederica contemplating Stephanie and Marcus, "the still and passive pair on the sofa. That was not an end, but since it went on for a considerable time, is as good a place to stop as any." And, indeed, it is not the end of Frederica's story.

Byatt's next novel, *Still Life* (1985), the second in the Potter quartet, begins with a prologue that again takes readers forward to a time in advance of the central action, here to 1980. Paralleling the opening of *The Virgin in the Garden*, Frederica again meets Wedderburn, now an old friend, and Daniel, her brother-in-law, in London. This time it is in the Royal Academy of Arts to view the Vincent Van Gogh paintings. The Dutch artist and his sun-bright French landscapes function symbolically throughout the novel, a contrast to the dark tones with which Byatt paints the events in the Potter siblings' lives.

In the present time of *Still Life* Frederica spends the summer of 1953, before going to university, in Provence with a French host family, the Grimauds. Though still fancying herself a bit in love with Alexander, she goes to bed with another man, for whom she feels no strong emotional attachment. Once installed at Cambridge, at Newnham College, Byatt's alma mater, Frederica finds it difficult to make friends with other women students, but she is "greedy for variety" among the men. "Sex was a problem, and partly a threat." She has affairs with several male students, experiences something of the English upper classes, and suffers a serious crush on the poet-lecturer Raphael Faber. While Frederica does well academically in her study of English literature, she also learns much about the difficulties of

Dust jacket for the U.S. edition of Byatt's novel about a modern couple who uncover a clandestine love affair between two Victorian poets

about the breadth of knowledge required by a reader in order to match Byatt's own. For instance one sentence alone, a description of Frederica's bedroom in France, assumes familiarity with postimpressionist art and classic motion pictures: the room's "walls were painted a bright dark blue—a colour that reminded her of a postcard of Van Gogh's *Starry Night* and even more of the colour behind the fleurs de lys on the banners in Olivier's 1944 film of Henry V."

Byatt intrudes into the narrative frequently in *Still Life,* commenting upon the characters, the making of the book itself, and the larger ideas under consideration, in the manner of a Victorian author. Well into *Still Life* Byatt confesses: "I had the idea that this novel could be written innocently, without recourse to reference to other people's thoughts, without, as far as possible, recourse to simile or metaphor. This turned out to be impossible." Such metafictional asides annoyed some readers and delighted others. A reviewer in the 30 August 1985 *Publishers Weekly* writes of *Still Life,* "It is a bountiful, even overloaded book, very much one for those who enjoy novels that probe philosophical concepts, tap profound emotions and raise provocative questions." In the 1991 Stout interview Byatt seemed to answer the criticism of her difficult, overly intellectual novels: "All my heros wrote long sentences. . . . I like people who are interested in the way the mind puts the world together."

At the time, however, Byatt abandoned Frederica and produced her first collection of short fiction, *Sugar and Other Stories* (1987). The somber narratives, about loss and possibility, reflect her still-painful mourning for her dead son. The stories were written quickly, Byatt later admitted, and are so autobiographical that she gave a copy of the collection to interviewer Stout "to help with the factual background of her Yorkshire childhood and family relationships."

One of the stories in the collection, "The July Ghost," has been much anthologized; it concerns a woman who resists mourning the death of her son and is therefore denied the solace of his comforting ghost. Another story, "Precipice-Encurled," recounts an imagined incident in the life of Robert Browning, discovered in the poet's letters by a fictional scholar, anticipating in many ways Byatt's next novel.

If many were surprised by the popular success of Byatt's fifth novel, *Possession: A Romance* (1990), she was not. The book, however, had a difficult publishing history in the United States; "Nobody wanted it," Byatt recalled in a 1996 interview with John F. Baker. Only after the novel had appeared in

emotional detachment and resistance to romantic entanglements.

Meanwhile, her sister Stephanie delivers her first child, named William for the Wordsworth she read during her pregnancy. Near the end of *Still Life* Stephanie, after having borne Mary, a second child, is killed in an accident while attempting to save a sparrow that has gotten into the house. Marcus, living with the Ortons since his breakdown, is there at the time and must try, in his slow, painful way, to understand what happened to his sister and his inability to prevent it.

The final chapter of *Still Life* has a lengthy meditation upon death, grief, and survival, Byatt's personal concerns at the time of the writing of the book. As the novel comes to a close, Daniel is faced with raising his two small children without Stephanie. Once again the story is left open-ended.

Still Life was received by the critics much as was *The Virgin in the Garden,* with praise for Byatt's obvious skill and artistry but with reservations

England and won both the coveted Booker Prize and the *Irish Times*-Aer Lingus International Fiction Prize did Random House accept it. Moreover, Byatt had to resist efforts by the editors to make major changes in the manuscript in order to render it more appealing and more accessible, they insisted, to American readers. When the novel appeared, still intact, *Possession* made the bestseller list, where it remained for nearly six months.

Byatt told Stout in her 1991 interview, "I knew people would like it. It's the only one I've written to be liked, and I did it partly to show off." And, indeed, it is a literary tour de force. Stout describes it as "a good-natured mix of genres: detective saga and romance novel, campus satire, Grimm fairy tale and Norse myth, post-Freudian deconstructionist riddle and, most satisfying, a philosophical exploration of love and possession, replete with invented love letters and original pseudo-Victorian verse."

Possession involves the intertwined stories of two couples: a pair of contemporary literary scholars, Roland Michell and Maud Bailey, on a quest to substantiate a clandestine affair between two long-dead Victorian poets; and the poets, Randolph Henry Ash and Christabel LaMotte. Ash's poetry (as written by Byatt) resembles that of Robert Browning, while LaMotte's owes much to Emily Dickinson and Christina Rossetti. Byatt has also fabricated correspondence and diaries from the period, autobiography, and scholarly articles by 1980s admirers of the two poets. A postmodern mixture of genres, styles, and voices, *Possession* is a pastiche of a high order. It is also a ripping good story.

The novel begins in the London Library when Roland, a postdoctoral researcher at Prince Albert College, discovers drafts of an urgent personal letter Ash, himelf a married man, wrote to a young woman whom he had just met. Roland is so intrigued, so possessed by the desire to learn more, that he behaves in a most unscholarly manner and steals the drafts, meaning to return them later. Although hapless and without prospects, Roland is basically a good man, a sort of English antihero cast as a questing knight.

Roland's employer, Professor James Blackadder, presides in the basement of the British Museum over the Ash factory, which is a long-standing scholarly enterprise in assembling all known facts about the Victorian poet. Blackadder once had aspirations to be a poet himself but was discouraged at university by critic F. R. Leavis, who "did to Blackadder what he did to serious students: he showed the terrible, the magnificent importance and urgency of English literature and simultaneously deprived him of any confidence in his own capacity to contribute to

or change it." Blackadder has done the same to Roland, which echoes the experience of Byatt herself at the hands of Leavis and, later, Helen Gardner.

Roland, purloined letters tucked into his copy of Ash's collected works, makes guarded inquiries at the Ash factory as to the woman's identity. Further textual research convinces him that she must be LaMotte, who had previously been thought to be exclusively lesbian. In his hunt for more details about the two poets Roland meets Maud Bailey, a LaMotte scholar at Lincoln University and a distant relative of "the fairy poet," as she is called by Sir George Bailey, in whose country house the complete Ash-LaMotte correspondence is uncovered, literally, in the bottom of LaMotte's dolls' bed.

Maud and Roland, as are so many of Byatt's characters, are both wary of personal emotional entanglements. Maud is ashamed of her beauty and hides it beneath head scarves and intellectual seriousness; Roland, feeling out of his class and out of his depths, is intimidated by her. They work uncomfortably together as they learn about the growing passion of the Ash-LaMotte affair. The scholars are soon thwarted in their research by legal questions concerning ownership and access to the letters. At the same time they are being pursued by two rival Americans who want to know more about their find: Mortimer Cropper, representative of a wealthy foundation at Robert Dale Owen University in New Mexico, eager to buy up, to possess, anything remotely connected with Ash; and Leonora Stern of Tallahassee, a flamboyant feminist scholar who longs to possess Maud as well as any new information about LaMotte. Byatt appears to be having great fun with these characters, parodying the Americans' speech, aggressiveness, and acquisitiveness.

What drives Roland and Maud is something more powerful than the others' motives: Byatt calls it "narrative curiosity," something more basic to readers and less sophisticated than current literary theory is likely to acknowledge. Roland and Maud suspect from reading the letters of Ash and LaMotte that they traveled together to the Yorkshire coast in June 1859. Possessed by their nineteenth-century counterparts, the modern couple flee from their pursuers to the seaside town of Whitby, matching details of the landscape, place names, and local legends to references in the later work of both poets. The irony here is particularly strong: two young people, living in a sex-obsessed, post-Freudian culture, reading erotic feminist literary criticism, are staying in separate bedrooms and avoiding sex altogether. In contrast, Byatt has Ash and LaMotte, products of the sexually repressive Victorian age, sharing a bed during their "honeymoon" in Yorkshire and enjoying sex together, fully and freely.

The question of the virgin LaMotte's previous sexual experience rises briefly in Ash's mind. Even after the journal and letters of LaMotte's housemate, Blanche Glover, are presented to readers, the true nature of the two women's relationship defies simple definition. That they are emotionally, even spiritually, close is indisputable; Glover commits suicide when she learns the extent of LaMotte's involvement with Ash. As Brenda K. Marshall says in the May 1991 *Women's Review of Books,* "the strongest attachment between Blanche and LaMotte is clearly their desire to live autonomous, independent lives, outside of the control, financial or personal, of men." That autonomy is threatened and ultimately destroyed by Ash's amorous pursuit of LaMotte.

After a brief separation during which Roland and Maud return to their respective homes, a series of fortuitous events reveal two more texts related to their scavenger hunt: another stolen letter, this one to Stern from a French literary researcher, and the recovered journal of LaMotte's cousin Sabine in Brittany. Roland and Maud undertake a second journey, this time through France, followed by Cropper and Stern and Blackadder. Roland and Maud visit the locale where LaMotte secretly gave birth, in early 1860, to Ash's baby, which raises the unanswered and seemingly unanswerable question: What became of the child?

Back in London, Roland and Maud consult the journals of Ash's wife, Ellen, with the assistance of Beatrice Nest, the scholar who has been patiently and protectively cross-referencing them for the last twenty-five years in the Ash factory. They find that when Ash was dying, a sealed letter within a letter arrived for Ellen from LaMotte. Sensing its contents, Ellen left the sealed letter unopened and placed it, along with other mementos, in a metal box, which she dropped into her dead husband's grave on top of his coffin. The desire to know the contents of that mysterious letter draws the mixed group of British and American scholars and other interested parties to an inn in rural Sussex, near the churchyard where Ash and his wife are buried.

Here Byatt self-consciously shifts genres, turning the intricate plot from quest/romance to race and chase. On a furiously stormy night Randolph and Ellen's grave is robbed by the wickedly possessed Cropper, with the help of one of Ash's collateral heirs, but before they can escape with the metal box, the rest of the group prevent their leaving. When the contents of the box are examined back at the inn, the question of what became of the child is

answered, and Maud finds herself the legitimate owner of all of the Ash and LaMotte correspondence, being descended from both poets.

In the end Roland and Maud return to where they began, the quest journey complete; both are changed and charged to begin anew. Roland, after researching the lives and works of Ash the Victorian poet, has discovered and begun to release the poet within himself. Maud has overcome her frigidity and fear of attachment and tells Roland that she loves him. Their romance continues, a story yet to be written. The nineteenth-century story's circle is completed with a postscript that reveals the poignant single meeting of Ash and his daughter, a young child who is unaware of his identity.

In a 24 February 1996 interview in the online magazine *Salon1999* Byatt says, "The nice thing about a novel is that everything can go into it, because if you've got the skill between sentence and sentence, you can change genre, you can change focus, you can change the way the reader reads. And yet you can keep up this sort of quiet momentum of narration. It's a wonderful form." In *Possession* Byatt demonstrates that, undeniably, she has the skill, generating a variety of texts by a range of fictitious writers; peopling the story with a Dickensian mob of major and minor characters; and packing the book with fairy tales, folklore, mythic symbols, countless cross-references and literary allusions, and recurring images of fairies, mermaids, peacocks, dragons, eggs, gloves, keys and keyholes, castles, knights, and more.

As well as having created a witty, literate, and exciting novel, Byatt, in *Possession,* also invites consideration of some serious intellectual matters: whether current theories of linguistic indeterminacy are as important as what language can do and say; how self-interest and devotion to theory may distort one's reading of literature; the primacy of the text; and the limitations of retrieving the truths of the past, except through narrative.

Possession won praise from critics and lay readers alike. Richard Jenkyns wrote in the 2 March 1990 *Times Literary Supplement,* "Intelligent, ingenious and humane [it] bids fair to be looked back upon as one of the most memorable novels of the 1990s." As a complex postmodern work of scholarship and artifice, the novel continues to attract scholarly examination and is the subject of many articles and graduate theses. In addition to the celebrity *Possession* brought to its author, in 1990 Byatt was included in the Queen's Honors List and was named a Commander of the Order of the British Empire (C.B.E.).

As she had in the past, Byatt followed her novel with a book of nonfiction, a collection titled *Passions of the Mind: Selected Writings* (1991). The essays, some of them previously published, are "an illuminating guide to writers she admires," according to Merle Rubin in *The New York Times Magazine* (26 May 1991). The collection covers an astonishing range, from George Eliot to Toni Morrison and the French feminist Monique Wittig. In addition to literature Byatt writes knowledgeably about Van Gogh, Sigmund Freud, and French literary theory. She says in the introduction, "Novelists sometimes claim that their fiction is a quite separate thing from their other work. . . . I have never felt such separation. . . . From my early childhood, reading and writing seemed to me to be points on a circle."

Critical responses to *Passions of the Mind* raised the old issue of Byatt's flaunting her considerable learning. Suzanne Berne said in *The New York Times Book Review* (22 March 1992) that the book "will delight the very literary and intimidate everyone else." Michele Roberts, in *The New Statesman and Society* (9 August 1991), contends, "Reading [the essays] evokes all the pleasures of lounging indefinitely in a well-stocked library at one end of which a large table groans with a delicious buffet supper." Still, after the virtuoso performance of *Possession,* Byatt's fans waited eagerly to see what fiction she would produce next.

Angels and Insects (1992) was hailed by the 16 October 1992 *Times Literary Supplement* as Byatt's "best work to date." But its lush Pre-Raphaelite descriptions and musings upon philosophical concerns did not please all the reviewers; Rubin wrote in *The Christian Science Monitor* (25 May 1993) that it is "an exquisitely executed, intelligent, and diverting diptych that lacks only the final touch of inspiration to transform it from reflective mirror into illuminating lamp."

The pair of tenuously linked fictions that comprise *Angels and Insects* have as their foundations the Victorians' anxiety in the face of scientific inquiry, which called religious faith into question, and the increasing materialism of the age. For Byatt the two novellas are a natural follow-up to *Possession.* The first story, "Morpho Eugenia," is reminiscent of Ash, his preoccupations, and his poetry, with its focus on natural history and Darwinism. And "The Conjugial Angel," the second story, echoes LaMotte's involvement with spiritualism.

"Morpho Eugenia," set in 1859, tells of a young naturalist, William Adamson, recently returned from ten years of studying insects in the Amazonian jungle. Shipwrecked on his return voyage to England, he has lost nearly all his belongings

Dust jacket for the U.S. edition of Byatt's interconnected novellas about entomology and spiritualism in the Victorian period

and is left homeless and without prospects. The Reverend Harald Alabaster, an ardent but indiscriminate collector of natural curiosities, invites William to reside at his home, Bredely Hall, and assist him in ordering his collection and in writing a book about Darwinism and Christianity.

William brings with him his few salvaged specimens, among them a rare butterfly, *Morpho eugenia.* The Alabaster family also has its Eugenia, the eldest of three equally pale and beautiful daughters, who captivates William. He writes in his diary, "I shall die if I cannot have her." Penniless, arising from the wrong social class, William nevertheless attempts to win Eugenia with a gift only he can provide; he arranges a cloud of butterflies for her in the conservatory. They flutter around her, tremble on her outstretched hands. Eugenia says, "They are so light, so soft, like coloured air. . . . You are a miracle-worker."

To his surprise and delight Eugenia agrees to marry him. Their wedding night signals readers, if they are not already aware, that something sinister lurks beneath the surface of the picture that the Alabaster family presents of mannered and mannerly landed gentry. William seems unable to recognize that anything is amiss as Eugenia presents him with child after child, all of whom are pale, blond replicas of the Alabasters.

Meanwhile, Lady Alabaster, herself the mother of a large number of children, suggests that William instruct the younger ones in natural history. With the able assistance of Matty Crompton, a poor dependent of the family, William sets up a study of an ant colony on the grounds of the estate. Matty encourages him to write a book about the ants, which she will illustrate. While observing and writing about the ants with Matty's help William recognizes the parallels between the insects' social organization and behavior and that of the Alabaster household, with its army of scurrying servants below stairs, and the whole class-rigid Victorian society. He comes to realize that his position in the hierarchy of Bredely Hall is analogous to that of the male ants, whose only function is to impregnate the queen of the colony. Increasingly William finds himself attracted to Matty; while playing a parlor game of anagrams he passes her the letters forming *insect,* and she returns them rearranged as *incest*—his first clue to Eugenia's dark secret. Soon after, William and Matty escape the insidious Alabasters and sail back to South America on a ship captained by a man named Arturo Papagay. In 1995 the novella "Morpho Eugenia" was adapted for the screen by British movie director Philip Haas, who retitled it *Angels & Insects.*

"The Conjugial Angel," the second story in *Angels and Insects,* embodies the Victorian fascination with spiritualism. In *Possession* LaMotte, although a professed Christian, defends her belief in séances, ectoplasmic manifestations of the dead, automatic writing, and the like. She writes in a letter to the debunking Ash: "We are grossly materialist—and nothing will satisfy us but material proofs—as we call them—of spiritual facts—and so the spirits have deigned to speak to us in these crude ways—of rapping—and rustling—and musical hummings—such as once were not needed—when our Faith was alight and alive in us–."

Such rationalization explains the situation in "The Conjugial Angel"; a group of sturdy upper-middle-class Victorians convene regularly, amid lace curtains and glass-fronted cases, potted palms and William Morris upholstery, for séances conducted by Lilias Papagay and her assistant, Sophy Sheekhy. Members of the circle hope to make contact with their dearly departed loved ones. For Lilias it is her husband, Captain Papagay, last seen at the end of "Morpho Eugenia," now lost at sea, presumed dead these last ten years. Mrs. Hearshaw, in perpetual deep mourning, pathetically seeks some sign from the five babies she has borne and buried. The spirit most eagerly sought, desired by Mrs. Jesse, is that of Arthur Hallam, friend of Tennyson and subject of his poem *In Memoriam* (1850). Emily Jesse, Tennyson's younger sister, had been engaged to marry Hallam at the time of his sudden death.

Emily meditates upon her brother's memorial verses and comes to the angry conclusion that they have stolen her grief, and yet the power and great popularity of Tennyson's poetry had raised expectations that she would remain forever the virgin widow, "the heroine of a tragic story." Even though she has now been married for thirty-three years to Captain Jesse, she is still emotionally bound to Hallam and works at séance after séance, with the aid of the two mediums, to call him up in order to be released from that bondage.

The story includes discussions of the philosophy of the eighteenth-century religious mystic Emanuel Swedenborg. It was his belief that for each person there exists a single soul mate, "one perfect other half, whom we should seek ceaselessly"; an angel, he said, will bring the two halves together in "conjugial love"– Swedenborg's spelling—hence, the title of the novella.

During one séance Sophy has a vision of such an angel. Lilias urges her to describe it more fully; Sophy says, "A lot of the colours don't have names." Later it is Sophy, the genuine psychic, to whom the shade of Hallam comes, a rotting corpse unable to die because those still living love him too much. In Sophy's arms Hallam is "unmade, undone." And by the end of the novella Lilias's "conjugial" other half, Captain Papagay, returns in the kind of joyously happy ending beloved by Victorian readers.

But despite its nineteenth-century setting *Angels and Insects* is not imitation Victorian literature. Byatt's is a postmodern sensibility, examining such matters as evolutionary theory and the loss of religious faith from a late-twentieth-century perspective. Neither are the two novellas the fictional pastiche that *Possession* is. Marilyn Butler suggested in *The Times Literary Supplement* (16 October 1992) that Byatt "has not stayed with fiction precisely, nor moved to faction, but developed a form (ficticism?) which has allowed her to be herself."

Michael Levenson, in *The New Republic* (2 August 1993), dubbed Byatt a "postmodern Victorian" and observed that "she is undeterred in the belief that the road into the twenty-first century winds exactly through the middle of the nineteenth." Modernism, with its rejection in the early twentieth century of so much that was seen as repressive and hopelessly outdated, threw out too many babies with the Victorian bathwater. In the process of making it new, as Ezra

Pound urged, too many vital discussions were closed off, some of which Byatt now chooses to re-open.

The Matisse Stories (1993) followed shortly after *Angels and Insects*. Byatt had told Stout, "I'd like to write the way Matisse paints." In this triptych of short stories she does just that. Each is based upon a work by Matisse, and each story is a carefully drawn picture of a woman in midlife beset with rage and despair. The narratives are built up of layer upon layer of significant detail, much as a painter works, and the colors used are bold and lively.

The first story, "Medusa's Ankles," concerns Susannah, a university professor, who is attracted to a beauty salon by a reproduction of Matisse's *Rosy Nude* (1935) hanging over the coat rack: "pure flat colour, but suggested mass. She had round breasts, contemplations of the circle, reflections on flesh and its fall." Susannah enters the shop to have her hair styled, to somehow revive her spirits and relieve her worries about her own body, aging, and experiencing its own fall.

The shop decor amplifies the Matisse: "like the interior of a rosy cloud, all pinks and creams." Lucian, the hairdresser-owner, admits to buying the nude not out of any appreciation for it as a work of art but because "it went with the colour-scheme I was planning." He advises a short and bouncy hairstyle for Susannah, and in the ensuing months, instead of being "the new healer," as a salon magazine had promised, Lucian inverts their relationship. He becomes the patient as he forces Susannah into the role of psychiatrist, confiding in her each week the details of his love life. He is in the midst of crisis, torn between loyalty to his wife and a passion for his young girlfriend. Over time his domestic situation becomes more tangled; his teenage daughter is distressed; and he lives sometimes with his family, sometimes with his lover. He confesses to Susannah that he is afraid to make the decision to break away or stay. She listens to his problems but remains largely detached. Then during one appointment Lucian tells her the salon will be closed for a month while he goes on holiday to Greece.

The next time Susannah comes to have her hair done the salon has been completely redecorated, all gray and maroon and high-tech steel and tinted glass that "made even bright days dull ones." Her face in the mirror looks gray and dull as well, and the Matisse is gone, replaced with "photographs of girls with grey faces, coal-black eyes and spiky lashes." Lucian tells her he has decided to divorce his wife; he says, "It's her own fault. She's let herself go altogether. She's let her ankles get fat."

As Susannah thinks about Lucian's wife, a woman not unlike herself, she's filled with rage and erupts into savage violence. She throws cosmetic jars, shatters mirrors, upsets bottles of hair dye, smashes cream into the tape deck playing heavy metal music. When she stops, her hands are bleeding, and the shop is "full of glittering fragments and sweet-smelling rivulets and puddles of venous-blue and fuchsia-red unguents, patches of crimson-streaked foam and odd intense spills of orange henna or cobalt and copper"—the full Matisse palette. At home Susannah's husband tells her, affectionately, that she looks twenty years younger, that she should have her hair done more often, an ending that is witty, ironic, and wickedly satisfying.

The second story, "Art World," delineates another sort of female revenge. The cast of characters includes Robin Dennison, a full-time painter; Debbie, his wife, who has given up her own art to be an editor of a woman's magazine in order to support the family; and Mrs. Brown, their middle-aged black cleaning woman. Robin has the entire top floor of the house as his studio, imposes strict rules about noise when he's working, and complains that Mrs. Brown moves things in tidying his studio so that he cannot find them, thus interfering with his creative process. He is particularly upset when he finds she has dropped into a blue bowl some odds and ends—paper clips, thumb tacks, a cuff link—recovered during her cleaning. The bowl, he insists, "as anyone can see, is a work of art," not "a kind of dustbin for things they were too lazy to put away or carry off. . . . " He complains to his wife, "Her habits are filthy."

This is a ritual exchange, and Debbie, caught in the middle, is required to soothe her husband and not offend Mrs. Brown, without whose help she would be unable to do her editorial work at home and keep an eye on the children. She suspects that Mrs. Brown does secretly interfere with Robin's things as one of her "modes of silent aggression." Another is the way she dresses, in outfits she creates herself from garishly colored, mismatched castoffs: "plush curtains, Arab blankets, parachute silk . . . fringes and braid and bizarre buttons" in magenta and vermillion, salmon pink and lime green, acid yellow and swimming-pool blue.

By contrast, Robin paints neorealist still lifes of what he calls "fetishes": china flowers, glass balls, feathers, "nothing alive." His paintings are of "small bright things in large expanses of grey and buff and beige." He often delivers unsolicited lectures to Mrs. Brown on color theory and rants about the inappropriateness of the color combinations that she chooses for her clothing and for the knitted garments she makes for the Dennison children.

Robin has yet to become successful. Because of a magazine article she has written Debbie is able to arrange for an art dealer, Shona McRury, to look at his paintings. McRury is unimpressed. Later the Dennisons receive an invitation to an exhibition by a new artist called Sheba Brown at McRury's gallery, where Mrs. Brown's "squashy sculptures" in rainbow colors are a triumph.

The stifling mentor (the ghost of Gardner), previously depicted in Byatt's *Shadow of a Sun* and *Possession,* is reincarnated in Robin. The third story features yet another manifestation. "The Chinese Lobster" follows Gerda Himmelblau, dean of women at a London college, through an uncomfortable lunch in a Chinese restaurant with visiting professor Perry Diss. A distinguished authority on Matisse, Diss also has a reputation as a womanizer, and Peggi Nollett, an art student whose graduate project he is supervising, has accused him of sexual harassment. Before she can do anything, Gerda must sort out what actually happened.

The student's letter of complaint is a greasestained jumble of misspelled words, frantic underlinings, and tiny drawings. It is a diatribe about Diss's response to her work—a feminist deconstruction of Matisse through the defacing of reproductions of his work—and contains accusations about Diss's personal comments about her body and the way she dresses: "He put his arm about me and hugged me and said I had too many clothes on. He said they were a depressing colour and he thought I ought to take them all off and let the air get to me."

Diss's response to her charges is to attack Peggi's work, or nonwork, her lack and intellectual or artistic ability, and to make it clear that he was defending his beloved Matisse from her debasement. Gerda knows that Peggi is emotionally distressed, probably suicidal, and the older woman begins to understand that whatever Diss may have said or done, it is the colorful, joyous, life-affirming Matisse that the student is feeling assaulted and exhausted by. Peggi is like the black lobster, dying, gasping for breath, that Gerda had noticed in the glass case on entering the restaurant.

When they leave after lunch, Gerda sees that the lobster is almost dead, and a sense of her own mortality overtakes her, replacing her earlier concerns about the student. Diss, in parting, tells Gerda, offhandedly, to take care of herself, and she replies, "Oh, . . . I will. I will."

Reviewers praised Byatt and *The Matisse Stories* for the most part; the short stories were called stunning, beautiful, painterly. The old charge of intellectual elitism surfaced, however—in *The Times Literary Supplement* (14 January 1994), Alex Clark wrote that "the emotional impact that Byatt has the power to make is lessened by an oppressive sense that the author is superior to the reader."

Byatt's production of short fiction continued. *The Djinn in the Nightingale's Eye: Five Fairy Stories* was published in Britain in 1994 (the American edition would not appear until 1997). Two of these fairy tales for adults, "The Glass Coffin" and "Gode's Story," were previously included in Byatt's *Possession;* they purported to be entertainments that LaMotte created for her niece, Maia Thomasina Bailey, who was actually LaMotte's natural daughter. In the novel the two fables functioned intertextually as variations upon the quest motif and as reflections of LaMotte's and Ash's letters and poetry. Removed from that context, the stories set the theme of the new collection: narrative as a way of knowing and as a means for women to rewrite their lives.

The three new fairy tales in the collection are "The Story of the Eldest Princess," "Dragon's Breath," and "The Djinn in the Nightingale's Eye." All are concerned with the quest, the archetypal structure of folk and fantasy narratives. In "The Story of the Eldest Princess," a crisis threatens the kingdom: the sky is changing from blue to green, and the king's oldest daughter must go forth and bring back the silver bird from the garden of the Old Man of the Mountain, which is guarded by poisonous thorns and fiery snakes. The princess, a reader of stories, recognizes that it is the third seeker who always prevails in traditional trials of this kind. She says to herself, "I am in a pattern I know, and I suspect I have no power to break it, and I am going to meet a test and fail it, and spend seven years as a stone." But with that knowledge she is able to break the pattern; she refuses to sacrifice herself unnecessarily and, thus, survives. In the other stories spunky tailors, swineherds, and the like find themselves in classically strange situations and deal with them in ways that the Brothers Grimm would never have considered.

The title story, "The Djinn in the Nightingale's Eye," although it begins with the old-fashioned "Once upon a time," brings the genre up to date. The heroine, Gillian Perholt, a middle-aged English academic and a scholar of storytelling, attends a narratology conference in Ankara, Turkey. Its subject is "Stories of Women's Lives," and Gillian delivers a paper on Griselda, the fabled long-suffering wife. In true postmodern fashion, stories nest inside stories like Russian dolls. The central incident of her stay in the Middle East is Gillian's purchase of a bottle made of a swirled blue-and-white glass called the nightingale's eye. Back at her hotel she removes the bottle's stopper and falls into something like *A Thousand and One Nights.* A genie who has been trapped in the bottle since 1850 emerges and offers her the customary three wishes.

Dust jacket for Byatt's novel about a divorce case and an obscenity trial, the third part of her
projected tetralogy chronicling life in England during the 1950s and 1960s

Wise and well-read, Gillian considers her choices carefully. She wishes "for my body to be as it was when I last really liked it." Her wish is granted even though the djinn prefers her just the way she is. After the djinn tells the stories of his previous incarnations, recounting other women's wishes, Gillian responds with her own life story. Then she makes her second wish; she tells the djinn, "I wish you would love me." And their love-making is elaborate, shape shifting, and mythical in its extravagance.

In great demand as a speaker, Gillian flies to conferences around the world, always taking the djinn in his bottle with her in her carry-on luggage. Finally Gillian is ready to make her final wish. She tells the djinn: "I wish you could have whatever you wish for–that this last wish may be your wish." This reversal confounds the djinn. He does not want to go. When he leaves, as he must, he leaves with the hope that he will return during Gillian's lifetime, the narrative left open-ended for more possible tale telling in the future.

Once more Byatt followed a work of fiction with a nonfiction book; next, she wrote *Imagining Characters: Six Conversations about Women Writers* (1995) in collaboration with Ignes Sôdré, a Brazilian psychologist practicing in London. This collection of dialogue essays examines their individual readings of books that the two women admire: Jane Austen's *Mansfield Park* (1814), Charlotte Brontë's *Vil-*lette (1853), Eliot's *Daniel Deronda* (1876), Willa Cather's *The Professor's House* (1925), Murdoch's *An Unofficial Rose* (1962), and Toni Morrison's *Beloved* (1987). Sôdré makes the point that "the human mind needs 'fictions' . . . to create narratives which represent aspects of the internal world in symbol form." Dreams and stories meet that need. Not surprisingly given the nature of Byatt's recent fiction, she and Sôdré discuss the fantasy, fairy-tale, and mythic elements in the six novels. Lorna Sage noted in *The Times Literary Supplement* (26 January 1996) that "It's a level of interpretation that enables them to claim kin and continuity with the nineteenth century." Byatt and Sôdré also talk about the characters in the novels as if they were real people, which for devoted readers they are. And according to Sage, "they do it marvellously. . . . It's great fun, all this perceptive talk about unreal people."

Babel Tower (1996) takes up Frederica's story in the 1960s, but Byatt does not return to the linear third-person narrative employed in *The Virgin in the Garden* and *Still Life,* the first two novels in the planned quartet. After the pitch-perfect ventriloquism of *Possession* she chose a similar form, a self-consciously postmodern assemblage of texts. The novel opens with an embodiment of one of its themes, the power and inadequacy of language: "It might begin . . . or it might begin. . . ." The rest of the book is a cacophony of stories making themselves heard.

The central metaphor of *Babel Tower* is the Old Testament structure built by Noah's descendants in an attempt to reach heaven; God punished their hubris by causing them to speak different languages so that confusion halted their enterprise. Among the voices raised above the din of the 1960s is Frederica's. She has married a classmate from Cambridge, Nigel Reiver, a violent, brutish member of the anti-intellectual gentry who has kept her a virtual prisoner in his country home. For Frederica the sexual attraction is incredibly strong, but when, in a jealous rage, Nigel threatens her with an axe, she escapes with their four-year-old son, Leo. In London she shares a house with another single mother. Included in the novel is a charming, J. R. R. Tolkien–like fantasy that Frederica's housemate writes for her daughter and Leo; one of the many stories within the story, it demonstrates again Byatt's interest in folk and fairy tales as narratives necessary to understanding the world.

The trial transcripts and other legal documents concerning Frederica's divorce from Nigel and her petition for custody of Leo are also included in the novel. Frederica deals with the stress and shame of the battle for her freedom and for her son by cutting up letters from her husband's lawyer and rearranging them into collages, which defuses their power under her control of the fragments. Her notebooks also include quotations from the trendy gurus of the 1960s: Norman O. Brown, R. D. Laing, Timothy Leary, and Allen Ginsberg. Surrounding her characters, inescapably influencing their lives and their thinking, Byatt re-creates that period when the medium was the McLuhan message, the Beatles were more popular then Jesus, and London was the swinging, patchouli- and pot-scented place to be.

Daniel, clergyman husband of Frederica's late sister Stephanie, has come down from Yorkshire and is staffing a London suicide hotline. There he deals with an ascetic poet named Jude Mason. Like a slightly deranged biblical prophet, Mason has written a cautionary novel, *Babble Tower: A Tale for the Children of Our Time,* which reflects and condemns the radical social changes and the unfettered behavior of the young. This novel within the larger novel depicts a group of survivors of the French Revolution who close themselves off in a distant tower and form an ideal society where no restrictions are placed upon its members. If the Old Testament tower is at the core of Mason's (and Byatt's) novel, so is the Marquis de Sade's *The 120 Days of Sodom* (1784). Liberty turns to license, and the utopian dream become a dystopian nightmare.

Frederica, in order to support herself and her son, teaches literature to reluctant art students and is a part-time publisher's reader; she recommends Mason's novel to her employer. Subsequently its publication results in an obscenity trial, the details and documents of which Byatt also fabricated for *Babel Tower.* The novel's many texts, layered and overlapping, are as multivocal as the builders of the biblical tower were. In addition, Frederica and her intellectual circle of friends talk and talk about the serious issues of the day–the death of God, sexual freedom, genetic research, educational reform, libertarianism, women's roles, nuclear power, the egotism and cruelty of the young, and more.

The ending of *Babel Tower* finds the *Babble Tower* obscenity case won on appeal by the defense and Frederica freed from a bad marriage and having gained custody of her son. Her story, however, is not yet ended. Byatt has already let slip the title of the fourth novel in the quartet, "A Whistling Woman." What will become of Frederica by the close of the decade is yet to be seen, but, as in the earlier novels of the Potter family, Byatt will, without doubt, continue to explore the pain and intensity of love and the struggle to balance connection and independence. Readers may also expect Byatt to deal with her ongoing philological and philosophical concerns about the power of language to convey and distort truth and literature's relationship to the lived life.

Critical response to *Babel Tower* was mixed; many readers were daunted by the complexity of the novel. J. M Coetzee, in *The New York Review of Books* (6 June 1996), lists its failings: "a multiplication of data, a failure to push narrative situations to their limits . . . many of its situations . . . are contrived as occasions for the discussion of ideas." In a 5 May 1996 review in *The Sunday Times* (London), however, Lucy Hughes-Hallett wrote, "*Babel Tower* is tartly funny, emotionally engrossing and headily intelligent."

Once more Byatt was both praised and criticized for her intellectual scope, her intelligence, and her willingness to deal with difficult ideas. In Byatt's prizewinning novel *Possession* the fictional professor Blackadder says that Ash "wanted to understand how individual people at any particular time saw the shape of their lives–from their beliefs to their pots and pans. . . . He thought carefully and didn't make up his mind in a hurry. He believed knowledge mattered." The same must be said for A. S. Byatt.

Interviews:

Mira Stout, "What Possessed A. S. Byatt?," *New York Times Magazine,* 26 May 1991, pp. 13–15, 24–25;

"Ant Heaps and Novelists," *Salon1999* [online magazine], 8 (24 February 1996);

John F. Baker, "A. S. Byatt: Passions of the Mind," *Publishers Weekly* (20 May 1996): 235–236.

References:

Ann Ashworth, "Fairy Tales in A. S. Byatt's *Possession,*" *Journal of Evolutionary Psychology,* 15 (March 1994): 93–94;

Malcolm Bradbury, "On from Murdoch," *Encounter* (July 1968): 72–74;

Jackie Buxton, "'What Is Love Got to Do with It?': Postmodernism and *Possession,*" *English Studies in Canada,* 22 (June 1996): 199–219;

Jane Campbell, "The Hunger of the Imagination in A. S. Byatt's *The Game,*" *Critique: Studies in Modern Fiction,* 29 (Spring 1988): 147–162;

Campbell, "'The Somehow May Be Thishow': Fact, Fiction, and Intertextuality in Antonia Byatt's 'Precipice-Encurled,'" *Studies in Short Fiction,* 28 (Spring 1991): 115–123;

Catherine Civello, "George Eliot: From *Middlemarch* to Manhattan," *George Eliot Fellowship Review,* 20 (1989): 52–56;

Charlotte Clutterbuck, "A Shared Depository of Wisdom: Connection and Redemption in *Tiger in the Pit* and *Possession,*" *Southerly: A Review of Australian Literature,* 53 (June 1993);

Tess Cosslett, "Childbirth from the Woman's Point of View in British Women's Fiction: Enid Bagnold's *The Squire* and A. S. Byatt's *Still Life,*" *Tulsa Studies in Women's Literature,* 8 (Fall 1989): 263–286;

Joanne V. Creighton, "Sisterly Symbiosis: Margaret Drabble's *The Waterfall* and A. S. Byatt's *The Game,*" *Mosaic,* 20 (Winter 1987): 15–29;

Juliet Dusinberre, "Forms of Reality in A. S. Byatt's *The Virgin in the Garden,*" *Critique: Studies in Modern Fiction,* 24 (Fall 1982): 55–62;

J. Stephen Fountain, "Ashes to Ashes: Kristeva's Jouissance, Altizer's Apocalypse, Byatt's *Possession* and the 'Dream of the Rood,'" *Literature & Theology: An International Journal of Theory, Criticism and Culture,* 8 (June 1994): 193–208;

Guiliana Giobbi, "Know the Past, Know Thyself: Literary Pursuits and Quests for Identity in A. S. Byatt's *Possession* and in Francesca Duranti's *Effetti Personali,*" *Journal of European Studies,* 24 (March 1994): 41–54;

Julian Gitzen, "A. S. Byatt's Self-Mirroring Art," *Critique: Studies in Contemporary Fiction,* 36 (Winter 1995): 83–95;

Frederick M. Holmes, "The Historical Imagination and the Victorian Past: A. S. Byatt's *Possession,*" *English Studies in Canada,* 20 (September 1994): 319–334;

Ann Hulbert, "The Great Ventriloquist: A. S. Byatt's *Possession: A Romance,*" in *Contemporary British Women Writers,* edited by Robert E. Hosmer Jr. (New York: St. Martin's Press, 1993), pp. 55–65;

Del Ivan Janik, "No End of History: Evidence from the Contemporary English Novel," *Twentieth Century Literature,* 41 (Summer 1995): 160–189;

Kathleen Coyne Kelly, *A. S. Byatt* (New York: Twayne, 1996);

Olga Kenyon, "A. S. Byatt," in her *Women Novelists Today: A Survey of English Writing in the Seventies and Eighties* (New York: St. Martin's Press, 1988), pp. 51–84;

Michael Levenson, "The Religion of Fiction," *New Republic,* 209 (2 August 1993): 41–44;

Peter Lewis, "The Truth and Nothing Like the Truth: History and Fiction," *Strand Magazine,* 27 (Spring 1986): 38–44;

Roger Lewis, "Larger Than Life," *New Statesman,* 109 (28 June 1985): 29;

Mark F. Lund, "Lindsay Clarke and A. S. Byatt: The Novel on the Threshold of Romance," *Deus Loci: Lawrence Durrell Journal,* 2 (1993): 151–159;

Daphne Merkin, "The Art of Lying," *New Leader* (23 April 1979): 16;

Victoria Sanchez, "A. S. Byatt's *Possession:* A Fairytale Romance," *Southern Folklore,* 52 (Spring 1995): 33–52;

Thelma J. Shinn, "'What's in a Word?': Possessing A. S. Byatt's Meronymic Novel," *Papers in Language and Literature: A Journal for Scholars and Critics of Language,* 31 (Spring 1995): 164–183;

Richard Todd, *A. S. Byatt* (Plymouth: Northcote House, in association with the British Council, 1997);

Todd, "The Retrieval of the Unheard Voices in British Postmodernist Fiction: A. S. Byatt and Marina Warner," in his *Liminal Postmodernisms: The Postmodern, the (Post-) Colonial, and the (Post-) Feminist* (Amsterdam: Rodopi, 1994), pp. 99–114;

Caroline Webb, "History through Metaphor: Woolf's *Orlando* and Byatt's *Possession: A Romance,*" in *Virginia Woolf: Emerging Perspectives,* edited by Mark Hussey and Vera Nerverov (New York: Pace University Press, 1994), pp. 182–188;

Louise Yelin, "Cultural Cartography: A. S. Byatt's *Possession* and the Politics of Victorian Studies," *Victorian Newsletter,* 81 (Spring 1992): 38–41.

Bruce Chatwin
(13 May 1940 – 18 January 1989)

John J. Su
University of Michigan

BOOKS: *Animal Style Art from East to West,* by Chatwin, Emma C. Bunker, and Ann R. Farkas (New York: Asia Society, 1970);

In Patagonia (London: Cape, 1977; New York: Summit, 1979);

The Viceroy of Ouidah (London: Cape, 1980; New York: Summit, 1981);

On the Black Hill (London: Cape, 1982; New York: Viking, 1983);

Patagonia Revisited, by Chatwin and Paul Theroux, illustrated by Kyffin Williams (Salisbury: Michael Russell, 1985; Boston: Houghton Mifflin, 1986); republished as *Nowhere Is a Place: Travels in Patagonia,* with new foreword and photographs by Jeff Gnass (San Francisco: Sierra Club, 1991);

The Songlines (London: Cape, 1987; New York: Viking, 1987);

Utz (London: Cape, 1988; New York: Viking, 1989);

What Am I Doing Here (London: Cape, 1989; New York: Viking, 1989);

Bruce Chatwin: Photographs and Notebooks, edited by David King and Francis Wyndham, introduction by Wyndham (London: Cape, 1993); republished as *Far Journeys: Photographs and Notebooks* (New York: Viking, 1993);

The Attractions of France (London: Cape, 1993);

Anatomy of Restlessness: Selected Writings, 1969–1989, edited by Jan Borm and Matthew Graves (London: Cape, 1996; New York: Viking, 1996).

OTHER: Osip Mandelstam, *Journey to Armenia,* translated by Clarence Brown, introduction by Chatwin (London: New Editions, 1980);

Howard Hodgkin, *Indian Leaves,* introduction by Chatwin (New York: Petersburg, 1982);

Robert Mapplethorpe, *Lady, Lisa Lyon,* text by Chatwin (London: Blond & Brigg, 1983);

Werner Herzog, *Cobra Verde: Filmbuch,* includes diary by Chatwin (Schaffhausen: Edition Stemmle, 1987);

Bruce Chatwin (photograph by Paul Kasmin)

Sybille Bedford, *A Visit to Don Otavio,* introduction by Chatwin (London: Folio Society, 1990).

"I have a compulsion to wander and a compulsion to return—a homing instinct like a migrating bird," Bruce Chatwin wrote in a letter to Tom Maschler. "True nomads have no fixed home as such; they *compensate* for this by following unalterable paths of migration. If these are upset it is usually by interference from the civilised or semi-civilised half-nomads. The result is chaos." Chatwin considered this conflict between settling and wandering "instincts" to be the central struggle of human existence, epitomized in the story of Cain and Abel. The profound restlessness in his own life and work suggests the enduring attraction of both instincts. By turns novelist, journalist, tourist, art dealer, and archaeologist, Chatwin traveled the globe over the course of his short lifetime. Known as a travel writer of the exotic and remote, Chatwin nonetheless was concerned deeply with preserving connections to home and past traditions. His novels depict expatriates in Patagonia and Dahomey and the nomads of Africa and Australia; they also portray rural Welsh and Eastern Europeans who refuse to wander and who reject the flux of modern life. Even the novel that most clearly espouses Chatwin's "nomadic alternative" to sedentary civilization, *The Songlines* (1987), demands the preservation of sacred aboriginal landmarks, places to which individuals must return periodically and reconnect with their past.

Born 13 May 1940 in Sheffield, Bruce Charles Chatwin spent his earliest years on the move. He and his mother, Margharita, shuttled about England, staying with friends and relatives during World War II. Charles Leslie Chatwin, his father, was away during this period, serving aboard a Royal Navy minesweeper in Cardiff harbor. Chatwin described home during his earliest years as "a serviceman's canteen or a station platform piled with kit bags." The love of wandering for which Chatwin would become famous began at this time, when along with his maternal grandfather, Sam Turnell, he took long walks over the moors of Derbyshire. By his own account Chatwin became infected with Charles Baudelaire's "la grande maladie: horreur du domicile" (the great sickness: dread of staying home) at the end of the war, shortly after the family eventually settled in Birmingham. Horreur du domicile proved to be a condition from which he would never recover.

Like many of his postwar contemporaries, Chatwin could discover and articulate a vision of Englishness only outside of England: "I find I can be English and behave like an Englishman only if I'm not here," he told Michael Ignatieff in an interview. The economic and social upheaval produced by the eclipse of the British Empire marked Chatwin as he grew up. Throughout his career his writing would reflect these anxieties of impending loss. Early in his *In Patagonia* (1977) Chatwin relates how fears of nuclear holocaust inspired him and his fellow schoolmates to travel: "We started an Emigration Committee and made plans to settle in some far corner of the earth. We pored over atlases, and we fixed on Patagonia as the safest place on earth." In a later essay reflecting on his lifelong desire to travel to Patagonia, Chatwin describes a recurring childhood nightmare of nuclear war. Patagonia represented a place outside the horrors of civilization and nuclear war. Only in such lands could Chatwin find respite from the omnipresent reminders of a decaying West.

Chatwin's fascination with nomadic peoples—the first book he attempted to write was titled "The Nomadic Alternative"—needs to be understood in light of his fears that sedentary civilization inevitably decays and yields to violence. What initially attracted Chatwin to nomads was their "irreverent and timeless vitality": to a twenty-six-year-old traveling through Africa to recover from job-related eye problems, the nomadic alternative did not simply represent another way of life but the only possibility for future existence. During his travels through the Sahara, Chatwin speculated as to why nomads possess the capacity to continue "while the empires come crashing down." He concluded that settled societies lack constructive outlets for channeling human restlessness. Without a satisfactory release mechanism, this pent-up energy periodically explodes into violence. Nomadic peoples disperse their restless energy through wandering along the migratory pathways of their ancestors.

Although he enjoyed a typical middle-class upbringing after his father resumed his law career, Chatwin decided not to attend university after finishing at Marlborough College, his boarding school. Rather than pursuing the traditional family profession of architecture, Chatwin moved to London in 1959 and became a porter at the art auction house of Sotheby and Company of Bond Street. Shortly thereafter he began a meteoric climb within the firm, becoming the head of the Impressionist Department at the age of twenty-five and one of Sotheby's youngest partners ever. It was there that Chatwin met his future wife, Elizabeth Chanler, secretary of Peter Wilson, Sotheby's chairman.

His years at Sotheby's were not happy ones, however, instilling in Chatwin a fascination with and aversion to art collections and museums. In an interview with Colin Thubron, Chatwin described museums as morgues, saying that Sotheby's was a "rather superior funeral parlour." The beginning of the end of his career at Sotheby's came when he perceived something sinister about the act of collecting: "I began to feel that works of art were literally going to kill me, there and then." Although art did not in fact kill him, it did blind Chatwin. While staying with friends in Ireland, Chatwin woke one morning completely blind. He regained sight in one eye later that day but his eye specialist warned him against examining artwork too closely. According to an apocryphal story possibly spread by Chatwin, his doctor prescribed travel in Africa rather than glasses. The truth of the story is less important than how it encapsulates Chatwin's vision of the good

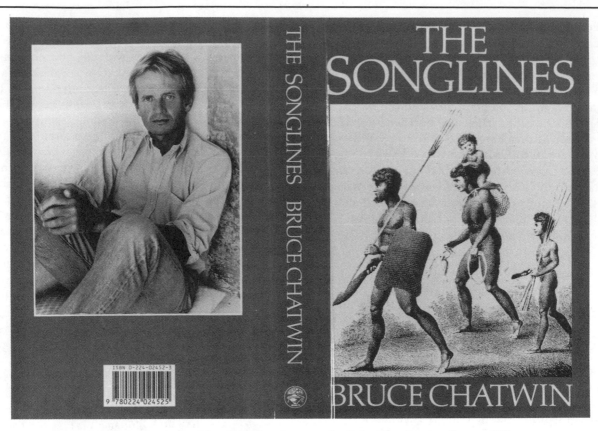

Dust jacket for the novel in which Chatwin argues for the benefits of a nomadic way of life

life: roaming across the wide landscapes and living the ascetic life are conceived of as remedies for disorders attributed to sedentary, civilized life.

Nonetheless, Sotheby's and the world of art collecting would have a lasting influence on Chatwin. The collector and his or her artifacts figure prominently throughout his works. *In Patagonia* opens with a description of a piece of skin (which Chatwin's grandmother believes to be a piece of a brontosaurus) that Chatwin's grandmother's cousin Charley Milward had brought back from Patagonia. The twins Lewis and Benjamin Jones, in *On the Black Hill* (1982), become fervent antique collectors in reaction to postwar modernization. Francisco Manoel da Silva becomes, in *The Viceroy of Ouidah* (1980), the most loathsome form of collector and dealer, a trader of human slaves. Utz's obsession with Meissen porcelain, in the eponymous novel, prevents him from fleeing Communist Czechoslovakia: the government will not allow him to emigrate with his collection, and he cannot bear to be parted from it.

While Chatwin asserts that art museums are immoral and approves of a New York art critic's suggestion that people who are attracted to art are psychopathic, he nonetheless acknowledges a genuine human need to acquire and possess at least a minimal number of objects. For instance, Chatwin's

engagement ring was a late-fifth-century Greek electrum ring acquired from the grand chamberlain of the king of Albania. Objects are valuable because they contain stories commemorating moments of the past. But because they are never adequate to what they purport to represent, possessions ultimately instill restlessness.

The problem of possession, then, is to satisfy both the longing for freedom and the need for a point of orientation or home. In "The Morality of Things" Chatwin offers his role model: a traveling salesman in Africa who lives out of a suitcase, having neither relatives nor friends. The only other possessions the man owns are kept in a solicitor's black tin deed box in the London office safe. Four times a year he returns to London and for half an hour examines the contents of the box: a teddy bear, a photograph of his father, a swimming trophy, and several other items of English middle-class life. What Chatwin admires most about the man is that he would bring one new thing from Africa each time and also throw out one thing from the box. In this way the man preserved the delicate balance between freedom and possession.

During his own travels in Africa, Chatwin thought that he had found an alternative to the Western collector: the ascetic nomads of the Sahara.

Like his traveling salesmen, the nomads possessed a hardy vitality and the ability to travel lightly. Chatwin sincerely believed that the restlessness of humankind arose from the suppression of instinctive migratory habits. Nomads were less violent and hardier than settlers because they were more attuned to the biorhythms of our species. The nomad refuses the settled existence altogether, following instinctive migratory pathways.

Africa forever altered Chatwin's sense of priorities: shortly after his return to England in 1966 he quit Sotheby's and began studying archaeology at Edinburgh University. During this period Chatwin started work on his never-to-be-finished book, "The Nomadic Alternative." The university experience proved unsatisfying to Chatwin. His theories of human migratory instincts met resistance and dismissal by the archaeology faculty at Edinburgh. More and more Chatwin found himself driven abroad during term breaks, traveling across Africa, Asia, and the Soviet Union. In many respects Chatwin found that archaeology resembled too closely the art scene he had left at Sotheby's. Chatwin became engrossed with the stories that must have escaped the archaeological record, the stories that objects did not preserve. Archaeology focused too exclusively upon artifacts of settled societies, on monumental histories, and not personal stories.

By his own admission "penniless, depressed, and a total failure at the age of 33," Chatwin might never have started his writing career if Francis Wyndham, then editor of *The Sunday Times* (London), had not offered him a job as a freelance writer. The resulting pieces, some of which are collected in *What Am I Doing Here* (1989) and *Anatomy of Restlessness: Selected Writings, 1969–1989* (1996), are a fascinating set of cameos ranging from Indira Gandhi to André Malraux and Nadezhda Mandelstam (the widow of the poet Osip Mandelstam). In these pieces Chatwin developed his Hemingway-like style ("concise and often epigrammatic," as Nicholas Murray puts it) and his facility for storytelling. Chatwin remained with *The Sunday Times* for two years, until Hunter Davies became the magazine section's new editor. Shortly thereafter, according to Chatwin, he simply sent the editors a telegram declaring: GONE TO PATAGONIA FOR SIX MONTHS.

The fruit of his South American travel, *In Patagonia,* is one of the most intriguing pieces of English travel literature. Broken up into ninety-seven short sections, *In Patagonia* ostensibly centers on Chatwin's journey to the cave where Charley Milward found the "brontosaurus" skin. However, the work avoids the common trap of travel literature, that of focusing exclusively upon the tourist's experience of a place. Instead Chatwin seeks to unearth the uncollected stories of Patagonia. He becomes an archaeologist of the personal, seeking stories from the inhabitants of famous figures such as Butch Cassidy (who is said to have gone into semiretirement there) and local heroes such as the revolutionary Antonio Soto. *In Patagonia* certainly has descriptions of the land itself, but the central focus is on the recovery of stories. The connection between land and story is made explicit when Chatwin describes his experience of listening to a local storyteller: "For the next two hours he was my Patagonia." The themes of exile, wandering, and collecting that pervade Chatwin's works are all found in germinal stage here. In the opening pages Chatwin characterizes the history of Buenos Aires as "a story of exile, disillusion and anxiety behind lace curtains." Expatriates from all over the world came to Patagonia, fiercely proud and protective of their ethnic identities. As Chatwin records their stories, he increasingly discovers the value of retelling experiences of separation and exile: stories of loss provide a means of recovering and preserving cultural traditions. Perhaps the most compelling tale of cultural preservation, however, concerns the story of Thomas Bridge's "Yaghan Dictionary," an unfinished attempt to record the language of a "primitive" people. The dictionary becomes a monument to the Yaghans, whose culture subsequently has been suppressed. Native Americans who might never otherwise have learned the language of their ancestors could do so with the aid of Bridge's work. Furthermore, the dictionary presents a people of philosophical sophistication equal to that of Western Europeans and from which Western thought could learn much.

Although *In Patagonia* received high acclaim upon publication, winning the Hawthornden Prize and the E. M. Forster Award of the American Academy of Arts and Letters, and continues to be popular, it and Chatwin's subsequent work have been criticized in recent years for appropriating non-Western European cultures. To characterize nomadic peoples as concerned with spiritual over physical issues and even the very characterization of a people as "nomadic" may be construed as allowing Western European powers a cultural justification for imperialism. This vision conceives of non-Westerners as having moved "beyond" material concerns, thereby leaving the West free to exploit material resources. Further, the act of elegizing a "fading" culture potentially creates a narrative of progress in which Western European forms of modernization appear as inevitable and appropriate.

Assessing Chatwin's culpability is by no means an easy task. Chatwin retains his defenders.

David C. Estes, for instance, argues that *In Patagonia* does not elegize the passing of Native Americans but satirizes the concept of the Western European explorer as hero in the figure of Charley Milward. Chatwin applies this same satire to himself by framing his entire journey as the attempt to rediscover the location of a skin that was not from a brontosaurus but probably a sloth. He at least appears never to have intentionally appropriated other cultures for the purposes of demeaning them. If he places foreign peoples within a Western conceptual framework, Chatwin nonetheless attempts to understand their visions of the world.

Chatwin found the material for *The Viceroy of Ouidah,* during his second trip to the West African nation of Dahomey in 1978 (he had first traveled there in 1971). Transformed by a Marxist coup since his previous visit and renamed the People's Republic of Benin, the country displayed all the political chaos and random violence that Chatwin associated with settled societies. During his stay Chatwin was mistaken for a foreign mercenary, brought before a mock firing squad, and jailed briefly (a fictionalized version of his experiences appears in his 1984 piece "A Coup–A Story"). This same senseless violence is apparent in *The Viceroy of Ouidah*. In Ouidah, the former slave port of Dahomey, a recently installed and still unstable Marxist government casts a looming if farcical shadow over the present-time scenes. Chatwin is at pains to point out that the violence brought by Marxism only perpetuates an historical cycle: in his prefatory note Chatwin states that in the nineteenth century "the Kingdom of Dahomey was a Black Sparta, and their only source of income was the sale of their weaker neighbors." The success and affluence of the kingdom were dependent upon military domination and ruthlessness. The present internal discord and civil strife are inevitable outcomes of Benin's inability to continue to project its violent impulses onto neighboring states.

The Viceroy of Ouidah opens with a description of the descendants of Francisco Manoel da Silva celebrating a requiem mass on the 117th anniversary of his death. Da Silva, or Dom Francisco to his descendants, became the viceroy of Ouidah and enjoyed a monopoly on the slave trade in Dahomey in exchange for supplying the king with the firearms necessary to maintain regional military superiority. Dom Francisco has become a legend for his descendants, with a shrine erected to him in what was his bedroom. As befits a legend, tales of his life, death, and possible hidden fortune circulate wildly among the "mourners." The next four sections of the book represent a Chatwinian archaeology of Dom Fran-

cisco; again Chatwin concerns himself with the stories that history never relates yet which drive the events that history records. Throughout his early life in Brazil the young man who would become the viceroy of Ouidah devotes himself to wandering, finding happiness only in departing: "Believing any set of four walls to be a tomb or a trap, he preferred to float over the most barren of open spaces." Abandoning his wife shortly after the birth of their child, Dom Francisco volunteers to travel to Ouidah and resuscitate the slave trade, which had fallen off because of the "madness" of the king of Dahomey. Dom Francisco's life in Ouidah transforms the footloose wanderer into a patriot longing for recognition from home even as he finds himself slipping "into the habits of the natives." Recognition can never be given, however, because the slave trade has been made illegal, first by Britain and later by Brazil itself. His frustrated longing to return instills in him an obsession with the passage of time. Dom Francisco takes up collecting watches: he sets each at a different hour in hopes of mastering time. Instead the timepieces become reminders that time is running out and that he is forever separated from the world that made these devices. Ultimately falling out of favor with the new king, Dom Francisco dies alone and unloved, accompanied only by his collection. The final section of the book consists of a daughter's horrified memories of Dom Francisco's burial ("it was not to be a Christian funeral," the narrator remarks) juxtaposed with the present-time radio broadcast of the president spewing propaganda. The juxtaposition serves to link the senseless violence of the two events: Chatwin refuses to moralize overtly on the connection but implicitly suggests that the senseless violence upon which civilization builds itself is not just part of a distant past but remains ever present. Werner Herzog's 1987 motion picture, *Cobra Verde,* is based loosely on *The Viceroy of Ouidah.*

Chatwin's third book, *On the Black Hill,* represents a radical departure from his earlier work, focusing on the twins Lewis and Benjamin Jones and their lives in rural Wales. If his first two books concern the "compulsion to wander," then his third addresses the compulsion to return. Although he never lived there himself, Chatwin said in a television interview that he considered the Welsh Black Mountains to be a personal "home base." The novel centers on the struggle of the Jones family to hold onto a home: to purchase their own farm despite a vengeful neighbor, to maintain it, and finally to find an heir to pass it on to. Perhaps what is so remarkable about the novel is that its characters ask nothing more than to live quotidian lives in extraordinary times, across two world wars, the Cold War, and economic depression. Chatwin refuses to depict pioneers, heroes, and romantic adventurers, focusing instead upon mundane lives and everyday trials.

On the Black Hill shares with Chatwin's earlier work a concern for the destructive aspects of technological modernization. Modernization encroaches upon and threatens to transform the traditional modes of life for the Welsh farmers. On the night after the bombing of Nagasaki, the twins have an identical nightmare: "their bed-curtains had caught fire, their hair was on fire, and their heads burned down to smoldering stumps," imagery almost identical to that Chatwin had used to describe his own recurring nightmare after the bombing. Ultimately the technology of war not only inhabits the imagination of the Welsh farmers but also physically enters into their world. Late in their lives the twins witness jet fighters flying overhead during military exercises. A fear of technology prevents the twins from even purchasing a tractor for their farm until after World War II. Their fears are not wholly misplaced, however; in the penultimate section of the novel Lewis dies when his tractor overturns.

Their fear of the future is only exacerbated by the fact that neither twin marries, and after their decades of toil they have no children to inherit the farm. The knowledge that their memories may not be preserved by an heir inspires in the twins an impulse to collect. They become avid collectors as they age. Their collections of antiques represent an attempt to suppress the flow of time, to hold onto the lost past, especially to the memory of their mother: "Nothing—not even a teacup—was replaced; and the house began to look like a museum." What were once daily objects become artifacts in a world of modern appliances and headset radios. Lewis and Benjamin, in an attempt to stave off death, turn their home into a museum, preserving everything as it was at the moment their mother died.

Chatwin presents an ambivalent attitude toward modernization and change. The fulfillment of Lewis's lifelong dream of flying shortly before his death seems to offer a sort of reconciliation between the human and the technological, though technology, in the form of the tractor, kills him only a few pages later. Nonetheless, "for ten magnificent minutes, he had done what he wanted to do," seemingly compensating for years of hopes and expectations that the rural life never satisfied. And although technology represents the most insidious agent of change, the culture imported from England and its colonies also represents a challenge to the traditional Welsh way of life. The twins' mother, Mary, herself introduces elements from the outside world,

Dust jacket for the last novel Chatwin completed before his death in 1989

coming from a middle-class and cosmopolitan background before marrying Amos Jones. The latter's parochialism becomes obvious when he smashes the dishes after Mary serves a mild Indian curry: "I want none of your filthy Indian food." Certainly the threat of intellectual and cultural suffocation amid such intolerance is present throughout the book. But Chatwin also depicts the grim potential for the complete dissolution of Welsh culture by outside influences. When military officers come to recruit for the war effort, their appeal is based upon the duties citizens owe to England. A question about the duties owed to Wales is studiously ignored and silenced.

It is perhaps his genuine concern for the Welsh people that has made *On the Black Hill* a cult classic in Wales. The novel was also a critical success, receiving the 1982 Whitbread Literary Award for best first novel (apparently *The Viceroy of Ouidah* was not considered a novel) and the James Tait Black Prize. Scholars consider *On the Black Hill* a regional novel in the tradition of Thomas Hardy's *Woodlanders* (1887), and perhaps because of its regional focus, for many it remains Chatwin's most beloved work. The 1987 motion-picture version, directed by Andrew Grieve, only renewed the popularity of the novel.

Five years elapsed between the publication of *On the Black Hill* and Chatwin's comprehensive treatise on wandering, *The Songlines*. Chatwin said that he took inspiration from the eighteenth-century dialogue novel, particularly Denis Diderot's *Jacques le fataliste* (1796). *The Songlines* is structured around a series of dialogues between the narrator, Bruce, and a Russo-Australian, Arkady. Bruce has come to Australia hoping to learn about the aboriginal songlines. According to aboriginal mythology the continent was created by totemic beings who wandered over the land singing out the name of everything they came across, "singing the world into existence." Tribes could subsequently trace their way across the land by repeating the correct song as they traveled. A song thus acts as both map and direction finder. Aboriginal trade, the novel asserts, centered on the exchange of songs rather than goods because of their invaluable utility. But beyond their mapping function, songs are sacred because they have the ability to create the world and the individual. Each individual knows the songs corresponding to a particular region that centrally defines and links him or her to the land and ancestors. Land-rights activists such as Arkady seek to preserve aboriginal sacred sites because development on them disrupts the songlines and represents the partial uncreation of the world.

The struggle between the racist white Australians and the spiritual Aborigines provides the impetus for the philosophical discussions between Arkady and Bruce. Here as nowhere else Chatwin puts forth his case for the nomadic alternative (about a third of the book is a collection of epigrams, many taken from "The Nomadic Alternative"). The possession of material goods is declared self-destructive: "Things filled men with fear: the more things they had, the more they had to fear." Material possessions, in eliciting compulsive devotion, prevent spiritual growth. Returning to "original simplicity" represents not a naive solution but the only solution to the crisis of modernity: "The world, if it has a future, has an ascetic future."

After establishing the superiority of the aboriginal way of life, the narrator, Bruce, proceeds to establish the universality of such an existence. The novel suggests not only that some form of "original simplicity" existed but also that it was common across human cultures. Looking to the roots of Judaism, Bruce argues that Yahweh is "a God of the Way," a God of deserts and wandering, favoring Abel's nomadic life over Cain's settled version. But because Jews and Christians no longer prefer nomadism to settled civilization, they no longer identify with communities such as the Aborigines. If

they were to return to the nomadic roots of Judeo-Christian religion, however, they would find a renewed spirituality. Chatwin associates wandering with a pilgrimage that returns individuals to a closer relationship with God. He remarked in an interview shortly after the publication of *The Songlines* that the "act of walking through a wilderness was thought to bring you back to God." Chatwin envisions songlines as extending back across space and time to the beginning of human self-awareness. If individuals repeat the songs, they can reconnect with the origins of a universal human spirit.

Beyond spiritual health, Chatwin asserts that there is a biological imperative for wandering. Just as a sedentary gene pool leads to a dying species, so does a sedentary lifestyle. He employs a variety of examples from nature to suggest an instinctive desire for movement. Instincts are important because without them humankind has no basis for morality. Physical health is thus equated with spiritual fitness. Revising Fyodor Dostoyevsky's dictum that without religion everything is permissible, Chatwin argues that without "instinct, everything would be equally permissible." By following instinct individuals will perform good and moral actions. To ignore these instincts leads not only to disease but also to moral failure.

Chatwin's ruminations on human nature and aboriginal life proved immensely popular. *The Songlines* was on the top-ten best-seller list in *The Sunday Times* for nine months. Critical reception has been quite mixed, however. Ruth Brown's critique of the novel is perhaps the most succinct. For Brown, Chatwin absolves the colonial center of blame for the history of imperialism by shifting racist behavior solely on the shoulders of the white Australians. This critique is simply an extension of that brought against *In Patagonia*: by declaring himself a neutral observer Chatwin increases his narrative credibility and excuses his appropriation of local culture. Chatwin's status as "observer" further conceals his intimate relationship with the colonial and racist policies of England. His privileged status is only possible because of a history of exploitation. A second criticism of the novel is that it is loosely structured, which can be attributed directly to Chatwin's declining health. Suffering from what he claimed was a rare bone-marrow disease acquired while traveling through China, Chatwin considered himself to be in a race against time to complete *The Songlines*.

Chatwin completed one more short novel, *Utz* (1988), before his untimely death in 1989 from an illness rumored to have been AIDS. The novel opens with the funeral of Kasper Joachim Utz, an obsessive collector of Meissen porcelain whom the narrator had

Dust jacket for a posthumous collection of Chatwin's journalistic pieces and short stories

met back in 1967 while in Prague. Attempting to write a study of the psychology of the compulsive collector, the narrator was directed to Utz, whose obsession with collecting made him a contemporary version of the mad seventeenth-century emperor Rudolf II. The strange events surrounding the funeral and the mysterious disappearance of Utz's entire collection spark a familiar Chatwinian archaeology of the individual. For Utz, public museum collecting was immoral, denaturing objects as zoos denature animals: "Ideally, museums should be looted every fifty years, and their collections returned to circulation." The touch of the passionate collector restores life to the object, re-creating the relationship between maker and made. This link between collector and artifact is so powerful that Utz cannot defect from Czechoslovakia because he cannot leave his collection behind. Utz prefers to endure a world of unhappiness to one of separation.

Central to the novel is the examination of endurance as a means of resisting tyranny and oppression. Utz focuses his life on his collection, refusing to acknowledge the communist government. He does not actively rebel but endures, ignoring the government and its policies when possible. The narrator is told that the true heroes of this impossible situation are those such as Utz who use their silence to "inflict a final insult on the State, by pretending it does not exist." The collection itself becomes a model of endurance and resistance. Its continued existence and value stand as a refutation of socialist utility and the attempts by the communists to eradicate all markers of the bourgeois past. Utz's claims about the idolatry of collecting, its connection to sacrilege (Utz declares himself a Jew and then gleefully pronounces that *porcelain* and *pork* derive from the same root word), and his ultimate claim that porcelain is the antidote to decay all seek to establish the enduring subversiveness of his act. Such everyday acts of subversion will ultimately triumph over the most repressive regimes because tyranny is self-destructive; one need only endure and "in the end, the machinery of repression is more likely to vanish, not with war or revolution, but with a puff, or the voice of falling leaves."

What is most striking about the novel is not the claim for the resistance of objects that remain but the resistance that comes from the ephemerality of stories. About midway through the novel the narrator's confident sense of Utz's story breaks down. He begins to realize that he has never perceived the complexity of the man. Utz's most fascinating aspects were those that remained outside history and public view, including his secret marriage to his servant, Marta. What remains hidden cannot be co-opted by totalitarian forces, the novel seems to assert. Only through a genuine engagement with the world of the subject can he or she be understood. This assertion grows out of Chatwin's fascination with an archaeology of the personal. The historical record preserves only a particular vision of the past, usually that of the conquerors. But the lives of the others—expatriates, rurals, aborigines—continue despite the most oppressive tyrannies, and the stories of their lives call out to Chatwin. The conclusion of *Utz* suggests that such stories are recoverable, that they continue to endure if one only knows where to look: the narrator manages to locate Marta, who in the last words of the novel identifies her true self by revealing that she is really "die Baronin von Utz"—the baroness von Utz.

If *Utz* lacks the scale of *The Songlines,* it is nonetheless Chatwin's finest work. Chatwin's friend and contemporary Salman Rushdie (whom Chatwin proclaimed as the model for Arkady in *The Songlines*) argues that *Utz* represented the beginning of a "new, light-spirited phase of flight" for Chatwin after having released himself of the burden of *The Songlines.* The novel has not received the popular acclaim that *The Songlines* did but has received more-uniform critical approval and was short-listed for the Booker Prize. *Utz* manages to interweave narrative and philosophical concerns where *The Songlines* failed to do so. Further, the political dimension of the Chatwinian archaeology in *Utz* develops upon that in earlier works, supporting the argument that his work does not appropriate but helps to preserve threatened cultures. A 1992 motion-picture version of *Utz,* directed by George Sluizen, failed to capture the mystery and ambiguity that are central to the latter half of the novel.

Two collections of Chatwin's shorter works have been published since his death, *What Am I Doing Here* and *Anatomy of Restlessness.* The former book was approved by Chatwin on his deathbed while the latter was edited after his death by Jan Borm and Matthew Graves. Both collections include journalistic pieces and short stories, though Borm and Graves's inclusion of several essays on nomadism in *Anatomy of Restlessness* seems intended to emphasize Chatwin as philosopher rather than Chatwin as storyteller. For precisely this reason the first collection proves far more satisfying. Chatwin is a brilliant storyteller and a less-than-rigorous philosopher. He proves too willing to make universal assertions about human nature and in-

stincts with the slightest evidence. This led him to a politics that even his friend Rushdie describes as "simple." Chatwin's great strength, and what his work will be remembered for, was his ability to use objects, places, and people to weave intricate and moving stories that had seemingly been effaced by history. He managed to speak to the contradictory longings for freedom and home that have haunted twentieth- century thought.

Interviews:

Michael Ignatieff, "An Interview with Bruce Chatwin," *Granta,* 21 (Spring 1987): 23–37;

Michael Davie, "Heard between the Songlines," *Observer* (London), 21 June 1987, p. 18;

Lucy Hughes-Hallett, "Songs of the Earth," *Evening Standard,* 24 June 1987, p. 33;

Colin Thubron, "Born under a Wandering Star," *Daily Telegraph* (London), 27 June 1987.

References:

David Birch, "Strategy and Contingency," in *Twentieth-Century Fiction: From Text to Context,* edited by Peter Verdonk and Jean Jacques Weber (London: Routledge, 1995), pp. 220–234;

Ruth Brown, "*The Songlines* and the Empire That Never Happened," *Kunapipi,* 13 (1991): 5–13;

Susannah Clapp, "The Life and Early Death of Bruce Chatwin," *New Yorker,* 72 (23 and 30 December 1996): 90–101;

Clapp, *With Chatwin: Portrait of a Writer* (London: Cape, 1997);

David C. Estes, "Bruce Chatwin's *In Patagonia:* Traveling in Textualized Terrain," *New Orleans Review,* 18 (1991): 67–77;

Graham Huggan, "Maps, Dreams, and the Presentation of Ethnographic Narrative: Hugh Brody's 'Maps and Dreams' and Bruce Chatwin's 'The Songlines,'" *Ariel: A Review of International English Literature,* 22 (1991): 57–69;

Peter Levi, *The Light Garden of the Angel King* (London: Collins, 1972; revised edition, London: Penguin, 1984);

Patrick Meanor, *Bruce Chatwin* (New York: Twayne, 1997);

Karl Miller, *Doubles* (Oxford: Oxford University Press, 1985), pp. 402–409;

Nicholas Murray, *Bruce Chatwin* (Bridgend: Seren, 1993);

John Pilkington, *An Englishman in Patagonia* (London: Century, 1991);

Salman Rushdie, *Imaginary Homelands* (London: Granta, 1991), pp. 226–231, 232–236, 237–240.

Roddy Doyle

(8 May 1958 –)

Marco Abel
Pennsylvania State University—University Park

BOOKS: *The Commitments* (Dublin: King Farouk, 1987; London: Heinemann, 1988; New York: Vintage, 1989);

War (Dublin: Passion Machine, 1989);

The Snapper (London: Secker & Warburg, 1990; New York: Penguin, 1992);

The Van (London: Secker & Warburg, 1991; New York: Viking, 1992);

Brownbread; and, War (London: Secker & Warburg, 1992; New York: Penguin, 1994);

The Barrytown Trilogy: The Commitments, The Snapper, The Van (London: Secker & Warburg, 1992; New York: Penguin, 1995);

Paddy Clarke, Ha-Ha-Ha (London: Secker & Warburg, 1993; New York: Viking, 1994);

The Woman Who Walked into Doors (London: Cape, 1996; New York: Viking, 1996).

PLAY PRODUCTIONS: *Brownbread,* Dublin, SFX Centre, September 1987;

War, Dublin, SFX Centre, September 1989.

MOTION PICTURES: *The Commitments,* screenplay by Doyle, Dick Clement, and Ian La Frenais, Beacon Communications, 1991;

The Snapper, screenplay by Doyle, British Broadcasting Corporation/Miramax, 1993;

The Van, screenplay by Doyle, Deadly Films/Fox Searchlight/British Broadcasting Corporation, 1996;

Famine, screenplay by Doyle, Crom Films, 1998.

TELEVISION SCRIPT: *Family,* script by Doyle, British Broadcasting Corporation, 4 episodes, summer 1994.

OTHER: "Republic Is a Beautiful Word," in *My Favorite Year: A Collection of New Football Writing,* edited by Nick Hornby (London: Witherby, 1993), pp. 7–21; republished as "Jacko's Army," *Observer,* 7 November 1993, p. 29;

Clement Cairns, ed., *The Stranger and Other Stories,* introduction by Doyle (Cork: Fish, 1996).

Roddy Doyle (photograph by Amelia Stein)

Among the generation of Irish writers who emerged in the 1980s, Roddy Doyle is one of the most popular both at home and worldwide. While his popular appeal has been undisputed from the moment his privately published first novel, *The Commitments* (1987), became widely available when it was republished by William Heinemann in 1988, Doyle's status among critics was initially less clear. Whereas his work found immediate approval with the literary establishments in England and the United States, his use of four-letter words in his dialogue and his cinematic style led Irish critics to conclude that Doyle was catering to a voyeuristic Anglo-American audience eager for the perpetuation of the stereotypical foul-mouthed, illiterate, working-class Irishman. With the publication of his fourth novel, *Paddy Clarke, Ha-Ha-Ha* (1993), however, many of these critics finally agreed that Irish literature had produced yet another major talent. This assessment was underlined when *Paddy Clarke, Ha-Ha-Ha* won the Booker Prize, making Doyle the

*Dust jacket for the U.S. edition of Doyle's novel about two
unemployed friends who try to start their own business*

1971 and at St. Fintan's Christian Brothers School
in Sutton from 1971 to 1976. He graduated from
University College, Dublin, in 1979 with a bachelor's degree in English and geography. For the next
fourteen years he taught those subjects at Greendale
Community School in Kilbarrack; he was known to
his students as "Punky Doyle" for his leather-
jacket-and-jeans rock-and-roll outfits. He was a
member of the Irish Socialist Party from 1978 to
1982.

After contributing short articles to student
magazines such as *In Dublin* Doyle decided in 1982
to make a more serious attempt at writing. An enthusiastic fan of popular music, Doyle said in an unpublished interview that his decision to start writing
was like that of an air-guitar player who finally decides to pick up a real instrument. Reading Flannery
O'Connor's *Wise Blood* (1952), E. L. Doctorow's
Ragtime (1975), and John Irving's *The World According to Garp* (1978) gave him the idea that he, too,
could write. Doyle characterizes these works as using simple, straightforward language to produce
complex and engaging narratives—a description that
characterizes Doyle's own style, which strives for
clarity but not simplicity.

All of Doyle's work is set in Barrytown, the fictional counterpart of Dublin's Northside. Here his
mostly uneducated working-class characters, many
of whom are unemployed or underemployed, struggle with finding the material means necessary for
survival. But while their economic situation is dire,
they are not defeated: a peculiar sense of joie de
vivre runs throughout Doyle's narratives. Although
the characters are aware of their precarious situations, they have a healthy sense of humor, try to
overcome unpleasant circumstances with the help of
communal networks, and display unmitigated pride
in their regional dialect, with all of its *eijits, fucks,* and
shites. Foul language functions as a means of defying
the conventions created by those who oppress them;
using *fuck*—even between syllables—allows these
working-class characters to assert a sense of independence.

As Gail Caldwell argues in *The Boston Globe*
(19 December 1993), Doyle's brilliant ear for dialogue allows him to capture and promote "a modern
working-class Ireland with a near boisterous affection for language." Whereas James Joyce, Doyle's
predecessor as a chronicler of Dublin life, criticized
Dubliners' inability to use language properly, Doyle
puts a positive value on this so-called shortcoming
and even exaggerates it. The issue is not whether
real working-class people talk as Doyle depicts them
(that they do, however, is implied by some critics'
objection that Doyle merely walks into a local pub

first Irish author ever to receive the prestigious
award; it was the largest-selling winner of the prize
to that time. Doyle gained further critical acclaim
with the publication of *The Woman Who Walked into
Doors* (1996). Representing much of the criticism
Doyle has received over the past ten years, Mary
Jordan wrote in *The Washington Post* (4 February
1995) that there "is no other writer documenting
modern Ireland—the new Ireland of the European
union, a land more U2 than lovelorn tenor, more
working man than Quiet Man—the way Roddy
Doyle is."

The third of four children—two girls and two
boys—of Rory and Ida Bolger Doyle, Roddy Doyle
was born 8 May 1958 in Dublin. He grew up in Kilbarrack, a working-class district six miles north of
Dublin's city center, where his father was a printer
for the government and then an employee of an
agency for the coordination of apprentices; his
mother was a secretary for a lawyer. Doyle was educated at a National School in Raheny from 1963 to

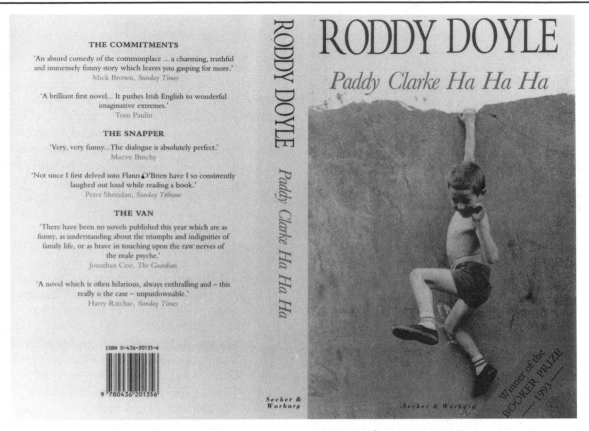

THE COMMITMENTS

'An absurd comedy of the commonplace ... a charming, truthful and immensely funny story which leaves you gasping for more.'
Mick Brown, *Sunday Times*

'A brilliant first novel... It pushes Irish English to wonderful imaginative extremes.'
Tom Paulin

THE SNAPPER

'Very, very funny...The dialogue is absolutely perfect.'
Maeve Binchy

'Not since I first delved into Flann O'Brien have I so consistently laughed out loud while reading a book.'
Peter Sheridan, *Sunday Tribune*

THE VAN

'There have been no novels published this year which are as funny, as understanding about the triumphs and indignities of family life, or as brave in touching upon the raw nerves of the male psyche.'
Jonathan Coe, *The Guardian*

'A novel which is often hilarious, always enthralling and – this really *is* the case – unputdownable.'
Harry Ritchie, *Sunday Times*

ISBN 0-436-20135-6

RODDY DOYLE

Paddy Clarke Ha Ha Ha

Winner of the BOOKER PRIZE 1993

Dust jacket for Doyle's novel in which a ten-year-old boy tries to make sense of his world

with a tape recorder and transcribes what the people say); rather, Doyle understands that their localized language enables the characters to affirm their independence, self-respect, and self-worth. As does Jack Kerouac, Doyle works hard at providing his prose with an oral, musical rhythm; in an unpublished 1997 interview he said that he spends "a lot of time rejecting words and taking in others because of the rhythm as much as the meaning of individual words. It is a little bit like editing a film."

After a failed attempt at a novel, "Your Granny's a Hunger Striker"–which, he insists, will never be published–in 1985, Doyle completed *The Commitments* in 1986. When he could not find a publisher for the work, he and his friend John Sutton formed their own company, King Farouk, solely for the purpose of privately printing the book. Using borrowed money, they printed three thousand copies and distributed them to local bookstores. Heinemann, the London publishing firm, took notice of the book, bought the rights to it, and published it to great success. Doyle and Sutton then dissolved King Farouk, which stands as a real-life example of the kind of innovative lo-

cal entrepreneurship in which many of Doyle's characters engage in Barrytown.

Chronicling the up-and-down trajectory of the less-than-mediocre Dublin soul band that gives the book its title, *The Commitments* is primarily the story of Jimmy Rabbitte Jr., who forms and manages the group. Jimmy organizes band practice, arranges a few local gigs, and does his best to keep the band members from literally killing each other. He views the Commitments not merely as yet another local band playing third-rate rock and roll but as a vehicle for political statements. In the novel's memorable opening scene Jimmy articulates to his friends their real reason for being in a band:

> "Yis want to be different, isn't tha' it? Yis want to do somethin' with yourselves, isn't tha' it? . . . Yis want to get up there an' shout I'm Outspan fuckin' Foster . . . An' I'm Derek fuckin' Scully, an' I'm not a tosser. Isn't tha' righ'? That's why yis're doin' it. Amn't I righ'?

Since the band is supposed to be playing cover songs of old soul classics, Jimmy continues his pep talk by dismissing "All tha' mushy shite abou' love an' fields an' meeting mots in the supermarkets an'

McDonald's" as "bourgeois" and opting instead for songs that are about "Sex an' politics."

Asked to elaborate on what he means by "politics"—the "sex" part is easy for his friends to comprehend—Jimmy responds with a speech that includes a quote from the soul singer James Brown:

> "Yeah, politics.—Not songs abou' Finna fuckin' Fail or anythin' like tha'. Real politics. . . . Where are yis from? . . . Dublin. . . . Wha' part o' Dublin? Barrytown. Wha' class are yis? Workin' class. Are yis proud of it? Yeah, yis are. . . . Who buys the most records? The workin' class. . . . Your music should be abou' where you're from an' the sort o' people yeh come from.—Say it once, say it loud, I'm black an' I'm proud . . . . The Irish are the niggers of Europe, lads. . . . An' Dubliners are the niggers of Ireland. . . . An' the northside Dubliners are the niggers o' Dublin."

Although Jimmy wants to make a political impact on his community, he has a typical late-twentieth-century cynicism about politics. As he explains to his band, "Party politics . . . means nothin' to the people. . . . Soul is the politics o' the people."

Although the band ultimately fails because of its members' inability to overcome their personal differences, Jimmy and two of the members immediately start to form a new one. While it seems unlikely that they will improve musically, Doyle's point appears to be that it is the effort that counts. While some critics accuse Doyle of ignoring the darker aspects of working-class life in contemporary Dublin, most reviewers agree with Peter Conrad's contention in *The Independent* (14 April 1996) that Doyle's novels "celebrate imagination's power to alter and overcome a constricting reality." *The Commitments* was made into a movie in 1991, with a screenplay coauthored by Doyle, Dick Clement, and Ian La Frenais.

Doyle married Belinda Moller in 1989; the couple has two children, Rory, born in 1991, and Jack, born in 1992. After writing two plays, *Brownbread* (1987) and *War* (1989), Doyle continued his Barrytown saga with *The Snapper* (1990); he claims that his main inspiration for writing the work came from reading Doris Lessing's novel *A Proper Marriage* (1954). The novel begins with Jimmy Rabbitte's sister Sharon informing their parents, Jimmy Sr. and Veronica, that she is pregnant as the result of having been raped by a friend's father; she refuses, however, to reveal his name. While all of the Rabbittes are curious about the rapist's identity, Jimmy Sr. becomes obsessed with the question. He uses every trick he knows to elicit the name; when all fail, he punishes Sharon for her disobedience by refusing to talk to her.

With the help of books from the local library, Sharon educates herself about her body and the changes it will undergo during her pregnancy. Her father, who is spying on her in an attempt to uncover the rapist's identity, finds the books, reads them, and discovers—to his amazement and the pleasure of his wife—many facts about the female body of which he had previously been unaware. Sharon, on the other hand, seizes the unexpected chance to create a niche of her own within the claustrophobic space of the family by remaining always one step ahead of her father's curiosity. Ultimately, father and daughter realize that they have to work together: Sharon needs her father's emotional and financial support, and Jimmy Sr. needs his daughter's sympathy, love, and cooperation if he is to maintain his already fragile position as patriarch. Although Sharon all but confirms his suspicions, he finally accepts the fact that he will never know for sure the identity of his first grandchild's father.

Sharon also comes to terms with Mr. Burgess, the man who raped her. When she hears that he has been bragging about her being a "ride," she visits him at his home and threatens to expose him if he ever speaks about her in such a way again. Sharon realizes that Burgess is afraid of her, and she rejoices inwardly because she has "never felt power like this before."

Jimmy Sr. learns an important lesson from his experience with his daughter's pregnancy. Having understood the necessity for family members to support each other, he announces to his youngest son, Darren, an avid cyclist, that he has "been thinkin' that I should get involved in somethin'—for the kids—an' the community" and that he intends to form a cycling club. *The Snapper* was filmed in 1993, with a screenplay by Doyle.

The final, and darkest, installment of the Barrytown Trilogy, *The Van* (1991), was short-listed for the Booker Prize in 1991. Jimmy Sr. and his best friend, Bimbo, have joined the ranks of the unemployed. As the prospect of regaining a job grows dimmer, Jimmy becomes increasingly passive; but Bimbo refuses to give in to despair. Astutely calculating the potential inherent in his fellow citizens' stomachs, he invests in an old "chipper van" (mobile fish-and-chips stand). The enterprise fails; not only do they encounter problems with the health authorities, but they also find that "capitalism with a human face"—Bimbo and Jimmy are to share equally the profits even though Bimbo paid for the van—is more easily envisioned than achieved: Bimbo's entrepreneurial drive, encouraged by his wife, almost ruins his relationship with his best friend, who is content with what they have. *The Van* was filmed in

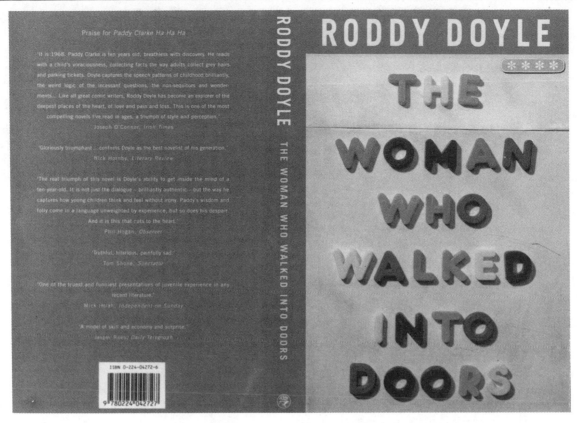

Dust jacket for Doyle's novel about an abused wife

1996; Doyle wrote the screenplay and served as coproducer.

Set in Dublin in 1968, *Paddy Clarke, Ha-Ha-Ha* views the deterioration of the marriage of ten-year-old Paddy's parents through the boy's eyes. Because Doyle was also ten in 1968, some critics assumed that the novel was autobiographical. In a 1994 interview with Desmond Ryan, however, Doyle insisted that even though the "geography of the place where Paddy lives, the fields and things like that are autobiographical and part of my memories . . . it's not me."

The novel is Doyle's most complex narrative to date. Although the story is told from Paddy's perspective, the boy has not developed an intellectual repertoire that would allow him to understand his parents' behavior. Paddy has other problems, as well: he is losing his status among his peers as children from newly built housing projects begin to bully him. Thus, he has to cope not only with the loss of his father, who eventually abandons the family, but also with finding himself an outcast among his former friends. Paddy recounts the events in a fragmented narrative consisting of free association, flashbacks, and internal monologue that spirals to-

ward a chilling end. Doyle's understanding of child psychology is movingly demonstrated in the scenes in which Paddy tries to alter his parents' behavior toward each other by telepathically telling them to stop. Doyle perfectly captures children's tendency to take upon themselves the guilt for the marital problems of their parents. The challenge of reading the work is that of making sense of the confused and unreliable memories of a young boy who does not comprehend the strange world of adulthood. As Ryan remarks, *Paddy Clarke, Ha-Ha-Ha* is an "unforgettable novel about childhood and memory."

After the publication of *Paddy Clarke, Ha-Ha-Ha* Doyle was able to quit teaching to concentrate on his writing. Today he treats writing as a job that he pursues until five o'clock on weekdays, when he stops to help his wife prepare dinner.

While Doyle merely hints at domestic violence in *Paddy Clarke, Ha-Ha-Ha,* he made spousal abuse an explicit theme in his next two projects: the television miniseries *Family* (1994), for which he wrote the script, and *The Woman Who Walked into Doors,* a novel in which the same characters appear. Colin Lacey notes that the "series was addressed in the Dail [the Irish Parliament], occupied inches of newspaper and magazine columns and was debated at length on every radio and television chat show in the country. In delineating the brutal vocabulary of marital violence in a representative Irish setting, Doyle has exposed a tender national nerve, and much of his audience was displeased."

While in the television series the family's struggles are told from the perspectives of four of its members, *The Woman Who Walked into Doors* presents only the viewpoint of Paula Spencer, the abused wife. Many critics agree that with Paula, Doyle has created one of the most compelling female voices in contemporary literature; how well he has imagined Paula's situation is indicated by the response he received from actual victims of marital violence. Paula tells her story through a series of flashbacks in which she describes the stages of her disintegrating marriage, the development of her alcoholism, and her abuse by her husband, Charlo; but she also remembers the good times with Charlo, whom she married to escape her abusive father. Despite the graphic descriptions of Charlo's violent behavior, the most disturbing passage in the novel is the one that explains the title: embarrassed to explain the real cause of her bruises, Paula tells the nurses and doctors that she has walked into yet another door. Instead of challenging her statement and helping her to get out of her predicament, the hospital personnel look the other way, thus perpetuating the problem.

In the end, however, Paula—like the working-class protagonists of Doyle's Barrytown Trilogy—takes control of her situation. Not only does she retaliate against her husband, hitting him over the head with a pan and throwing him out of the house, but she also reconstructs her life through recounting her story, inventing a new past that she can accept as her own. Like the Rabbittes, Paula realizes that blaming others and retreating into stasis are unproductive choices. Once again Doyle shows in his fiction that individuals can overcome the oppressive forces that dominate their lives. Because Doyle's characters choose activity over passivity, the laughter that is a major element even in his darker tales appears to be justified. Based on his work so far, one can agree with John McRae's evaluation in the *New Straits Times* (7 August 1996) that Doyle "is a master of the balancing act between comedy and concern, between pathos and pungent social commentary."

Interview:

Desmond Ryan, "Profit without Honors?," *Philadelphia Inquirer,* 20 January 1994, pp. E1, 7.

References:

Peter Conrad, "The Smiler Makes a Killing," *Independent,* 14 April 1996, p. 32;
Colin Lacey, "Roddy Doyle: Ruffling Feathers, after a Booker," *Publisher's Weekly* (25 March 1996): 55–56.

Alice Thomas Ellis
(Anna Margaret Haycraft)
(9 September 1932 –)

Catherine Burgass
Staffordshire University

BOOKS: *Natural Baby Food: A Cookery Book,* as Brenda O'Casey (London: Duckworth, 1977); republished, as Anna Haycraft (London: Fontana, 1980);

The Sin Eater (London: Duckworth, 1977);

Darling, You Shouldn't Have Gone to So Much Trouble, by Ellis, as Haycraft, and Caroline Blackwood (London: Cape, 1980);

The Birds of the Air (London: Duckworth, 1980; New York: Viking, 1981);

The 27th Kingdom (London: Duckworth, 1982);

The Other Side of the Fire (London: Duckworth, 1983; New York: Viking, 1984);

Unexplained Laughter (London: Duckworth, 1985; New York: Harper & Row, 1987);

Home Life (London: Duckworth, 1986);

Secrets of Strangers, by Ellis and Tom Pitt-Aikens (London: Duckworth, 1986);

The Clothes in the Wardrobe (London: Duckworth, 1987);

More Home Life (London: Duckworth, 1987);

Home Life Three (London: Duckworth, 1988);

The Skeleton in the Cupboard (London: Duckworth, 1988);

The Fly in the Ointment (London: Duckworth, 1989);

Loss of the Good Authority: The Cause of Delinquency, by Ellis and Pitt-Aikens (London: Viking, 1989);

Home Life Four (London: Duckworth, 1989);

The Inn at the Edge of the World (London & New York: Viking, 1990);

A Welsh Childhood, photographs by Patrick Sutherland (London & New York: M. Joseph, 1990);

The Summerhouse Trilogy (London: Penguin, 1991); republished as *The Summer House: A Trilogy* (New York: Penguin, 1994)—comprises *The Clothes in the Wardrobe, The Skeleton in the Cupboard, The Fly in the Ointment;*

Pillars of Gold (London & New York: Viking, 1992);

Cat among the Pigeons: A Catholic Miscellany (London: Flamingo, 1994);

The Evening of Adam (Harmondsworth: Viking, 1994);

Alice Thomas Ellis (photograph by Fay Goodwin)

Serpent on the Rock (London: Hodder & Stoughton, 1994);

Fairy Tale (London: Viking, 1996).

OTHER: Mary Keene, *Mrs. Donald,* edited by Ellis (London: Chatto & Windus, 1983);

Wales: An Anthology, edited by Ellis (London: Collins, 1989).

Alice Thomas Ellis (Anna Margaret Haycraft) has written eleven novels, a collection of short stories, and several nonfiction works. Her novels, all of which are short, are peopled largely by middle-class characters whose mores and manners are the butt of the mordant wit that is often noted by reviewers. Most of the novels contain at least an element of the mystical or the supernatural. Ellis's novels are not simple social comedies; she shares with Iris Murdoch a preoccupation with the nature of good and evil that is informed by her conservative Catholicism. Her fiction has been compared to that of another contemporary Catholic-convert writer, Muriel Spark. Her heroines—male characters are generally of lesser importance—tend to be acquainted with the deadly sin of pride but often possess a spiritual awareness that is contrasted with the hypocrisy of her more sanctimonious but less moral characters, and they frequently act as mouthpieces for Ellis's comments on what she considers the declining state of the Catholic Church. Ellis's novels, which are both well crafted and entertaining, can best be described as "middlebrow" women's fiction. Her work occupies the gray area between popular and "high" literary fiction; thus, while she receives good reviews in the quality and literary press she has, so far, prompted little academic criticism.

Ellis was born Anna Margaret Lindholm on 9 September 1932 in Liverpool but spent a significant part of her childhood in Penmaenmawr, Wales, where her mother had relatives. She retains a close sentimental attachment to Wales, which forms the setting for many of her novels. She was educated at Bangor County Grammar School in Gwynedd and at Liverpool School of Art. Brought up an Anglican, she converted to Catholicism in her late teens and entered the Convent of Notre Dame de Namur in Liverpool as a postulant at nineteen but had to leave after suffering a slipped disk. In 1956 she married Colin Haycraft, the chairman and managing director of the Duckworth publishing house, for which Ellis worked as fiction editor. They had seven children, two of whom died young. In addition to her books, Ellis has written columns for the *Spectator,* the *Universe,* and *The Catholic Herald.*

Ellis has said that after years of raising her family she realized that there were things that she wanted to say, so she wrote them down. Her first novel, *The Sin Eater* (1977), is dedicated to her son Joshua, who at the time she wrote the work lay in a coma after falling off a roof. It is set in Wales and revolves around the visit of Michael and his wife, Angela, who are visiting Michael's childhood home, the Plâs, where his father is dying. Resident at the Plâs are Michael's brother, Henry, and sister-in-law, Rose; their twin sons; and three generations of domestic staff: the efficient but sour Phyllis; her son, "Jack the Liar"; and

her illegitimate grandson, the stupid and repellent Gomer. Also returning home is Michael and Henry's sister, Ermyn, the first of Ellis's characters whose otherworldliness—in this case marked by a preoccupation with death, religious leanings, and a sense of dislocation from ordinary human affairs—is combined with an unusual awareness of the evil and hostility that are at large in the world. The story is told from multiple points of view, and Ermyn's thoughts are represented in substantial passages, but Rose, the first of Ellis's sinful heroines, is the real protagonist of the novel. A Catholic, Rose "much preferred to honour the letter of the old law, rather than submit herself to the vague dispensations and ill-defined freedoms of the spirit of Vatican II." She devotes a considerable amount of effort to, and derives an equal amount of entertainment from, causing trouble within the family. Her primary means of mischief-making is the preparation of food, which Rose uses to manipulate events, parody her less-sophisticated guests, and safeguard the well-being of her children. The descriptions of these culinary masterpieces are lent a sinister flavor by the "sin eater," a figure who in Welsh tradition consumes the sins of the dead along with the crumbs of the funeral feast.

The central event of the story is a cricket match between "the house" and the village, a tradition instituted by Michael's father to foster relations between the local gentry and outsiders who are vacationing in the village. The cricket match gives Ellis scope for social comedy as the mutual suspicions and hostilities of the various layers of the class system become increasingly apparent. Ellis said in a 1996 interview with Peter Stanford:

> The rise of moral relativism has made the task of the novelist extremely difficult. The denial of the existence of the Devil implies the non-existence of angels, and . . . of God himself. This position makes fiction, as well as everything else, pointless. The grey avowal that "we are all guilty" and pretty well much of a muchness does not make for a ripping yarn.

God and his opposite number are often included among Ellis's dramatis personae; here the devil presides over the events. A contrast is drawn between Rose's calculated malice and the hypocrisy of Michael and Angela. Angela pursues an affair with the weak-chinned Edward, a school friend of Michael; the night of the cricket match culminates in licentious chaos during which Michael is caught by Ermyn in a compromising position with Gomer behind a hedge. The aftermath is less comic or farcical than tragic; at the close of the novel the scene is set for disaster.

In *The Sin Eater,* as in the majority of her novels, Ellis combines pedestrian prose with lyrical passages, and elements of magic and mysticism are included within the broadly realistic presentation. Characterization is subsumed to social comedy and to the didactic purpose of the work, but *The Sin Eater* is a dense and event-filled first novel that was well received by reviewers and won a Welsh Arts Council Award.

Ellis's next novel, *The Birds of the Air* (1980), which won another Welsh Arts Council Award, is also dedicated to Joshua, who by this time had died. The family of the widowed Mrs. Marsh is gathering at her house for Christmas. Mrs. Marsh's daughter Mary had already returned home from Melys y Bwyd, the family cottage in Wales, incapable of looking after herself after the death of her son, Robin. Barbara Lamb, Marsh's other daughter, has just discovered that her husband, Seb, is having an affair with one of his university colleagues; as revenge Barbara has decided to seduce Hunter, his publisher. Seb and Barbara bring with them to Mrs. Marsh's their winsome and precocious daughter, Kate, and their sullen, adolescent son, Sam. Mrs. Marsh hopes that a family Christmas will help Mary recover from her grief, but chaos erupts: Sam dyes his hair green; uninvited guests descend; and Barbara's attempt at seducing the homosexual Hunter fails, and she is left drunk, disheveled, and hysterical.

Again there is an element of social comedy: Seb has married "beneath" him, and in "the Close," where Mrs. Marsh and Mary live, infinitesimally small class differences are magnified by the residents. This is, however, the most poignant of Ellis's novels: she has spoken of losing a son as a type of madness that removes the sufferer from everyday reality, and she conveys this experience in her depiction of the acute and isolating pain that has left Mary longing for death so that she might see Robin again. Although Ellis, who has also lost a baby daughter, has said that grief cannot be shared, the lyrical description of Robin's funeral under a blazing sun, Hunter's perception of Mary as a sick animal, and Mary's awareness of the bathetic aspect of death evoke what Ellis has described as the "almost unbearable" pain of loss. Barbara's angst over her unfaithful husband and Mrs. Marsh's stoic attitude to her own bereavement, while less dramatic, are presented with a degree of sympathy.

Bird imagery pervades the novel. There are the conventional associations of the robin with Christmas, and Robin's death was been foretold by a bird knocking on the window of Melys y Bwyd. Mary thinks that "The birds of the air should mourn for Robin and all the vast hordes of the dead." Seb's mistress is known as "The Thrush," and Barbara discovers their affair when she sees him lasciviously place a

Dust jacket for the U.S. edition of Ellis's novel about two sisters, one of whom must cope with the death of a son and the other with an unfaithful husband

slice of damp turkey in the woman's mouth. Her own fixation on Hunter is likened to the imprinting of a newly hatched goose on its parent. Just before Christmas dinner Mary remembers an aboriginal Welsh myth in which a Christmas feast, whose centerpiece is a swan stuffed with other birds, is interrupted by a strange visitor. The man casts a spell that brings the birds back to life, just as Mary desires the resurrection of Robin. Again, lyrical description is interwoven with pedestrian narrative and dialogue, social comedy with highly emotive passages, and the mythical with the mundane. As well as noting Ellis's wit, reviewers acknowledged her "verbal grace" and "dense, compacted prose." In *The Anglo-Welsh Review* (1981) Martin Haslehurst criticizes a certain one-dimensionality in some of the characters, concluding that "*The Birds of the Air* is not a work of genius . . . but it is a very accomplished novel."

The 27th Kingdom (1982), which was short-listed for the Booker Prize, is a modern fairy tale set in bohemian Chelsea in the 1950s. The action centers on

Dust jacket for Ellis's novel about a middle-aged woman's infatuation with her stepson

Dancing Master House, the home of Aunt Irene; her nephew, Kyril, a boy of great physical beauty and equal capacity for evil; and Focus, an anthropomorphized swimming cat. At the opening of the novel Irene is awaiting the arrival of a new boarder, Valentine, a would-be nun who has been temporarily sent away from a convent by Irene's sister, the Reverend Mother, because an apple she picked refuses to rot. Earlier, Valentine's sister, Joan, had been killed, as a result of her own carelessness, in a boating accident; a female tourist had also died. Only the tourist's husband survived.

Valentine, who is black, radiantly beautiful, and perfectly good, attracts the attentions of devils who have taken the form of pigeons and an attempt at seduction by Kyril. The O'Connors, a Cockney family whose matriarch is Irene's friend, are professional criminals, but that they are not truly evil is shown by their ability to appreciate Valentine's saintliness and by Mrs. O'Connor's correct identification of the pigeons. Irene's cleaning lady, Mrs. Mason, thrown on hard times by her husband's drinking, ex-

hibits a painful degree of gentility that overlies some less savory traits, notably snobbery and racism. Her middle-class preoccupation with appearances is contrasted unfavorably with Irene's and the O'Connors' "aristocratic" disregard for convention and the law. At the end of the novel the O'Connors chase a man into the Thames in the belief that he is a tax inspector on Aunt Irene's trail. The man drowns but is miraculously revived by Valentine blowing into his nostrils; he is discovered to be the sole survivor of the boating accident. In spite of this miracle the apple in the Reverend Mother's desk finally rots. Reviewing the novel in the *Times Literary Supplement* (2 July 1982), Linda Taylor said that "Ellis's skill lies in surface detail rather than in depth." The social satire loses its edge in the incongruous setting of a fairy tale in a specific, but finally unrealized, time and place.

The Other Side of the Fire (1983) returns to the countryside. Although the novel includes references to magic, human drama takes precedence over the supernatural. The middle-aged and middle-class Claudia Bohannon, whose children are at boarding school, falls in love with her stepson, the raven-haired Philip. This infatuation is contrasted unfavorably to the emotional equilibrium of Claudia's friend Sylvie, who has abjured men and lives alone in a cottage in the woods with her dog, Gloria. Although Claudia is the protagonist of the novel, Sylvie is a more typical Ellis heroine: not only is she self-sufficient, but she also has the requisite attitude toward death, which she regards as "a satisfactory conclusion to the vagaries of life." The scales finally fall from Claudia's eyes when Sylvie's bright but tactless daughter, Evvie, unwittingly reveals that Philip is a homosexual. At the end of the novel Claudia has attained something of Sylvie's ironic detachment from the passions.

A subplot involving Evvie's writing of a cliché-ridden romantic novel set on a windswept Scottish island allows Ellis to make some comments about fiction. Evvie thinks that the ancient Roman poet and satirist Horace, with his "endless interest in people's antics," would have made an excellent novelist, and she describes the "happy ending" as a triumph of bourgeois values demanded by the readership. Sylvie, for whom "Life was like a novel that she knew by heart: a novel crammed with minor characters whose names she couldn't remember and whose fates did not interest her," tells Evvie that only neurotic people write novels. When Philip expresses scorn for Evvie's novel, she replies that his opinion is irrelevant since it is women who buy books. In a review in the *Times Literary Supplement* (18 November 1983) Pat Raine compared Ellis to Spark for the way that "the fortuitous correspondences between art and life,

God's gifts to the novelist, and the weird sense of omniscience which sometimes overtakes the author of fiction, are given a comic showing." Raine also commended Ellis's "enchanting and exhilarating style."

In *Unexplained Laughter* (1985) Lydia has retreated from London to her cottage, Ty Fach, in rural Wales to recover from an unhappy love affair. She is accompanied by her friend, the unattractive but faithful Betty. Lydia's nearest neighbors are the farmer Hywel; his wife, Elizabeth; and his sister, Angharad, who is mute and thought to be insane. The remainder of the limited dramatis personae comprises Beuno, Hywel's brother, who is training for the priesthood, and the lecherous Dr. Wyn, who is having affairs with Elizabeth and with April, the daughter of the newcomers Lil and Sid. At first Lydia, who bears similarities to Rose in *The Sin Eater,* regards the community as a kind of soap opera, and she sets out to exploit its entertainment value. In spite of her malice and arrogance, however, Lydia possesses an instinctive moral awareness; she despises the modernization of the church and opposes the ordination of women. Those who hear the unexplained laughter of the title—Lydia and Beuno—are marked by a certain spiritual superiority.

The third-person narration is interrupted by substantial italicized passages in the first person that represent Angharad's thoughts. These passages, which are marked by a particularly formal and stylized diction, were described by Julia O'Faolain in the *Times Literary Supplement* (6 September 1985) as "embarrassing flights of fey eloquence." Although Lydia undergoes some small spiritual advancement, the plot is lacking in dynamism. O'Faolain, however, asserted that "in the end the novel cannot be summarized and this is a proof of its excellence." Other reviewers also praised its brilliance, and it won the *Yorkshire Post* Novel of the Year Award.

In *The Inn at the Edge of the World* (1990) Eric has left a successful executive position in Telford to become the landlord of an unprofitable pub on a remote Scottish island; his sullen and dissatisfied wife, Mabel, is nostalgic for their former lifestyle. Eric decides to host a nonfestive Christmas at the inn. His advertisements in the London newspapers attract five guests, each with his or her own reason for avoiding the conventional yule: Harry, a former military man for whom life has been meaningless since he lost his wife and son; Jessica, a newly successful actress who is escaping yet another failed relationship; Jon, an attractive but unstable young man who is pursuing Jessica; Anita, a spinster who works in a stationery store, where Christmas begins in August; and Ronald, an emotionally stunted psychiatrist

Dust jacket for Ellis's novel about tangled relationships in the Welsh countryside

whose wife has just left him. The inhabitants of the island form two camps. Those who were not born there include Eric; the "professor," a lecherous dentist; and the equally libidinous Mrs. H. The indigenous population, which includes Finlay and his laconic sister-in-law, have an unusually strong bond with the sea, even for seafaring people. Eventually Finlay reveals to the visitors and Eric that the island people are descended from seals who came ashore to dance but whose skins were stolen, leaving them unable to return to the water. As Harry and Jessica discover an affinity for each other, and Anita makes a play for the hopeless Ronald, Jon, in the grip of his unreasonable and unrequited passion, turns to thoughts of murder. Harry reveals to Jessica that his wife, who drowned at sea, was a local woman, and that his seventeen-year-old son also drowned in a boating accident just offshore of the island. Jon, whose psychosis is worsening, takes a boat out to sea in treacherous weather. Harry, who places no value on his own life, goes out in an unsuccessful attempt to save him and is claimed by his wife and son, who rise out of the water. (In *The Other Side of the Fire* Evvie describes a scene in her trashy novel in which the hero and heroine are "united in death in the Halls of the Sea King or the water kelpie or something—you know the sort of muck.") In an anticlimactic counterpoint to Harry's reunion with his family, Ronald fails to respond to Anita's overtures. In the final line of the novel Finlay says to Eric's wife, Mabel, who, it turns out, possesses the webbed fingers characteristic of the islanders: "Och, . . . ye all come back in the end." Christopher Wordsworth said in *The Guardian* (5 September 1990) that only Ellis could "get away with two ghostly revenants and these magic sealpeople." The novel won the Writers' Guild Best Fiction Award.

The Summerhouse Trilogy is set in the London suburb of Croydon and consists of three novels, each of which relates the same situation—the impending marriage of the unenthusiastic ingenue Margaret to Syl, a forty-year-old roué and mama's boy—from a different character's point of view. The first volume, *The Clothes in the Wardrobe* (1987), which was made into a movie, *The Summer House* (1992), is narrated by Margaret. Margaret, who has no desire to marry Syl, describes the match as having been arranged by Syl and her mother, Monica. Prior to her engagement she had been sent to Egypt, where Monica had also gone to school, to learn French and acquire some sophistication. There she had had a disastrous first love affair with Nour, the half-Egyptian son of one of her mother's school friends. She had witnessed Nour's murder of a fortune-teller and had helped him dispose of the body. Before her affair with Nour she had wanted to become a nun, but she now feels that she has betrayed God and fears that she is damned. She says: "I seldom speak now. There is no need for speech"; the mother superior of the Egyptian convent had told her that the Virgin Mary "seldom spoke. She had no need for speech." Into Margaret's colorless world comes the exotic half-English, halfEgyptian Lili, another school friend of her mother, who has come to oversee her artist husband's exhibition. She recognizes Margaret's religious vocation and saves her from marriage by seducing Syl and contriving to gather the wedding guests at the summerhouse to witness their lovemaking. The novel closes with Margaret, in the convent, contemplating Lili's gift of salvation.

Clothes are important symbols in the novel. Monica insists that Margaret wear her old bridal gown, which is both literally and metaphorically unfitting since her own marriage failed. Margaret compares old clothes stuffed in closets with useless memories, contrasting the former with a nun's "blessed, sure and unobtrusive" habit and the latter, by implication, with the nun's clear conscience. Monica has to change her entire wardrobe every year or so, an indication of superficiality, while Lili's style of dress is timeless, suggesting the virtuousness that underlies her flamboyant and free-living exterior.

The Skeleton in the Cupboard (1988) is narrated by Syl's mother, Mrs. Monroe. Although Syl still lives at home, she communicates better with their smelly old pug dog, whom she dislikes, and the cleaning lady, Mrs. Rafferty. Mrs. Monroe is shocked when Monica tells her of Lili's arrival: she once caught her habitually faithless husband, now dead, and a much younger Lili in flagrante delicto in the summerhouse. She comes to appreciate Lili's intelligence, however, and their increasing intimacy leads to the major revelation—the "skeleton in the cupboard"—of the novel: Margaret's sexual abuse by her father. After seeing Margaret in a state of ecstasy in church, Mrs. Monroe, like Lili, recognizes the girl's religious vocation; she is herself nostalgic for her Catholic childhood among northern farmers who "took the Faith for granted, like air and bread."

The Fly in the Ointment (1989) is narrated by Lili, who reveals that her promiscuous hedonism is a slightly manic attempt to keep herself from falling into a black depression. Her narrative style is sometimes conversational, sometimes dramatic with breathless ellipses; she also has a tendency, shared with Margaret, toward archaic biblical-sounding forms of expression. While the comic or farcical aspects of her public seduction of Syl in the summerhouse are presented in the first two novels, in Lili's account the scene has elements of tragedy. Reviewers have described the novel as elegant, malicious, and darkly comic.

A theme that runs through the trilogy is the fallibility of memory. In *The Clothes in the Wardrobe* Margaret remembers seeing a dead kingfisher; it is revealed in *The Skeleton in the Cupboard* that the bird was actually described to her by Mrs. Monroe on the night of Margaret's father's departure. A much more significant memory lapse is Margaret's forgetting of her abuse by her father. In the elderly Mrs. Monroe's narrative recent events are often described in an indistinct fashion, reflecting short-term memory loss, while scenes from her childhood are recounted in vivid detail. The three novels were republished in one volume in England in 1991 as *The Summerhouse Trilogy* and in the United States in 1994 as *The Summer House: A Trilogy*. Reviewing the latter, Gabriele Annan asserted in *The New York Review of Books* (23 June 1994): "Each of the three first-person narrators alters our viewpoint and adds to our insights, but it's not until the end that we discover exactly who did what to whom and why."

Pillars of Gold (1992) is set in Camden, where the bored middle-class housewife Scarlet and her working-class friend, Constance, realize that another friend, Barb, a promiscuous feminist, is missing. They read in the paper that the body of a woman has been found in a canal, but they are too overcome by inertia to attempt to find out whether it is Barb. Class, gender, and generation relations are explored in the novel: Scarlet, the daughter of arty bohemians, is full of middle-class angst and admires Constance's family, who have Gypsy blood, because they show "their feelings artlessly, with simple language and gestures." (The narrator quickly disabuses the reader of this romanticized view of Constance's family.) Brian, Scarlet's petulant and childish husband, as a product of the upper working class both despises and fears Constance and her family. Constance functions as a mouthpiece for Ellis's disenchantment with modern Catholicism: "But the one true faith . . . have gone and fallen for that codswallop. Can you *believe* it? They prance around with their eyes closed, speaking in tongues. They've gone charismatic." Scarlet's rebellious teenage daughter, Camille, and her friends become interested in Barb's whereabouts. It eventually transpires that Barb is not dead but has taken off to do good works. Ellis was praised by reviewers for the irony and wit with which she treats her themes although Claire Messud in *The Guardian* (10 April 1993) described the moral message as "heavy handed."

In 1994 Ellis's husband died suddenly of a stroke, leaving her with business debts and precipitating a nervous breakdown. In 1996 she found herself at the center of a media row sparked by the reactionary line she took in her column in *The Catholic Herald*. Rather than attacking what she sees as the general degeneration of Catholic practices, as she does in her fiction, she specifically accused the recently deceased archbishop of Liverpool, Derek Worlock, of weakening the Catholic message through his support of ecumenicism and of being responsible for declines in church attendance, conversions, and vocations. *The Catholic Herald* fired Ellis, who declared herself delighted with the response her attack elicited.

Nevertheless, Ellis's next novel, *Fairy Tale* (1996), is unusually quiet on the subject of Catholicism. Seventeen-year-old Eloise, who is in the thrall of the hippie guru Moonbird, has moved to a cottage in rural Wales with her boyfriend, Simon, to commune with nature. While sewing in her garden she

suddenly decides that she wants to have a baby; the following day, as she is drying antique lace, she is visited by four immaculately attired men. Simon is disconcerted both by the men's appearance and by Eloise's desire for a baby, which he does not share. He telephones Eloise's mother, Clare, who cannot come immediately and dispatches her friend Miriam in her place. On the day Clare does arrive, with the disquieting information that a sex offender is at large in the vicinity, Eloise comes home in the pouring rain bone dry—a fact that is noticed only by Miriam. Miriam is curious about the history of the cottage, which is recounted to her in the language of legend by some locals. Eloise grows progressively odder until, one day, she returns home with a silver-haired, green-eyed baby; since she is able to nurse it, everyone assumes that it is her natural child. The cat, however, will not remain in its presence; strange people visit, claiming to be doctors and social workers; the forest encroaches on the cottage. Finally Miriam comes to the conclusion that the baby is a changeling and that the locals are the *Tylwyth Teg* (Welsh fairies). The baby is eventually given to the fairy people, and the humans return to their proper environment—taking with them the cat, who has given birth to a green-eyed kitten.

This novel lacks the complexity of *The Inn at the Edge of the World,* which treats a similar theme. Although there are some amusing scenes built around the problems of communication between humans and fairies and some vivid descriptions of dark and sinister forces, the novel is unleavened by Ellis's familiar acerbic edge. In *The Guardian* (5 September 1996) the novelist Philip Hensher compared *Fairy Tale* unfavorably with Ellis's earlier works, pointing to her reliance on stock characters and "the banal femininity of her writing, which—unlike the femininity of good women writers—seems to limit what she can achieve. Her world is too bounded by domesticity."

While Alice Thomas Ellis's novels do demonstrate something of what Hensher calls "banal femininity"—that is, a preoccupation with the domestic—their primary virtue is the skillful interweaving of social satire with highly emotionally charged passages, pedestrian dialogue with lyrical prose, and the descriptive detail characteristic of domestic realism with a deeper symbolism. As one reviewer has said, Ellis's novels are the exception to the rule that the most readable novels are seldom the best written.

Interview:
Peter Stanford, "Who Put Sin in Sinister?," *Guardian,*
	1 April 1996, p. 4.

Penelope Fitzgerald

(17 December 1916 –   )

Philip Harlan Christensen
State University of New York at Suffolk County Community College

See also the Fitzgerald entry in *DLB 14: British Novelists Since 1960.*

BOOKS: *Edward Burne-Jones: A Biography* (London: M. Joseph, 1975; revised edition, Stroud, U.K.: Sutton, 1997);

The Knox Brothers: Edmund ("Evoe") 1881–1971, Dillwyn 1883–1943, Wilfred 1886–1950, Ronald 1888–1957 (London: Macmillan, 1977; New York: Coward, McCann & Geoghegan, 1977);

The Golden Child (London: Duckworth, 1977; New York: Scribners, 1978);

The Bookshop (London: Duckworth, 1978; Boston: Mariner Books/Houghton Mifflin, 1997);

Offshore (London: Collins, 1979; New York: Holt, 1987);

Human Voices (London: Collins, 1980);

At Freddie's (London: Collins, 1982; Boston: Godine, 1985);

Charlotte Mew and Her Friends (London: Collins, 1984; Reading, Mass.: Addison-Wesley, 1988);

Innocence (London: Collins, 1986; New York: Holt, 1986);

The Beginning of Spring (London: Collins, 1988; New York: Holt, 1989);

The Gate of Angels (London: Collins, 1990; Garden City, N.Y.: Doubleday, 1992);

The Blue Flower (London: Flamingo, 1995; Boston: Mariner Books/Houghton Mifflin, 1997).

OTHER: William Morris, "The Novel on Blue Paper," introduction by Fitzgerald, *Dickens Studies Annual: Studies on Victorian Fiction,* 10 (1982): 143–150;

William Morris, *The Novel on Blue Paper,* edited, with an introductory essay, by Fitzgerald (London: Journeyman Press, 1982; New York: AMS, 1982);

Margaret Oliphant, *The Rector and The Doctor's Family,* introduction by Fitzgerald (London: Virago, 1986; New York: Penguin, 1986);

Penelope Fitzgerald (photograph by Tara Heinemann)

Oliphant, *Salem Chapel,* introduction by Fitzgerald (London: Virago, 1986; New York: Penguin, 1986);

Oliphant, *The Perpetual Curate,* introduction by Fitzgerald (London: Virago, 1987; New York: Penguin, 1987);

Oliphant, *Miss Marjoribanks,* introduction by Fitzgerald (London: Virago, 1988; New York: Penguin, 1989);

Oliphant, *Phoebe Junior,* introduction by Fitzgerald (London: Virago, 1988; New York: Penguin, 1989).

Penelope Fitzgerald's novels are described by Frank Kermode in the *London Review of Books* as "the kind of fiction in which perfection is almost to be hoped for." Louis B. Jones, in *The New York Times Book Review* (1 March 1992), places Fitzgerald firmly in the tradition of Jane Austen, whose sentence structure is "built on the ruins of Latin rhetoric," while A. N. Wilson, in the *Evening Standard,* writes: "Fitzgerald possesses what one can only call the purest imagination." Better known in England, where one of her novels received the prestigious Booker Prize and three others were short-listed for the Booker, Fitzgerald also enjoys considerable devotion from American readers, whose numbers have been limited only by the difficulty in obtaining several of her titles in the United States.

Penelope Mary Knox was born on 17 December 1916 in Lincoln. Her father, Edmund George Valpy (E.V. or "Evoe") Knox, edited *Punch* magazine for twenty-five years. Her mother, Christine Hicks Knox, was, according to *The Feminist Companion to Literature in English,* "a moderate suffragette." Fitzgerald graduated from Somerville College, Oxford, in 1939 with first-class honors in English. In 1941 she married Desmond Fitzgerald. Although she devoted much time to her husband and three children, Fitzgerald has worked, among other occupations, as a bookshop clerk, RPA (Recorded Programmes Assistant) for the British Broadcasting Corporation, a teacher (part-time with Westminster tutors), and a journalist, contributing frequently to the *London Review of Books* and *The New York Times Book Review.* Her first published book was a biography of the English artist Edward Burne-Jones (1975).

The majority of Fitzgerald's fictional characters can be identified with occupations, often jobs that she has held. Fitzgerald's novels have often been praised for their fluid, spare style, but there is an undertow beneath this seemingly smooth surface. Set within historical contexts characterized by economic, political, or cultural upheaval, her novels acknowledge the loss of paradise, with an awareness that what passes for innocence in this world is, at best, a self-serving parody of its ancient precursor. As does the novelist Evelyn Waugh, Fitzgerald describes this "decline and fall" in terms of venerable institutions and families.

A Christian, she nonetheless refrains from moralizing. Her villains are rarely without charm, while her heroes often thrive despite themselves and their misguided intentions. The endings of Fitzgerald's novels rarely exhibit closure, and they usually leave the reader uncertain as to whether muddle or order, self-interest or agape, will finally prove ascendant.

In 1976 her husband died. The following year she published another biography, this time of her father and her uncles: *The Knox Brothers: Edmund ("Evoe") 1881–1971, Dillwyn 1883–1943, Wilfred 1886–1950, Ronald 1888–1957.* Also published in 1977 was *The Golden Child,* Fitzgerald's first novel, which explores how value, power, and authority are interrelated. The setting is a London museum hosting a loan exhibition of the "Golden Treasure" of the Garamantes, an ancient North African civilization. Modeling her fictional exhibit on the enormously popular Tutankhamen exhibition at the British Museum in 1971–1972, Fitzgerald contrasts the crowds who wait patiently for a glimpse of the "golden boy" with the museum staff, ensconced within inner chambers, whose lives are bureaucratically dedicated to running the museum and protecting their careers.

The museum bureaucrats must deal with a double crisis when they learn that the artifacts are fake and the veteran archaeologist Sir William Simpkin, discoverer of the treasure, is found pinned between movable steel shelves, "a body in the library." The museum's director, Sir John Allison, is faced with a choice, aptly defined by Jean Sudrann as "either to maintain the integrity of the Museum by concealing the 'great swindle' of the modern replicas . . . or to maintain that integrity by telling the truth and closing down the Exhibition."

Waring Smith, a junior exhibition officer, is also drawn into the intrigue. Like the innocents in Fitzgerald's later novels, he is preoccupied not with thoughts of great moment but rather with quotidian concerns, such as how he will pay his mortgage or whether he will be reconciled with his estranged wife. When Sir John sends Smith to Moscow to seek evidence that the treasure is authentic, he identifies the crowds queued up to see "the embalmed head and hands, and the ghastly evening dress suit, of Lenin" with the crowds outside the London exhibition and begins to fear that his whole life has been shaped by such "shoddy undertakings."

Critics have praised *The Golden Child* for its social satire and its parody of everything from bureaucratic memorandums to spy literature. Responding to the charge that the novel's plot is overcomplicated, Bruce Bawer writes in *The New Criterion* that Fitzgerald "is less interested in devising jigsawlike plots than in exploring the perplexities of the human condition."

The Bookshop (1978) was Fitzgerald's first novel to receive a Booker Prize nomination. Regrettably, it was long unavailable in the United States and, despite its warm British reception, difficult for American readers to find. The novel is set in the later

1950s in the East Anglian village of Hardborough, its name an indication of the cultural and economic atrophy that often characterize such insular communities. The local ruins of bungalows and small villas are reminders of the danger of building on sand: "Before anyone had come to live there the sandy cliff had given way and the houses had begun to totter and slide." Florence Green, an innocent whose inexperience makes her vulnerable, has "a kind heart, though that is not of much use when it comes to the matter of self–preservation." She decides that Hardborough must have a bookshop and that she will open one in the historic, and undoubtedly haunted, Old House at the center of town. Florence becomes something of a local celebrity when she decides to sell Vladimir Nabokov's *Lolita* (1955), though she does not show even the slightest interest in reading it: "I haven't been trained to understand the arts ... I don't know whether a book is a masterpiece or not."

Florence does have allies, such as Mr. Brundish, a descendant of one of Suffolk's ancient families, but she underestimates Violet Gamart, a relative newcomer who opposes Florence and who has proclaimed herself leader of Hardborough society. Resolved that Old House should be converted into "some sort of ... arts centre," she makes every effort to thwart Florence and her plans. One of her tools is a nephew, "a brilliant, successful, and stupid young man," who guides through Parliament a bill making Ancient Buildings "subject to compulsory purchases even if ... occupied at the moment." As does *The Golden Child*, *The Bookshop* explores the workings of influence and power in the hands of the foolish and the petty.

Fitzgerald's third novel, *Offshore* (1979), a Booker Prize winner, is set in London in the 1960s, but in a London far removed from that familiar to armchair travelers. The novel focuses on a community of barge dwellers living in the shadow of Battersea Bridge who are "creatures neither of firm land nor water." Although Fitzgerald playfully suggests that this community, in more than one sense, is "overlooked by some very good houses," even here, among these outcasts, there is evidence of a social and economic hierarchy.

Richard Blake, an investment counselor who lives on the "converted *Ton* class minesweeper" *Lord Jim,* is the undisputed leader of the community. Everything he touches is shipshape, though his wife Laura, who reads *Country Life,* dreams of a life onshore. Other members of the community, not quite so respectable, include Willis, a sixty-five-year-old marine artist who is trying to sell his leaky barge, and Maurice, a homosexual prosti-

tute, whose barge is used by an acquaintance as a repository for stolen goods: "record-players, electric guitars, transistors, electric haircurlers, electric toasters ... the strange currency of the 1960's."

The hero of *Offshore,* Nenna James, is thirty-two and a single mother whose private thoughts often take "the form of a kind of perpetual magistrate's hearing." When her husband left for Central America to find work, she took all that she had left and bought "a houseboat ... the barge *Grace.*" Both from within and from without, Nenna confronts witnesses who try to persuade her that it is time she put her feet on solid ground, for her two girls, Martha and Tilda, if not for herself. In the early morning hours Nenna often shares hushed conversations with Maurice, who at such moments praises the virtue of indecision: "When you decide, you multiply the things you might have done and now never can."

In the end *Grace* has its way, though it is clear that no one, not even Richard Blake, has a firm hand on life's tiller. Nenna faces changes that will take her from "the river's edge, where Virgil's ghosts held out their arms in longing for the farther shore," and her husband, recently returned to London, is swept out to sea with, of all people, Maurice.

Human Voices (1980) has yet to be published in the United States. Set at the BBC's Broadcast House (BH) during World War II, the novel evokes both BH, standing "headed on a fixed course south," with radio broadcasts "scattering human voices into the darkness of Europe," and blitz-wracked London at night, its inhabitants huddled for shelter in overcrowded underground stations while T. S. Eliot attends to the fire watch at his publisher's office, moving "in measure, like a dancer."

Sam Brooks, RPD (Director of Recorded Programmes), has slipped into midlife and appears spiritually comatose: he "felt no resentment and, indeed, very little recollection of what he had suffered the day before." He is generally found in his office running volume tests to a recording of *The Teddy Bears' Picnic*. Although Sam has a reputation for being overly attentive to his female assistants, his self-absorption is disturbed by his newest, fifteen-year-old Annie Asra, "the kind of girl to whom people give a job, even when they didn't originally intend to."

Jeffrey Haggard, DPP (Director of Programme Planning), is the inventor of "the ten-second cue," but he "had run through three wives and had lost his digestion into the bargain." As Jeff gazes at the front of Broadcast House, decorated with carvings of Prospero and Ariel, he asks himself what it means to be aligned with Ariel, "a liar, pretending that someone's father was drowned full fathom five." Jeff also wonders if this island, too, will inevitably revert to Caliban. Although drawing on her own experience working for the BBC during World War II, Fitzgerald is here once again concerned with larger notions of truth and human relationships.

Fitzgerald's next novel, *At Freddie's* (1982), set in London's theater district in the 1960s, concerns Temple School, dedicated to training children for juvenile roles in plays by William Shakespeare and the classics. The school sits in Baddeley Street "in the middle of Covent Garden," where the Opera House and the Theatre Royal "rose majestically, beset with heavy traffic, above a wash of fruit, flowers, and vegetables." Presiding over Temple School is Frieda Wentworth, or Freddie, whose smile betrays "a certain lopsidedness," her voice "a croak suggestive of long suffering." With the assistance of Miss Blewett ("the Bluebell"), an odd-job man, and a beleaguered accountant Freddie holds forth in an office whose aroma hints at "a church vestry where old clothes hang and flowers molder in the sink." She had begun her theatrical career working for Lilian Baylis at the Old Vic. Despite increasing pressure on her to change the school and prepare children to act in television commercials, Freddie stands firm for tradition.

At the beginning of the novel Freddie hires two young teachers. Hannah Graves is a young girl of twenty for whom "backstage was the enchantment." Pierce Carroll, thirty, is painfully honest and is someone who, Freddie detects, "was never likely to earn much money, or even expect to." Despite his decency, Pierce Carroll is basically unqualified to teach Freddie's children, who are "feverishly competitive, like birds in a stubble field, twitching looks over their shoulder to make sure they were still ahead." Hannah, who has caught the attention both of Pierce and of one Boney Lewis, a veteran of the stage, must decide between Pierce, a young man who understands that "most teachers are a good deal more competent than I am" and who proposes to her by, quite literally, drawing "a rough map," and Boney, an actor who drowns in alcohol any realization that he is past his prime.

Freddie faces the formidable challenge of a proposed National Junior Stage School, affiliated with the National Theatre and endowed with public funds. Understanding that she "fulfilled the one sure condition of being loved by the English nation . . . she had been going a very long time," Freddie launches an offensive through letters in the *Times,* responses to which are headed "At Freddies." Temple School even receives an unexpected visit from the Master, Noel Coward. While Miss Wentworth proves herself more than up to the challenge, the real surprise of the novel comes at the end when she reveals to businessman Joey Blatt, who has long sought to turn Temple School into a private limited company with himself as director, the love that truly lies at the heart of this venerable institution.

In the 1980s Fitzgerald was involved in several projects as an independent scholar. She edited and wrote an introduction for William Morris's previously unpublished *Novel on Blue Paper* (1982). In 1984 she published a biography of the early twentieth-century poet Charlotte Mew. Beginning in 1986, she wrote the introductions for the Virago/Penguin editions of nineteenth-century novelist Margaret Oliphant's *Chronicles of Carlingford* novels.

For her own sixth novel, *Innocence* (1986), Fitzgerald chose to abandon her familiar English setting in favor of that of Florence in the 1950s. The plot revolves around two families. The story of one, the aristocratic Ridolphis, begins earlier, in the sixteenth century; the story of the other, the working-class Rossis, starts in the formative years of Italian Marxism, the 1920s. British characters who appear in the novel are the Harringtons, an expatriate couple whose lives become briefly entangled with Ridolphi family matters, and a brash, outspoken schoolgirl, Lavinia "Barney" Barnes. As its title implies, *Innocence* explores more pervasively a theme that earlier novels had dealt with in a limited way: the vulnerability of innocents. As characters fall prey to their own ways of seeing, they become inscrutable to others and dangerous to themselves.

The novel opens with a record, taken from 1568, of a midget Ridolphi who married another midget. When a daughter was born, also a midget, the parents made arrangements to protect their daughter's feelings by bringing another young midget girl, a mute, to the villa as a companion for their daughter. In time this companion, Gemma, began to grow. Because the parents could not reveal to their daughter that they had deceived her, they allowed her to believe that it was her companion who was the freak. After several weeks of praying for her companion, the young Ridolphi was shown the only way to "protect" Gemma from the intrusions of the outside world: her eyes were put out and her legs cut off at the knees.

This misguided "beneficence" survives well into the twentieth century in a family with a tendency "towards rash decisions, perhaps always intended to ensure other people's happiness, once and for all." Count Giancarlo, sixty-five and born in a society where "Italian nobility had been put in their place," has survived a failed marriage with a wealthy American and is determined "to outface the last part of his life, and indeed of his character, by not minding about anything very much." His sister Maddalena, whose marriage to an English husband has also ended disappointingly, has created a "Refuge for the Unwanted," where toothless old women care for homeless infants. Giancarlo's daughter Chiara, seventeen and fresh from Holy Innocents convent school in England, falls in love with a young surgeon, Dr. Salvatore Rossi, whom she meets at the opera. In the eyes of Barney, Chiara's English schoolmate, Chiara is a hopeless innocent "who hopped into bed with the first man [she] saw when [she] got out of the convent."

Chiara's lover, Rossi, is a thirty-year-old neurologist from the southern village of Mazzata who had determined early that he would live free of constraints imposed by others. An avowed skeptic, he flees from both the faith of his mother, an ardent Catholic who had named him "in honour of the Saviour," and the politics of his father, a devoted follower of Antonio Gramsci, one of the founders of the Italian Communist Party. Early on, Salvatore determines that he must live free of the constraints imposed by others' wishes and be "self-created, self-determined, forewarned and unclassifiable." Despite his successes as a physician, he is unable to free himself from the certainty that his life is somehow false, false because his behavior, even his very thought, is shaped by everyone else, from a new wife and her aristocratic family to his own neighbors back in the unbeautiful village of Mazzata.

After Chiara suffers a miscarriage, she leaves Salvatore to go recuperate with friends. Despairing of ever living an authentic life, Rossi concludes that his wife and others have been out "to cut down a grown man" and that suicide may be the way to cure his soul. Driving out to the Valsassina estate, the home of Chiara's cousin Cesare, Rossi sees the reclusive young vintner working carefully, as had generations before him: "the vinestocks were like massed rows of stunted patients, each waiting for a few minutes' attention." In response to Rossi's insistence that things cannot possibly continue as they are, Cesare responds: "We can go on exactly like this for the rest of our lives."

Fitzgerald's seventh novel, *The Beginning of Spring* (1988), was also short-listed for the Booker Prize. Like *Innocence,* it is set on foreign soil: Moscow, five years before the revolution. While Angela Huth, writing for the *Sunday Telegraph,* acknowledged the courage of an English writer who dares "to enter Russian territory," Monique Charlesworth observed in the *Daily Telegraph* that Fitzger-

ald's novel "spans a few weeks, yet it evokes a whole life."

As in *Offshore, The Beginning of Spring* celebrates lives that are vulnerable to tides of change. Frank Reid is a second-generation English expatriate who has inherited his family's greatly diminished printing business. Given to self-scrutiny, Frank is a man who is unsettled in virtually every aspect of his life. An Englishman, he has come to see "dear, slovenly, mother Moscow" as his home. A nominal Anglican who struggles with unbelief, Frank nonetheless honors with his presence his employees' religious ceremonies. A devoted husband and father, he makes love to an unsettling young woman who has recently come into his house as a *nanka* (nanny).

A man in his forties, Frank has suddenly discovered that the very foundations of his life are coming undone. His wife Nellie, having caught a train for parts unknown (perhaps England), has sent back their three children. His relationship to a Russian merchant, Arkady Kuriatin, is strained after an incident that compromises the safety of Frank's children. A new accountant at the print works, Bernov, sees "the business . . . as an undeclared war against every employee below the rank of cost accountant," in sharp contrast with his old accountant Selwyn, an expatriate poet and an ardent disciple of novelist and philosopher Leo Tolstoy, who represents a spiritual dimension that Frank has long denied himself. No atheist, Frank has concluded, "Because I don't believe in this . . . that doesn't mean it's not true," but his own Anglican chaplain can offer no more encouragement to worship than to wave "sheets of paper at him in ironic invitation."

To Frank, who has come to feel "the winter of his discontent," young Lisa, who has taken Nellie's place at the dinner table, appears as an angel of life and rejuvenation. However, there are surprises yet in store as winter begins reluctantly to release Moscow from its grip, and the children return from a visit to their dacha, under whose veranda "there was much animal and vegetable life." The yardman, preparing for spring, chisels away the putty. The windows are opened wide, and "the sounds of Moscow broke in . . . and with the noise came the spring wind." For Frank Reid, too, this may be just the "beginning of spring."

Fitzgerald's eighth novel, *The Gate of Angels* (1990), was also short-listed for the Booker Prize. The setting is in 1912 at the fictional St. Angelicus, "a very small college" at Cambridge, founded in the fifteenth century by the antipope Benedict XIII. The novel's title may allude to the "twelve gates, and at the gates twelve angels" of the New Jerusalem mentioned in the Book of Revelation. Unlike those gates that "shall not be shut at all by day: for there shall be no night there," the tall, narrow "gate of Angels" has been found standing open only twice since the small college's founding.

John Bayley, writing for the *New York Review of Books* (9 April 1992), marveled at the "mesmeric insouciance" with which she re-creates a university and market town. With wry humor the narrator reminds the reader that "the way to Cambridge," despite the university's persistence in acting as though it had no connection to the outside world, takes one "up Mill Road past the cemetery and the workhouse."

In this bastion of tradition winds of change must blow with such force that cows are literally swept off their feet in "a scene of disorder, tree-tops on the earth, legs in the air, in a university city devoted to logic and reason." Angelicus, which "resembled a fortress, a toy fortress, but a toy of enormous strength," is the embodiment of contradictions. Because it was confirmed by an antipope, Benedict XIII, it enjoys "no real existence at all."

Angelicus is dedicated to science; but one of its leading physicists, Professor Flowerdew, denies the existence of atoms and, as a consequence, the research of Ernest Rutherford and C. T. R. Wilson upon which modern physics is founded. Moreover, Angelicus continues to maintain certain clerical traditions that go back to the Middle Ages. Fellows, for instance, are not permitted to marry, and "no female animals capable of reproduction were allowed on the college premises." At meetings of the Disobligers' Society, members must argue for positions opposite to what they actually believe. The master of Angelicus is blind. Nonetheless, his junior fellows understand that they are firmly under his control: "I know the voices of everyone in the college. I also know their steps."

Fred Fairly, a junior fellow at Angelicus, serves under Professor Flowerdew, whose empiricism denies belief in anything the naked eye cannot see. Fred, a rector's son, undergoes a loss of faith, but he discovers in this godless universe anything but freedom. For junior fellows at Angelicus, "you don't have to make up your mind . . . you are choiceless." As the novel opens, Fairly is writing a letter to a Miss Saunders, a young woman with whom he has recently shared a bed. Both Fred and Miss Saunders had been knocked unconscious in a bicycle accident involving a collision with a farmer's cart. A Mrs. Wrayburn, who had mistakenly assumed that Miss Saunders was "Mrs. Fairly," had placed them in the same bed, though nothing had happened between them. As Fred writes to Daisy, he is trying to sort out what he really thinks about a young woman with whom he had been in such close proximity but barely knows.

Raised by a single, working-class mother in the south of London, Daisy "had always been used to there being too many people." She "grew up to be tall and slender, but solid. She had substance to her." Understanding early on that an unattached young woman must earn her own way, she also knows that she could fall prey to "carny" employers intent on wheedling sexual favors. To discourage such advances Daisy takes to wearing on her wedding finger a gold ring that her Aunt Ellie had given her.

Following the death of her mother, Daisy enters nursing at Blackfriars Hospital as an "ordinary probationer." Though conscientious, she gets into trouble when she takes the treatment of a suicidal patient into her own hands. Having violated hospital policy, she loses her position and, in the process, catches the attention of Thomas Kelly, a sleazy journalist who offers her a night at "a hotel in Cambridge, quite near the station." When Kelly puts his arm round her waist, Daisy thinks: "What a pair we make. . . . He doesn't deserve any better, no more do I."

Daisy does deserve better, as most readers will agree. However, in this world good people do suffer and individuals as disparate as Fred Fairly, rector's son and Cambridge junior fellow, and Daisy Saunders, working girl from South London, are rarely united in happy endings. The novel's conclusion leaves many questions unresolved: will Fred resign himself to the life of bachelor don? What lies ahead for Daisy after her brief interlude in the arms of Kelly? For Fred, Daisy, and even the blind master of St. Angelicus the answers lie beyond "a door as narrow as a good-sized crack, standing wide open."

Fitzgerald's most recent novel, *The Blue Flower* (1995), was widely praised in Britain and short-listed for the *Irish Times* International Fiction Prize. Though one of Fitzgerald's most thoroughly researched novels and one of her longest, *The Blue Flower* is built of short chapters whose juxtapositions create an elliptical narrative. The novel is set in Saxony in the final years of the eighteenth century, a time and place largely unfamiliar to English readers. The protagonist of the novel is the German Romantic poet Friedrich von Hardenberg, who later wrote under the pseudonym Novalis. While it is not, in the strictest sense, an historical novel, *The Blue Flower* responds to Novalis's own challenge that "Novels arise out of the shortcomings of history." Frank Kermode, in the *London Review of Books*, marvels at "the sureness and economy with which the setting is established."

Dust jacket for Fitzgerald's novel about the German poet Novalis

At the beginning of the novel Fritz (as Fitzgerald calls him) has brought a university friend, Jacob Dietmahler, home to meet his family. Freiherr von Hardenberg, Fritz's father, is a man of Moravian piety and a ferocious temper. An impoverished aristocrat, he depends for his livelihood on his post as director of the Salt Mining Administration. Fritz's mother, the Freiherr's second wife, has borne her husband numerous children but suffers silently, not knowing "how she was going to get through the rest of her life." She tries, once, to share her feelings with Fritz, but he fails to comprehend the depth of his mother's despair.

Following studies at the universities at Jena, Leipzig, and Wittenberg, Fritz is sent by his father to Tennstedt, where Kreisamtmann Coelestin Just, a local presiding magistrate and tax collector, will teach Fritz what he needs to know to become a trainee clerk in the Directorate of Salt Mines. After he meets Just's twenty-seven-year-old niece, Karoline, Fritz likens their souls to "two watches, set to the same time." He shares with her his poetry and, on one occasion, a fragmentary narrative about a knightly hero who lies restless, stirred by inexpressible longings for the subject of a stranger's tale: a blue flower. When Karoline can only tell Fritz what this "blue flower" is *not,* she feels that she has let him

down. Fritz turns his attentions to another, and Karoline suffers in silence.

While studying under Kreisamtmann Just, Fritz is introduced to Rockenthiens, a former captain in the prince's army who lives with his wife and her children by a former marriage at her house at Grüningen. From the time he first meets her, Fritz is passionately devoted to Rockenthiens's twelve-year-old stepdaughter, Sophie von Kühn.

Apart from Fritz's brother Erasmus, who himself initially describes her as "a very noisy, very young girl," no one appears to see Sophie as Fritz sees her. When Fritz tells Dietmahler that Sophie's complexion "is like a rose," his friend responds that a physician has described it as yellowish. Fritz likens her to a Raphael self-portrait and calls her his "Philosophy," but Sophie writes in her diary little more than a sentence a day, usually concluding that "nothing much happened." She is capable of "raptures, absolutely genuine" over the gift of a box of sweets, but Sophie responds to Fritz's knight-hero in the narrative of the blue flower by saying "Why should he care about a flower? . . . He is not a woman, and he is not a gardener."

Sophie contracts tuberculosis and undergoes several operations, all painful, as anesthesia has not yet been invented. Erasmus, desperate for a lock of her hair (Sophie's only undisputed asset), learns that she is now bald. When Sophie worsens, her elder sister, Friederike von Mandelsloh, serves as her constant companion and nurse. Separated from her officer husband and with little joy for the future, Friederike faces the tasks of caring for Sophie with silent courage and determination.

Having set aside the austere Christianity of his father, Fritz has declared: "The external world is the world of shadows. The universe, after all, is within us." His muse is "artless" Sophie, and it is to her that he prays "be my spirit's guide." Nonetheless, Fritz, as Sophie languishes, cannot bear to dress her wounds. Leaving her to the care of Friederike, he suffers apart. Having sold all that he had, Novalis may be left not with a pearl of great price but with "a blue flower."

Penelope Fitzgerald's career as a novelist began late, when she was already nearly sixty, and she has enjoyed only moderate commercial success since then, with most of her novels largely unavailable in the United States and British editions often allowed to go out of print quickly. Her critical reputation in Great Britain has risen steadily, however, with her 1979 winning of the Booker Prize confirming her status as one of the most important contemporary British writers, a status that subsequent works have confirmed. The eighty-one-year-old Fitzgerald was named a judge on the 1998 Booker panel, a prestigious post previously held by such writers as Rebecca West, Philip Larkin, and A. S. Byatt. Her American reputation seems to be on the ascent as well. *The Blue Flower,* published in the United States in 1997, has won for Fitzgerald many new American readers and was awarded the twenty-first Annual Fiction Prize by the National Book Critics Circle in 1998, the first year non-U.S. citizens were eligible for this significant award.

References:

Bruce Bawer, "A Still, Small Voice: The Novels of Penelope Fitzgerald," *New Criterion,* 10, no. 7 (1992): 33–42;

Jean Sudrann, "'Magic or Miracles': The Fallen World of Penelope Fitzgerald's Novels," in *Contemporary British Women Writers: Texts and Strategies,* edited by Robert E. Hosmer Jr. (London: Macmillan, 1993), pp. 105–127.

Michael Frayn

(8 September 1933 -   )

Malcolm Page
Simon Fraser University

See also the Frayn entries in *DLB 13: British Dramatists Since World War II* and *DLB 14: British Novelists Since 1960.*

BOOKS: *The Day of the Dog* (London: Collins, 1962; Garden City, N.Y.: Doubleday, 1963);

The Book of Fub (London: Collins, 1963); republished as *Never Put Off to Gomorrah* (New York: Pantheon, 1964);

On the Outskirts (London: Collins, 1964);

The Tin Men (London: Collins, 1965; Boston: Little, Brown, 1965);

The Russian Interpreter (London: Collins, 1966; New York: Viking, 1966);

At Bay in Gear Street (London: Fontana, 1967; London & New York: S. French, 1970);

Towards the End of the Morning (London: Collins, 1967); republished as *Against Entropy* (New York: Viking, 1967);

A Very Private Life (London: Collins, 1968; New York: Viking, 1968);

The Two of Us (London: Fontana, 1970; London & New York: S. French, 1970)—comprises *Black and Silver, The New Quixote, Mr. Foot,* and *Chinamen*;

Sweet Dreams (London: Collins, 1973; New York: Viking, 1974);

Constructions (London: Wildwood House, 1974);

Alphabetical Order (London & New York: S. French, 1976);

Donkeys' Years (London & New York: S. French, 1977);

Alphabetical Order and Donkeys' Years (London: Eyre Methuen, 1977);

Clouds (London: Eyre Methuen, 1977; London & New York: S. French, 1977);

Make and Break (London: Eyre Methuen, 1980; London & New York: French, 1980);

Noises Off (London: Methuen, 1982; London & New York: S. French, 1982; revised edition, London: Methuen, 1983);

Michael Frayn (photograph © Jillian Edelstein)

The Original Michael Frayn: Satirical Essays, edited by James Fenton (Edinburgh: Salamander, 1983; London: Methuen, 1990);

Benefactors (London: Methuen, 1984; London & New York: S. French, 1984);

Plays: One (London: Methuen, 1985)—comprises *Alphabetical Order, Donkeys' Years, Clouds, Make and Break,* and *Noises Off*;

Clockwise: A Screenplay (London: Methuen, 1986);

Balmoral (London: Methuen, 1987);

First and Last (London: Methuen, 1989);

The Trick of It (New York & London: Viking, 1989);

Jamie on a Flying Visit and Birthday (London: Methuen, 1990);

Listen to This (London: Methuen, 1990);

Look Look (London: Methuen, 1990);

Audience (London & New York: S. French, 1991)

A Landing on the Sun (New York & London: Viking, 1991);

Plays: Two (London: Methuen, 1991)—comprises *Benefactors, Balmoral,* and *Wild Honey*;

Now You Know [novel] (New York and London: Viking, 1992);

Here (London: Methuen, 1993);

Now You Know [play] (London: Methuen, 1995);

Speak after the Beep: Studies in the Art of Communicating with Inanimate and Semi-Animate Objects (London: Methuen, 1995).

PLAY PRODUCTIONS: *Zounds!,* by Frayn and John Edwards, music by Keith Statham, Cambridge, May 1957;

The Two of Us, London, Garrick Theatre, 30 July 1970;

The Sandboy, London, Greenwich Theatre, 17 September 1971;

Alphabetical Order, London, Hampstead Theatre Club, 11 March 1975;

Donkeys' Years, London, Globe Theatre, 15 July 1976;

Clouds, London, Hampstead Theatre Club, 16 August 1976;

The Fruits of Enlightenment, adaptation of a play by Leo Tolstoy, London, National's Olivier Theatre, 14 February 1979;

Liberty Hall, London, Greenwich Theatre, 24 January 1980; revised as *Balmoral,* Bristol, Bristol Old Vic, 8 May 1987;

Make and Break, Hammersmith, Lyric Theatre, 18 March 1980;

Noises Off, Hammersmith, Lyric Theatre, 11 February 1982;

Benefactors, London, Vaudeville Theatre, 4 April 1984;

Wild Honey, adaptation of a play by Anton Chekhov, London, National's Lyttleton Theatre, 19 July 1984;

Number One, adaptation of a play by Jean Anouilh, London, Queen's Theatre, 24 April 1984;

Three Sisters, translation of a play by Chekhov, Manchester, Royal Exchange Theatre, 11 April 1985;

The Seagull, translation of a play by Chekhov, Watford, Palace Theatre, 7 November 1986;

Uncle Vanya, translation of a play by Chekhov, London, Vaudeville Theatre, 24 May 1988;

The Sneeze, adaptation of works by Chekhov, London, Aldwych Theatre, 19 September 1988;

Exchange, translation and adaptation of a play by Yuri Trifonov, Southampton, Nuffield Theatre, 21 November 1989;

Look Look, London, Aldwych Theatre, 30 March 1990;

Here, London, Donmar Warehouse, 29 July 1993;

Now You Know, London, Hampstead Theatre, 19 July 1995;

La Belle Vivette, adaptation, with book and lyrics by Frayn, of Jacques Offenbach's *La Belle Helene,* London, English National Opera, 11 December 1995;

Copenhagen, London, National Theatre, 28 May 1998.

MOTION PICTURES: *Clockwise,* screenplay by Frayn, Moment Films/Thorn EMI, 1986;

Remember Me?, screenplay by Frayn, Talisman Productions/Channel Four Films, 1997.

TELEVISION SCRIPTS: "What the Papers Say," 35 episodes, Granada, 1 March 1962–28 January 1966;

"Second City Reports," 6 episodes, by Frayn and John Bird, Granada, March–May 1964;

Jamie on a Flying Visit, "Wednesday Play," BBC, 17 January 1968;

One Pair of Eyes, BBC, 26 October 1968;

Birthday, BBC, 12 February 1969;

"Beyond a Joke," by Frayn, Bird, and Eleanor Bron, 6 episodes, BBC, April–May 1972;

Laurence Sterne Lived Here, "Writers' Houses," BBC, 9 August 1973;

Imagine a City Called Berlin, BBC, 1 March 1975;

Making Faces, 6 parts, BBC 2, 25 September–30 October 1975;

Vienna: The Mask of Gold, BBC 2, 1 May 1977;

Three Streets in the Country, BBC, 2 February 1979;

The Long Straight, "Great Railway Journeys of the World," BBC, 6 November 1980;

Jerusalem, BBC, 1984;

Magic Lantern: Prague, BBC, 2 November 1993;

First and Last, BBC, 12 December 1989;

A Landing on the Sun, BBC, 8 June 1994;

Budapest: Written in Water, BBC, 22 April 1996.

OTHER: Alan Bennett and others, *Beyond the Fringe,* introduction by Frayn (London: Souvenir, 1963; New York: Random House, 1963);

John B. Morton, *The Best of Beachcomber,* selected, with an introduction by Frayn (London: Heinemann, 1963);

Timothy Birdsall, *Timothy,* edited by Frayn and Bamber Gascoigne (London: M. Joseph, 1963);

"Festival," in *The Age of Austerity, 1945–51,* edited by Michael Sissons and Philip French (London: Hodder & Stoughton, 1963), pp. 330–352;

"Australia: The Long Straight," in *Great Railway Journeys of the World* (London: BBC, 1981; New York: Dutton, 1982), pp. 71–95;

Bennett and others, *The Complete Beyond the Fringe,* edited by Roger Wilmut, introduction by Frayn (London: Methuen, 1987).

Dust jacket for the U.S. edition of Frayn's novel about an English student who serves as interpreter for a mysterious businessman in Moscow

TRANSLATIONS: Anton Chekhov, *The Cherry Orchard* (London: Methuen, 1978);

Leo Tolstoy, *The Fruits of Enlightenment* (London: Eyre Methuen, 1979);

Chekhov, *Three Sisters* (London: Methuen, 1983);

Chekhov, *Wild Honey* (London, Methuen, 1984);

Jean Anouilh, *Number One* (London: S. French, 1985);

Chekhov, *The Seagull* (London: Methuen, 1986);

Chekhov, *Uncle Vanya* (London, Methuen, 1987);

Chekhov, *Plays* (London: Methuen, 1988)—comprises *The Cherry Orchard, The Seagull, Three Sisters, Uncle Vanya,* and four one-act plays;

Chekhov, *The Sneeze: Plays and Stories* (London: Methuen, 1989)—comprises translations of four one-act plays and adaptations of four short stories;

Yuri Trifonov, *Exchange* (London: Methuen, 1990).

SELECTED PERIODICAL PUBLICATION–
UNCOLLECTED: "Oh Father, Look on Your Child with a Favourable Beak," *Sunday Telegraph,* 3 December 1995, Review section, p. 9.

Michael Frayn's versatility has prevented his full recognition in any of the areas he has worked in during a forty-year career: novelist, comic novelist, lay philosopher, humorist, translator of classic plays, and writer for the stage, film, and television. He is a shrewd observer of the way people live, with a distinctive philosophical turn of mind. Equally, he has mastered a distinctive vein of comedy–observant, whimsical, linguistic–treated in ways that range from unashamed farce to a deceptively light tone. Chronologically, Frayn's major work falls into four phases: five novels between 1965 and 1973, nine stage plays between 1970 and 1984, three more novels between 1989 and 1992, and five more stage plays between 1990 and 1998.

Michael Frayn was born on 8 September 1933 in Mill Hill in north London; his mother was the former Violet Alice Lawson, and his father, Thomas Allen Frayn, was a salesman for an asbestos company. When Frayne was eighteen months old the family moved to Ewell, on the southwest fringe of London. Frayn says: "Everyone puts down the suburbs but they're very pleasant places to live. It's quite amazing how little they've changed in 40 years. They should be taken more seriously." He attended what he describes as "a dreadful private day school at Sutton, where the headmaster used to cane about 20 boys every morning after prayers." He went on to Kingston Grammar School, which he found "merely rather dull and shabby, an imposing brick facade disguising an awful lot of corrugated iron."

He left with a state scholarship to Emmanuel College, Cambridge, but first had to do his two years of national service, from 1952 to 1954. Starting out in the Royal Artillery, he was recruited into the Intelligence Corps and taught Russian–fourteen hours a day for eighteen months, billeted in villages near Cambridge. Instructors reminded him: "At any time, any time, you may be parachuted behind the Russian lines. You do understand that?" In his first year at Cambridge he read Russian and French but found that though "he got on well with the language, when it came to the literature he couldn't see for the life of him what to write down." For his remaining two years he changed to moral sciences (philosophy). He wrote prolifically at Cambridge, producing columns in both *Varsity* and *Granta,* as well as a weekly cartoon strip for *Varsity;* he also wrote most of *Zounds!,* the 1957 Footlights show, a revue staged annually in May Week. He remarked that in those years "the art-forms most passionately aspired to were musical comedy, revue, jazz, singing to a guitar, posters–anything that was predominantly entertaining and stylish. Our brand of humour was what was then called by its admirers 'off-beat,' which meant whimsical; carefully artless sub-Thurber cartoons, fantasies based, in what was hoped to pass for the style of Paul Jennings, upon archaic railway regulations and the like."

After leaving Cambridge he joined *The Guardian* as a reporter; although he was based in Manchester, in 1959 he spent a month in Moscow covering Prime Minister Harold Macmillan's visit to that city. The same year he moved to London with the task of writing a column, "Miscellany," three times a week. "As Frayn saw it, his job with Miscellany was to write cool, witty interviews with significant film directors passing through, but there were never enough film directors so he started making up humorous paragraphs to fill," explains Terry Coleman. He invented for the column the Don't Know Party and such characters as the trendy Bishop of Screwe; Rollo Swavely, a public relations consultant; and the ambitious suburban couple, Horace and Doris Morris. In 1962 his move from *The Guardian* to *The Observer* (London), where his only duty was a weekly column, gave him more time for his own writing. The tone of the column, which he continued until 1968, slowly changed to a more serious examination of the contemporary urban liberal. Four collections of his columns were published in book form: *The Day of the Dog* (1962), *The Book of Fub* (1963), *On the Outskirts* (1964), and *At Bay in Gear Street* (1967). In 1960 he married Gillian Palmer; with their three daughters, Jenny, Susanna, and Rebecca, they eventually settled in Blackheath, in southeast London. He divorced his first wife in 1989 and married Claire Tomalin, well known as a biographer, in 1993.

The whimsical tone of his first novel, *The Tin Men* (1965), is almost that of a sustained column from *The Guardian*. The book is set in the William Morris Institute of Automation Research; its plot revolves around the financing and opening of a new wing. The collection of odd characters includes the sports fanatic who tries to be responsible for security, the would-be novelist who cannot get further than writing the blurb and reviews for his nonexistent book, and the researcher who reads everything backward, "setting himself and solving outrageous problems of comprehension in every paragraph." Most of the fun involves computers: the automating of football because the director believes "the main object of organised sports and games is to produce a profusion of statistics"; the programmed newspaper, which prints the core of familiar stories such as "I Test New Car" and "Child Told Dress Unsuitable by Teacher"; and Delphic I, the Ethical Decision Machine, which expresses the depth and intensity of its moral processes in units called pauls, calvins, and moscses. The story ends: "Epoch IV is a computer that writes books and *The*

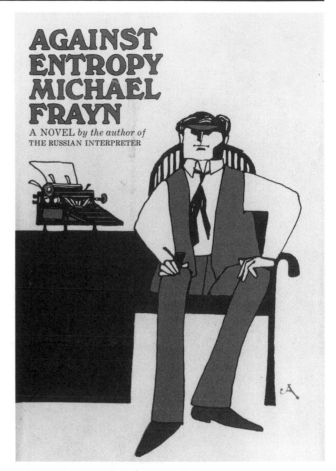

Dust jacket for the U.S. edition of Frayn's comic novel about the tribulations of a newspaper editor

Tin Men is its first novel." Amid the clever jokes there is a kernel of anxiety about the dangerous potential of computers and the limitations of the men responsible for them.

Most critics, such as Francis Hope of *The New Statesman,* found the book good fun: "Frayn's gifts include a Wodehousian felicity: the whole Institute rings with 'the bongling and goingling of steel scaffolding poles being thrown down from a great height.'" Similarly, Peter Buckman in *The Nation* noted, "It's farce from start to finish, without even a straight character against whom the weirdies can be compared." Julian Gloag in *Saturday Review* was more scornful: "You'll smile all right at *The Tin Men,* but it'll be the smile you give to a good joke you've heard before." The *Times Literary Supplement* faulted the framework: "The story is flimsy and ordinary... Frayn's mind, his sense of the ridiculous and his actual writing are all too good to be trivialized in this way." William Trevor in *The Listener* inevitably judged the book as "like a particularly good Frayn piece blown up to size, with extra bits added and a plot thrown in." He praised Frayn, however, as "the only hatchet man of

Dust jacket for the U.S. edition of Frayn's fantasy about life in the future

contemporary letters to combine a consistent attack with something that looks like a purpose."

Frayn's second novel, *The Russian Interpreter* (1966), is about an English research student in Moscow. He serves as interpreter for a mysterious businessman who seeks ordinary Russians for exchange trips, and they become involved with a Russian girl. Though the streets and weather are carefully described, the action soon moves swiftly. Books are stolen and sought; someone is tricking someone else; espionage or smuggling is occurring; and the reader continues, waiting for the explanations. Even when the two Englishmen are imprisoned the tone remains cheerful, and the book predictably ends with their release and flight home to England. The novel won Frayn a Somerset Maugham Award for 1966 (the prize money being spent on travel in the United States) and the Hawthornden Prize in 1967.

Critics treated the book gingerly, uncertain whether it deserved to be taken seriously. R. G. G. Price in *Punch* dismissed it as "just another novel making mild fun of cold war melodrama," and P. M.

of *The Christian Science Monitor* saw only "an atmosphere of self-righteous dullness." Bill Byrom of *The Spectator* was amused: "There are eleven good belly-laughs, and the rest is trim and shipshape and elegant." The *New Yorker* reviewer, on the other hand, thought the humor harmed the novel: because it "is a comedy, nobody comes to grief—or even looks as if he might—which rather eliminates the possibility of suspense." The *Times Literary Supplement* was earnest, calling it "a rather mournful story about the shabby half-world of deceit that surrounds dealing, on even the most personal level, between East and West."

The American title of Frayn's third novel, *Against Entropy* (1967), points to opposing inertia and conformity; the British one, *Towards the End of the Morning* (1967), points to the growing sense of life's being circumscribed that comes in one's mid thirties (the hero "had spent his youth as one might spend an inheritance, and he had no idea of what he had bought with it"). Frayn's thirty-seven-year-old protagonist is a features editor, gathering crosswords and the columns for "Meditations" and "The Country Day by Day." Endlessly worried about repairs to his Victorian house in London and about his West Indian neighbors, he dreams of escape and believes that appearing as a television panelist could make this possible. The comic plot centers around a newspaper office, and the story ends farcically as the man desperately tries to get a plane back from the Middle East in time for his television appearance. Some passages suggest that Frayn perhaps intended more, a fuller study of his hero's marriage and serious focus on the future of newspapers, but these possibilities are not pursued. Of his sources for the book, Frayn remarked: "About two per cent is based on my time on *The Guardian,* two on *The Observer* and 96 on my imagination."

Some critics concentrated on the account of life in a newspaper office. Philip Howard wrote in *The Times* (London) that the novel "catches the quirks and eccentricities of newspapers better than any previous book . . . In parts it is uncannily like home life in our dear old Printing House Square. . . . Nobody has ever recorded so truthfully and so funnily the facts about the nutters who besiege the front door of a newspaper with messages from God, expenses, . . . galley proofs, and freebies." The *Times Literary Supplement* reviewer, however, recognized that more important was "the more serious and delicate theme of the journalists' home lives . . . Frayn shows the private relationships within the public relations." Stephen Wall in *The Observer* admired the characterizations of the women: "the clueless Tessa, Bob's girl, and Dyson's wife—are treated with much gentleness. The Dyson marriage, in fact, comes through with remarkable solidity." The theme for the *Times Literary Supplement* reviewer, finally, "is time, is change, is quite simply the business of people, institutions and society growing older."

A Very Private Life (1968) is written in future tense, beginning "Once upon a time there will be a little girl called Uncumber." In this world, "inside people" spend their entire lives in windowless houses, making contact by "holovision" and receiving supplies by tube and tap. During their long lives they use drugs (such as Pax, Hilarin, and Orgasmin) for every experience. In chapters of two and three pages Frayn explains how life has grown more private: first through physical isolation, then through the reliance on drugs to cope with anger and uncertainty. The opening pages set the scene slowly; then Uncumber, unhappy with her life, seeks out a man on the other side of the world whom she has met through a wrong number on holovision. Found, he turns out to be an "outside person," speaking a language unknown to her, living in a decaying palace by the sea, and going out daily to work. Eventually leaving him, she is lost in a jungle and spends a night with some bandits before being found by the Kind People and then rehabilitated as an "inside person."

The story is compelling: part fairy tale, as the opening implies; part fantasy; and part morality tale. Certain details echo both Aldous Huxley's *Brave New World* (1932)—"decanted" babies—and the distant future of H. G. Wells's *The Time Machine* (1895), with weak Top People dependent on slaves. The *Times Literary Supplement* reviewer pointed out the relevance of Frayn's topics: "drugs, both medical and hallucinogenic, longevity, the treatment of personality, penology ('We don't think in terms of *guilt* and *innocence*. We just ask: are you happy, or are you unhappy?'), mass communications dropping-out, the reduction of so many aspects of life to numbers or to strips of magnetic tape." Frayn's concern with where society is headed is focused on technology's making possible a new kind of isolation that excludes uncomfortable realities. He is still intent on telling a good story, however, and the moralizing remains discreet.

Critics were impressed with both theme and form in this fable. Stephen Wall noted in *The Observer:* "Frayn has realised that what technology looks like making possible is a new kind of isolation. When all needs can be satisfied by impersonal agencies a man can become an island quite happily." Wall, however, was bothered by the style: "Its literary quality is uneven. The prose is sharpest when it's critical—when it has a bantering relationship

John Cleese in a scene from the movie Clockwise, *for which Frayn wrote the screenplay*

with current clichés of thought and word; it is less impressive as an instrument of narrative." Frederick P. W. McDowell in *Contemporary Literature* identified different faults: "A thinness of line and elaboration perhaps obtrudes. Progression in the tale is always linear, and the complexities of Uncumber's problems are not all adequately delineated. Moreover, the characters lack the complexity which the inhabitants of his less allegorical satires reveal." Malcolm Bradbury in *The Guardian,* however, had high praise: "The book's ultimate virtue is the rigorous, brilliant intelligence with which Frayn holds its stuff within a totally consistent universe."

Published in 1973, *Sweet Dreams* focuses on a typical middle-class, thirtyish, liberal Londoner who is killed and goes to heaven. He discovers that he can fly, speak any language, be any age, and find things he had thought irretrievable. Assigned to create the Matterhorn, he is then sent back to England

Dust jacket for Frayn's epistolary novel about a literary scholar who marries a writer

"if one does occasionally wish for more acid and even for more discussion these are witty dreams and not uninstructive." In *The Guardian* P. J. Kavanagh stressed the humor: "All this is extremely gloomy and very funny. Packed with jokes, parodies and asides, most of them on slow fuses so you catch them a beat late. . . . Frayn has the gift of making you laugh at someone, then he stands back mildly to watch whether you notice the joke is also on you." Margaret Drabble in *The New York Times Book Review* had only praise: "It is lucid, intelligent, delightful, stylish, extremely funny." Christopher Hudson of *New Society* also had no hesitations: the novel was "a small masterpiece, beautifully written, funny, perceptive."

For the rest of the 1970s and most of the 1980s Frayn concentrated on writing plays, both for television and for the stage, winning several awards, including an Emmy in 1990 for *First and Last* (1989). His translations and adaptations of several of Anton Chekhov's plays were also staged, and in 1986 a motion-picture comedy starring John Cleese, *Clockwise,* for which Frayn wrote the screenplay, was released.

With *The Trick of It* (1989) Frayn returned once more to the novel. The book is cast in the form of the letters of RD, a young lecturer in English, to a friend in Australia. He specializes in the work of a woman novelist, JL. He invites her to speak at his obscure university, then spends the night with her, though realizing he has found a new taboo, "against intercourse with an author on your own reading list. . . . Somewhere in common or statute law there must be a distant parallel; illicit sexual relations with a reigning monarch, perhaps." They fall in love, marry, and move to the country; then RD impulsively gives up his job, and the couple moves to Abu Dhabi. His wife's next novel displeases RD, and he suggests improvements, which are ignored. She then writes about his mother without mentioning him: now she is feeding off his world. She will not read his writing. He attempts a novel: "I don't see why the great castle of fiction should remain the exclusive preserve of the privileged few. I don't see why it shouldn't be made over to the National Trust, and thrown open to the populace at large. It's a trade, writing, that anyone can learn, not a Masonic mystery. Part of my aim is to demonstrate that any bloody fool can do it." He fails, for he has not "the trick of it." He comes to value his letters (which comprise the novel), then discovers that the recipient has lost them. Ultimately, he is an unreliable narrator, about both JL and himself.

The Trick of It is essentially playful. The novel is a university story, similar to those of David

to compose a report on its condition, then retires to the countryside only to rebound as right-hand man to God—who is rich, brilliant, and upper-class and says things such as "To get anything done at all one has to move in tremendously mysterious ways." The reader slowly realizes that the hero's heavenly progress is nearly identical to his earthly one, in this deceptively charming tale told with wit and flourish.

Julian Symons in *The Sunday Times* admitted to uncertainty: "It is difficult, though, to know just how to take Mr. Frayn, who offers without discernible irony a travel-brochure Heaven. . . . Frayn's intentions are probably more serious than his manner, which is almost too light in its butterfly flitting from subject to subject." Janice Elliott in *The Sunday Telegraph* concluded that "there are two elements missing: rage and love. . . . Within the limits of his humanity, man . . . is infinitely more various and flexible than Mr. Frayn would have us believe." The *Times Literary Supplement* reviewer was cautiously balanced, calling Frayn's characterizations "deft" if a "little indulgent" and remarking

Lodge and Malcolm Bradbury. Frayn displays an awareness of contemporary literary criticism (a student is referred to as "my female Foucault from Flixwich.") More seriously, Frayn demonstrates how the mysteries of the creator are beyond the cleverest speculations of the academic. The novelist can do without the critic; the critic needs the author.

Lawrence Osborne, writing in *The Spectator,* was one of the few reviewers to dislike the novel, calling it "a preciously twisted idea" that might have worked with "a more tense, more chilling style," but not Frayn's, which he termed "bantering intellectualised badinage" with a plot that "peters out feebly in self-indulgent pathos, amateurish parables and vacant profundity."

A more typical response came from Andrew Davies in *The Listener:* "The narrator, being an academic, prefers his novels to be highly self-conscious and 'ludic,' well kitted out with distancing ironic frameworks. He'd be well pleased with this one, which is as ludic as they come (and a lot funnier than most books which parade their playfulness), eminently decodable, mouth-wateringly allusive, as crafty as Nabokov." Bradbury was enthusiastic in *The Sunday Times:* "Like William Golding's *The Paper Men,* this is a book about who owns the livingness of the living writer; it is funny, moving, intricately constructed and done with an observant wisdom. . . . The book is about what makes writing living, and it lives. . . . I have not encountered such easy and delightful wit and wisdom in a new work of fiction in years."

While most reviewers emphasized just the humor in the novel, Anthony Burgess wrote in *The Observer* that "*The Trick of It,* at the end anyway, very nearly made me weep. And yet it is one of the few books I have read in the last year that has provoked laughter."

A Landing on the Sun (1991) is again hugely ingenious. A dull civil servant, Jessel, is asked to investigate the death sixteen years earlier of Summerchild, found dead after a fall from the Ministry of Defence building: was it really an accident? With a television enquiry starting, the file on Summerchild is reopened. Jessel proceeds to discover the attic used by Summerchild, transcripts of conversations, and then a biscuit tin of tapes. The conventions thus far are those of a spy novel. Summerchild, however, was heading a new Policy Unit to look "at the quality of life we should be working towards for our people." He had sought the help of an Oxford philosopher, Elizabeth Serafin. While the task had at first been seen in terms of devices such as washing machines, Serafin changed the issue to the nature of happiness. Jessel gradually grasps that Summerchild

Dust jacket for the U.S. edition of Frayn's novel about the fleeting nature of happiness

and Serafin had fallen in love and found happiness, a brief "landing on the sun." Jessel comes to relive three past lives: his own and the two he is studying.

Ronald Bryden, in his review for *The New York Times,* observed that this was the first work by Frayn "to combine most of the skills from all his careers. It is a very funny satire on bureaucracies, particularly the British Civil Service, and partly a spy novel or whodunit, sewn with small Hitchcock shivers. . . . In part, it turns into a play, or at least a dialogue to which the protagonist is audience." Several critics remarked on the satire, among them Michael M. Thomas in *The Washington Post:* "No one sends up the chatter of the chattering classes—talk-show pundits, civil service types, academics—better than Frayn, but he does other voices, too."

Frayn continues here his examination of the art of the novel and the novelist begun in *The Trick of It,* but the greatest strength of *A Landing on the Sun* is its exploration of the condition of happiness. Frances Hill notes in *The Times:* "Frayn suggests that happiness is a fleeting condition, never experienced in isolation from its opposite, but by contrast to it and mixed with it."

Dust jacket for the U.S. edition of Frayn's novel about the slippery nature of truth

Frayn wrote the script for the television adaptation of *A Landing on the Sun,* which was broadcast by the BBC in June 1994. His next novel, *Now You Know,* similarly appeared in multiple forms, as a novel in 1992, as a stage play three years later, and then published as a play (1995).

Matthew Parris in *The Times* remarks on how closely the novel *Now You Know* resembles drama, with its structure of "time-consecutive, on-the-spot reports" as characters take turns to narrate the story, and the novel "becomes a play without stage directions or even direct dialogue, with player after player stepping forward onto the stage apron and taking the audience into their confidence with a personal soliloquy."

Technique underlines the main theme of *Now You Know,* the slipperiness of truth. Terry, a devious though likeable Cockney, runs OPEN, dedicated to the principle of open government. Having scrutinized the Treasury and Ministries of Defence and the Environment, he moves on to the Home Office and the case of an Asian found dead in a police cell. Hilary, a pretty young civil servant, leaks important information on the case to Terry. They become lovers though Terry has a long-term mistress, Jacqui. As Francis King observes in *The Spectator:* "Frayn neatly contrasts Terry's demands for open government with the secrecy with which he is careful to shroud his own emotional life." Nearly everyone in the novel is dishonest at some level.

Other critics chose to focus on the astute comic observation. Peter Reading remarks in the *Times Literary Supplement* that the interest in the novel lies in its "cast of diverse and diverting humanity" successfully evoked by Frayn but adds that mainly "it's Terry's homespun analyses of himself and his world on which the reader is privileged to eavesdrop."

By constructing *Now You Know* as a collection of monologues, Frayn avoided a problem that novel writing had always presented for him: "One of the pleasures of writing plays is that you never speak in your own voice. You speak through the voices of your characters. But novels have to be written in your voice alone." Frayn has also remarked, however, that "The form chooses you, not the other way round. An idea comes and is already embodied in a form."

Frayn briefly resumed the role of columnist for *The Guardian* in 1995, with the resulting pieces collected later that year in *Speak after the Beep: Studies in the Art of Communicating with Inanimate and Semi-Animate Objects.* In 1998 he returned to the London stage, with two new plays scheduled for production, *Copenhagen* and *Alarms (and Excursions).*

Frayn's lasting contributions to literature include his translations of Anton Chekhov; his funniest dramatic pieces, notably *Clockwise* and the perennial repertory favorite, *Noises Off;* his undervalued comedy of philosophical concepts, *Here* (1993); and the shrewd, lightly moralistic plays *Make and Break* (1980) and *Benefactors* (1984).

Frayn's search in his novels is for a comic framework of accurate study of human beings that will allow him to comment socially and philosophically in witty and elegant language. The fables, *A Very Private Life* and *Sweet Dreams,* are complete, self-contained, unrepeatable successes. The three latest novels reveal Frayn more completely integrating his serious meditations, his comic gifts, his flair for precise yet satirical observation, and his ability to invent original plots.

Interviews:

John Grigg, "More Than a Satirist," *Observer,* 11 June 1967;

Terry Coleman, "Towards the End of Frayn's Morning," *Guardian,* 1 October 1968, p. 6;

Hugh Hebert, "Letters Play," *Guardian,* 11 March 1975, p. 12;

Ian Jack, "Frayn, Philosopher of the Suburbs," *Sunday Times* (London), 13 April 1975, p. 43;

Russell Davies, "Michael Frayn, Witty and Wise," *Observer,* 18 July 1976, p. 8;

Ray Connolly, "Playwrights on Parade," *Sunday Times* (London), 27 January 1980, p. 32;

Craig Raine, "The *Quarto* Interview," *Quarto,* 4 (March 1980): 3–6;

Pendennis, "Tom Frayn's Son," *Observer,* 27 April 1980, p. 44;

"Why Frayn Went to Mock and Stayed to Pray," *Guardian,* 6 February 1982,

Benedict Nightingale, "Michael Frayn: the Entertaining Intellect" *New York Times Magazine,* 8 December 1985, pp. 66–68, 125–128, 133;

David Kaufman, "The Frayn Refrain," *Horizon,* (January–February 1986): 33–36;

Lesley Thornton, "Funny You Should Say That . . ." *Observer,* 23 February 1986, 24–26;

Miriam Gross, "A Playwright of Many Parts," *Sunday Telegraph,* 30 November 1986, p.17;

Mark Lawson, "The Mark of Frayn," *Drama,* 3 (1988): 7–9;

Mick Martin, "A Not So Cosy Bear," *Plays International* (September 1988): 18;

Mark Lawson, "The Man Who Isn't Ayckbourn," *Independent Magazine,* 17 September 1988, pp. 40–42;

Blake Morrison, "Front Legs and Back Legs," *Observer,* 17 September 1989;

Penny Perrick, "The Adaptability of Michael Frayn," *Sunday Times* (London), 17 September 1989, G8–9;

Heather Neill, "Bleak Comedy of a Changing World," *Times* (London), 24 October 1989, p. 15;

Stephen Pile, "The Other Mr. Frayn," *Daily Telegraph Magazine,* 31 March 1990, pp. 17–21;

Heather Neill, "A Philosopher Speaks," *Times* (London), 17 April 1990;

Robert Hewison, "A Last Look," *Sunday Times* (London), 6 May 1990, E1;

John L. DiGaetani, *A Search for a Postmodern Theatre* (New York: Greenwood Press, 1991), pp. 73–81;

Patrick Stoddart, "The Play's Still the Thing," *Times* (London), 8 June 1994, p. 22.

Bibliography:

Malcolm Page, comp., *File on Frayn* (London: Methuen, 1994).

References:

John Bull, *Stage Right* (London: Macmillan, 1994), pp. 156–177;

Richard Allen Cave, *New British Drama in Performance on the London Stage, 1970–1985* (Gerrards Cross: Colin Smythe, 1987), pp. 61–66, 103–104;

Albert-Reiner Glaap, "Order and Disorder on Stage and in Life: Farce Majeure in Frayn's Plays," in *Studien zur Asthetik des Gegenswartstheaters,* edited by Christian W. Thomsen (Heidelberg: Carl Winter, 1985), pp. 195–208;

Vera Gottlieb, "Why This Farce?," *New Theatre Quarterly*, no. 27 (August 1991): 217–228;

Christopher Innes, *Modern British Drama 1890–1990* (Cambridge: Cambridge University Press, 1992), pp. 312–324;

"Michael Frayn," in *The Observer Book of Profiles,* edited by Robert Low (London: W. H. Allen, 1991), pp. 170–173;

Katherine Worth, "Farce and Michael Frayn," *Modern Drama,* 16 March 1983, 47–53.

Alasdair Gray
(28 December 1934 –)

Anne Margaret Daniel
Princeton University

BOOKS: *The Comedy of the White Dog* (Glasgow: Print Studio Press, 1979);

Lanark: A Life in Four Books (Edinburgh: Canongate, 1981; New York: Harper & Row, 1981);

Unlikely Stories, Mostly (Edinburgh: Canongate, 1983; New York: Penguin, 1984);

1982 Janine (London: Cape, 1984; New York: Viking, 1984);

The Fall of Kelvin Walker: A Fable of the Sixties (Edinburgh: Canongate, 1985; New York: Braziller, 1986);

Lean Tales, by Gray, James Kelman, and Agnes Owens (London: Cape, 1985);

Saltire Self-Portrait 4 (Edinburgh: The Saltire Society, 1988);

Old Negatives: Four Verse Sequences (London: Cape, 1989);

McGrotty and Ludmilla; or, The Harbinger Report: A Romance of the Eighties (Glasgow: Dog and Bone, 1990);

Something Leather (London: Cape, 1990);

Poor Things: Episodes from the Early Life of Archibald McCandless M.D., Scottish Public Health Officer (London: Bloomsbury, 1992; New York: Harcourt Brace Jovanovich, 1992);

Why Scots Should Rule Scotland (Edinburgh: Canongate, 1992); revised as *Why the Scots Should Rule Scotland 1997* (Edinburgh: Canongate, 1997);

Ten Tales Tall and True (London: Bloomsbury, 1993);

A History Maker (Edinburgh: Canongate, 1994; revised edition, San Diego: Harcourt Brace, 1996);

Mavis Belfrage: A Romantic Tale; with Five Shorter Tales (London: Bloomsbury, 1996);

Working Legs: A Play for People without Them (Glasgow: Dog and Bone, 1997).

OTHER: *The Anthology of Prefaces: A Short History of Literate Thought in English Taken from Writers of Four Nations,* edited by Gray (London: Bloomsbury, forthcoming 1999).

Alasdair Gray (photograph by Renate von Mangoldt)

PLAY PRODUCTIONS: *Dialogue,* Edinburgh, Pool Lunchtime Theatre, 1971;

Homeward Bound, Pool Lunchtime Theatre, Edinburgh, 1971;

The Fall of Kelvin Walker, 1972;

The Loss of the Golden Silence, Edinburgh, 1973;

McGrotty and Ludmilla, Glasgow, Tron Theatre, 1975;

Tickly Mince, by Gray, Tom Leonard, and Liz Lochhead, Glasgow, Tron Theatre, Edinburgh, and The Pleasance, 1982;

The Pie of Damocles, by Gray, Lochhead, Leonard, and James Kelman, Glasgow, Tron Theatre, and Edinburgh, and The Pleasance, 1983;

Working Legs: A Play for People without Them, Cumbernauld, Alpha Project, 1998.

TELEVISION SCRIPTS: *Under the Helmet,* BBC TV, 1965;

The Fall of Kelvin Walker, BBC 2 Television, 1968;

Dialogue, Granada Television, 1972;

Martin, Scottish BBC Schools, 1972;

Agnes Belfrage/Cholchis/Triangles, Granada Television, 1972;

Today and Yesterday, BBC TV Scotland, 1972;

The Man Who Knew about Electricity, BBC Television, 1973;

Honesty, Granada Television, 1974;

Henry Prince, as Martin Green, Granada Television, 1976;

The Gadfly, Granada Television, 1977;

The Story of a Recluse, adapted from the story by Robert Louis Stevenson, BBC 2 Television, 1987.

RADIO SCRIPTS: *Quiet People,* BBC Radio Scotland, 1968;

Dialogue, BBC Radio, 1969;

Thomas Muir of Huntershill, BBC Radio Scotland, 1970;

The Night Off, BBC Radio Scotland, 1971;

The Loss of the Golden Silence, BBC Radio Scotland, 1974;

The Harbinger Report, BBC Radio, 1975;

McGrotty and Ludmilla, BBC Radio, 1975;

The Vital Witness, Scottish BBC Radio, 1979;

Near the Driver, West Deutsche Rundfunk, 1983.

Dust jacket, with drawing by Gray, for his novel in which sadomasochism does not figure until the last chapter

"Alasdair Gray," writes Gray at the beginning of his tale *A History Maker* (1994), "is a fat old asthmatic Glaswegian who lives by painting and writing." Gray's summation does not intimate the extremely high critical regard in which he has been held since the appearance in 1981 of *Lanark: A Life in Four Books.* Gray had begun writing the novel in the early 1950s while a student at the Glasgow School of Art, and on its publication he found himself touted by Anthony Burgess and many others as the first great Scottish writer since Sir Walter Scott. He remains a vital and towering figure on the increasingly populated Scottish literary and artistic landscape, writing everything from fantastic historical fiction to plays, poetry, and political polemics, and illustrating his own books and those of others with his dark and distinctive pen drawings.

Alasdair James Gray was born in Glasgow on 28 December 1934 to Alexander Gray, who worked in a cardboard-box factory, and Amy Fleming Gray. In 1939, during World War II, Alasdair, his mother, and his younger sister, Mora Jean, were evacuated to Lanarkshire; they were reunited with Alexander Gray in Wetherby, Yorkshire, in 1941. In Yorkshire, Gray wrote a short play based on Homer's *Odyssey;* when it was performed by Gray and his classmates at the Church School in Wetherby, he took the role of the blinded Cyclops, Polyphemus. After the war the family returned to Glasgow, where Gray was a member of the choir at Whitehill Senior Secondary School. As a teenager he wrote a version of one of Aesop's *Fables* and several poems and read them on a BBC children's program; his drawings and writings were published in the *Whitehill School Magazine.*

Gray left Whitehill with high grades in art and English and enrolled at the Glasgow School of Art, where he specialized in murals. Around this time he began, under the working title "Thaw," the

150

pictures were handsomer and less comic than anyone
else, unless they were newly rich. These thoughts were stopped
by noisy shouts and clattering hooves. Three galloping
horses brought a peculiar carriage ~~along the quay~~
lurching along the quay. They   were pulled to a halt
at the end of our gangway. Out climbed one of the
well-dressed, handsome people I had been puzzling
over in Punch. As he came aboard past the Russian seamen
and officers I nearly laughed aloud — his thin stiff
figure, stiff face, glossy top hat and neat frock coat
looked so comically English.

      Bell Baxter likes meeting new people.
Wedder will not eat outside   our cabin so last
night I tied a clean linen napkin round my poor man's
neck, settled him with his dinner tray and headed
for the dining saloon. I am now a well-known
character on this ship, and passengers who speak
English are always placed at my table. Last night
I   had   only two. Both had boarded at Odessa.
One was a stout, brown-faced American called Doctor Abraham
Stetson; the other was the obvious Englishman. He
said his name was — Astley! I got very excited. I.
said, "Do you work for a London firm called Lovel
and Co?"
"I am on the board of directors."
"Are you a cousin of Lord Pibroch?"
"I am."
"How wonderful! I am a friend of a great friend of
yours, a lovely little Russian gambler who drifts
around the German betting shops in a very poor way —
he has even been to jail, but not for anything very
nasty. The odd thing is, I do not know his name, but
he thinks of you as his best friend because you have
been so very good to him."

Page from the manuscript, and an illustration by the author, for Gray's novel Poor Things *(Collection of Alasdair Gray)*

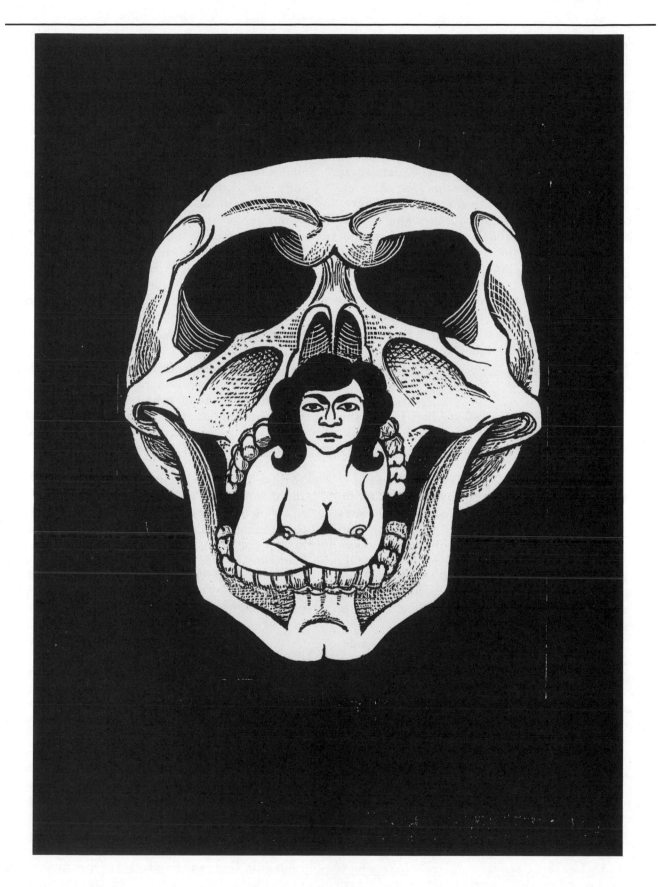

novel that would be published as *Lanark*. In 1957 he made his first extended trip out of Scotland, traveling to Spain on an art-school scholarship, but his stay was cut short by a violent asthma attack. Characteristically, a year after his return he made the dreadful experience the basis of a story, "A Report to the Trustees of the Bellahouston Traveling Scholarship," which appears in *Lean Tales* (1985) which Gray coauthored with James Kelman and Agnes Owens. Returning to Scotland, he obtained his diploma and went on to teach art in Lanarkshire and paint murals for churches and a synagogue; some of these paintings have been destroyed along with the buildings, but his best-known public work, on the walls of Glasgow's Ubiquitous Chip restaurant, remains. In 1961, while working as a cabaret comedian in a nightclub at the Edinburgh Festival during the school holidays, Gray met and married Inge Sorensen. He gave up teaching to work as a scene painter for two theaters and attempted, without success, to publish the first part of *Lanark*. His son Andrew was born in 1963.

Gray's teleplay *The Fall of Kelvin Walker,* the saga of a young Presbyterian nihilist from Glaik, Scotland, who triumphs in and then is crushed by the swinging London of 1967, was produced by the British Broadcasting Company in 1968. In the next ten years Gray had a series of plays accepted for radio, television, or stage performance; sometimes the same work would be adapted for two, or even all three, of these media. Many of these plays—including *The Fall of Kelvin Walker, Agnes Belfrage* (1972), and *McGrotty and Ludmilla* (1975)—would be revised and published as novellas or short stories in the 1980s and 1990s, after the long-delayed appearance, and success, of *Lanark*.

Lanark is a double bildungsroman, two side-by-side stories of young artists becoming men, aging, and confronting death in bizarrely parallel decaying worlds. The "real-world" hero is Duncan Thaw, an art student and writer; his reincarnation in the bleak, disease-ridden dystopia of Unthank is named Lanark. Thaw, trapped in the postwar depression of 1940s Glasgow, wishes that he could make his city into something new, beautiful, and imaginative. Given a second chance after his death as Lanark, in the dying, machine-dominated world of Unthank, he devotes his energies primarily to his fellow human beings and is rewarded by the rebirth of the city. *Lanark* has been compared to works by Laurence Sterne and James Joyce and is credited with launching a new generation of experimental fiction by Scottish writers, including the Booker Prize winner (and good friend of Gray's)

James Kelman; Liz Lochhead; Agnes Owens; and Irvine Welsh, whose 1993 novel *Trainspotting* was filmed to great success in 1996. In an interview with Mark Axelrod published, along with other articles by and about Gray, in *The Review of Contemporary Fiction* (Summer 1995) the author said of his best-known work: "my continuity of discontinuous people springs from a socialist democratic faith in all of us incarnating the eternal imagination—differently. Forget the discontinuities, enjoy the range!" The range of *Lanark* includes its illustrations, which were executed by Gray and are an integral part of the text. All of Gray's subsequent works include his art on the dust jackets and covers and in the marginal drawings and tailpieces. His prose and poetry cannot be appreciated fully without the drawings, which not only illustrate but also often comment on the writing.

Unlikely Stories, Mostly (1983) includes stories that were written as early as 1951 ("The Star") but not collected until after the success of *Lanark*. Many of the stories have an historical or scientific tenor that adds to their humor. "The Crank That Made the Revolution" sets the beginning of the Industrial Revolution in a swamp, "neither beautiful nor healthy," near Glasgow. Here Vague McMenamy, who was born in 1707, the year of the last Scottish Parliament, encases first a flock of ducks and then his aged grandmother in contraptions designed to improve their efficiency. His invention of the crankshaft "dealt a deathblow to the cottage knitting industry, and laid the foundations of the Scottish Textile Trade." "Five Letters from an Eastern Empire" describes "etiquette government irrigation education clogs kites rumour poetry justice massage town-planning sex and ventriloquism in an obsolete nation" not unlike some nations Gray implies, that are flourishing today (such as Britain). "Logopandocy," one of Gray's better-known short works, is a mosaic of seventeenth-century texts woven into a Jacobite polemic. The Republican John Milton and the Royalist Thomas Urquhardt agree on the primacy of language—that is, conversation—in social improvement.

In a 1997 interview with Miranda France, Gray identified *1982 Janine* (1984) as his favorite among his books. France noted that while Gray's other works may be "irreverent," *1982 Janine* is "obscene." Its title character is the sexual fantasy of Jock McLeish, whose midlife crisis has drawn him into divorce, drinking, soul-searching, conversations with God—and bondage. He spends a painful, sleepless night trying *not* to see that his work as a supervisor of security systems has warped his imagination and destroyed his marriage.

Shortly after the publication of *1982 Janine* Gray announced his intention to give up fiction to paint full-time. Nevertheless, he converted two of his plays from the late 1960s, *The Fall of Kelvin Walker* and *McGrotty and Ludmilla,* into novellas in 1985 and 1990, respectively. In the latter work McGrotty is a naive young Scotsman who is a minor servant to Sir Arthur Shots, the corrupt British prime minister. A secret report falls into his hands that enables him to blackmail the government. He marries Shots's daughter, Ludmilla, and becomes prime minister himself.

Gray's next new work of fiction, *Something Leather,* appeared in 1990. An essay by S. J. Boyd, "Black Arts: *1982 Janine* and *Something Leather*" and included in *The Arts of Alasdair Gray* (1991), edited by Robert Crawford and Thom Nairn, begins: "The publication of *Something Leather* confirms beyond doubt what was already strongly suggested by *1982 Janine:* Scotland's greatest living literary light is a pornographer." Not as critically successful as its predecessor, *Something Leather* has as its central character the mild-mannered June, who decides that she wants a leather skirt. She is then sexually subjugated for much of the rest of the novel by the skirt's makers, Senga and Donalda, and their friends. The sadomasochism that is forecast in chapter 1 is not depicted until the final chapter; each of the intervening ten chapters constitutes a short story in itself and includes no pornographic elements at all. The narrative includes such symbolically named characters as Miss Cane.

Gray followed *Something Leather* with *Poor Things: Episodes from the Early Life of Archibald McCandless M.D., Scottish Public Health Officer* (1992), a postmodern revision of the Frankenstein story set in Glasgow at the end of the nineteenth century. Replete with medical illustrations, reproduced engravings, and Gray's original art, the novel is the story of two doctors and the gorgeous Bella Caledonia, whom they construct from body parts and who ends up becoming a doctor herself under the name Victoria McCandless. While the original Frankenstein turned his creation into a monster by hating and neglecting it, *Poor Things* shows that love and a good education can produce a caring benefactor. The novel is dedicated to Gray's second wife, Morag McAlpine, whom he married in 1991 (his first marriage had ended in divorce in 1971). It won both the Whitbread and the *Guardian* awards for fiction.

A History Maker is the saga of Wat Dryhope, hero of border wars between England and Scotland in a rather medievally depicted twenty-third century. Pursued by women ages sixteen to sixty after his accidental triumph in battle, Wat wants only to escape the machine-dominated, matriarchal society and

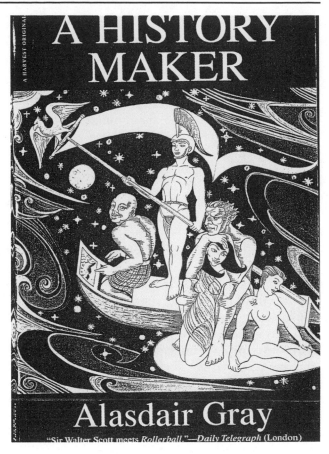

Dust jacket, with illustration by Gray, for his novel about life in the twenty-third century

build a house far from the "public eye"—which is, literally, a floating surveillance device and disseminator of information. Wat is ruined, however, when he meets the rapacious revolutionary Delilah/Lulu/Meg, who seduces him and leaves him with no purpose in life but to find her again. In the final line of his extensive notes on the text, Gray mentions that Meg is Wat's sister. The story suggests that by using fewer machines, men can achieve self-respect through productive manual labor and will no longer need to fight each other.

Meg is one of the most memorable of Gray's strong women: she, Ludmilla in *McGrotty and Ludmilla,* and Mavis Belfrage, the eponymous character of the title novella in *Mavis Belfrage: A Romantic Tale; with Five Shorter Tales* (1996) share intelligence, sensuality, and a lack of concern for the feelings of men. Mavis, a lovely, enigmatic graduate student, seduces, moves in with, destroys, and leaves a lonely professor, liberating him for a healthier life. In the other stories in the volume women, drink, and money ruin men, and children are neglected. The final story in the volume, "The Shortest Tale," ends with a schoolboy being beaten and mocked. Gray notes at the conclusion of the story that other "tales in this book have sour endings but none as bad as this because the others are fiction."

Gray is a strong advocate of Scottish independence from England. This theme recurs in his fiction, most prominently in *A History Maker,* and manifests itself in his letters to newspapers, public appearances, and interviews. *Why the Scots Should Rule Scotland 1997,* revised from its 1992 edition and republished just in time for the general elections of May 1997 in England, Scotland, and Northern Ireland, purports to be a history of Scotland from the days of Roman rule to the year 2020; it is also, as its title makes clear, a political statement opposing the legal binding of Scotland to England. Joyce McMillan in *The Scotsman* (6 April 1997) found the 1997 edition "more verbose, slightly darker, a little more bitter, more obsessed with the past, less hopeful for the future, less merrily self-mocking, and tinged with a sense of grief and loss that was almost entirely absent from the 1992 version." In a piece written for the same issue of *The Scotsman* Gray says: "The following article is not favourable to England but I promise it is written against none but the Scots. We are to blame for our condition. . . . when a political party grows big in Westminster the Scots members come to love Big Brother as much as the English do—he pays them such a fair minimum wage."

Lanark continues to be Gray's best-known work. Allan Massie in *The Daily Mail* (22 March 1997) said that "there is no doubt *Lanark* is a remarkable work, which set Scottish literature in a new direction, and gave every Scottish writer something to aim at." Kelman and Welsh are among those who have aimed and scored, and they acknowledge their debt to the artist, writer, and poet who has become, in Alastair Clark's words, the "avuncular uncle in the Scottish arts scene."

Interviews:

Keith Bruce, "Alasdair Gray Has Remarkable Visions," *Glasgow Herald,* 31 October 1995, p. 25;

Miranda France, "The Auld Sangs Are the Best," *Daily Telegraph,* 18 January 1997.

References:

William Boyd, "The Theocracies of Unthank," *Times Literary Supplement,* 27 February 1981, p. 219;

Bruce Charlton, "An Introduction to Alasdair Gray's *The Loss of the Golden Silence,*" *Bete Noire,* 12–13 (Autumn 1991–Spring 1992): 231–252;

Alastair Clark, "Song Lines," *Scotsman,* 6 December 1996, p. 18;

Dominique Costa, "Decadence and Apocalypse in Gray's Glasgow: *Lanark,* a Postmodern Novel," *Scotia,* 18 (1994): 22–34;

Costa, "In the Scottish Tradition: Alasdair Gray's *Lanark* and *1982 Janine,*" *Literature of Region and Nation,* 2 (November 1990): 2–7;

Robert Crawford and Thom Nairn, eds., *The Arts of Alasdair Gray* (Edinburgh: Edinburgh University Press, 1991);

Douglas Gifford, "Private Confession and Public Satire in the Fiction of Alasdair Gray," *Chapman,* 10 (Summer 1987): 101–116;

Gifford, "Scottish Fiction 1980–81: The Importance of Alasdair Gray's *Lanark,*" *Studies in Scottish Literature,* 18 (1983): 210–252;

Alison Lumsden, "Innovation and Reaction in the Fiction of Alasdair Gray," in *The Scottish Novel Since the Seventies: New Visions, Old Dreams,* edited by Gavin Wallace and Randall Stevenson (Edinburgh: Edinburgh University Press, 1993), pp. 115–126;

Isobel Murray and Bob Tait, eds., *Ten Modern Scottish Novels* (Aberdeen: Aberdeen University Press, 1984);

Review of Contemporary Fiction, 15 (Summer 1995): 103–198;

Richard Todd, "The Intrusive Author in British Postmodern Fiction: The Cases of Alasdair Gray and Martin Amis," in *Exploring Postmodernism,* edited by Matei Calinescu and Douwe Fokkema (Amsterdam: Benjamins, 1987), pp. 123–137.

Papers:

Collections of Alasdair Gray's manuscripts are at the National Library of Scotland, Edinburgh; the Mitchell Library, Glasgow; and the Hunterian Museum, Glasgow University.

Kazuo Ishiguro

(8 November 1954 –)

D. Mesher
San José State University

BOOKS: *A Pale View of Hills* (London: Faber & Faber, 1982; New York: Putnam, 1982);
An Artist of the Floating World (London: Faber & Faber, 1986; New York: Putnam, 1986);
The Remains of the Day (London: Faber & Faber, 1989; New York: Knopf, 1989);
The Unconsoled (London: Faber & Faber, 1995; New York: Knopf, 1995).

TELEVISION SCRIPTS: *A Profile of Arthur J. Mason,* 1984;
The Gourmet, 1986.

OTHER: "A Strange and Sometimes Sadness," "Waiting for J," and "Getting Poisoned," in *Introduction 7: Stories by New Writers* (London: Faber & Faber, 1981), pp. 13–51;
"A Family Supper," in *Firebird 2* (Harmondsworth: Penguin, 1983), pp. 121–131.

Kazuo Ishiguro (photograph by Nigel Parry)

Kazuo Ishiguro's literary reputation was established by three novels published over seven years: *A Pale View of Hills* won the Royal Society of Literature's Winifred Holtby Prize for the best first novel of 1982; *An Artist of the Floating World* won the 1986 Whitbread Book of the Year Award, the largest cash prize for literature in Britain; and *The Remains of the Day* received the 1989 Booker Prize, Britain's highest literary award. As impressive as the prizes he received during that period, however, is Ishiguro's passion for re-creating his art. He distanced himself from the "new internationalism" in British literature, an association prompted in part by the Japanese settings of his first two novels, by focusing his third on that most English of archetypes, the butler. Then, rejecting the mistaken praise for that work's "realism," Ishiguro invented an unquestionably surreal world for his fourth novel, *The Unconsoled* (1995). These diverse fictions are linked, nonetheless, by the author's consistent interest in narrative unreliability, a technique he has used with great effect in the development of his plots, in the complex-

ity of his characters, and in the manipulation of his readers.

Kazuo Ishiguro was born in Nagasaki, Japan, on 8 November 1954 and moved with his parents to Guilford, Surrey, in 1960, where his father, an oceanographer, was to be temporarily employed by the British government. Though the family left with the expectation of returning to Japan after a year or two, the assignment was repeatedly renewed, until they found themselves settled in England permanently, and Ishiguro's first trip back to Japan came only in 1989.

Ishiguro was educated at the Woking County Grammar School for Boys in Surrey, then studied American literature at the University of Kent, taking an honors degree in English and philosophy in 1978. He found employment as a social worker, first in Glasgow and, after graduating from Kent, in London. While working in London, Ishiguro pursued an interest in fiction by enrolling in the creative-writing program at the University of East Anglia, where he received an M.A. in 1980. Ishiguro continued as a social worker until 1983, a year after the publication of his first novel, when he found he could support himself as a writer of television scripts, book reviews, and fiction. In 1986 he married Lorna Anne MacDougall; they live in London. He has received honorary degrees from both the University of Kent and the University of East Anglia. In 1995 the Order of the British Empire was conferred on him for "services to literature."

The quantity of Ishiguro's output as a writer has always been modest. When, for example, the editors of *Esquire* magazine wanted to run a short story by the author for their March 1990 issue, following the success of *The Remains of the Day,* they eventually settled for "A Family Supper," a seven-year-old piece that had already been published twice before. Ishiguro first appeared in print in the Faber and Faber anthology *Introduction 7: Stories by New Writers,* (1981) with three stories that were produced for his creative-writing degree. The longest of these, "A Strange and Sometimes Sadness," was developed into his first novel, *A Pale View of Hills.* During the 1980s Ishiguro completed three relatively short novels—a book every three or four years, each somewhat longer than the previous one. But the critical and popular success of those three works was remarkable: by the end of the decade Ishiguro's fiction had won the most prestigious literary awards in Britain. The wait for *The Unconsoled,* Ishiguro's fourth novel and almost as long as the first three put together, was six years, and the critical reaction was not nearly as encouraging.

Ishiguro has said that his initial interest in writing fiction was as a way of preserving memories of Japan that were beginning to fade, and he attributes his meteoric rise, in part, to his Japanese name and the Japanese subject matter in his first two novels. His first novel was published a year after Salman Rushdie's *Midnight's Children* won the 1981 Booker Prize and, as Ishiguro recalled in a 1991 *Mississippi Review* interview, "everyone was suddenly looking for other Rushdies. . . . Usually first novels disappear, as you know, without a trace. Yet I received a lot of attention, got lots of coverage, and did a lot of interviews. I know why this was. It was because I had this Japanese face and this Japanese name and it was what was being covered at the time." But he has also had to deal with assumptions made by numerous critics and readers based solely on his ethnicity. "I often have to battle to speak up for my own individual territory against this kind of stereotyping," Ishiguro said, discussing comparisons between his fiction and Japanese literature. "Now if I wrote under a pseudonym and got somebody else to pose for my color jacket photographs, I'm sure nobody would think of saying, 'This guy reminds me of that Japanese writer.'" Moreover, Ishiguro made it clear that the images of Japan in his early novels were not intended to be historically accurate: "I did very little research. . . . I just invent a Japan which serves my needs. And I put that Japan together out of little scraps, out of memories, out of speculation, out of imagination." Nor was this problem entirely solved by using a European setting for his third and fourth novels, since reviewers such as David Gurewich continued to compare, for example, the narrator's description of the English countryside in *The Remains of the Day* to the "Japanese criteria for beauty" and his emphasis on ritual, duty, and loyalty to "prominent aspects of the Japanese collective psyche."

In a personal way, however, Ishiguro's early experiences in leaving Japan have, indeed, colored his art. "I had very strong emotional relationships in Japan that were severed at a formative age," he told Maya Jaggi in an interview for *The Guardian.* "I've only recently become aware that there's this other life I might have had, a whole person I was supposed to become." His first novel deals directly with the results of such a severing, but all of his fictions touch at least indirectly on the "other lives"—imagined, denied, repressed, or projected—of their narrators.

Another consistent element in Ishiguro's first four novels is his fascination with narrative unreliability, which he takes considerably beyond the familiar techniques of writers such as Joseph Conrad and Ford Madox Ford, where the narrators' account of events can be trusted, if not their interpretations or explanations of those events. In his first novel, *A Pale View of Hills,* for example, Ishiguro's narrator fabricates not only motives but also actions and even characters. In his later fictions Ishiguro's challenge is to surprise the reader with some unanticipated permutation of unreliability, which he achieves through multiple levels of complexity. In *An Artist of the Floating World* the narrator's unreliability seems to involve his initial denial of wrongdoing in prewar Japan, and only after he has recalled and accepted responsibility for those increasingly reprehensible activities does the reader grasp that the activities themselves never took place. In *The Remains of the Day* this greater level of complica-

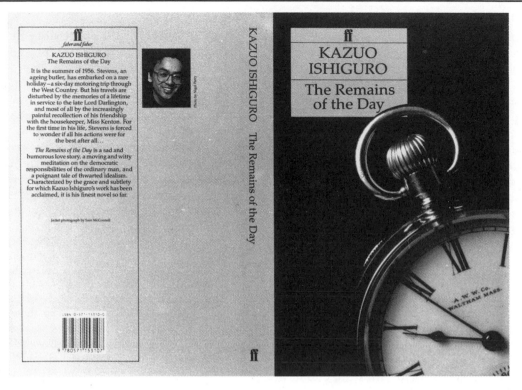

Dust jacket for Ishiguro's novel about an emotionally repressed butler

tion is achieved through the narrator's memories of two involvements, one a reluctantly revealed romantic relationship and the other an even more guarded political venture, which both transpired at Darlington Hall over the same fourteen-year period. And in *The Unconsoled* Ishiguro subverts even physical laws by expanding the realm of unreliability from the past to the present in order to make the external world a projection of the narrator's contorted psychology.

A Pale View of Hills is narrated by Etsuko, a Japanese woman who has married a British man in occupied Japan and returned with him to live in England, accompanied by her daughter from an earlier marriage, Keiko. In England they have a daughter, named Niki as a compromise between the father, who wants a Japanese name, and Etsuko, who wants an English one, "perhaps out of some selfish desire not to be reminded of the past." Now, decades later, Keiko's suicide makes revisiting that past unavoidable for Etsuko. Living alone since the death of her husband, Etsuko is visited by Niki, who comes, the mother thinks, "to tell me that things were no different now, that I should have no regrets for those choices I once made. In short, to reassure me I was not responsible for Keiko's death." The nature of those choices—whether they only encompass her second marriage and their removal to England,

or whether they also involve when and why Etsuko's marriage to Jiro, Keiko's father, ended—is never made clear in the novel. These concerns, however, are the psychological background of Etsuko's narration, which recounts the details of Niki's visit, because "it was during that visit," Etsuko says, "I remembered Sachiko again after all this time. I never knew Sachiko well. In fact our friendship was no more than a matter of some several weeks one summer many years ago." Etsuko's account of that summer in Nagasaki and her past relationship with Sachiko, interspersed with brief descriptions of Niki's present-day visit, becomes the story of *A Pale View of Hills*.

A connection between the events of that summer and Keiko's suicide is quickly established. Sachiko, the somewhat neglectful mother of a young girl, Mariko, moves into "the derelict house by the river" and becomes the talk of the neighborhood because of her relationship with an American soldier, Frank. Etsuko, living in the apartment building but feeling estranged from the other women there, is in her "fourth or fifth month of pregnancy by then" with her first child and suffering "every kind of misgiving about motherhood." From the beginning Etsuko feels "a kind of sympathy for Sachiko," based on an intuitive understanding of "that aloofness I had noticed about her when I had watched her from afar." Having doubts about her own fitness as a mother, Etsuko is also concerned about the lack of parental supervision for Mariko and about Sachiko's plans for them to move to America with Frank. Sachiko responds to this concern impatiently, asserting that America "is a better place for a child to grow up. And she'll have far more opportunities there, life's much better for a woman in America." As the novel progresses, however, and her hopes to emigrate with Frank are alternately dashed and then renewed, Sachiko eventually contradicts her claim that her "daughter's interests come first" and asks Etsuko, "Do you imagine for one moment that I'm a good mother to her?"

Sachiko's fitness as a mother is significant because of Etsuko's defense of her own decision to bring Keiko to Britain. Despite Niki's reassurances that she was not responsible for Keiko's suicide, Etsuko is obviously feeling guilty about Keiko's unhappiness and death. At first, echoing Sachiko, Etsuko asserts, "My motives for leaving Japan were justifiable, and I know I always kept Keiko's interests very much at heart." Not until the end of the novel does Etsuko admit, "I knew all along that she wouldn't be happy over here. But I decided to bring her along just the same." Shortly thereafter, however, another revelation ties Etsuko and Sachiko even more closely together. As the novel concludes Etsuko tells Niki that she has been remembering a "day-trip" to "those hills over the harbour" in Nagasaki. This is apparently a trip taken with Sachiko and Mariko, while Etsuko was pregnant, but when Niki asks what was special about that day Etsuko replies, "Oh, there was nothing special about it. I was just remembering it, that's all. Keiko was happy that day. . . . No, there was nothing special about it. It's just a happy memory, that's all."

The implications of this climactic revelation—that Keiko was already born at the time of the trip and therefore that Sachiko and Mariko are merely projections from Etsuko's troubled mind of herself and her daughter at that period—only confirm Etsuko's status as an unreliable narrator. Many indications of this unreliability appear earlier in the novel, including specific disclaimers by Etsuko herself about the accuracy of her recollections. "Memory," Etsuko realizes, "can be an unreliable thing; often it is heavily colored by the circumstances in which one remembers, and no doubt this applies to certain of the recollections I have gathered here." Indeed, the entire "memory" of the summer with Sachiko and Mariko is a product of the guilt Etsuko is enduring as a result of her daughter's suicide. In thus undercutting the "factual" nature of most of his novel, Ishiguro moves Etsuko beyond conventional narrative unreliability where the reader is invited to reconstruct the "truth" of the story by disregarding the narrator's misleading interpretations of otherwise accurately represented events. *A Pale View of Hills* defies such a literal resolution: once the characters of Sachiko and Mariko are shown to be figments of Etsuko's guilty conscience, any factual reconstruction or rereading of the novel is excluded.

According to Ishiguro, however, this is not exactly the effect he had sought. In an interview with Gregory Mason the author explained that the ending could work the way he intended only

> if the rest of the book had built up to that kind of ambiguity. But the trouble is that the flashbacks are too clear, in a way. They seem to be related with the authority of some kind of realistic fiction. It doesn't have the same murkiness of someone trying to wade through their memories, trying to manipulate memories, as I would have wanted. The mode is wrong in those scenes of the past. They don't have the texture of memory. And for that reason, the ending doesn't quite come off. It's just too sudden. I intended with that scene for the reader finally to realize, with a sense of inevitability, "Of course, yes, she's finally said it." Instead, it's a shock. I didn't quite have the technical sophistication to pull it off, and the result is that it's a bit baffling. Fortunately, a lot people enjoy being baffled.

Ishiguro's dissatisfaction with his handling of the "murkiness" of *A Pale View of Hills* shaped the texture of future works, especially *The Unconsoled,* just as his use of the unreliable narrator has been recast in each of his first four novels, following a clear progression from one to another. And there are other connections between the novels. The subplot involving Etsuko's first husband, Jiro, and his father, Ogata, in *A Pale View of Hills,* for example, contains the germ of Ishiguro's second novel, *An Artist of the Floating World*. In the Mason interview Ishiguro apologized for the problematic nature of the Ogata passages: "Let's just say I was a less experienced writer at that point, and I think that one of the things that happens to less experienced writers is that you cannot control the books, as more experienced writers can." Ishiguro reworked the dispute between Ogata and Jiro—representative of the conflict between the generation that brought Japan into World War II and the one that succeeded it and rejected many of its values—into the central theme of *An Artist of the Floating World,* also set in Japan in the years following the war and again recounted by an unreliable narrator.

Masuji Ono, the narrator of Ishiguro's second novel, like Ogata in his first, undergoes postwar scrutiny for his earlier attitudes and activities. The novel's present is the period between October 1948 and June 1950, during which Ono, now retired, attempts to arrange a marriage for his younger daughter, Noriko. The delicate negotiations surrounding the engagement make Ono increasingly aware of his unresolved past; the greatest obstacles to the marriage, Ono comes to believe, are himself and his wartime conduct. Through an interrelated series of memories Ono reconsiders his career as a painter, teacher, and government propagandist, until he is ready to admit his personal and political wrongdoing. But Ishiguro gives the unreliability screw another turn here. The reader believes Ono's admissions of past transgressions the more readily because they are slow in coming and unpleasant in nature. But those reluctant admissions—the sort that might prompt a reader's realization, "Of course, yes, he's finally said it"—are later countered by hints that Ono has exaggerated his past and inflated his record of villainy. Even more than in *A Pale View of Hills,* because of the complex narrative of *An Artist of the Floating World,* the reader is left with little certainty about any of the concrete details of Ono's life but with a clear sense of one individual's tortured psychology.

Ono's recollections of his past highlight "the exaggerated respect my pupils always had for me" and the "high regard" in which he was held "by people in this city"—assertions undercut by the false modesty of his disclaimer, "I have never had a keen awareness of my own standing." But Ono's reminiscences recount a long series of rebellions and betrayals of his own mentors, pupils, and friends. Most notable among these are Ono's breaks with his father, his art teacher Seiji Moriyama, and his protégé Kuroda—episodes in which similarities suggest parallels or confusion in Ono's memories of paintings burned and harsh words exchanged. When he describes the rebellion of his own predecessor as Moriyama's protégé, for example, Ono weighs both the natural aspirations of a superior student and the often unforgiving response of a teacher:

> it is this same leading pupil who is most likely to see shortcomings in the teacher's work, or else develop views of his own divergent from those of his teacher. In theory, of course, a good teacher should accept this tendency—indeed, welcome it as a sign that he has brought his pupil to a point of maturity. In practice, however, the emotions involved can be quite complicated. Sometimes, when one has nurtured a gifted pupil long and hard, it is difficult to see any such maturing of talent as anything other than treachery, and some regrettable situations are apt to arise.

In dealing with his own protégé, Kuroda, Ono is excessive and vindictive. During "the winter be-

Anthony Hopkins as Stevens in a scene from the 1993 motion-picture adaptation of The Remains of the Day *(Derrick Santini © MIP/Columbia Pictures)*

fore the outbreak of war" Ono, a "member of the Cultural Committee of the Interior Department" and "an official adviser to the Committee of Unpatriotic Activities," informs against his former pupil and then attends a raid on Kuroda's house, which results in the burning of Kuroda's art and the imprisonment of Kuroda. Though at the time he only "suggested to the committee someone come round and give Mr. Kuroda a talking-to for his own good," Ono has in mind his responsibility for Kuroda's suffering and loss in publicly acknowledging his personal guilt at Noriko's *miai,* or betrothal, ceremony: "There are some who would say it is people like myself who are responsible for the terrible things that happened to this nation of ours. As far as I am concerned, I freely admit I made many mistakes. I accept that much of what I did was ultimately harmful to our nation, that mine was part of an influence that resulted in untold suffering for our own people. I admit this."

But has Ono, in fact, anything to admit? Ono's turn from the indulgent art of Japan's "floating world" of geishas and pleasure districts to propagandistic paintings adorned with naive political slogans coincides with Japan's growing nationalism and explains his rise in influence and later feelings of guilt. Whatever his predilections as a painter, however, Ono's narrative reveals him to be still an artist of a floating world, who indulges his emotions in the enclosure of his own invention and whose version of events is consistently undercut within the novel.

Once again, in Ishiguro's next novel the narrator's present circumstances force him to reflect on his prewar activities. But in *The Remains of the Day* Ishiguro brings that issue home for his British reader, first by moving the setting from Japan to England and then by progressing in narrative duplicity from an innocent man only claiming to be a war criminal to someone with a rather dubious past—despite his vocation as that paragon of traditional English conduct, a butler—claiming to be a completely honorable man. The narrator is Stevens, for thirty years the butler at Darlington Hall. In the present, 1956, Stevens is employed by Mr. Farraday, the new American proprietor of Darlington Hall, who prefers an informal, bantering relationship with his butler that Stevens finds disconcerting. Farraday is planning a trip to the States and has encouraged Stevens to "take the car and drive off somewhere for a few days" while he is gone. Such a sightseeing trip would be extraordinary for Stevens, who has rarely left Darlington Hall but believes that he and others of his profession "did actually 'see' more of England than most, placed as we were in houses where the greatest ladies and gentlemen of the land gathered." Nevertheless, Stevens decides to mix business with pleasure by driving to the West Country to visit Miss Kenton, the housekeeper from 1922 to 1936, whose recent letter, "her first in almost seven years if one discounts the Christmas cards," contains "an unmistakable nostalgia for Darlington Hall, and—I am quite sure of this—distinct hints of her desire to return here." The assertion "I am sure of this" is an example of Ishiguro's favorite way of emphasizing narrative unreliability and suggests here that Stevens has not been entirely forthcoming about his relationship with Miss Kenton.

Miss Kenton begins work at Darlington Hall "at more or less the same time" as Stevens's own father does, "that is to say, the spring of 1922," and the elder Stevens's "declining abilities" become an issue as a result of the pressures of an important international conference to be held there in March 1923, the first of "many more events of equal gravity over the fifteen years or so that followed." Near the other end of that period, in 1936, Miss Kenton tells Stevens about her engagement and imminent departure in her parlor, while upstairs at Darlington Hall "the British Prime Minister, the Foreign Secretary and the German Ambassador" are huddled with Lord Darlington, who is apparently promoting the policy of appeasement toward Hitler that would culminate so disastrously two years later in the Munich Pact.

Darlington's pro-German sentiments and his misguided involvement in the quest for "peace in our time" are what Stevens is hiding from the reader as he sets out on his trip. When, for example, Stevens gives his address as "Darlington Hall" to the landlady on his first night in Salisbury, he comments on her look of "trepidation, assuming no doubt that I was some gentleman used to such places as the Ritz or the Dorchester and that I would storm out of her guest house on being shown my room." But it is just as likely that the landlady's reaction is due to Lord Darlington's infamy as a Nazi supporter. Later in the novel Stevens feels called upon repeatedly to defend his former employer against "the sort of foolish speculations concerning his motives" that one hears "all too frequently these days." Yet Darlington is made to appear all the more guilty by the nature of Stevens's defense and its qualifications: that Darlington was not alone "in believing Herr Ribbentrop an honourable gentleman and developing a working relationship with him," nor was he alone "in receiving hospitality from the Nazis on the several trips he made to Germany during those years." Further, Darlington was not really involved with the British Union of Fascists, whose leader dined at Darlington Hall on "three occasions at the most"; nor was he ever himself anti-Semitic, "except, perhaps, in respect to one very minor episode in the thirties," the dismissal of two women from the staff of Darlington Hall during the summer of 1932 because they were Jews. Indeed, while Stevens continues to maintain, "my chief satisfaction derives from what I achieved during those years," the most telling condemnation of Darlington comes from Stevens's own denials, in two recent instances, of ever having been "in the employ of Lord Darlington," lies he explains away "as the simplest means of avoiding unpleasantness."

But Stevens's thoughts are not wholly occupied by Lord Darlington's politics, and if it seems at first that the narrator is "avoiding unpleasantness" by focusing on his personal life, the situation is reversed later in the novel, with Stevens's personal behavior rather than his allegiances the greater disgrace. That first important conference in 1923, for example, is also the scene of the death

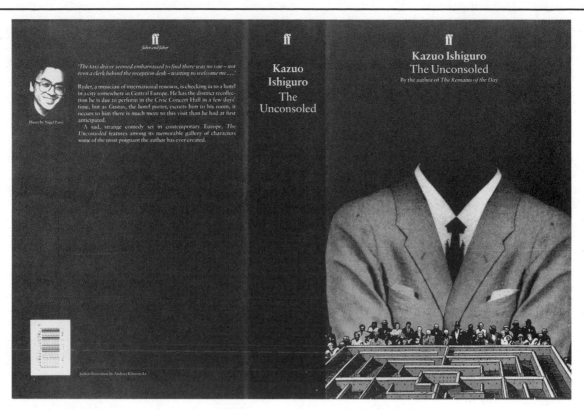

Dust jacket for Ishiguro's novel about an amnesiac pianist

of Stevens's father, yet on being informed by Miss Kenton that his father has just passed away, Stevens decides to continue with his work, saying, "Miss Kenton, please don't think me unduly improper in not ascending to see my father in his deceased condition just at this moment. You see, I know my father would have wished me to carry on just now."

The awkwardly formal and emotionless tone of this remark is a wonderful evocation of Stevens's insensitivities and insecurities. Yet he continues to view that episode as "a turning point in my professional development" because in carrying on with his duties Stevens believes he "did perhaps display, in the face of everything, at least in some modest degree a 'dignity'" akin to that of the "'great' butlers of our generation." As a result Stevens concludes, "for all its sad associations, whenever I recall that evening today, I find I do so with a large sense of triumph."

There is a similar end to the scene in which Miss Kenton gives notice, during the 1936 diplomatic meeting at Darlington Hall. There, too, Stevens relies on his sense of personal dignity and professional manners—two topics much on his mind during the trip to the West Country—to avoid the messy, emotional side of life. It is the moment outside her room shortly after Miss Kenton has informed him of her engagement which,

Stevens says, "has remained so persistently lodged in my memory—that moment as I paused in the dimness of the corridor, the tray in my hands, an ever-growing conviction mounting within me that just a few yards away, on the other side of that door, Miss Kenton was at that moment crying." But instead of acting on his emotions Stevens returns to his usual post upstairs, where he stands with absolutely nothing to do for the next hour.

At first, my mood was—I do not mind admitting it—somewhat downcast. But then as I continued to stand there, a curious thing began to take place; that is to say, a deep feeling of triumph started to well up within me. I cannot remember to what extent I analysed this feeling at the time, but today, looking back on it, it does not seem so difficult to account for. I had, after all just come through an extremely trying evening, throughout which I had managed to preserve a "dignity in keeping with my position"—and had done so, moreover, in a manner even my father might have been proud of.

Unlike Masuji Ono, the narrator of *An Artist of the Floating World,* who apparently has done nothing of which to be ashamed, Stevens should rightly be ashamed of doing nothing. At best Stevens does nothing to dissuade Darlington from his promotion of fascism—even when those abhorrent policies invade Stevens's own sphere, as in the firing of the two Jews from the staff of Darlington Hall. In acquiescing in their dismissal Stevens betrays his own vocation, which he sums up with the credo "we butlers should aspire to serve those great gentlemen who further the cause of humanity." And it is for this dubious calling that Stevens has sacrificed his relationship with Miss Kenton. He has embarked on this trip to the West Country in the unspoken hope of salvaging what he can of a wasted life by recapturing Miss Kenton's affections. But after a brief and restrained reunion with Miss Kenton—who is, in fact, Mrs. Benn and has been so for some twenty years—Stevens again finds himself unable to assess his personal failures directly and so ends up making a tearful confession to a stranger, on the pier at Weymouth, about his time with Lord Darlington: "You see, I *trusted*. I trusted in his lordship's wisdom. All those years I served him, I trusted I was doing something worthwhile. I can't even say I made my own mistakes. Really—one has to ask oneself—what dignity is there in that?" And so Stevens heads back to Darlington Hall and his new American employer, with the hope that "in bantering lies the key to human warmth."

Despite—or because of—the critical and popular success of *The Remains of the Day,* Ishiguro has chafed when his work is misread as essentially realistic. In an interview with Allan Vorda and Kim Herzinger, Ishiguro identified this as the one point about which he felt "an element of frustration. . . . In Britain, I suppose I'm still slightly locked into this realist reader and I recognize that a part of that is my own responsibility. I hate to use the word fantastic, but the book is still too realistic for the metaphorical intentions to be obvious if the people actually come from the society which the book superficially resembles." *The Unconsoled* is Ishiguro's solution to that frustration, a novel that forces even the most "realist reader" to recognize its narrative unreliability.

Mr. Ryder, the narrator of *The Unconsoled,* is a famous pianist on a visit to an unnamed European city. On arrival Ryder can remember neither his schedule nor the purpose of his visit, and he is too embarrassed by this lapse to request precise information. Though he never does acquire a schedule, Ryder comes to understand that this city, where music seems to be the chief public and personal measure of success, has pinned its hopes on the rehabilitation of Brodsky, a once-promising musician whose career has collapsed into alcoholism. Ryder is there to witness the miracle of Brodsky's professional rebirth or, perhaps, to perform a miracle himself. His ignorance of his own situation makes Ryder less like a conventional narrator than a reader, who also has

no memory of the world of the text and must understand the past and future from information and hints garnered in the present, or a writer, who must invent the present in such a way as to make that past and future recognizable; even his name, Ryder, seems a combination of *reader* and *writer*.

When, for example, Gustav, the hotel's aging porter whom Ryder has apparently never met before, asks him to speak to the porter's estranged daughter Sophie, Ryder seeks her out in a local café. But before he can broach the subject of her father, Sophie addresses him warmly about a house she has found that "might be exactly what we've been looking for." Ryder describes his reaction: "She began to give me more details about the house. I remained silent, but only partly because of my uncertainty as to how I should respond. For the fact was, as we had been sitting together, Sophie's face had come to seem steadily more familiar to me, until now I thought I could even remember vaguely some earlier discussions about buying just such a house in the woods."

Sophie turns out to be Ryder's long-time lover and the mother of his son, Boris, in the first of many such episodes that reveal Ryder to be either the most unreliable of narrators or someone caught in a dreamlike fantasy in which information expands rapidly. Ishiguro uses this technique of expansion to differentiate between logical possibility and literary realism. Later that night, for example, the narrator is taken by the hotel manager, Mr. Hoffman, to a reception at a house in a distant residential district. On arriving Ryder is, as usual, ignorant as to the nature of the scene he has just entered and is left to understand it on his own: "I noticed there was an odd quality to the whole atmosphere in the room—something forced, even theatrical about its conviviality—though I was unable immediately to put my finger on it." Soon, however, he recognizes what he has been missing, "that the occasion was not a cocktail party at all, but that in fact all these people were waiting to be called into dinner," a dinner that "should have been served at least two hours earlier." At that point Ishiguro's narrative takes an incredible turn when Ryder claims "to realise just what had taken place before our arrival" and then spends nearly four pages recounting those events. Ryder's slow recollection of his relationship with Sophie could be accounted for, though implausibly, by some physical or emotional trauma or defect, but this expansion of the narrative into the scene before Ryder's arrival, about which his detailed knowledge is inexplicable, is clearly impossible. As in other postmodern fiction the reader is challenged here to suspend disbelief while remaining conscious of that suspension.

That challenge takes place on many levels in *The Unconsoled,* where absurdity and impossibility mix easily with burlesque and bathos. Ryder, for example, has arrived at the reception, where everyone else is in formal attire, wearing only a dressing gown. When he stands up to make a speech, following glowing tributes to Brodsky's Bruno, "the greatest dog of his generation," Ryder's dressing gown opens, "displaying the entire naked front" of his body. Yet no one seems to notice or care. A little later, when Ryder complains of being tired, Hoffman's son Stephan offers to walk back with him. Though Ryder had described being driven to the reception by the hotel manager and "speeding through the darkness for some time," he suddenly recognizes that the reception is being held "in the atrium of the hotel" as if the physics of Ryder's world were based on an M. C. Escher print, where physical distances are as mutable as memory and logic.

Ryder's conveniently expanding memory and collapsing universe are part of Ishiguro's attempt, as he explained to Jaggi, to "move away from a recognizably real setting and create an alternative world—physical, temporal, behavioral—with a new set of rules. . . . It's a biography of a person, but instead of using memory and flashback, he bumps into other versions of himself." In *The Unconsoled* Ryder discovers versions of himself everywhere: in Brodsky's self-destructive behavior, in Stephan Hoffman's insecure aspirations, even in his son Boris's sense of rejection. At the beginning of the novel Ryder recalls a time playing as a boy with toy soldiers on a torn mat when, during one of his parents' many fights, he realizes "that the blemish that had always threatened to undermine my imaginary world could in fact be incorporated into it." And Ryder never overcomes this childish practice, brought on by the pain of his parents' quarreling: his imaginary world, the world of his narration, continually incorporates his own flaws into itself, enabling him to avoid seriously confronting his repressed unhappiness or present shortcomings. At the end of the novel, having disappointed almost everyone, including himself, Ryder still manages to claim, "Things had not, after all, gone so badly. Whatever disappointments this city had brought, there was no doubting that my presence had been greatly appreciated—just as it had everywhere else I had ever gone." As long as he continues to incorporate real blemishes into an imaginary world, Ryder will remain among the unconsoled.

Throughout his writing Ishiguro has returned again and again to such complex themes as guilt, self-deception, and the subjectivity of narrative truth. Yet his artistic vision and imaginative storytelling have attracted a wide audience, made wider still by the Merchant-Ivory motion-picture production of *The Remains of the Day,* with a script by Ruth Prawer Jhabvala, which was released in 1993 and garnered eight Academy Award nominations. Named by *Granta* magazine that same year as one of the "Twenty Best British Novelists," Ishiguro has secured for himself, within a relatively short period of time, status as one of the leading figures of contemporary British literature. With his works translated into more than twenty-five languages, he has also emerged as an important figure in contemporary world literature.

Interviews:

Gregory Mason, "An Interview with Kazuo Ishiguro," *Contemporary Literature,* 30, no. 3 (1989): 335–346;

Kenzaburo Oe, "Wave Patterns: A Dialogue," *Grand Street,* 10, no. 2 (1991): 71–91; reprinted as "The Novelist in Today's World: A Conversation," *Boundary 2,* 18 (Fall 1991): 109–122;

Allan Vorda and Kim Herzinger, "An Interview with Kazuo Ishiguro," *Mississippi Review,* 20, no. 1–2 (1991): 131–154;

Maya Jaggi, "A Buttoned-Up Writer Breaks Loose," *Guardian,* 29 April 1995; reprinted in *World Press Review,* 42, no. 4 (1995): 45.

References:

David Gurewich, "Upstairs, Downstairs," *New Criterion,* 8, no. 4 (1989): 77–80;

Susie O'Brien, "Serving a New World Order: Postcolonial Politics in Kazuo Ishiguro's *The Remains of the Day,*" *Modern Fiction Studies,* 42, no. 4 (1996): 787–806;

John Rothfork, "Zen Comedy in Postcolonial Literature: Kazuo Ishiguro's *The Remains of the Day,*" *Mosaic,* 29, no. 1 (1996): 79–10;

Brian W. Shaffer, *Understanding Kazuo Ishiguro* (Columbia: University of South Carolina Press, 1997);

Kathleen Wall, "*The Remains of the Day* and Its Challenges to Theories of Unreliable Narration," *Journal of Narrative Technique,* 21, no. 1 (1994): 18–42.

Ruth Prawer Jhabvala

(7 May 1927 –   )

Jackie Turton
University College Chester

See also the Jhabvala entry in *DLB 139: British Short-Fiction Writers, 1945–1980.*

BOOKS: *To Whom She Will* (London: Allen & Unwin, 1955); republished as *Amrita* (New York: Norton, 1956);

The Nature of Passion (London: Allen & Unwin, 1956; New York: Norton, 1957);

Esmond in India (London: Allen & Unwin, 1957; New York: Norton, 1958);

The Householder (London: John Murray, 1960; New York: Norton, 1960);

Get Ready for Battle (London: John Murray, 1962; New York: Norton, 1963);

Like Birds, Like Fishes and Other Stories (London: John Murray, 1963; New York: Norton, 1964);

A Backward Place (London: John Murray, 1965; New York: Norton, 1965);

A Stronger Climate: Nine Stories (London: John Murray, 1968; New York: Norton, 1968);

An Experience of India (London: John Murray, 1971; New York: Norton, 1972);

A New Dominion (London: John Murray, 1972); republished as *Travelers* (New York: Harper & Row, 1973);

Savages: A Film, by James Ivory, from a Screenplay by George Swift Trow and Michael O'Donoghue; and Shakespeare Wallah: A Film, by James Ivory, from a Screenplay by R. Prawer Jhabvala and James Ivory (London: Plexus, 1973; New York: Grove, 1973);

Heat and Dust (London: John Murray, 1975; New York: Harper & Row, 1976);

Autobiography of a Princess, Also Being the Adventures of an American Film Director in the Land of the Maharajas, by Jhabvala, James Ivory, and John Swope (New York: Harper & Row, 1975; London: John Murray, 1976);

How I Became a Holy Mother and Other Stories (London: John Murray, 1976; enlarged edition, New York: Harper & Row, 1976);

Ruth Prawer Jhabvala (photograph © Jerry Bauer)

In Search of Love and Beauty (London: John Murray, 1983; New York: Morrow, 1983);

Out of India: Selected Stories (New York: Morrow, 1986; London: John Murray, 1987);

Three Continents (London: John Murray, 1987; New York: Morrow, 1987);

Poet and Dancer (Garden City, N.Y.: Doubleday, 1993; London: John Murray, 1993);

Shards of Memory (London: John Murray, 1995; Garden City, N.Y.: Doubleday, 1996).

MOTION PICTURES: *The Householder,* screenplay by Jhabvala, Merchant-Ivory Productions, 1963;

Shakespeare Wallah, screenplay by Jhabvala and James Ivory, Merchant-Ivory Productions, 1965;

The Guru, screenplay by Jhabvala and Ivory, Merchant-Ivory Productions, 1969;

Bombay Talkie, screenplay by Jhabvala and Ivory, Merchant-Ivory Productions, 1970;

Autobiography of a Princess, screenplay by Jhabvala, Merchant-Ivory Productions, 1975;

Roseland, screenplay by Jhabvala, Oregon Four/Merchant-Ivory Productions, 1977;

Hullabaloo over Georgie and Bonnie's Pictures, screenplay by Jhabvala, Merchant-Ivory Productions/London Weekend Television, 1978;

The Europeans, screenplay by Jhabvala, adapted from the novel by Henry James, Levitt/Merchant-Ivory Productions/Pickman, 1979;

Jane Austen in Manhattan, screenplay by Jhabvala, Merchant-Ivory Productions, 1980;

Quartet, screenplay by Jhabvala and Ivory, adapted from the novel by Jean Rhys, Merchant-Ivory Productions/Lyric International, 1981;

Heat and Dust, screenplay by Jhabvala, adapted from her novel, Merchant-Ivory Productions, 1983;

The Bostonians, screenplay by Jhabvala, adapted from the novel by James, Merchant-Ivory Productions/Almi Pictures, 1984;

A Room with a View, screenplay by Jhabvala, adapted from the novel by E. M. Forster, Merchant-Ivory Productions/Cinecom, 1985;

Madame Souzatzka, screenplay by Jhabvala and John Schlesinger, adapted from the novel by Bernice Rubens, Cineplex Odeon Films, 1988;

Mr. and Mrs. Bridge, screenplay by Jhabvala, adapted from the novels *Mr. Bridge* and *Mrs. Bridge,* by Evan S. Connell, Cineplex Odeon Films/Merchant-Ivory Productions/Miramax Films, 1990;

Howards End, screenplay by Jhabvala, adapted from the Forster novel, Merchant-Ivory Productions, 1992;

The Remains of the Day, screenplay by Jhabvala, adapted from the novel by Kazuo Ishiguro, Merchant-Ivory Productions/Columbia Pictures, 1993;

Jefferson in Paris, screenplay by Jhabvala, Merchant-Ivory Productions/Touchstone Pictures, 1995;

Surviving Picasso, screenplay by Jhabvala, Merchant-Ivory Productions/Wolper/Warner Bros., 1996.

While Ruth Prawer Jhabvala is not British by birth, lived in England for only twelve years, and is no longer a British subject, she can be regarded as a British novelist for several reasons. First, during the period in which she produced the fiction that established her reputation, she did hold British citizenship. Second, the setting and subject matter of those books reflect the continuing British preoccupation with India that has made that country a subject for writers as various as Rudyard Kipling, E. M. Forster, and Paul Scott. And third, irony is a well-established weapon in the arsenal of British humor, and Jhabvala, whose wit is reinforced by a deceptively simple style, ranks among its most expert handlers.

Jhabvala's work has evolved through three stages. Initially she looked at Delhi middle-class Indian life and the tensions between the indigenous culture and imported Western values. The increasing—and often superficial—Western interest in Indian spirituality during the 1960s and 1970s, which coincided with the author's growing ambivalence toward India, provided her with a new avenue to explore: the Western experience of Indian life. V. S. Pritchett says that Jhabvala "probably knows more about India and feels it more strongly, in terms of personal conflict, than any other novelist writing in English," and John Updike, reviewing her novel *Heat and Dust* (1975) in *The New Yorker* (5 July 1978), described her as an "initiated outsider." William Walsh echoes this assessment, saying that her work "combines the unblurred perception of the outsider with the intimate familiarity of the inhabitant." Since moving to America in 1975 she has extended her subject matter beyond the Indian scene although she has continued to address problems of alienation and identity.

Jhabvala, it seems, was destined from the beginning to be a cultural and social outsider. In an interview with Ramlal G. Agarwal that originally appeared in *Quest* (September–October 1974) and was republished in his *Ruth Prawer Jhabvala: A Study of Her Fiction* (1990), she observed that "I was practically born a displaced person, and all any of us ever wanted was a travel document and a residential permit. One just didn't care as long as one was allowed to live somewhere." The daughter of a Polish Jewish lawyer, Marcus Prawer, and Eleonora Cohn Prawer, Ruth Prawer was born on 7 May 1927 in Cologne, Germany. In 1939 she fled with her parents and her older brother to England to escape Nazi persecution. The family settled in Coventry and later moved to a London suburb, where Marcus Prawer opened a clothing business. Ruth was educated at the local grammar school and was naturalized as a British subject in 1948, the same year her father, whose family had perished in the Holocaust, committed suicide. She received an M.A. from London University in 1951; her thesis was "The Short Story in England." Also in 1951, on 16 June, she married a young Indian architect, Cyrus S. H. Jhabvala, by whom she was to have three daughters, and moved with him to New Delhi. Again she was an outsider: not only was she a European, but her husband's family were Parsis, members of an ethnic group of Persian origin that retained a distinctive culture in India.

Jhabvala's first books reflect an optimism born of new experience. These early novels, as she acknowledges, have much in common both stylisti-

Scene from the motion-picture adaptation of Jhabvala's novel The Householder, *for which she wrote the screenplay
(Subrata Mitra © MIP)*

cally and in subject matter with those of Jane Austen. Comedies of manners centered on the themes of romantic love and arranged marriage, they explore tensions between the generations, particularly through the conflict of modern Western ideas with traditional Indian mores.

The title of Jhabvala's first novel, *To Whom She Will* (1955), is taken from an injunction in the Hindu epic *Panchatranta* that one should marry off daughters at an early age to protect their reputations. The story revolves around the determination of an emancipated young woman, despiter her family's opposition, to marry for love. The tensions between family obligation and individual freedom are satisfactorily resolved. In *Silence, Exile and Cunning: The Fiction of Ruth Prawer Jhabvala* (1983) Yasmine Gooneratne remarks that the incorporation of the structures of eighteenth-century English drama and fiction into the novel is somewhat jarring. Jhabvala's tendency to explain the motives and feelings of characters who are substantial enough to exist without

such narrative elaboration also betrays her inexperience.

These faults were quickly overcome. *The Nature of Passion* (1956), whose title is taken from a verse of the *Bhagavad Gita* (circa 1785), demonstrates Jhabvala's growing confidence and shows an impressive grasp of the Indian cultural and social background. Again the story revolves around the difficulties of the young—this time the indulged favorite daughter and the youngest son of a self-made Punjabi businessman—striving to escape traditional family-imposed restrictions. Whereas *To Whom She Will* depicts the resistance to change of what Agarwal describes in *Ruth Prawer Jhabvala* as the "last vestiges of sterile aristocracy," *The Nature of Passion* examines the values of the new middle classes. In her *Silence, Exile and Cunning* Gooneratne describes the novel as "a satiric exposure of worldliness on the one hand, and . . . a celebration of India's indestructible vitality of spirit on the other." The novel's epigraph explains that in Hindu thought *rajas* (pas-

Jhabvala in the Bikaner palace in Rajasthan, India, scouting locations for the movie The Guru
(photograph by James Ivory)

sion), is the active force that maintains equilibrium between the base and noble states of the human personality: "While the activities of a sattvika temperament are free, calm and selfless, the rajasa nature wishes to be always active and cannot sit still and its activities are tainted by selfish desires." The businessman Lala Narayan Das Verma, known as Lalaji, whose personality dominates the book, is of a decidedly rajasa temperament. His household is organized—to the chagrin and embarrassment of his "modern" daughter, Nimmi—along traditional lines, and he is not averse to using long-established and somewhat dubious business methods. It is to Jhabvala's credit that she succeeds in making him not only a credible but also an engaging character. His innate warmth and courtesy and his regard for his extended family are in marked contrast to the attitudes of his eldest son, a civil servant, and the son's wife, Kanta, whose dependence on her father-in-law's generosity for the maintenance of her lavish and Westernized lifestyle does nothing to decrease her aversion to his uncouth manners and outdated attitudes. The possibility of his being exposed in a corruption scandal is of concern to her only because of the threat it poses to her family's social position. Lalaji, Nimmi, Kanta, Lalaji's sons, and the various hangers-on hoping for patronage all pursue their own interests while demonstrating the common human capacity for self-deception and self-justification.

Asked by Agarwal about the "note of bitterness" that appears in her third novel, *Esmond in India* (1957), Jhabvala said:

I loved everything during my first years here. . . . I was wildly excited by it and never wanted to go away from here. But later that changed. I saw a lot I didn't like. I'll go further: a lot that horrified me. . . . All those Indian paradoxes and comical situations that Western writers especially like to exploit and make fun of . . . well, perhaps one laughs at first . . . but afterwards you see that it is not comic at all but quite the opposite. Then one stops laughing: at which point perhaps one's writing opens up?

Although the complacency and materialism of upper-middle-class Delhi society and the problems of young love are satirized once again in *Esmond in India,* a Chekhovian sense that, as Jhabvala put it in the interview with Agarwal, "what is ludicrous on the surface may be tragic underneath" is now apparent; it would become increasingly characteristic of her work. The psychological impact of India on Europeans living there is, for the first time, a prominent theme. Esmond Stillwood, whose intellectual and aesthetic understanding of Indian culture earns him some prestige and a modest living in middle-class Indian, as well as European, circles, finds the reality of India—epitomized for him in his unimaginative, indolent, superficially compliant but fundamentally implacable Indian wife—more and more intolerable. In his increasingly unbalanced mind India is, like his wife, a repellent snare from which he sees no escape.

It is not only Esmond who finds the reality of India falling short of the ideal. Ram Nath and his family, who had been active in the campaign for independence, look back with nostalgia to the days of their struggle. Modern India, it seems, has no place for Ram Nath. With no political role to play, he draws what solace he can from his unblemished moral integrity. Whereas his family lost everything in the fight to free India, his old university friend Har Dyal, directed by his coolly pragmatic wife to be somewhat more circumspect in his loyalties, has not only retained his family wealth but is now reaping the rewards of political influence. Jhabvala, ever the mistress of the ironic style, shows Har Dyal as vain, complacent, and—in his shallow intellectual posturing—faintly absurd.

Jhabvala's Indian characters are generally drawn from the stratum of society with which, as the wife of an architect, she was most in contact; the family of her husband's Punjabi business partner was particularly invaluable in giving her entrée into affluent Hindu circles. In *The Householder* (1960), however, she departs from the upper-middle-class milieu to address circumstances at a somewhat lower social level. The novel charts the sexual and emotional adjustments of a young couple in the months following their arranged marriage. The story is recorded almost entirely from the perspective of the husband, Prem, an underpaid teacher at a third-rate college. The title of the book refers to the second of four stages of personal development in Hindu tradition, that of the "householder." Although Prem finds temporary respite from his problems through visits to a guru, his present duty, as the title indicates, lies in engagement with the world, not in avoidance of it.

Get Ready for Battle (1962) is the last of Jhabvala's novels to deal almost exclusively with the lives of Indians. The title is taken from a verse of the *Bhagavad Gita* in which Krishna urges the reluctant warrior Arjun to abandon his objections and fight: it is a divine injunction to the individual to detach himself from personal desires and loyalties, no matter how creditable, to meet the greater obligations of caste duty and obedience to God. Most of the novel's characters might be said to be preparing for battle, though on a less lofty plane: almost invariably, self-interest determines their actions. The businessman Gulzari Lal, content with the status quo and his mistress, is reluctant to obtain a divorce from his estranged wife, Sarla Devi, because he believes that doing so will compromise his social standing. His son, Vishnu, trapped in an arranged marriage as discordant as his father's love match has proved to be, is torn between the example of his successful father and the fiercely uncompromising moral integrity of his mother. An idealistic, impoverished friend wants his support in founding a school; Vishnu guiltily harbors a preference for investing in a partnership to produce fountain pens. Only Sarla Devi is a warrior in the spirit of the *Bhagavad Gita.* Constantly struggling against her desire to leave the world to its own devices and find spiritual fulfillment, she is led by her sense of duty to continue campaigning on behalf of the poor. But the poor, who, as Jhabvala told Agarwal, "are there *indirectly*—the great mass of India beneath these middle class lives," are not idealized. Jhabvala's realism does not allow her to equate poverty with virtue: all levels of society are subject to the same critical but benevolent gaze. An element of social comedy is always present in Jhabvala's Indian novels, and it is comedy with a sharp edge: propriety, rather than morality, is what the world requires; moral adjustment is more comfortable both for the individual and for society than are moral imperatives that require self-sacrifice.

In *A Backward Place* (1965) Jhabvala returns to the theme she had first explored in *Esmond in India:* the difficulties faced by Europeans in India. For Judy marriage has meant exchanging a stultifying and insular upper-working-class existence in London for what is, by Western standards, a quite modest standard of living, but the warmth of her extended Indian family compensates for her financial anxieties. Clerical work at the Cultural Dais enables her to provide for Bal, her husband, who aspires to be an actor, and their two children. For the German Hochstadts, on a two-year academic exchange from London, admiration for Indian culture is affordable; they are merely visitors, and their position and income are secure. The Hungarian Etta, on the other hand, frantically

Dust jacket for Jhabvala's novel about a group of emotionally isolated New Yorkers

attempting to deny middle age and to retain the relatively sophisticated lifestyle that her looks and her well-heeled lovers—who are now less in evidence and less physically appealing themselves—had once ensured, finds herself trapped in a country whose culture and climate she detests. She has stayed too long and has neither the means nor the contacts in Europe to enable her to return there. In contrast, Clarissa, an upper-middle-class Englishwoman who has rejected Western materialism for Indian spirituality, indiscriminately embraces all that is Indian.

The failure of engagement between East and West is a fruitful area for satire in the novel. The Cultural Dais's preposterously amateurish Hindi production of Henrik Ibsen's *A Doll's House* can be regarded as a highly satisfactory event if judged by the degree of high-level social intercourse it generates: important politicians are present, including the Indian prime minister and the Norwegian ambassador, "who had seen the occasion as one more link in the chain of friendship that so closely bound the peoples of India to those of Norway."

Jhabvala's irony is not always so immediately evident. As Laurie Sucher has observed, "with Ruth Jhabvala's allusions, investigation is rewarded." Knowledge of both the Western and Eastern cultural contexts within which she writes is necessary if one is to appreciate fully Jhabvala's subtlety. Gooneratne remarks, for example, that Dr. Hochstadt's quoting from E. M. Forster's *A Passage to India* (1924) when

expounding on the "rhythm" of Indian life only demonstrates his inability to recognize the universal significance of Forster's message. Hochstadt's theoretical view of Hindu culture is in marked contrast to reality, not only for those Europeans such as Judy and Etta who live in India but also for many Indians.

It is no coincidence that Dr. Hochstadt's observations are followed by a summary of the somewhat trying circumstances of Sudhir Bannerjee's life. Sudhir, the Dais's young general secretary, is one of what Gooneratne has called Jhabvala's "inconspicuous and unsung, but gallant, nonconformists." Intelligent, educated, and principled, he has been forced, by financial obligations to his family and lack of influential contacts, to lower his ambitions. The faintly formal wording Jhabvala uses to describe his efforts suggests the gulf between the real and the ideal: she says that he has been obliged "to spend patient hours outside great men's offices" in order to be rewarded with an obscure job in some remote district of Orissa, suggesting an ironic reversal of the Hindu idea of the devout and eager disciple sitting at the feet of his teacher. These "great men" are no expounders of spiritual truths but men of wealth and influence. It is not enlightenment that the reluctant Sudhir has sought, but the means of earning a living.

Immediately after finishing *The Householder* Jhabvala adapted the book for the screen; the movie appeared in 1963. Since then she has alternated between writing fiction and writing screenplays, mostly for the Ismail Merchant-James Ivory partnership (in *Who's Who* she lists "writing film-scripts" as her single recreation). Writing screenplays not only introduced her to new subjects on which to draw for her fiction but also sharpened her already disciplined style; Walsh has remarked that through her film work "Jhabvala's prose, always flexible and adaptable, became . . . even more expert in concision, elision and implication, as we see particularly in her short stories." The first of her volumes of short stories, *Like Birds, Like Fishes and Other Stories* (1963), was published shortly after *The Householder* was released and is dedicated to the movie's producer, Merchant, and its director, Ivory. A second collection, *A Stronger Climate: Nine Stories,* appeared in 1968. By 1970 Jhabvala had written the scripts for three more motion pictures: *Shakespeare Wallah* (1965) and *The Guru* (1969) are about Europeans in India, the first based on the real-life experiences of a troupe of traveling English actors and the second a wry account of two young seekers after Eastern wisdom; *Bombay Talkie* (1970) looks at the Indian movie industry. Jhabvala had already cast a searching eye over the somewhat tawdry Indian film business in *A Backward Place,* and her third collection of stories, *An Experience of India* (1971), includes two tales, "A Star and Two Girls" and "Suffering Women," that indicate her increasing familiarity with this world. Jhabvala's short stories were originally published in periodicals such as *London Magazine, Encounter,* and *The New Yorker* and include satirical studies of Indian life and attitudes and accounts of Westerners who are seeking spiritual, intellectual, and emotional fulfillment in India or whose enthusiasm for the country has been eroded by experience. A later collection, *How I Became a Holy Mother and Other Stories* (1976), also includes stories dealing with the Western experience of India. The title story is a humorous exposure of the shallowness of cultish Hinduism, which in the 1960s and 1970s was increasingly exploiting a naive Western obsession with finding self-knowledge through Eastern pseudoreligious practices.

Jhabvala's introductory essay in *An Experience of India* is a carefully crafted account of the author's ambivalence about India: she says that what interests her now is not India itself but "myself in India" or, more particularly, "my survival in India." Jhabvala's view of herself—"I am a central European with an English education and a deplorable tendency to self-analysis. I am irritable and have weak nerves"—carries a suggestion of self-mockery that Ron Shepherd, writing in the *Commonwealth Review* (1990–1991), overlooks. What he calls her "apparent failure of self-knowledge," evidenced by her blaming the Indian climate and Indian poverty for her distress, is actually quite the reverse: it is a wry recognition of her own helplessness. By describing a cycle of Western response to India that parallels the Hindu concept of existence—"first stage, tremendous enthusiasm . . . ; second stage, everything Indian not so marvelous; third stage, everything Indian abominable"—she reinforces the message of the individual's impotence in the face of an implacable cultural force. The only option for the Westerner is to live "with the blinds drawn and the air-conditioner on."

A New Dominion (1972) and *Heat and Dust* (1975) are the last of Jhabvala's novels set entirely in India. In them she goes beyond Delhi and the mainly domestic and interior settings of her earlier books to place a greater emphasis on landscape and climate. The hostile physical environment symbolizes a damaging cultural force: for the European, India is potentially destructive both physically and psychologically.

A New Dominion suggests that for all but the most resilient and selfless, surviving India requires abandoning it. The elderly English missionary has the fortitude to stay; for the aesthetic and morally scrupulous Raymond, suppressing his homosexual attachment to Gopi, it is time to go. For the young Englishwomen in thrall to an exploitative cult, to remain is to choose total subjugation and, in one case, death. The guru here is not the relatively benign figure of *The Householder* but a hedonistic and sadistic manipulator intent on the physical and emotional domination of his followers.

Pritchett finds echoes of Forster's *A Passage to India* in *A New Dominion:* the relationship of Raymond and the young Gopi is similar to that of Fielding and Aziz, while the English girls seeking self-knowledge through Indian spirituality recall the disturbed Mrs. Moore. As Pritchett observes, it is the Indian characters in Jhabvala's novel who are the most complete and convincing: the vain, egotistical, and utterly materialistic Gopi and his seductress, Asha, an aging aristocratic beauty from a family that has also seen better days who repeatedly veers between self-indulgence and self-loathing. It is an ironic touch to have Asha and her elderly female spiritual guide find in the shallow Gopi a modern representation of the god Krishna.

After finishing *A New Dominion,* her most ambitious novel to that date, Jhabvala told Agarwal that it would probably be some time before she wrote another. Two years later, however, she had written *Heat and Dust,* the novel that did the most to establish her reputation and for which she received the Booker Prize.

'A writer of genius ... a writer of world class ...
a master storyteller'
THE SUNDAY TIMES

'Master of her craft'
ANNE TYLER, BOSTON GLOBE

'Each book has her hallmark of balance, subtlety,
wry humour, and beauty'
RUMER GODDEN, THE NEW YORK TIMES

RUTH PRAWER
JHABVALA

Shards of Memory

JOHN
MURRAY

Dust jacket for Jhabvala's novel that examines the ambiguous nature of identity

Structurally, Jhabvala's novels were becoming increasingly complex. *A New Dominion* had employed an omniscient narrator to express the viewpoints of the various characters, who were gradually linked within the plot. *Heat and Dust* interweaves a modern-day first-person account with the record of an affair half a century earlier between Olivia, the young first wife of a district officer–the narrator's grandfather–and an Indian prince. Olivia's letters provide the basis for the narrator's journal as she visits the places in which the events took place. The double narrative suggests both parallels and contrasts between the circumstances of the anonymous traveler in independent India and those of the elusive woman whose life in the days of the raj she attempts to uncover and, increasingly, to emulate. The narrator comes to India to learn and to discover herself; Olivia comes as a member of a governing elite. Olivia's pregnancy, which is terminated, is probably the result of her liaison with her aristocratic lover; the narrator's pregnancy is the consequence of a casual affair with a lowly government officer. When Olivia abandons the oppressive and restricted life of a colonial wife, she also abandons all contact with her past. Ultimately, she remains elusive; her chosen exile and eventual life of seclusion in the hills leave no clue to the psychology of the woman. The narrator, too, elects for the unknown, her quest for truth transmuted into a desire to embrace spiritual certainties that may demand

the negation of her individual identity. Her prospects for psychological survival, like Olivia's fate, remain undetermined.

Heat and Dust and the screenplay for *Autobiography of a Princess* (1975), both set in the present but with characters who have emotional links with the India of the past, were written almost simultaneously. Novel writing, Jhabvala told John Pym in an interview, provides her with the necessary "strength of background" for her film writing. Screenplay writing, in turn, has exerted a strong influence not only on her short stories but also on her novels. The change from the third-person narrative style of her earlier work to the more experimental form of *Heat and Dust* and her increasing use of counterpoint, already evident in *A Backward Place,* owe much to her experience in the other medium. In an interview with Anna Rutherford and K. H. Petersen, excerpted in their article in *World Literature Written in English* (1976), she said of her procedure in composing *Heat and Dust:* "I wrote great blocks of present time and then great blocks of 1923. Then afterwards I cut them up and put them together to set each other off. So I have learnt a lot technically from film."

While Jhabvala's Indian novels have met with general acclaim in the West, the response to her work in India has been less enthusiastic. An outsider whose experience of the country was largely shielded from the harsh economic realities faced by

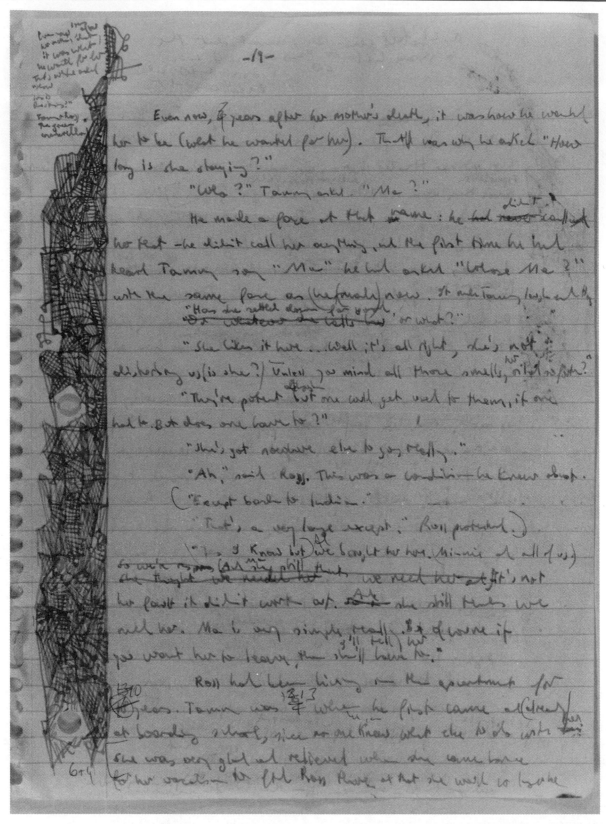

Pages from the manuscript for Jhabvala's "The Temptress," to be published in a forthcoming collection of her short stories
(Collection of Ruth Prawer Jhabvala)

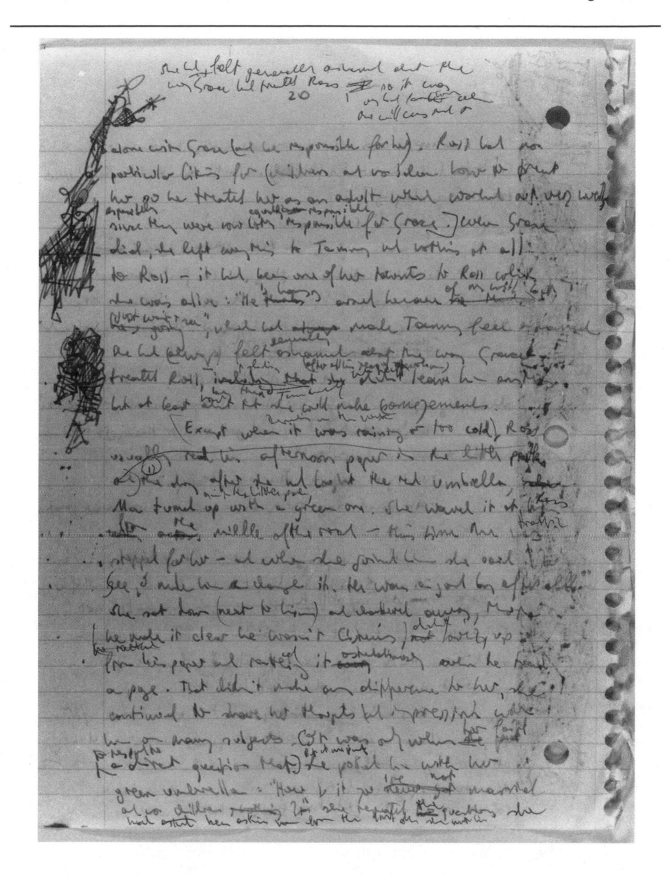

much of the populace, she has been seen by some as ill equipped to comment on life there. One of her most vitriolic critics, Eunice De Souza, has said that in Jhabvala's writing "there is no progress towards a deepening of insights about the social forces at work . . . no striving to understand them." De Souza describes Jhabvala's characters as "one-dimensional stereotypes" and adds that she "reduces language to the same threadbare quality." Jhabvala's observations, De Souza insists, "always remain superficial," and her mind "consistently fails to analyze what it observes."

That Jhabvala does not see India, in Walsh's words, simply "as a case to be explained by history, politics or sociology" does little to endear her to those who believe that she should emphasize Indian achievements in the face of adversity. Political, economic, and cultural change only concern her insofar as they are reflected in the circumstances and preoccupations of her characters. She is, as Walsh observes, "free . . . from any defensiveness about life in India, and freer than any British writer on India from guilt, overt or latent, about India's imperial past"; this freedom gives her a remarkable objectivity and allows her to treat her Indian and European characters equally dispassionately. Jhabvala responds to her cool reception in India with equanimity. She does not expect to be widely read there: there is no tradition of fiction writing in India, and books are expensive. Furthermore, she told Agarwal, "I write differently from Indian writers because my birth, background, ancestry and traditions are different. If I must be considered anything, then let it be as one of those European writers who have written about India."

In 1975 Jhabvala moved to New York City although she continued to spend the winters in Delhi with her husband. The move brought both a change of focus to Jhabvala's film and fiction writing and wider recognition to her work. New York is the setting for the Merchant-Ivory movies *Roseland* (1977) and *Jane Austen in Manhattan* (1980). *Hullabaloo over Georgie and Bonnie's Pictures* (1978) was again set in India, as was, of course, the adaptation of *Heat and Dust* (1983), for which Jhabvala was awarded Britain's National Film Critics Award and the British Academy of Film and Television Arts Award. The Booker Prize for the novel version of *Heat and Dust* was followed by a Guggenheim Fellowship in 1976, a Neil Gunn international fellowship in 1979, and a MacArthur Foundation Fellowship in 1984. In 1983 her alma mater, London University, awarded her an honorary doctorate of letters. Jhabvala became an American citizen in 1986.

Although India was no longer central to Jhabvala's writing, the themes of exile and alienation that had preoccupied her since 1965 continued to dominate her work. The novel *In Search of Love and Beauty* (1983) focuses on three generations of an émigré German-Jewish group in New York who are seeking to invest their indulgent and rootless lives with some significance; they find it through yet another guru figure, a dubious "psycho-spiritual" therapist named Leo Kellerman.

A retrospective collection of short stories, *Out of India* (1986), was followed by perhaps Jhabvala's blackest novel, *Three Continents* (1987). The book's three-part structure and its themes—the search for identity and the need to invest life with significance, and the emotional and physical seduction of a twin sister and brother by a charismatic charlatan peddling a pseudo-Eastern philosophy—are reminiscent of *A New Dominion*. That the narrator, Harriet, can be aware of the corruption and betrayal in which she is involved and yet can simultaneously deny it is a masterly achievement. Reviewing the novel in *Newsweek* (24 August 1987), Laura Shapiro wrote: "In its geographical scope, its large and far-flung cast and its relentless scrutiny of both sexual and intellectual thralldom, it is Jhabvala's most ambitious and impressive work."

During the six years that elapsed between the publication of *Three Continents* and Jhabvala's next novel, she continued to write screenplays. Despite her stated preference for writing original scripts, she adapted two of Henry James's novels as *The Europeans* (1979) and *The Bostonians* (1984), as well as Jean Rhys's *Quartet* (1981). With John Schlesinger, the movie's director, she adapted Bernice Rubens's 1962 novel *Madame Souzatzka* (1988)—her only movie not produced by Merchant-Ivory. Her understated style had already resulted in a sympathetic screen interpretation of Forster's *A Room with a View* (1985), and, following the adaptation of two Evan S. Connell novels as *Mr. and Mrs. Bridge* (1990), her version of Forster's 1910 novel *Howards End* was filmed in 1992. Both Forster movies won Academy Awards. Kazuo Ishiguro's novel *The Remains of the Day* (1989) was adapted by Jhabvala and released as a movie in 1993.

Jhabvala's enthusiasm for structural experimentation in her novels, prompted by film techniques, has occasionally been exercised at the expense of characterization. *Poet and Dancer* (1993), an exposé of the limitations of Western—particularly New York—individualism, is a case in point. The characters live and work in close proximity yet avoid meaningful contact. The egotistical and emotionally immature Dr. Hugo Manarr, whose reputation rests on his methods of "self-perfection," cannot deal with his own daughter Lara's psychological disintegration. Angel, the one character capable of emotional involvement, befriends Lara. But her selfless commitment involves a different type of avoidance, of responsibility to herself, and proves to be equally destructive. That these figures appear representative rather than real detracts from the force of the author's message: it is the minor players in *Poet and Dancer*—the maid, the cab driver, the waiter—all poor, vulnerable, and as emotionally isolated as the central characters, who most effectively engage the reader's sympathy.

The dense and complex *Shards of Memory* (1995), Jhabvala's most recent novel, examines the ambiguous nature of identity and shows that there is no single truth but only fractured accounts and interpretations. Henry, the great-grandson of a long-time disciple of the dead "Master" of a movement whose nature is unclear, bears an uncanny physical resemblance to the Master. Whether this resemblance is coincidental or, as Henry's mother suggests, an unfathomable transference of the Master's qualities to her son is left unresolved in the novel. Henry searches through his family's involvement in the history of the movement not only to uncover the Master's elusive nature but also to clarify his own role as a possible successor.

Although there is continuity in her novels—the human propensity for self-deception and self-justification is a recurring theme—the increasingly innovative nature of Ruth Prawer Jhabvala's work has come at the cost of the humor, warmth, and rounded characterizations that are so much a part of her Indian novels. Those novels, however, will stand as a lasting achievement. Jhabvala was made a companion of the British Empire in 1998.

Interviews:

Alex Hamilton, "The Book of Ruth," *Guardian,* 30 November 1975, p. 12;

John Pym, "Where Could I Meet Other Screenwriters? A Conversation with Ruth Prawer Jhabvala," *Sight and Sound,* 48 (Winter 1978/1979): 15–18.

References:

Ramlal G. Agarwal, *Ruth Prawer Jhabvala: A Study of Her Fiction* (New York: Envoy Press, 1990);

Agarwal, "Two Approaches to Jhabvala," *Journal of Indian Writing in English,* 5, no. 1 (1977): 24–27;

Eunice De Souza, "The Blinds Drawn and the Air Conditioner On: The Novels of Ruth Prawer Jhabvala," *World Literature Written in English,* 17 (1978): 219–224;

Yasmine Gooneratne, "Film into Fiction: The Influence of Ruth Prawer Jhabvala's Early Cinema Work upon Her Fiction," in *Still the Frame Holds: Essays on Women Poets and Writers,* edited by Sheila Roberts (San Bernardino, Cal.: Borgo Press, 1993), pp. 173–209;

Gooneratne, "Irony in Ruth Prawer Jhabvala's *Heat and Dust," New Literature Review,* 4 (1978): 41–50;

Gooneratne, *Silence, Exile and Cunning: The Fiction of Ruth Prawer Jhabvala* (London: Sangham, 1983);

V. S. Pritchett, "Ruth Prawer Jhabvala: Snares and Delusions," in his *The Tale Bearers: Essays on English, American and Other Writers* (London: Chatto & Windus, 1980), pp. 206–212;

Anna Rutherford and K. H. Petersen, "*Heat & Dust:* Ruth Prawer Jhabvala's Experience of India," *World Literature Written in English,* 15 (November 1976): 373–378;

Ron Shepherd, "The Need to Suffer: Crisis of Identity in the Fiction of Ruth Prawer Jhabvala," *Commonwealth Review,* 2, nos. 1–2 (1990–1991): 196–203;

Laurie Sucher, *The Fiction of Ruth Prawer Jhabvala: the Politics of Passion* (Basingstoke & London: Macmillan, 1989);

William Walsh, *Indian Literature in English* (London: Longman, 1990);

Haydn Moore Williams, "Strangers in a Backward Place: Modern India in the Fiction of Ruth Prawer Jhabvala," *Journal of Commonwealth Literature,* 6 (1971): 53–64;

Williams, "The Yogi and the Babbitt: Themes and Characters of the New India in the Novels of R. Prawer Jhabvala," *Twentieth Century Literature: A Scholarly and Critical Journal,* 15, no. 2 (1969): 81–90.

James Kelman
(9 June 1946 –)

Cairns Craig
University of Edinburgh

BOOKS: *An Old Pub Near the Angel and Other Stories* (Orono, Maine: Puckerbush Press, 1973);

Three Glasgow Writers, by Kelman, Alex Hamilton, and Tom Leonard (Glasgow: Molendinar Press, 1975);

Short Tales from the Nightshift (Glasgow: Print Studio Press, 1978);

Not Not while the Giro and Other Stories (Edinburgh: Polygon, 1983);

The Busconductor Hines (Edinburgh: Polygon, 1984);

A Chancer (Edinburgh: Polygon, 1985; Monroe, La.: Subterranean, 1985);

Lean Tales, by Kelman, Agnes Owens, and Alasdair Gray (London: Cape, 1985);

Greyhound for Breakfast (Edinburgh: Polygon, 1987; New York: Farrar Straus Giroux, 1988);

A Disaffection (London: Secker & Warburg, 1989; New York: Farrar Straus Giroux, 1989);

Fighting for Survival: The Steel Industry in Scotland (Glasgow: Clydeside Press, 1990);

The Burn (London: Secker & Warburg, 1991):

Hardie and Baird and Other Plays (London: Secker & Warburg, 1991);

Some Recent Attacks: Essays Cultural & Political (Stirling & San Francisco: AK Press, 1992);

How late it was, how late (London: Secker & Warburg, 1994; New York: Norton, 1994);

Busted Scotch: Selected Stories (New York: Norton, 1997).

OTHER: *East End Anthology,* selected, with an introduction by Kelman (Glasgow: Clydeside Press, 1988);

George Elder Davie, *Scottish Enlightenment and Other Essays,* foreword by Kelman (Edinburgh: Polygon, 1991).

Since the publication in 1983 of *Not Not while the Giro,* his first major collection of short stories, and of his first novel, *The Busconductor Hines,* in 1984, James Kelman has been one of the most influential—and one of the most controversial—of modern Scottish writers. His stylistic techniques for render-ing the consciousness of his solipsistic working-class characters have opened the way for a generation of younger Scottish writers, including Janice Galloway, Irvine Welsh, and Duncan MacLean, "to write about their own world in the way that they speak." In an interview with MacLean, Kelman said that the problem for working-class and regional writers is

to discover how to talk before we're allowed to write about subjects, and then we think it's surprising that we can't write about certain subjects because we don't have the right voice! They obviously don't realise that language is culture—if you lose your language you've lost your culture, so if you've lost the way your family talk, the way your friends talk, then you've lost your culture, and you'd be divorced from it.

In his insistence on the primacy of the spoken language as the foundation for contemporary expression Kelman has provided for other Scottish writers an effective model of how to revitalize in a modern context the dialect writing which has been, since the makars of the late medieval period, the foundation of an independent Scottish literary identity. Kelman set out to write stories which, as he recalled in "Artists and Value," "would derive from my own background, my own socio-cultural experience. I wanted to write as one of my own people, I wanted to write and remain a member of my own community." At the same time, as he said in the published version of his acceptance speech for the Booker Prize in 1994, he sees his writing as part of the movement "towards decolonisation and self determination" based on "the validity of indigenous culture" and "the right to defend it in the face of attack."

Kelman has claimed to know little of Scottish writers before him, but his status as "working-class intellectual" puts him in a long tradition of self-taught Scottish writers going back to Robert Burns and James Hogg, of whom the most notable in the twentieth century was the poet Hugh MacDiarmid. Kelman insists that "the literate class isn't logically distinct from the working class . . . folk read and

James Kelman (photograph by Douglas Robertson)

write literature from every social position," and his own life is proof of that fact, for he was born on 9 June 1946 into a family of five (he has four brothers) that lived first in Govan, in a traditional inner-city tenement, and then were rehoused in Drumchapel, one of the postwar "schemes" built to alleviate Glasgow's terrible working-class housing conditions. His family, however, was more artisan than proletarian, since his mother was a teacher and his father ran a one-man business making and gilding picture frames, a trade handed down from Kelman's grandfather.

Kelman's background was, therefore, one in which, to put it in his own negative terms, the arts were not absent, and in which "books were not unknown"; his family included relatives who had "white collar occupations—even distant relatives who were school teachers"—so that "social mobility certainly existed as a concept."Nonetheless, Kelman left Hyndland School at the age of fifteen without qualifications and spent two years apprenticed as a

compositor. He then spent nearly ten years in a variety of jobs in England and Scotland, jobs that ranged from bus conducting to laboring in a copper mill, some of which, along with periods on the dole, would provide the background for his novels and stories, and one of which—as an asbestos mixer in Manchester—would lead him to become, in the early 1990s, an unpaid welfare-rights officer for Clydeside Action on Asbestos, fighting for compensation for workers whose lives have been blighted by contact with the chemical. Between the ages of fifteen and nineteen Kelman's reading developed from Louis L'Amour, the American Western novelist, through Jack Kerouac ("it wasn't a great jump") to Albert Camus.

In American writing, Kelman believes, young British writers are "really amazed at the freedom they find" from the class-bound language of English writing, and if accounts of Kelman's work tend to focus on his rejection of traditional literary forms for a realistic presentation of working-class voice, the most profound influence on his writing is none-theless the "existential tradition," and particularly the work of Franz Kafka, whom Kelman regards as "a supreme realist." Kelman's characters may be drawn from an intensely local Glaswegian experience, but he sees his writing in a European and existential tradition, and his working-class characters inhabit a world where existential angst is not discovered in dramatic confrontation with death but in the constricting confines of the daily struggle for survival: he has commented that "the most ordinary person's life is fairly dramatic; all you've got to do is follow some people around and look at their existence for 24 hours, and it will be horror. It will just be horror. You don't need any beginning, middle and end at all. All you have to do is show this one day in maybe this person's life and it'll be horror."

It is on this basis that James Wood has suggested that Kelman's work is "a kind of prison literature"—related to works by Camus, Aleksandr Solzhenitsyn, and others—a literature characterized by a "luxurious oppressiveness whereby the smallest things . . . . are subjected to intense scrutiny. Eventually, these small things become the only things, and hence metaphysically important and narratologically suspenseful." Wood equates this to the "Biblical inversion of being rich in poverty."

But Kelman's characters are more prisoners in their own minds than prisoners of the material world, no matter how constricted their environment. In an early story, "The Paperbag," which appeared in *Lean Tales* (1985) the protagonist reflects on a condition that Kelman will explore with ever-increasing intensity in his novels:

> Imagine being a dog but—murder! people taking you wherever they like and you don't have a say in the matter. Here boy, here boy. I would hate to be a dog like that, getting ordered about by cunts without knowing what for, not having a genuine say on the matter. Horrible, really fucking horrible. And then getting put down for christs sake sometimes for nothing, no reason, just for doing what dogs do. Biting people!

> Crazy, walking along the road thinking about such stuff. Absolute fucking nonsense. Mongrels by christ! But that's what happens. And thinking of that is better than thinking of nothing. I would say so anyway. Or would I? The trouble with being useless is thinking; it becomes routine, you cannot stop yourself. I think all the time, even when I'm reading my newspaper. And the things I think about are fucking crazy.

Kelman's characters are obsessed with an imagined "other" in which they might be trapped and which would be far worse than their own, apparently hopeless, conditions; their destiny is an emptiness in which their thoughts spiral endlessly, tormented by their ability to reverse every assertion ("Or would I?") and to invent endless hypothetical worlds, tormented finally by the impossibility of ceasing to think.

Kelman came to his characteristic style quickly after he started writing in the late 1960s at the age of twenty-two, when he was working in England and when, he has said, it was as though his subconscious flicked a switch and "it was time to go out, buy the paper and start." By the time he and his wife Marie had reestablished themselves in Glasgow in the early 1970s, with their two daughters (born in 1970 and 1971), Kelman had already written most of the stories that were to be published in his first full collection of short stories in 1983.

At the age of twenty-nine Kelman enrolled at the University of Strathclyde, which, as a mature student, he was able to enter without standard qualifications. He claims to have gone for purely economic reasons and to have left uncertain whether he did or did not get a degree. What he did leave with was a profound distaste for "English Literature" and "the Anglo-American canon," which he has been fighting ever since. According to Kelman the academic establishment claims to "own" literature and seeks to disenfranchise those who do not share their value systems. He has said that

> When I was at uni I was studying literature, but that doesn't necessarily mean that you become a part of the establishment, only if you want it to be. Anybody who wants to study literature is entitled to do so, because it doesn't belong to anybody, you know. So when you're going there, you're not going to study what it is to be one of the middle classes—not unless you want to do that. . . . I mean I spent four years trying to find an argument for that really; ultimately what I wanted to be able to do was to say "Right, Eliot is a good writer but he's a bad artist." I wanted to get to some kind of position like that, you know. I wanted to be able to define things and say "Right, what does it mean to say that this is a good poem."

In Glasgow, however, Kelman met several writers, including Alasdair Gray, Tom Leonard, and Liz Lochhead, who were engaged in a similar exploration of Glasgow life and of the local voice. For Kelman the discovery of what came to be known in the second half of the 1980s as "the Glasgow group" provided a sense of solidarity, a solidarity he was to repay by his own efforts in leading writers' groups in Glasgow that were to produce works such as Jeff Torrington's novel *Swing Hammer Swing!* (1992), winner of the Whitbread Book of the Year Prize in 1993. Torrington was an unemployed former car-factory worker whose novel of working-class life in the 1960s in the Gorbals—the slum district of Glasgow inhabited largely by immigrants or their offspring—was recommended by Kelman to his own publishers.

What has made Kelman controversial, however, is his refusal to engage in what he regards as the censorship of the Glasgow working-class language out of which he writes by the suppression of its use of swearwords. The controversy is sometimes instigated by Kelman himself when he challenges newspapers and the media not to censor his work by suppressing its nonstandard language: his view is that "BBC and ITV; the film, theatre, newspaper and mainstream magazine industry; all exercise censorship, they collude in suppression"; on other occasions the controversy is instigated by critics who, like Julia Neuberger when she challenged the appropriateness of awarding Kelman the Booker Prize for fiction in 1994, regarded it as unacceptable that a "serious" novel should use the word *fuck* four thousand times. For Kelman, however, the issue of the suppression of the actualities of people's speech is part of a wider cultural and political issue to do with power and control in society: writing, in his view, must begin as a challenge to the "literary" as a particular mode of suppression and censorship, one that bears down especially on people from a working-class city such as Glasgow. In English literature, Kelman contends, Glaswegians were traditionally reduced to brutish stereotypes, and characters meant to be working-class or from "any regional part of Britain" were similarly linguistic caricatures:

> Every time they opened their mouth out came a stream of gobbledygook. Beautiful! their language a cross between semaphore and morse code; apostrophes here and apostrophes there a strange hotchpotch of bad phonetics and horrendous spelling—unlike the nice stalwart upperclass English hero . . . whose words on the page were always absolutely splendidly proper and pure and pristinely accurate, whether in dialogue or without. And what grammar! Colons and semicolons! Straight out of their mouths! An incredible mastery of language.

What Kelman finds most interesting about these traditional heroes is that their "mastery" was not confined to language but was over the narrative; they were in possession of "the place where thought and spiritual life exists," excluding those outside "the parameters of their socio-cultural setting." Kelman, identifying with these excluded figures, says, "We all stumbled along in a series of behaviouristic activity; automatons, cardboard cut-outs, folk who could be scrutinised, whose existence could be verified in a sociological or anthropological context. In

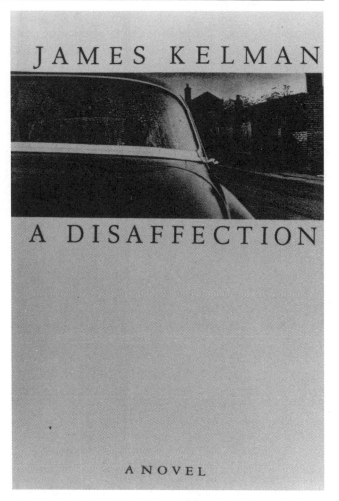

Dust jacket for the U.S. edition of Kelman's third novel, winner of the James Tait Black Prize in 1990

other words, in the society that is English Literature, some 80 to 85 percent of the population simply did not exist as ordinary human beings."

Kelman's insistence is not only that working-class people do have a spiritual life, which it is his job to present, but that they also have an intellectual life, an intellectual life which he participates in and contributes to as a working-class intellectual: "I don't think it's usual to meet books written from a working class experience that is total. Total in the sense that the character can be at the same time an intellectual and still be a *bona fide* member of the working class." It is the bona fide member of the working classes who is nonetheless an intellectual (of sorts) who is the protagonist of Kelman's first novel, *The Busconductor Hines* (1984). Hines is an inversion of the Scottish tradition of the "lad o' pairts," the working-class boy who makes good by progressing through the educational system. Hines has refused the opportunities of the educational system, and although he hates being a bus conductor, he cannot decide to be anything else, even when he knows that the job will soon disappear as the company introduces "one man" buses. The bus conductor journeys outward only to return to the same place, and Hines's job is a metaphor for a life tethered endlessly to the same point. Hines continually imagines alternatives for himself (promotion, change of job, emigration) which he knows he will never seek in actuality. The novel traces Hines's increasing mental torment as he faces the prospect of the breakup of his marriage, and through his consciousness Kelman develops the dialogic technique that will become typical of his "interior monologues," a technique in which competing voices with different linguistic registers engage each other in endless debate:

> There are parties whose attention to a variety of aspects of existence renders life uneasy. It cannot be said to be the fault of Hines that he is such a party. A little leeway might be allowed him. A fortnight's leave of absence could well work wonders. A reassembling of the head that the continued participation in the land of the greater brits
>
> Fuck off.
> Hines is forced into situations a dog wouldn't be forced into. Even a rat. It is most perplexing Hines has a wean and he treats this wean as a son, i.e. a child, a fellow human being in other words yet here is he himself being forced into a situation whence the certain load of shite as an outcome, the only outcome such that it is not fair. It is not fucking fair. Hines is fucking fed up with it.

Kelman uses none of the usual markers of difference between the spoken and unspoken, between public dialogue and inner self-reflection, so that his language is able to move back and forth between third-person and first-person points of view and between vernacular and standard modes of speech. The significance of this in a Scottish context is that it allows him to overcome what has been one of the most problematic technical issues for Scottish writers since the time of Sir Walter Scott: the division between a narrative voice in standard English and characters who speak in Scots dialect. Is there a narrator describing Hines's life? Is Hines describing himself in the third person? The result is a style like the protagonist himself: it renders reading "uneasy":

> This isnt Hines who's talking. It's a voice. This is a voice doing talking which he listens to. He doesn't think like it at all. What does he think like. Fuck off. He thinks like anybody else, anybody else in the circumstances, the circumstances which are oddly normal.

A "voice doing talking which he listens to" describes the inner nature of Kelman's major characters: their ear is turned inward toward consciousness as a space in which many voices, from within and without, reverberate, so that they can address themselves in the second or the third person and can challenge themselves with an alternative voice as though they were altogether another.

In his second published novel, *A Chancer* (1985), most of which had been written before *The Busconductor Hines*, Kelman eschewed the inner processes of the character's thinking by a rigorous presentation of the life of a young working-class man in a style that deliberately excludes the reader from the character's thought and presents him only through his actions. This is Kelman's version of Roland Barthes's "writing degree zero," in which the reader has to guess at the motivation and intention of a character who seems, much of the time, unable to define the reasons for his own actions: "He had less than £40 in his trouser pocket. The horse he fancied was paper favourite and it appeared as favourite when the actual betting started. He was going to do it for £5 but when he wrote out the line he had written it for £20; and when he passed it beneath the grille he paid the additional £2 tax in advance."

The narrative moves from "he was going to do it" to "he had written it," and the point of decision is erased from the text. Kelman has attributed this strange quality of *A Chancer* to the fact that he wrote it when he was twenty-three or twenty-four, and although he rewrote it at thirty-eight, he had denied himself techniques that he had discovered in the interim. He challenged himself "to be absolutely concrete" and "to do nothing that was abstract, nothing that was internal." The objectivist technique of *A Chancer* casts into darkness the relationship between thought and action. Tammas, the gambling protagonist, lives for the moment when the world conforms or fails to conform to his predictions of it, when the event of a horse race or a dog race is decided beyond his control and yet within the scope of the pattern that he has tried to impose on it "He had backed it and that was that, the money was running on and there was nothing he could do about it, either the horse would win or it would lose. There was not anything in between."

Kelman's self-denying technique—the novel is almost barren of metaphors—brings into focus precisely what can never be presented to the reader, the "not anything in between" that defines an action, the elusive instant when future possibility turns into past certainty. The novel, like Tammas, accepts the rigor of its self–limitation: "You had to make a selection and stick to it. There was nothing else you

BY THE SAME AUTHOR

GREYHOUND FOR BREAKFAST

'Sheer art and wild wit ... hilarious genius for detail'
New York Times Book Review

A DISAFFECTION

'James Kelman's *A Disaffection* caught me from the very
first sentence. As a portrait of a romantic obsession it
made me laugh and cry. Brilliant'
Scotland on Sunday

THE BURN

'One of the most enjoyable writers around'
Guardian

ISBN 0-436-23292-8

WINNER OF THE 1994 BOOKER PRIZE

JAMES
KELMAN

How late it was, how late

How
late
it was,
how
late

Secker & Warburg

Dust jacket for Kelman's controversial novel about one week in the life of a blind, drunken, small-time thief in Glasgow

could do. There was nothing else, nothing at all. A mistake even to think like that."

Kelman investigates the conflict between the cultural establishment of power and real cultural creativity in his third, and what many critics believe is his best, novel, *A Disaffection,* published in 1989. The protagonist, Patrick Doyle, is a Glasgow schoolteacher, obsessed with the destructiveness of his role as a member of the cultural "polis" (Scots for "police") who are employed by the state to impose order on people's lives ("how come they wound up with a boy who went in for his Highers and then went to uni and became a member of the polis"), and his desire to be a member of a free and democratic "polis" (Greek for "community"). He is entangled in a hopeless relationship with a married woman who is also a teacher in his school, a relationship that consciously copies that of Werther, protagonist of Goethe's *The Sorrows of Young Werther* (1774), because Doyle is obsessed with the generation of 1770 (Friedrich Hegel, Friedrich Hölderlin, Ludwig van Beethoven, William Wordsworth, James Hogg), the last generation who could look

forward to the possibility of a liberated imagination within a liberated society and the European generation that had to see the promise that the American Revolution of 1776 held for them fail in the autocratic aftermath of the French Revolution. Doyle is trapped within the consequences of that failure, the failure to make "culture" liberating, the development of culture as an entrapment in hierarchy, and an exclusion of the mass of the people. Doyle, university educated and yet a member of the working classes in origin and sentiment, is enmeshed in a situation in which his efforts to liberate his pupils lead only to their greater entrapment: "I'm sick of being alone and being a teacher in a society I say I detest all the time, to the extent that the term 'detest' isni really appropriate christ because it's a form of obscenity."

A Disaffection was nominated for the Booker Prize and won the James Tait Black Prize in 1990, but if Kelman resists participating in a society that he sees as an "obscenity," it was the obscenities of his fourth novel, *How late it was, how late*, which were to attract the greatest attention when it was awarded the Booker Prize in 1994. The novel is an account of the struggles of Sammy Samuels, small-time Glasgow crook, after he is beaten up by the polis, goes blind, and is thrown out onto the streets to find his way around. It is rendered in Sammy's voice, a voice which cannot speak without the word *fuck* and which tells us that "It didny fucking matter about the story. Even if it was all fucking junk. All he was doing was telling her he had changed. That was fucking all." Reviewing it in *The Independent* (2 April 1994), Janet Hospital Porter celebrated its intensity and powerful use of language, saying "This, in a nutshell, is the astounding achievement of Kelman's latest novel: that you are stuck, for 374 pages, inside the befuddled hung-over mind and the unshaven none-too-clean skin of a blind drunk who achieves nothing in a week beyond the fact of surviving it, but you are never bored."

Others, however, were to consider the novel a betrayal of standards: Simon Jenkins, leading columnist of *The Times* (London), complained (15 October 1994) that Kelman "is totally obsessed with the word [*fuck*]. He sometimes writes it over and over again when he cannot think of anything else with which to fill a line." Jenkins declared that awarding the Booker Prize to Kelman "is literary vandalism . . . I can only assume that the judges were aspiring to some apogee of political correctness . . . . They wanted to give awfulness a break. Here was a white European male, acceptable only because he was acting the part of an illiterate savage. Booker contrived both to insult literature and patronise the savage."

Such responses to Kelman's work replicated the comments of Richard Cobb, a Booker Prize judge of 1984, who thought *The Busconductor Hines* was one of the two worst books he had read that year and commented at the award ceremony that "there was even one novel written entirely in Glaswegian!" In his Booker Prize acceptance speech Kelman pointed out that for such critics any writer who uses "vernaculars, patois, dialects, gutter-languages might well have a place in the realms of comedy . . . but they are inferior linguistic forms and have no place in literature"; the consequence, he concluded, is that "*a priori* any writer who engages in literature of such so-called language is not really engaged in literature at all." Kelman's view of the forces which he has to oppose has been justified to the extent that many of those in positions of power in the literary world, and not just in the metropolitan culture of London, have reacted with extreme hostility to his writings. In Scotland his novels have been challenged as pandering to the worst

versions of outsiders' view of Scotland; *The Sunday Times* of 16 October 1994 reported reaction to his winning of the Booker Prize under the headline "Scots bewail 4,000-expletive blot on the national character." Kelman has also been accused of leading a left-wing literary establishment in Scotland that is entirely out of touch with the realities of modern Scottish life. Gerald Warner, for instance, argued in *The Sunday Times* (25 September 1994) that

> The basic premise of the modern Scottish "serious" novel is that the section of the population which really matters, the "working class," has been victimised and deprived of its authentic "culture" by the combined forces of the English, Toryism and American influence.

> It is this sinister axis which has deprived the Scottish proletariat of its birthright: the privilege of breaking sweat daily by metal-bashing in some rust-bucket industry. . . . Add to this an obsession with violence and poverty, complemented by a disdain for any aspect of history or contemporary life that smacks of tartan and romance, and you have the ground rules laid down by the cosy coterie of socialist nostalgia freaks who form the mutual-admiration society that is the Scottish literary set.

For Kelman, on the other hand, literature is both ordinary and, at the same time, necessarily a challenge to the existing order of things. In his introduction to *East End Writers' Anthology* (1988), a collection of writing by people from some of the most deprived areas of Glasgow, Kelman argued that "many folk will be startled to discover" that the "realistic portrayal of the lives of ordinary people" could be "classed as 'literature,'" and the reason was that "the vast majority of those who have studied literature at an advanced level, including English teachers, university lecturers and professors, have never created one piece of literary art in their lives." Against the weight of establishment views of what counts as literature, he went on,

> Writers have to develop the habit of relying on themselves. It's as if there's a massive KEEP OUT sign hoisted above every area of literature. . . . The very idea of literary art as something alive and lurking within reach of ordinary women and men is not necessarily the sort of idea those who control the power in society will welcome with open arms. It is naive to expect otherwise. Literature is nothing when it isn't being dangerous in some way or another and those in positions of power will always be suspicious of anything that could conceivably affect their security.

In the effort to provide a context in which literature can be "dangerous in some way or another," Kelman was involved in the establishment in the 1980s of what was known as "The Free University of Glasgow," a "university" consisting of those who wanted to come together to teach and to learn on a basis of equality and mutuality. This anarchistic challenge to the established university of Glasgow, like Kelman's participation in 1990 in "Workers City"–an organization that sought to provide an alternative to the official celebrations of Glasgow's year as "European City of Culture"–was designed to reclaim as "culture" the experiences of a community that Gerald Warner had dismissed as being "not properly a 'culture,' but the primeval vortex of undevelopment that precedes culture."

The focus on Kelman's "obscenity" and his resistance to traditional literary values has, however, obscured the real strength of his development as part of the existential tradition. His characters may be "low," but what they dramatize is the world where all knowledge has become uncertain. Doyle is the "bloke who can show Goedel's theorem to a first year class in a sentence," but the sentence he is condemned to is the endless groundlessness of all truth that is implied in Goedel's theorem. The world constantly dissolves under him, all its meanings and fulfilments in the past, all the power of imagination capable only of creating hypotheses that will be proved redundant at some point in the future.

Kelman's protagonists, far from being simply the inhabitants of a downtrodden social world, are questers after an existential Being that forever evades them. The reader learns of Hines that

> The position in which he is to be finding himself is no worse than that of countless others whose efforts are no longer negotiable but that that position, that position might yet have become tranquil that they could have multiplied inasmuch, in asmuch as Hines could eventually, he could have become

> He was wanting that becoming.

The "becoming" that, for existentialism, makes humanity different from any thing that has an essence is what Hines desires, but he desires equally that the world of "give us an aye or give us a naw–because in betweens no longer exist in any scheme of the world that Hines, that he might be said to be participating within." He is trapped in the essence of a social definition ("the busconductor") without which he is nothing and yet which he resists because it is a denial of his "becoming."

Equally, Doyle, in *A Disaffection,* realizes the impossibility of his relationship with Alison when he uses the word *arse* in conversation with her: "It was the word, of course, arse, she didn't like it hadni been able to cope when he had said it. It was an odd word right enough. Arse. There aren't many odder words. Arse. I have an arse. I kicked you on the arse. This is a load of arse. Are–s. It was an odd word."

Readers who focus on Kelman's use of such words, who are not "able to cope," may miss the way in which his protagonists kick against the "Ares" of the world, kick against "Being." Kelman's aim is to kick the reader into an awareness that language is culture, that literature is not always "splendidly proper and pure." He acknowledges that the way he uses language can be seen as "an attack on literature or somehow a negation. But it isn't at all, it's just an attack on the values of the people who own literature–or the people who think they own literature. . . . They think it attacks literature, but it's not, because literature doesn't belong to anybody at all."

Interviews:

Kirsty McNeill, "Interview with James Kelman," *Chapman* (Edinburgh), 57 (Summer 1989): 2–10;

Julia Llewellyn Smith, "'The Prize Will Be Useful. I'm Skint'; James Kelman; Booker Prize," *Times* (London), 13 October 1994, p. 17;

"The Speech He Had No Time To Make at the Booker Ceremony; James Kelman," *Sunday Times* (London), 16 October 1994, Scottish Section, p. 21;

"K Is for Culture: Interview with Scottish Writer James Kelman," *Scottish Trade Union Review,* 68 (January/February 1995): 24–29.

Duncan McLean, "James Kelman Interviewed," in *Nothing Is Altogether Trivial: An Anthology of Writing from Edinburgh Review,* edited by Murdo MacDonald (Edinburgh: Edinburgh University Press, 1995), pp. 100–123.

References:

Cairns Craig, "Resisting Arrest: James Kelman," in *The Scottish Novel Since the Seventies,* edited by Gavin Wallace and Randall Stevenson (Edinburgh: Edinburgh University Press, 1993): 99–114;

Macdonald Daly, "Gray Eminence and Kelman Ataxy: A Reply To H. Baum," *Gairfish,* 8 (1995): 23–35;

Daly, "Your Average Working Kelman," *Cenerastus,* 46 (Autumn 1993): 14–16;

Keith Dixon, "Notes from the Underground: A Discussion of Cultural Politics in Contemporary Scotland," *Etudes Ecossaises,* 3 (1996): 117–128;

Dixon, "Punters and Smoky Breath: The Writing of James Kelman," *Ecosse,* 9 (1990): 65–78;

Douglas Gifford, "Discovering Lost Voices," *Books in Scotland,* 38 (Summer 1991): 1–6;

H. Gustav Klaus, "1984 Glasgow: Alasdair Gray, Tom Leonard, James Kelman," *Etudes Ecossaises,* 2 (1993): 31–40;

Michael McCormick, "For Jimmy Kelboats," *Chapman* (Edinburgh), 83 (1996): 30–34;

Karl Miller, "Glasgow Hamlet," in his *Authors* (Oxford: Clarendon Press, 1989), pp. 156–162;

Drew Milne, "James Kelman: Dialectics of Urbanity," in *Writing Region and Nation: Proceedings of the Fourth International Conference on the Literature of Region and Nation,* edited by James A. Davies, et al (Swansea: Department of English, University of Wales, 1994): 393–407;

Alastair Renfrew, "Them and Us?: Representation of Speech in Contemporary Scottish Fiction," in *Exploiting Bakhtin,* edited by Renfrew (Glasgow: Department of Modern Languages, University of Strathclyde, 1997), pp. 15–28;

Roderick Watson, "The Rage of Caliban: The 'Unacceptable' Face and the 'Unspeakable' Voice in Contemporary Scottish Writing," in *Scotland to Slovenia: Proceedings of the Fourth International Scottish Studies Symposium,* edited by Horst W. Drescher and Susanne Hagemann (Frankfurt am Main: Peter Lang, 1996): 53–69.

Papers:
A collection of James Kelman's manuscripts is at the Mitchell Library, Glasgow.

Hanif Kureishi

(5 December 1954 –   )

Peter Childs
John Moores University

BOOKS: *Borderline* (London: Methuen, 1981);

Outskirts, The King and Me, Tomorrow–Today! (London: Calder / New York: Riverrun Press, 1983);

Birds of Passage (Oxford: Amber Lane Press, 1983);

My Beautiful Laundrette and The Rainbow Sign (London & Boston: Faber & Faber, 1986);

Sammy and Rosie Get Laid: The Script and the Diary (London: Faber & Faber, 1988; New York: Penguin, 1988);

The Buddha of Suburbia (London & Boston: Faber & Faber, 1990; New York: Viking, 1990);

London Kills Me (London & Boston: Faber & Faber, 1991);

London Kills Me: Three Screenplays and Four Essays (New York: Penguin, 1992);

The Black Album (London: Faber & Faber, 1995; New York: Scribners, 1995);

Love in a Blue Time (London: Faber & Faber, 1997; New York: Scribners, 1997);

My Son, the Fanatic (London: Faber & Faber, 1997);

Intimacy (London: Faber & Faber, 1998).

PLAY PRODUCTIONS: *Soaking up the Heat,* London, 1976;

The Mother Country, London, Riverside Studios, 1980;

The King and Me, London, Soho Polytechnic, 1980;

Borderline, London, Royal Court Theatre, 1981;

Outskirts, London, Royal Shakespeare Company Warehouse, 1981;

Cinders, adapted by Kureishi from a play by Janusz Glowacki, London, Royal Court Theatre, 1981;

Tomorrow–Today!, London, Royal Court Theatre, 1983;

Mother Courage, adapted by Kureishi from the play by Bertolt Brecht, Royal National Theatre, London, 1984.

MOTION PICTURES: *My Beautiful Laundrette,* screenplay by Kureishi, Working Title Films, 1986;

Sammy and Rosie Get Laid, screenplay by Kureishi, Working Title Films/Channel Four Films/Cinecom Pictures, 1987;

London Kills Me, screenplay by Kureishi, directed by Kureishi, Working Title Films/Channel Four Films/PolyGram Filmed Entertainment, 1991;

My Son, the Fanatic, British Broadcasting Corporation/UDC DA International/Zephyr Films/Arts Council of England, 1998.

TELEVISION SCRIPT: *The Buddha of Suburbia,* by Kureishi and Roger Michell, British Broadcasting Corporation, 1993.

RADIO SCRIPTS: *You Can't Go Home,* 1980;

The Trial, adapted by Kureishi from the novel by Franz Kafka, 1982.

OTHER: *The Faber Book of Pop,* edited by Kureishi and Jon Savage (London & Boston: Faber & Faber, 1995).

SELECTED PERIODICAL PUBLICATIONS–
UNCOLLECTED: "Finishing the Job," *New Statesman and Society,* 1 (28 October 1988): 19–24;

"England, Your England," *New Statesman and Society,* 2 (21 July 1989): 27–29;

"A Long, Cool Glance," *Guardian,* 4 November 1989, pp. 15–16;

"Boys Like Us," *Guardian,* 2 November 1991, pp. 4–7;

"Wild Women, Wild Men," *Granta,* 39 (Spring 1992): 171–180;

"A Wild Dance to a Dangerous Tune," *Independent on Sunday,* 24 May 1992, p. 22.

Hanif Kureishi is not only a leading contemporary novelist but also a prominent playwright, essayist, and screenwriter. He has also directed his own screenplay for the movie *London Kills Me* (1991). His script for the director Stephen Frears's *My Beautiful Laundrette* (1986) was nominated for an Academy Award; one of his early plays, *Outskirts* (1981), won the George Devine Award. His *The Buddha of Suburbia* (1990) received the Whitbread Prize for best first novel, and the reviewer for the *Independent* on Sunday called it "one of the sharpest

Hanif Kureishi (photograph by Jacques Prayer)

satires on race relations in this country that I've ever read." Kureishi celebrates the counterculture and is largely anti-Establishment in his views; when he said on a Radio 4 program that he thought the anti-poll-tax riots in London were a good thing, the BBC switchboards were jammed with complaints. Reviewing his second novel, *The Black Album* (1995), the London magazine *Time Out* said that "Kureishi is an extraordinarily gifted creator of human characters and a shrewd observer of human folly." The leading literary and cultural critic Colin MacCabe has called him "one of the great talents of the past 25 years." Kureishi also has his detractors, ranging from Establishment figures to Britons of Asian descent. His adaptation of his story "My Son, the Fanatic" (1994) as a movie in 1998 has been attacked by Islamic leaders as a negative and unrepresentative portrayal of Muslim beliefs and behavior.

Kureishi's father came to England from Bombay when the subcontinent was partitioned into India and Pakistan in 1947; his mother is English. Born 5 December 1954 in Bromley, Kent, Kureishi attended the same local school in south London (though not at the same time) as one of his heroes, the rock star David Bowie, who would write the music for the television adaptation of *The Buddha of Suburbia*. The only Asian boy at the school, Kureishi also found himself caught between the working-class life of his friends and the privileged background from which

his father came. His prominent memories of school are of casual, institutional racism (one of his teachers habitually called him "Pakistani Pete") and of a growing disillusionment with his studies. After the age of fourteen Kureishi, whose father had also wanted to be a novelist, spent much of his time at school thinking about his creative writing and most of his free time working on it. His other early passion was music, and he would coedit *The Faber Book of Pop* in 1995. He studied philosophy at King's College, London, from which he received a B.A., while working at the Royal Court Theatre, where he first had a play performed when he was nineteen. He went on to write plays for fringe theaters, supplementing his income by writing pornography. His 1984 adaptation of Bertolt Brecht's play *Mother Courage* has been performed by the Royal Shakespeare Company and the Royal National Theatre. He was appointed writer in residence at the Royal Court Theatre in 1981 and again in 1985–1986. His breakthrough came with the movie *My Beautiful Laundrette;* since then he has consistently produced thoughtful and challenging fiction and drama although *Newsweek* said, more simply, that "he lives to offend."

Hanif Kureishi is not only a leading contemporary novelist but also a prominent playwright, essayist, and screenwriter. He has also directed his own screenplay for the movie *London Kills Me* (1991). His script for the director Stephen Frears's *My Beautiful Laundrette* (1986) was nominated for an Academy

Daniel Day-Lewis as Johnny and Gordon Warnecke as Omar in My Beautiful Laundrette,
the first movie for which Kureishi wrote the screenplay (photograph by Mike Laye)

Award; one of his early plays, *Outskirts* (1981), won the George Devine Award. His *The Buddha of Suburbia* (1990) received the Whitbread Prize for best first novel, and the reviewer for the *Independent on Sunday* called it "one of the sharpest satires on race relations in this country that I've ever read." Kureishi celebrates the counterculture and is largely anti-Establishment in his views; when he said on a Radio 4 program that he thought the anti-poll-tax riots in London were a good thing, the BBC switchboards were jammed with complaints. Reviewing his second novel, *The Black Album* (1995), the London magazine *Time Out* said that "Kureishi is an extraordinarily gifted creator of human characters and a shrewd observer of human folly." The leading literary and cultural critic Colin

MacCabe has called him "one of the great talents of the past 25 years." Kureishi also has his detractors, ranging from Establishment figures to Britons of Asian descent. His adaptation of his story "My Son, the Fanatic" (1994) as a movie in 1998 has been attacked by Islamic leaders as a negative and unrepresentative portrayal of Muslim beliefs and behavior.

Kureishi's work is largely autobiographical. In his essay "The Rainbow Sign" (1986) he says that the derision heaped on Pakistanis in England led him to deny that side of himself for a long time. A sense of hybridity is constant in Kureishi's work. On the first page of *The Buddha of Suburbia* the narrator proclaims: "I am an Englishman born and bred, almost . . . Englishman I am (though not proud of it), from the Lon-

Francis Barber and Ayub Khan Din as the title characters in Sammy and Rosie Get Laid, *for which Kureishi wrote the screenplay (British Film Institute)*

don suburbs and going somewhere. Perhaps it is the odd mixture of continents and blood, of here and there, of belonging and not, that makes me restless and easily bored." The major tone of his writing is one of irony; Kureishi said in a November 1996 BBC Radio interview with Sue Lawley, "Irony is the modern mode, a way of commenting on bleakness and cruelty without falling into dourness and didacticism."

Kureishi began his career not as a novelist but as a playwright. He says in the introduction to *Outskirts, The King and Me, Tomorrow–Today!* (1983), a collection of three of his plays:

> A festival of "happenings" and new plays by performance-oriented groups was called "Come Together" after a Beatles song. And dozens of young people were working in this "alternative" or "fringe" theater. The plays, when they were about anything, concerned left and anarchist politics, sex roles, rebellion and oppression. They flourished all over London, in basements, above pubs, in tents, in the street and even in theaters. They used nudity, insult, music, audience participation and comedy. They attacked the Labour Party from the Left. This was good enough for me.

Kureishi's early play *Borderline* (1981), researched in the Asian community in Southall and developed in the theater with the Joint Stock Company, explores the forces acting on Indians in postimperial Britain: the abuse and violence they suffer from whites on the one hand and the cross-generational tensions between an Asian and a Western life on the other. *The King and Me* (1980) focuses on the aspirations and arguments of a young English couple fascinated with Elvis Presley. *Birds of Passage* (1983) shows the effects of the recession of the early 1980s on a lower-middle-class family who have to sell their house to a former lodger, an Asian.

Outskirts, probably Kureishi's most successful early play, concerns two former school friends, Del and Bob, who have drifted apart over the years. Del, now a teacher, is still haunted by an attack they thoughtlessly made on an Asian when they were teenagers; Bob, who is unemployed, leans toward the racist National Front. Bob's wife, Maureen, has an abortion rather than bring a child into their moneyless and hopeless lives.

Kureishi's first screenplay, *My Beautiful Laundrette,* is an unconventional rite-of-passage story. Set in south London, the movie looks at racial violence, cross-generational tensions, and young people faced with the choice between a life of hard work and entrepreneurial endeavor or one of lassitude and unemployment among childhood friends. The movie had its origin in the advice of a family friend who owned a chain of self-service laundries and insisted at the beginning of the Margaret Thatcher decade that a boy such as Kureishi could do well running a small local business. Drafted during a visit with his father's relatives in Karachi and revised while Kureishi was working on his adaptation of *Mother Courage,* the script confronts racial and sexual stereotypes in its depiction of a homosexual relationship between two boys, an Asian and a white neo-Nazi, who successfully renovate and run a laundrette they call "Powders."

Sammy and Rosie Get Laid (1987), also directed by Frears, is a satirical look at Britain in the Thatcher years. Rafi Rahman, a former official of an oppressive Pakistani regime, comes to London to visit his son, Sammy, a young accountant who lives in Brixton with Rosie Hobbs, an English social worker. Rosie, Sammy, and Rafi have various sexual encounters amid scenes of riots, drug dealing, and promiscuity, all quite different from the imperial metropolis that Rafi remembers from his student days there.

The largely autobiographical hero of Kureishi's first novel, *The Buddha of Suburbia,* Karim Amir, grows from a bored schoolboy in Kent into an aspiring actor in London and New York against a 1970s background of hippies and punks, drugs and sex.

Karim wants to be English, not Indian; he cannot see that he has any connections with Indian culture. But the other characters will not allow him to be English. He is constantly addressed as an Indian—by his teachers, by racists in the streets, by theater directors. The book's liberals want Karim to be Indian because he is their shortest route to the India that they want to experience in suburban England. Similar pressures are placed on Haroon, Karim's father, to be the "Buddha of suburbia," and on Karim's friend Jamila to be a dutiful Muslim daughter. Karim finally realizes that he can be both English, like his mother, and Indian, like his father. At the end of the book he decides that he has spent his life denying a part of his identity, that Indians are "his people." At the same time Karim, like Kureishi, realizes that he does not have the kind of Indian identity that is demanded by those around him, one that is rooted not in England but in India. He says: "If I wanted the additional personality bonus of an Indian past, I would have to create it," and he invents an Indian past for himself at the same time as he is creating a character for a stage performance.

Karim's father, Haroon, is a British civil servant and part-time oriental mystic. His idea on coming to England was to follow the path of Mohandas Gandhi and Jawaharlal Nehru: "Dad would return to India as a qualified and polished English gentleman lawyer and an accomplished ballroom dancer." Instead, he becomes the "Buddha of suburbia" and never returns home. Haroon, who has spent his life becoming "more of an Englishman," exaggerates his accent and manner to seem more Indian when he is cast in the role of spiritual leader of his neighborhood. Karim goes through the same transformation when he is asked to change his accent and manner to play Mowgli in a stage adaptation of Rudyard Kipling's *The Jungle Book* (1894).

Another character who exploits his national identity abroad is Karim's friend Charlie. Charlie is the object of Karim's desire for most of the book although for a period this fixation is transferred to Eleanor, another actor. Both represent an ideal for Karim, and both are quintessentially English. Charlie is a cold and beautiful street punk based on the rock star Billy Idol, with whom Kureishi went to school. Charlie moves to New York, where he adopts a Cockney accent. Eleanor, by contrast, represents effortless English power, privilege, influence, and culture. Karim explains the attraction women such as Eleanor hold for him and his friends of Asian extraction: "we pursued English roses as we pursued England; by possessing these prizes, this kindness and beauty, we stared defiantly into the eye of the Empire and all its self-regard. . . . We

Roshan Seth as Haroon and Naveen Andrews as Karim in the television play The Buddha of Suburbia, *adapted by Kureishi from his novel (BBC, London)*

became part of England and yet proudly stood outside it." Karim's friend Jamila is the character who is most sure of who she is and what she wants to achieve. The differences among the characters are most strikingly revealed at the book's conclusion. It is 1979, and the Labour government is about to give way to Thatcher's dominance of British politics throughout the 1980s. The novel ends on the night of the election that brings the Conservatives to power. Generally, the characters are oblivious to this shift in values, but most of them, nevertheless, reflect it. Karim celebrates his new job in a soap opera; he will abandon the left-wing theater and compromise his artistic aspirations but will earn a great deal of money. Haroon and his girlfriend Eva, the Bohemian couple of the 1970s, announce that they are going to get married. In London, "Everyone was smartly dressed, and the men had short hair, white shirts and baggy trousers held up by braces." Only Jamila continues her alternative lifestyle: she lives in a squat, forms a lesbian relationship, has an illegitimate child, and spends the evening of the novel, when Karim and the others are at a restaurant, campaigning for the Labour Party.

Some reviewers saw Karim as a picaresque hero and compared him to protagonists in novels by Richard Wright, James Baldwin, and Ralph Ellison (all of whom Kureishi had read avidly as a teenager); others viewed him as similar to H. G. Wells's Mr. Polly or Kipps, or Kingsley Amis's Lucky Jim. The novel has been translated into twenty languages; it was adapted by Kureishi in 1993 as a miniseries for the BBC and was widely acclaimed.

Less autobiographical, Kureishi's 1991 movie, *London Kills Me,* deals with homelessness and drugs in the English capital, which he damned in the interview with Lawley as "an intolerant, racist, homophobic, narrow-minded, authoritarian rathole." Clint, who lives in a squat above a Sufi center with his drug-posse friends Muffdiver and Sylvie, is trying to get a job as a waiter, for which he needs a pair of smart-looking shoes. Covering a weekend in the lives of the characters, the familiar Kureishi story line explores the forces pulling Clint toward drugs and continued homelessness on the one hand and toward employment and respectability on the other. Written and directed by Kureishi, the movie was not a critical success.

Kureishi's second novel, *The Black Album,* follows Shahid Hasan's first months at a London college, to which he has come to study under a young cultural-studies lecturer, Deedee Osgood. Shahid is an aspiring author engaged in writing a novel about his early life. He begins an affair with Deedee, a white liberal, and the two discuss black history and contemporary culture, take drugs, attend raves, and explore each other sexually. Shahid also becomes friendly with a group of activist Muslim students. When Deedee tries to stop the students from burning a copy of Rushdie's *The Satanic Verses* (1988) and defends the book on the grounds of freedom of speech, the students accuse her of racism.

Shahid finds himself agreeing with his friends when he is with them, but at other times the world seems more complex to him. The novel takes its title from a rare 1994 album by Prince, made in response to accusations that he was losing touch with his black musical roots; the title of that album, in turn, is indebted to the 1968 Beatles record popularly known as "The White Album." For Kureishi these two cultural reference points represent the best of black and white pop music. Throughout the narrative Shahid oscillates between the two sets of values offered to him by his black friends and his white lover. His dilemma represents the position of many members of the Pakistani community in Britain.

Kureishi's "My Son, the Fanatic," first published in *The New Yorker* (28 March 1994), appears in his first collection of short stories, *Love in a Blue Time* (1997); Kureishi's screenplay for the movie version of the story was published in 1997, and the picture was released in 1998. "My Son, the Fanatic" returns to some of the themes of Kureishi's second novel while again exploring father-son relationships as in *The Buddha of Suburbia.* Parvez, a Punjabi taxi driver in England, becomes concerned by the eccentric behavior of his son, Ali. When confronted, Ali accuses his father of being "too implicated in Western civilization" by eating pork, drinking alcohol, and consorting with prostitutes. Ali becomes more and more fixed in his views, finally declaring that he will work with "poor Muslims who were struggling to maintain their purity in the face of corruption." The story ends with Parvez physically assaulting Ali while the latter is at prayer because the boy has offended Bettina, Parvez's prostitute friend. Ali responds by asking, "So, who's the fanatic now?" Thus the conflict between Western and Muslim values results in intolerance and violence, and a family with roots in two cultures is torn apart.

In 1998 Kureishi published his third novel, *Intimacy,* in which Jay, a successful television scriptwriter, is preparing to leave his partner, Susan, and their two sons for a woman named Nina. The book focuses on the dilemmas of middle-aged men who feel caught between responsibilities and passion, between overfamiliar love and new desire.

Kureishi himself recently left a relationship and now lives alone in London. He teaches creative writing and continues to work as a novelist, playwright, and moviemaker.

Interviews:

Ria Julian, "Brecht and Britain: Interview with Hanif Kureishi," *Drama,* 1 (Spring 1985): 5–7;

Sheila Johnston, "Plain Dealing," *Independent,* 7 March 1991, p. 15;

Philip Dodd, "Requiem for a Rave," *Sight and Sound,* new series 1 (September 1991): 8–13.

References:

John Clement Ball, "The Semi-Detached Metropolis: Hanif Kureishi's London," *Ariel,* 27 (October 1996): 7–27;

Alamgir Hashmi, "Hanif Kureishi and the Tradition of the Novel," *International Fiction Review,* 19 (1992): 88–95;

Gayatri Spivak, "In Praise of *Sammy and Rosie Get Laid,*" *Critical Quarterly,* 31 (Summer 1989): 80–88.

David Lodge

(28 January 1935 –)

Dennis Jackson
University of Delaware

and

William M. Harrison
State University of New York, College at Geneseo

See also the Lodge entry in *DLB 14: British Novelists Since 1960*.

BOOKS: *About Catholic Authors* (London: St. Paul Press; Dublin: Browne & Nolan, 1957);

The Picturegoers (London: MacGibbon & Kee, 1960; London & New York: Penguin, 1993);

Ginger, You're Barmy (London: MacGibbon & Kee, 1962; Garden City: Doubleday, 1965; afterword by Lodge, Harmondsworth & New York: Penguin, 1984) ;

The British Museum Is Falling Down (London: MacGibbon & Kee, 1965; New York: Holt Rinehart & Winston, 1967; introduction by Lodge, London: Secker & Warburg, 1981; New York: Penguin, 1989);

Language of Fiction: Essays in Criticism and Verbal Analysis of the English Novel (London: Routledge & Kegan Paul; New York: Columbia University Press, 1966; revised edition, London & Boston: Routledge & Kegan Paul, 1984);

Graham Greene, Columbia Essays on Modern Writers Series (New York & London: Columbia University Press, 1966);

Out of the Shelter (London: Macmillan, 1970; revised edition, London: Secker & Warburg, 1985; New York: Viking Penguin, 1989);

The Novelist at the Crossroads and Other Essays on Fiction and Criticism (London: Routledge & Kegan Paul, 1971; Ithaca: Cornell University Press, 1971);

Evelyn Waugh, Columbia Essays on Modern Writers Series (New York & London: Columbia University Press, 1971);

Changing Places: A Tale of Two Campuses (London: Secker & Warburg, 1975; Harmondsworth & New York: Penguin, 1979);

The Modes of Modern Writing: Metaphor, Metonymy, and the Typology of Modern Literature (Ithaca: Cornell University Press, 1977; London: Arnold, 1977);

How Far Can You Go? (London: Secker & Warburg, 1980; republished as *Souls and Bodies* (New York: Morrow, 1982);

Working with Structuralism: Essays and Reviews on Nineteenth and Twentieth-Century Literature (London & Boston: Routledge & Kegan Paul, 1981);

Small World: An Academic Romance (London: Secker & Warburg, 1984; New York: Macmillan, 1985);

Write On: Occasional Essays '65–'85 (London: Secker & Warburg, 1986);

Nice Work: A Novel (London: Secker & Warburg, 1988; New York: Viking, 1989);

After Bakhtin: Essays on Fiction and Criticism (London & New York: Routledge, 1990);

The Writing Game: A Comedy (London: Secker & Warburg, 1991):

Paradise News: A Novel (London: Secker & Warburg, 1991; New York: Viking, 1992);

The Art of Fiction: Illustrated from Classic and Modern Texts (London: Secker & Warburg, 1992; New York: Viking, 1993);

Therapy: A Novel (London: Secker & Warburg; New York: Viking, 1995);

The Practice of Writing: Essays, Lectures, Reviews and a Diary (London: Secker & Warburg; New York: Viking, 1996).

PLAY PRODUCTIONS: *Between These Four Walls* [revue], by Lodge, Malcolm Bradbury, and James Duckett, Birmingham, Birmingham Repertory Theatre, 19 November 1963;

David Lodge (photograph by Fay Godwin–Network/Matrix)

Slap in the Middle [revue], by Lodge, Bradbury, Duckett, and David Turner, Birmingham, Birmingham Repertory Theatre, 1965;

The Writing Game: A Comedy, Birmingham, Birmingham Repertory Theatre, 12 May 1990.

TELEVISION SCRIPTS: *Big Words . . . Small Worlds,* 1987;

Nice Work, 4 episodes, BBC2, 1989;

The Way of St. James, 1993;

Martin Chuzzlewit, 5 episodes, BBC2, 1994;

The Writing Game, Channel 4, 1996.

OTHER: Charles Kingsley, *Alton Locke,* edited by Herbert van Thal, introduction by Lodge (London: Cassell, 1967);

Jane Austen: "Emma." A Casebook, edited by Lodge (London: Macmillan, 1968; Nashville: Aurora, 1970; revised edition, London: Macmillan, 1991);

Jane Austen, *Emma,* edited, with an introduction, by Lodge (Oxford & New York: Oxford University Press, 1971);

Twentieth Century Literary Criticism: A Reader, edited by Lodge (London & New York: Longman, 1972);

George Eliot, *Scenes of Clerical Life,* edited, with an introduction, by Lodge (Harmondsworth & Baltimore: Penguin, 1973);

Thomas Hardy, *The Woodlanders,* edited by Lodge (London: Macmillan, 1974);

Ring Lardner, *The Best of Ring Lardner,* edited, with an introduction, by Lodge (London: Dent, 1984; Rutland, Vt.: Tuttle, 1993);

Henry James, *The Spoils of Poynton,* edited by Lodge (Harmondsworth: Penguin, 1987);

Malcolm Bradbury, *My Strange Quest for Mensonge: Structuralism's Hidden Hero,* foreword and afterword by Lodge (London: Deutsch, 1987);

Modern Criticism and Theory: A Reader (London & New York: Longman, 1988);

Kingsley Amis, *Lucky Jim,* foreword by Lodge (New York: Penguin, 1992).

David Lodge is the author of some of the most clever, ambitious, and funny fiction written in England during the past four decades. His fifth novel, *Changing Places: A Tale of Two Campuses* (1975), won the Hawthornden Prize and the *Yorkshire Post* Fiction Prize for 1975, and his sixth novel, *How Far Can You Go?* (1980), was selected as the Whitbread Book of the Year for 1980. He has combined the writing of fiction with a keen interest in its theory and, in addition to his novels, has written eleven books of literary criticism and scores of articles for academic journals. Such writings on literary theory as *Language of Fiction: Essays in Criticism and Verbal Analysis of the English Novel* (1966) and *The Modes of Modern Writing: Metaphor, Metonymy, and the Typology of Modern Literature* (1977) have made him one of the foremost critical speculators on the novel form. While carrying on this prolific writing career he worked as a professor of English literature at the University of Birmingham until his early retirement in 1987.

Since then he has worked full-time as a freelance writer.

Lodge's novels have all focused largely on his own experiences and on the environments he has known best—lower-middle-class Catholic family life in a South London suburb; a childhood spent in wartime England and an adolescence in austerity-ridden postwar London; life as a graduate student and as a literature professor; married life; and life inside the Catholic Church after World War II. For his characters and for his settings he seldom ventures from academia or the Catholic Church. In most of his novels his protagonists are literature students or college professors, and a majority of them are also enlightened Catholics. The author himself is "a believing Catholic of a very liberal kind theologically," and most of his novels have at least some Catholic statement set in them. Taken as a whole, his fiction forms an interesting chronicle of the vast changes that took place in the Catholic Church and in the attitudes of the Catholic community in the years following the war. One crucial area of such change involved individual Catholics' attitudes toward official church teachings regarding sex and birth control, and one of the recurrent themes in Lodge's stories is the struggle of his Catholic characters to reconcile their spiritual and sensual desires.

He is undoubtedly at his best as a writer of comic fiction, one very much in the British comic tradition of Evelyn Waugh and Kingsley Amis. (Lodge signaled his admiration for Amis in 1992 when he wrote an insightful introduction to a new Penguin edition of Amis's *Lucky Jim* (1954)—the first "campus novel" of the sort that Lodge was to make his own reputation writing.) Unlike many contemporaries, Lodge retains his faith in traditional realism as a vehicle for his fiction, and his stories never veer off into fantastic or apocalyptic visions of life such as those found in so many other postwar novels. His rhetoric is usually unobtrusive, and his style is crisp and conversational. As an academic critic and teacher of literature with a particular interest in prose fiction, he is inevitably self-conscious about matters of narrative technique, and his fiction, like his criticism, shows a deep sensitivity toward language. Further, his novels often reflect his interest in critical theories; this is especially true of *The British Museum Is Falling Down* (1965), *Changing Places, How Far Can You Go?, Small World: An Academic Romance* (1984), and *Nice Work* (1988), where his theoretical interest in the problematic relation of art to reality is built into the fiction itself.

Born on 28 January 1935 in South London, David John Lodge was the only child of a lower-middle-class couple. His father, William Frederick

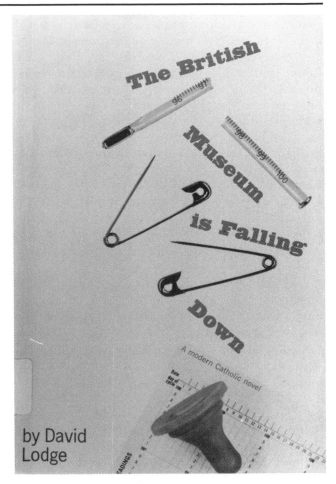

Dust jacket for the U.S. edition of Lodge's comedic novel of a postgraduate student who becomes convinced that his life is imitating the novels he has been studying in the British Museum

Lodge, worked as a saxophonist and clarinetist in dance bands. Though he had little formal education, Lodge's father liked to read—early Charles Dickens, Waugh, Jerome K. Jerome, P. G. Wodehouse, and other British humorists—and years later the son acknowledged that his father's "rather mellow" literary tastes had likely influenced his own fictional style. His mother, Rosalie Marie Murphy Lodge, came from an Irish-Belgian background and was a Roman Catholic. During much of the Blitzkrieg he was in London, but he and his mother spent over two-thirds of the war years living in the country in Surrey or Cornwall. He later fictionalized that period of his life in his fourth novel, *Out of the Shelter* (1970). At age ten, as soon as the war ended, he was enrolled at St. Joseph's Academy, a Catholic grammar school in Blackheath, London, and it was there that he first became vitally interested in Catholicism, as it was taught by the Delasalles, the order of religious teaching brothers who ran the school. He first showed an interest in creative writing at age fifteen, when he began writing poems and stories.

After graduation from St. Joseph's in 1952, Lodge went to University College, London, where he took a B.A. in English (with honors) three years later. After his first year of college, at eighteen, he attempted his first novel, "The Devil, The World and The Flesh." A publisher to whom he submitted it responded encouragingly but advised against publication. He took the advice. As in several of his later novels, "The Devil, The World and The Flesh" focused both on Catholic characters living in a seedy suburban section of London and on certain religious interests. Several episodes from the work were later incorporated into *The Picturegoers* (1960), his first published novel.

During undergraduate days at University College, Lodge met Mary Frances Jacob, another English student. She was the third eldest of seven children in a large Catholic family whom Lodge often visited at their home fifteen miles from London. He later used them as a rough model for the warm and happy Mallory family in *The Picturegoers*. Four years after finishing his B.A. degree he married her.

In 1955 he began his national service, working during most of his two-year stint as a clerk at Bovington Camp in Dorset (a Royal Armoured Corps training camp). He bitterly resented military life, and several years later, as an "act of revenge," he wrote *Ginger, You're Barmy* (1962), his second published novel, recounting in near-documentary fashion the brutality and tedium of army camp existence.

During his final year in the army, in the spring of 1957, he began work on *The Picturegoers*. A novel about Catholics set in the dingy suburb of Brickley, its action occurs mainly in three locales–a decaying cinema (the Palladium), a Catholic church, and a large Catholic household on Maple Street. The story relates the changes in the lives of more than a dozen characters over a year's time but focuses on the gradual return to faith of one lapsed Catholic, a young English literature student named Mark Underwood.

Mark's conversion is effected rather ironically through the influence of Clare Mallory, one of the seven children of a family with whom he lodges while he finishes college. Mark longs to possess her "flawless torso," and Clare, a former novice in a convent, longs to help him rediscover the Catholic faith. Gradually she falls in love with him, and her own piety becomes less intense; when she at last offers herself in passionate embrace, however, he rejects her and soon after announces his own plans to enter the priesthood. The ironic see-saw of their attitudes provides much of the story's dramatic tension as the two young people struggle toward self-awareness. Like Mark and Clare, several of the more-engaging minor figures in *The Picturegoers* are also caught in a conflict between their spiritual and carnal desires.

Lodge defines nearly every character in the novel in terms of his or her responses to the cinema. For a pathetic teddy boy named Harry, for instance, the cinema fuels romantic fantasies of one day making the "big time," of having money, cars, and big-bosomed "tarts" such as he views on the Palladium screen. For Mark Underwood, by nature contemplative and analytical, the cinema provides much food for deep thought. He decides that "picture-going" has become a "substitute for religion" and frequently draws parallels between "Mother Cinema" and the Catholic Church. In an ironic way such musings over the cinema draw him back toward the church.

Lodge attempts to orient the whole book around his characters' trips to the cinema. Early in the novel he describes the Palladium's habitués one by one as they enter on a Saturday night; he describes their individual responses to the current film, often pausing to offer exposition through flashbacks on their lives; and he describes how the characters go home thinking about the movie in relation to their own life dreams. But the Palladium ceases to be such an important structural peg in the second half of the book, and the plot becomes rather disconnected.

There are other problems. Some scenes appear extraneous; the reader is asked to remember too many characters (more than a dozen), a few of them only tenuously related to the plot; further, there is little dramatic interplay between some of the characters and others in the story. But for a first novel *The Picturegoers* is eminently lively and readable, and most reviewers in 1960 acknowledged these qualities even while noting the book's flaws. Many of the novel's passages clearly show Lodge's promising future as comic novelist and prose stylist. His alternation of diction, tone, and rhythm as he shifts from his description of the inner thoughts of one character to those of another seems particularly impressive. Such alternation of styles–which he had learned by reading James Joyce's novels and which he was to employ again in later novels–enables him to delineate sharply the inner lives of a broad range of contrasting characters.

Certain mannerisms in *The Picturegoers* indicate Graham Greene's influence on Lodge's style. Lodge had read with special interest the works of Greene, Waugh, and other Catholic writers. After his mili-

Dust jacket for Lodge's fifth novel, a wide-ranging satire of youth culture, academia, and critical theories of literature in the 1970s

tary service ended, he returned to University College, London, to take an M.A. degree and did his thesis on "Catholic Fiction Since the Oxford Movement: Its Literary Form and Religious Content."

After finishing his M.A. work he married Mary Jacob on 16 May 1959. Unable to find a university post, he took a temporary job with the British Council's Overseas Students Center in London, where he taught English and literature to foreign students and organized various cultural activities. In 1960, while living in Battersea, he and Mary had their first child, Julia, and in that same year MacGibbon and Kee published *The Picturegoers.*

Lodge began immediately to write another novel, *Ginger, You're Barmy,* drawing significantly upon his experiences in the British army. The story's first-person narrator, Jonathan Browne, records the difficulties he encounters after he is wrenched out of his sheltered existence as an English student at a London university and is thrust into a crass, dehumanizing military world in which his assets—intelligence, critical judgment, and culture—become liabilities. The book interestingly describes all the

universals of soldiering, especially of basic training, with its "quality of realism, of nightmarish unreason," but the novel is kept from becoming just another stale army tale by the narrator's detached and often ironical observations and his keen attention to detail.

As Lodge later acknowledged, *Ginger, You're Barmy* is closely patterned after Greene's *The Quiet American* (1955). As in Greene's novel, the narrative alternates between two time frames: in one Browne recalls episodes from his months in basic training in Catterick Camp in the Midlands, and in alternate sections he narrates events from his final week in the national service, when he is a clerk in the Royal Armoured Corps at Badmore Camp in Dorset. *Ginger, You're Barmy* also resembles *The Quiet American* in its themes, characterizations, and plot. Both stories treat the theme of treachery and betrayal. Jon Browne, like Greene's narrator, Fowler, is an intellectual, cynical, detached man, not at all willing to become involved in life. Like Fowler also, Browne steals his best friend's woman and ultimately betrays him. His friend is Mike Brady, another conscript, who, like Greene's "quiet American" Pyle, is a Christian and idealist willing to fight for what he thinks is right or just in life. In contrast to the self-centered and unfeeling Browne, Brady is a passionate man, a man of conscience and compassion. When a shy, frail, bumbling boy named Percy is bullied by other soldiers, Brady nobly defends him. When Percy accidentally kills himself, Brady works to make sure that the dead boy—who is, like himself, a Roman Catholic—is not "stigmatized as a suicide" and hence denied Christian burial, and he later retaliates against a corporal whose harsh reprimands had helped cause Percy's death. Near the story's end Brady becomes involved in yet another cause as he helps the Irish Republican Army raid a British armory at Badmore. He is captured through information provided by Browne and is consequently sent to prison. The novel focuses on the changing nature of Browne's relationship with Brady and on a "small advance" that Browne claims he has made as a person—by story's end he has, like Greene's Fowler, finally become engagé and has found a new generosity of spirit (a change of heart that some critics found less than convincing).

Not long after he began writing *Ginger, You're Barmy* in 1960, Lodge accepted a one-year job teaching English literature at a Midlands redbrick university, the University of Birmingham. A year later he was rehired as an assistant lecturer and then began a steady rise through the academic ranks, culminating in his promotion in 1976 to the rank of professor of modern English literature.

During his first four years at the university he worked on material that formed his first academic critical book, *Language of Fiction: Essays in Critical and Verbal Analysis of the English Novel*. After its publication in 1966 it became one of the most widely read of contemporary books on the novel. In it Lodge argues that the novelist's language (image patterns, "key-words," and other features of the "verbal texture" of novels) deserves the same kind of close critical attention customarily given to poetry. He first offers a long argument toward a poetics of fiction and then puts his poetics into practice in seven essays dealing with the use of language in the works of seven English novelists.

Over the next fifteen years Lodge established a reputation as one of the ablest critics and theorists of the novel at work in England. During that time he produced dozens of journal articles and five more books of criticism: *Graham Greene* (1966), a short biographical-critical monograph in the Columbia Essays on Modern Writers series; *Evelyn Waugh* (1971), another Columbia monograph; *The Novelist at the Crossroads and Other Essays on Fiction and Criticism*

(1971), which collected fourteen of his essays, many of them reaffirming what he had said in *Language of Fiction* regarding the "primacy of language in literary matters"; *The Modes of Modern Writing: Metaphor, Metonymy and the Typology of Modern Literature*, in which he argues the need for "a comprehensive typology of literary discourse" and proposes that such a typology might be based upon Roman Jakobson's theory of the metaphoric and metonymic poles of language; and *Working with Structuralism: Essays and Reviews on Nineteenth- and Twentieth-Century Literature* (1981), another collection of his critical articles.

During the 1960s and 1970s Lodge also edited and wrote introductions for Jane Austen's *Emma* (1971), George Eliot's *Scenes of Clerical Life* (1973), and Thomas Hardy's *The Woodlanders* (1974), and he edited *Jane Austen: "Emma." A Casebook* (1968) and *Twentieth Century Literary Criticism: A Reader* (1972). The idea for the latter text he had gotten while teaching courses on literary criticism at Birmingham. He had in the 1960s often collaborated in teaching such courses with his friend and colleague, the novelist and critic Malcolm Bradbury.

He also had collaborated with Bradbury in 1963 in writing a satirical revue titled *Between These Four Walls*. With a third writer, a talented English student named James Duckett, they accepted a commission by a Birmingham repertory theater to write a series of short humorous sketches and comic topical songs. The revue ran for a month.

That experience and his continued association with Bradbury, among other things, inspired Lodge to try his hand at a comic novel, and in late spring 1964, just after he had completed *Language of Fiction*, he began writing *The British Museum Is Falling Down* (1965). He had for several years been considering a novel about a postgraduate English student whose life keeps taking on the quality of the novels that he is studying in the British Museum, and when he got an idea for a comic novel about the dilemma of Catholics over birth control, he soon found a way of linking the two stories. The church's teaching on contraception was a topical issue. A pontifical commission was studying problems associated with the family, population, and birth control, and the Catholic world was buzzing with the possibility that the church's teaching on contraception, which had formerly been thought of as absolutely unchangeable, might, indeed, change. Lodge and his wife themselves experienced in 1964 some of the strains that the church's teaching imposed on married people (their second child, Stephen, had been born in 1962), and the author hoped that with his new novel he might in some way affect the winds of change

Dust jacket for Lodge's novel chronicling how church reform affects the lives of a group of British Catholics from just after World War II until the 1970s

that were already blowing in the Roman Catholic Church.

The novel's hero, Adam Appleby, and his wife, Barbara, have already lost three rounds of "Vatican Roulette" using the rhythm method, and, as *The British Museum Is Falling Down* starts, they are fearful, despite a house full of ovulation charts, calendars, and thermometers, that a fourth child may be on the way. Amid this "surging sea of fertility" Appleby is struggling to finish his Ph.D. thesis (on modern British novels) and is suffering great anxiety over his need to find a job soon. *The British Museum Is Falling Down* tells the story of one day of pandemonium in his life. It is a day he had planned to spend doing quiet research inside the British Museum, but during the roughly eighteen-hour span of the novel he fails to open a single book: he runs back and forth for telephone calls home to see if his wife has started her menstrual period; he discusses contraceptives at a Catholic meeting; he raises a false fire alarm that throws the British Museum into a panic; he gets drunk and disgraces himself at a gathering of academics; he negotiates with a stately

Catholic matron who wants to sell him some literary relics and with her not-so-stately daughter who agrees to give him valuable manuscripts if he will take her virginity; he watches as his scooter explodes and sends the treasured manuscripts up in flames; he at last lands a job as a book buyer for a fat American who has come to England hoping to buy the British Museum in order to relocate it to the Colorado Rockies; and he returns triumphantly home to make love to his wife, who immediately thereafter starts her period.

These events of one zany day are all structured very much according to the scheme of James Joyce's *Ulysses* (1922), and the imprint of that book is everywhere seen (usually to comic effect) through *The British Museum Is Falling Down*. Like Leopold Bloom, Adam—because of the domestic and academic pressures he is facing—becomes increasingly disoriented as his day progresses, and his perceptions of life around him become increasingly phantasmagoric. Like Bloom also, Lodge's hero keeps his mind constantly fixed throughout the day on his home and his wife; he suffers because of his religion; and he has fantasies of grandeur (which, like Bloom's, are always followed by some sort of comic diminution). Among the numerous other explicit *Ulysses* parallels, the most obvious is the "Epilogue," a ten-page parody or pastiche of Molly Bloom's unpunctuated monologue, wherein Barbara Appleby rehearses, in a flowing stream-of-consciousness style, her love life with Adam. She records her husband's triumphant return to the house in Battersea, and, as does Molly's in *Ulysses,* her monologue forms an optimistic and life-affirming end for the story.

Of all writers, Joyce had the greatest influence on Lodge's fiction. The kind of realism seen in Joyce's treatment of Catholic lower- and middle-class life in *Dubliners* (1914) and *A Portrait of the Artist as a Young Man* (1916) is reflected in Lodge's early novels, and Joyce's stylistic variations in *Ulysses* had an even stronger influence on Lodge's later books, especially *The British Museum Is Falling Down* and *Changing Places.* In *The British Museum Is Falling Down* Lodge changes the style and technique from one section to another, and also much in Joycean fashion, he frequently shifts the language of the story into pastiches or parodies of various other novelists, among them Joseph Conrad, Ernest Hemingway, Virginia Woolf, Amis, Greene, Baron Corvo, Henry James, and C. P. Snow. Through such a parody technique Lodge subtly weaves into his novel's fabric his hero's own professional interest in literary language and modes. Lodge's critical interest in the "language of fiction" had led him to examine various authors' styles closely, and that research made it easier for him to create the parodies when he came to writing *The British Museum Is Falling Down.* As he later observed, *Language of Fiction* and the novel had "a kind of jokey relation to each other." The parodies also help demonstrate the novel's subsidiary theme that "life imitates art," and they are expressive projections of Adam's own neurotic notion that the events of his life are following the shape of certain scenes from novels he has read.

The British Museum Is Falling Down is unceasingly and vigorously funny; there are frequent flashes of Lodge's natural wit and endless literary jokes, but, more often than not, the humor is of a broad, farcical sort. Yet throughout the book serious undertones give emphasis and point to the author's general levity. His comic and satiric treatment of the current Catholic indecision over family planning is not a frontal attack on the church itself but rather a good-natured jibe meant to provoke both laughter and a serious new consideration of the effect of the Catholic ban on artificial contraception on couples such as the Applebys. Lodge's satire extends also to the academic world, and he takes more than a few pokes at the petty jealousies, pretentiousness, and absentmindedness exhibited by professors in Adam's English department. Much of the comedy, tone, and atmosphere of *The British Museum Is Falling Down* is reminiscent of *Lucky Jim* (Lodge had noted in *Language of Fiction* a "strange community of feeling" he shared with Amis), but that earlier novel has a more savage satiric edge. Lodge's treatment of academe is gentler, more the lighthearted raillery and ridicule of a member of the family than the heavy-handed attack by a bitter defector such as Amis's hero.

The British Museum Is Falling Down received more favorable commentary from more reviewers than Lodge's two previous novels had, and it represented a real development in his career as a writer of fiction. Despite the frequent parodies, Lodge gave evidence in *The British Museum Is Falling Down* that he was finding his own "voice," his own fictional style, and he mined a high comic vein in the novel that was later to be acknowledged as one of the most notable features of his fiction.

Lodge took the first chapter of *The British Museum Is Falling Down* with him in August 1964 when he went to the United States on a Harkness Commonwealth Fellowship. He went first to Brown University in Rhode Island to study American literature, and during his six months there he completed the novel (by early 1965). Soon afterward he, Mary, and their two children launched a slow journey by automobile across the southern United States, arriving in San Francisco for a three-month stay in the summer of 1965. After that "fairly euphoric year" in America he returned home to Birmingham and again collaborated on a satirical revue with Bradbury and Duckett (this time they were joined by a playwright named David Turner). *Slap in the Middle* was produced in a Birmingham repertory theater in the fall of 1965.

In 1966 Lodge began writing another novel, *Out of the Shelter* (1970), which focuses on two crucial periods in the early life of its protagonist, Timothy Young—his childhood in wartime London and his 1951 holiday trip to Germany (when he is sixteen). The story includes frequent humorous episodes that recall *The British Museum Is Falling Down,* but *Out of the Shelter* is a comparatively sober treatment of several themes, the most prominent being the sexual maturation of the rather priggish young English Catholic boy.

As in *The Picturegoers* Lodge's main characters in *Out of the Shelter* are members of a working-class Catholic family in South London. In an opening chapter more than a little like the beginning of

Joyce's *A Portrait of the Artist as a Young Man,* Lodge describes the developing consciousness of young Timothy (in a third-person narrative style that simulates a child's syntax and diction) and relates the profound effects of the war on the Young family. Following the war the shy, intellectual youth prospers as a student at St. Michael's Catholic grammar school in London, and his life is "safe, orderly" for a time. The novel's first section is titled "The Shelter"—referring not only to an Anderson air-raid shelter, where Timothy had felt "warm and safe" during the Blitzkrieg, but also by extension to the "shelter" of his home, parents, school, and the Catholic Church. In section 2, "Coming Out," sixteen-year-old Timothy fearfully prepares to embark for the "exotic" land of Germany, where he will spend the summer with his twenty-seven-year-old sister, Kate, who works as a secretary for the American occupation army. (Lodge had made a similar journey to Germany in 1951 to visit his mother's sister.) This holiday, as Timothy himself later observes, is a "turning-point" in his life, and more than two-thirds of the novel relates his experiences on the Continent, his slow emergence from and his life out of "the shelter" of his former existence in London.

His "Coming Out" involves his adaptation to several kinds of changes in his life—geographical, cultural, social, and sexual. He ventures into "the Germany of his imagination," into the land of the recent enemy, but ironically, during his stay there he experiences culture shock less from the German natives than from "the American way of life" he encounters. Coming from austerity-ridden postwar England, the naive youngster is thrust headlong into an "environment of excess" among Kate's hedonistic American friends in Heidelberg (most of them civilians working for the American occupation army) and joins them in their endless rounds of sunbathing, drinking, dancing, gambling, and dashing around various fancy resorts in the Bavarian Alps. Gradually he enters into their "spirit of excess" and begins to realize the limitations of English life as he had known it in a Catholic household of the 1940s, a life of dreariness and repression where one had lived always "in anticipation and recollection, never by impulse." However, he never fully accepts the "abundantly pleasurable," insouciant, and free life that he and Kate identify as "the American way"; he only goes, as he says, "sort of half-way." But his journey to Germany does result in a significant testing and readjustment of his values.

Out of the Shelter focuses largely on the way its young hero advances "half-way" toward sexual maturity. The book lacks intensity; it has no sharply drawn conflict or dramatic tension; and for most of

Dust jacket for Lodge's 1991 novel, which mixes the story of a former Catholic priest who finds salvation in Hawaii with a satire on British tourists abroad

the story the only real suspense has to do with this question of how and when Timothy will learn about sex. As in *The Picturegoers* and *The British Museum Is Falling Down,* Lodge frequently links the sexual interests of *Out of the Shelter* with certain religious interests. Timothy constantly relates his developing sexual knowledge to the teachings of the Catholic Church. His own religion seems a strange mixture of fear and superstition. He believes that extramarital sex is a "mortal sin," that "if you died with it on your soul you went to Hell," and after he and a half-nude sixteen-year-old named Gloria have touched each other's genitals, he immediately thinks to himself, "I must get to confession before I leave for home tomorrow. Trains could crash, ships could sink."

He never quite gets "out of the shelter" of the Catholic Church, and neither does his sister, Kate. While in Germany, Timothy fears that Kate has become a "lapsed" Catholic, and he worries over her soul. But in an epilogue (an awkward and contrived effort to tie up some of the plot's loose ends), when he visits his sister in America fourteen years later, she tells him, "I've gone back to the Church.... As you get older, I think you feel the need for something." In a significant way Lodge was to return to that theme—of man's "need for something" (which the church has to offer)—in his sixth novel, *How Far Can You Go?*

Out of the Shelter was finished in 1968 and was published two years later by Macmillan. Lodge completed the book just before he moved his family (then numbering five, son Christopher having been born in 1966) to America, where for two academic quarters he was a visiting associate professor of English at the University of California, Berkeley.

The spring of 1969 was a turbulent time in America; among other troubles, the country was at war in Vietnam, and its university campuses were in turmoil caused by the student revolution. For a time during Lodge's first quarter at Berkeley, normal university activities were virtually shut down by a "Third World Students' Strike," and during his second quarter there the campus was disrupted by a bloody controversy over the "People's Park," where a group of young radicals had seized a plot of university land, and the National Guard eventually was dispatched to the campus. Not by nature an activist, Lodge generally remained on the sidelines during all this activity, although he did join a vigil by the Berkeley English faculty in late spring protesting the presence of armed police and troops on campus. He had been witness to a much milder form of student revolution before coming to Berkeley. At Birmingham the previous autumn, students demanding a stronger voice in the government of the university had occupied an administration building. But such disturbances in England had been much less bloody and less explosive and a great deal less political than the Berkeley protests, which involved the whole community and not just students and faculty.

Lodge was intrigued by dissimilarities in how the revolution of the young was playing out in America and Europe, and his fifth novel, *Changing Places,* which he began writing in 1971, grew out of his desire to explore that cultural contrast. The public revolution pictured in the novel serves as background to a more important "duplex chronicle" of the private lives of two literature professors, one from a prestigious California university and the other from a redbrick British university, who exchange jobs (and ultimately cars, houses, children, and wives) for six months. Each of Lodge's heroes gets caught up in the student rebellion in some fashion. Philip Swallow, who goes to the United States as a visiting professor at the State University of Euphoria, stands in a vigil and unknowingly aids a group of radicals involved in the "People's Garden" protest (the "People's Park" episode at Berkeley is recounted in the novel virtually as it had happened). He views firsthand the fierce and bloody conflict between the "University-Industrial-Military Complex" and the "Alternative Society of Love and Peace" on the American campus. His counterpart, an American scholar named Morris Zapp, goes to the Midlands to the University of Rummidge, where he eventually becomes the chief mediator who brings a confrontation between British students and the administration to a peaceful resolution.

But the primary focus of the book is on the personal lives of the two academics who, approaching middle age, find new identities as a result of their moves to new environs. (*Changing Places* is, like *The British Museum Is Falling Down,* a comic "campus novel," with the same sort of zany characters and events depicted in the earlier novel.) Each of the two college professors depicted in *Changing Places* is, at the time of the transatlantic swap, forty years old; each has, for various reasons, a failing marriage and a career that has gone stale. Swallow is a dull, routinized, weak-kneed man. He has published little scholarly writing and has little chance for promotion at Rummidge. But his "pilgrimage" to the American West results in a "liberation" of sorts for him and ends some of his self-doubts. He finds himself (mostly by accident) a hero of Euphoria campus politics and a radical philosopher. In California, Swallow gradually loses his inhibitions: he commits adultery for the first time (with Zapp's college-age daughter) and later moves in with Zapp's liberated wife, Désirée, thus becoming a "new man." Similarly, Philip's submissive wife Hilary Swallow is attracted to Morris Zapp's take-charge tactics, and Zapp too becomes a "new man" as a result of the strange marital exchange that occurs in the story. In many ways Zapp is the antithesis of Swallow. He is rakish, vain, sarcastic, and brilliant, and he is *"the Jane Austen man,"* author of five books. But like his British counterpart he has reached a point of midlife crisis: he has written very little for the past several years; he has found it hard to hold the attention of students increasingly hostile to traditional academic values; he does not want the divorce Désirée is seeking; and he has experienced some recent sexual failures. But with Hilary in the Swallow household and with the low-key British academics at Rummidge, he no longer feels threatened and begins to project a future for himself in the dark gray Midlands.

Exactly what that future will be, the reader never learns. When the two couples reunite in a Manhattan hotel (as the two parallel plots finally merge), Hilary wonders aloud: "Where is this all going to end?" No one—not even the author himself—ever gets an answer to the question. The four characters sit in the hotel room searching for an ending, like "scriptwriters discussing how to wind up a play." Lodge floats a series of possible endings to his story, but before the reader learns which option the characters choose, the story abruptly concludes. Philip is addressing "the question of endings" when, with a movie-script notation that "the camera stops, freezing him in mid-gesture," *Changing Places* simply ends. With this conclusion Lodge is poking a little fun at postmodernist fiction by parodying the strangely ambivalent endings that many postmodern writers have given to their stories. The final pages of *Changing Places* are, in a fashion, a comic version of endings such as that which John Fowles gives his 1969 novel *The French Lieutenant's Woman,* where the novelist invites his readers to choose between alternative endings to his story. (Lodge discusses Fowles's book and other postmodernist endings in *The Modes of Modern Writing.*)

Lodge is also, in the ending of this novel, taking a playful poke at some theorists of modern fiction, among them Robert Scholes, the author of the 1967 study *The Fabulators.* Scholes had there argued that the cinema has superseded the mimetic possibilities of literature, that the camera has rendered literary realism redundant. Consequently, Scholes has decided, the novel is "dying," and contemporary narrative writers are turning to "fabulations," or nonrealistic literary modes. But Lodge had disagreed, and in his 1969 essay "The Novelist at the Crossroads" he had countered that such "obsequies" over the novel are "premature," and he had affirmed his "faith in the future of realistic fiction." He is further challenging Scholes's ideas in *Changing Places* (and once again his fiction stands in a sort of "jokey relation" to his own critical writings). On the novel's penultimate page Lodge has Swallow subscribe to those arguments of Scholes and other theorists who believe that methods of conventional realistic imitation are all no longer adequate to portray "illusory" contemporary life. In the Manhattan hotel Philip views a television picture of a protest march of young California radicals, and he declares: "There *is* a generation gap. . . . Our generation—we subscribe to the old liberal doctrine of the inviolate self. It's the great tradition of realistic fiction, it's what novels are all about. The private life in the foreground, history a distant rumble of gunfire, somewhere offstage. . . . Well, the novel is dying, and us with it. . . . It's an unnatural medium for [young people's] experiences. Those kids . . . are living a film, not a novel." Lodge presents the whole last chapter of *Changing Places* in the form of a movie script. But that represents no capitulation on his part to Scholes's (and Swallow's) theory that the cin-

ema has superiority over realistic fiction when it comes to representing modern "reality"; to the contrary it is merely a rhetorical strategy. Lodge invokes the visual medium (television as well as film) merely in order to reinforce a verbal communication—a novel, obviously, and one which sensitively registers the many discords of contemporary experience and does so without stretching too far beyond the parameters of a realistic vision of life.

Changing Places, even more than *The British Museum Is Falling Down,* expresses Lodge's interests in the nature of fictional form. The novel's style becomes a major source of its comedy as the manipulating author tries out various techniques. Three chapters are told from a third-person "privileged narrative altitude (higher than that of any jet)," but three other chapters shift narrative gears—one is presented in epistolary style; another is a Joycean gathering of newspaper items, press releases, underground press publications, handbills, and classified ads; and the final chapter is cast as a movie script. The novelist thus often renegotiates his narrative position. *Changing Places* is, in frequently comic ways, a reflexive novel. His characters often consider the aesthetic problems Lodge is facing in writing his fiction. Zapp, for instance, reads a book titled *Let's Write a Novel,* one passage of which declares: "There are three types of stories, the story that ends happily, the story that ends unhappily, and the story that . . . doesn't really end at all." The last one, it is declared, is "the worst kind." This and other references to *Let's Write a Novel* serve as a comic commentary on Lodge's own novel, which has no ending at all. The difficulty of the novel writer's task ultimately becomes, in the closing chapter of *Changing Places,* Lodge's subject, and readers are there made to participate in the aesthetic and philosophical decisions that the novelist must make at the end of his story. In its final chapter, at least, *Changing Places* becomes an example of what Lodge in "The Novelist at the Crossroads" calls the "problematic novel," the "novel-about-itself."

Lodge finished *Changing Places* in summer 1973. As soon as Secker and Warburg published the novel in February 1975, it elicited favorable responses from almost all reviewers. The book won both the *Yorkshire Post* Fiction Prize and the Hawthornden Prize for 1975. In 1976 Lodge was invited to become a fellow of the Royal Society of Literature. Increasingly through the 1970s he was sought after as a lecturer at universities and at literary conferences across Europe. In 1977 he served as Henfield Writing Fellow at the University of East Anglia during the summer months.

He began writing his sixth novel, *How Far Can You Go?*, in summer 1976, and it was finished by autumn 1978. In a sense Lodge was circling back over thematic grounds covered in his earlier novels. As in *The Picturegoers, The British Museum Is Falling Down,* and *Out of the Shelter,* the focus in *How Far Can You Go?* is on the sexual and religious concerns of English Catholic characters. In *Changing Places* he had treated the political, social, and sexual revolutions taking place in the 1960s; in *How Far Can You Go?* he narrows that focus and treats the effect of those and similar revolutions on English Catholics of his generation. The book presents a panoramic view of the vast changes effected inside the church during the era spanning the 1950s up to Pope John Paul II's installation in the late 1970s. Especially in the years following the Second Vatican Council, traditional attitudes of Catholics toward authority, sex, worship, pastoral practice, and other religions changed radically; the traditional Catholic metaphysic faded; and the church came no longer to represent a sort of monolithic, unified, uniform view of life as once it had done.

To chronicle such changes, Lodge in *How Far Can You Go?* traces the fortunes of a group of ten enlightened Catholics over a quarter century of their adult lives (the group includes, among others, a priest, a nun, a physician, a Cambridge historian, and an English professor). He uses an early morning mass in the gloomy Church of Our Lady and St. Jude in London to introduce his ten principal characters (at a time when most of them are University of London students) and to outline the Catholic "world-picture" that these young people had been taught to believe in, the complex "synthesis of theology and cosmology and casuistry" that "situated individual souls on a kind of spiritual Snakes and Ladders board," in the "game" of salvation. Lodge significantly sets this mass on Valentine's Day. At a party later one of the students recites the woeful tale of St. Valentine as another mimes an "extravagant display of passion" on a sofa nearby. The irony comes in the fact that Lodge's young Catholics know such a great deal more about the figure of St. Valentine in his aspect as a Christian martyr than they do about his being the patron saint of lovers. A later chapter, "How they lost their virginities," gives a case-by-case rundown of how the repressed young Catholics all fare in their first sexual encounters, either in motels or in marriage beds. Most fare poorly. Lodge's point, one he repeats for emphasis throughout the novel, is that Catholic youths have generally been ill prepared for sex, for accepting lovemaking as something pleasurable.

Most of Lodge's Catholic couples spend the 1960s producing "babies, babies" in spite of "strenuous efforts not to," and Lodge launches a vigorous discussion of a subject he had covered before in *The British Museum Is Falling Down*—the problems of conscience that married Catholics face because of the church's teaching on birth control. *The British Museum Is Falling Down,* written at a time when Lodge and other Catholics were hopeful that a pontifical commission was about to change the church's ban on contraception, was lighthearted in its treatment of Vatican Roulette; but in *How Far Can You Go?,* written after Pope Paul VI's 1968 *Humanae Vitae* had produced no change in church doctrine, the author speaks bitterly, with righteous indignation, about the church's failure to change its stance on birth control. Lodge blames the rhythm method for having caused great ills in Catholic marriages—among them, frigidity in wives fearful of pregnancy and hideous gynecological complications caused by excessive childbearing. Moreover, he suggests that the breakdown of marriages among the Catholic couples in his story is due significantly to the church's past reticence and repression concerning sexual love.

Changing Places had dramatized the growing permissiveness in Western secular society in the 1960s; *How Far Can You Go?* traces the challenge that this new permissiveness gave specifically to the Roman Catholic ethos, then and later. In lively fashion Lodge first shows the struggles of his characters to overcome their inbred fear that contraception would be a grave sin in the "spiritual game of Snakes and Ladders"; he depicts their subsequent pursuit of erotic fulfillment through "postural variations" during coitus, blue movies, sex "games" and the like; and he finally focuses on the way they all weather the sexual upheavals of middle age (some commit adultery, others are tempted by group sex). With a few exceptions the characters seem, by the story's end, to have made a fairly satisfactory compromise between their sensual and spiritual longings.

The novel stresses the far-reaching effects that the crisis over birth control had in the church. Most significant, the debate over contraception caused Catholics to begin reexamining and redefining their views on other fundamental issues, and some of the results of this process are made evident in the novel's final chapter, in the description of a "Paschal Festival" sponsored by a liberal Catholic group. Lodge presents this festival in the rather contrived form of a transcript (supposedly written by one of his characters, a literature professor named Michael) based on a videotape of a television documen-

Dust jacket for Lodge's 1995 novel, a comic look at modern attempts to deal with spiritual crises

tary called "Easter with the New Catholics." This transcript reads "like a coda to everything that had happened" to Lodge's Catholic characters "in matters of belief," and it is, in effect, a recapitulation of the novel's primary themes. The Easter-weekend festival is a "showcase for the pluralist, progressive, postconciliar Church," and the participants represent well the wide range of special interests (for instance, the "Charismatic Renewal" and the "new theology" of sexual love as something "self-liberating . . . life-giving and joyous") that engaged Catholics in the years following the Second Vatican Council. Through the Paschal Festival transcript Lodge dramatizes numerous issues affecting the church over the two previous decades—the fading of the Catholic metaphysic; the growing ecumenism; the democratization of the church; certain liturgical experiments; and other similar matters.

Hovering over the festival and over the whole novel is the question of "how far can you go?" It has numerous applications. It applies particularly to the problems of Catholics in regard to sex—to youngsters who during religious instruction ask, "Please,

Father, how far can you go with a girl?" and to older Catholics who must decide "how far" to go in the pursuit of erotic fulfillment and how far to go in challenging the church's teaching on sex. In a broader sense the question applies to the important issue of changes taking place inside the church—for example, to the matter of how far progressive theologians could go in demythologizing the Bible, or to the problem of how far the official church could go in condoning the "new theology of sex" in the 1970s.

To all these questions Lodge responds, "well, you can go pretty far, but . . . ," and it is that *but* that makes the novel engaging. The author finds the recent changes in the church on the whole "agreeably stimulating," but he also finds them "slightly unnerving" and expresses throughout *How Far Can You Go?* his anxiety that in their new attitudes toward sex, the church, and the matter of faith itself, modern Catholics may be going a bit too far.

Several times in the novel an ingenious analogy is drawn between religious belief and the imagination involved in the reading or writing of fiction.

When describing how disturbed his Catholic protagonists become over the "ebbing away" of the "old dogmas and certainties," Lodge observes: "We all like to believe, do we not, if only in stories. People who find religious belief absurd are often upset if a novelist breaks the illusion of reality he has created." And he extends this faith-fiction analogy: "In matters of belief (as of literary convention) it is a nice question how far you can go" in the process of discarding old beliefs and old practices "without throwing out something vital."

That "nice question" is never definitively answered in *How Far Can You Go?* nor is that of how far a novelist can go in destroying the "illusion of reality" in fiction, but Lodge proposes at least a partial answer to the latter query in the way he writes his novel. First, he carefully creates the "illusion of reality" in the story by rendering his characters' personalities and actions with such specific, evocative, and interesting details as to make them real to readers and by interleaving his fiction with a journalistic rehearsal of key historical events of the 1960s and 1970s (thereby lending the story a certain atmosphere of authenticity). And yet the author is forever shattering this "illusion of reality" that he has labored to create. He stops, for example, to lecture readers on the novel as it develops, and he pauses to help them interpret the symbolic codes involved in the names and physical appearances of his characters (the fiction is thus both itself and an academic commentary on itself). Further, his readers become involved in the process of his art, for example, when the author writes into the novel his own indecision concerning the selection of a name for a character or when he halts the story to discuss the problematic nature of his art. He admits openly that his protagonists are only "fictional characters, they cannot bleed or weep" but asserts that "they stand here for all the real people" who lived during the era of crumbling faith and growing sexual permissiveness he is chronicling. (His ten major figures are indeed "types," and the whole book is in effect a fictionalized essay, with the individual characters' stories serving as symbols or parables exemplifying and animating the novel's ongoing discussions of faith.) But despite his repeated baring of the devices of his art, Lodge manages—especially through his ever-present wit and playful irony—to maintain a strong hold on the reader's attention throughout.

Reviewers greeted the novel favorably after Secker and Warburg published it in England in April 1980, and it soon won the Whitbread Literary Award for book of the year in 1980. It was then published in the United States in 1982 as *Souls and Bodies.* Both *Changing Places* and *How Far Can You Go?*

marked significant advances in Lodge's artistic development. In neither were there the overplayed and wasted scenes, the crude epilogues, or the shaky (and often imitative) narrative structures that had occasionally marred his 1960s fiction. By the time Lodge came to write these two novels he had developed his own strong, original, self-confident, narrative voice, one capable of great modulation, and he had gained a firmer control of his material.

Lodge continued to demonstrate this modulation and control in his sequel to *Changing Places, Small World,* published in 1984. The latter novel, however, has a much more ambitious scope than its predecessor, for here Lodge introduces the concept of the (pre-Internet) global campus. As Morris Zapp explains to romantic protagonist (and hapless academic) Persse McGarrigle,

> There are three things which have revolutionized academic life in the last twenty years, though very few people have woken up to the fact: jet travel, direct-dialling telephones and the Xerox machine. Scholars don't have to work in the same institution to interact, nowadays: they call each other up, or they meet at international conferences. And they don't have to grub about in library stacks for data: any book or article that sounds interesting they have Xeroxed and read it at home. Or on the plane going to the next conference. I work mostly at home or on planes these days. I seldom go into the university except to teach my courses.

This "campus novel," therefore, avoids university grounds as *Small World* takes place at those conferences—and during the often prolonged and complex travel in between them.

Of course, Zapp's nomadic academic existence might be the result of his marriage's collapse; he and Désirée are divorced, and her novel *Difficult Days* depicts Zapp as a horribly domineering husband. (Ironically, the portrayal perversely motivates some women to proposition Zapp, including the Italian Marxist critic Fulvia Morgana, whose proposed threesome with Zapp and her husband, Ernesto, is too much for Zapp's libido.) Apparently Lodge decided that the indeterminate ending of *Changing Places* needed a more realistic conclusion after all.

According to one of the characters, the elderly Sybil Maiden, the grail legend "was only superficially a Christian legend, and . . . its true meaning was to be sought in pagan fertility ritual," or to put it another way, "[i]t all comes down to sex, in the end." In *Small World* almost every character seeks the sexual grail in one form or another; for Lodge, even the global pursuit of academic success seems invariably to lead to some surprising sexual encounter. Lodge furnishes a noble, romantic knight-errant, Persse McGarrigle. Persse meets Ph.D. candidate Angelica Pabst, who is working on a dissertation about romance and who becomes Persse's highly elusive grail figure. Persse ultimately cannot succeed in his quest of winning Angelica's love, a quest complicated by the existence of Angelica's identical twin sister, Lily, and a series of confusing coincidences because, as Lily reminds him, "[y]ou were in love with a dream." By novel's end, however, Persse moves on to pursue someone else, this time an airline ticket agent who may really care about him. But Lodge does not reveal whether or not Persse will find her.

Lodge has written a novel that is more about searching and wandering than about finding and concluding (a repetitive narrative plotting that is, as Angelica argues trenchantly at the Modern Language Association Convention, the very structure of romance). Another major plot strand focuses on the competition for the UNESCO Chair of Literary Criticism (Maiden calls it "the Siege Perilous"). Zapp and Morgana are contenders, as are the mysterious German reader-response critic von Turpitz (he insists on affectedly wearing a leather glove on his right hand), the gay French structuralist Michel Tardieu, and—coincidentally—Rummidge's own Philip Swallow. None of the candidates wins the chair, for in a moment of resurrection alluding to T. S. Eliot's *The Waste Land* (1922), Persse asks a simple question that inspires UNESCO judge Arthur Kingfisher (the fisher king of *Small World*) to assume the chair himself.

This is not the only loss Swallow faces in *Small World*. A significant story line concerns Swallow's reunion with Joy Simpson, a woman with whom he had a wondrous sexual experience years ago. However, Swallow has mistakenly believed she had died in a plane crash (her name erroneously appeared in a passenger manifest). He meets her again in Turkey, where Swallow is giving a lecture on William Hazlitt. Their relationship rekindles, and Swallow becomes more assertive, confident, and happy in her presence. Lodge clearly represents their romance as a transformative experience for Philip, yet the academic lacks the courage to break off his marriage with Hilary (although Swallow makes sure that Joy attends a conference in Israel so that they may continue their affair). However, Joy soon knows that Philip will never make the necessary sacrifice in order to keep them together. By the end Swallow confesses to Persse his failure "in the role of the romantic hero. I thought I wasn't too old for it, but I was. My nerve failed me at a crucial moment." Despite Swallow's new celebrity for even being considered for the UNESCO chair, the novel essentially records his defeat—Philip literally misses his chance for joy (Joy). More than any of the novel's other subplots, Swallow's story invests *Small World* with a sense of real, mournful loss.

Small World received excellent reviews, both on first publication and when the paperback edition appeared. In 1984 the novel was short-listed for the prestigious Booker Prize, and it has been discussed in several academic articles. Indeed, this ambitious novel, in combination with *Changing Places,* cemented Lodge's reputation as a leading comic novelist and the contemporary master of the "academic novel."

In 1986 Lodge collected thirty-two previously published personal and critical pieces in *Write On: Occasional Essays '65–'85.* His foreword indicated that royalties would go to Cottage and Rural Enterprises (CARE), a charity operating sheltered communities for mentally handicapped adults. His advocacy for CARE grew out of his experiences as the parent of a mentally handicapped child. After Lodge's youngest child, Chris, was born in 1966 with Down's Syndrome, a health official had predicted that the child would never learn to read or write and encouraged the parents to place him in a mental hospital. But the Lodges persisted in keeping Chris at home while sending him to state special schools, and by the time the young man entered his twenties, he was relatively active and independent. (The Lodges' older children meanwhile achieved academic success, with Julia taking a doctorate in microbiology and Stephen earning a degree in political studies.)

The foreword to *Write On* made it clear that Lodge was finding it increasingly difficult to "keep the muscles of composition exercised" fully as he maintained his "double life" as a professor-academic author at the University of Birmingham and as a creative artist. Entering his fifties, he was finding a stronger need to devote his full attention and energies to writing. He notes in a 1990 essay, "Prized Writing," that he used his 1980 Whitbread award of £5,000 to take an unpaid leave of absence from Birmingham to begin *Small World*. This led him to become, after 1981, a part-time academic. But various concerns—not the least being his need to finance Chris's special education—kept Lodge employed in academe, reluctant to break away completely. By 1987, however, he was willing to "go freelance" as he put it. Prime Minister Margaret Thatcher's budget cutbacks were forcing British universities to eliminate faculty jobs, and when Lodge was offered early retirement (and a pension), he took it. Since 1987 he has been honorary professor of modern English literature at Birmingham.

By the time he left his university post he was working on his next novel, *Nice Work*. It focused significantly on England's financial woes and the depressing effects of Thatcher's economic austerity program. In the mid 1980s the city of Birmingham was caught in a deadening recession, with many local engineering firms faltering and unemployment rising. Seeking facts for his fiction, Lodge persuaded a friend, an industrial executive, to let him follow him around through several workdays. To explain Lodge's presence they told people that he was "shadowing" the manager as part of a government-ordained "Industry Year" promotion.

Thus was born the premise for Lodge's new novel, where a junior-level English professor from Rummidge University agrees (grudgingly) to participate in a "Shadow Scheme" designed to foster greater understanding between those who work in academe's ivory towers and those who toil in industry's dark satanic mills. Lodge thus again has his characters "change places"; in this binary scheme cultures clash and readers watch with delight as the novelist skewers the language, manners, pretensions, and warped values of both worlds. In this case the opposing worlds of town and gown are each operating under the belt-tightening pressures of Thatcherite cutbacks.

Lodge combines his familiar campus novel with the Victorian "industrial novel" genre. *Nice Work* self-consciously mimics the "Condition of England Novel" in the same way that *Small World* had mimicked traits of the quest-romance genre. This is set up by quotations throughout the narrative from industrial novels such as Dickens's *Hard Times* (1854), Benjamin Disraeli's *Sybil* (1845), and Elizabeth Gaskell's *North and South* (1855) and especially by a deconstructionist lecture delivered by Rummidge professor Robyn Penrose. (More than half of *Nice Work* is narrated from her point of view—the first time Lodge has used a woman character's perspective so pervasively in a novel.) Robyn explains that Condition of England Novels were so labeled because they dealt with the nation's social and economic problems and described the nature of capitalism and industrialism, all in the context of the lives of characters who debate these topics while pursuing love and careers. Her lecture is followed by just such a novel—albeit one that often plays off that genre in comic ways.

Robyn Penrose is a "tall trendy leftist feminist" with an impressive Cambridge doctorate, a successful book on Victorian industrial fiction, a broad familiarity with poststructuralist literary theory, and no permanent job. Her three-year Rummidge lectureship shows little promise of being ex- tended. At thirty-two she faces the fearful prospect that she will not be able to pursue her dream of "nice work" teaching college. Her relationship with Charles, a fellow Cantabrigian, is dysfunctional—they are into "non-penetrative sex" and enjoy discussing sex more than performing it.

In her lecture "Condition of England Novels" she explains that "industrial capitalism is phallocentric," a male-dominated world for which the "most commonplace metonymic index" is the phallic factory chimney. She has written a thesis and book on industrialism but soon discovers—as a one-day-a-week "Arts Faculty Shadow" to an engineering executive—that she knows nothing about real industry. On arriving in the "Dark Country" of grimy factories outside Rummidge, she is first disappointed to learn that the factory at J. Pringle & Sons Casting & General Engineering possesses not one chimney. More such discoveries follow, shattering her naive, untested feminist and Marxist notions about the industrial world.

Her counterpart from that world, Vic Wilcox, is a mechanical engineer who works as Pringle's managing director. Like Robyn he suffers anxiety over his job security; Pringle's has sharply reduced its workforce, too, and he is charged with keeping the ailing company afloat. He is beset on all sides—he is powerless to do anything with his three lazy and ungrateful children or his menopausal, Valium-drugged wife, Marjorie, who lives to shop and to decorate their house in an affluent Rummidge suburb.

Wilcox, a culturally unenlightened graduate of Rummidge College of Advanced Technology, is a hard-nosed pragmatist and staunch capitalist, and inevitably he knocks heads with the idealistic young female scholar sent to shadow (and torment) him. They clash immediately over the value of literary studies: he recalls his hatred of *Julius Caesar* in school, expresses dismay over how schools grant degrees in "women's studies" and the study of "ideas, feelings" that, as he says, will not "pay the rent," and seems wholly consternated by the idea of academic tenure ("You mean, they've got jobs for life?"). She, on the other hand, is shocked by the appalling conditions of factory life—the noise, the dirt, the "mindless, repetitive work"—and by what she perceives as the exploitation of immigrant labor. During her first day she inspires a labor-halting walkout by the company's Asian and Caribbean foundry workers.

She and Vic hotly debate social, educational, and economic issues, struggling each to understand the other's jargon-riddled professional language. But slowly they develop a grudging admiration for each other and even begin to use the other's ideas and language (she embraces his notions concerning inefficient business practices at universities, and he removes the "sexist" nude calendars hanging at Pringle's). They indulge in a highly implausible sexual liaison during a trip to a trade show in Germany (where her knowledge of German helps him pull off a negotiating coup in the purchase of a giant molding machine). She fully dominates the "captain of industry" during their night of sex, and he emerges from the encounter avowing "love" for her, but she insists that love is merely a "bourgeois fallacy." To woo her he begins reading literature and volunteers to shadow her work at the university.

In typical Lodgean fashion the novelist builds the ending(s) of *Nice Work* into its beginning. In her opening lecture on industrial novels, Robyn scorns the slick contrivances by which such books were concluded: "all the Victorian novelist could offer as a solution to the problems of industrial capitalism were: a legacy, a marriage, emigration or death." This discussion serves as a comic preparation for Lodge's own novel that has many endings—or, as in the case of *Changing Places,* no ending at all. Robyn is offered all sorts of "solutions"—two offers of marriage, a surprise legacy from a rich Australian relative, and an opportunity to immigrate to a job at Euphoric State University in America. She rejects marriage, risks her legacy by investing it in Vic's new business venture of manufacturing "spectometers" (he has lost his job at Pringle's following a corporate merger), and rejects the job in America, gambling that Rummidge will eventually keep her on.

This improbably happy series of possible endings is accompanied by more-somber reflections on the enduring racial, class, and economic divisions in British society. This too is prepared for by one of Robyn's lectures, this one on the deconstructionist critics' "favourite trope" of *aporia.* As she explains to (no doubt perplexed) undergraduate students, aporia in classic rhetoric referred to a "pathless path" that, for example, leads one up a mountain to a ledge where he or she is unable to go backward or forward. It is, she explains, a term deconstructionists use to explain the "defeat of the reader's expectations in a text." There are aporia aplenty at the close of *Nice Work,* not the least in the way Robyn recognizes that the "values of the university" cannot be reconciled with "the imperatives of commerce." Despite her utopian daydreams of a world in which factory workers travel from the "Dark Country" to the pastoral setting of a university to be embraced by its inhabitants, she realizes that there really is no communication between races or classes in England: "Physically contiguous, they inhabit separate worlds." Like the Condition of England Novels *Nice Work* ultimately offers no solution to the serious problems of industrialism or to the country's other social and financial dilemmas.

Readers are cheered, however, by the cameo appearances of two old friends from Lodge's earlier fiction: Philip Swallow, as hapless as ever, still resides at Rummidge (as dean of the arts faculty), and the cigar-chomping powerhouse of American academe, Morris Zapp, touches down in Rummidge briefly en route to Yugoslavia, Austria, Italy, and points beyond as he continues junketing from one scholarly conference to another. The appearance of these two figures from his earlier novels continues the sort of intertextual playfulness that Lodge readers have come to expect.

Nice Work forcefully critiques the profession from which Lodge had just retired—it is as much about the "condition of English" as the "condition of England." Robyn's lover, Charles, resigns his job teaching college English and in a letter declares: "Poststructuralist theory is a very intriguing philosophical game for very clever players. But the irony of teaching it to young people who have read almost nothing except . . . *Adrian Mole,* who . . . cannot recognise an ill-formed sentence . . . the irony of teaching them about the arbitrariness of the signifier in . . . their first year becomes in the end too painful to bear." One suspects there is much of Lodge's own feeling in these words. His frustrations as an educator are also no doubt laid bare in the somber discussion that Swallow has with his faculty over the problems facing their profession. Swallow notes that in the past "there was a single syllabus, essentially a survey course on Eng. Lit. from Beowulf to Virginia Woolf." But in the 1960s and 1970s multiple "new ingredients" were added—linguistics, media studies, American and Commonwealth literature, literary theory, women's studies, and so forth—"without subtracting anything from the original syllabus." Meanwhile, budget cuts reduced the number of faculty available to teach that mushrooming curriculum. The result is that "we are trying to do too many things at the same time and not doing any of them particularly well." It is, he says, "like a three-masted ship with too many sails aloft and a diminishing crew" who are exhausting themselves trying to "keep the damn thing from capsizing." Swallow's comments may express some of Lodge's own reasons for abandoning ship himself in 1987.

Nice Work was widely reviewed and generally hailed by critics. They often pointed out its "mechanical" plot and its typically Lodgean tendency toward caricature. Many also noted that the humor in *Nice Work* is darker, not the boisterously funny stuff that had made *The British Museum, Changing Places,* and *Small World* such treats. But most agreed with the reviewer for *The New York Times* who called *Nice Work* a "funny, intelligent, superbly paced social comedy."

Lodge finished the book in early 1988. It made the shortlist for the Booker Prize and won the *Sunday Express* Book of the Year Award for 1988. Later, as a paperback, it climbed the British best-seller lists. To coincide with the publication of *Nice Work* in America in 1989, Viking Penguin published *Out of the Shelter* for the first time in the United States, where Lodge's reputation was slowly growing. He had been a popular novelist in England since *Changing Places* but had not drawn substantial attention in America until the publication of *Small World.*

With *Paradise News* (1991) Lodge returns to the concerns of his major earlier work—sensual and spiritual longings. In this novel, however, he demonstrates a new way of thinking about the essential conflict between sexual fulfillment and Catholicism. He exchanges the progressive Catholic position of *The British Museum Is Falling Down* and *How Far Can You Go?* for a more secular, sentimentally agnostic position. While Lodge abandons the Catholic Church's rules and rituals—those sacramental trappings so important to his earlier characters' religious life—he still concerns himself with issues of spirit, duty, and love. And in exploring an agnostic existence Lodge apparently cannot escape the eschatological framework Catholicism has provided him. The novel's title, *Paradise News,* suggests an allusion to the New Testament Gospels and their promise of heavenly salvation. But while *Paradise News* is in a sense a conversion narrative, the novel's paradise is Hawaii, and the spiritual salvation it offers lies in making deep personal connections with loved ones: family, friends, and lovers.

Paradise News chronicles the unusual Hawaiian journey of Bernard Walsh, a former Catholic priest turned part-time theology lecturer for the South Rummidge Colleges. Bernard's expatriate aunt, Ursula, has been diagnosed with advanced terminal melanoma, and now facing a quick death, she requests Bernard's presence at her bedside in her Waikiki home. Ursula also asks that Bernard bring along his father, the cranky and staunchly Irish Catholic Jack, so that the two siblings can reconcile some long-standing family hostilities. Of course, Bernard's relations with his family, especially his father, have been strained since he resigned the priesthood, but out of service to his aunt, Bernard manages to convince his father to accompany him on the trip. (The fact that Ursula spends part of her life savings on their airfare also helps motivate Jack.) To

keep everything within budget, Bernard finds that a package tour provides the cheapest and most convenient fare, which transforms the devotional trip to Ursula's deathbed into an unusual form of holiday.

At this point in the novel Lodge reveals his secondary plotline, a satire of British vacationers, for the fellow passengers Bernard and his father meet on their flight reappear throughout their Hawaiian visit. (Lodge represents Waikiki as a kind of enclosed vacationland in which tourists are forever bumping into one another.) While the tourist characters never quite become anything more than stereotypes (a duo of single women looking for "Mr. Nice," a lower-middle-class husband attached to a video camera, two arguing newlyweds, an ineffectually regimented and dissatisfied family of four), the comedic aspects of *Paradise News* are well controlled overall. Never does the novel threaten to turn into a macabre black comedy, exploiting Ursula's illness for laughs. Rather, Lodge deftly presents Ursula as a noble, pragmatic, and courageous old woman. It is, in fact, her strength of character that helps motivate Bernard into reaching out to his father, his sister Tess, and Yolande Miller, an American woman Bernard meets and falls in love with after she hits his father with her car.

Bernard's salvation comes through an agnostic spiritual enlightenment and a physical awakening. While Bernard may be "an honest man" according to Yolande, he still needs saving. After leaving the priesthood for a woman's love, Bernard found his new sexual life too stressful to encourage his libido, long suppressed by priestly devotions; his resulting impotence drove the unsuccessful lovers apart, and now he seems unable "to have an ordinary, friendly relationship with a woman." Similarly, every time he and Yolande spend time together, in situations that seem increasingly romantic by his own devising, Bernard reflexively retreats from any suggested intimacy, physical or emotional. In desperation Bernard writes out his story in a journal (a narrative device that makes up the second section of *Paradise News*) and leaves it on Yolande's doorstep for her to read. Understanding Bernard's textual "cry for help," Yolande mentors him in the ways of sensual pleasure, guiding him through three days of touching and loving, slowly working up to actual intercourse. His honesty and her kindness provide them both with what promises by novel's end to be the basis for a successful, loving relationship.

Bernard clearly overcomes the fear and hesitancy Catholicism has instilled in him, yet Lodge significantly balances Bernard's overt critique of the church with the old-fashioned faith of Ursula and Jack. Yolande suggests this balance as well when in a letter to Bernard she describes Ursula's oceanside funeral service: "it seemed hard to believe that Ursula was totally extinct, gone forever. I suppose everybody has these moments of doubt—or should I say, faith?" According to Lodge, faith and doubt are intertwined, each dependent on the other. Agnosticism, he seems to say, is in and of itself a state of deeply religious and spiritual attention and perhaps the best that modern people can hope for. Lodge also reinforces this linkage between faith and doubt analogically by means of the dual plotlines of *Paradise News.* One of the vacationers, Roger Sheldrake, is in fact an undercover anthropology professor deconstructing the tourist trade, and to him "sightseeing is a substitute for religious ritual" to such an extent that "tourism is the new world religion." While Lodge certainly means for the academic's propositions to be humorous, Sheldrake's investigations invest the tourists' harried activities with a kind of urgent importance, as if the resort were a manufactured shrine for a world without religion yet still with faith, however misplaced.

But it is how faith brings people together that Lodge finds most important. Jack and Ursula's Catholic faith means little in *Paradise News* apart from its ability to allow them to bond and forgive. Likewise, Yolande's and Bernard's faith in each other really provides the promise of an earthly paradise—a loving relationship of uncertain future.

Lodge's latest novel, *Therapy* (1995), further explores the nature of human spiritual crisis and the difficulty in finding a healing, therapeutic solution to such a crisis. Protagonist Laurence "Tubby" Passmore suffers from undiagnosable, untreatable, and possibly psychosomatic knee pain. Apparently the overweight and balding fifty-eight-year-old feels vague but unyielding alienation and angst despite being a successful writer-creator of a long-running television situation comedy, wealthy (with suburban house and luxury car, the "Richmobile"), and the husband of a beautiful woman with whom he has raised two now-adult children. But the nagging knee leads Laurence to try various treatments: cognitive behavior therapy (a form of psychological analysis), physiotherapy, aromatherapy, acupuncture—even high-tech knee surgery. None of the treatments relieves Laurence, so being something of a curious autodidact, he turns to Søren Kierkegaard's theological philosophy for succor.

Sadly, as Laurence explores Kierkegaard's texts he achieves what the philosopher termed the "aesthetic" sphere of existence, the abstractly intellectual life of the speculative thinker lost in the immediacy of his own thought. And Laurence is lost indeed; his surprisingly entertaining engagement with the philosopher's life and work—an interest that quickly progresses into a mania—absorbs all Passmore's concentration. Consequently, Laurence starts to withdraw from his life—and his wife, Sally. He finds himself in trouble for not listening to the things his wife tells him. At first Laurence merely forgets to stay home when Sally invites some boorish Tory neighbors over for drinks (an understandable and perhaps unconscious oversight), but the problem intensifies to the point that when Sally informs him that their daughter is pregnant, Laurence cannot remember what exactly his spouse has just told him. Finally, Laurence is shocked when Sally must remind him that they are through: "Sally just came into my study to tell me she wants a separation. She says she told me earlier this evening, over supper, but I wasn't listening. I listened this time, but I still can't take it in."

Despite the serious intellectual and philosophical aspects of *Therapy,* Lodge still invests the novel with exceptional humor. Laurence is a truly sympathetic and pleasantly self-deprecating comic character. Lodge even plays a substantial formalist joke in the novel's second section. The first part of *Therapy* is in the form of Laurence's journal, but in the next section Lodge presents six different sketches describing Laurence's post-separation insanity, each written from the perspective of one of the work's other characters: a gay tennis coach Laurence suspects of having an affair with Sally; Laurence's "platonic mistress," Amy, from whom he now begs sex (culminating in a pathetic holiday tryst at Tenerife); Louise, an American film producer who four years earlier propositioned Laurence and now finds him back in Los Angeles; Ollie, a British television executive who has heard Laurence pitch an unmarketable series on Kierkegaard's life; the attractive "script doctor" Samantha, whose implicitly sexual getaway with Laurence to Copenhagen devolves (much to her surprise) into a chaste pilgrimage to Kierkegaard's house and grave; and finally Laurence's estranged wife, Sally. The segments are among Lodge's best and funniest writing, and the various perspectives add significant detail to Laurence's character. Some ten pages into section three, however, Lodge reveals that the sketches are the work of Laurence himself, written at his analyst's request. This clever narrative joke is a remarkable example of Lodge's postmodernism.

The final section of *Therapy* impels Laurence to a quest to rediscover his first sweetheart, Maureen Kavanagh, a Catholic girl from his old South London neighborhood. In this form of Kierkegaardian repetition Laurence needs to contact Maureen and apologize for betraying her love. When their rela-

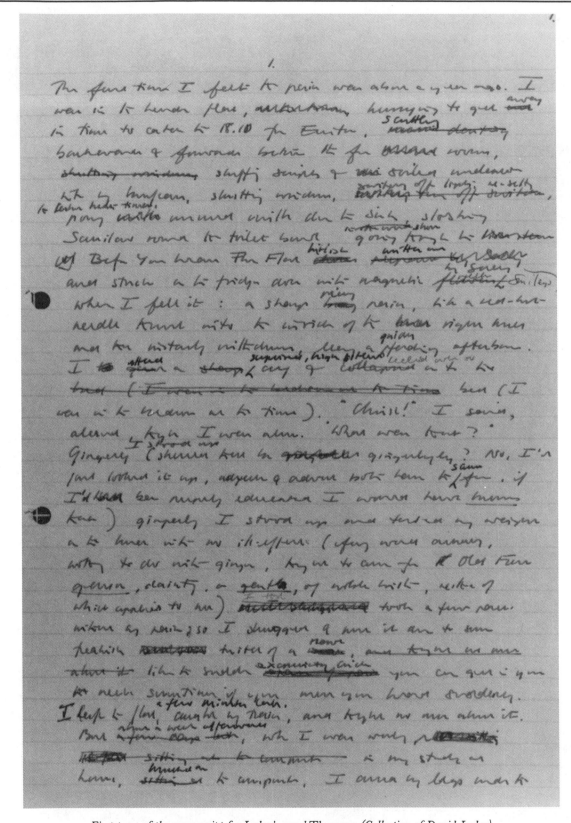

First page of the manuscript for Lodge's novel Therapy *(Collection of David Lodge)*

tionship cooled, Laurence created a situation in which she was forced to make the choice to end it—and since then he has lacked that ability to choose that Kierkegaard finds so important for worthwhile existence. Through a series of rather unbelievable but charming events, Laurence and Maureen are reunited on a Spanish pilgrimage to Santiago de Compostella. Maureen has married Laurence's adolescent rival, Bede, but since her mastectomy Maureen and her husband have had a marriage without sex. Laurence and Maureen complete the pilgrimage together, and afterward they make transcendent love in a Spanish hotel. Upon his return to England (and free of knee pain) Laurence abandons hope of reuniting with Sally, and he and Maureen—and Bede—"are the best of friends." Laurence and Maureen sleep together "every now and then," but the sex does not betray Bede. Laurence even plans another Copenhagen Kierkegaardian pilgrimage for the threesome to unite them further.

Reviewers generally praised *Therapy* for its masterful characterization and ingenious structure although several noted the novel's rather improbable ending. However, in many ways the final, morally unorthodox bonding between Laurence and Maureen (and Bede) suggests a kind of secular equivalent to Kierkegaard's "religious" sphere of existence in which an individual escapes the relative values of the social order. Certainly, Lodge is not reinforcing any real sense of theological dogmatism in *Therapy,* for there is little fear or trembling by the novel's end. Instead, Lodge appropriates Kierkegaard's philosophy for his own, and in *Therapy* he tries to postulate a potentially radical method of transcending the angst of modern life. As in *Paradise News,* personal connections made within a loving relationship seem to be the best for which humanity can hope.

Since 1985, when Lodge sold the television rights for *Small World* to Granada, he has shown an intensifying interest in writing for television and stage. *Small World* (adapted by another writer) aired in fall 1988 in a six-part serialization on British television. Lodge had relished writing satirical theatrical revues in the 1960s, and as he watched the development and production of "Small World," his appetite for writing drama was again whetted. In 1985 he wrote a play, "The Pressure Cooker," but no theater at the time was willing to stage it. After abortive efforts to adapt *Out of the Shelter* and *How Far Can You Go?* for British television, Lodge in April 1988 succeeded in getting a commission from the BBC's Birmingham Centre to write the screenplay for a televised version of *Nice Work*. It aired in 1989 in

four episodes, ultimately winning the Royal Television Society's award for best drama serial of 1989 and a Silver Nymph at the 1990 International Television Festival in Monte Carlo. The experience was an extremely pleasurable one for Lodge. (Clearly, he drew upon this and his other television experience when depicting Laurence Passmore's job in *Therapy*.) He later accepted a commission from BBC2 to adapt Dickens's massive novel *Martin Chuzzlewit* (1842–1844). From April to August 1993 he laid aside the manuscript of *Therapy* to work on a five-episode serialization; he delivered a revised (six-hundred-page) script to BBC2 before Christmas, spent several weeks in 1993 working with actors during rehearsals, and watched with satisfaction as the miniseries aired in 1994. He later wrote: "In many ways the collaborative activity of making television drama has replaced the collegiate activity of university teaching in my life."

His first full-length stage play, *The Writing Game: A Comedy,* was first performed on 12 May 1990 at the Birmingham Repertory Theatre. (This play, a reworking of "The Pressure Cooker," was published in 1991.) On 18 February 1996 his screenplay of *The Writing Game* aired on British television, with George Segal in a leading role. The production drew more than a million viewers, but the few journalists who noticed the play gave it mixed reviews. Nonetheless, Lodge declares in *The Practice of Writing: Essays, Lectures, Reviews, and a Diary* (1996) that "It is no exaggeration to say that participating in the production of *The Writing Game* has been the most intensely interesting experience of my literary career to date."

Since leaving his academic career Lodge has been even more productive as a writer, producing an astonishing number of high-quality essays and book reviews alongside his imaginative work. In 1990 he collected thirteen of his previously published essays in *After Bakhtin: Essays on Fiction and Criticism*. Most of these pieces were influenced by the ideas and methods of Mikhail Bakhtin, the Russian literary critic. Lodge especially appreciates Bakhtin's affirmative arguments for "the writer's creative and communicative power." Structuralist studies of the 1960s and especially the deconstructionist studies of the 1970s had sought to "de-center" texts and see their meaning as produced more by the reader than by any creative design of the author; Lodge (himself a creative writer) naturally dissented from such a view.

Frequently in *After Bakhtin* he laments the "barrier of non-comprehension" that poststructuralist theories have erected between scholars and the broader literary culture of readers outside the academy (an issue raised fictionally in *Nice Work*). As Lodge acknowledges, he had himself long kept "a foot in both camps" of discourse: he had embraced the ideas of contemporary literary theorists as he produced his critical essays while, almost simultaneously, he had satirized those same theorists and theories in his novels.

In a fashion, however, *After Bakhtin* represented Lodge's goodbye to all that, to the sort of academic literary criticism and theory he had published so often and so impressively in learned journals and books. Now he denounces such criticism. It seems, he suggests, to have exhausted itself even among its most-fervid practitioners. "[A] vast amount" of what he now reads in scholarly journals and books no longer seems to him a genuine "contribution to human knowledge" (such as that made by Bakhtin) but instead seems merely a translation of "known facts into more and more arcane metalanguages." He declares that unlike the essays in *After Bakhtin* his future literary criticism will be much less "academic." Indeed, the pieces he later collected in *The Art of Fiction: Illustrated from Classic and Modern Texts* (1992) and *The Practice of Writing* do reflect a shift away from Lodge's engagement with structuralist and poststructuralist critical theory toward a more intense preoccupation with what in the later book he calls "the stresses and strains of the writer's life," particularly his own struggles with the craft of fiction and drama writing. The personal, often anecdotal essays in *The Practice of Writing*–most aimed at "demystifying" and illuminating "the creative process"–are more relaxed than Lodge's previous literary criticism.

Most of Lodge's novels are now available in popular paperbacks. His books have been translated into twenty languages. By 1997 he had been the focus of at least six critical books, scores of scholarly essays, and a growing number of dissertations by novice scholars obviously fascinated by his "double life" as a critic and creative writer. By the 1990s he had established a solid worldwide reputation as a very good minor novelist–and that should not be taken as dismissive, for as Lodge himself observed in one of his essays, "to be a *good*

minor novelist is no dishonorable ambition and no mean achievement."

Interview:

Bernard Bergonzi, "David Lodge Interviewed," *Month,* 229 (February 1970): 108–116.

Bibliography:

Norbert Shürer, *David Lodge: An Annotated Primary and Secondary Bibliography* (Frankfurt am Main: Lang, 1995).

References:

Daniel Amman, *David Lodge and the Art-and-Reality Novel* (Heidelberg: Winter, 1991);

Bernard Bergonzi, "A Conspicuous Absentee: The Decline and Fall of the Catholic Novel," *Encounter,* 55 (August–September 1980): 44–56;

Bergonzi, *David Lodge,* Writers and Their Work Series (Plymouth: Northcote House in Association with the British Council, 1995);

Fredrick M. Holmes, "The Reader as Discoverer in David Lodge's *Small World,*" *Critique: Studies in Contemporary Fiction,* 32 (1990): 47–57;

Park Honan, "David Lodge and the Cinematic Novel in England," *Novel: A Forum on Fiction,* 5 (Winter 1972): 167–173;

Siegfried Mews, "The Professor's Novel: David Lodge's *Small World,*" *MLN,* 104 (1989): 713–726;

Robert A. Morace, *The Dialogic Novels of Malcolm Bradbury and David Lodge* (Carbondale & Edwardsville: Southern Illinois University Press, 1989);

Merritt Moseley, *David Lodge: How Far Can You Go?,* Milford Popular Writers of Today Series (San Bernardino, Cal.: Borgo Press, 1991);

Ingrid Pfandl-Buchegger, *David Lodge als Literaturkritiker, Theoretiker und Romanautor* (Heidelberg: Carl Winter, 1993).

Papers:

A collection of David Lodge's manuscripts is at the University of Birmingham Library.

Patrick McCabe
(27 March 1955 –)

Tim Middleton
University College of Ripon and York, St. John

BOOKS: *The Adventures of Shay Mouse: The Mouse from Longford* (Dublin: Raven Arts Press, 1985; Chester Springs, Pa.: Dufour, 1994);

Music on Clinton Street (Dublin: Raven Arts Press, 1986);

Carn (Henley on Thames: Aidan Ellis, 1989; New York: Dell, 1997);

The Butcher Boy (London: Pan, 1992; New York: Fromm International, 1993);

The Dead School (London: Picador, 1995; New York: Dell, 1995).

MOTION PICTURE: *The Butcher Boy,* screenplay by McCabe and Neil Jordan, Warner Bros./ Butcher Boy Films/Geffen Pictures, 1998.

Patrick McCabe came to prominence with the publication of his third adult novel, *The Butcher Boy,* in 1992; the book was shortlisted for the Booker Prize in Britain and won the *Irish Times*-Aer Lingus Prize for fiction. McCabe's strength as an author lies in his ability to probe behind the veneer of respectability and conformity to reveal the brutality and the cloying and corrupting stagnation of Irish small-town life, but he is able to find compassion for the subjects of his fiction. His prose has a vitality and an anti-authoritarian bent, using everyday language to deconstruct the ideologies at work in Ireland between the early 1960s and the late 1970s. His books can be read as a plea for a pluralistic Irish culture that can encompass the past without being dominated by it.

Patrick McCabe was born on 27 March 1955 in Clones, County Monaghan; like his fictional Carn, Clones is a few miles from the Irish Republic's border with Northern Ireland. In 1969 he attended St. Patrick's College in Drumcondra, County Kildare, but, like Des in his novel *Music on Clinton Street* (1986) and Malachy Dudgeon in *The Dead School* (1995), he appears to have been more interested in the rock culture of the time than in his studies. He held several part-time teaching jobs in Dublin before obtaining a full-time position at a primary school in Longford in 1974. For three years he played keyboard with a

Patrick McCabe (photograph © Paul Pringle)

country-and-western group, Paddy Hanrahan and the Oklahoma Showband, which makes a fleeting appearance in his novel *Carn* (1989). In 1980 he became a teacher at the Kingsbury Day Special School in London. The following year he married Margot Quinn; they have two daughters.

McCabe's first book was a story for children, *The Adventures of Shay Mouse: The Mouse from Longford* (1985). His first adult novel, *Music on Clinton Street,* weaves Irish history, from the movement for Catholic Emancipation in the early nineteenth century to "the Troubles" of the early 1970s, through the lives of its main characters: a rebellious schoolboy named Des and a young priest, Philip, the junior dean at Des's school, St. Xavier's College. *Music on Clinton Street* is particularly alert to the ways in which nostalgia provides a convenient means of glossing over the difficulties of the present. The novel seems to want to pack in too much—the well-evoked but distracting account of Des's mother's life and the depiction of Des's brother James's descent into drug-induced

Dust jacket for McCabe's novel about a boy's descent into madness and murder

madness, for example—and one is left uncertain as to where the novel's central interest lies. Rüdiger Imhof, in one of the few academic assessments of McCabe published to date, describes the book as "a state of Ireland novel . . . an examination of a society in violent and bewildering transition."

Carn begins in the late 1950s with the eponymous town facing isolation and economic decline as the railway is closed; then traces its boom years in the 1960s, resulting from the development of a meat-processing plant, and its decline in the 1970s and early 1980s. As a border town Carn is caught up in the sectarian violence of Northern Ireland from the late 1960s onward, and bombings frequently disrupt the lives of the citizens. The main characters are Josie Keenan, Benny Dolan, and Sadie Rooney. Josie has been abused throughout her life: as a child by her father and later by the men she services as a prostitute in England. Josie returns to Carn when she is too old to practice her profession, and she provides McCabe with a means of registering how far the town and Ireland have changed since she left. Her story also points up the stasis that lies behind the town's facade of success and the hypocrisy with which Irish culture approaches sexuality. Benny's family has long supported the nationalist cause—his grandfather is remembered locally as a hero—and thus he is weighed

down with expectations based on a history that initially appears remote to him but, as "the Troubles" intensify, comes to seem relevant as a guide for his own actions. Sadie is a product of the new transatlantic youth culture. In the second half of the novel the cloying community against which Benny and Sadie rebel is replaced by a hollow culture in which all that appears to be shared by the people of Carn are the plot lines of imported television programs such as *Dallas*. *Carn* ends dramatically with a botched Irish Republican Army raid; Benny murders the manager of the local football team who stumbles on the raid, and Josie dies in the fire the raiders set off. This rather lurid ending sits uneasily with the novel's evocation of small-town life, and the closing pages try to restore this perspective by focusing on Sadie's isolation.

Carn sounds many of what would become the dominant notes in McCabe's work: the loss of national self-certainty in the face of a hegemonic transatlantic culture, small-town hypocrisy, the ease with which reverence for the past can stagnate into self-destructive nostalgia, and the tension between conformity and self-determination. The *Times Literary Supplement* (19 May 1989), mistakenly referring to it as McCabe's first novel, offered a generally positive evaluation while sounding warning notes about "lurid touches" and overcharged social comment. *The Guardian* found the novel "didactic." Imhof praises the work, comparing the narrative tone with that of Ivan Turgenev and arguing that its cyclical structure suggests that violence is endemic across the generations in Ireland.

The Butcher Boy is narrated retrospectively by Francie Brady from the mental institution in which he was placed after murdering his neighbor, Mrs. Nugent. Francie's memories of days by the river with his best friend, Joe Purcell, when life was as "clear as polished glass," are at odds with the reality of an adolescence in which he experienced his mother's suicide, the death of his father from alcoholism, and sexual abuse at the hands of the priest, Father Sullivan. *The Butcher Boy* may also be read as a commentary on the social tensions that emerged in Ireland in the late 1960s. For families such as the Purcells and the Nugents, the period was a time of improving living standards and relative affluence; others, such as the Bradys, were cut off from the period's urban-based economic growth. Francie is handicapped not only by his limited intelligence and small-town upbringing but also by slipshod and corrupt educational and social-welfare systems. McCabe explores the tensions of late-1960s Ireland in a consistently dark but often bleakly humorous fashion.

Dust jacket for McCabe's novel about two Irishmen who come of age in different times and with contrasting values

At the heart of the novel is the contrast between the modern, suburban Nugents, recently returned from England, and the small-town, economically declining Bradys. The contrast is made particularly stark in the deeply disturbing scene early in the novel in which Francie breaks into the Nugents' house and dresses up in Philip Nugent's school uniform. In this fantasy of being someone he is not, he imagines Mrs. Nugent forcing him to her breast; suddenly enraged at the betrayal of his own mother implicit in this fantasy, he smashes the mirror in which he has been admiring his assumed "Francie Nugent" self. Francie's fantasy continues as, imagining himself as Philip, he defecates on the bedroom carpet—thereby forcing a "pure" Nugent to act like an "uncivilised" Brady and eradicating the distinction between the socially acceptable Nugent household and his own. In *The Butcher Boy* McCabe offers contrasting representations of Ireland and Irishness, and these provide readers with a basis for discriminating, in Richard Kearney's words, "between the ideals which keep [the Irish] . . . imprisoned in a dead past and those which [could] liberate [them] . . . into a living future."

While Philip grows from a prim private-school boy into a confident, sophisticated young man, Francie remains locked in a childish world of rhymes, name-calling, and blood feuds. The violent, childlike, and intensely loyal Francie represents the Irishman who is unable to adapt to the changed circumstances of the new Ireland of the late 1960s.

In the *Times Literary Supplement* (24 April 1992) Phil Baker praised McCabe's "sensitive treatment of personal and communal nostalgia" but was less convinced by the depiction of Francie's descent into madness; "The second half of the book is a study in abjection that rapidly descends into Guignol." In *Newsday* Francine Prose drew parallels between the novel and classical tragedy. Imhof calls the book "utterly astonishing" and Francie "one of the most impressively realised narrators in recent fiction." A movie version of *The Butcher Boy,* directed by Neil Jordan from a screenplay by Jordan and McCabe, was released in 1998; McCabe appears in the movie in the minor role of Jimmy-the-Skite.

The phenomenal success of *The Butcher Boy* allowed McCabe to give up teaching to write full time.

He returned to Ireland in 1995 and now lives in Dublin.

McCabe's most recent novel, *The Dead School*, tells the intertwined stories of two Irishmen who are products of different eras. Raphael Bell comes of age in the 1930s; he is sober, responsible, and respectful of tradition and authority. He tries to fulfill the ideal of Irish manhood that is promoted in the church-dominated education he receives and is exemplified by his father, Mattie, a caring husband and loving parent who is brutally murdered by a Black and Tan soldier before his son's eyes. Raphael's idealism sees him through school and college, where he excels academically and in sports, and into a teaching career, in which he is soon promoted to headmaster. By the early 1970s, however, many of his beliefs have been called into question: the indiscriminate violence of the new Irish Republican Army conflicts with the political ideals he inherited from his father, while radio and television talk shows reveal that a new set of values, particularly in regard to sexuality, has become widespread.

Malachy Dudgeon is Raphael's antithesis: the product of a home riven by his mother's adultery and his father's resulting suicide, Malachy drifts into teacher training and bluffs his way into a job at Raphael's school. Raphael is unable to see through Malachy's deception; such dishonesty would be unthinkable for him, and he is unable to recognize it in others. Raphael is also unprepared when his old friend Father Stokes supports the chairwoman of the school's new Parents' Committee against him. The final blow comes when a child in Malachy's class drowns while on a school outing. Raphael resigns his headmastership and slides into alcoholism, madness, and suicide. The end of Malachy's story is only marginally less bleak: he fails as a teacher and as a lover and gives in to drug abuse and despair. At the conclusion of the novel all he has left are his pitiful fantasies, the daily round of caring for his invalid mother, and memories of happier times.

The novel is told by a mocking, wisecracking, omniscient narrator. In a 1995 interview with Kate Kellaway, McCabe talked about the effort that went into creating this voice, noting that the narrator is "a wolfish Cassandra, oracular . . . [but also] a voice which you might encounter in the early afternoon in Ireland, in a pub." The tone veers from bleak comedy to poignant descriptions of Raphael's plight to touching evocations of his youthful idealism and of the young lovers Malachy and Marion in college. The work is organized into 136 sections, ranging in length from a single paragraph to several pages; this structure allows for a productive series of juxtapositions that illustrate the breakup of Irish culture. In a

1995 interview with Liam Fay, McCabe said that the style he adopted in *The Dead School* was a deliberate attempt to write for a young audience:

> If you are competing with video, take it on. Get as many people as you can as fast as you can. The days of expecting people to pore over ten subjunctives are gone. . . . My feeling is that this is the way to go because the lives people lead nowadays are so different. They're reading three or four pages on a tube train or a bus. There's music everywhere. Books have to compete with that.

The Dead School uses music to signify nodal points in its characters' lives. For Raphael the song "Macushla," by Count John McCormack, comes to stand for all that was pure and has now been lost; for Malachy the seemingly asinine "Chirpy Chirpy Cheep Cheep" comes to take on more-sinister tones as the novel unfolds.

In *The Guardian* (26 May 1995) the writer Philip MacCann noted that the intrusive third-person narration sustains a mood of "intelligent pessimism." He characterized the novel as "confined to surface," "uncertain," and dominated by a "wistful naturalism" but claimed that

> it's meant to be like this. McCabe is vandalising aesthetic structure because it fails us in life. His unreliable narrative steadily deconstructs itself, emphasises the illusion of narrative authority. The novel is committed to anti-aestheticism, and suffers willingly from its own ugliness. . . . The novel collapses into genuine rather than artistic disorder. . . . It deliberately allows itself to fail in order to express real desperation.

Aisling Foster, writing in *The Times* (1 June 1995), noted that Raphael's and Malachy's stories suggest that "Irish people . . . have been institutionalised too long; they cannot distinguish dream from reality." Sean O'Brien in the *Times Literary Supplement* (26 May 1995) argued that the characters are destroyed by a specifically Irish modernity and that McCabe is "dancing on a grave long after the other mourners have gone, in order to make it absolutely certain that what it contains is dead."

Interviews:

Liam Fay, "Welcome to the Cheapseats," *Hot Press*, electronic edition, 1995;

Kate Kellaway, "Master Class," *Observer* (London), 21 May 1995, Review Section, p. 15.

References:

Rüdiger Imhof, "The Fiction of Patrick McCabe," *Linen Hall Review*, 9, no. 2 (1992): 9–10;

Richard Kearney, *Transitions: Narratives in Modern Irish Culture* (Dublin: Wolfhound Press, 1988).

Ian McEwan
(21 June 1948 –)

Merritt Moseley
University of North Carolina at Asheville

See also the McEwan entry in *DLB 14: British Novelists Since 1960.*

BOOKS: *First Love, Last Rites* (London: Cape, 1975; New York: Random House, 1975);

In Between the Sheets, and Other Stories (London: Cape, 1978; New York: Simon & Schuster, 1978);

The Cement Garden (London: Cape, 1978; New York: Simon & Schuster, 1978);

The Imitation Game: Three Plays for Television (London: Cape, 1981); republished as *The Imitation Game and Other Plays* (Boston: Houghton Mifflin, 1982);

The Comfort of Strangers (London: Cape, 1981; New York: Simon & Schuster, 1981);

Or Shall We Die? Words for an Oratorio Set to Music by Michael Berkeley (London: Cape, 1983);

The Ploughman's Lunch (London: Methuen, 1985);

The Child in Time (London: Cape, 1987; Boston: Houghton Mifflin, 1987);

Soursweet (London: Faber & Faber, 1988);

Move Abroad (London: Picador, 1989)—comprises *Or Shall We Die?* and *The Ploughman's Lunch*;

The Innocent (London: Cape, 1990; New York: Doubleday, 1990);

Black Dogs (London: Cape, 1992; New York: Nan A. Talese/Doubleday, 1992);

The Daydreamer, illustrated by Anthony Browne (New York: HarperCollins; London: Cape, 1994);

The Short Stories (London: Cape, 1995);

Enduring Love (London: Cape, 1997; New York: Nan A. Talese/Doubleday, 1998).

MOTION PICTURES: *The Ploughman's Lunch,* screenplay by McEwan, Greenpoint/Samuel Goldwyn, 1983;

Soursweet, screenplay by McEwan, British Screen/Film Four/Zenith, 1989;

The Good Son, screenplay by McEwan, 20th Century Fox, 1993;

The Innocent, adaptation by McEwan from his novel, Lakeheart/Miramax/Sievernich, 1993.

Ian McEwan (photograph © Jerry Bauer)

PLAY PRODUCTION: *Or Shall We Die?* (oratorio), London, Royal Festival Hall, 6 February 1983.

TELEVISION SCRIPTS: *Jack Flea's Birthday Celebration,* script by McEwan, BBC, 1976;

The Imitation Game, script by McEwan, BBC, 1980;

The Last Day of Summer, adaptation by McEwan from his short story, BBC, 1983.

RADIO SCRIPT: *Conversation with a Cupboardman,* adapted by McEwan from his short story, BBC Radio, 1975.

Ian McEwan first came to public notice in 1975; he was immediately recognized as an important and new voice on the fictional scene. Along with Martin Amis and Julian Barnes, his contemporaries, he is one of the most esteemed novelists of his generation. Having at first achieved fame, or even notoriety, because of the edgy nature of his subject matter, he has moved into longer, deeper, and more engaged work in the late 1980s and 1990s. Above all a serious novelist—serious about his craft, about life and politics, about the important things in life such as love and marriage—he stands among the most important of contemporary British fiction writers.

Born on 21 June 1948 in Aldershot, Kent, the son of David McEwan, a career soldier, and Rose Moore McEwan, Ian Russell McEwan spent part of his childhood in Singapore and North Africa, where his father was posted. His siblings were considerably older, and he describes himself as "psychologically, an only child." Returned to England for schooling, he attended Woolverstone Hall in Suffolk, then the University of Sussex (B.A. in English, 1970) and the University of East Anglia (M.A. 1971). At the University of East Anglia he took courses in creative writing taught by Malcolm Bradbury and Angus Wilson. Following the periodical publication of some of his fiction, his first book, *First Love, Last Rites* (1975), collected eight stories, originally written as his dissertation at the University of East Anglia, most of them macabre or surreal; his second book was another collection of stories, *In Between the Sheets* (1978). Since then he has published six novels, written screenplays for films and television, composed the lyrics for an oratorio, and written a children's book.

McEwan has been a well-regarded and successful writer since the early 1970s. His range has increased; the seriousness and maturity of his writing have grown; and, certainly, the political concerns of his fiction have noticeably sharpened. His *First Love, Last Rites* won the Somerset Maugham Award in 1976, and two of his novels have been finalists for the Booker Prize: *The Comfort of Strangers* in 1981 and *Black Dogs* in 1992. *Enduring Love* was a finalist in the Whitbread Book of the Year competition in 1997–1998.

McEwan's work first attracted public attention because it was unsettling and disturbing. He initially appeared as a highly accomplished short-story writer. The stories in *First Love, Last Rites* have a high quotient of evil, particularly eroticized evil and evil involving children. There is a nasty quality to the contents, made more striking, and to some readers more shocking, because of the unemotional language of the writing. There is a perverted sex murderer telling his own story of violating a young girl

and dumping her in the canal. There is a tale of sexual initiation among a commune of children without parents. There is an odd story of a man with a pickled penis in a jar who turns his wife into a Möbius strip. Mixed with the startling and the macabre is a surprising amount of humor. Without question, a new voice had joined the chorus of postwar British fiction.

McEwan was twenty-seven when *First Love, Last Rites* was published. His apparent precocity along with his willingness to affront conventional decorum aligned him with Amis, another assured young talent, whose debut, *The Rachel Papers,* had appeared in 1973, when he was only twenty-four years old. Amis and McEwan are now friends and have formed (in the minds of many readers at least) something of a "school" of writing with their contemporary Barnes, who began publishing fiction in 1980.

McEwan's collection *In Between the Sheets* contains a greater variety of fiction but still plenty of unsettling material, and *The Cement Garden,* his first novel, which appeared in the same year, amply confirmed some expectations. The sensational account—rendered in unnaturally unsensational prose, courtesy of a first-person narrator partly responsible for the horrors he narrates—of a family of solitary children who occupy themselves with hiding the body of their mother, regression to infancy, and incest, it seems to confirm the assessment of Jack L. Slay Jr., focusing particularly on the early work, that "McEwan's writing is characterized by a literature of shock, a conscious desire to repel and to discomfit the reader. It is a fiction inundated with incest, regression, brutality, perversion, and murder." McEwan, by the way, has repudiated the suggestion that he wrote out of "conscious desire" to shock and has expressed a—perhaps disingenuous—wonder that his stories seemed too upsetting to some readers: he told John Haffenden, "I don't sit down to think about what will unsettle people next" and testified to his surprise when critics were shocked by his stories. Kiernan Ryan refers to the "received wisdom"—from which he disassociates himself—that "McEwan started out in the seventies as a writer obsessed with the perverse, the grotesque, the macabre," and the "myth of his devotion to depravity."

Whatever his conscious desire, his obsession, or his devotion, there is little doubt that McEwan's early work has much violence, unconventional sex, and bleakness in it. What seems to have been new was the combination of these elements with social concern and artistic integrity. Bradbury, looking back from the early 1990s, provided this account of the place of Amis and McEwan in English letters:

By the turn into the Eighties, both Amis and McEwan had established themselves as major writers, troubling, self-conscious, experimental visionaries of a world where the methods of the grotesque, the mechanisms of fantasy and extremity, seemed all that would serve to encompass the disordered psychic and social landscape of an age where actuality leaked into the world of the thriller, self leaked into social disorder, and the moral wholeness of the times was set in doubt. Both displayed a new attitude growing in fiction, as writers crossed its known frontiers and broke its limits, attempting to link the social aspects of British fiction with the underground psychic and sexual realms where the sense of contemporary crisis was most strongly felt.

It is undoubtedly an oversimplification to describe his development since the late 1970s as a "growing up" out of an "adolescent" desire to shock into a mature concern with broader subjects though neither is wholly inaccurate. McEwan told Haffenden: "I had begun to feel rather trapped by the kinds of things I had been writing. I had been labelled as the chronicler of comically exaggerated psychopathic states of mind or of adolescent anxiety, snot and pimples."

His later novels lack the full shock value of his early work though he continues to write commandingly about evil, and no one could accuse the author of *The Innocent* (1990), with its harrowing account of sawing up a body to fit it into suitcases, of having become squeamish. His early fictions are nonpolitical except insofar as they examine sexual politics; his later work is increasingly concerned with late industrial society and its discontents, with systematic inequalities between men and women, and with the poisonous effects of Conservative rule on the present and, by implication, the near future. Most obviously in his television play *The Imitation Game* (1980) but less overtly elsewhere he has also invoked a feminist ethos. D. J. Taylor comments on this process, perhaps unfairly, since there is no reason to doubt McEwan's sincerity: "In some ways he is the first male English writer to hook himself on to the feminist lobby, a progress not without its inconsistencies and bruising encounters (McEwan gives an amusing account of the reaction to his attempt to analyse sado-masochism at a feminist conference)."

Since the early 1980s McEwan has increasingly explored forms of writing other than those of the short story and the novel. He has written television plays, movie scripts (both original and adapted from the fiction of others), children's literature, and the words for an oratorio. He is now one of the most versatile (though not one of the most prolific) English authors of his generation.

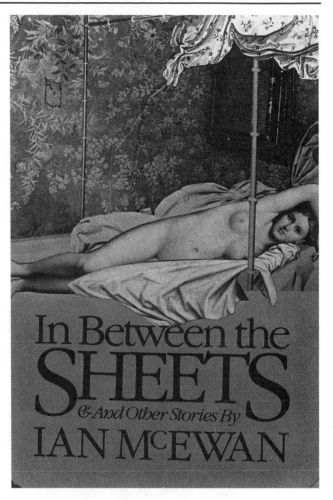

Dust jacket for the U.S. edition of McEwan's first short-story collection

First Love, Last Rites declares its striking combination of Eros and Thanatos, its extreme and slightly facetious linking of disparate elements, in its title. It contains eight stories. Of these, "Cocker at the Theatre" is a lightweight conceit about actors in a play such as "Oh, Calcutta" getting carried away into real, rather than feigned, sex; "Butterflies" is a disturbing account by a deranged sex murderer; "Conversation with a Cupboard Man" gives the affecting story of a man suffering from a disorder that recurs in McEwan's fiction—regression. (It formed the basis both for a 1975 radio play by McEwan and for *Rozmowa z czlowieckim z szafy,* a 1993 Polish film by Mariusz Grzegorzek). The title story presents a coming-of-age story of two young lovers in which the central act is the somewhat nauseating killing of a rat.

"Solid Geometry" is a peculiar account of a preoccupied man whose obsession with his grandfather's journals and the nagging of his wife lead him to "disappear" her by turning her in on herself like a

Dust jacket for the U.S. edition of McEwan's spy thriller set in Berlin during the Cold War

Möbius strip; on his desk is a pickled penis in a jar, a detail that caused problems when the BBC proposed to broadcast an adaptation of this story. "Disguises" and "Last Day of Summer" are both about childhood or adolescent sexuality, with regression and gender confusion added in "Disguises." In some ways the most astonishing story in the collection is "Homemade," a first-person account of brother-sister incest. The narrator believes that his ability to say "I have fucked" makes him a man—

> I felt proud, proud to be fucking, even if it were only Connie, my ten-year-old sister, even if it had been a crippled mountain-goat I would have been proud to be lying there in that manly position, proud in advance of being able to say "I have fucked," of belonging intimately and irrevocably to that superior half of humanity who had known coitus, and fertilized the world with it.

This odd and amoral declaration of the privileges of manhood and sexual experience helps to justify Ry-

an's diagnosis of this book as being pervaded by a "sense of masculinity in crisis."

Three years later the second collection, *In Between the Sheets,* appeared. There is more variety here, including "To and Fro," which must be considered an exercise in style and squalid atmosphere, and "Psychopolis," the story of an Englishman in Los Angeles based on McEwan's time there. "Two Fragments, Saturday and Sunday, March 199–" is a dystopian future vision that foreshadows *The Child in Time* (1987). "In Between the Sheets" is about incest, again, though this time the much more unambiguously wrong father-daughter kind; it is in imagination rather than act, but a father attributes an adult sexuality to his daughter in a way that seems his fear but is arguably his desire. "Reflections of a Kept Ape" is narrated by, in fact, an ape, who has been the lover of a woman but is now bereft. In "Dead as They Come" a man is in love with a department-store mannequin; he eventually becomes jealous of her and "kills" her. The strongest story in this collection is "Pornography," about a despicable vulgarian named O'Byrne, a pornography dealer and abuser of women justly punished when his two female victims act together against him.

In the same year McEwan published his first novel, *The Cement Garden.* Its concerns (incest, murder or at least murderousness, infantilism, gender confusion) had all been foreshadowed in the stories. The first-person narrator, a fourteen-year-old boy named Jack, opens the novel with the remark "I did not kill my father, but I sometimes felt I had helped him on his way." In fact he wished his father dead, and his father died while the boy was masturbating, having taken a break for this purpose from helping his father pave the back garden; his father moves heavy bags of cement by himself and is felled by a heart attack—so there is an Oedipal angle. When the mother also dies, the children—two boys and two girls, isolated and friendless—bury the body without reporting her death and live on together, descending into greater and greater strangeness. The younger brother is, for all practical purposes, turned into a baby girl by his sisters (regression again); the older sister begins to dominate, with the help of a snooker-playing boyfriend; and at the climax of the novel the body is discovered, and the police are arriving as the narrator and his sister consummate their incest in a baby bed.

It is easy to see how, coming after the two books of stories, *The Cement Garden* enabled reviewers to sum up the author as perverse, a pornographer, a clever young man determined to worry and disgust his readers. In addition, *The Cement Garden* has a wonderful way with neo-Gothic atmosphere (the children live in a big, awkward house away from any neighbors) and succeeds in making the succession of bizarre developments believable and, if not sympathetic and certainly not inviting, at least not wholly repellent. Andrew Birkin wrote a screenplay based on the novel, also directing the motion picture, which was released in 1993.

The Comfort of Strangers appeared in 1981 after McEwan had done some television writing. Set in a Venice used less for its romantic or historic properties than as a place of menace and distortion and curdled Mediterranean machismo, it tells about an English couple, Colin and Mary, on holiday. Their time there is a dreamy, hardly real stay, not idyllic, though comfortable enough. One night they lose their way and fall in with a local man named Robert who eventually involves them in his own life and that of his wife, Caroline; eventually he brings about the death of Colin.

There is a tone of brooding menace over the events of this short novel. Robert is both repellent and, somehow, attractive; Colin and Mary are repelled by him almost as much as they are drawn to him. They disapprove of his male chauvinist bombast (both of them are feminists), but having met him enhances their sex life. They never fully understand the relationship between Robert and Caroline, which is sadomasochistic but apparently contains more than sadomasochism. From feeling that they have accidentally fallen in with the Italian couple, they come to learn that they have been stalked.

Robert is a fascinating portrait. For one thing he is an unreconstructed male supremacist: much of his diagnosis of current conditions is contempt for confused sex roles, and his oddly excessive idealization of his father is framed around his father's manliness. Progressive Colin and Mary recognize Robert as "the enemy." A longer view might recognize him as another of McEwan's characters spoiled or ruined by a deforming childhood environment; Randall Stevenson has even pointed to this as evidence for McEwan's limited scope, limited by his focus on childhood and adolescence. Though his capacity for violence is implicit throughout the book, the murder, when it comes, is breathtakingly moving. This is an elegant and troubling novel. Released in 1990, the motion-picture version of *The Comfort of Strangers,* adapted by Harold Pinter and starring Christopher Walken, was only moderately successful.

While he was turning from short stories to longer fictions, McEwan was also turning to dramatic forms. His collection *The Imitation Game: Three Plays for Television* was published in 1981; it contains three plays written in the late 1970s. The first of

Dust jacket for the U.S. edition of McEwan's novel about the persistence of evil in the twentieth century

these, *Jack Flea's Birthday Celebration,* was written in 1974, making it contemporary with the last stories in *First Love, Last Rites* and prefatory to *The Cement Garden,* with which it shares some concerns. Here is the infantilism, the grown man in a baby bed; here is the uncertainty about gender. In this case the setting is a dinner party in which the parents of a twenty-year-old man named David are entertained by him and his older lover, Ruth. The dinner turns into a power struggle between David's mother, who asserts her claim to be David's mother no matter how old he is, and Ruth, who in her view is his new mother. David plays the infant with apparent enjoyment. He is Jack Flea.

Solid Geometry is a dramatization of the story of the same name published in *First Love, Last Rites* and, because of the decision of the BBC to cancel its broadcast in 1979, something of a cause célèbre. The reason for the cancellation decision seems to have been the pickled penis used as one of the props though the broader content of the play might also be seen as disturbing to a mass audience.

The strongest and most thoughtful play in this collection is *The Imitation Game,* produced in 1980. An historical play set in the beginning of World War II, it concerns a deeply unsatisfied young woman whose desire to live fully and to contribute to the war effort are frustrated by her father's rigidity and then by the masculinist restrictions encoded into the security system she joins. She ends up in prison, literarily, though we are to understand that she has been metaphorically imprisoned throughout. This play has attracted a good deal of attention because it is here that McEwan seems most openly to "hook on" (to use the suspicious analysis) to the women's movement. He explains in the introduction to the volume of three plays:

> My novel *The Cement Garden* was in certain respects a synthesis of some of the concerns of my short stories, and after I had finished it, in August 1977, I felt I had written myself into too tight a corner; I had made deliberate use of material too restricted to allow me to write about the ideas that had interested me for some years. The Women's Movement had presented ways of looking at the world, both its present and its past, that were at once profoundly dislocating and infinite in possibility. I wanted to write a novel which would assume as its background a society not primarily as a set of economic classes but as a patriarchy.

He admitted to Haffenden that the male characters were stereotypes but explained that part of his point was that women are often stereotyped without men understanding this. It is a strong play, no matter how "fair," and McEwan's most political text up to that point.

Theatrical work helped to occupy the author in the years between *The Comfort of Strangers* and *The Child in Time. Or Shall We Die?* (1983) and *The Ploughman's Lunch* (1985) are two of McEwan's more overtly political works. *Or Shall We Die?,* an oratorio with words by McEwan (set to music by Michael Berkeley), was written at a time of mounting anxiety over the threat of nuclear war, sharply accelerated in Britain by the election of Ronald Reagan as president of the world's greatest nuclear power. It contains some feminist concerns, as well, in its treatment of science as masculine and the feminine principle as humanity's potential salvation. McEwan, who favors unilateral nuclear disarmament, intended for the oratorio to support the Campaign for Nuclear Disarmament.

The Ploughman's Lunch is a mordant condition-of-England work, somewhat reminiscent of the work of playwright David Hare. It depicts a coarse, opportunistic, false society that is explicitly Thatcherite (the Falklands War is an important part of the play, with stressed parallels to the 1956 Suez Crisis, also under a Conservative government, throughout). Perhaps McEwan's strongest indictment of the society he depicts is that it is dishonest. The "ploughman's lunch," which pretends to be an ancient rural meal but was actually invented by marketing men in the 1960s to get people to eat lunch in pubs, is a symbol of meretricious modernity while the antinuclear women at Greenham Common represent integrity.

The Child in Time, one of McEwan's most powerful works, is a sort of futuristic fantasy, though set in a world that is meant to be like Margaret Thatcher's Britain carried a bit further. For example, the streets are full of licensed beggars.

In a contemporary interview with Amis (in which Amis twitted McEwan about being sick, evil, twisted, and unable to write without pickled penises on his desk), McEwan explained that setting novels in the future may be related to an insecurity about whether there will be a future but added that he did so in this case only to permit himself some satirically distorted liberties with the present. He went on to explain:

> Time certainly isn't sequential and linear. . . . Novelists have always played tricks with time, and the novel itself, though you read it sequentially page after page, when you come to think of it—any novel—you have to think of it as a structure all at once, as an architecture, and that's a strange trick with time, too.

McEwan's titles are always significant, and *The Child in Time* is perhaps more so than most. It indicates the two main concerns of this novel: time and children. Playing tricks with time is part of McEwan's point; he violates duration and sequence in order to have Stephen Lewis, the main character, observe his own parents in a pub on the day he (Stephen) was conceived. More striking is the moving concern with children in the book. Stephen and his wife, Julie, have suffered a tragedy when their daughter, Kate, was snatched from a supermarket. She has never returned. The marriage has broken up as a result, and Stephen is never able to stop thinking about Kate. He is part of a task force developing guidelines for child rearing, at the behest of the conservative government.

The differences between *The Child in Time* and the earlier novels are impressive. One is that it assumes a normal relationship between a normal child and her loving parents. There is no whiff of pedophilia, preternatural eroticism, or violence. Another is the mature politics of the novel. And the most striking is the happy ending—hardly joyous, not without complications, but an ending with some hopefulness for the future and for Stephen and Julie. Amis, in the recorded interview, asked McEwan if it was difficult, for fear of sentimentality, to write a happy ending, and McEwan concurred: "Yes, it's a great difficulty for writers in this century." That he has managed it is one of the strengths of this novel, which may be McEwan's best work.

McEwan's next screenplay was an adaptation of Timothy Mo's 1982 novel *Sour Sweet* (1989). The screenplay was published as *Soursweet* in 1988. In his introduction to *Soursweet* McEwan explains both that he enjoys screenplays and that adapting "a novel you admire, particularly if it is the sort of novel you could never write yourself, can feel like brutal, arrogant work." Oddly, considering that he is explaining why he turned it into something else (and lesser?), he includes this tribute to the novel itself: "*Sour Sweet* is one more example of the novel's capacity to investigate character, to provide intimate access to private states of mind, to show how difficult it is for people to understand one another and tell each other what they feel."

Published in 1990, *The Innocent* represented another new departure for the author; Slay calls it a move "into the mainstream genre of the espionage thriller, an area where such writers as John LeCarré and Tom Clancy currently reign." Most likely this summary overstates the thriller qualities of *The Innocent* and badly understates its intelligence. Nevertheless it (like *The Child in Time*) is more public in its concerns than the early work, more world-historical in importance. Set in Cold War Berlin, it is the story of a mild-mannered British telephone technician involved in spying on the Soviet sector; he is also having an affair with a German woman that leads to the murder of her husband and the dismemberment, transportation, and hiding of the husband's body. The account of how Leonard Marnham and his lover, Maria, saw up Otto's body is harrowing. (McEwan is reported to have completed extensive medical research for this scene.) Marnham then hauls the body around, stuffed into two suitcases, for a long time, looking for somewhere to stash it.

Leonard Marnham is an ordinary man caught up in extraordinary events; somewhat accidentally involved in the spying game because of his technical expertise, he gets in over his head, first with American secret agents, then with Maria. McEwan carefully traces his development. The most important change is in his capacity for violence; the killing of Otto (shown to be almost inevitable) has nevertheless been prefaced by Leonard's odd decision that he should rough Maria up a bit—it seems to him that

Dust jacket for McEwan's philosophical novel about different kinds of love and obsession

that would be the manly thing to do. He is ineffectual at carrying this out, but it makes him, already, like Otto, an abusive husband to Maria in the past.

The Innocent is a rich book. Not only is the historical background well developed (including the ending, which flashes forward a considerable period) and the characterization of Leonard and Maria well accomplished (the secondary characters less so, perhaps), but also it does what *The Child in Time* did so well and what *Black Dogs* will do again: fuse the private, personal, individual story with a larger, public, political, even philosophical dimension that feels natural, supports the personal plot, and deepens the book. Some have suggested that McEwan writes allegories; this is far too harsh, but, at least after about 1980, his books always have a meaning that goes far beyond the interaction of the characters—without rendering that secondary. It is a nice balance. McEwan also wrote the motion-picture adaptation, released in 1993.

Black Dogs is also at least in part about Berlin. *The Innocent* showed us Cold War Berlin at its strangest and most unnatural; in *Black Dogs* some of the characters visit a Germany where the wall is coming down, where decades-old political divisions are becoming meaningless. This novel has at its heart (its private heart, anyway) an odd triangle. The narrator, Jeremy, describes himself as irresistibly drawn to other people's parents because earlier he lost his own. In this case it is his wife's parents, June and Bernard Tremaine. He is writing about June, who lies dying; with Bernard he visits Berlin to see the wall come down.

June and Bernard are an odd couple. They were once both Marxists; however, June was transformed into a mystic by an experience on her honeymoon in France in 1946. Bernard is still a rationalist, a scientist (amateur entomologist), an atheist, and a politician, now a socialist. Jeremy, an agnostic, relays the epistemelogical concerns of the novel, which he describes this way: "Rationalist and mystic, commisar and yogi, joiner and abstainer, scientist and intuitionist, Bernard and June are the extremities, the twin poles along whose slippery axis my own unbelief slithers and never comes to rest."

And in fact it never does come to rest. If Bernard and June are thesis and antithesis, there is no synthesis. Jeremy moves toward a disclosure of what happened to June on her honeymoon; it turns out to have been an encounter with enormous, monstrous black dogs that are rumored (somewhat implausibly) to have been trained by the Nazis to rape women. She escapes this fate, but the dogs also escape, back into the hills.

They function as a symbol of the omnipresence of evil, as do skinheads encountered by Bernard and Jeremy in Germany and a man who mistreats his children. The novel, then, broods over evil and its irruptions, in a way that is closer to *First Love, Last Rites,* perhaps, than it first appears.

McEwan's one book for children is *The Daydreamer* (1994). This is a novel about transformations (with an epigraph from Ovid's *The Metamorphoses*), featuring a series of fantastic adventures by a ten-year-old boy named Peter. It is beautifully written.

It is amusing to try imagining this ten-year-old Peter in the context of the children of "Homemade." Presumably Peter too, like all the characters in McEwan's fiction, has unexplained and unexplored depths, is capable of cruelty, is a sexual being; but (perhaps due to his own fatherhood) the author has recently focused on children who are childlike and on adults who have adult desires, hatreds, confusions, and woes. The movement is toward a deeper, richer, certainly less sensational but more thoughtful fiction.

Enduring Love amply continues this trend. This novel begins with one of the most brilliant passages in McEwan's work and perhaps in recent fiction. Joe Rose, the narrator, describes a joyful reunion with his wife Clarissa after a trip, a birthday celebration, a picnic in the country; then events take control of their lives as they see a man and a child struggling to control a hot-air balloon. As Joe and several other men try to hold the balloon down (the boy is in it, his father helping to drag on it), they drop off, one by one, until only one man still clings to the ropes; as the balloon sweeps over an escarpment and across a valley, he falls to his death.

Joe is shaken, naturally, by what has happened; more, he worries about his failure (and everyone else's) to hang on—who turned loose first? If they had all held on would the weight have kept the balloon on the ground?—and about what it was like for the dead man, John Logan, who endured and died.

But the novel then takes a strange turn as Joe begins to be stalked by Jed Parry, another of the helpers, an unbalanced religious enthusiast and homosexual. Clarissa cannot see the threat of Parry—nor can anyone else—and it more and more seems that Joe is unhinged. His wife moves out; his work as a science journalist is affected; and he buys a gun.

A secondary plotline concerns the dead man, John Logan, whose wife is persuaded that he was in position to assist with the balloon only because he was having an affair. When this turns out to be wrong—another professor admits to having the affair himself, and Logan was just as selfless as he seemed—the professor tells Mrs. Logan, "He was a terribly brave man. . . . It's the kind of courage the rest of us can only dream about. But can you ever forgive us for being so selfish, so careless?" and she responds desperately, "Of course I can. . . . But who's going to forgive me? The only person who can is dead." Joe Rose's story ends more happily, with Parry locked away and Clarissa restored to him; the novel actually concludes with some mock documentation including a letter Parry wrote from the mental hospital and an article, complete with bibliography, about "de Clérambault's syndrome," which is the diagnosis of Jed Parry's own disturbed form of enduring love. *Enduring Love* has the "happy ending" that McEwan told Amis was so hard to write; it has philosophical depth and complication in the form of speculation about chance and causation and the meanings of events, and it has deep and powerful emotion.

Interviews:

Ian Hamilton, "Points of Departure," *New Review,* 5 (Autumn 1978): 9–21;

Christopher Ricks, "Adolescence and After," *Listener* (12 April 1979): 526–527;

John Haffenden, *Novelists in Interview* (London: Methuen, 1985), pp. 168–190;

Amanda Smith, "Ian McEwan," *Publishers Weekly,* 232 (11 September 1987): 68–69;

"Ian McEwan with Martin Amis," *Writers Talk: Ideas of Our Time,* ICA Video, 1989.

References:

J. R. Banks, "A Gondola Named Desire," *Critical Quarterly,* 24 (Summer 1982): 27–31;

Christina Byrnes, "Ian McEwan–Pornographer or Prophet?," *Contemporary Review,* 266 (June 1995): 320–323;

Byrnes, *Sex and Sexuality in Ian McEwan's Work* (Nottingham: Pauper's Press, 1995);

Marc Delrez, "Escape into Innocence: Ian McEwan and the Nightmare of History," *Ariel,* 26 (April 1995): 7–23;

Paul Edwards, "Time, Romanticism, Modernism and Moderation in Ian McEwan's *The Child in Time,*" *English,* 44 (Spring 1995): 41–55;

Laurie Muchnick, "You Must Dismember This: Ian McEwan's Shock Treatment," *Village Voice,* 35 (28 August 1990): 102;

Kiernan Ryan, *Ian McEwan,* Writers and Their Work Series (Plymouth: Northcote House in association with the British Council, 1994);

David Sampson, "McEwan/Barthes," *Southern Review* (Adelaide), 17 (March 1984): 68–80;

Jack L. Slay Jr., *Ian McEwan,* English Authors Series (New York: Twayne, 1996; London: Prentice Hall, 1996);

Slay Jr., "Vandalizing Time: Ian McEwan's *The Child in Time,*" *Critique,* 35 (Summer 1994): 205–218;

Randall Stevenson, *The British Novel Since the Thirties: An Introduction* (Athens: University of Georgia Press, 1986), pp. 185–193;

D. J. Taylor, *A Vain Conceit: British Fiction in the 1980s* (London: Bloomsbury, 1989), pp. 55–59.

Timothy Mo

(30 December 1950 –)

Aiping Zhang
California State University, Chico

BOOKS: *The Monkey King* (London: Deutsch, 1978; Garden City, N.Y.: Doubleday, 1980);

Sour Sweet (London: Deutsch, 1982; New York: Vintage, 1985);

An Insular Possession (London: Chatto & Windus, 1986; New York: Random House, 1987);

The Redundancy of Courage (London: Chatto & Windus, 1991; New York: Vintage, 1992);

Brownout on Breadfruit Boulevard (London: Paddleless Press, 1995).

Since the publication of his first novel, *The Monkey King,* in 1978, Timothy Mo's reputation has been rising steadily. He has won several prestigious literary awards and has established himself as a leading novelist. As a writer of dual cultural heritage, Mo is fascinated by the clash of Western and Eastern civilizations. His novels create fictional worlds in which individuals find themselves straddling two cultures while belonging to neither. Mo's style embraces both conventional forms and modernist, or even postmodernist, inventions.

The son of Peter Mo Wan Lung, a Cantonese local solicitor, and Barbara Helena Falkingham, an Englishwoman, Mo was born in Hong Kong on 30 December 1950. His parents were divorced soon afterward. When he was ten he moved to England with his mother. After grammar school Mo went to St. John's College, Oxford, where he majored in history. Later he took M.A. courses in creative writing at the University of East Anglia in Norwich. He has worked for various newspapers and magazines in London and has contributed reviews to periodicals, including the *New Statesman* and *The Times Educational Supplement*. He has fought as a bantamweight boxer and has also written for *Boxing News*.

A dedicated recluse in London, Mo strenuously avoids public attention. Although he speaks only a little Cantonese and cannot write Chinese, Mo visits Hong Kong occasionally. Mo does not regard himself as a "Hong Kong writer" but as a

Timothy Mo (Spooner/Gamma-Liaison)

writer whose work addresses universal issues and concerns.

Mo made his debut as a novelist with *The Monkey King,* which won the Geoffrey Faber Memorial Prize. Set in Hong Kong during the 1950s, the novel displays the real ambience of the city largely unknown to outsiders. In Chinese legend, the Monkey King is a figure of wit, virtue, and independence; but it is restrained by its Buddhist master, who can make the monkey's head spin by activating the magic power of an iron band encircling its head. While staying loyal to his master, the Monkey King tries to act according to his free spirit and good conscience through his unusual gifts and mischievous

216

tricks. In many ways this legend parallels the rise of Wallace Nolasco, the hero of the novel.

Raised in the Western tradition by his father in Macau, Wallace is disdainful of Chinese culture but believes that "The English were a nation of crafty hypocrites as well." As a Portuguese half-caste he does not have much choice when he is "instructed" to marry May Ling, the daughter of the second concubine of the powerful Poon family. Forced to submit to the tyranny of his father-in-law, constant reproaches from his sisters-in-law, the innocent imbecility of his wife, and the cultural and moral emptiness of Hong Kong, Wallace is able neither to maintain his own cultural identity nor to transform himself into a valuable member of the extended Poon family. Things start to change when he is sent to run one of Mr. Poon's businesses in the New Territories, where he learns about the old Chinese culture and discovers the value of his own dual cultural affinities. What begins as an "exile" turns out to be a rare opportunity for Wallace to show his business acumen and leadership qualities. As he realizes the importance of cultural compromises, Wallace matures steadily by adopting his Chinese ancestry, modifying Western practices, and nurturing a true companionship with his wife, May Ling, who becomes Westernized with his encouragement. Wallace scores his ultimate triumph when Mr. Poon, the dying patriarch, summons him back to Hong Kong to take control of the family dynasty. Wallace thus becomes the legendary Monkey King who outsmarts everyone else with his intelligence and resilience.

Mo reveals the shortcomings of both Chinese culture and Western imperialism, evoking the reader's disgust toward the old Chinese hierarchical system while underscoring the hypocrisy and cruelty of the Western colonists.

Mo dramatizes cultural clashes from a new angle in his second novel, *Sour Sweet* (1982). This time he creates the dismal world of Chinese immigrants in London, a mileu that had never before been portrayed in English fiction. The novel was short-listed for the Booker Prize, the most prestigious literary award in England, and won the Hawthornden Prize from the Society of Authors in 1982. The popularity of the novel led to a 1989 motion-picture adaptation, with a screenplay by novelist Ian McEwan.

The Chens' dilemma is clearly enunciated in the opening of the novel: "The Chens had been living in the UK for four years, which was long enough to have lost their place in the society from which they had emigrated but not long enough to feel comfortable in the new." After Mr. Chen quits his job as a waiter and opens his own carry-out Chinese food

Dust jacket for Mo's fictional treatment of the invasion of East Timor by Indonesia

business in a suburban area, the family's fortunes start to change. The Chens learn through interacting with their English customers that they cannot shut themselves off in the Chinese subculture but have to acculturate themselves. Mr. Chen is a phlegmatic and reticent hard worker who conducts his life based on the precepts he acquired in China. Lily, his wife, is a devoted and strong-willed woman who is loyal to her Chinese heritage but is willing to learn about Western ideas. Chen's sister-in-law, Mui, who was a compliant, dutiful, and submissive woman before coming to help the couple with their business and their newborn son, Man Kee, is eager to adapt to the English way of life. The differences in their cultural perceptions are revealed in their views about the education of Man Kee. Lily sends him to a Chinese school once a week so as to "train his character, foster diligence, teach him discipline and obedience." Mui believes that such an education will impose on him the same dilemma of cultural duality that has troubled the older generation. Lily's slow change from resentment of Mui's new

Dust jacket for Mo's novel about an international conference in the Philippines

China was trying to consolidate its isolation and stop the widespread use of opium among its populace. Mo traces the events that led to the British invasion and annexation of Hong Kong as "an insular possession" of the British Empire.

In contrast to his first two novels, Mo focuses not on individuals' experiences but on the collective perspective of a huge cast of characters. Though Mo particularly condemns the hypocritical British traders, especially the missionary clergy who "go up the coast in opium-clippers and distribute Bibles with the drug," his scornful irony is extended to both sides.

Mo resorts to various experimental devices of modernist fiction. The main narrator speaks with the tone of a historian presenting formal commentaries and conclusions; this voice is often replaced by those of the cynical American daguerrotypist, Walter Eastman, and the seventeen-year-old American Sinophile, Gideon Chase, who quit their jobs at an American trading company and founded a newspaper, *The Lin Tin Bulletin and River Bee,* to fight against the view of the *Canton Review* on the opium trade. In addition to the patchwork division of the narrative, there are official records, court transcripts, extracts from newspapers, letters, diaries, memoirs, and discussions of journalism, painting, photography, and drama. This documentary format, which makes up more than half of the novel, is a barrier that may prevent many from reading through it.

Nonetheless, this richly textured work retains some of the finest qualities of Mo's writing. The image of the Canton River with which the novel starts is a sustained metaphor for the tide of history: "The river succors and impedes native and foreign alike; it limits and it enables, it isolates and it joins." The color of the river when it reaches the sea is "yellow-brown, the color of tea as drunk in London"; historical truth is just like the surface of the water, "half-transparent, brittle, yet in the end opaque to our discernment." Mo provides rich descriptions of details such as a Chinese barber's inner-eyelids scraping, a coolie killed by a snake, a wrestling match between sailors, brothel visits, and fierce battles.

The Redundancy of Courage (1991) put Mo on the Booker Prize shortlist for the third time in ten years. The story takes place on a fictional island, Danu, which, like the real East Timor, is a former Portuguese colony north of Australia. The island, which had been granted independence some time before, is invaded and occupied by the "Malais." But as the narrator, Adolph Ng, finishes his neatly compressed flashback about the peacefulness before and the

Western ideas to acceptance of an English-style education for her son may signify Mo's hope that the future will be easier and brighter for the new generation of immigrants. The story, however, ends tragically with the disappearance and subsequent death of Mr. Chen at the hands of the Triad, the Chinese Mafia-like organization in London to which he turned when he was in financial trouble. Such plot twists like this shape *Sour Sweet* into what Jonathan Yardley in *The Washington Post* (31 March 1985) called "a work filled with wonders, surprises and rewards."

Mo's third book, *An Insular Possession* (1986), is an epiclike experimental novel based on massive research in London, Hong Kong, and mainland China. The novel was short-listed for the Booker Prize. The work is set during the first opium war between China and England in the early nineteenth century, when Britain was forcing opium into China to pay for Asian goods and colonial expansion and chaos after the invasion, the focus of the story is shifted to Ng's own struggle for survival. Danuborn and Canada-educated, Ng becomes the owner of the only decent hotel on the island just before the sudden invasion. As a member of the left-wing resistance group FAKOUM Ng becomes an expert in guerrilla warfare. Mo incorporates facts about Indonesia's 1975 occupation of East Timor and its suppression of the island's independence movement into a riveting account of oppression, brutality, and depravity.

Brownout on Breadfruit Boulevard (1995), Mo's fifth novel, has attracted more attention for the dispute between Mo and his publisher over the size of his advance than for its literary merit. Mo, offended by his publisher's offer and suggestions for changes in the novel, established his own publishing firm, Paddleless Press, to bring out the work. The move has been assessed as everything from a heroic act against the philistinism of the publishing industry to an act of arrogance and greed. Except for a few sketchy reviews the novel has not received the interest bestowed on his earlier works. Set in the fictional city of Gobernador de Leon in the Philippines, the novel begins with a prologue in which Detleg Pfeidwengeler, an obese German professor, enjoys a vulgar romp with a prostitute that includes enemas and defecation. The professor then disappears from the novel. In part 1, Mo presents some inhabitants of the city, including Boyet, a newspaper columnist who visits the brothel regularly without his wife's knowledge until an infection gives him away, and Victoria Init, the strong-willed wife of an influential congressman who considers herself "the real boss" because she "had been used to living in a man's world and to getting her own way in it." In part 2 international delegates to the "Dragons' Conference," a meeting organized under Mrs. Init's supervision, face each other in a discussion of "Asian Values in the 20th Century Contexts" and exchange harsh remarks about each other's cultures. The epilogue of the novel moves twenty-seven years into the future, tracing the lives of some of the delegates after the conference.

The novel's structure, with the prologue and epilogue and the clear division into chapters, is more fragmentary than it appears. The only part of the narrative that produces real excitement is the conference; but this portion constitutes less than one-third of the novel. Elsewhere the narrative shifts randomly among characters of various profes-

sions and cultures. In the *Times Literary Supplement* (7 April 1995) Nicholas Clee noted that Mo sees the novel as a comedy: "But the comedy is for those who find farts funny."

Timothy Mo has made for himself an important place in contemporary British literature. In each of his novels he experiments with fresh issues, structures, and devices. His touching dialogue, vivid descriptions, straight-faced irony, and farcical character portraits have few rivals in contemporary British fiction.

Interview:

Julia Wilkinson, "On the Rails," *All Asia Review of Books,* 1 (September 1989): 6–7.

References:

Elaine Yee Lin Ho, "How Not to Write History: Timothy Mo's *An Insular Possession,*" *Ariel,* 25 (July 1994): 51–65;

Bruce King, "The New Internationalism: Shiva Naipaul, Salman Rushdie, Buchi Emecheta, Timothy Mo and Kazuo Ishiguro," in *The British and Irish Novel Since 1960,* edited by James Acheson (New York: St. Martin's Press, 1991), pp. 192–211;

Hermione Lee, "Saga of the Opium Wars," *Observer* (London), 11 May 1986, p. 24;

Jill McGivering, "Timothy Mo Buries Hong Kong," *World Press Review,* 38 (August 1991): 56;

Victor J. Ramraj, "The Intertices and Overlaps of Cultures," in *International Literature in English: Essays on Major Writers,* edited by Robert L. Ross (New York: Garland, 1991), pp. 475–485;

John Rothfork, "Confucianism in Timothy Mo's *The Monkey King,*" *Tamkang Review,* 18 (Autumn 1987): 403–421;

Rothfork, "Confucianism in Timothy Mo's *Sour Sweet,*" *Journal of Commonwealth Literature,* 24, no. 1 (1989): 49–64;

Kaud Sorensen, "Pastiche and Anachronism in Timothy Mo's *An Insular Possession,*" *Studies in Modern Fiction,* 18 (1990): 123–130;

Rajiva Wijesinha, "Timothy Mo's *The Redundancy of Courage:* An Outsider's View of Identity," *Journal of Commonwealth Literature,* 28, no. 2 (1993): 28–33;

Jonathan Yardley, "Dinner at the Chinese Restaurant," *Washington Post,* 31 March 1985, pp. 3, 8.

Iris Murdoch
(15 July 1919 –)

Cheryl Bove
Ball State University

See also the Murdoch entry in *DLB 14: British Novelists Since 1960.*

BOOKS: *Sartre, Romantic Rationalist* (Cambridge: Bowes & Bowes, 1953; New Haven: Yale University Press, 1953); republished with a new introduction by Murdoch (London: Chatto & Windus, 1987);

Under the Net (London: Chatto & Windus, 1954; New York: Viking, 1954);

The Flight from the Enchanter (London: Chatto & Windus, 1956; New York: Viking, 1956);

The Sandcastle (London: Chatto & Windus, 1957; New York: Viking, 1957);

The Bell (London: Chatto & Windus, 1958; New York: Viking, 1958);

A Severed Head (London: Chatto & Windus, 1961; New York: Viking, 1961);

An Unofficial Rose (London: Chatto & Windus, 1962; New York: Viking, 1962);

The Unicorn (London: Chatto & Windus, 1963; New York: Viking, 1963);

The Italian Girl (London: Chatto & Windus, 1964; New York: Viking, 1964);

A Severed Head: A Play in Three Acts, by Murdoch and J. B. Priestley (London: Chatto & Windus, 1964);

The Red and the Green (London: Chatto & Windus, 1965; New York: Viking, 1965);

The Time of the Angels (London: Chatto & Windus, 1966; New York: Viking, 1966);

The Italian Girl [play], by Murdoch and James Saunders (London & New York: S. French, 1968);

The Nice and the Good (London: Chatto & Windus, 1968; New York: Viking, 1968);

Bruno's Dream (London: Chatto & Windus, 1969; New York: Viking, 1969);

A Fairly Honourable Defeat (London: Chatto & Windus, 1970; New York: Viking, 1970);

The Sovereignty of Good (London: Routledge & Kegan Paul, 1970; New York: Schocken, 1971);

An Accidental Man (London: Chatto & Windus, 1971; New York: Viking, 1971);

Iris Murdoch (photograph © Mark Gerson)

The Black Prince (London: Chatto & Windus, 1973; New York: Viking, 1973);

The Three Arrows and The Servants and the Snow: Plays (London: Chatto & Windus, 1973; New York: Viking, 1974);

The Sacred and Profane Love Machine (London: Chatto & Windus, 1974; New York: Viking, 1974);

A Word Child (London: Chatto & Windus, 1975; New York: Viking, 1975);

Henry and Cato (London: Chatto & Windus, 1976; New York: Viking, 1977);

The Fire and the Sun: Why Plato Banished the Artists (Oxford: Clarendon Press, 1977);

The Sea, The Sea (London: Chatto & Windus, 1978; New York: Viking, 1978);

A Year of Birds: Poems (Tisbury, Wiltshire: Compton, 1978; London: Chatto & Windus/Hogarth, 1984);

Nuns and Soldiers (London: Chatto & Windus, 1980; New York: Viking, 1981);

The Philosopher's Pupil (London: Chatto & Windus/Hogarth, 1983; New York: Viking, 1983);

The Good Apprentice (London: Chatto & Windus, 1985; New York: Viking, 1986);

Acastos: Two Platonic Dialogues (London: Chatto & Windus, 1986; New York: Viking, 1987);

The Book and the Brotherhood (London: Chatto & Windus, 1987; New York: Viking, 1988);

The Message to the Planet (London: Chatto & Windus, 1989; New York: Viking, 1990);

Metaphysics as a Guide to Morals (London: Chatto & Windus, 1992; New York: Allen Lane/Penguin, 1993);

The Green Knight (London: Chatto & Windus, 1993; New York: Viking, 1994);

Joanna Joanna: A Play in Two Acts (London: Colophon Press with Old Town Books, 1994);

Jackson's Dilemma (London: Chatto & Windus, 1995; New York: Viking, 1996);

The One Alone (London: Colophon Press with Old Town Books, 1995);

Existentialists and Mystics: Writings on Philosophy and Literature, edited by Peter J. Conradi (London: Chatto & Windus, 1997; New York: Allen Lane, 1998);

Poems by Iris Murdoch, edited by Yozo Muroya and Paul Hullah (Japan: University Education Press, 1997).

PLAY PRODUCTIONS: *A Severed Head,* by Murdoch and J. B. Priestley, Bristol, Theatre Royal, 7 May 1963;

The Italian Girl, by Murdoch and James Saunders, Bristol, Bristol Old Vic, 29 November 1967;

The Servants and the Snow, London, Greenwich Theatre, 29 September 1970;

The Three Arrows, Cambridge, Arts Theatre, 17 October 1972;

Art and Eros, London, Olivier Theatre, 2 April 1980;

The Black Prince, London, Aldwych Theatre, 25 April 1989.

RADIO SCRIPT: *The One Alone,* BBC Radio 3, 13 February 1987.

OTHER: "Something Special," in *Winter's Tales,* 3 (London: Macmillan, 1957; New York: St. Martin's Press, 1957): 175–204;

The Servants: Opera in Three Acts, libretto by Murdoch, music by William Mathias (London: Oxford University Press, 1981).

SELECTED PERIODICAL PUBLICATIONS–UNCOLLECTED: "Nostalgia for the Particular," *Proceedings of the Aristotelian Society,* 52 (1952): 243–260;

"Vision and Choice in Morality," *Proceedings of the Aristotelian Society: Dreams and Self-Knowledge,* Supplement 30 (1956): 32–58;

"The Sublime and the Good," *Chicago Review,* 13 (Autumn 1959): 42–55;

"A House of Theory," *Partisan Review,* 26 (Winter 1959): 17–31;

"The Sublime and the Beautiful Revisited," *Yale Review,* 49 (December 1959): 247–271;

"Against Dryness: A Polemical Sketch," *Encounter,* 16 (January 1961): 16–20;

"Art Is the Imitation of Nature," *Cahiers du Centre de Recherches sur les Pays du Nord et Nord-Ouest,* 1 (1978): 59–65.

One of the prominent writers of postwar British literature, Iris Murdoch has published twenty-six novels, five philosophical books, five plays, a book of poetry, and most recently two edited volumes of previously uncollected work–another book of poetry and a book of essays. She has also worked in such far-ranging genres as the short story, a play for radio, a pamphlet, a cantata, and the libretto for an opera by William Mathias, *The Servants* (1981), based on her play *The Servants and the Snow* (1973). In his introduction to *Iris Murdoch* (1986) Harold Bloom remarks, "No other contemporary British novelist seems to me of Murdoch's eminence. . . . She . . . has the style of her age." Her literary awards include the Black Memorial Prize for *The Black Prince* (1973), the Whitbread Literary Award for fiction for *The Sacred and Profane Love Machine* (1974), and the Booker McConnell Prize for *The Sea, The Sea* (1978). She was named Dame of the Order of the British Empire in 1987, made a Companion of Literature by the Royal Society of Literature that same year, and was awarded the New York National Arts Club Medal of Honor for literature in 1990.

Iris Jean Murdoch was born 15 July 1919 in Dublin to Anglo-Irish parents, Wills John Hughes Murdoch and Irene Richardson. Her father, a second lieutenant in King Edward's Horse, had been in the civil service prior to military service and returned to it following the war. Murdoch has described her father as a good man who loved books. Although she invents characters rather than taking models from real life, Murdoch has admitted to Ivan Rowan in a 26 November 1978 interview for the *Sunday Telegraph* that when Charles Arrowby describes his father in *The Sea, The Sea,* he is describing her own father. Irene Richardson was trained for the opera before her marriage, and music has played an important part in Murdoch's life and in those of her characters. The family moved to London when Murdoch was a young child, but Ireland remained a force in their lives through frequent holiday visits to relatives. She has written an early short story set in Dublin, "Something Special" (1957), and two novels have Irish settings: *The Red and the Green* (1965), an historical novel about the 1916 Dublin Easter Rebellion, and *The Unicorn* (1963), which is set in a landscape similar to County Clare. Murdoch described herself to Lorna Sage in a University of East Anglia video (20 October 1976) as feeling "thoroughly Irish" but said that she found it difficult to write about Ireland today because the current troubles were "too terrible."

Murdoch grew up in the Hammersmith and West Chiswick districts of London while Hughes Murdoch continued with his post as a civil servant. As an only child Murdoch claims that she received the education that a brother would have had. She attended the Froebel Institute in London and boarded, from age twelve to age eighteen, at Badminton School in Bristol, which she describes in a Dutch interview for *Opzij* (October 1986) as "rather left wing," with "enlightened liberal views." Her classmates included Indira Gandhi, whom she also saw later at Oxford, and Jewish girls from London as well as refugees from Europe with whom she became good friends.

She went up to Somerville College, Oxford, to study English, but the Somerville classics don read her general paper and persuaded her to study Greek and Latin. Her Somerville instructors were Mildred Hartley and Isobel Henderson. She also attended Eduard Fraenkel's *Agamemnon* class and has written a poem about this experience, "Agamemnon Class 1939."

While at Oxford, Murdoch was a frequent contributor of poems, essays, and reviews to *The Adelphi, The Cherwell,* and *Oxford Forward.* She also became involved in liberal student politics and joined the Communist Party, then one of the few voices of dissent against the Nazi Party; but she left the party a year later, claiming ideological differences. This brief connection with communism may have directed her career. Following the war she received a graduate fellowship from Vassar College but was denied a student visa based on her former membership in the Communist Party. Even today, unlike most citizens of Great Britain who are automatically granted visas by the United States, Murdoch must apply for a visa each time she visits America.

She received a first-class degree in Greats (Latin and Greek languages, literature, history, and philosophy) in 1942 and was immediately admitted into the civil service as an assistant principal in the Treasury. Her Whitehall experience and familiarity with the civil service is evident in her novels, particularly in her characters and in such novels as *A Word Child* (1975), which has a London and Whitehall setting, and *Henry and Cato* (1976), in which the bomb shelters of the administration buildings figure. Murdoch lived near the St. James's Park tube station during the war; she told Angela Lambert in a 1992 interview in the *Independent* that she worked a five-and-one-half day week during the war and that the bombs kept her awake all night. She worked as an administrative officer with the United Nations Relief and Rehabilitation Administration in London, Belgium, and Austria from 1944 to 1946. These experiences can be seen in the many displaced Eastern Europeans in her novels. Her Continental experiences also contributed to her interest in French writers and existentialism. While working in Belgium she became caught up in the excitement about existentialism and was able to read, for the first time, Jean-Paul Sartre's *Being and Nothingness* (1943), unavailable in England during the war. She met Sartre in Brussels, where he had the fame and magnetism of a cinema star. In 1986 she told interviewer Didier Eribon that she was never a disciple of Sartre; however, his *Being and Nothingness* stimulated her turn to philosophy. Even though she objected to much of the book, she found it thrilling. During this time she also met and became friends with Raymond Queneau, the French novelist and poet to whom she dedicated *Under the Net* (1954).

These experiences also affected the direction of her career. Before this time, Murdoch's interests had been in archaeology, and she had even thought about becoming a painter; but now she turned to philosophy, and in 1947 she accepted a fellowship at Newnham College, Cambridge, to study that discipline. In 1948 she was named a tutor in Philosophy and fellow of St. Anne's College, Oxford. Philosophy at Oxford then emphasized linguistic analysis, which is reflected in Murdoch's novels through discussions about and demonstrations of the inadequacy of language for conveying truth. Murdoch, however, prefers moral philosophy and regrets that there is so little interest in that field today. She retired from full-time teaching in 1963 in order to spend more time on her writing and became an honorary fellow of St. Anne's College upon her retirement; however, she continued teaching philosophy part-time at the Royal College of Art in London until 1967.

Before the war Murdoch had been engaged to a classmate, Frank Thompson, who was killed early in the war; she was later engaged to the poet Franz Steiner, a Jewish refugee who died of a heart attack at an early age. In 1956 she married critic John Bayley, then an Oxford don, who apparently saw her bicycling across campus one day and fell in love with her. Their marriage gave rise to many jokes about their combined brainpower, but their close relationship has obviously benefited their long and productive careers. Although Bayley does not read her novels in progress, she does consult him about technical matters such as weapons or aircraft, and they do discuss aesthetic issues. Her concern with characterization has often been credited to his influence and is a focus of his work *The Characters of Love* (1960). The Bayleys maintain a Kensington residence but live in north Oxford.

For a contemporary writer Murdoch has an unusual method of invention and writing. She shuns word processors and typewriters and always writes her entire drafts in longhand. The novels are planned entirely in her head before she begins writing. The plot usually evolves from an incident, such as the car accident in *An Accidental Man* (1971), from which a set of characters emerges. Each character is then attached to his or her own circle of acquaintances, and so on, until all of the figures of the novel develop. Once the novel has been entirely written in her mind, she produces a first draft using pen and notebooks or loose-leaf paper, leaving wide margins for notes. During a second draft entire pages of the loose-leaf may be replaced with revisions. The novel is then ready to be handed to the publisher for typing, and she permits no changes or editing by her publishers. This policy has drawn repeated complaints from critics who feel that the later, quite lengthy novels could have benefited from some artful pruning.

While working on her 1992 philosophical work, *Metaphysics as a Guide to Morals* (unusual in that it was in progress for some ten years), she wrote philosophy in the morning and her novels in the afternoon. She has maintained a formidable publication rate of nearly a novel a year and pauses scarcely one-half hour between completing one novel and beginning the next. Her prolific output has brought the criticism that she is repeating the themes and characters of earlier novels, but she simply replies that she must write about what she knows and that each novel she brings out, while necessarily imperfect, works to correct the mistakes of the last.

Murdoch believes that she writes in the English realist tradition, and her writing has been compared to that of George Eliot; however, she is also frequently compared to Fyodor Dostoyevsky, whose illustrations of the struggle between good and evil have influenced her writing. Her greatest contribution to the development of the novel has been in the area of characterization, an area addressed by many early critical essays including "The Sublime and Beautiful Revisited" (1959), in which she identifies the creation of character as the greatest problem confronting the modern novelist. She believes it is the artist's duty to create real, free characters who behave according to human nature, not merely as the puppets of their creators. To this end she focuses on the inner life of her people, which projects their spiritual awareness and explains their actions.

It is difficult to consider Murdoch's aesthetics without also addressing her interrelated moral philosophy. Her first published work, *Sartre, Romantic Rationalist* (1953), a critical study of Sartre's writings, establishes a relationship between aesthetics and philosophy. Here Murdoch distances herself from Sartre's existentialism and concludes that Sartre fails as a great novelist because he "has an impatience which is fatal to a novelist proper, with the *stuff* of human life." Ultimately he is more interested in issues than in people, and thus his readers are left with "a sense of emptiness" with regard to his characters. In establishing distinctions between her own and Sartre's vision of the novel—for Sartre the novel is a political device, but for Murdoch the emphasis on the political message interferes with the writer's freedom to present free and various characters—Murdoch places the novel firmly within the realist tradition. Both Sartre and Murdoch connect art with morality but do so in different ways. For Sartre, transmitting an ideological commitment is necessarily a moral act; for Murdoch, a just portrayal of reality is a virtuous act. This monograph presents, for the first time, her view of the artist's duty to convey truth—to show the world as it is—and the attending duty of the reader to judge the work independent of "his resentments, his fears, and his lusts in order to put himself at the peak of his freedom."

Another of her essays, "Against Dryness" (1961), discusses the alternatives that dominated literature at the time Murdoch was beginning to write, and critics now identify her early novels as falling into one or the other of the types addressed in this essay—the crystalline novel or the journalistic story. The crystalline is associated with the symbolist movement (T. S. Eliot, Paul Valéry); in its admiration of myth and symbol, however, it fails to incorporate the accidental happenings of life. Its alternative, the journalistic story, is "a large, shapeless quasi-documentary object . . . telling with pale con-

Dust jacket for the U.S. edition of Murdoch's novel about accepting responsibility for one's actions

ventional characters some straight forward story enlivened with empirical facts." Murdoch believes that neither type fully presents the human personality. Here and earlier Murdoch faults Sartre for picturing the individual as lonely and self-contained. Real people break away from myth, and imagination, not fantasy, is necessary for truth. Readers should see people "against a background of values, of realities, which transcend [them]." A. S. Byatt, whose pioneering *Degrees of Freedom: The Novels of Iris Murdoch* (first published in 1965) has profoundly influenced Murdoch studies, views this essay as crucial to an understanding of Murdoch's view of personality: "This individual human person lives in a world where there are degrees of freedom, he is 'free and separate' but 'related to a rich and complicated world from which as a moral being he has much to learn.'" These ideas are put into perspective with Byatt's claim that all of Murdoch's novels can be seen, in an important way, as "studies of the 'degrees of freedom' available to individuals."

Her fusion of aesthetics and moral philosophy is evident in her essay "The Idea of Perfection" (included in *The Sovereignty of Good,* 1970). Murdoch recognizes great art can be a means for conveying truth and thus a means for moral improvement. In this context the artist has a duty to his/her audience to convey truth by means of an "unsentimental, detached, unselfish, objective attention." For this reason she believes that political statements should be made in pamphlets rather than in novels.

The title essay of that 1970 volume, "The Sovereignty of Good over Other Concepts," continues to develop art as a means for discovering reality—an idea that will be central to Murdoch's aesthetics. Murdoch also states the ends of her moral philosophy: "Ethics . . . should be a hypothesis about good conduct and how this can be achieved." She then defines virtue and establishes humility as the virtue closest to the Good. Like Plato, Murdoch believes that few people know truth, but she believes one can move toward it by just and loving attention. Two fundamental assumptions—that human beings are naturally selfish and that human life has no external point—make moral improvement difficult to achieve. If there is no hope of reward nor fear of punishment, what will entice solipsistic humans to a higher moral level? These are the issues that her novels probe. She holds out optimism that people can learn to be good without the ulterior motive of reward. The good person who acquires humility undergoes an "unselfing" process that allows him to view others as something besides an extension of himself. Rare in life, such people are also rare in her novels, which are filled with self-centered and egoistic people.

"The Sovereignty of Good over Other Concepts" also establishes a relationship between the proximity of death and the recognition of truth that is illustrated in several novels. According to Murdoch, "The acceptance of death is an acceptance of our own nothingness which is an automatic spur to our concern with what is not ourselves." However, in keeping with her view of human nature, the epiphany alone is insufficient to alter behavior. When characters with a low spiritual awareness recognize truth, they are unable to sustain this vision, and they return to their former egoistic state after the danger that is often associated with awareness has passed.

The dense texture and multifaceted nature of Murdoch's aesthetics and moral philosophy attract considerable scholarly attention, and Murdoch is regularly taught in contemporary British courses in universities throughout the world. However, her apparent lack of conformity with the feminist position has brought adverse criticism from that quarter. Feminists object to the male point of view in her novels, particularly her preponderance of first-person male narrators, and question the decentering of the voice of women in these novels. Murdoch's refusal to write "as a woman" and her insistence on presenting "the human condition" are consistent with her aesthetics. She feels she is presenting the world as it is, and in doing so Murdoch critiques a male-oriented society by undercutting the reliability of her male narrators, who are frequently egoists. Decentering the female voice is a valid concern, yet a female character such as Ann Peronett, who is the focus of much of *An Unofficial Rose* (1962), is consistent with Murdoch's moral philosophy in which good characters lack power. Murdoch does not recognize gender distinctions and told Jean-Luis Chevalier at a 1978 conference in Caen that people are "at a higher level" androgynous—thus she presents several characters in her novels with names and physical traits that initially leave the reader in doubt about the character's gender. Lindsay Rimmer has a dual role in *An Unofficial Rose*—secretary-companion-love interest for Emma Sands and lover of Randall Peronett. The spritelike female Julian Baffin-Belling is initially mistaken for a young boy by Bradley Pearson in *The Black Prince;* and in *The Message to the Planet* (1989) Alfred Ludens is confounded by Irina Vallar's gender and age when he first stumbles upon her during the night, mistaking her for a child of ten or twelve, "more probably a boy."

Critics such as Deborah Johnson have tried to develop Murdoch's position as a feminist, and many would like to say that the basis of the relationship between men and women in Murdoch's novels is power; but power is the basis of all relationships in Murdoch's novels, and she has repeatedly denied any partisanship. According to Murdoch, one of the reasons men are in more positions of power than women is that they are better educated. She would hate to see Women's Studies lead women to ignore some of the great works that have been written by men, and she has expressed an interest, during a 1982 interview with Heide Ziegler and Christopher Bigsby, in "just having studies." Nevertheless, two later novels reveal subtle changes in her views and offer representations of women that are more extensive and varied than earlier novels, in part because these later works are narrated to a greater extent through the consciousness of their women characters—Rose Curtland and Tamar Hernshaw in *The Book and the Brotherhood* (1987) and Franca Sheerwater, Irina Vallar, and Maisie Tether in *The Message to the Planet.*

Religion and experimentation with beliefs that would accommodate the ideas presented by the contemporary world have been important issues in Murdoch's novels. Her father's background was evangelical Quaker, and she was reared in the Church of England; yet she has repeatedly stated that she does not believe in a personal God or in an afterlife—views that are compatible with her early Marxism. Her moral philosophy, however, has continually involved her in the religious debate, and most of Murdoch's later novels show an increased interest in religion, particularly in the unselfing aspects of Quakerism and Buddhism that relate to her moral philosophy. Murdoch has often called herself a sort of "Christian-Buddhist" and claims that she is drawn to these religions because they are concerned with losing one's ego. She also considers unorthodox religious issues because they are a part of the search for meaning in life. During a 1989 interview with David Gerard, Murdoch agreed that her work has a sense of religion. That same year she told Rosemary Hartill in a 20 July BBC Radio 4 interview that religion disappearing from people's lives would be a terrible thing; instead, she would advocate a move toward demythologization in theology and has experimented with such conditions in her novels. Indeed, the later novels, particularly, include several unconventional priests or clergy, and she has lately expressed a keen interest in the views of the more radical Oxford clergy.

In a 1954 review for the *Spectator* Kingsley Amis declared *Under the Net* "a winner, a thoroughly accomplished first novel." It is difficult to read Murdoch's first published novel, a picaresque adventure with a philosophical backdrop, without becoming caught up in the youthful exuberance of its feckless narrator, Jake Donaghue, the first of Murdoch's failed artists. Following a series of comic episodes, Jake ends the novel where he began—with little money and no place to stay—but he has learned something about himself, about love, and about life (although he will still make mistakes in these areas), and he resolves to abandon his job as a literary hack who translates second-rate novels in order to try his own writing talents.

The philosophical background of the novel continually evaluates language, and language theory is taken up by all of the characters in the book—from the philosopher, Dave Gellman, to the compulsive liar, Sadie Quentin. Cambridge was still under the influence of Ludwig Wittgenstein when Murdoch studied philosophy there; in *Iris Murdoch: The Saint and the Artist* (first published in 1986), Peter

Conradi points out that the title of the novel comes from Wittgenstein's *Tractatus Logico-Philosophicus* (1921) and refers to the "net of discourse behind which the world's particulars hide." The net is comprised of language and theory which reveal and conceal the world simultaneously. Wittgenstein's influence can also be seen in other novels, including *Nuns and Soldiers* (1980), where he is a topic of conversation.

Another major theme in Murdoch's fiction, the capacity of art to tell truth, is also taken up by the characters in the novel—even the extreme of silence in a mime theater in an effort to circumvent the lies of speech. Here Murdoch's aesthetics merge with her moral philosophy, for while great art has the capacity to reveal the truth about the world, mediocre art does not. Jake Donaghue so embellishes with falsehood his record of the dialectics he has had with Hugo Belfounder that when the conversations are published as *The Silencer,* Hugo does not even recognize his ideas in the book.

The existentialism of this period is also evident in *Under the Net,* with its dedication to her friend Queneau. Murdoch has often expressed her great admiration for Samuel Beckett and Queneau and has told Harold Hobson that in *Under the Net* she was consciously imitating their styles; she even thinks the French translation of her novel sounds like Queneau's *Pierrot mon ami* (1943). The characters, as in any existential novel, can be judged by their actions—Jake in his change from literary hackwork to original work and Hugo in his divesting himself of his material possessions. Another common plot motif of unlikely love interests, much like a drawing-room comedy, begins in *Under the Net:* Jake Donaghue loves Anna Quentin, who loves Hugo Belfounder, who loves Sadie Quentin, who loves Jake.

In an unusual move, not repeated with later novels, the first American edition of *Under the Net* was discreetly modified, apparently for the assumed interests of an American audience. Chapter 2 is missing part of a discussion about British philosophy, and in chapter 8 some 274 words have been cut from a conversation about Marxism and English socialism that takes place between Jake and Lefty Todd, the leader of the National Independent Socialist Party.

Dedicated to Elias Canetti, *The Flight from the Enchanter* (1956) has been influenced by Canetti's *Auto da Fe* (1946). The major themes of the novel address the destructiveness of power and the problem of displacement. Although this is the second of Murdoch's published novels, Murdoch was working on it before the publication of *Under the Net,* and the major characters in the novel were initially meant to be displaced persons.

Murdoch has repeatedly objected to any classification as a Gothic writer; she told Chevalier, "I would not like to be labeled as a Gothic novelist. I would regard this as limiting in a slightly derogatory sense." However, *The Flight from the Enchanter,* as well as *The Unicorn, The Italian Girl* (1964), *The Time of the Angels* (1966), and *Bruno's Dream* (1969), certainly fall into that category. What Murdoch appears to be doing in this form is exploring the concept of power, and the enclosed circumstances of these novels lend themselves to this dark genre. The enchanter figures that recur in Murdoch's novels have their origin in the aptly named Mischa Fox of *The Flight from the Enchanter,* a newspaper magnate who is a source of fear and attraction for the other characters. Fox is often described in satanic terms, as in the references to the "extra ordinary flexibility of his feet and ankles" and in discussion about his odd eyes. He exerts considerable control over the lives of his fellow characters with the aid of his associate and "alter ego," Calvin Blick, who is described as "the dark half of Mischa's mind." When Rosa Keepe contemptuously tells the malevolent Blick that she cannot understand why Fox did not kill him years ago, Blick replies softly: "Mischa did kill me years ago." The enslaved character performs his master's bidding after having been broken by him, thus continuing the cycle of power and suffering.

Murdoch told Chevalier that "characters who want to be manipulated by others" interest her. People who put themselves in others' power avoid truth and live safely without responsibility; in so doing they continue the illusions with which they are comfortable. The immigrants in *The Flight from the Enchanter* also continue this cycle. Although victims of power, they often resort to power themselves. The refugees Jan and Stefan Lusiewicz try to stabilize their positions by intimidating Rosa Keepe. Yet when power is exerted by Fox in an attempt to remove them from Rosa's life, it has not only that effect but also the unintended effect of the suicide of another illegal immigrant, Nina.

The dark tone of the novel is relieved, as in many Murdoch novels, by comedy. Here the humor involves an amusing (some may feel too lighthearted) treatment of the struggle between Mischa Fox and the surviving founders of *The Artemis,* a suffragette publication that he intends to acquire. In a similar pull between the genders, civil servant John Rainborough finds himself relentlessly and romantically pursued by his personal assistant at

SELIB (Special European Labour Immigration Board), Agnes Casement. The bureaucracy at SE-LIB, carried out by a band of "female harpies" that quite alarm Rainborough, would rival that of Charles Dickens's Circumlocution Department.

While not highly acclaimed critically, in part because of its rather romantic story line, *The Sandcastle* (1957) nevertheless demonstrates the connection between truth and moral virtue while addressing issues such as aesthetic preference and permanence in art. It also presents one of Murdoch's few characters of the good, the art master Bledyard, a Platonist who illustrates Plato's disgust for representational art and points the way to an ideal—in art and in morality. Importantly, *The Sandcastle* raises a problematic question in Murdoch's aesthetics—is it necessary for an artist to be good in order to convey truth? While Murdoch has declined actually to take this position on the basis that there are too many counterexamples from real life, it is a position that is regularly suggested in her novels. The May-December romance in *The Sandcastle* takes place between Bill Mor, a teacher at St. Bride's school who has a wife and two children, and Rain Carter, a young painter who has been commissioned to paint a portrait of St. Bride's former headmaster, Demoyte. Bledyard believes the affair will damage Carter's ability to paint and tells Mor, "You are diminishing her by involving her in this. A painter can only paint what he is. You will prevent her from being a great painter." Indeed, Carter believes she can improve the painting only after she breaks off her affair with Mor: "I must finish this. I want to repaint the head. I see what to do now. I must go on working."

The Bell (1958) considerably increased Murdoch's standing with the critics. William Van O'Connor's remark in *Critique* (1960) is typical: "With *The Bell* Murdoch emerges as the best of the young novelists." James Gindin also grouped Murdoch with Amis, Angus Wilson, and John Wain as one of the young British writers who assert the dignity and worth of the individual and who voice social grievances through comedy. The novel is often cited for its veracity of character and well-paced plot, and its description of the raising of the fourteenth-century bell, Gabriel, from the bottom of a lake is typical of the complicated mechanical processes that appear in later Murdoch novels.

The novel is set in Gloucestershire, where a religious lay community, Imber Court, resides alongside a cloistered Benedictine Anglican abbey. The members of the lay community try to live a contemplative life and attempt to love others but prove unable to sustain this utopian community. Murdoch explores the idea of spirituality through various characters' interpretations of the ideal life. James Tayper Pace and Michael Meade present opposing views of the moral life through sermons that they deliver to the community. James advocates living by simple rules and truth-telling, but Michael's view of the good life involves an awareness of self: "The chief requirement of the good life is that one should have some conception of one's capacities" and should act in the best way one can. Byatt equates their visions with positions taken by Murdoch in "Against Dryness," with James having many things in common with the Ordinary Language Man of convention and Michael purporting similar views as the Totalitarian Man of Sartre, who has surrendered to neurosis.

Near the beginning of *A Severed Head* (1961) its narrator, Martin Lynch-Gibbon, returns home from an assignation with his mistress, Georgie Hands, to whom he has lied about the expected arrival time of his wife, Antonia, so that he might enjoy some quiet time by himself. He introduces himself to the reader with these remarks: "In almost every marriage there is a selfish and an unselfish partner. . . . In my own marriage I early established myself as the one who took rather than gave. Like Dr. Johnson, I started promptly upon the way in which I intended to go on." The Murdoch reader will recognize that such complacency in the hands of a master of irony must soon change, and Martin immediately finds himself in a storm of turmoil when his wife returns home to announce that she wishes to leave him for her psychiatrist (and Martin's best friend), Palmer Anderson. This witty, satirical comedy of manners includes the pairing and switching of partners in almost every conceivable situation among a small cast of characters that includes Martin's brother, Alexander, and Palmer's half sister, Honor Klein. The novel is a delightful spoof of Freudian theory, with situations involving incest, sibling rivalry, and homosexual jealousy, all evoking many of the sexual complications associated with the Greek myths of Oedipus, Electra, Medusa, and Candaules and Gyges. Despite these relationships the novel forwards a theme of sterility. There are no children in the novel; Antonia is barren and Georgie had an abortion when she discovered herself pregnant with Martin's child. The thought of children devastates both women, and the absence of children appears to prompt the characters' parental behavior toward one another and, perhaps, their childish behavior.

The subsequent stage version of *A Severed Head* (the most successful stage adaptation of any of Murdoch's novels) resulted from a collaboration between Murdoch and J. B. Priestley. In *Essays in The-*

Dust jacket for the U.S. edition of Murdoch's novel about unorthodox religious beliefs and the importance of individual goodness

atre (1985), John Fletcher enumerates the reasons for its success: it "has all the speed, elaboration and stylisation of a Restoration comedy, and develops an action which, if not particularly credible, never fails to sustain the audience's interest and involvement." After a provincial tryout at the Theatre Royal, Bristol, in 1963, the play ran for two and one-half years at the Criterion in London. It also ran for about three weeks at the Royale Theatre in New York. The play was published in a reading edition by Chatto and Windus as *A Severed Head: A Play in Three Acts* (1964), and an acting edition was also published in 1964 by Samuel French. Further testimony to the success of the play are the Italian (1965), German (1966), and Japanese (1967) editions; the play was also performed in the Netherlands in a Dutch translation, and a motion picture based on the novel and the play was released by Columbia Pictures in 1971 with a cast that included Lee Remick, Richard Attenborough, and Ian Holm.

An Unofficial Rose opens with the funeral of Fanny Peronett. At her burial Fanny's husband, Hugh, catches sight of his old mistress, Emma Sands, for whom he had failed to leave his wife. Hugh would like to rekindle their romance, but Emma, now a popular detective-fiction writer, has other plans. Although more benign than Mischa Fox in *The Flight from the Enchanter,* Emma has much in common with him as an enchanter figure, and she wants to meet (and manipulate) Hugh's children and grandchildren.

As with other Murdoch novels, iconography is an important element in the plot. Here it revolves around a Tintoretto nude, described as "an earlier version of the figure of Susannah in the great Susannah Bathing in Vienna. . . . It was a picture which might well enslave a man, a picture round which crimes might be committed." Hugh may have married Fanny because he coveted the painting, and their son, Randall, now expects his father to sell the Tintoretto in order to finance his liaison with Lindsay Rimmer, Emma's secretary-companion, primarily because Hugh had lacked the courage to elope with his mistress in his own youth. The Shakespearean doubling of circumstances (here taking place one generation later with Randall actually leaving his wife), is a recurring motif in Murdoch's later fiction.

This novel also attends to the concerns of the artist and the saint through the characters of Randall and his wife, Ann. A horticulturist, Randall has the creative energies of an artist: "It was his patient work which had produced the series of new roses, most of them now well known, by which the name of Peronett would be remembered." A Peter Pan figure who has never grown up, Randall would like both his freedom and the assurance that his wife will maintain their home should he decide to return. Ann, the good character in the novel, has the humility and selflessness required for perfection. She has a courtly suitor, Felix Meecham, whom she loves, but she eventually sends him away and decides to wait for Randall. Murdoch has cited Ann as an example when discussing the difficulty of presenting dynamic good characters. The figures with powerful and active egos stand out in the novels, but the good figures have a tendency to recede into the background because they do not demand attention from others.

The Irish landscape of *The Unicorn* conforms to that of County Clare, with its immense cliffs of black sandstone overlooking a dark coastline and a cold, killing sea. A nineteenth-century lodge built over the ruins of an eighteenth-century house and surrounded by wrecked gardens, Gaze Castle sequesters Hannah Crean-Smith, a beautiful young woman who has been imprisoned there for seven years after an unsuccessful attempt to kill her husband-cousin, Peter, during an argument over her affair with their neighbor Pip Lejour. Peter has gone away to America, and one of his lovers, Gerald Scottow, enforces Peter's wish. Hannah is attended by various courtly lovers, including Effingham Cooper, who is visiting at Riders, the Lejour estate. A local man reported to be related to fairies, Denis Nolan, performs the duties of a page. Another outsider, Marian Taylor, comes to Gaze Castle to tutor Hannah in French. The plot revolves around the outsiders' botched attempt to rescue Hannah, a rescue that appears unwelcome to her.

In a 1983 *Gáeliana* interview Murdoch said that the "germ for this book came . . . when I first saw the Cluny tapestries." The motifs of these medieval tapestries include a woman and a unicorn—the symbol for both purity and suffering. Hannah initially appears to be the unicorn of the title; however, her suffering acts as a form of consolation and illustrates Simone Weil's development of the Greek concept of Até. In the novel Murdoch explains this concept and its association with power and with good:

> Até is the name of the almost automatic transfer of suffering from one being to another. Power is a form of Até. The victims of power, and any power has its victims, are themselves infected. They have to pass it on, to use power on others. . . . [I]t is in the good that Até is finally quenched, and when it encounters a pure being who only suffers and does not attempt to pass the suffering on.

Denis Nolan, a curious composite of a Christ figure who also has connotations of the ritual fisher king, is better seen as the pure being who perfects his suffering, thereby making it an effective means for expiating guilt. Although he ultimately kills Peter when the latter returns, Denis begins atonement for his transgression, as well as those of the household, with his decision to leave Gaze at the end of the novel and take the suffering with him.

Effingham Cooper has a Platonic recognition of the meaning of love and death that is expressed in his momentary unselfing: "This then was love, to look and look until one exists no more, *this* was the love which was the same as death." But Cooper's spirituality is such that he cannot maintain his vision of unity, and he leaves Gaze after Hannah's suicide, trying "to forget what he had briefly seen."

Some critics feel that *The Italian Girl,* Murdoch's least successful novel, may be an earlier manuscript published out of sequence. Like *The Flight from the Enchanter,* this novel has displaced persons at its center; Elsa and David Levkin are

Russian Jews who are obsessed with their heritage and feel they must suffer because of it. As the novel begins, the narrator, Edmund Narraway, returns home for his mother's funeral, and his reunion with the other inhabitants of the household develops two other recurring motifs in Murdoch's fiction—sibling rivalry and the Oedipal complex. Edmund's brother, Otto; his wife, Isabel; and their daughter Flora live in the family home. Also present are the Levkins and Maria Magistretti (Maggie), the title character, who was Edmund's old nurse. Throughout the course of the novel Edmund, a writer, and Otto, a stonemason, come to terms with their artistic abilities and their feelings for Lydia, their domineering mother. Lydia had jealously and alternately loved each of her sons and then her grandchild, Flora, causing alienation and estrangement for all of them. Isabel and Flora both have affairs with David Levkin, who impregnates them, and Elsa Levkin has an affair with Otto because he is a "monster and a ruin." Isabel looks to Edmund, the outsider, as the only one who can heal the family, but Edmund feels (and indeed initially proves) himself unworthy of that role.

In an Oedipal ending to the novel, Edmund forms a romantic attachment with Maggie, the nurse of his youth. Maggie has possibly had a lesbian relationship with Lydia, but she replaces Lydia in a positive way by teaching Edmund how to love others. After he demonstrates a new awareness of others, Maggie becomes for Edmund "the one person in the world for whom [he] could be complete." Part of the difficulty with this novel is that Edmund's reformation appears unconvincing even though he speaks the correct words for such a change: "I certainly now, and with a fresh sharpness, saw Maggie as a separate and private and unpredictable being. I endowed her, as it were, with those human rights, the right of secrecy, the right of surprise." The Levkins' desires for self-destruction are also unconvincing. Following Elsa's death in a fire, David returns to Leningrad, where he faces certain grief, explaining that he cannot forsake his heritage and must suffer in his own place. Perhaps the reader remains unconvinced about the motives of this bizarre group of characters because the novel lacks the depth to develop the motives for their actions adequately and convincingly.

This novel does not enjoy the large world and scope of Murdoch's more successful novels, and though it was adapted for the stage by Murdoch and James Saunders in 1967 and published in an acting version the following year, it was largely unsuccessful. Murdoch has commented in a 4 April

1968 *Listener* interview with Ronald Bryden that the collaboration was rushed and that the play turned out more comic than the novel had been. She also felt that the staging clearly brought out the weaknesses of the novel—three rather cardboard characters and a structural weakness about two-thirds of the way through.

The framework of *The Red and the Green* (1965), Murdoch's only historical novel, concerns the Easter Rebellion in support of Home Rule that took place in Dublin in April 1916 when Irish nationalists (Sinn Fein) took control of the Dublin Post Office and replaced its British Union Jack with a green flag bearing the words *Irish Republic.* The main theme of initiation is shown through Andrew Chase-White, an Anglo-Irish officer who has been commissioned in King Edward's Horse (as Murdoch's father had been) and is in Ireland on leave before going to the front during World War I. Although he is a British officer, his loyalties are confused: "Andrew had grown up in England and more especially in London, and felt himself unreflectively to be English, although equally unreflectively he normally announced himself as Irish." Andrew, who somehow connects his sexual initiation with his death and expects to die at the front, is later killed at Passchendaele. He has proposed to an Irish girl, Frances Bellman, but she refuses his proposal because she is secretly in love with Andrew's cousin Pat Dumay.

Other themes in the novel are carried forward by Barnabas Drumm, a promising medieval scholar and former priest whose scholarship and marriage suffer because of the conflicting demands of celibacy and religious scruples that he still retains. All of the characters in the novel are affected by Irish nationalism, whether they support it or not. Hilda Chase-White, Andrew's mother, remarks that the Irish are obsessed with history, a topic that is seldom discussed among her set in England. Many of Andrew's relatives are Irish nationalists, particularly Frances's father, Christopher Bellman, and Andrew's cousins, the Dumays. An Irish enthusiast, Bellman is an expert on Irish antiquities and is familiar with Gaelic; Pat Dumay takes part in and is killed during the Easter Rebellion; and his younger brother, Cathal, later joins the Irish Republican Army and is killed during the 1921 Irish civil war.

Within this pervading atmosphere of nationalism, the novel explores Andrew's confusion about his loyalties, his sexual insecurity and initiation (with his aunt, Millie Kinnard), and his loss of honor as a British officer when he does not reveal what he knows about the planned uprising. Millie has unusual, masculine traits—wearing trousers, smoking cigars, and taking target practice. Her unconventional, promiscuous behavior produces an unforgettable evening that results in a highly comic Murdoch muddle: during the course of the evening four men (Pat, Andrew, Barnabas, and Christopher) bicycle the fifteen miles from Dublin to Rathblane expecting assignations with her.

One difficulty with the novel is that the many historical figures associated with the Easter Rebellion have all become folk heroes, and Murdoch's treatment of them appears idealized and sentimental. Murdoch too has found herself in Andrew's position of feeling thoroughly Irish and yet also thoroughly English.

The atheistic Anglican priest in *The Time of the Angels* (1966), who is another of Murdoch's dark figures of power, has a pervading desire to break away from the restraints of authority and convention and wishes a freedom unencumbered by moral obligations or consciousness of others. Described variously as "a witch doctor," "a man of power," and a "neurotic . . . unbalanced, psychotic, and a thoroughly evil man," Father Carel Fisher imposes his will upon others with little resistance on their part. To initiate an affair with Pattie, his black housekeeper, Carel merely calls her to him and slips out of his cassock. He offers no explanation, and Pattie expects none. His "great dark night eyes" and "white teeth" identify him as a Gothic protagonist; he is also the fisher king gone wrong, the estranged "saver" of souls who rules from a virtual wasteland. His parish, St. Eustace Watergate, is located in an abandoned war-torn area of London, and the rector's lodging is the only building left standing in a parish whose structure has been destroyed—both figuratively and literally. Subterranean passages in the novel belong to the Underground railway whose ever-present rumblings disturb the sleep of the household and lend an ominous atmosphere to a setting that is continually shrouded in fog.

The secluded maiden in the novel, Carel's daughter, Elizabeth (originally thought to be his orphaned niece), remains confined to her room throughout the novel, incapacitated by a mysterious back ailment that resists treatment. Elizabeth's cousin, Muriel, wanting to force some involvement with the outside world for Elizabeth, tells two Russian immigrants (the rectory porter Eugene Peshkov and his son Leo) about her. Ironically, when Muriel agrees to help Leo look into the room of this "beautiful virgin," they discover an incestuous relationship between Carel and his daughter.

Throughout the novel Murdoch raises a fundamental question concerning her moral philosophy—what is the moral order for a world that no longer believes in God? This topic is taken up by several people in the novel, including Carel's rather conventional brother, Marcus, who is writing "a philosophical treatise upon morality in a secular age," and Carel's bishop, who accepts the doctrine of demythologization. Marcus is a spokesman for rationality, and he tries to construct an argument for the continued existence of goodness and morality and concern for others, even in an unordered world; however, Carel replies with an existential view: "No, no, we are creatures of accident, operated by forces we do not understand." Unsettled and appalled by what he calls the consolations of "milk-and-water modern theism," Carel remains seared by the possibilities entailed in the death of God. The title of the novel refers to the angels, the other spiritual powers, who take over the vacuum caused by the death of God: "The disappearance of God does not simply leave a void into which human reason can move. The death of God has set the angels free. And they are terrible." Carel cannot accept a spiritual world that offers only torment and no consolation, so he resorts to the only form of consolation available to him—the use of power. His threadbare carpet and constant pacing are symbolic of his desire to escape his unsettling spirituality, and his use of power evidences his will to wrestle these manifestations into an order over which he has control. When these efforts fail to release him from his torments, Carel finally escapes to an unknown world by suicide.

Many college instructors find *The Nice and the Good* (1968) an excellent introduction to Murdoch's mature works as the novel successfully integrates her moral philosophy, aesthetics, and characterization. As the title indicates, the characters can easily be ranked according to awareness of others, clear vision, and appropriate action; however, many scholars agree that there are no "good" characters in the novel. Two characters, John Ducane and Theodore Gray, have intimations of the good, and Theo recognizes the vast disparity between the spiritual states indicated by the title of the novel, but no one achieves that end.

The main settings of the novel are a Whitehall department in London and the Dorset seaside estate to which the department head, Theo's brother Octavian Gray, and his fellow civil servant, Ducane, retreat on weekends. Sacred and profane love, the seductive nature of power, the evil that power produces, justice, and forgiveness concern the characters in their efforts to achieve good lives.

Sleaze and sex are thrown into the mix when the quiet reserve of Whitehall is disturbed by a gunshot—the suicide of Joseph Radeechy, who, it is sub-

sequently discovered, had been conducting black masses in the Whitehall vaults (complete with pigeon sacrifices and a naked woman in attendance). Ducane, an expert on Roman law whose ambition is "to lead a clean simple life and to be a good man," investigates the suicide and finds himself drawn further and further into a moral muddle.

The iconography of the novel involves Agnolo Bronzino's sixteenth-century painting *An Allegory (Venus, Cupid, Folly, and Time)*, in which Cupid stoops to give his mother, Venus, an erotic kiss while Folly spreads rose petals over the couple and Time stands in the background watching the scene. Murdoch incorporates the jealousy, masks, deceit, eroticism, and various guises of love shown in the painting into the plot of her novel. Richard Biranne, another civil servant, and his former wife, Paula, identify most closely with the painting and are reunited through it; however, all of the characters in the novel love badly and present false images of themselves.

As with other characters faced with near-death experiences, Ducane learns the truly important things in life when trapped by a rising tide in a cave while attempting to save the son of the woman he marries, Mary Clothier: "If I ever get out of here I will be no man's judge. Nothing is worth doing except to kill the little rat [ego], not to judge, not to be superior, not to exercise power, not to seek, seek, seek. To love and to reconcile and to forgive, only this matters." Notable too is Willy Kost, a Jewish refugee-scholar who, like Theo, quietly lives in his own private hell. Lending a lighter touch to the novel are nine-year-old twins, Edward and Henrietta Biranne—perhaps Murdoch's most successful portrayal of children—and the Grays' unforgettable pets, Mingo and Montrose.

Malcolm Bradbury notes that "by the end of the 1960s it was clear that Iris Murdoch had become a very different kind of novelist from the one whose first book had seemed so much to match the mood of the 1950s." Murdoch has made the change from bohemian to middle-class characters, and the problems in her novels no longer have clear ethical resolutions. Many critics see in this movement a turn toward bleakness, yet there is general praise for *Bruno's Dream* (1969), the subject of which is the relationship between love and death.

The novel concerns the spiritual awakening of the dying Bruno Greensleave and some of his family members, including his estranged son, Miles, a failed poet whose visits to Bruno appear to be prompted by his interest in Bruno's valuable stamp collection. Bruno is attended to by Danby Odell, the widower of Bruno's daughter, Gwen. Nigel Boase and his cousin, Adelaide, a maid with whom Danby has had a casual affair, live with Danby. Nigel acts as companion and nurse to Bruno and teaches him about the significance of love. He also writes to Danby, with whom he is in love, about the "thought that anyone is *permitted* to love anyone and in any way he pleases," a tenet of many Murdoch novels.

With the exception of Nigel all of the characters in the novel love selfishly. Bruno has never forgiven himself for failing to respond to the calls of his dying wife nearly forty years ago—he was afraid she might curse him instead of forgiving him for an affair she had discovered. Miles too has a warped perception of love. Although married to Diana, he is still obsessed with his deceased first wife, Parvati, and unable to bring himself to forgive Bruno for disapproving of their marriage; yet Miles also harbors a secret love for Lisa Watkins, Diana's sister. Near death, Bruno has a vision of love and realizes his own loves have been solipsistic failures: "He had loved only a few people and loved them so badly, so selfishly. . . . Was it only in the presence of death that one could see so clearly what love ought to be like? If only the knowledge which he had now, this absolute nothing-else-matters, could somehow go backwards and purify the little selfish loves and straighten out the muddles."

A Fairly Honourable Defeat (1970) continues the high achievement—a merging of idea, technique, and incident—that marks the next two decades of Murdoch's career. Writing for *The New York Times* (30 January 1970), Christopher Lehmann-Haupt praised the comic spirit and double twists of irony in the novel, calling it "the most entertaining Iris Murdoch I've read in years." The novel concerns the struggle between good and evil that takes place in everyday life. The cast of characters includes Hilda and Rupert Foster, a middle-aged idealistic couple. Hilda performs good works, and Rupert has been writing a book about virtue and morals for the past eight years. Hilda's sister, Morgan, a linguistic theorist who is estranged from her husband, Tallis Browne, has been living in America with Julius King, a biochemist involved with developing nerve gas. The Fosters' son, Peter, an antisocial layabout, lives with Tallis and Tallis's father, Leonard. Rupert's younger brother, Simon, and his lover, Axel Nisson, complete the family group. Tallis, a social worker living a muddled but altruistic life, is one of Murdoch's clearly developed good figures. Julius King (formerly Kahn) had been in a concentration camp and exhibits Weil's idea that the victim of suffering can find relief from his/her suffering by causing suffering in others—an idea that was also considered at length in *The Unicorn*.

The main plot evolves from a wager between Julius and Morgan. When Julius claims that he can divide anybody from anybody, Morgan bets him ten guineas that he cannot. They fix on separating Simon Foster and Axel Nilsson. Axel and Simon are unusual in traditional literature: they are a sympathetically portrayed homosexual couple. Murdoch told Chevalier that one of her intended goals in *A Fairly Honourable Defeat* was to portray a happy homosexual relationship; she has known many such couples and wanted to show this situation in her novels. Murdoch sensitively establishes Simon and Axel as a believable, worthy, and normal couple whose love for each other allows them to survive the jealousy and doubt that Julius maliciously plants in their lives. However, the wager does have the result of separating another couple, and it has the tragic consequence of Rupert's death.

In an alternate allegorical reading of the novel suggested by Murdoch herself, this struggle also involves spiritual beings. At an Amsterdam conference (recalled in *Encounters with Iris Murdoch*, 1988), Murdoch told Diana Phillips that she identifies Julius King with the "devil" and calls Tallis "not exactly a Christ-figure, I think, but what in the East would be called a 'high incarnation.' He is a good person who's turned up, as they perhaps do every now and then in the world, but he is also a spiritual being." Murdoch explains that Leonard, "if you want to carry the allegory a litle bit further into a kind of absurdity, is God the Father. He's Tallis's father, and he's constantly making the remark: 'It all went wrong from the start.'" Peter Conradi agrees that "Morgan represents the human soul over which the two spiritual magnates are battling."

An Accidental Man, a dark novel that still retains Murdoch's wit, has motifs of power, pain, guilt, alienation, suffering, redemption, and forgiveness; however, its consideration of the contingencies of life and its few redemptive characters present a horrific life vision. In a *Listener* review (28 October 1971) Frank Kermode comments on its "compulsively elaborate plot" yet concludes that the novel "represents a major development in the career of a major novelist."

Critics debate the identity of the title character, with most critics, including Conradi, giving that place to Austin Gibson Grey, who identifies himself as such in the novel. Described as "a huge fat egoist, as fat as a bull-frog," Austin exemplifies the vagaries of the world: he has been fired without a pension and appears to have been unlucky with two wives. His first wife, Betty, drowned, or may have been murdered by a jealous Austin; his next wife, Dorina, is kept sheltered throughout the novel from the object of Austin's jealousy and hatred, his brother Matthew, and she is eventually electrocuted in the bath. Ludwig, an American student living in London and avoiding the American draft through the technicality of being born in England, faces a moral dilemma—taking up his Oxford appointment and marrying the girl he loves, Gracie Tisbourne, or returning home to America to face draft-evasion charges.

These men's lives are intertwined through Austin's son, Garth, who is Ludwig's friend. An absolutist with existential leanings, Garth had studied philosophy at Harvard and had been concerned with freedom, correct choice, and action but gave up philosophy because he felt it had no meaning in his life. He had witnessed a murder on the streets of New York, did not interfere, and felt no guilt for this failure to act. Garth recorded his experience in a novel in which the hero's suicide coincides with Garth's own spiritual death. In Murdoch novels those who cannot endure spiritual hardships engage the material world instead. Eventually Garth grasps for wealth and happiness by marrying Ludwig's former fiancée, Gracie. Ludwig, however, determined to suffer for his opposition to the Vietnam War, returns to America, where he is imprisoned.

Readers who are unfamiliar with Murdoch's work would do well to begin with *The Black Prince* (1973), winner of the James Tait Black Memorial Prize for fiction and (with *The Sea, The Sea*) the most critically acclaimed of Murdoch's novels. Careful plotting, fully realized characterization, and attention to details are joined to a murder mystery of sorts through postscripts that suggest various postmodern readings of the novel. Throughout this closely structured novel Murdoch again relates the life of the artist whose work has been impacted by Eros.

Bradley Pearson, the narrator of *The Black Prince,* is a fifty-eight-year-old civil servant with limited literary publications who is taking an early retirement in order to satisfy a lifelong creative urge to write his "great work," intended to be a commentary on art and love. His best friend, Arnold Baffin, is a successful and prolific writer, and together they represent both extremes of the French symbolist debate about how truth can be told: should art be crystalline and compact or journalistic and loosely written?

Before Pearson can leave London, he receives a telephone call from Baffin, who reports that he has just murdered his wife, Rachel, with a blow from the fireplace poker. Baffin's attempt on Rachel's life is not successful, however, and eventually their roles reverse and Rachel telephones Bradley for help, ac-

tually having succeeded in murdering her husband with this same instrument. Pearson rushes over to the Baffins' home to help and console Rachel, but he is soon arrested for Arnold's murder and convicted. During his time in prison Pearson recounts the events between these two telephone calls in his own "book within a book," *The Black Prince—A Celebration of Love,* which becomes his literary masterpiece. It is a book that Bradley could not have written without the experiences which that telephone delay brought—including his love affair with the Baffins' daughter, Julian.

An "Editor's Foreword" by one P. Loxias, who claims to have been responsible for the publication of Pearson's book, makes the connection between art and Eros. Although Murdoch provided a clue to Loxias's identity when she asked a friend to draw a head of the statue of Apollo at Olympia for the dust jacket of the novel, critics misread the reference in the title. "*The Black Prince,* of course is Apollo—most critics who reviewed the book in England didn't appear to realize this, even though there was a picture of Apollo on the front!" she noted during a conference in Caen. Instead, critics identified Bradley Pearson (B.P.) as Hamlet (known as the Black Prince due to his sable robes of mourning). Bradley also gives Julian Baffin a *Hamlet* tutorial, a wonderful piece mixing brilliant criticism with a bizarre Freudian interpretation of the play, and he is able to consummate their affair (described almost as a rape) only after she dresses up as Hamlet.

Conradi points out that Apollo is named Luxius and Lycean in Sophocles's *Oedipus Rex*. Further, the myths surrounding Apollo include rape and murder. Murdoch has long associated the destruction of the ego, or sublimation of self, with the artist's creativity. She reiterated this position by choosing Titian's *The Flaying of Marsyas* as the background painting for her own portrait which now hangs in the National Portrait Gallery. The doubling of the Apollo-Marsyas myth can be seen in the novel in Pearson's supposed murder of his fellow artist and friend, in his forceful consummation of his affair with Julian, and in his own suffering and death as necessary for the production of his work of art, the novel *The Black Prince*. The subtitle of the novel, "A Celebration of Love," indicates that through the painful process of loss of self Pearson has achieved truth.

Postscripts by four of the characters (Pearson's former wife, Christian; Pearson's former brother-in-law, Francis Marloe, a quack psychiatrist; Rachel; and Julian) follow the novel. These clever extensions of the plot offer alternative read-

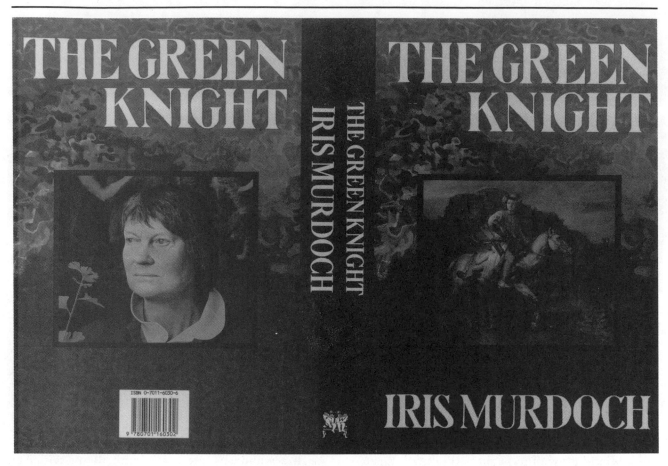

Dust jacket for the novel in which Murdoch mixed a modern-day story of sibling rivalry with a retelling of the medieval tale of Sir Gawain and the Green Knight

ings of Pearson's version of events and are consistent with the characterization of the individuals that were developed within the novel. Finally, the "Editor's Postscript" discloses Pearson's death and critiques the other postscripts, pointing out each individual's egoistic concerns. P. Loxias, Apollo—the god of art and Eros—directs the reader back to the truth that great art can reveal if the reader will attend properly. Readers are left with a novel that satisfies the criteria of both of its artists and advances the aesthetics of its author: "Art is not cosy and it is not mocked. Art tells the only truth that ultimately matters. It is the light by which human things can be mended. And after art there is, let me assure you all, nothing."

The Black Prince was successfully staged in the Aldwych Theatre in London in 1989, directed by Stuart Burge and produced by Josephine Hart. Ian McDiarmid played Bradley Pearson, and his interior monologues were staged as soliloquies.

In her review of *The Sacred and Profane Love Machine* (1974) for the *New Review* (April 1974), Lorna Sage remarked, "Iris Murdoch has become . . . a figure of comfort and almost ceremonial assur-

ance on the fictional scene. Her freshness, her refusal to dry up, now seem more odd and outstanding than the plotty perversities that would once have distinguished her." And in *The New York Times Book Review* (22 September 1974), speaking about the "most well-worn of all subjects," the plot of a man with two women, John Wain exclaimed: "She handles this theme with such power and authority as to make one feel that one is reading about it for the first time."

The iconography for the novel, Titian's painting *Sacred and Profane Love,* represents the dual nature of love, divine and human; but, as in real life, these characters best exemplify the profane and cannot endure the ideal. Blaise Gavender, an unqualified psychotherapist with a penchant for dream interpretation, has a wife (Harriet) and a son (David) living in the country, and a mistress (Emily McHugh) and their autistic son (Luca) living in a mean flat in Putney. Like the men in similar circumstances in *An Unofficial Rose, The Black Prince,* and *The Message to the Planet,* Blaise would like to maintain both relationships, and it initially appears that his wife, a saintly figure, will agree to the extended "family." Harriet takes the unwanted Luca under her care, much like the menagerie of homeless dogs she has collected, but the strain of her situation proves too great and leads to tragedy.

Imperfect love is also shown through the Gavenders' neighbor, writer Montague Small, who is both obsessed with and oppressed by the women in his life. Supposedly in anguish over the death of his beloved wife, Sophie, Monty has actually strangled her in order to avoid the prolonged suffering of watching her die from cancer. Seemingly released from one painful relationship, Monty begins receiving love letters from his mother, who had nearly smothered him with attention as a child and now wants him back in her life again.

As usual, Murdoch's characters have ample room to display their misery, and the dark denouement of the novel holds little promise for redeeming love in the future. While a pregnant Emily has replaced Harriet at Hood House, readers wonder what quality of love can be expected for this next child when Luca, who has been the object of so little concern and who had been able to communicate only with Harriet and with animals, has now been institutionalized by his relieved parents.

Kermode had strong praise for *A Word Child* (1975) in his 17 April 1975 *Listener* review of the novel: "It would be difficult to speak too highly of the extraordinary skill and confidence here displayed. . . . [I]n its own dazzling way, it is as problematic as *Mansfield Park*." The narrator and title character, Hilary Burde, is an emotionally abused orphan who has grown up feeling he was unlovable. He lives a maimed existence, repeating the mistakes of his past. Ironically, Hilary has highly developed linguistic skills, but they function mechanically and not as a basis for communication with others. While at Oxford, Hilary had fallen in love with Anne Jopling, the wife of Gunnar, a history don in his college. When Anne, pregnant with her husband's child, tells Hilary that she wants to break away from him, Hilary causes an automobile accident that kills Anne. Following this incident Hilary leaves Oxford and takes a dead-end job with the civil service. In order to control his life and minimize human interaction, Hilary has carefully compartmentalized his routine, visiting friends and his sister, Crystal, only on certain days of the week. He also selfishly controls his sister's life, keeping her lonely and sequestered. So programmed is Hilary's isolation that, when not attending to this routine, he spends his spare time surrounded by strangers, riding beneath central London on the Inner Circle Line of the Underground. The days of the week actually become a structural framing device for the novel, for all of the

chapters except the last two—which take place following the death of Lady Kitty, Gunnar's second wife, when there are "no more days"—are titled as days of the week.

Gunnar Jopling cannot bring himself to forgive Hilary for Anne's death, for the loss of the expected child, or for the later suicide of an older son, Tristram. When Jopling takes over as head of civil service, Lady Kitty initiates meetings with Hilary, trying to effect a reconciliation, but their relationship eventually repeats the cycle of pain with Lady Kitty's own accidental death. The main themes of the novel, all of which its narrator painfully comes to realize, are the debilitating consequences (alienation and sterility) of the failure to love, the importance of forgiving oneself and others for mistakes of the past, and the importance of spiritual redemption.

Henry and Cato (1976) was written after Murdoch returned from a year of teaching at Washington University, St. Louis, and it evokes the iconography of the paintings of German Expressionist Max Beckmann, which she had seen in St. Louis. This novel again enacts the themes that Murdoch has been discussing in her moral philosophy: forgiveness, redemption, love, and death as the great teacher. Henry Marshalson returns home from America to claim his inheritance and plans to give his family estate away in order to spite his mother, who preferred his elder brother, Sandy. When Henry, an art historian who has been working on a book about Beckmann for the past nine years, eventually has a life experience that actually reflects the fear and suffering depicted in Beckmann's paintings, he finds it too horrific to embrace; instead, he chooses to live a worldly and mediocre life.

This same incident also involves the other title character, Cato Forbes, Henry's childhood friend and a failed priest who lost his faith when he became enamored of a street thug, Beautiful Joe Beckett. When Beautiful Joe attacks Cato's sister, Colette, after kidnapping her and Cato and mutilating Henry, Cato kills him; that act results in Cato's spiritual destruction. Cato had held moral promise in the novel because his mentor, Brendan Craddock, is one of Murdoch's few saints.

Craddock, a Platonist whose ideas about shadowed vision, love, death, suffering, and the use of power echo Murdoch's own writings, explains why spiritual awareness is so difficult to maintain: "Death is what instructs us most of all, and then only when it is present. . . . Those who can live with death can live in the truth, only this is almost unendurable. . . . Death is the great destroyer of all images and all stories, and human beings will do anything rather than envisage it." In the final section of the novel, titled "The Great Teacher," many of the characters, including the gifted but failed poet Lucius Lamb, experience an awareness that comes with the proximity of death. After suffering a stroke, Lucius realizes that he has not fulfilled his promise because he lacked courage. In one final haiku Lucius writes: "So many dawns I was blind to. / Now the illumination of night / Comes to me too late, O great teacher."

The Sea, The Sea was awarded the 1978 Booker Prize and met with nearly universal critical praise. Margaret Drabble, writing in *Saturday Review* (6 January 1979), remarked, "Here is a novelist whose books glitter and expand with exhilaration and joy, like the sea itself." Sally Cunneen, in *Commonweal* (9 November 1979), called it representative of Murdoch's recent works "in its fusion of moral vision and literary form." The novel illustrates the human compulsion for illusion in various forms—the illusion of the theater, Tibetan powers that degenerate into magic, and the fantastic workings of the imagination. Murdoch draws from the worlds of theater and art to develop these themes. A realistic set piece at the Wallace Collection museum in London provides the iconography for the novel, primarily associating two of the paintings in the collection, Titian's *Perseus and Andromeda* and Rembrandt's *Titus,* with people and events in the novel. The magic and power evident in William Shakespeare's *The Tempest* (1611) also figure prominently in the plot, and Murdoch is surely making much of Plato's objections to the illusory qualities of art.

As with *The Black Prince,* the novel is itself a literary device. Its narrator, Charles Arrowby, an actor, playwright, and famed director who is known as a "Shakespeare man," claims to have written this work to repent his life of egoism. Much like Prospero, Charles hopes to retire from his life of power and magic; but like Prospero, he finds it difficult to relinquish his manipulation of others.

Throughout his memoir Charles reveals his envy of his cousin, James, a Buddhist and a retired general. The cousins strive for virtuous lives but have been hindered in their quests by their use of power; Charles had enjoyed considerable control as a theater director, and James had developed paranormal abilities in the course of studying Buddhism. Both must relinquish their powers and come to terms with their pasts in order to avoid repeating their previous mistakes.

Although Charles has withdrawn to a seaside house, Shruff End, in order to write, most of his former friends and lovers reenter his life there, and his interaction with them and with his cousin pro-

vides the context for Murdoch's consideration of the moral and aesthetic issues. The novel also stresses the interconnectedness of all things, the consequences of actions, and the necessity for acting with humility through the character of James, whose vanity cost him a beloved friend and sent him, according to Buddhist teaching, back to the wheel to perfect himself. James had been setting aside worldly things, preparing for death, when he contacted Charles to effect a reconciliation between them. James appears as a spokesman for Murdoch when he observes, "Goodness is giving up power and acting upon the world negatively."

A Year of Birds (1978), including twelve of Murdoch's poems accompanied by wood engravings by Reynolds Stone, was published by Compton Press in a limited edition of 350 signed copies and republished (with textual variants) by Chatto and Windus (1984). The poems, titled with the months of the year, were originally meant to be used in a calendar form. Sir Malcolm Williamson adapted the work for soprano and orchestra as a symphonic song cycle that premiered on 19 August 1995 at the Royal Albert Hall in London.

When *Nuns and Soldiers* appeared in 1980, Victoria Glendinning remarked in *The Listener* (4 September 1980) that the novel "is written with a happy pressure of purpose and great confidence; the old black magic is in perfect working order." Rosemary Dinnage, writing for the *Times Literary Supplement* (5 September 1980), complained about "too much mechanism" but concluded that "one is gratified that the Murdoch world exists."

The opening chapter focuses on the death of Guy Openshaw, a kind and generous half-Jewish scholar. His pain illustrates one of the themes of the novel: the suffering of the just. In many ways all of the characters in the novel suffer, and, once again, Murdoch considers the extent to which their suffering acts as consolation. The nuns and soldiers of the title refer to all of the characters, who are in some way withdrawn from the world or soldiering on with their disappointments and duties; but the two characters who specifically fulfill these title roles are Anne Cavidge (a former nun) and Wojciech Szczepanski (Peter, the count), who vicariously identifies with the suffering of the Polish freedom fighters.

Gathering around to support the dying Guy and his wife, Gertrude, are a collection of upper-middle-class relatives and friends (the "Ebury Street set") and two characters who are peripheral to this group: Tim Reede and his mistress, Daisy Barrett, failed painters who live in a bohemian area of London, north Soho. Following Guy's death, Gertrude becomes a sort of Penelope figure, attracting almost all of the available men as suitors, and she enjoys the attention. As an act of kindness, Gertrude offers to let Tim become caretaker of her Provence house, but after she arrives there unexpectedly, they fall in love and decide to marry. The objections from the Ebury Street group can be imagined, and these are complicated by the lies that Tim has told in order to satisfy both Daisy and Gertrude. Not since *Under the Net,* with its scenes of the carefree Paris of her youth, has Murdoch so powerfully evoked the French landscape in her novels. Here the magnificence of the sun-struck wilds of Provence counterpoint the closely detailed London settings. The French landscape is seen as enchanting, for only here can Tim and Gertrude's relationship flourish, and the plotting follows the tradition of the staid British being captivated and transformed by the more relaxed atmosphere of France.

Perhaps the most controversial set piece in any Murdoch novel to date involves a beatific vision of Jesus Christ that Anne Cavidge experiences. Her enlightenment from this visitation is similar to one Theodore Gray had experienced in a Buddhist monastery in *The Nice and the Good:* "Theo had begun to glimpse the distance which separates the nice from the good, and the vision of this gap had terrified his soul." Like Theo, Anne learns that she must work toward the good alone, without consolation from the world or from faith.

In his 1 May 1983 review of *The Philosopher's Pupil* (1983) for the *Sunday Observer,* Martin Amis praised Murdoch's fiction as "habit-forming," yet he also raised a point about which critics have complained for years: "Miss Murdoch's characters inhabit an eroticised world, untouched by the usual anxieties of health, work and money." In his *Contemporary Review* essay, however, John Elsom identified some of the reasons why Murdoch's work has remained a powerful force in British fiction for so many decades: "Far from dwindling away, Iris Murdoch [has come] into her own, having discovered how best to blend those elements of passionate thought, cool (even comic) observation and narrative surprise which had been present in her novels since the early 1950s."

In writing about *The Philosopher's Pupil* for *The Friend* (7 October 1983), Diana and John Lampen pointed out the enormity of Murdoch's task: in the tradition of George Eliot's *Middlemarch* (1871–1872) she "has evoked a whole world in the form of a small town, peopled it, and given it a unique history and geography." The world presented in *The Philosopher's Pupil* is the small spa town of Ennistone, to which the philosopher John Robert Rozanov returns in order to refine his understanding of his field

and to complete his great work on moral philosophy. Rozanov faces a situation similar to many of Murdoch's thoughtful academics (possibly even including Murdoch herself): formulating the sum of his knowledge and experience in a single work. *The Philosopher's Pupil* begins a series of lengthy commentaries upon art and life that present a mature reevaluation of the complexities of Murdoch's vision. The reader finds in this work (as well as in *The Good Apprentice* [1985], *The Book and the Brotherhood* [1987], and *The Message to the Planet,* [1989]) a sense of adjustment and summary. All of these later novels demonstrate the interconnected nature of all life and the futility of attaching oneself to substitute gods.

Some of the particular concerns in *The Philosopher's Pupil* are moral improvement, artistic duty, and religion. Murdoch explores the concept of the artist's duty to his work and his duty to others through Rozanov's relationships with the title character, George McCaffrey, and with his grandchild, Hattie Meynell. Father Bernard Jacoby's eccentric religious beliefs are revealed in a dialectic with Rozanov, and a good figure, William Eastcote, expresses Quaker humility and the necessity for love.

Rozanov serves as a father figure for the malevolent McCaffrey, who feels that his life can become whole again if he can make his former teacher notice him; but Rozanov, disgusted by this interference with his work, utterly rejects McCaffrey. Throughout his life Rozanov has refused to allow others to intrude upon his time. Following the early death of his wife, Linda, Rozanov ignored his daughter and concentrated on his publications. When his daughter also died, leaving her daughter, Hattie, Rozanov absolved himself of responsibility for her by hiring a governess and later by sending Hattie away to private schools and trying to arrange for her marriage.

One eccentric religious figure in the novel, Father Bernard Jacoby, is a high Anglican priest who had been a convert from Judaism. Although Jacoby does not believe in God, he meditates, using a mixture of Christian and Buddhist beliefs. A religious experience in Greece leads him to believe that "the essential and only question of our age [is] the absolute denial of God." His beliefs are contrasted with those of the devout Eastcote, who sees a flying saucer and equates it with parallel life-forms on other planets because he believes all things are related. A revered and gentle person who performs good works, counsels wisely, and speaks ill of no one, Eastcote is a character of the good.

In a 12 January 1986 review of *The Good Apprentice* for *The New York Times Book Review,* Bloom included that book with *Bruno's Dream, The Black Prince,* and *A Word Child* as the best of Murdoch's novels. Forgiveness and healing through the acceptance of responsibility are the subjects of *The Good Apprentice,* a painful work about the consequences of the failure to attend to others. The referent in the title of the novel is ambiguous, and critics assign the role to either of two motherless stepbrothers in the novel, Edward Baltram and Stuart Cuno. The action centers around Edward, who is suffering from guilt and depression over his responsibility for the death of his friend Mark Wilsden. Edward had slipped a drug into Mark's sandwich and then watched as Mark experienced what Edward felt would be a "happy journey." Then, after Mark fell asleep, Edward slipped out of their apartment to meet Sarah Plowmain and left Mark locked in the flat. When he returned Edward found the window in their flat open and Mark's crushed body on the pavement below. For Edward, Mark's death signifies the wretched ending of all past innocence and promises a future forever maimed by the manner of its loss.

Stuart, an absolutist, exasperates his friends with his moral talk and his impracticality. He has given up a coveted teaching post at a London college in order to try to live a moral life. Stuart will play a part in Edward's recovery by trying to convince Mrs. Wilsden to stop writing hateful letters to Edward. Also central in the novel are Midge and Thomas McCaskerville. Midge is having an affair with Harry Cuno, Stuart's father, and Thomas is a psychiatrist who is trying to help Edward. The McCaskervilles' neglected young son, Meredith, is given a sense of worth by his relationship with Stuart.

The Prodigal Son, the biblical allusion that also acts as the title of the first part of the novel, is given an unusual reading. The novel begins, "I will arise and go to my father, and will say unto him, Father I have sinned against heaven and before thee, and am no more worthy to be called thy son." The connection in the novel, however, is with Edward and Jesse Baltram, the father who deserted Edward's mother before his birth. After attending a séance in which he receives a message telling him to seek spiritual healing from his natural father, Edward begins searching for Baltram. His search leads to the discovery of another stepmother, May, and two stepsisters, Betinna and Ilona, as well as an infirm and crazed Jesse Baltram. Edward's healing begins when he reconciles with his father and begins to take care of him. When he focuses on the needs of others, Edward's attention is drawn away from his own grief, and he is then able to seek forgiveness from Mark's sister, Brenda. Edward's true salvation comes after he has seemingly lost everything through the death of his father and the engagement of Brenda to Giles Brightwalton;

only then can he perceive his place in the world and his connection to others.

Stuart's journey to goodness takes the form of his duty to others. Thomas McCaskerville tells him, "You want to be like the Prodigal Son's elder brother, the chap who never went away!" And Stuart replies, "Exactly—except that he was cross when his brother was forgiven." Stuart's actions as the dutiful elder brother coincide with the quiet, saintly virtues displayed by Murdoch's good characters. He is initially frustrated in his attempts to help his brother, and his efforts on Meredith's behalf to save the McCaskerville marriage result in rejection by his father, Harry. At an extreme moment of isolation and futility he experiences an epiphany while watching a mouse in the tracks of the Underground station at Oxford Circus: "The mouse ran a little way along beside the wall of the pit, then stopped and sat up. It was eating something. Then it came back again, casting about. It was in no hurry. It was not trapped. *It lived there.*" This last thought comes as a revelation to Stuart, and he experiences a "peaceful joy" at recognizing his place in the world. Following this experience Stuart decides to return to teaching; he wants to use language and literature to give young children "an idea of what goodness is, and how to love it."

Perhaps the strongest of Murdoch's later novels, *The Book and the Brotherhood* is a well-paced and dynamic novel that brings together parts of her Oxford past and her earlier Marxist ideology. In a review for the *Observer* (13 September 1987) Anthony Burgess praised the "naturalistic dialogue" and "minimum of aesthetic display" in the novel, and Stuart Evans, writing in the London *Times* (10 September 1987), called it "thoroughly gripping, stimulating, and challenging fiction." The novel opens with an Oxford Commem Ball, where a circle of Oxford friends, now middle-aged, evaluate their lives and reconsider the politics of their youth, particularly their financial support of one member of their group, David Crimond, who is writing a book about Marxism. Speaking about this novel with Jo Thomas in *The New York Times Book Review* (31 January 1988), Murdoch said that the main theme of the novel is Marxism. She continued, "I ceased being a genuine Marxist or a serious Marxist when I was about 20—it was an early flirtation. Then I felt increasingly hostile" toward it—as do the characters in the Brotherhood of this novel.

The Brotherhood, a society that consists of Gerard Hernshaw, Rose Curtland (sister of Sinclair Curtland, Gerard's former friend and lover), Jenkin Riderhood (one of Murdoch's saints), and Gulliver Ashe (a failed artist), had agreed to support Crimond so that he could complete his great work without the distraction of earning a living. Unfortunately, the work was not completed while the friends were still Marxists, and Crimond, a demon figure, alienated the group by eloping with Jean Kowitz, the wife of Duncan Cambus. A fight between the two men has left Duncan with seriously impaired vision, and Jean leaves Duncan for Crimond a second time the evening of the Commem Ball. Jean and Crimond are the center of an absorbing dramatic set piece, once again demonstrating Murdoch's skill in mechanical descriptions, when they attempt suicide by driving their cars toward each other on a deserted Roman road.

The Commem weekend evokes a sense of loss when Gerard visits his former classics professor, Levquist, who asks him to read aloud from the *Iliad* for him. Gerard chooses the passage in which the immortal horses weep after the death of Patroclus, and both Levquist and Gerard, separately, remember the genius and promise of Sinclair Curtland, who had died at a young age in a glider accident.

The novel also considers women's social situation through several of the characters whose problems are resolved in quite ambiguous ways. Tamar Hernshaw, a young student, is forced to leave Oxford to go to work to support her mother, Violet, who is incapable of holding a job. Tamar becomes pregnant as a result of her attempt to comfort Duncan about Jean's elopement; she then has an abortion that leaves her seared in spirit and crippled by guilt. Angus McAlister, another of Murdoch's curious ecclesiastics, combines the dogmas of high Anglican and Methodist evangelical; he and the saintly Riderhood are the only characters who attempt to help Tamar out of her despair. Following her religious conversion, Tamar is described as "ruthless" in her dismissal of her mother and "ready to trample on anyone," and Father McAlister worries, "Have I liberated her not into Christ, but into selfish uncaring power?" Jean Kowitz Cambus also possesses intelligence equal to the men in the Brotherhood and has an Oxford degree, but her self-destructive attraction to Crimond limits her from realizing her potential. Finally, Rose Curtland, an intellectual in her own right, has wasted her life waiting for Gerard, and in the closing chapters of the novel Gerard finally realizes that he needs her—but only as a research assistant for a book that will answer Crimond's book. With the restoration of Gerard's creativity it appears that the cycle treated in the book may begin anew; besides answering Crimond's book point by point, Gerard wants his work to represent the present views of the old circle of Oxford friends.

The Message to the Planet continues the ruminations on religion and the importance of being good and reconsiders unorthodox religious positions through the cult figure Marcus Vallar, a Sephardic Jew. Peter Kemp, writing in the *Sunday Times* (1 October 1989), referred to the novel as "an anthology of her earlier effects, characters, situations and themes." Like David Crimond of *The Book and the Brotherhood*, Vallar is an intellectual demon with an alternative vision of life; and like James Arrowby of *The Sea, The Sea*, Vallar has spiritual powers that may degenerate into magic. Vallar had once been a brilliant mathematician but then began experimenting with other arts. He solved the dilemma of the artist whose personal life detracts from his art by quarreling with his friends and then denouncing them. Two former friends, in particular, suffered from Vallar's denunciation: Gildas Herne and Patrick Fenman. When Marcus suggested that Gildas leave the priesthood because he did not have the faith that he professed, Gildas did so; and Patrick, a superstitious, failed Irish poet, became convinced that Marcus had cursed him during a quarrel, and believed he would die from the curse. After a time, Vallar left England for California and joined a religious group that combined meditation with extraordinary physical feats; he then went on to the Far East, where he hoped to discover a unity principle for the universe.

When Patrick lapses into a coma, historian Alfred Ludens locates Vallar, now back in England and living in seclusion in the countryside, and asks him to try to save Patrick's life. In an extraordinary descriptive passage that illustrates Murdoch's technical skill, Vallar revokes his curse and revives Patrick. This recovery gains Vallar a reputation as a healer, and Ludens urges him to try to formulate his thoughts and write them down as some sort of message of universal understanding; however, Vallar's daughter, Irina, believes that her father has no message for the world. She calls him "a helpless solitary person with a thoroughly confused mind."

Irina takes her father to a sanitarium for rest, but his status as a religious figure grows, and members of a cult called the Stone People arrange flowers and pebbles as propitiatory offerings for Vallar. He tries, but finds the role as savior too difficult and tells the onlookers that he cannot help them. Following his death on Midsummer Day, various open-minded religious figures, including Father O'Harte, Rabbi Daniel Most, and Mr. Richard Talgarth, recognize Vallar as a spiritual man.

Vallar's death leaves Ludens to state his universal message: "One must try to be good—just for nothing." Murdoch herself made a similar remark

Dust jacket for the U.S. edition of Murdoch's novel about love and remorse in the English countryside

during a National Public Radio interview with Linda Wertheimer (26 February 1990): "The message is—everything is contingent. There are no deep foundations. Our life rests on chaos and rubble, and all we can try to do is be good."

Many of the academics in Murdoch's novels who spend the latter part of their lives straining to articulate the sum of their thinking into one great piece of art discover their works are failures. Not so for Murdoch. The publication of *Metaphysics as a Guide to Morals* (1992) culminated at least ten years of concentrated work on moral and aesthetic issues that Murdoch views as important for our existence as a world community, and it has been greeted with universal acclaim. Galen Strawson described its contents in *The Independent on Sunday* (11 October 1992): "This book is based on the Gifford Lectures that Iris Murdoch gave in Edinburgh in 1982, and is a grand elaboration of her earlier *The Sovereignty of Good* (1970). It is a great congested work, a foaming sourcebook, about life, imagination, tragedy, philosophy, morality, religion and art." With *Metaphysics as a Guide to Morals* Murdoch brings together

the issues that have preoccupied and profoundly influenced her fiction for the past forty years, and in doing so she provides a discussion of an area that she finds sadly missing from contemporary philosophic study: moral philosophy.

When *The Green Knight* (1993) opens, the characters in the novel are worrying about the disappearance of Lucas Graffe; the reader soon learns that Lucas has fled because he has attempted to kill his younger brother, Clement, with a baseball bat—mainly because Lucas was unable to overcome his envy of his brother. A stranger passing them at this fateful moment had intervened and blocked the blow; in a fit of pique, Lucas then turned the bat on the stranger, Peter Mir. Thus far the age-old tale of sibling rivalry appears realistic enough. However, the critics and reading public were completely dismayed as Murdoch then began to thread parts of the medieval tale *Sir Gawain and the Green Knight* into her novel. *Sir Gawain* is a tale of magic whereby a larger-than-life Green Knight appears to challenge the honor of King Arthur's Court by suggesting a trade of blows from his huge ax. Gawain accepts his challenge and decapitates the Green Knight—who then retrieves his head and reminds Gawain of his promise to accept a blow the following year. Gawain, facing sure death in a return blow from the magic figure, dutifully rides out a year later in search of the Green Knight but manages to compromise the hospitality of his host by accepting kisses and other gifts from the host's wife. When the host turns out to be the Green Knight in disguise, he exacts a remarkably light punishment on Gawain—a nick on his neck with the ax—and offers Gawain forgiveness and his wife's green girdle to wear as a reminder of the adventure. In Murdoch's novel the recipient of the blow is Peter Mir, who apparently dies from the blow and then, following a police hearing on the case in which Lucas's lawyer indicates that Lucas thought he was being robbed, returns to life. Most readers are incredulous about a police hearing that exonerates Lucas for the death of a man who has not died.

Mir, who has lost his memory and his ability to work, desires revenge. While awaiting Lucas's return, Mir watches Clement's activities and discovers the circle of friends on which the novel centers: Louise Anderson and her three daughters, Aleph, Sefton, and Moy, who appear to belong more to the nineteenth century than to the contemporary world; Bellamy James, who has relinquished his worldly goods—including his dog, Anax—because he plans to join a monastery; and Harvey Blacket, whom Louise considers a son. Mir wants to become a member of their "family" and is taken in by them until he is "retrieved" by his psychiatrist and returned to a sanitarium, where he actually dies.

In an article for the *Iris Murdoch News Letter* (an annual publication of the International Iris Murdoch Society) Priscilla Martin says of *The Green Knight:* "Like the Middle English poem, the novel modulates from justice to mercy (the subtitles of the second and third parts) as Mir's desire for 'restitution' . . . gives way to reconciliation." This part of the novel works well, provided the reader can suspend belief about Mir's "death." Unfortunately, the book includes few sympathetic characters, perhaps due to long unedited passages of self-absorbed complaint by several of them, especially Harvey Blacket.

Bellamy James, a seeker of the good, intends to improve morally by renouncing material goods and comforts; his mentor, Father Damien, turns out to be another of Murdoch's doubting priests and eventually leaves the monastery because of his loss of faith. Despite this circumstance Father Damien gives Bellamy sound advice—telling him that he should take back his dog and discover his path by helping others. Damien's counsel, "do not be miserable seeking for moral perfection," echoes the lesson of Michael Meade in *The Bell* (1958), who must learn to live the best life he can, given the person that he is.

In a denouement that disgusted the critics and even many faithful readers, the women end up making rather unusual matches—the worst being Aleph's elopement to America with Lucas Graffe. Lucas has proven himself a power figure throughout the novel, and his prior position as Aleph's tutor, as well as their considerable age difference, makes their marriage repugnant.

Jackson's Dilemma (1995), Murdoch's most recently published novel, is a surprisingly short compendium of Murdoch novels. Although descriptive and promising, the novel ultimately leaves the reader disappointed in a story that has little development. Such a wide range of critical reception followed its publication that Anne Rowe, in compiling an overview of the reviews for the Autumn 1995 *Iris Murdoch News Letter,* initially considered sorting the critiques into three groups—commendatory, dismissive, and ambivalent: "This soon had to be extended on either side with columns for 'ecstatic' and 'downright rude.' The exercise became impossible when the whole range of responses was frequently to be found in one review."

In a plot resembling a Shakespearean comedy, the novel opens with a broken engagement (between Edward Lannion and Marian Barran). Edward, the master of a country house called Hatting Hall, had met Marian at a gathering at nearby Penndean after reconciling a feud that his grandfather had had with the Penndean neighbors. The current owner of Penndean, Benet Barnell, lives there with his elderly Uncle Tim. Like many of Murdoch's truth-seekers, both Edward and Benet are writing books—Edward an historical novel and Benet a study of Martin Heidegger. Benet's manservant, the title character, does not appear until well into the novel. An ambiguous figure with a mysterious background, Jackson is associated with Shiva, Caliban, the Fisher King, and Rudyard Kipling's Kim. His dilemma is whether he should give Marian a note from her secret lover, an Australian named Cantor Ravnevik; this decision could mend or deepen the crisis between Edward and Marian.

The subjects of the novel are love and remorse, and, as usual, Murdoch rearranges her characters in unexpected patterns at the end of the story, including several marriages. Elizabeth Dipple establishes the importance of this novel in the canon when she points out that it continues the third-person restricted narration with which Murdoch has been experimenting since the 1978 publication of *The Sea, The Sea;* this narrative structure forces Murdoch's readers to act as "decoders and participators in her novels." Unfortunately, due to illness, it seems unlikely that Murdoch will publish any more novels; but whether she does or not, her position as a significant figure of modern British literature is secure.

Interviews:

Harold Hobson, "Lunch with Iris Murdoch," *Sunday Times* (London), 11 March 1962, p. 28;

Frank Kermode, "House of Fiction: Interviews with Seven English Novelists," *Partisan Review,* 30 (Spring 1963): 62–82;

Stephanie Nettle, "Iris Murdoch: An Exclusive Interview," *Books and Bookmen,* 11 (September 1966): 14–15;

W. K. Rose, "Iris Murdoch, Informally," *Shenandoah,* 19, no. 2 (1968): 3–22;

Martin Jerritt Kerr, "Good, Evil and Morality," *CR: Quarterly Review of the Community of the Resurrection,* 265 (Michaelmas 1969): 17–23;

A. S. Byatt, *Talking to Iris Murdoch* (London: National Sound Archives tape no. T33963, 26 October 1971);

Iris Murdoch in Conversation with Malcolm Bradbury (British Council tape no. RS 2001, 27 February 1976);

Sheila Hale and Byatt, "Women Writers Now: Their Approach and Apprenticeship," *Harpers and Queen* (October 1976): 178–191;

Rein Zondergeld and Jorg Krichbaum, "De Filosofie van Iris Murdoch," *Hollands Diep* (December 1976): 30–34;

Michael O. Bellamy, "An Interview with Iris Murdoch," *Contemporary Literature,* 18 (Spring 1977): 129–140;

Jack I. Biles, "An Interview with Iris Murdoch," *Studies in the Literary Imagination,* 12, no. 2 (1978): 115–125;

Jean-Louis Chevalier, ed., *Rencontres avec Iris Murdoch* (Caen: Centre de Recherches de Littérature et Linguistique des Pays de Langue Anglaise de l'Université de Caen, 1978);

Heide Ziegler and Christopher Bigsby, eds., *The Radical Imagination and the Liberal Tradition: Interviews with English and American Novelists* (London: Junction Books, 1982), pp. 209–230;

"Discussion sur *The Unicorn,*" *Gáeliana,* no. 5 (1983): 195–210;

John Haffenden, "John Haffenden Talks to Iris Murdoch," *Literary Review,* 58 (April 1983): 31–35;

Byatt and Murdoch, *Writers Talk: Ideas of Our Time,* series no. 9, *Guardian Conversations* (London: ICA Video, 1984);

Didier Eribon, "Iris Murdoch romancière philosphe: Les pavés d'Oxford," *Le Nouvel Observateur,* 3–9 January 1986, pp. 4–5;

David Gerard, "Iris Murdoch," in *Women Writers Talk: Interviews with 10 Women Writers,* edited by Olga Kenyon (Oxford: Lennard, 1989), pp. 133–147;

Jeffrey Meyers, "The Art of Fiction CXVII: Iris Murdoch," *Paris Review,* 32 (Summer 1990): 206-225;

Angela Lambert, "In the Presence of Great Goodness," *Independent,* 8 September 1992, p. 18.

Bibliographies:

Laraine Civin, *Iris Murdoch: A Bibliography* (Johannesburg: University of the Witwatersrand, 1968);

Thomas T. Tominaga and Wilma Schneidermeyer, *Iris Murdoch and Muriel Spark: A Bibliography* (Metuchen, N.J.: Scarecrow Press, 1976);

Kate Begnal, *Iris Murdoch: A Reference Guide* (Boston: G. K. Hall, 1987);

John Fletcher and Cheryl Bove, *Iris Murdoch: A Descriptive Primary and Annotated Secondary Bibliography* (New York & London: Garland, 1994).

References:

Harold Bloom, ed., *Iris Murdoch* (New York: Chelsea House, 1986);

Cheryl Bove, *Understanding Iris Murdoch* (Columbia: University of South Carolina Press, 1993);

Malcolm Bradbury, *No, Not Bloomsbury* (New York: Columbia University Press, 1988);

John J. Burke Jr., "Canonizing Iris Murdoch," *Studies in the Novel,* 19 (Winter 1987): 115–129;

A. S. Byatt, *Degrees of Freedom: The Novels of Iris Murdoch,* second edition (London: Vintage, 1994);

Byatt and Ignês Sodré, *Imagining Characters: Six Conversations about Women Writers,* edited by Rebecca Swift (London: Chatto & Windus, 1995), pp. 152–191;

Peter Conradi, *Iris Murdoch: The Saint and the Artist,* first edition (Basingstoke, U.K.: Macmillan, 1986);

Elizabeth Dipple, *Iris Murdoch: Work for the Spirit* (Chicago: University of Chicago Press, 1982; London: Methuen, 1982);

John Elsom, "Iris Murdoch," *Contemporary Review,* 247 (December 1985): 311–315;

John Fletcher, "A Novelist's Plays: Iris Murdoch and the Theatre," *Essays in Theatre,* 4, no. 1 (1985): 3–20;

James Gindin, "Images of Illusion in the Work of Iris Murdoch," in his *Postwar British Fiction: New Accents and Attitudes* (Berkeley: University of California Press, 1962), pp. 178–195;

David J. Gordon, *Iris Murdoch's Fables of Unselfing* (Columbia & London: University of Missouri Press, 1995);

Angela Hague, *Iris Murdoch's Comic Vision* (Selinsgrove, Pa.: Susquehanna University Press/London & Toronto: Associated University Presses, 1984);

Barbara Stevens Heusel, *Patterned Aimlessness: Iris Murdoch's Novels of the 1970s and 1980s* (Athens: University of Georgia Press, 1995);

Deborah Johnson, *Iris Murdoch* (Bloomington: Indiana University Press, 1987);

Priscilla Martin, "Sir Gawain and *The Green Knight,*" *Iris Murdoch News Letter,* 9 (Autumn 1995): 11–12;

Darlene D. Mettler, *Sound and Sense: Musical Allusion and Imagery in the Novels of Iris Murdoch* (New York: Peter Lang, 1991);

Modern Fiction Studies, special Murdoch issue, 15 (Autumn 1969);

Patricia O'Connor, *To Love the Good: The Moral Philosophy of Iris Murdoch* (New York: Peter Lang, 1992);

William Van O'Connor, "Iris Murdoch: The Formal and the Contingent," *Critique,* 3, no. 2 (1960): 34–46;

Diana Phillips, *Agencies of the Good in the Work of Iris Murdoch* (Frankfurt am Main / New York: Peter Lang, 1991);

Suguna Ramanathan, *Iris Murdoch: Figures of Good* (New York: St. Martin's Press, 1990);

Lorna Sage, *Women in the House of Fiction: Post-War Women Novelists* (London: Macmillan, 1992);

Hilda Spear, *Iris Murdoch* (New York: Macmillan, 1995);

Richard Todd, *Iris Murdoch: The Shakespearian Interest* (New York: Barnes & Noble, 1979);

Todd, ed., *Encounters with Iris Murdoch* (Amsterdam: Free University Press, 1988);

Lindsey Tucker, *Critical Essays on Iris Murdoch* (New York: G. K. Hall, 1992).

Papers:
The manuscript and typescript drafts of most of the novels, together with other papers both published and unpublished, are held in Special Collections at the University of Iowa Library, Iowa City. The Bodleian Library, Oxford, possesses the manuscript of the Romanes lecture (revised and published as *The Fire and the Sun: Why Plato Banished the Artists*). There are also manuscript letters at the following libraries: the Eugene Barker Texas History Library, University of Texas Archives, Austin; the Harry Ransom Humanities Research Center, University of Texas, Austin; George Washington University Library, Washington, D.C.; Washington University Library, St. Louis, Missouri; the University of Reading; the Brotherton Library, Leeds University; University of Bristol Library, Bristol; Department of French, Adam Archive, King's College, London; University College Library, London; the University of Sussex Library, Brighton; Brynmor Jones Library, University of Hull; Eton School Library, Eton; John Rylands University Library of Manchester; Northamptonshire Record Office, Northampton.

Jane Rogers

(21 July 1952 –   )

Rob Spence
Edge Hill University College

BOOKS: *Separate Tracks* (London: Faber & Faber, 1983; Boston: Faber & Faber, 1985);
Her Living Image (London: Faber & Faber, 1984; Garden City, N.Y.: Doubleday, 1986);
The Ice is Singing (London & Boston: Faber & Faber, 1987);
Mr Wroe's Virgins (London & Boston: Faber & Faber, 1991);
Promised Lands (London & Boston: Faber, 1995).

TELEVISION: *Dawn and the Candidate,* 1989;
Mr. Wroe's Virgins, BBC 2, 24 February, 3 March, 10 March, 17 March 1993.

Jane Rogers has established a reputation as a writer of novels that deal uncompromisingly with raw emotions in a variety of settings. Although most of her work is set in contemporary England, she is becoming increasingly interested in exploring historical settings. Her early novels, *Separate Tracks* (1983) and *Her Living Image* (1984), both use an intense style to examine the inner lives of her female protagonists. The latter won the prestigious Somerset Maugham Award in 1985. *The Ice is Singing* (1987) chronicles the thoughts of a runaway woman in a series of bleak and graphically described urban and rural landscapes. *Mr. Wroe's Virgins* (1991), which she also used as the basis for a television play, takes an historical account of a religious cult in early-nineteenth-century Lancashire, using the voices of the eponymous acolytes to tell the story of oppression in the midst of political upheaval. Her most recent work, *Promised Lands* (1995), employs a dual narrative that switches between present-day England and eighteenth-century Australia to explore the nature of morality. Indeed, it is true to say of all her work that she engages with the big issues, unflinchingly examining the workings of relationships, and often the ways in which they fail.

Jane Rogers was born 21 July 1952 in London, but her life has been spent in many locations, a factor that perhaps influences her frequent portrayal of characters without roots. Her father, Andrew W. Rogers, was a professor, her mother, Margaret Farmer Rogers, a nurse. Coming from an academic family, she moved around as a child, living by turn in London, Birmingham, Oxford, Copenhagen, and New York. She read English at Cambridge, and during that time her family immigrated to Australia when her father was offered a professorial chair at Adelaide. After graduating from Cambridge in 1974, she qualified as a teacher at Leicester University in 1976. She then worked as an English teacher in secondary schools and further education as well as in a children's home and a mental hospital. She became a full-time writer when her first child was born, which coincided with the publication of *Separate Tracks*. She married the playwright Michael Harris in March 1981 and lives in Manchester in the north of England, with frequent visits to her family in Australia. She has worked as a writing fellow on university and college creative-writing courses in the north of England and continues to work with budding writers.

Rogers's reputation has continued to grow. She is regularly mentioned as a possible contender for the various prestigious literary prizes, though the Somerset Maugham Award remains her only official recognition for her novels. She was joint winner of the Samuel Beckett Award in 1989 for her television play *Dawn and the Candidate*. Her work, which suffered somewhat in the early years of her career from being labeled "women's writing," is now acknowledged as powerful, universal, and deeply committed. The close focus on women's lives remains a feature of her work, but the canvas has broadened, especially with the introduction of the historical dimension that features in both of her last two published novels.

Separate Tracks clearly draws on Rogers's experience as a secondary-school teacher of English and as a worker in a children's home. The novel charts the relationship between an ill-matched young pair, Orph (the name derives from his status as an or-

Jane Rogers (photograph by Jason Bell)

phan) and Emma (from a privileged middle-class background). In the early chapters, scenes from their childhoods are described alternately by an omniscient narrator. The focus is on significant moments that will resonate later in their lives, and each incident is balanced by a corresponding incident in the other protagonist's life. When the novel opens, Orph, abandoned as a baby by his mother, becomes an isolated and difficult inmate of a children's home. Orph's abandonment is balanced by a chapter describing Emma's parents' frantic search for her after she becomes detached from them on a beach. Orph suffers at school because of his poor reading, whereas Emma develops quickly and soon reads voraciously. The reader witnesses Orph failing to come to grips with the culture enshrined in his reading primer, where a classic middle-class family enjoys the sort of lifestyle granted to Emma but entirely alien to Orph. Emma develops a clandestine obsession with the formulaic romances in cheap women's magazines, surreptitiously reading them to avoid her mother's scorn. It is this susceptibility to the romantic that will draw Emma to Orph.

They first encounter each other at the children's home. Emma, successful in her education, has a university position but is taking a year out in order to give something back to society. Rogers emphasizes the strangeness of her new environment. Although the council estate where Orph has spent

his life is in Emma's hometown, it is somewhere she has never ventured. A lyrical passage describing Emma's journey home for a weekend break from her live-in job emphasizes the degradation of the conditions under which Orph lives.

Orph becomes Emma's project—written off by the manager of the home, he represents a challenge to her do-gooder middle-class sensibilities, assuming heroic proportions in her eyes, although it is the protagonist of Albert Camus's novel *L'étranger* (1942), Meursault, to whom she compares him rather than the handsome heroes of the cheap romances of her childhood. Rogers, however, balances Emma's idealized vision of Orph with a relentlessly downbeat description of his life and attitude. When Orph unexpectedly disrupts Emma's cozy student household, events are set in motion that reach a frightening and bloody climax. Rogers anatomizes contemporary Britain in this novel, juxtaposing the comfortable, concerned middle class represented by Emma and her student friends and the underclass represented by Orph. The result is a disturbing and impressively frank narrative. Reviewers were impressed with the dramatic power of the story and the harshly realistic tone. The frankness of the portrayal of deprivation was particularly effective, coming as it did at a time when Britain's disaffected youth were making their presence felt in a series of urban riots. Rogers had become estab-

Dust jacket for Rogers's historical novel about a nineteenth-century prophet and his female followers

lished as a major new voice in English fiction and quickly consolidated her success with the publication of *Her Living Image* (1984).

Her Living Image is more self-consciously experimental than the previous work. The central conceit of the novel is to entwine two narratives, both centered on a young woman who is involved in a car accident in the opening pages. One narrative follows the course of her early adulthood after the accident, documenting the effect her chance meeting in the hospital with the radical Clare has on the somewhat timid schoolgirl, while the other describes the life she might have had if the accident had not occurred. The woman, Carolyn, becomes two separate people, and the two narratives develop separately although the two lives become entwined through Alan, boyfriend to Carolyn and lover to her alter ego, Caro.

Rogers uses the simple typographical device of putting Carolyn's story in italics while the story of Caro remains in regular font. The arrangement pro-

vides Rogers with plenty of opportunity to contrast the lives of the two women and to comment on the ways in which society shapes women's lives and gives them roles. In the narrative of Carolyn an early marriage, the result of an unplanned pregnancy, leads to genteel desperation in the suburban home she makes with her erstwhile boyfriend and now husband, the architect Alan. Caro becomes radicalized in the atmosphere of the communal home presided over by Clare and soon becomes involved in community issues, such as working at a women's refuge with the other inhabitants of Clare's house. In contrast, Carolyn's life revolves increasingly around her children as she and Alan drift further apart.

Both stories are well realized. The atmosphere of 1990s Britain, epitomized in the contrasting lives of the two women, is expertly suggested. Jane Rogers uses her characters to show the class differences that were exacerbated in Britain at the time by the polarizing of the political parties. Alan and Carolyn's comfortable middle-class existence in their mock-Tudor house is contrasted with the radical lifestyle of the all-woman household lived in by Caro, where trips to Greenham Common—site of a long and contentious women's protest against nuclear weapons—and protests in support of local community initiatives against the interests of business are the order of the day.

As is the case with *Separate Tracks,* one of the most striking features of *Her Living Image* is the way contemporary society in Britain is analyzed, not through polemic, but through the interaction of characters who exemplify many aspects of the class warfare that continues to be a major aspect of British life. In *Separate Tracks* Emma is involved with the antiracist movements that came to prominence in the early 1980s; Caro finds herself committed to the creation of a city park in derelict land; Carolyn, left at home as a middle-class housewife, finds herself increasingly isolated by Alan's moods and infidelities.

The final third of the novel, which is set five years after the narratives that unfold following the accident, increasingly interweaves the stories of Carolyn and Caro as Alan becomes involved in Caro's life. Eventually the tangled lives of the central characters are resolved, though not without some emotional bloodletting.

Her Living Image is a tour de force of sharp, observant writing, highly original in concept and wonderfully detailed in execution. The technique of multiple narrative becomes a staple of Rogers's art following this novel, and is perhaps best observed in *Mr. Wroe's Virgins.* The reception of *Her Living Image* was extremely positive. Critics praised the boldness and ambition of the work and its precise observation of the minutiae of the lives of ordinary people.

The experimental prose that is so much a feature of this novel is developed further in *The Ice is Singing*, which presents her bleakest portrait yet of life in contemporary Britain.

The Ice is Singing is a short novel that comprises the journal of a woman, Marion, who is escaping from the constraints of her life by traveling through the winter landscape of mid-1980s England, and interpolated stories "written" by Marion, which focus on the relationships between parents and children and are by turns brutal, tender, and always unsettling.

What is remarkable about the novel is the graphic, ruthlessly honest way the writer approaches her subject matter. Nothing is taboo as Marion, perhaps attempting a cathartic release, examines the depths to which relationships can plunge and in particular considers the treatment women receive at the hands of a patriarchal society. The novel is painful to read and powerful in its effect. The winter landscape is used as a metaphor for the emotional wasteland in which Marion finds herself, and the novel returns relentlessly to the familiar themes of the previous novels, particularly the pains of motherhood. The style is even more terse than in the previous novels, and the overall effect is of an anguished voice yearning for a hearing. In her journals Marion often refers to herself in the third person, adding to the sense of lonely isolation with which she is invested. A kind of closure is achieved at the end, but the unsettling images of this novel live long in the reader's memory, ensuring that there is no sense of an easy answer to the problems encountered by ordinary women in contemporary life.

In a recent interview Rogers revealingly said that

> If anybody asked me, "What's been the most important and interesting experience of your life?" it would have to be: having children. Motherhood is the thing we do that's most red in tooth and claw, we with our easy lives in the Western world. The terrors we have for our children . . . I've not known such terrors on my own behalf. Having children has led me into extremes of emotion. I think motherhood borders on lunacy a lot of the time.

Those concerns are clearly to the fore in *The Ice is Singing* and in her most recent novel, *Promised Lands*. The successor to *The Ice is Singing* is not so obviously concerned with motherhood though it certainly touches heavily on notions of nurture and patriarchy.

Mr. Wroe's Virgins is the first Rogers novel with a noncontemporary background. It concerns a real historical circumstance, the arrival of the self-proclaimed prophet John Wroe in the Lancashire

Dust jacket for Rogers's novel set in eighteenth-century Australia and modern-day England

mill towns of the early nineteenth century. The novel centers on the household Wroe gathers around himself, consisting entirely of seven local women, the "Virgins" of the title. Each of the women has a voice in the novel, and the story unfolds from multiple perspectives. Rogers is adroit at differentiating the voices of the women, and in each case, the character is fully revealed in the style of the monologue. The seven range from the credulous Joanna to the knowing Leah, from the animal-like Martha to the prim Hannah. Rogers adeptly sketches the background of mill-town life in the 1830s, lending the narrative a credibility it might otherwise have lacked. As the author observes in an historical note appended to the novel, there is no record of the seven women, although there is plenty of documentary evidence pertaining to Wroe and his Christian Israelite church. This allows her the freedom to develop a rich cast of characters and to demonstrate her virtuosity in portraying those characters through their individual voices. The novel has been the best received of all Rogers's works, aided by the 1993 BBC television adaptation (for which she wrote the script), which appeared in time to boost paperback sales.

Promised Lands has an obvious affinity with *Mr. Wroe's Virgins* in that it has its roots in historical events and uses multiple narrators. It too is concerned with the relationships between powerful men and subjugated women and touches on many typical Rogers themes, especially motherhood and education. Once again the idea of physical and psychological dislocation is a key feature.

The novel opens with an apparently straightforward third-person account of the arrival of the first settlement of British forces and convicts at Sydney, Australia, in 1788. The focus is on the young Christian idealist Lt. William Dawes, whose scrupulous moral standards will be tested by the conditions in which he finds himself. Soon, however, two other narrative voices appear: Stephen, a present-day history teacher (who, in a neat twist, is the "author" of the opening passage), and Olla, his Polish-born wife. The three narratives interweave, creating an intricate pattern wherein images emerge and resurface later in another narrative. The eighteenth century comments on the twentieth, and vice versa. Rogers uses structural devices to bind the narratives, the most obvious one being Stephen's authorship of the Dawes narrative, but also the reader's attention is drawn to frequent correspondences between the accounts. For example, Olla first encounters Stephen when she is working as a hotel chambermaid where he is staying and attempts to steal his watch. He takes pity on her, and their relationship develops from there. In the 1788 narrative a prostitute who tempts Dawes is there because she was sentenced to seven years' transportation—for stealing a watch.

In many respects, this is a story of lost innocence. Instead of Dawes's new promised land in Australia, the amoral culture of the convicts infects the aboriginal population with physical disease and moral decay. Stephen's personal promised land was the school he helped to radicalize where the ideals of 1960s liberalism would show the world a better way. It is the ignominious failure of his project that draws him to the story of Dawes, another weak man trying to do good in an indifferent world. Olla's promised land resides in her severely brain-damaged baby. She invests him with mysterious messianic power and jealously excludes her husband from him.

The three narratives develop in different ways. The Australian story is the most conventional: a closely plotted, tautly structured narrative revolving around a series of moral dilemmas for the naive Dawes, who is unable to impose his Christian vision on the chaotic world of convicts, prostitutes, and natives. In the end Stephen's narrative of his life intercuts with his own interior monologue, and the two characters are strangely drawn together by Stephen's impulsive and doomed decision to go to Australia in order to find the spirit of Dawes. The novel ends with a surreal melding of the two worlds and with many of the moral problems raised but not solved.

The historical narrative is the most successful of the three—Stephen's and Olla's voices sometimes strike the wrong note, especially when Stephen addresses himself in the third person. This is nevertheless a major achievement by a novelist maturing with every book and from whom more important work may confidently be expected.

Promised Lands confirms Jane Rogers as a novelist of major stature and one who cannot with any legitimacy be classified as being a writer for women. Her new novel, which she is currently writing, returns to an earlier theme—the mother-daughter relationship—but again deals with the big issues in people's lives in a remarkably candid manner. She firmly rejects the idea that she is a women's novelist. Her canvas is a broad one, becoming ever more encompassing, and her engagement is total.

Interviews:

Ailsa Cox, "Mothers and Virgins," *Metropolitan,* 1 (Winter 1993–1994): 19–21;

Christina Koning, "Take One Good Man . . . ," *Guardian,* 14 August 1995, p. G25;

Angela Lambert, "Please Remember My Name: Jane Rogers," *Independent,* 15 September 1995, Arts section, p. 8.

Salman Rushdie
(19 June 1947 -   )

Cynthia Ho
University of North Carolina at Asheville

BOOKS: *Grimus* (London: Gollancz, 1975; Woodstock, N.Y.: Overlook Press, 1979);
Midnight's Children (London: Cape, 1981; New York: Knopf, 1981);
Shame (London: Cape, 1983; New York: Knopf, 1983);
The Jaguar Smile: A Nicaraguan Journey (London: Pan / Cape, 1987; New York: Viking, 1987);
The Satanic Verses (London: Viking, 1988; New York: Viking, 1989);
Two Stories (London: Sixth Chamber Press, 1989);
Is Nothing Sacred? (London: Granta, 1990);
In Good Faith (London: Granta, 1990);
Haroun and the Sea of Stories (London: Granta, 1990; New York: Viking, 1990);
Imaginary Homelands: Essays and Criticism, 1981–1991 (London: Granta, 1991; New York: Viking, 1991);
The Wizard of Oz (London: British Film Institute Publishers, 1992);
East, West: Stories (London: Cape, 1994; New York: Pantheon, 1994);
The Moor's Last Sigh (London: Cape, 1995; New York: Knopf, 1995).

TELEVISION SCRIPTS: *The Painter and the Pest,* 1985;
The Riddle of Midnight, Channel 4, 27 March 1988.

OTHER: Rudyard Kipling, *Soldiers Three and In Black and White,* introductory essay by Rushdie (New York: Penguin, 1993);
Angela Carter, *Burning Your Boats: The Collected Short Stories,* introductory essay by Rushdie (New York: Holt, 1996);
The Vintage Book of Indian Writing, 1947–1997, edited by Rushdie and Elizabeth West (London: Vintage, 1997); republished as *Mirrorwork: 50 Years of Indian Writing, 1947–1997* (New York: Holt, 1997).

SELECTED PERIODICAL PUBLICATIONS—
UNCOLLECTED: "The Empire Writes Back with a Vengeance," *Times* (London), 3 July 1982, p. 8;

Salman Rushdie (photograph © 1989 by Horst Tappe)

"Dynasty and Democracy: The Idea of India after the Death of Mrs. Gandhi," *New Republic* (26 November 1984): 17–20;
"The Press: International Viewpoints; India," *Times Literary Supplement,* 21 February 1986, p. 190;
"Goodness—The American Neurosis," *Nation,* 242 (22 March 1986): 344–346;
"Zia Unmourned," *Nation,* 247 (19 September 1988): 188–190;
"Rushdie on Censorship," *New Republic,* 203 (8 October 1990): 31–40;
"The Oxford Guide to Card Games," *Times Literary Supplement,* 16 November 1990, pp. 1239–1240;
"My Decision," *Index on Censorship* (February 1991);

"Out of Kansas," *New Yorker,* 68 (11 May 1992): 93–104;

"Reservoir Frogs (or, Places Called Mama's)," *New Yorker,* 72 (23 September 1996): 104–105;

"On Leavened Bread," *New Yorker,* 72 (23 December 1996): 72–73.

Salman Rushdie embodies in his own life and in his writings the conundrums of the postcolonial author, writing within the tradition of Indo-English literature while simultaneously appealing to the conventions and tastes of a worldwide, especially Western, audience. The condemnation and support surrounding the death sentence issued against him by Iran epitomize the postcolonialist's delicate and constant battle to balance the demands of conflicting cultures. Not only must the postcolonial writer contend with these external struggles, but he must also deal with the interior conflicts of colonial identity, living as a permanent outsider, searching for personal authenticity in one or many cultures. In the role of the South Asian expatriate author Rushdie also finds himself a spokesman for the peoples of the subcontinent, whether he or they would wish it so. Throughout his career Rushdie has struggled to speak to the mainstream in both Britain and Asia while mimicking and critiquing that same mainstream from the margins. The culturally and religiously diverse worlds of both India and Great Britain offer Rushdie a wealth of concerns and themes that consistently reflect and refract throughout his works.

Ahmed Salman Rushdie was born into the liberal and prosperous Muslim family of Anis Ahmed Rushdie and Negin Rushdie in Bombay, India, on 19 June 1947, the year Pakistan divided from India at the end of British colonialism in South Asia. Rushdie has said of the relaxed religious climate in his home, "Although I came from a Muslim family background, I was never brought up as a believer, and was raised in an atmosphere of what is broadly known as secular humanism." Despite the movements of Muslims north to Pakistan and Hindus and Sikhs south to India, Rushdie's family remained in Bombay during his childhood. Although the family later resided in Pakistan, it is India, and most especially Bombay, which is home to Rushdie's complex vision. India, as large as all of Europe, contains one-sixth of the human race. Within this country exists one of the most diverse human cultures: fifteen major languages and innumerable others are spoken by Indians of varied backgrounds including Hindu, Christian, Parsi, Muslim, and Sikh. Bombay, a city built by foreigners upon reclaimed land, epitomizes the Indian and subcontinental identity crisis of this native mélange overlaid with the powerful remnants of European colonialism. In 1961 at thirteen Rushdie went to England to be educated at Rugby. Ian Hamilton records Rushdie as saying that while at school he "had a pretty hideous time from my own age group: minor persecutions and racist attacks which felt major at the time . . . I never had any friends at school, and I don't now know a single person I was at school with." Incidents from these early years appear refigured in Rushdie's fiction, such as the kippered herring passage in *The Satanic Verses* (1988) in which Saladin's humiliation in front of the other boys because he is unable to bone his fish illustrates his uncomfortable sense of not fitting in.

From 1962 to 1964 Rushdie's family joined him in England, and their neighborhood in Kensington provides one of the settings of *The Satanic Verses.* Although they had become British citizens, his family moved to Karachi, Pakistan, and founded a family business, a towel factory. In 1965 Rushdie followed his father's precedent by studying at Kings College, Cambridge, where he received his M.A. in history with honors in 1968. Yielding to family pressure, he returned to Pakistan, where he worked in television production and publishing until instances of what he considered irrational government meddling with movie endings, essay publication, and television content convinced him to return to London. He details this experience later in "Censorship" in *Imaginary Homelands: Essays and Criticism, 1981–1991* (1991). During the 1960s, although occasionally on welfare, he had jobs in television, publishing, and advertising. His work with advertising executives, while writing television commercials for Ogilvy and Mather, inspired the character of the bigoted Hal Valance in *The Satanic Verses.*

In 1970 Rushdie met Clarissa Luard, whom he married in May 1976. During this time he completed his first two novels. In 1971 "The Book of the Pir" (parts of which reappear in other forms in *The Satanic Verses*) was rejected, but in 1975 *Grimus,* a science-fiction parody that mixes diverse Nordic and Asian mythologies, was published. *Grimus* was not, however, a success. In *Imaginary Homelands* Rushdie comments on his early efforts: "Before *Midnight's Children* [1981], I had had one novel rejected, abandoned two others, and published one, *Grimus,* which, to put it mildly, bombed." From this point on, however, he turned to the subject matter which he knows best and can handle most successfully: South Asia. He did retain what was best in *Grimus*—an experimental and playful use of language that he would develop more fully in later novels. From 1976 to 1983 Rushdie served as the executive member of the Camden Committee for Community Relations, assisting emigrants from Bangladesh. This experience in dealing with others' cultural displacement, along with other incidents about this time, sensitized him to the problem of racism in Britain. Here he saw the fractured identity of exiles, emigrants, and expatriates, their sense of loss. Their uncertainties confirmed his own questions about what he calls "the provisional nature of all truths." Rushdie also became sensitive to his own designation as "Indian," which simultaneously places him inside and outside of British culture. The British Indian community itself is varied and includes political exiles, first-generation migrants, affluent expatriates, naturalized Britons, and people born in Britain who may have never seen the subcontinent. Aware that his English accent and what he has called his "freakishly light skin" ironically made him seem less Indian than others, he battled with his Indo-English identity and his strong identification with his life in Britain. Rushdie comments:

> The phrase that really gets me angry is this thing about being "more English than the English." . . . It is used as if it should be offensive. I point out to these people that if there was an English person living in India who adopted Indian dress, who had learnt to speak Urdu or Hindi or Bengali fluently without an accent, nobody would accuse him of having lost his culture. They would be flattered and pleased that the language had been acquired so efficiently. And they would see it as a compliment to themselves. But they wouldn't accuse him of having betrayed his origins.

When *Midnight's Children,* the novel that many people feel is his best, was published in 1981, Rushdie gained fame in both Britain and South Asia. In contrast to some of his later novels, *Midnight's Children* was immediately embraced in India, and Rushdie was greeted as a major author, honored as a native son on his return home. With this universal acclaim Rushdie achieved his goal of speaking to both segments of his audience. *Midnight's Children* won the Booker Prize for fiction, a literary award from the English Speaking Union, the James Tait Black Prize, and finally the "Booker of Bookers," given to the best Booker-winning novel of the first twenty-five years of the Booker Prize. In a poll conducted by the *Guardian* newspaper of the favorite novels of the British public, *Midnight's Children* ranked twenty-fifth. *Midnight's Children* narrates the history of modern India from 1910 to the declaration of the emergency in 1976. The narrator, Saleem Sinai, is born at the stroke of midnight on 15 August 1947, an important moment for himself, for his family, and for India:

Dust jacket for the novel that led the Iranian leader Ayatollah Ruholla Khomeini to pronounce a death sentence on Rushdie for blasphemy

> I was born in the city of Bombay . . . once upon a time. No, that won't do, there's no getting away from the date: I was born in Doctor Narlikar's Nursing Home on August 15th, 1947. And the time? The time matters too. Well then: at night. No, it's important to be more. . . . On the stroke of midnight, as a matter of fact. Clock hands joined palms in respectful greeting as I came. Oh, spell it out, spell it out: at the precise instant of India's arrival at independence, I tumbled forth into the world.

Saleem and modern India are twin protagonists whom the narrative follows from their births—accompanied by fireworks, celebrations, and Prime Minister Nehru—to the unhappy death of hope. At midnight Saleem's parents gain ownership of their home, the British transfer power to the Indians in a ceremony of independence, and Saleem and the one thousand other children of midnight are born, a symbol of their country's transformations. Just as these new children are an amalgam of the old Raj and a new postcolonial entity, so the blue-eyed Saleem is the son of a departing Englishman but a citizen of the new India. After growing up in Bom-

Muslim demonstrators in Hyde Park, London, in May 1989 protesting the publication of The Satanic Verses

bay as a "relaxed Muslim," with a luxurious childhood, he becomes unhappy with the development of this new India, and he goes to Pakistan to meet even more disappointment in the fighting against both India and Bangladesh. His private, personal actions are mirrored in the public events and national affairs of his sibling India; both his life and his health are a labyrinthine tangle with those of his nation, "mysteriously handcuffed to history, my destinies indissolubly chained to those of my country." What is a family saga doubles as the history of a liberated and hopeful land at the end of the imperialist age. But the systematic disillusionment, murder, and diaspora of Saleem's midnight generation also represents India's movement from optimism to despair, although Rushdie claims in *Imaginary Homelands,* "It's not supposed to be a despairing view of India today but of that generation. In the book, the children are a kind of metaphor for potential destroyed, or hope betrayed, or whatever. And I think that's kind of true about what has happened in India since 1947. But the book implies that there's another generation on the way, you know."

Rushdie's own life and personal politics intersect with the novel and the history of India, much like Saleem's. Because he was born only eight weeks before independence day, his family joked that he occasioned the British departure, making him an almost–Midnight Child. Rushdie often refers to his contemporaries as "Midnight's Children," a term that has been used in Indian media for the generation of 1947. In his writings Rushdie has been a particular critic of the damage done to Indian life by the 1974–1977 "Emergency," Indira Gandhi's period of authoritarian rule. Rushdie contrasts the dictatorial atmosphere, jailing of opponents, forced sterilizations, and fevered pitch of communal discord with Gandhi's "State truth." Gandhi's insistence in her public announcements that bad things just did not happen during the Emergency provides *Midnight's Children* with a location to question the sources of truth and reality. Gandhi, then prime minister of India, did not appreciate her depiction in the novel and won a suit against Rushdie for libel which forced him to revise the book shortly before her assassination. Like the subsequent narrators in Rushdie's novels, Saleem, the narrator of *Midnight's Children,* has remarkable physical and metaphysical attributes which both bless and damn him. His amazing inherited sense of smell, which can even sniff out truth, allows him to tell his tale through his nose. In addition he is telepathic, a gift he discovered at nine years of age in his mother's laundry hamper. In his endowment he is like his one thousand siblings, all with special powers standing by to be used in their country's new age. While waiting for death in a Bombay pickle factory, Saleem begins his story at the end and then recalls the familial, sexual, and political adventures of his life. But he is suspect in his narration, for his mistakes about public (and, the reader must assume, private) history are numerous. (The Elephant God Ganesha did not sit at the feet of the poet Valmiki and write the *Ramayana;* Lata Mangeshkar could not have been on All-India Radio in 1946). These are neither the result of a stupid narrator nor his purposeful deceptions. The mistakes result from a fallible memory compounded by Saleem's idiosyncratic character. *Midnight's Children* was not meant to be an authoritative history of postindependence India even though some segments of Rushdie's South Asian public wanted to read it in that way. Instead, Saleem, the unreliable narrator, reflects the difficulty of really remembering what the truth is. Saleem, like his creator Rushdie, suggests that imaginative truth is both honorable and suspect. Rushdie often writes of the mirror reflecting the world, and Saleem here uses the broken mirror of memory, some fragments reflecting truthfully, others only refracting distortions, and some completely lost.

Rushdie has a lifelong avidity for motion pictures and often uses the metaphors of movie theaters to define the enigmas of postcolonial existence. Thus, Saleem offers the experience of the cinema screen to explain remembering and representing the past:

> Reality is a question of perspective; the further you get from the past, the more concrete and plausible it seems–but as you approach the present, it inevitably seems more and more incredible. Suppose yourself in a large cinema, sitting at first in the back row, and gradually moving up, row by row, until your nose is almost pressed against the screen. Gradually the stars' faces dissolve into dancing grain; tiny details assume grotesque proportions; the illusion dissolves–or rather, it becomes clear that the illusion itself is reality.

Although Rushdie at first believed *Midnight's Children* would be his definitive work on India, it instead became the first of three novels sharing the subject matter of twentieth-century British–South Asian history with a wild mix of Hindu, Islamic, postcolonial, linguistic, philosophical, and social issues embedded in the matrix. Many topics appear in *Midnight's Children* for the first time to be continually revisited throughout Rushdie's work: the history and construction of Islam, the multitudinous varieties of metamorphosis, the malleability and unreliability of time, and the pliability of the English language. After receiving the James Tait Black Memorial Prize in 1982 Rushdie appeared on the Channel Four television-station program *Opinions.* His talk (which appears in its entirety as "The New Empire Within Britain" in *Imaginary Homelands*) begins: "Britain isn't South Africa. I am reliably informed of this. Nor is it Nazi Germany. I've got that on the best authority as well. . . . I find it odd, however, that those who use such absences as defenses rarely perceive that their own statements indicate how serious things have become." Although many listeners praised the show, others were outraged. Rushdie said that his intention was to "tell the white majority how life in Britain all too often felt to members of racial minority groups," but some insisted that Rushdie attacked the racial politics of Great Britain too vigorously and thus alienated himself from the general British public. Later, when he was under attack for *The Satanic Verses,* his unpopularity over the Channel Four incident may have dampened some public shows of support. During this time he left his wife Clarissa Luard (Pamela Lovelace in *The Satanic Verses*) for a new love, Robyn Davidson (who also appears in *The Satanic Verses,* as the fearless mountain climber, Alleluia Cone).

Rushdie's next novel, which was awarded the French Prix du Meilleur Livre Etranger in postmodernist fiction, continues the investigation of postcolonial consciousness begun in *Midnight's Children. Shame* (1983) transpires in a fictional, remade version of Pakistan and takes care of what Rushdie calls "unfinished business" from *Midnight's Children. Shame* offers a thinly veiled critique of Pakistan's small ruling class of power brokers who, following the end of the Raj, exploited the colonizer's consolidation of power. For reviving the forbidden history of the late 1970s *Shame* was banned in Pakistan. The narrator had disingenuously argued, "I am only telling a sort of modern fairy-tale, so that's all right; nobody need get upset, or take anything I say too seriously. No drastic actions need be taken either." Some readers see this as Rushdie's most autobiographical work because the first-person narrator, who lives in London and infrequently visits Pakistan, seems to be a transparent persona for Rushdie. *Shame* slips back and forth from narrative fiction to seeming nonfiction essay, a dueling of genres that

Rushdie and his second wife, novelist Marianne Wiggins, shortly before they went into hiding to escape the decree of death pronounced on Rushdie (photograph by Terry Smith/Camera Press)

gives the sense of double meaning, a full and true exposition seen from all viewpoints. It also confirms the sense of the author closely directing the text. The narrator encounters various elaborations on the nature of the shame that begins to saturate his existence—in London and Pakistan, public and private, in himself and in others. In the newspaper he reads about Pakistani shame, first of a father who doubts his daughter's chastity and murders her and then of a girl, who might be his sister, molested in the subway and shamed into silence. For Rushdie shame is "a central method of organizing experience." The narrator learns how shame becomes overwhelming and leads to violence: "Looking at the smoking cities on my television screen, I see groups of young people running through the streets, the shame burning on their brows and setting fire to shops, police shields, cars. They remind me of my anonymous girl. Humiliate people for long enough and a wildness bursts out of them."

In *Shame* Rushdie examines the problematic nature of all languages, and the specific difficulties in speaking English. A protestor shouts: "Outsider! Trespasser! You have no right to this subject! . . . Poacher! Pirate! We know you, with your foreign language wrapped around you like a flag: speaking about us in your forked tongue, what can you tell but lies?" Postcolonial writers who use English do so with an awareness that it is an ambiguous choice: using the language of imperialism to fit their own postcolonial agendas. Many have noted that this linguistic strain reflects other important cultural struggles of accommodation and rejection in the culture, for entrapment in a foreign language mirrors the cultural entrapment of the immigrant. In addition, the choice of language indicates the audience for whom the writer writes and makes an assumption about the voice they wish to hear. English in India has a much more privileged position than in other postcolonial cultures, such as Africa, so much so that Rushdie argues that the British Indian does not really have the option of rejecting English. In their own countercolonization effort Indian speakers and Indo-English authors have conquered English by reuttering it in a dialect distinctly their own. Despite the fact that India, like many other English-speaking countries such as the United States and Australia, has developed its own standard forms of English, speakers and writers of Indian-English often have not had confidence in the suitability of their dialect. Consequently, Rushdie claimed in a 1996 *Salon1999* interview, they tend to write "a kind of classical Forsterian English that had nothing to do with the way they were speaking." Rushdie legitimatizes the spoken language by reflecting the Indianization of English. The dialects and phrasings Rushdie uses in his novels, however, are often as fictional as the works themselves. First he uses Indian terms meshed with English in daily Indian speech: *angrez* (an Englishman), *babuji* (a clerk/bureaucrat/semianglicized intellectual), and *bewaqoof* (idiot, fool). To Standard British English and its vocabulary he then adds Briticisms, puns, and his own coinages in a made-up Bombay dialect. This exciting and jumbled array of

Rushdie in the study of his London home, one of the last photographs taken of him before he went into hiding (photograph by Terry Smith/Camera Press)

language makes Rushdie's prose electrifying. An exasperated Epifania in *The Moor's Last Sigh* (1995) exclaims to her husband, "And then, when funds are frittered, and children are cap-in-hand? Then can we eatofy your thisthing, your anthropology?"

Rushdie explained in the *Salon1999* interview that his playfulness with language is "typical of Bombay, and maybe of India, that there is a sense of play in the way people use language. Most people in India are multilingual, and if you listen to the urban speech patterns there you'll find it's quite characteristic that a sentence will begin in one language, go through a second language and end in a third. It's the very playful, very natural result of juggling languages." To South Asian nationalists who protest against using the language of the colonialists, Rushdie might argue that Indians have now "colonized" the English language.

The fantastic elements of Saleem's existence and adventures reflect the magical realism that is so much a part of all of Rushdie's novels. In *Imaginary Homelands* Rushdie argues that realism as practiced in the nineteenth century is no longer "appropriate" to express the literary consciousness in "Third World" countries where political and cultural control have obliterated truth. Magical realism is intrinsically part of postcolonial literature because "It deals with what Naipaul had called 'half-made' societies in which the impossibly old struggles against the appallingly new problems of the nature of real-

ity." Merging fantasy and naturalism is one way of representing at least two separate realities, both of which are relevant and neither of which presents the complete truth. In the magical meshing of two cultures fantasy becomes real. Isabel Allende has said that magic realism is a true representation of the way some people see the world, and the narrator of *Shame* agrees; his is "a world thoroughly pervaded by miracles—so thoroughly, indeed, that the miraculous comes to appear routine."

During the next five years Rushdie produced two documentary films, *The Painter and the Pest* (1985) and *The Riddle of Midnight* (1988). His interest in motion pictures is deep, producing periodic critical pieces. A special interest is *The Wizard of Oz,* which appears in various ways in essays in his fiction and nonfiction. (Rushdie appeared with other writers in a 1993 BBC documentary, *In Search of Oz.*) Dorothy's desire to go home to Kansas (a black-and-white monotony compared to the multicolored Oz) crystallizes the ambiguous longings of the emigrant. In 1986 Rushdie traveled to Sandinista Nicaragua. *The Jaguar Smile: A Nicaraguan Journey* (1987) is a diary of that trip which mixes travel accounts with observations on the political problems then current in central America. Critics have complained that the political sentiments he expresses are unusually naive for Rushdie. In 1987 he was finally divorced from his estranged wife Clarissa and met the American writer Marianne Wiggins, whom he married in 1988 and divorced during the uproar over *The Satanic Verses*. While in India he was caught in Hindu-Muslim violence from the destruction of the Babri Masjid Mosque, the spot where according to local legend Rama was born and which is now a Muslim place of worship. In "The Riddle of Midnight, India, August 1987" in *Imaginary Homelands* Rushdie explains why this incident (which he incorporates into *The Moor's Last Sigh*) is indicative of the problems of plurality in the subcontinent. Also, later that year he reconciled with his dying father, much as does Saladin in *The Satanic Verses*.

Rushdie's already established propensity for writing novels that offend some segment of the public reached its peak on 26 September 1988, when Viking Penguin published the work that has brought him his greatest notoriety, *The Satanic Verses*. Groups were immediately polarized in their praise or condemnation of the book. On the one hand, *The Satanic Verses* brought Rushdie the Whitbread Prize in Great Britain and Germany's Author of the Year Award. On the other hand, many Islamic groups, including members of the Indian Muslim community, protested, and *The Satanic Verses* was quickly banned in India. After a London-based Saudi newspaper denounced Rushdie on 8 October, copies of the book were publicly burned. The protests then turned violent: five Iranians were killed outside the American Culture Center in Islamabad; sixty Indians were injured in a protest in Kashmir; and six Pakistanis were killed in riots. In February of 1989 the Ayatollah Khomeini, then leader of the Iranian revolution, denounced Rushdie in a *fatwah*, a judicial decree:

> I inform all zealous Muslims of the world that the author of the book entitled *The Satanic Verses*—which has been compiled, printed and published in opposition to Islam, the Prophet, and the Qur'an—and all those involved in its publication who were aware of its content, are sentenced to death. I call on all zealous Muslims to execute them quickly, wherever they may be found, so that no one else will dare to insult the Muslim sanctities. God willing, whoever is killed on this path is a martyr.

The current rulers of Iran continue to support the fatwah with a reward that has now escalated to $2.5 million. The book is banned in India, Pakistan, Iran, Bangladesh, South Africa, and Egypt. The threat is a real one: in 1991 the Japanese translator of *The Satanic Verses* was stabbed to death, and the Italian translator barely survived a separate stabbing attack, while the Norwegian publisher was ambushed in a 1993 shooting. After the fatwah announcement Rushdie and his British bodyguards went into hiding, although since 1996 he has made several public appearances. In 1989 *International Guerillas,* a Pakistani fantasy movie about Islamic militants who attempt to murder Rushdie, was initially refused entry into Great Britain but later allowed in through Rushdie's intervention. The Rushdie affair has generated conversation about the rights of free speech around the world, and Rushdie himself has sought help for his cause throughout the West. His essay "In Good Faith" incorporates his earliest and fullest defense of the novel and critique of his attackers. In addition to the effects of the ordeal on his personal freedoms, Rushdie has also undergone something of an examination of faith. In the final essay of *Imaginary Homelands,* "Why I Have Embraced Islam," Rushdie discusses his secular Muslim upbringing and explains that a Christmas Eve meeting in 1990 with six Muslim scholars convinced him to affirm "the two central tenets of Islam—the oneness of God and the genuineness of the prophecy of the Prophet Muhammad—and thus enter into the body of Islam after a lifetime spent outside it." This "re-affirmation of faith" did not last long, however. Asked by John Blades in a 1996 *Chicago Tribune* interview about his public embrace of Islam, Rushdie replied, "That was a depressed and despairing moment for me. I rapidly understood that it was a very foolish attempt at appeasing the opposition. I proceeded to admit that, and I've been admitting it ever since. I have no problem with people's religious beliefs. I just don't happen to have any."

The Satanic Verses begins with two Bombay men falling from grace and from an Air India plane blown up by Sikh terrorists over England. Gliding through the air, they begin a metamorphosis that unfolds throughout the novel: Gibreel Farishta, a Muslim Indian movie star who specializes in playing Hindu gods, becomes the angel Gabriel who whispered revelation to Mohammed; and his companion Saladin Chamcha, a voice-over artist proud of his British affectations, becomes a devil, complete with horns and revolting smell. Of all of Rushdie's novels, *The Satanic Verses* ends with the greatest sense of reconciliation with the world when Saladin Chamcha, much like his creator Rushdie, returns home to make peace with his dying father and rejects his Englishwomen to accept the embrace of his Indian lover. *The Satanic Verses* tells of the many kinds of human fragmentation. Saladin is the postcolonial divided man, halfway between India and England, while Gibreel is the Everyman, searching to be whole again through spiritual truth.

Dust jacket for Rushdie's 1994 collection of short stories

Alternating with the narrative of these metamorphizing Indians is the story of a prophet, Mahound, whose name Rushdie has taken from an obscure and insulting medieval European epithet for Muhammad. To this figure the archangel Gibreel and Shaitan dictate the Qur'an, including the errant "Satanic Verses." Herein lies the most offensive material to Muslims, for the original "Satanic Verses" were allegedly transmitted to the Prophet Muhammed to permit veneration and respect for pre-Islamic female deities. In the disputed tradition, Muhammad later realized that he had been tricked by Satan, and in consequence he withdrew the verses, substituting others in their place. Nearly all Muslims believe that the purported passages of the Qur'an on which this story is based are later forgeries and thus were never part of the genuine revelation. In addition to what was perceived as a parodic assault on the veracity of Islam's holy book, the novel also was seen as satirizing Muhammad's wives, as when Gibreel dreams that the inhabitants of a brothel take on the names of the wives of the Prophet Mahound in order to arouse their customers.

While *The Satanic Verses* may be seen as questioning the revelation that is the foundation of Islam and ridiculing how a merchant is metamorphized into a prophet, the novel also raises the issue of the immigrant who must metamorphose himself, or else be demonized by others, in the brutal world of British immigration. In *The Satanic Verses* a sanatorium full of immigrants and foreign visitors to England find themselves being transformed into various loathsome beasts. It is accomplished with words: "They describe us. That's all. They have the power of description, and we succumb to the pictures they construct." Many of the characters in the novel are British Muslims or Hindus struggling with the sense of being hybrids, the problem of fitting in while not losing cultural identity, and all the other issues of immigrants that Rushdie had presented in his earlier works. Metamorphosis has always been an important literary motif. One of Rushdie's characters quotes Ovid, and Ovidian mutations take place everywhere in his novels: Saleem's supersensitive nose, Sufiya Zinobia's spongelike ability to absorb shame; and Saladin Chamcha's goatness, which undoes all his careful English preening aimed at gaining the perfect English bride.

Once again the language of the immigrant takes center stage. The whole text mimics bits and pieces of cultures spliced together in the same way the main characters have made careers from imitation, from assuming false identities. Rushdie evokes bits and pieces of Indian culture vividly, using elements emblematic of the Indian diaspora, such as snatches of the song "Mera Joot Hai Japani," which reverberate in *The Satanic Verses* ("O my shoes are Japanese / these trousers English, if

Dust jacket for Rushdie's 1995 novel, a condemned man's history of his family, which parallels that of twentieth-century India

you please"). Despite the vibrancy of Indian English, Saladin emblematically suffers for decades of linguistic selfeffacement. He loses his job because his English voice does not fit his Indian reality: "They pay you to imitate them, as long as they don't have to look at you. Your voice becomes famous, but they hide your face." But English, the language he has embraced, causes him to betray his heritage. On a short return home Saladin learns that "Caught in the aspic of his adopted language, he had begun to hear, in India's Babel, an ominous warning: don't come back again. When you have stepped through the looking-glass you step back at your peril. The mirror may cut you to shreds."

In 1990 Rushdie took a seemingly different path with *Haroun and the Sea of Stories*, a children's book that he wrote for his own son. Written in the genre of *Thousand and One Nights,* from which it borrows some characters, *Haroun and the Sea of Stories* tells a fantasy tale that represents Rushdie's own dilemma of the continuing fatwah against him and the larger questions of storytelling that are an intrinsic part of the Arabic narrative tradition. In the story Haroun is the only child of an amazingly prolific and inventive storyteller, Rashid "The Shah of Blah," who depends on his subscription to the water from the Sea of Stories for his tale-telling magic. Rashid loses his voice

and his confidence, but Haroun, through a series of adventures with genies and a trip to Earth's other moon, is able to save Language from the evil cult leader Khattam-Shud, who is bent on imposing silence on the sea of stories. For this eloquent and entertaining plea for freedom of speech Rushdie won a Writer's Guild Award.

Imaginary Homelands collects the essays, interviews, and reviews Rushdie produced between each of his novels. This collection gives a glimpse at his other talents beyond the narrative as he offers his thoughts on an amazingly broad range of topics. The first three sections deal with subcontinental themes: section 1 discusses *Midnight's Children,* section 2 the politics of India and Pakistan, and section 3 Indo-English literature. The fourth deals with movies and television around the world. In particular, he critiques Raj fiction with its "zombie-like revival of the defunct empire" because it "propagates a number of notions about history which must be quarreled with, as loudly and as embarrassingly as possible." One such revisionist theory he decries is "the fantasy that the British Empire represented something 'noble' or 'great' about Britain; that it was, in spite of all its flaws and meannesses and bigotries, fundamentally glamorous." Section 5 contains five pieces about the experiences of migrants, primarily Indians to Britain. In addition to the somewhat infamous "The New Empire Within Britain" is "The Painter and the Pest," which tells the story of the discovery of the abstract expressionist Harold Shapinsky by Akumal Ramachander, a teacher of elementary English at an agricultural college in Bangalore, southern India. The stuff of this tale is also the subject of Rushdie's documentary movie of the same name. Section 6 contains three pieces also commenting on current problem areas in Britain. The rest of the book, excluding the conclusion, reviews the works of writers from Africa, Britain, South America, and the United States. The last three essays, "'In Good We Trust,'" "Is Nothing Sacred?," and "Why I Have Embraced Islam," deal with the crisis connected with the publication of *The Satanic Verses.*

East, West (1994) is a collection of short stories, many of which had already appeared elsewhere. The three parts of the work each have three stories. The first part, set in the East, begins with "Good Advice is Rarer than Rubies," first published in *The New Yorker.* A young Muslim woman learns from a bus driver how to flub her immigration interview intentionally and thus lose her chance to move to Great Britain. "The Free Radio" (originally in *The Atlantic*) tells about a young rickshaw driver who undergoes a vasectomy, for he mistakenly believes he will be rewarded with a free radio. When he discovers the contest is already over, he pretends he has the radio after all. "The Prophet's Hair" concerns a relic by that name. The second part, which is the least interesting of the three because it veers so far from Rushdie's most accurately imagined topics, is set in the West. It contains "Yorick," "At the Auction of the Ruby Slippers," and "Christopher Columbus and Queen Isabella of Spain Consummate their Relationship (Santa Fe, AD 1492)" (first appearing in *The New Yorker*). Critics have generally agreed that the third part, which features immigrants from the East living in the West, contains the best stories. Reflecting as they do Rushdie's own life of reconciling two cultural identities, they feature the material that continues to be his most successful. "The Harmony of the Spheres" narrates an Indian Cambridge student's tale of adultery, unfolding before the husband of his lover through a diary. One of the longest stories, "Chekov and Zulu," concerns two covert operatives of the Indian government's intelligence division in the days after the assassination of Indira Gandhi who have taken their code names from *Star Trek.* Much of the story centers on the conversations of these two old friends who debate such topics as

the appropriateness of British guilt in the colonial aftermath and the place of militant violence in the 1980s. "The Courter" returns to many of the autobiographical elements visited in the novels. Here the young narrator, born in Bombay but studying in England, clashes with his father whom he so much resembles. The title refers to the family's housekeeper, whose romance galvanizes her cultural struggles to love both West and East.

The Moor's Last Sigh, published in 1995, returns once again to Rushdie's controversial trademark issues of religion, miscegenation, and postcolonial angst. This novel was met with much of the same mixed, if much less violent, response as his previous novels: a winner of the Whitbread Novel of the Year Award and short-listed for the Booker Prize, *The Moor's Last Sigh* was nevertheless temporarily banned by Indian Customs. Set in Cochin, site of the first contact between India and the West, the novel opens with "a kind of science fiction moment, if you like, a meeting of two species." In a manner reminiscent of Saleem in *Midnight's Children,* the Moor—Moraes Zogoiby—sits in his grave and pours out a first-person retrospective of his four-generational family saga, which also parallels the history of twentieth-century India. His captor demands he write this family history before being killed, and so Moor writes a version as long and convoluted as possible, postponing his destiny: "He had made a Scheherazade of me. . . . As long as my tale held his interest he would let me live." The allusion here to writing under a death sentence makes the Moor a type of Rushdie, but the novel goes beyond the autobiographical.

The Moor's family mimics the chaotic diversity of South Asia. His father, Abraham Zogoiby, is a south-Indian Jew who claims descent from Boabdil, the last Muslim sultan of Granada, who abdicated in disgrace, while his Christian mother, Aurora da Gama, comes from a family proud of their illegitimate link with Vasco da Gama, the Portuguese navigator who brought European trade and colonialism to India. Throughout the narrative the Moor is pulled by conflicting racial, religious, familial, and sexual loyalties: "I, however, was raised neither as Catholic nor as Jew. I was both, and nothing: a jewholic–anonymous, a cathjew nut, a stewpot, a mongrel cur. I was—what's the word these days?—atomised. Yessir: a real Bombay mix." United in an illicit "pepper love," his parents personify the passionate attractions and repellents of the subcontinent's diversity. While his father parlays the family business into a corrupt megaempire of drugs and vice, the eccentric mother becomes India's greatest living artist. The Moor, like many of Rushdie's protagonists, battles with surreal and fantastic handicaps. He is burdened with a deformed, hammerlike right hand, which in its powerful grotesqueness makes him an emblem of the misappropriated power of new India. In addition he lives life "double-quick," even in the womb. In this way he is a contemporary man, racing at the constantly accelerating pace of life:

> I'll say it again: from the moment of my conception, like a visitor from another dimension, another time-line, I have aged twice as rapidly as the old earth and everything and everyone thereupon. . . . Premature? Post-mature is much more like it. Four and a half months in the wet and slimy felt much too long for me. From the beginning–from before the beginning–I knew I had no time to waste.

Rushdie turns from his previous examination of Islam's foundations and religious leaders to the problems of Hindu fanaticism. Through the character of Raman Fielding, a Hindu political demagogue with an underground army of thugs and toughs, Rushdie caricatures Bal Thackery, the leader of the Shiv Sena. This mockery of the Hindu fundamentalist strongman was the reason for the early banning of the book in India. Although the specific social abuses critiqued have changed from previous novels, Rushdie again presents the struggle between the forces of religious fanaticism and secular corruption. But which side is "good" in the battle between good and evil? None, according to the Moor. Using one of the defining metaphors of *The Satanic Verses,* the characters are falling from grace, either figuratively, from the heights of fame and power, or literally, from the top of Bombay's tallest skyscraper. The Moor himself falls in and out of love, and like all the protagonists of Rushdie's novels he forms romantic attachments that lead to betrayal and disappointment.

The Moor may have to suffer, but not in silence. *The Moor's Last Sigh* is about the power of language. "For several years I was preoccupied by defending the principle of freedom of speech," Rushdie has explained. "With *The Moor's Last Sigh,* I went back to practicing that freedom." "Freedom" expresses the exuberant mix of all the strands of his character's language. Puns are everywhere: Aurora nicknames her children Ina, Minnie, Mynah, and Moor; a famous Indian financial institution is Cashondeliveri. Allusions to everything imaginable–Shakespeare, James Joyce, "Bollywood" (the Bombay-based Indian movie in-

dustry), Popeye, the Lone Ranger and Tonto, and Martin Luther–seem to saturate the text. And once again the reported speech of an unknown dialect strikingly individualizes the characters. A young Aurora confides to a famous movie star, "O boy, what a handsome guy–too much sizzle, too much chilli, bring water. He may be a thief and a bounder, but that is some A-class loverboy good. And now look–you have gone and marry-o'ed him! What sexy lives you movie people leadofy." This wild tangle of Indian-English works to defeat the chaos of the characters' lives.

In his 1996 essay "Reservoir Frogs (or, Places called Mama's)" Rushdie emphatically stresses the importance of the title in the organic whole of a work. And indeed the title of *The Moor's Last Sigh* is nuanced and alluded to throughout the novel. Two of the many paintings in the story that have this name sit before Moor in his prison. One, painted by his mother Aurora, is the finale of her series of Moor paintings that feature her son; the other is a version of Sultan Boabdil's final departure from Granada, painted by his mother's erstwhile live-in lover and now Moor's jailer, Vasco Miranda. Moraes Zogoiby is left to contemplate the similarities and differences in these two visions–of himself and of the well-integrated culture of Alhambra that the historical Moor represented. And finally, the title refers to Moor's last breath, his story: "A sigh isn't just a sigh. We inhale the world and breathe out meaning. While we can. While we can."

Despite the restrictions placed on him by the continuing threat of the fatwah Rushdie has continued with his life and his work. He has been reported to be writing a screenplay for an adaptation of his short story "The Courter." The BBC is adapting *Midnight's Children* into a five-part serial called *Saleem's Story.* In 1997 he and his girlfriend of three years, Elizabeth West, published an anthology of Indian writing in English, timed to coincide with the fiftieth anniversary of the founding of India. He also celebrated his own fiftieth birthday, married West, and became a father once again. In November 1997 Indian newspapers reported that Rushdie had won a long lawsuit to reclaim ancestral property at Solan in Himidal Pradesh. His Indian attorney released a statement by Rushdie that said, in part, "I look forward to renewing the old family ties with Solan, and more broadly, my own deep connections with India in the near future."

Interviews:

"Fact, Faith and Fiction," *Far Eastern Economic Review,* 143 (2 March 1989): 11–13;

Gerald Marzorati, "Rushdie in Hiding," *New York Times Magazine,* 4 November 1990, p. 30;

James Fenton, "Keeping Up With Salman Rushdie," *New York Review of Books,* 38 (28 March 1991): 26–35;

Karsten Prager, "Free Speech Is Life Itself," *Time,* 138 (23 December 1991): 50–52;

Sybil Steinberg, "A Talk with Salman Rushdie: Six Years into the 'Fatwa,'" *Publishers Weekly,* 242 (30 January 1995): 80–83;

Maya Jaggi, "The Last Laugh," *New Statesman and Society,* 8 (8 September 1995): 20–22;

"When Life Becomes a Bad Novel," *Salon1999* [online magazine], 6 (27 January–9 February 1996);

John Blades, "An Interview with Salman Rushdie," *Chicago Tribune,* 28 January 1996, p. 3.

Bibliography:
Joel Kuortti, *The Salman Rushdie Bibliography: A Bibliography of Salman Rushdie's Work and Rushdie Criticism* (Frankfurt am Main & New York: Peter Lang, 1997).

Biography:
Ian Hamilton, "The First Life of Salman Rushdie," *New Yorker* (25 December 1995): 90–119.

References:
Lisa Appignanesi and Sara Maitland, eds., *The Rushdie File* (Syracuse, N.Y.: Syracuse University Press, 1990);

Timothy Brennan, *Salman Rushdie and the Third World: Myths of the Nation* (New York: St. Martin's Press, 1989);

R. K. Dhawan, *The Novels of Salman Rushdie* (New Delhi: Indian Society for Commonwealth Studies, 1992);

Fawzia Afzal Khan, *Cultural Imperialism and the Indo-English Novel: Genre and Ideology in R. K. Narayan, Anita Desai, Kamala Markandaya and Salman Rushdie* (University Park: Pennsylvania State University Press, 1993);

Leonard Williams Levy, *Blasphemy: Verbal Offense against the Sacred, from Moses to Salman Rushdie* (New York: Knopf, 1993);

Ian Richard Netton, *Text and Trauma: An East-West Primer* (Richmond, U.K.: Curzon Press, 1996);

Daniel Pipes, *The Rushdie Affair: The Novel, the Ayatollah, and the West* (New York: Carol, 1990);

Hans Semminck, *A Novel Visible but Unseen: A Thematic Analysis of Salman Rushdie's The Satanic Verses* (Ghent, Belgium: Studia Germanica Gandensia, 1993).

Graham Swift

(4 May 1949 -   )

Nicolas Tredell
University of Sussex, Brighton

BOOKS: *The Sweet Shop Owner* (London: Allen Lane, 1980; New York: Washington Square Press, 1985);

Shuttlecock (London: Allen Lane, 1981; New York: Washington Square Press, 1984);

Learning to Swim and Other Stories (London: London Magazine Editions, 1982; New York: Poseidon, 1982);

Waterland (London: Heinemann, 1983; New York: Poseidon, 1983);

Out of This World (London: Viking, 1988; New York: Poseidon, 1988);

Ever After (London: Picador, 1992; New York: Knopf, 1992);

Last Orders (London: Picador, 1996; New York: Knopf, 1996).

OTHER: *The Magic Wheel: An Anthology of Fishing in Literature,* edited by Swift and David Profumo (London: Picador in association with Heinemann, 1985).

SELECTED PERIODICAL PUBLICATIONS–
UNCOLLECTED: "Throwing off our Inhibitions," *Times* (London), 5 March 1988, p. 20;

"Siding with Mystery," *Sunday Times* (London), 16 February 1992, VII: 6–7.

Graham Swift is a spellbinding storyteller whose primary concerns, in his novels, are the experience of loss and the ways in which human beings try to come to terms with loss. Real and symbolic bereavements haunt his work: the death or estrangement of a partner, parent, or child; the effacement of a sense of history and of identity; and the collapse of faith. Swift belongs to the generation of highly talented novelists born around the middle of this century–such as Peter Ackroyd, Martin Amis, Kazuo Ishiguro, Timothy Mo, and Swift's close friend, Salman Rushdie–who came to prominence in England in the 1970s and 1980s and who are now in their maturity. Swift's work, now consisting of six novels and a collection of short stories, has garnered criti-

cal acclaim and literary prizes and has won a large and appreciative audience in England and abroad; he has been translated into more than twenty languages. Reserving his energies as a writer for his novels, Swift has written no nonfiction books and has rarely published articles. Although his success has inevitably brought him into the public eye, he is a private man who does not court publicity; he is said to dislike the business of promoting his books, and he is, apparently, not one to suffer fools gladly. His recreation is angling, an activity conducive to quiet contemplation, and in his only venture so far into editing he has compiled, with David Profumo, an anthology of fishing in literature, *The Magic Wheel* (1985).

Graham Colin Swift was born on 4 May 1949 in Catford in South London, the son of Lionel Allan Stanley Swift and Sheila Irene Bourne Swift. His father was a civil servant, and Swift's childhood was, as he told *The Times* (London) on 30 October 1996, "a very ordinary suburban existence." He was educated at Dulwich College, a prestigious public school (equivalent to a private school in the United States) in South London that has produced a variety of novelists–Raymond Chandler, C. S. Forester, P. G. Wodehouse–and went on to Queen's College, Cambridge University, to take a degree in English in 1970. He followed this up with an M.A. at York University (1970–1973), writing his thesis on "The City in Nineteenth-Century English Literature." Rejecting the option of a career in academia, Swift instead took teaching jobs in Greece and London while working on his fiction. His first novel, *The Sweet Shop Owner,* was published in 1980 and was well received; for example, Stuart Evans commended it in *The Times* (London) of 24 April 1980 as a "beautifully balanced novel" about "the arrangements, accommodations, pacts and treaties of our ordinary lives."

The Sweet Shop Owner tells the story of Willy Chapman, a widower who owns and runs a candy store and newsstand in South London. In contrast to Swift's later novels, the story is told in the third

Graham Swift (photograph by Mark Douet)

person, but much of it is related from Willy's point of view. The narrative, moving between present and past in a way that is characteristic of Swift, alternates an account of one working day in Willy's present life with his recollections of key moments of his past: his marriage to a beautiful and wealthy woman who bought him his shop and bore him a daughter but who, possibly traumatized by a sexual assault she suffered as a young woman, became a recluse and a permanent invalid. As Willy's working day progresses, the reader begins to realize that this is no ordinary day; it is not only the twenty-fifth birthday of his estranged daughter, whom he misses deeply, but also the last day of his life. The novel takes on the elegiac tone that pervades Swift's fiction. The imminence of Willy's death helps to focus the question: What has his life meant?

This question is pursued in relation to a theme which is important in this novel and in much of Swift's work: the relationship between an individual life history and the kind of grand history that is concerned with large-scale, world-historical change. If, in a sense, grand history is unavoidable—as Willy reflects, "History came to meet you"—it is still possible to live in its margins. An injury to his leg keeps Willy out of active service in World War II—that

historical event to which Swift's novels return again and again—and confirms his sense of noninvolvement: "Nothing touches you, you touch nothing." Since World War II, grand history has only entered his life through the headlines on the newspapers which he sells but does not read, through his daughter's troubled awareness of politics in her teenage years, and through his observations of the changing styles of dress and behavior in the people who pass and enter his shop. In terms of grand history Willy's life hardly counts at all, but it nonetheless has, as Swift's story makes clear, its triumphs and disasters: for example, the moment when, as a young man, he wins his future wife by going down a slide in a children's playground; or his desertion by his daughter, resentful at her mother's treatment of her while she was alive and at the stipulation in her mother's will that her daughter will come into her inheritance only when Willy himself dies. On this last day of his life Willy hopes that, having given his daughter the money she wants, she will come home, but he moves toward death still in doubt: "She will not come. She will come."

Swift's second novel, *Shuttlecock* (1981), is told in the first person by Prentis—his first name is never revealed—a civil servant in his early thirties who works in a department in London, attached to the police, that deals with "dead crimes"–crimes committed, or suspected to have been committed, some time ago, the files on which have been officially closed but not destroyed. Prentis is obsessed by his father, who was a secret agent in World War II and who later wrote a book–also called *Shuttlecock,* his wartime code name–about his resistance to a Gestapo interrogation and his daring escape from captivity. This heroic father is now, however, a mute resident of a mental home, in "a kind of language-coma." Prentis visits him regularly, but the only way Prentis has to understand his father is by reading and re-reading his book. Prentis's obsession harms his relationships with his wife and young sons, whom he bullies and frightens. He has problems at work, where he suspects his boss, Quinn, of removing certain files which should be available, and thus undermining Prentis's attempts to do his job, which involves finding links between different pieces of information. When Prentis finally summons up the courage to confront his boss, Quinn tells him that among the missing files is one that suggests that Prentis's father may, in fact, have broken under torture by the Gestapo and given away information that led to the deaths of British agents. He offers Prentis the choice of looking into the file or destroying it without reading it; Prentis chooses the latter option, and this seems to release him from his obsession and open up the possibility of better relationships with his wife and sons.

Swift's major themes in *Shuttlecock* are power and knowledge and the ways in which the possession of power and knowledge–even when they are bound up with benevolence and love–can lead to oppression. Analogies are established between Prentis's painful recollection of how, as a boy, he tortured a pet hamster that he loved and his bullying of his beloved wife and of his sons and between his boss's bullying and mystification of his staff and the Gestapo's torturing of Prentis's father. By making the father a supposed war hero–or perhaps a traitor–Swift creates in *Shuttlecock* a much more direct link than in *The Sweet Shop Owner* between individual history and grand history and between private, professional, and political oppression. The novel also explores the question that Quinn puts to Prentis: "Is it better to know things or not to know them? Wouldn't we sometimes be happier not knowing them?" *Shuttlecock* effectively dramatizes all these issues. In its structural and stylistic accomplishment and its engagement with crucial themes the novel marks a definite development beyond *The Sweet Shop Owner,* and it gained critical acclaim; for instance, John Coleman, writing in *The Sunday Times* (Lon-

don) of 20 September 1981, called it "An astonishing study of forms of guilt." *Shuttlecock* also won the prestigious biannual Geoffrey Faber Award for fiction.

In 1982 *Learning to Swim and Other Stories,* a collection of eleven of Swift's short stories, was published. All but one of the stories had previously appeared in magazines or anthologies of new writing. These concise tales are, with one exception, told in the first person and are written, for the most part, in a spare, dry style which implies, and sometimes intensifies, a deep pressure of emotion. Successful in their own right Swift's stories can also be related to his novels in their use of the storytelling voice and in their themes: for example the themes of the childless marriage in "Seraglio" and of father-daughter incest in "Hotel" are echoed in *Waterland* (1983), while the story of a son's discovery of his real paternity in "The Son" is taken up again in *Ever After* (1992). One of the most effective stories, however, "The Tunnel," deals with a topic–a young couple living in a rundown inner-city tenement–which has not, so far, found an echo elsewhere in Swift's fiction. But in general the stories in *Learning to Swim* are rather inhibited and could hardly have prepared the reader for the scope and exuberance of the novel which appeared the following year: *Waterland.*

Waterland remains Swift's most accomplished and wide-ranging work to date. The story is told by Tom Crick, a history teacher in his fifties living in Greenwich in London who is about to lose his job–both because the school at which he works is "cutting back on history" and because his childless wife, Mary, also in her fifties, has been convicted of stealing a baby from a local supermarket. Crick's story takes the form of a series of talks to his sixth-form class in which he not only ranges back over his own life and his traumatic early relationship with Mary–a relationship darkly shadowed by abortion and murder–but also extends his narrative to encompass the landscape and history of the flat, bleak, amphibious country of the English Fens from which both he and Mary come–the "waterland" of the novel's title. That history engages at times, more or less directly, with key moments in the broader narrative of English history, such as imperial expansion, the Industrial Revolution, and World War I. *Waterland* shows Swift at his most compelling. Landscapes, characters, and incidents, whether of the Fenland past or the London present, are powerfully evoked; chronological order is altered in order to create suspense and to provide striking connections between events widely separated in time. The narrative voice is captured with consummate skill, its insistent, repeated phrase "let me tell you" drawing the readers into the story, making them want to read on.

Two main themes of *Waterland* are the relationships between individual history, life history, and grand history and between the past, present, and future—the future symbolized in the novel by children and by the question of how to pass on to the rising generations the legacy, for better and worse, of the past. Whereas Swift's two previous novels had a largely urban setting, much of *Waterland* has a rural location, and this helps Swift to add a further dimension by dramatizing the relationships between human beings and the primal elements: earth, air, water, and fire. *Waterland* also tackles in a more explicit way the theme of human curiosity and desire raised in *Shuttlecock*. As in *Shuttlecock,* the dangers of curiosity and desire—represented in *Waterland* by the consequences of Mary's early sexual explorations—are acknowledged, but in this novel their force is also recognized and linked to a key theme of postmodernist thought: the limitations of grand history, of large narratives. As Crick says to his class at one point: "Have you ever considered that why so many historical movements, not only revolutionary ones, fail, fail at heart, is because they fail to take account of the complex and unpredictable forms of our curiosity. Which doesn't want to push ahead, which always wants to say, Hey, that's interesting, let's stop awhile, let's take a look-see, let's retrace—let's take a different turn? What's the hurry? What's the rush? Let's *explore*." This desire to explore is evident in the expansiveness and scope of *Waterland* itself.

As George P. Landow notes, Swift's novel echoes both the work of Charles Dickens, especially *Great Expectations* (1861) with its evocation of "the marsh country," and the work of William Faulkner, particularly *Absalom, Absalom* (1936) in its heady brew, unusual in English fiction, of murder, misalliance, and a strong sense of place. In contrast to Faulkner, however, Swift's personal knowledge of the area about which he wrote was minimal; many readers of *Waterland* were surprised to learn that he did not come from the Fens. The power of his evocation bears out his belief in the importance of the imagination in writing, and of the relationship between imagination and exploration, which he affirmed in an article in *The Times* (London) on 5 March 1988: "One often hears offered as indispensable advice to young writers: 'Write only about what you know about—write from your experience.' I could not agree with anything less. My maxim would be: for God's sake write about what you *don't* know about! For how else will you bring your *imagination* into play? How else will you *discover* or *explore* anything?" *Waterland* is a notable example of a more

Dust jacket for Swift's novel about a widower's attempt to reconstruct his past and that of a Victorian ancestor

general movement in English fiction in the 1980s away from the constraints which—apart from notable exceptions such as John Fowles—had seemed to inhibit it since World War II. Swift recalled in the March 1988 *Times* article that he wrote *Waterland* "at a time when I felt my own literary inhibitions were dropping away, and I wanted to write something ambitious, adventurous and energetic, where, if I erred I would err, like Dickens, on the side of too much colour rather than too little. . . . I wanted to perform. I wanted to 'show off.'" In fact, the novel succeeds triumphantly, without an undue sense of exhibitionism on the part of its author.

Waterland was short-listed for the 1983 Booker Prize, England's most highly publicized literary award, and there was some surprise that it lost out to J. M. Coetzee's *Life and Times of Michael K* (1983). Swift's novel did, however, win the *Guardian* Fiction Prize, the Winifred Holtby Memorial Prize for the best regional novel of the year, and, in 1987, the Italian Premio Grinzane Cavoure. *Waterland* more than justified Swift's inclusion in a controversial list of the twenty best young British novelists drawn up in 1983 by the Book Marketing Council, and it established him as a novelist of authority and range. In 1983 he became a full-time writer, and the following year he was elected a fellow of the Royal Society of Literature. But the success of *Waterland,* at a relatively early stage of his career as a novelist, was to create a problem for Swift: *Waterland* was a hard act to follow, and there was the risk that it might–as Swift, in the 30 October 1996 *The Times,* was quoted as saying–"haunt me in a disadvantageous way," setting an especially high standard by which his future work would be measured.

It was, in fact, five years before Swift's next novel, *Out of This World* (1988), was published, to mixed reviews. *Out of This World* engages with a range of major events in twentieth-century English and world history: for example, World War I, World War II, the Nuremberg trials, the Vietnam War, the Congo, the 1974 military coup in Greece, the IRA bombing campaign, and the conflict between Britain and Argentina over the Falkland/Malvinas islands in the South Atlantic which began in April 1982–significantly, the date at which the novel opens. Swift engages with this history by constructing, perhaps in a rather contrived way, two characters whose lives and careers have brought them into a close relationship with the global violence of the twentieth century. One of these characters is Robert Beech, who won a Victoria Cross and lost an arm in World War I, who later took over his family's armaments business, and who was killed in 1972 by a massive IRA bomb planted in his car. The other character is Robert's son, Harry, who had refused to follow his father into the arms trade and had pursued a successful career as a photojournalist capturing harrowing images from the world's trouble spots but who, after his father's violent death, gave up photojournalism for aerial photography of the landscapes of England–airplanes are significant symbols in the novel of the desire to get "out of this world." The story is told mainly through the first-person narratives of Harry and of his daughter, Sophie, from whom–like Willy in *The Sweet Shop Owner*–he is estranged. Sophie lives in New York with her husband and twin sons and has not communicated with Harry since the day of Robert's death, when she apparently saw him, immediately after the explosion, taking a photograph of the scene. Harry has now fallen in love with a young woman of twenty-three whom he intends to marry, and he has invited Sophie to the wedding; as the novel ends, it seems that she will go so that, in contrast to the mood at the end of *The Sweet Shop Owner,* there seems to be a real possibility of a reconciliation between father and daughter.

In *Out of This World* Swift is concerned with the relationships between representation and reality, telling and showing, the visual and the verbal. The novel brilliantly evokes and explores the predominantly visual global culture of today: "Have you noticed how the world has changed? It's become this vast display of evidence, this exhibition of recorded data, this continuously running movie." But paradoxically the visual image also blurs the distinction between reality and representation to such an extent that it may make us doubt whether there is any reality in the first place–as Harry says to his father, not quite jokingly, even the moon landing may have been faked in a studio. The distinction between the real and the aesthetic is also blurred. On the one hand, the photograph may seem to offer direct reality: Harry recalls that he thought, as he took a picture of a dying World War II pilot which was to become famous: "Let this have no aesthetic content, let this be only like it is, in the middle of things." On the other hand, the photograph may itself become an object seen as worthy of conservation and contemplation, as has happened with Harry's photographs. Moreover, if the photograph offers involvement, it also permits detachment: "If you exist in your vision, then nothing can hurt you, you need never be frightened of anything." The camera transforms history into spectacle–which does not mean that history ceases to hurt, as Robert's violent death and Sophie's subsequent trauma show. In a culture saturated with visual images Swift seeks to affirm, through the very act of his narrative, the human importance of telling as a vital way in which we apprehend the meaning of images and learn to live with them. It is significant that Sophie's monologue is presented as a series of sessions with her therapist, Dr Klein: it is by talking, by telling a story, whether or not this takes place in a formal therapeutic situation, that one may be able to come to terms with trauma. As Dr Klein, according to Sophie, says: "the answer to the problem is to learn how to tell. It's telling that reconciles memory and forgetting."

In 1992 a motion picture adaptation of *Waterland* was released starring Jeremy Irons and Sinead Cusack. Despite a few positive reviews, it was generally poorly received and did not succeed commercially. The same year, however, saw the publication–this time after a four-year gap–of Swift's sixth novel, *Ever After.* With *Ever After* Swift returns to a narrator, Bill Unwin, who, like Willy Chapman in *The Sweet Shop Owner,* has lived in the margins of history and is now a widower with a death wish–indeed, he has recently tried to commit suicide and feels that he is in a "curious post-mortal condition." In contrast to Willy's obscure, reclusive wife, however, Unwin's wife, Ruth Vaughan, was a celebrated stage and screen actress. There is also a similarity between *Ever After* and *Shuttlecock* in that mystery shrouds the narrator's father. But whereas

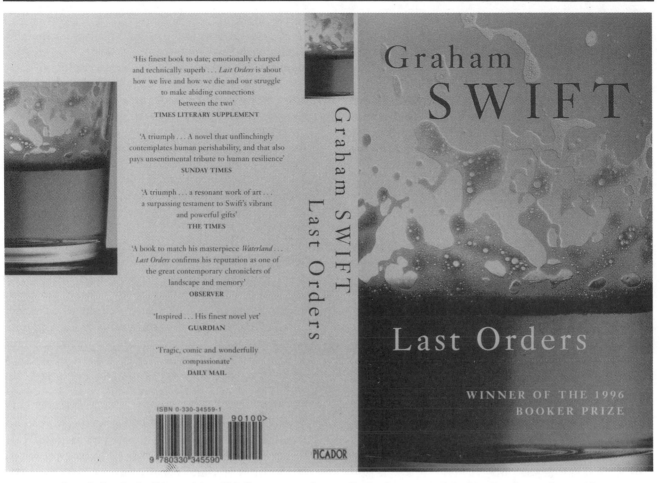

'His finest book to date; emotionally charged
and technically superb . . . *Last Orders* is about
how we live and how we die and our struggle
to make abiding connections
between the two'
TIMES LITERARY SUPPLEMENT

'A triumph . . . A novel that unflinchingly
contemplates human perishability, and that also
pays unsentimental tribute to human resilience'
SUNDAY TIMES

'A triumph . . . a resonant work of art . . .
a surpassing testament to Swift's vibrant
and powerful gifts'
THE TIMES

'A book to match his masterpiece *Waterland* . . .
Last Orders confirms his reputation as one of
the great contemporary chroniclers of
landscape and memory'
OBSERVER

'Inspired . . . His finest novel yet'
GUARDIAN

'Tragic, comic and wonderfully
compassionate'
DAILY MAIL

ISBN 0-330-34559-1

Graham SWIFT
Last Orders

Graham
SWIFT

Last Orders

WINNER OF THE 1996
BOOKER PRIZE

PICADOR

Dust jacket for Swift's novel in which four men travel across England to scatter their friend's ashes at the seaside

Prentis's father in *Shuttlecock* is alive though silent, Unwin's father in *Ever After* is dead, having shot himself when his son was nine, apparently because of his wife's infidelity with the American owner of a plastics firm, "Uncle Sam" Ellison. She subsequently married Ellison, whom Unwin for a long time conceived of as Claudius to his Hamlet—only to be told late in life by Sam that, according to his mother, his real father was a railway-engine driver who was killed in World War II. *Ever After* further resembles *Shuttlecock* in that it raises the issue of whether knowledge is desirable—is it better to know the truth if it brings unhappiness? The novel ranges back over key moments of Unwin's life but also, like *Waterland,* goes further back in time—in this case to the Victorian era through the notebooks of Unwin's ancestor Matthew Pearce that he discovered after his mother's death. Pearce was also a figure in the margins of history who, but for the notebooks, might have been unknown to posterity but who was linked with two great events of the nineteenth century—the building of the Great Western Railway from London to Cornwall, on which he worked as a

surveyor, and the erosion of Christian belief brought about by the writings of Sir Charles Lyell on geology and of Charles Darwin on evolution. In Pearce's case the skepticism induced by their writings was compounded by the death of his small son and led finally to a complete loss of faith, a total break with his clergyman father-in-law, and the irrevocable collapse of his marriage.

Ever After is about memory, mourning, imagination, change, and permanence. As Unwin remembers and in a sense re-creates his own life, possibly searching, as he suggests, for what he calls "anteriority," that is, "To know who I was," he also becomes aware of gaps and enigmas which he sometimes tries to close or resolve with acts of fiction-making, of imagination: "The past, they say, is a foreign country, and I fictionalize (perhaps) these memories of that afternoon. But then my mother is dead. With all the others. She doesn't exist. And fiction is what doesn't exist." He is led even further into fiction as he tries to reconstruct Matthew Pearce's life on the basis of the sporadic and questionable evidence provided by Pearce's notebooks: "What do I know of Matthew? I conjure him up, I invent him. I make him the protagonist . . . of this 'dramatized version.'"

Even if reliable knowledge of the past can be achieved, it is, Swift's novel suggests, a knowledge of change rather than of permanence—symbolized by the way in which Lyell called into question the very ground under the feet of his contemporaries. Moreover, the awareness of unreliability and change throws into question the very notion of posterity and survival, of enduring "ever after." What kind of survival is possible? For Unwin, for example, the posterity provided by the numerous photographs and videos of his famous late wife cannot speak to him of her reality; only memory and narration can do that, and the last part of the novel largely consists of his loving recollection of the first night on which they slept together.

Like Swift's previous novels, *Ever After* is compellingly written, engages in fascinating ways with images and examples of change and permanence, and brilliantly re-creates the past. But by the 1990s the fictional re-creation of the Victorian era had already become a stock technique of English fiction—notable examples are Fowles's *The French Lieutenant's Woman* (1969) and A. S. Byatt's *Possession* (1990)—so that there is a sense of Swift mining, though skillfully, an already well-worked vein. The chief weakness of *Ever After,* however, lies in its perfunctory characterization of Unwin's late wife, Ruth, and its failure to make their relationship sufficiently convincing. In contrast to Willy's wife in *The Sweet Shop Owner* Ruth is endowed with a successful career, but this is not evoked adequately; and although her relationship with Unwin is supposed to have been an intense love match, this does not come across. While the portraits of Unwin's mother, or even, more distantly, of Matthew Pearce's wife, are quite vivid—though stereotyped—Ruth is little more than a cipher. This exemplifies a recurring difficulty that Swift seems to have with the major women characters in his novels. It was not surprising that *Ever After,* like *Out of This World,* received mixed reviews; it did, however, win the French Prix de Meilleur Livre Etranger in 1994.

In his latest novel, *Last Orders* (1996), Swift returns to the world of small shopkeepers and tradesmen which he had explored in *The Sweet Shop Owner,* and, like that first novel, *Last Orders* is shadowed by mortality. It describes how four men carry out the last orders of London butcher Jack Dodds: that his ashes should be scattered at the seaside. The four men are a secondhand-car dealer, Vince, whom Jack had informally adopted as his son after Vince's real parents were killed in a bombing raid in World War II; an insurance clerk, Ray, who was Jack's wartime buddy and who later had an affair with Amy, Jack's wife; Lenny, a former boxer and fruit-and-vegetable trader; and Vic, the local undertaker. The story is mainly told through their alternating points of view and moves between their experiences of their journey and the memories of their lives, and of Jack's life, which the occasion provokes. The reader is also privy to the interior monologues of Amy and of Vince's wife, Mandy. Amy has not come on her husband's last journey because she wishes to make a final farewell visit to June, the couple's fifty-year-old daughter who has been disowned by Jack because she has been in a permanent vegetative state from birth.

In contrast to the conventionally literate styles he employed in his previous novels, Swift represents the thoughts and feelings of the characters of *Last Orders* in an expertly sustained vernacular mode which at times becomes poetic. Echoing the concern for the English past in his previous work, the journey of Vince, Vic, Ray, and Lenny from the capital of England to its coast is also a kind of journey through national history, taking in Rochester, the Naval Memorial at Chatham and—with an echo of Geoffrey Chaucer's pilgrims—Canterbury Cathedral. The novel ends—with another literary echo, seemingly not consciously inserted by Swift, of T. S. Eliot's *The Waste Land* (1922)—at Margate, where Jack's ashes are finally scattered: "and the ash that I carried in my hands, which was the Jack who once walked around, is carried away by the wind, is whirled away by the wind till the ash becomes wind and the wind becomes Jack what we're made of."

Last Orders received good reviews and secured for Swift the £20,000 Booker Prize which *Waterland* had failed to win thirteen years before, boosting sales: only three copies of the novel were sold in all of the United Kingdom the week before the prize was announced; the week following the Booker announcement saw the novel as number five on the best-seller list. The prize usually generates controversy, however, and this time it was sparked off by John Frow, professor of English at the University of Queensland in Australia, who, in a letter to the book review supplement of *The Australian* newspaper, quoted in the *Times Literary Supplement* (14 March 1997), said that *Last Orders* used "precisely the same structure" as William Faulkner's novel *As I Lay Dying* (1930), down to details such as having a chapter attributed to a dead person, a one-sentence chapter, and a chapter made up of numbered points. While some press reports interpreted Frow's criticisms as a charge of plagiarism, Frow, in an article in the London *Independent on Sunday* on 16 March 1997, was careful to make it clear that he had made no such charge and that "Close imitation does not constitute 'plagiarism' or 'theft'"; he did, however, claim that "The use that *Last Orders* makes of *As I Lay Dying* is . . . an inert borrowing." Swift, in an article in *The Times* on 10 March 1997, pointed out that the link with *As I Lay Dying* had already been noticed by Claire Messud in her 1996 *Times* review of *Last Orders;* he went on to argue, however, that the great number of reviews and commentaries which did not mention Faulkner suggested that the link with *As I Lay Dying* was not central to his novel and that while *Last Orders* could "understandably, be compared to Faulkner's," it "does not stand comparison to it. It's a different book."

The controversy, characteristically, improved the sales of *Last Orders*. It is unlikely to do any permanent harm to Swift's reputation or to inhibit his future work. As he told Scott Rosenberg in a 1996 interview: "I think that nothing does or will replace the storytelling urge. It's something that, from the receiver's end and the supplier's end, is so deep in human nature. The need to tell and be told stories is intrinsic to the creatures that we are." The appearance of a new novel by Graham Swift remains an event to which most serious readers look forward, knowing that his words will weave a compelling web of illusion as they engage with major themes in a way that is sophisticated yet accessible.

Interviews:

David Profumo, "The Attraction of the Pessimistic View," *Sunday Times* (London), 6 March 1988, G8–9;

Ludmila Lakshu, "The Writer and Inspiration: a Conversation with Graham Swift," *English Review,* 1 (1990): 36–39;

Scott Rosenberg, "Glowing in the Ashes," *Salon* [online magazine], 14 (6 May–10 May 1996).

References:

David Leon Higdon, "Double Closures in Postmodern British Fiction: The Example of Graham Swift," *Critical Survey,* 3 (1991): 89–95;

Del Ivan Janik, "History and the 'Here and Now': the Novels of Graham Swift," *Twentieth Century Literature,* 35, no. 1 (1989): 74–88;

George P. Landow, "History, His Story and Stories in Graham Swift's *Waterland,*" *Studies in the Literary Imagination,* 23 (1990): 197–211;

John Schad, "The End of the End of History: Graham Swift's *Waterland,*" *Modern Fiction Studies,* 38 (Winter 1992): 911–925;

Nicolas Tredell, "Feelgood Fiction: The Novels of Graham Swift," *Oxford Quarterly,* 4 (Spring/Summer 1997): 37–41.

Barry Unsworth
(10 August 1930 –   )

William F. Naufftus
Winthrop University

BOOKS: *The Partnership* (London: New Authors, 1966);

The Greeks Have a Word for It (London: Hutchinson, 1967);

The Hide (London: Gollancz, 1970; New York: Norton, 1996);

Mooncranker's Gift (London: Allen Lane, 1973; Boston: Houghton Mifflin, 1973);

The Big Day (London: M. Joseph, 1976; New York: Mason/Charter, 1977);

Pascali's Island (London: M. Joseph, 1980); republished as *The Idol Hunter* (New York: Simon & Schuster, 1980);

The Student's Book of English: A Complete Coursebook and Grammar to Advanced Intermediate Level, by Unsworth, John Lennox Cook, and Amorey Gethin (Oxford: Blackwell, 1981);

The Rage of the Vulture (London: Granada, 1982; Boston: Houghton Mifflin, 1983);

Stone Virgin (London: Hamish Hamilton, 1985; Boston: Houghton Mifflin, 1986);

Sugar and Rum (London: Hamish Hamilton, 1988);

Sacred Hunger (London: Hamish Hamilton, 1992; New York: Nan A. Talese/Doubleday, 1992);

Novels and Novelists in the 1990's (London: Random House, 1993);

Morality Play (London: Hamish Hamilton, 1995; New York: Nan A. Talese/Doubleday, 1995);

After Hannibal (London: Hamish Hamilton, 1996; New York: Nan A. Talese/Doubleday, 1997).

Barry Unsworth

TELEVISION SCRIPT: *The Stick Insect*, BBC 2, 1975.

In the twelve novels he has published since 1966 Barry Unsworth has explored his stated interest in "moral complexities and ambiguities" in a wide variety of genres and settings. Several of his books have been primarily comic or have mixed serious moral messages and tragic story lines with comic material. Half of his novels have been set, entirely or primarily, in Greece, Turkey, or Italy, often developing plotlines concerned with murder or political intrigue. Perhaps most significantly, he has participated in the recent rebirth of the British historical novel, dealing with periods as different as the late Middle Ages, the eighteenth century, and the last days of the Ottoman Empire but always providing messages clearly intended for modern times. The moral content of these messages often deals with the dangers posed to individuals by their own obsessive behavior. Another preoccupation of his work has been a broadly political concern for the fate of helpless "subaltern" people (individuals or races) at the mercy of brutal power. Once described as being on the fringes of the literary establishment, he has now moved close to the center: two of his novels have been short-listed for the Booker McConnell Prize, and in 1992 his *Sacred Hunger* shared that most prestigious of British literary prizes with Michael Ondaatje's *The English Patient.*

Barry Forster Unsworth was born 10 August 1930 in County Durham, the son of Michael Unsworth, a coal miner who became an insurance salesman, and Elsie Forster Unsworth. He attended Stockton-on-Tees Grammar School and the University of Manchester, graduating with a B.A. in English in 1951. After serving from 1951 to 1953 as a second lieutenant in the Royal Corps of Signals, in 1959 he married Valerie Irene Moor, with whom he had three daughters: Madeleine, Tania, and Thomasina. He and his growing family spent most of the 1960s in Greece and Turkey, where he served as British Council lecturer at the Universities of Athens and Istanbul, an experience that would provide him with settings for four of his novels.

His first novel, *The Partnership* (1966), however, deals with two art dealers in Cornwall. The creative partner, Foley, designs and makes statues of pixies, West Country fairy folk used as lawn decorations; the practical partner, Moss, takes care of the financial side of the business. Foley at first seems to be a success with women; Moss is a more or less latent homosexual who is attracted to Foley. The cast is filled out with various eccentric artistic characters who provide comic relief in a basically sad story about how the partnership is dissolved when the two men discover their own and each other's secrets. The limited critical reception the novel received was basically favorable. The reviewer in the 16 June 1966 *Times Literary Supplement* described it as "a comedy and a good one"; after voicing some minor complaints about the improbability and sentimentality with which Moss is treated, the review concluded that "on the whole this is a stylish, controlled and witty first book." B. A. Young in the 22 June 1966 issue of *Punch* said that "in a quiet way it's one of the funniest books I've read for a long time" and concluded that "Mr. Unsworth is well worth keeping an eye on."

The combination of the comic and the serious also marks Unsworth's second novel, published the next year. *The Greeks Have a Word for It* clearly draws on the author's own experience from 1960 to 1963 as an English language teacher in Athens, since this is also—loosely—the profession of the novel's comic protagonist, Brian Kennedy. Compared by one reviewer to the eponymous hero of Kingsley Amis's novel *Lucky Jim* (1954), Kennedy uses fraudulent credentials to attract private students, whom he pre-

pares for success by finding out the examination questions in advance. He needs a salary primarily to keep him in women and liquor, and he is doing quite well until he encounters Mitsos, the tragic protagonist, who is looking for revenge on the man who killed his father and raped his mother. Gillian Freeman in the 6 October 1967 *New Statesman* called the novel "competently written but dated. Fifties rather than Sixties." She also complained that "the merging of the twin plots doesn't quite come off." The reviewer in the 19 October 1967 *Times Literary Supplement* was more positive, calling the novel a tragicomedy. While granting that the comic half "is more convincing than the other," the reviewer concluded that the novel is "unusually successful" and "carves out a genuine area of its own in a difficult genre."

These first two novels introduce several of the hallmarks of Unsworth's fiction: sexual obsession; artists as subjects; the illegitimate acquisition of money; the mixing of comic and tragic; exotic settings; and protagonists haunted by past traumas. His third and fourth novels develop these themes. *The Hide* (1970), like *The Greeks Have a Word for It,* focuses on two characters, one Anglo-Saxon and deviant and the other exotic, primitive, and destructive. The Anglo-Saxon deviant is Simon, who habitually hides in a clump of bushes to stare through his binoculars at a housewife in a nearby cottage. He also hides in a tunnel he has been digging under the garden behind his sister's house and has been gradually moving his most important possessions into a subterranean chamber. Simon narrates half of the chapters, alternating with Josh, an unschooled young gypsy who works as gardener for Simon's sister Audrey. Audrey is a widow with artistic pretensions and is attracted to Josh, who in turn is attracted to Marion, Audrey's maid. This story line also involves Josh's sinister "educated" friend Mortimer and a rapist named Lionel, and the various love stories end unhappily. The main interest of the novel is Simon, the lunatic digger and inspired voyeur. He is, in his way, an artist or perhaps even a visionary. His problem is the mobility—the constant flux—of everything he watches so intensely: it will not stand still for him to focus on it sufficiently. He stares at insects, plants, and birds as well as the housewife, but they all move and ruin the experience.

Stanley Reynolds in the 24 April 1970 *New Statesman* remarked that although a summary of the novel's plot "must sound awful," nevertheless "the novel is a success." The review focused on Simon's voyeurism and concluded with the insight that "Barry Unsworth is perhaps more akin to modern kinetic artists than to contemporary writers." The *Times Literary Supplement,* on the other hand, gave the book a generally unsympathetic review on 28 May 1970. Granting that the "writing is both delicate and resourceful," the reviewer said that the characters "are conspicuously unreal behind the mask of [Unsworth's] clever prose, grotesques enacting oddly unmoving rituals of contrived and gratuitous nastiness."

In 1970 Unsworth brought his family back to England. They lived for most of the next decade in Cambridge, where Unsworth periodically taught at the Lennox Cook School of English, a private institution providing language instruction for foreigners. Both kinetic art and nastiness figure in *Mooncranker's Gift,* the 1973 novel that gave Unsworth undoubted critical success in the form of the Heinemann Fiction Award (after three novels that had provided a total of only £500 in royalties); in the following year he was elected a fellow of the Royal Society of Literature. The gift in the title of the book is a crucifix with the figure of Jesus made of sausages wrapped in bandages. The recipient of the gift is thirteen-year-old James Farnaby, who is going through a phase of pubescent religiosity that finds expression in ritual masturbation in a secluded garden before the crucifix, which was given to him by his middle-aged neighbor, Mr. Mooncranker. When he returns to the garden one day, Farnaby finds the sausages rotting and crawling with worms. He experiences angst compounded of guilt and fear, which ends his religious interests and gives him a sense of having been betrayed by the whole adult world.

The story of the gift is supplied in a flashback; the novel actually begins ten years later, when Farnaby is in Istanbul working on a thesis about Ottoman finance and again encounters Mooncranker, now an elderly alcoholic. Miranda, who ten years earlier had been the fifteen-year-old object of Farnaby's sublimated sexual interests, has just resigned as Mooncranker's secretary and mistress and departed for a spa in the Turkish interior, and Farnaby pursues her. The rest of the novel takes place there among an eccentric and tragicomic collection of mostly foreign hotel guests, who interact in primarily sexual ways with frequent frustration and considerable mutual incomprehension. One of the spa's guests is a German photographer named Plopl who, in language reminiscent of Simon in *The Hide,* talks endlessly about how he tries in his (usually pornographic) art to impose stasis and focus on the constant flux of life. The mythic associations and landscape of the hotel's healing thermal pool in the mountains are clearly symbolic, and at the end of the novel Farnaby comes to terms with his past and looks forward to a future with Miranda.

Unsworth's apparently unhappy experiences at the Lennox Cook School provided material for his next novel, *The Big Day,* published in 1976. The setting is the Regional College of Further Studies, a proprietary institution that awards baccalaureate degrees to almost any student, usually from overseas, who can pay the tuition. Cuthbertson, the college's founder and principal, is fond of making speeches about its importance and filling advertising copy with pompous clichés about the value of higher education. The "big day" of the title is the fortieth birthday of Mr. Cuthbertson's neglected wife Laura, who celebrates with a costume party at which she determinedly attempts to seduce anybody she can corner. The festivities are interrupted by a terrorist bomb, placing the comic idiocies of the college in the broader context of worldwide political violence in the 1970s.

Some of the comedy in the novel comes from the fraudulent absurdities of the college and—by extension—of higher education and capitalism in general. Even more is derived from the problems ill prepared foreign students have with the English language, a subject on which by this time Unsworth had stored up many funny anecdotes. Valentine Cunningham, writing in the 17 December 1976 *Times Literary Supplement,* praised the novel's unusual success as a black comedy: unlike even Evelyn Waugh's *Vile Bodies* (1930), he argued, *The Big Day* "is not least distinguished by its managing, on the whole, to fit its two tones together." On the other hand, he thinks that the character of Laura Cuthbertson is too tragically real "for her more comic destiny."

In the late 1970s Unsworth held an Arts Council creative writing fellowship at Charlotte Mason College, Ambleside. Looking a bit further into his own past and, for the first time, also into the historical past, he set his next (and perhaps best) novel, *Pascali's Island* (1980), on an island in the Aegean in 1908, during the few days just before and after the revolt of the Young Turks against the last Ottoman sultan. The entire novel is ostensibly a single monthly report to the sultan from his informer Basil Pascali, who has served for eighteen years on an unnamed island off the Turkish coast, where a corrupt pasha and his brutal garrison attempt, with uneven success, to contain the activities of Greek guerrillas in the interior. Pascali believes that this report will be his last because the Greeks have discovered his treachery, and he is particularly troubled by the fact that none of his previous reports seems to have accomplished anything. The suspicion grows that nobody is reading them; and since the sultan is addressed in quasi-religious language as the shadow of God on earth, the lack of response makes Pascali an existential anti-hero in an empty universe. He is also an artist who admits that he has been embroidering

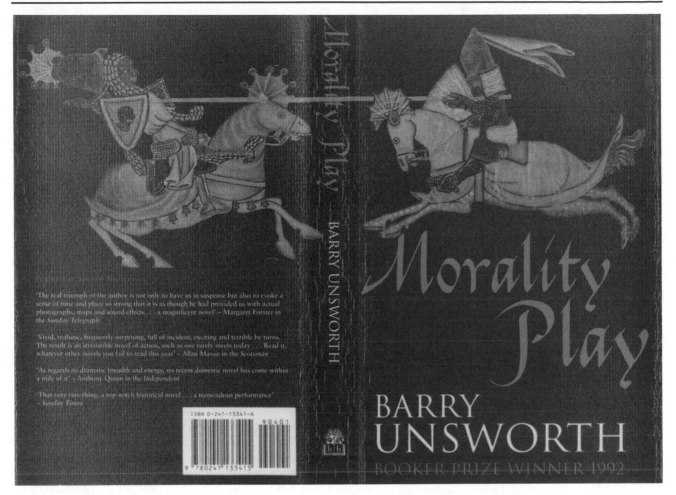

Dust jacket for Unsworth's historical novel about a fourteenth-century lapsed priest who sets out to solve a murder

the truth to create a better story; eventually he makes so many confessions that he realizes he can never send this report to the sultan. Most of the letter is devoted to the machinations of a seemingly honorable Englishman named Anthony Bowles, who has apparently come to the island to steal an ancient bronze statue that is buried in the hills. Bowles employs Pascali to assist him in disingenuous negotiations with the suspicious pasha, and a complicated series of masquerades and betrayals ultimately results in a nocturnal raid on Bowles's excavations, just as the statue is being hoisted out of the ground. The Turks open fire, killing Bowles and Lydia Neuman, an artist who is the subject of Pascali's romantic fantasies. The statue falls and breaks, leaving Pascali with "nothing really but questions . . . of fact, questions of interpretation." Bowles and Lydia remain mysteries, as does exactly what they were doing with the statue and what will happen to Pascali now that the sultan has been deposed.

This novel was not widely reviewed, but notices were all quite favorable. Michael Malone in the *New*

York Times Book Review (11 January 1981) praised the novel as a "marvelous lapidary creation," while a short notice in *The New Yorker* (23 February 1981) remarked on its "almost Conradian richness" and noted that "in the curious relationship of Pascali and the Englishman there is an interesting intimation of 'The Secret Sharer.'" The novel received its greatest praise, however, when it was short-listed for the Booker Prize. Other novels on that year's shortlist included Anthony Burgess's *Earthly Powers* and William Golding's *Rites of Passage* (which eventually won); being in such company substantially enhanced Unsworth's status as a writer. A motion-picture version of *Pascali's Island* appeared in 1988, with Ben Kingsley in the role of Pascali, Charles Dance as Bowles, and Helen Mirren as Lydia. James Dearden directed and wrote the screenplay for the movie, which was reasonably successful with critics but not at the box office.

The Rage of the Vulture (1982) in a sense repeats the same story from other perspectives. In the earlier novel the sultan seems to represent a god to whom prayers are useless since he seems not to exist. The second novel begins with Sultan Abdul Hamid, godlike in his hilltop palace, peering down through a telescope at Constantinople in the last year of his reign. At one point his gaze lights upon a garden party at the home of Capt. Robert Markham of the British Military Commission. Meanwhile, the captain's ten-year-old son, Henry, is hiding in the summerhouse spying on his father's guests as his father gazes up at the palace, plotting vengeance on his enemy the sultan. Like Simon, Plopl, and Pascali, these three characters are voyeurs or spies; and the chapters in the first half of the novel are seen from their individual perspectives. The sultan is spying on everybody who threatens either his empire or his life and is shown reading reports from spies like Pascali. In 1896, to distract popular attention from his misgovernment, he had instigated the massacre of an estimated 250,000 Armenians, one of whom was Robert Markham's fiancée Miriam. On the night of their engagement party she was raped and murdered before his eyes, while he saved himself by shouting that he was a British subject. Like Mitsos and James Farnaby, he is haunted by this horror from his past. Now, with British wife, son, and army commission, he has returned to Constantinople seeking healing and revenge.

The vultures in the novel's title are all the groups who seek to feed on the moribund Ottoman Empire, including the European powers, the revolutionary Young Turks, and even Armenian conspirators who seek an independent homeland. The domestic world of young Henry Markham and the public world of Sultan Hamid are both inhabited by Capt. Robert Markham, who spends the four hundred-plus pages of the novel trying to redeem his act of personal treason twelve years earlier. He has never told anybody about Miriam but needs to be understood by someone, ultimately confessing to a venal and reactionary Moslem journalist a few minutes before the journalist's murder by Armenian terrorists. Framed for this murder, Markham tries (unsuccessfully) to kill the sultan; after being horribly tortured he returns to England. An epilogue dated 1915 finds him there; his son is now serving on the western front, and Markham, now indifferent to almost everything, is reading about the new Armenian atrocities of the Young Turks and writing a vast, labyrinthine book about Balkan history and race theory. This novel lacks the compact elegance and sustained tension of *Pascali's Island,* but it is ambitious and engrossing and was favorably reviewed. *The New Yorker* (14 March 1983) praised it as "a very fine and haunting tale"; Thomas R. Edwards in the *New York Times Book Review* (13 March 1983) called it "a beautifully honest story of how life is both given

point and thwarted by its concern for self-definition through political commitment" and praises Unsworth "for having told it so scrupulously and vividly."

From 1982 to 1984 Unsworth was Northern Arts Literary Fellow at the Universities of Durham and Newcastle, and in 1984–1985 he was writer in residence at Liverpool University. In the early 1980s Unsworth made an extended visit to Venice to research its history, and this city replaces Constantinople as the setting of his next novel, *Stone Virgin,* published in 1985. Like Constantinople, Venice is the decaying scene of vanished imperial splendor; and like several other historical novels published in the 1980s, *Stone Virgin* moves back and forth among several time periods, specifically 1972, 1793, and 1432. All the narratives are united by a stone statue of the Virgin Mary at the moment when she learns that she is to be the mother of Christ. The novel begins and ends with the statue's fifteenth-century sculptor, Girolamo, imprisoned for the murder of his lover Bianca, a beautiful prostitute who served as the model for the virgin. In the last chapter it is revealed that Bianca was actually murdered by another lover, Federico Fornarini, a great feudal lord motivated by jealousy, who has framed Girolamo and visits him in his dungeon to gloat, as Girolamo looks forward to a painful death consoled by the realization that the statue will survive him.

The eighteenth-century story concerns Ziani, an aged and impoverished Cassanova-like aristocrat, who is composing his scandalous memoirs in the last decade of the Venetian Republic. He has now reached the events of 1743, a year in which he seduced (or was seduced by) Francesca, the young wife of his elderly nouveau riche employer Boccadoro. The seduction is, in a sense, brought about by the Stone Virgin, which was then in the garden of Boccadoro's palazzo, having been rejected for ecclesiastical purposes because of its scandalous history. The statue now glows with a preternatural light, and Francesca becomes more passionate and daring in its presence.

Most of the novel deals with Simon Raikes, a failed modern sculptor who has made a successful career in the less demanding field of restoring weathered statuary. He has been commissioned to remove the "bemonstering accretions of time and chemical pollution" from the surface of the Stone Virgin, which is now located on the facade of a church, thirty-two feet above the ground. As he proceeds with the painstaking work of restoration, Simon begins to experience hallucinations, visions of the dead Bianca floating in a canal and a general state of intense sexual excitement. Fearing that he might one day fall from the scaffolding as a result of these spells, he consults a neurologist, leading to various thoughts about the relationship of art and reality. This theme, which was introduced by the other Simon in *The Hide,* by Plopl's discussions of photography, and by the statue in *Pascali's Island,* would continue to appear in later Unsworth novels. Raikes also meets his own Bianca—or Francesca—in the person of Chiara, a descendant of Federico Fornarini and now the wife of a reclusive sculptor who lives on an isolated island in the Lagoon. When Chiara's husband dies mysteriously while she and Simon are making love—at her suggestion—in a hotel in Venice, Simon fears that she has arranged their romance simply to provide herself with an alibi and perhaps even the opportunity to frame him. Along with the question of the relationship of art to reality, the novel considers the masculine tendency to see women as either whores or Madonnas.

Reviews were mixed. Francis King, in a mostly favorable review in the 24 August 1986 issue of *The Spectator,* complained that the supernatural aspects of the novel "strained my credulity" but called Unsworth "a master stylist" and compares the novel, in form and theme, to the work of Lawrence Durrell. Katha Pollitt, on the other hand, in the 6 April 1986 *New York Times Book Review,* complimented Unsworth for his imaginative topic and vivid depiction of the statue but complained about faulty structure, a melodramatic prose style, and flat, stereotypical characters.

The late 1980s seem to have been difficult years for Unsworth. He had been publishing novels for more than two decades to generally good reviews, but major success had eluded him, and he seemed to have peaked in 1980. He felt little sympathy for the era of Margaret Thatcher; moreover, his daughters were growing up, and his marriage was breaking up. Viewing himself as a working-class liberal, he had never been entirely comfortable with the exotic settings and generally upper-middle-class characters in his novels, so the idea of a novel set in Liverpool and dealing with the iniquities of the slave trade was doubly appealing. As he said in a 1992 interview with Susannah Hunnewell, the glorification of the entrepreneurial spirit in Britain in the 1980s seemed to make that decade like the eighteenth century in its confident acquisitiveness. But the novel proved difficult to write, ultimately taking six years, though it would eventually result in his greatest success.

In the meantime he set it aside to make a lesser novel out of his difficulties in writing the major one. The result was *Sugar and Rum* (1988), which deals with Clive Benson, a novelist with writer's block who is doing research for a planned novel about the slave trade and who makes ends meet by hiring himself out as a creative-writing teacher to a series of unpromising

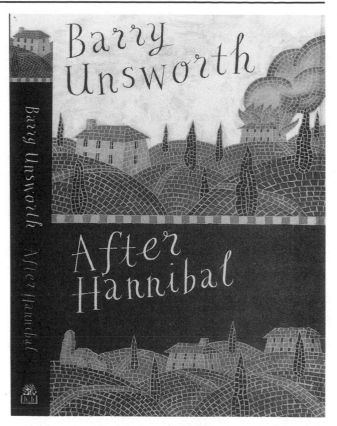

Dust jacket for Unsworth's novel about expatriates lving in the Umbrian countryside

misfits, whose failures mirror his own. The novel begins with Benson witnessing the suicidal leap of a black man from a high-rise, includes riots in Liverpool's black ghetto, emphasizes the decay of this once great maritime city, and concludes with two of Benson's old regimental comrades from World War II, one now a beggar and the other a brutally successful businessman. The novel is a protest against what Benson calls the "callous and short-sighted government," which he blames for anything that goes wrong in anybody's life. It was reviewed neither widely nor favorably, and it was the first Unsworth novel since *The Hide* that was not brought out in an American edition. The brief notice in the 7 October 1988 *Times Educational Supplement* praised Unsworth as "a writer of unusual depth and insight" but continued with the now familiar criticism that adding the "comic farce" of the creative-writing students to the tragic "Baudelairean city" of Liverpool "makes for an unsuccessful hybrid" and added that the novel "bears all the marks of having been written in all the haste of urgency."

In June 1987 Unsworth had moved to Scandinavia, where he would live for five years—first in Sweden and then in Finland. In Sweden he held a British Council visiting scholarship in 1988 at Lund University, where he did research on the eighteenth century and the slave trade. In Finland he finally finished *Sacred Hunger* (1992); there he also married Aira Pohjanvaara-Buffa in 1992 after his first marriage was dissolved in 1991. When *Sacred Hunger* won the Booker Prize in 1992, Unsworth finally achieved the literary recognition that had eluded him for so many years. This massive novel deals primarily with two cousins, Matthew Paris, a disgraced physician, and Erasmus Kemp, a wealthy merchant's son, both of whom, in a fashion familiar to readers of Unsworth, are haunted by traumatic experiences. As the novel opens, Paris has recently been condemned to the pillory for imprudently forcing his evolutionary theories on the bishop of Norwich, and his wife Ruth has miscarried and died when a mob ransacked their house. Now at the end of his tether, Paris signs on as surgeon to *The Liverpool Merchant,* the new ship that Erasmus's father is building for the slave trade. The descriptions of the slave trade are graphic and horrible, with Captain Thurso, "a simple man, being an incarnation, really, of the profit motive," becoming progressively more insane and more brutal; he eventually brings on a mutiny when he decides that the slaves will never live through the voyage and should be drowned so that 30 percent of their value can be collected through insurance fraud.

This mutiny occurs near the end of book one, which is set in 1752–1753. In this section attention alternates between Erasmus Kemp's comfortable world and the desperate one inhabited by Paris and the other members of the ship's crew, both before and after sailing. Erasmus is courting the daughter of a prosperous merchant and thus becomes unwillingly involved in her amateur theatrical rehearsals of *The Enchanted Island* (1690), Sir William Davenant and John Dryden's revision of William Shakespeare's *The Tempest* (1623). When *The Liverpool Merchant* fails to arrive in America with its cargo of slaves, it is assumed to have sunk. Erasmus's father, facing bankruptcy, commits suicide; Erasmus, now disgraced and traumatized, loses his fiancée and must spend the next twelve years paying his father's debts through marrying an unattractive heiress and working his way ruthlessly to the top of the sugar trade. Book 2, set in 1765, brings him the discovery that *The Liverpool Merchant* is not sunk but is, in fact, hidden in a dry streambed in southern Florida, where the mutinous crew and the slaves have established a utopian community in the jungle. Guided by a Rousseauistic French painter named Delblanc, who had joined the ship in Africa, they practice polyandry, egalitarianism, and racial harmony but have difficulty overcoming recalcitrant human nature. As Erasmus Kemp and British troops from St.

Augustine close in, Paris has already realized that his enchanted isle, complete with a Caliban-like sailor named Calley, shows signs of becoming another fallen Eden. Eventually the surviving mutineers are all hanged and the Africans and children enslaved, and the novel concludes with the exultations of Erasmus Kemp, whose belief in the absolute rightness of his own conduct, the sacredness of his hunger for wealth and power, is one of the most disturbing aspects of the story.

Reviewers were all enthusiastic about this enormous and somber novel. Janet Barron in the *New Statesman & Society* (16 October 1992) praised the novel for being "philosophical in its conception, teeming with the scents and sounds of the eighteenth century," and also "very much a reading of history from the E. P. Thompson perspective." Thomas Flanagan, writing in the *New York Times Book Review* (19 July 1992), began by calling the novel "wonderful and heartbreaking" and concluded that it "is a book of grace and meditative elegance, and of great moral seriousness."

After finishing *Sacred Hunger*, Unsworth had moved to Italy, settling in the Umbrian countryside near Perugia; his next novel, *Morality Play* (1995), is, however, set near his birthplace in the northeast of England. Like *Pascali's Island,* it is a fairly short historical novel narrated in the first person by a single character, here Nicholas Barber, a young runaway priest in the fourteenth century. Like other Unsworth characters, he is first seen hiding and spying on other people, in this case on a troupe of actors, one of whom is dying. He takes the dead man's place as the actors travel to Durham to perform at Christmas. Like Farnaby, Captain Markham, Pascali, and Simon Raikes, he sees himself as a failure and is troubled by guilt, in his case for having committed fornication and abandoned the priesthood. His redemption comes through the solution of the murder mystery that is central to the plot and has led this novel to be compared to such works as Umberto Eco's *The Name of the Rose* (1981) and Ellis Peters's Brother Cadfael stories.

When the players arrive in an unnamed town somewhere between York and Durham, they hear that a local boy named Thomas Wells has been robbed and murdered by a young woman. After they perform the *Play of Adam* at a local inn for a small and uninterested audience, their leader suggests that they need a new kind of play. The lavish productions of the town guilds now outclass performances of traditional plays by traveling players, he argues, and their only hope is to draw their subjects from contemporary life, specifically the murder of Thomas Wells. In gathering information for this play, they decide that the

In matters of this sort she never was.

3

** *and expressed it in the accents of the privileged. Apart from anything else, it impressed the people he did business with*

Harold stared. "So it is," he said after a moment. "A shrewd observation, sweetheart. April the 12th, 1995." He glanced at his watch. "Local time 8.43."

"No," she said. "I was talking about the poem you just quoted from. Its 'Oh, to be in England now that April's there'. Not Spring."

Harold thought briefly of disputing this. It was not that he ~~thought~~ *believed* Cecilia might be wrong. ~~His was an~~ *like all* intensely competitive ~~nature and~~ *people* he had learned ~~long ago~~ to *cede* ~~make grants~~ of land that lay beyond hope of conquest *and teh* He had assigned the marginal territories of literature and art to his wife from the early days of their marriage. Indeed he was proud to have a wife who possessed such exotic knowledge. ** But to be caught out, to be corrected, that was a different matter. He glanced quickly at his wife's face. Small-boned, softly molded, rather squeamish about the mouth, it bore the loving expression it always did when she felt she was making him a gift. She said, "Browning, the poet's name."

"Well, I know that much," Harold lied, and smiled his tight smile again. Spring, April, what the hell?" he said.

They were dressed and ready for breakfast, but Harold had paused to admire the view, thus naturally requiring that Cecilia should pause too. He was giving *en* to counting his blessings which in practice meant listing *the* his assets, natural enough in one who had made quite a lot of money buying and selling them in the form of residential and office properties in Dockland London.

The view from their holiday villa in Umbria, recently acquired, came under the heading of asset, without a doubt, since a man in some measure possesses what he can see from his house and also of course it has a bearing on the market value of the property considered as a whole. Harold, partly to assuage the chagrin his blunder had occasioned him, found himself making - yet again - an inventory: there was the curve of the road, the ancient olives, the stiff green shoots of the half-grown maize. Above this the land rose in terraces of vines, bare still between their tall posts. Then the beautiful

Page from the manuscript for After Hannibal *(Collection of Barry Unsworth)*

boy was murdered by a priest employed at the castle that dominates the town; the woman was framed because her father is a troublesome religious radical. After considerable discussion of the relation of art to truth, the company performs the play for a large and enthusiastic audience but is arrested and taken to the castle, where Nicholas discovers that the priest had merely been a procurer for the son of de Guise, the local lord. This young knight, who had seemed to be the flower of chivalry, is actually a homicidal pederast and is infected with the plague to boot. Rather oddly for an Unsworth novel, this story ends with Nicholas escaping from the castle and succeeding in bringing about some limited justice by telling his story to the king's magistrate, who finds this murder a useful weapon to use against de Guise. The power structure remains corrupt, but at least the woman is exonerated; the actors are freed; and Nicholas returns to the church.

Morality Play was short-listed for the Booker Prize and widely and favorably reviewed. Harry Mount in *The Spectator* (23 September 1995) complained about the unconvincing medievalisms of Nicholas's speech but praised the mystery story, calling it "tight and sophisticated enough to grip to the end." Janet Burroway in the 12 November 1995 *New York Times Book Review* was troubled by the discrepancy between the novel's somber tone and happy ending but concluded that it is "a bravura performance." Bernard O'Donoghue, in the *Times Literary Supplement* (8 September 1995), called it "a parable for our times, like those of Golding and Conrad" and, rather improbably, judged it "Unsworth's best book yet."

Unsworth's most recent novel is *After Hannibal*, published in late 1996. Most of its characters are neighbors, usually expatriates, living in the Umbrian countryside outside Perugia, like Unsworth himself. The Greens are an unworldly retired American couple who have bought a dilapidated farmhouse, which is being badly renovated by Stan Blemish, a predatory British confidence man who is himself trying to finance a ghastly faux-medieval restaurant for his wife. Anders Ritter is that familiar Unsworth character, a man haunted by debilitating youthful trauma, in his case the realization that some careless words to his father during World War II had resulted in the arrest and probable execution of his childhood friend by German troops in Rome. Monti is an Italian historian who has been abandoned by his wife and wanders around Perugia examining medieval and Renaissance buildings in the hope of discovering the truth about the brutal historical characters who constructed or inhabited them. Fabio is a former race-car driver who has been abandoned by his homosexual lover Arturo, who is trying to swindle him out of his house and land. Cecilia Chapman is an artistically inclined Englishwoman who, at the end of the novel, abandons her aggressive, materialistic husband Harold, who is himself engaged in a bitter legal dispute with their Umbrian neighbors, the Checchetti family, over the responsibility for the destruction of a stone wall. All of these characters (except the Checchettis) have come after Hannibal as invaders of Umbria, and almost all of them have occasion to consult the devious lawyer Mancini, who resembles Abdul-Hamid as he sets in motion all sorts of strategies which he watches from a safe distance.

The concept of the house as an expression of personality, as the embodiment of dreams, is central to this novel, and the earthquake that destroys the Greens' already undermined house suggests the fragility of these dreams. The focus on the layers of history that lie beneath the current landscape is also characteristic of Unsworth's fiction. While clearing his land Ritter finds signs of a guerrilla skirmish during the last days of World War II. When Monti drives through the countryside he visits the scene of Hannibal's victory at Lake Trasimene, and Harold Chapman feels like Hannibal as he watches the Checchettis through his binoculars, an act which reminds us of the long line of furtive watchers in Unsworth's fiction. Critical reaction to this relatively slight novel reflects perhaps more of Unsworth's current high stature than the actual merits of the book. The *Times Literary Supplement* called it "a beautifully written novel"; *The Spectator* (24 August 1996) concluded: "There's very little a reviewer need say about his fiction, except: read it."

As of 1998 Barry Unsworth's career is on an upswing. Between 1993 and 1996 Norton published paperback editions of seven of his novels and a new hardcover edition of *The Hide*. Unsworth is still living in Umbria, trying to negotiate motion-picture contracts for *Sacred Hunger,* and *Morality Play* and writing a novel about Lord Nelson. As an author, he has usually been at his best with historical subjects, and since he has so often been compared to nautical writers like Conrad, this new novel sounds quite promising.

Interview:

Susannah Hunnewell, "Utopia Then and Now,"*New York Times Book Review*, 19 July 1992, p.23.

Marina Warner
(9 November 1946 –   )

Kari Boyd McBride
University of Arizona

BOOKS: *The Dragon Empress: The Life and Times of Tz'u-hsi, Empress Dowager of China, 1835–1908* (London: Weidenfeld & Nicolson, 1972; New York: Macmillan, 1972);

Alone of All Her Sex: The Myth and the Cult of the Virgin Mary (London: Weidenfeld & Nicolson, 1976; New York: Vintage, 1983);

In a Dark Wood (London: Weidenfeld & Nicolson; New York: Knopf, 1977);

The Crack in the Teacup: Britain in the 20th Century (London: Deutsch; New York: Clarion, 1979);

Queen Victoria's Sketchbook (London: Macmillan; New York: Crown, 1979);

Joan of Arc: The Image of Female Heroism (London: Weidenfeld & Nicolson; New York: Knopf, 1981);

The Impossible Day (London: Methuen, 1981);

The Impossible Night (London: Methuen, 1981);

The Skating Party (London: Weidenfeld & Nicolson, 1982; New York: Atheneum, 1984);

The Impossible Bath (London: Methuen, 1982);

The Impossible Rocket (London: Methuen, 1982);

The Wobbly Tooth (London: Deutsch, 1984);

Monuments and Maidens: The Allegory of the Female Form (London: Weidenfeld & Nicolson; New York: Atheneum, 1985);

The Lost Father (London: Chatto & Windus, 1988; New York: Simon & Schuster, 1989);

Into the Dangerous World: Some Reflections on Childhood and Its Costs, Counterblast 5 (London: Chatto & Windus, 1989);

The Absent Mother, or, Women Against Women in the Old Wives' Tale (Hilversum: Verloren, 1991);

Indigo, or Mapping the Waters (London: Chatto & Windus; New York: Simon & Schuster, 1992);

L'Atalante (London: British Film Institute, 1993; Bloomington: Indiana University Press, 1994);

Mermaids in the Basement (London: Chatto & Windus, 1993);

Managing Monsters: Six Myths of Our Time (London: Vintage, 1994); republished as *Six Myths of Our*

Marina Warner (photograph by Ifeoma Onyefull)

Time: Little Angels, Little Monsters, Beautiful Beasts, and More (New York: Vintage, 1994);

From the Beast to the Blonde: On Fairy Tales and Their Tellers (London: Chatto & Windus, 1994; New York: Farrar Straus Giroux, 1995).

PLAY PRODUCTIONS: *The Queen of Sheba's Legs,* libretto by Warner, music by Julian Grant, London, English National Opera Bayliss Programme, 1992;

In the House of Crossed Desires, libretto by Warner, music by John Woolrich, toured Britain July–December 1996.

MOTION PICTURES: *Joan of Arc,* screenplay by Warner, 1984;

Cinderella, screenplay by Warner, 1986;

Imaginary Women, screenplay by Warner, 1986.

TELEVISION SCRIPT: *Tell Me More,* Channel 4, 1991.

OTHER: Christine de Pizan, *The Book of the City of Ladies,* translated by E. J. Richards, introduction by Warner (New York: Persea Books, 1982);

"In the Garden of Delights: Helen Chadwick's 'Of Mutability,'" in *Helen Chadwick* [exhibition catalogue] (London, 1986); republished in *Enfleshings,* by Helen Chadwick (London: Secker & Warburg, 1989; New York: Aperture, 1989);

Leonora Carrington, *The House of Fear: Notes from Down Below,* introduction by Warner (New York: Dutton, 1988; London: Virago, 1988);

Carrington, *The Seventh Horse and Other Stories,* introduction by Warner (New York: Dutton, 1988; London: Virago, 1988);

"Fighting Talk," in *The State of the Language,* edited by Leonard Michaels and Christopher Ricks (London: Faber & Faber, 1989), pp. 100–109;

"Personification and the Idealization of the Feminine," in *Medievalism in American Culture,* edited by Bernard Rosenthal and Paul E. Szarmach (New York: Center for Medieval and Early Renaissance Studies, 1989), pp. 85–111;

"Signs of the Fifth Element," in *The Tree of Life* [catalogue], South Bank Centre Touring Exhibition (London, 1989);

"The First Epistle of Paul the Apostle to Timothy," in *Incarnation: Contemporary Writers on the New Testament,* edited by Alfred Corn (New York: Viking, 1990), pp. 76–82;

"Laughter and Hope in the Old Wives' Tale," in *La Cenerentola* [program], Royal Opera House (London, 1991);

"Leonora Carrington's Spirit Bestiary; or, The Art of Playing Make-Believe," in *Leonora Carrington* [catalogue] (London, 1991);

The Second Virago Book of Fairy Tales, edited by Angela Carter, introduction by Warner (London: Virago, 1992);

"Rich Pickings," in *The Agony and the Ego: The Art and Strategy of Fiction Writing Explored,* edited by Clare Boylan (London: Penguin, 1993), pp. 27–33;

"A Sense of Things," in *Richard Wentworth* [catalogue for traveling exhibition] (London: Serpentine Gallery, 1993; New York: Thames & Hudson, 1994);

"The Uses of Enchantment," "Through a Child's Eyes," and "Women Against Women in the Old Wives' Tales," in *Cinema and the Realms of Enchantment: Lectures, Seminars and Essays by Marina Warner and Others,* edited by Duncan Petrie (London: British Film Institute, 1993), pp. 13–84;

Wonder Tales: Six Tales of Enchantment, edited by Warner (London, Chatto & Windus; New York: Farrar Straus Giroux, 1994);

"Angela Carter: Bottle Blonde, Double Drab," in *Flesh and the Mirror: Essays on the Art of Angela Carter,* edited by L. Sage (London: Virago, 1994);

"The Searcher of the Woods," in *David Nash: Voyages and Vessels* [exhibition catalogue], edited by Graham William John Beal (Omaha: Joslyn Art Museum, 1994);

"The Rebel at the Heart of the Joker: Bobby Baker," in *Take a Peek* [performance catalogue], Royal Festival Hall (London, 1995);

"Through the Narrow Door," in *David Nash: Forms Into Time* (London: Academy Editions, 1996), pp. 8–24;

The Trial of Joan of Arc, introduction by Warner (Evesham: Arthur James, 1996).

SELECTED PERIODICAL PUBLICATIONS– UNCOLLECTED: "The Wronged Daughter," *Grand Street,* 7 (1988): 143–163;

"Bush Natural/Wie die Welden," *Parkett,* 27 (1991): 6–21;

"Penis Plenty Phallic Lack: Exit Mister Punch/Füllhorn Penis oder phallische Leere: Abtritt Mister Punch," *Parkett,* 33 (1992): 8–19;

"Marlene Dumas: In the Charnel House of Love/ Marlene Dumas: Im Beinhaus der Liebe," *Parkett,* 38 (1993): 76–87;

"Stolen Shadows, Lost Souls: Body and Soul in Photography," *Raritan: A Quarterly Review,* 15 (1995): 35–58;

"Annals of Religion: Blood and Tears," *New Yorker,* 72 (8 April 1996): 63–69.

Marina Warner, cultural critic, novelist, historian, and children's author, has made significant contributions to fields as diverse as religious studies, contemporary art, and the history of the fairy tale. Her fiction has ranged over many genres, from novels and short stories to children's books, movie scripts, and opera librettos. Her work appears in a variety of venues and media, including popular and scholarly journals, television, and exhibition catalogues. Uniting this remarkably creative and various corpus is an interest in women: the mythic figures of history, such as Joan of Arc, the Empress Dowager of China, and Queen Victoria; the heroines of fairy tale and story, such as Mother Goose and the Queen of Sheba; women as symbols, from the Virgin Mary to the Little Old Lady of Threadneedle Street; and the ordinary women

Dust jacket for Warner's feminist history of the fairy tale

who populate the streets, lanes, and boulevards of her novels and short stories. Warner's fiction provides the reader with a challenging and ultimately satisfying combination of writerly prose; strongly drawn, complex characters; compelling plots; and an erudite handling of history. Her books have been translated into many languages, and she has held several prestigious visiting lectureships at universities around the world. She has received numerous awards for her literature; *The Lost Father* was nominated for the Booker Prize in 1988 and won the Regional Commonwealth Writers' Prize and the PEN/Macmillan Silver Pen Award.

Marina Sarah Warner was born on 9 November 1946 in London to an Italian mother and a British father: Emilia Terzulli Warner, a teacher, and Esmond Pelham Warner, a bookseller. She was educated at Les Dames de Marie in Brussels (1953–1959) and then at St. Mary's convent in Berkshire (1959–1963). She was runner-up for the W. H. Smith Children's Poetry Prize in 1964. She studied at Lady Margaret Hall, Oxford, taking a B.A. in Modern Languages (French and Italian) in 1967 and an M.A. in 1968. While at Oxford, Warner was the editor of the University magazine, *Isis*. She continued to work as a journalist following her graduation, freelancing for the *Daily Telegraph Magazine* (1967–1970), working as features editor

for *Vogue* (1970–1972), and publishing in many journals and newspapers at this time. From 1970 to 1975 Warner worked in broadcasting as well. Warner was named Young Writer of the Year in 1971 by *The Daily Telegraph;* early in 1972 she married William Shawcross, a journalist, by whom she had one son, Conrad. That marriage was dissolved, and she married John Dewe Mathews, a painter, in 1981.

Warner's first books were studies in cultural criticism and history. *The Dragon Empress: The Life and Times of Tz'u-hsi, Empress Dowager of China 1835–1908* (1972) proved to be a precursor of many of her later works, offering rich detail and cultural critique. The book provides a portrait of this remarkable woman who began as a concubine and outlived both the emperor and her royal son to become a key player in the international games of diplomacy between French, English, and Chinese interests fighting to control political power, the opium trade, and religion. The book combines perceptive insights about the anomalous position of a politically powerful woman with an almost voyeuristic fascination with the minutiae of everyday life, from diet to dress to sexual practice. The book received polite reviews praising its journalistic handling of secondary materials, its readability, and its generous illustrations.

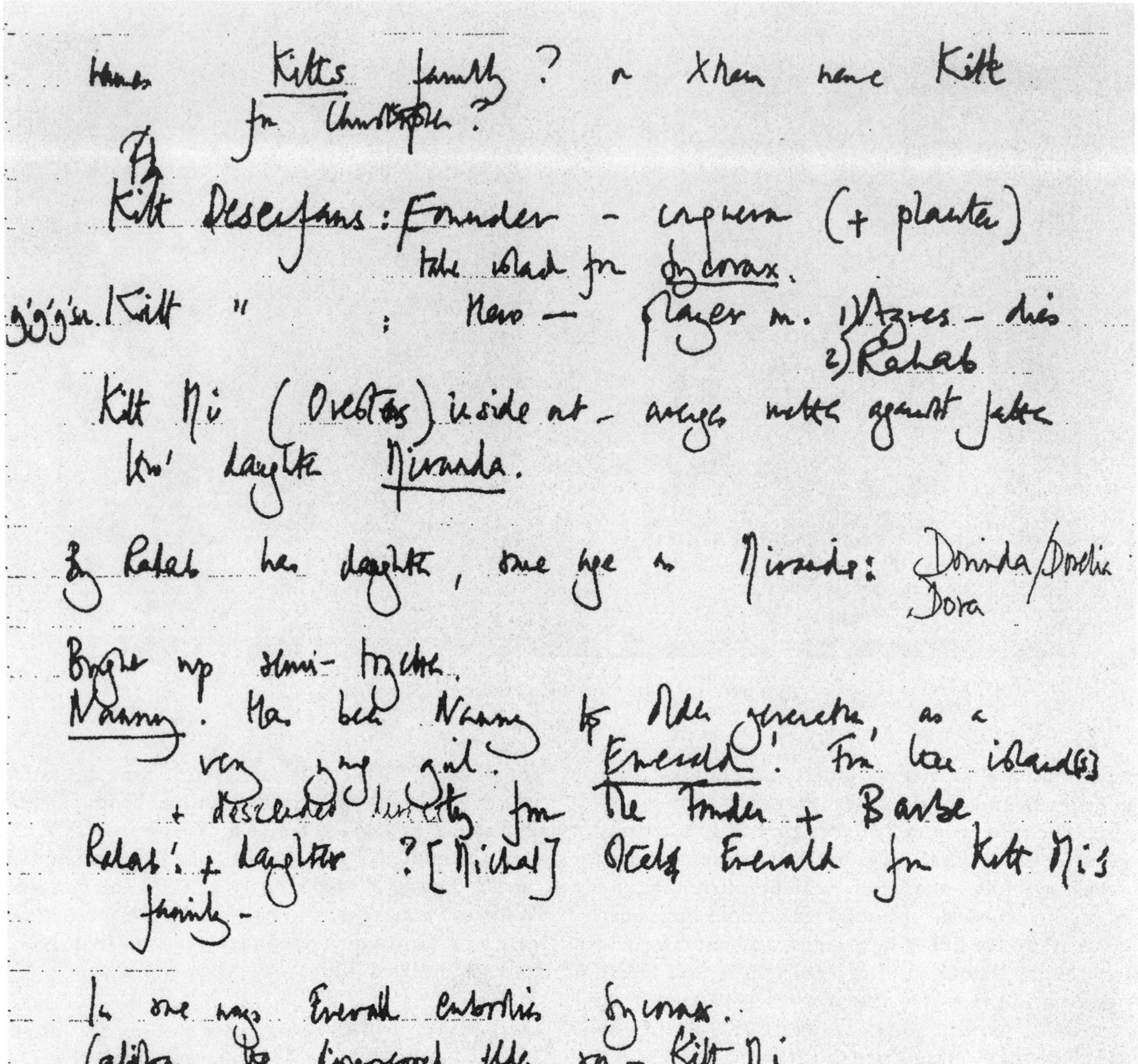

[Handwritten notes, partially legible]

Kitts family? a then name Kitt
for Christopher?

Kitt Descendants: Founder — conqueror (+ planter)
take island from Sycorax.

[illegible] Kitt   "   ;   Heir — player m. 1) Azores — dies
2) Rahab

Kitt [Ni] (Overseas) inside [out] — avenger works against false
[knowing] daughter _Miranda_.

By Rahab her daughter, same age as Miranda: Dorinda/Dorelia
Dora

Brings up semi-together.
Nanny: Has been Nanny to older generation, as a
very young girl. Emerald! From the island(s)
+ descended [directly] from the Founder + Barbe.
Rahab's + daughter ? [Michael] Otello Emerald for Kitt Ni's
family —

In one way Emerald establishes Sycorax.
Caliban the imprisoned slave son — Kitt Ni.

Who should be the Learner?

Pages from Warner's notes for her novel Indigo *(Collection of Marina Warner)*

Fine Arts: Would it be possible to lecture on, like
The Tempest? I'm building in the island: The first
nodes :   •   childhood of Hero
            •   son of Hero — touching foot —
   No   •   rage in fog / race ? (day out)
            •   2 girls hang the — grown-up.
            •   building of island + open day in garden.

_____

Make produce her own organ? A stimulant into
     another name? cf. opium?
2 experts: the game of the subsistence, — acid drink made
from potatoes = "Nicknobby" or "Hobby" or "Naby"
    Tom I — takes island for Sycorax. C

native mother looks like dies too — ?
does

— Sycorax witch taking of Thomas / Kitt

Her body is returned by her people: tree grows, opens
for bones, which promises storage; Emerald now at loss
     to strengthen her charges?
Nurses what part in Rebel's daughter?
Or raises her to be avenger?

This book was followed by the work for which she is best known in academic circles, *Alone of All Her Sex: The Myth and the Cult of the Virgin Mary* (1976). Against the emerging opinion of some feminist theologians, Warner argued that despite the significance of the Virgin Mary as archetypal symbol of female divine empowerment, she serves as a poor model for women's actual positioning and voice in the church and in society because she, "alone of all her sex," is both virgin and mother; all other women fall short. Rather than a model for empowerment, Warner suggests that the Virgin Mary has been used as a tool against women in the service of clerical hierarchy and dominance. Furthermore, any impact the quasi-deification of Mary may have had on the social, political, or religious position of women is now moot, for the myth embodied in the Virgin Mary is no longer functional in the modern world.

Critics praised Warner's painstaking scholarship but faulted her for her critique of the Catholic Church. Garry Wills, in the 24 October 1976 *New York Times Book Review,* accused Warner of "show[ing] an eye for conspiracy to shame the most devout critics of the Warren Commission." He also criticized the book's attention to the artifacts of devotion to the Virgin, calling it "a kind of Hebraic fervor in reverse on the subject of graven images–she would save all the statues, and only smash the Ideal." However, Joan M. Ferrante, in *The Nation* (11 September 1976) found the book's detail an asset: "the work is never dry or tedious because the material is so fascinating." Warner's book has become a standard reference for the study of the cult of the Virgin; in addition it has had a significant impact on the development of Christian feminist theologies and inspired similar scholarly treatments of other religious icons, including Mary Magdalene.

In 1979 Warner published her first children's book, *The Crack in the Teacup: Britain in the 20th Century,* a volume written at the zenith of the socialist/welfare state for the "Mirror of Britain" series of histories for young readers. As is typical of Warner's works, the book teems with material detail and anecdotes of everyday life and is lavishly illustrated with quotations and photographs. Warner's thesis articulates an indictment of the racism inherent in empire and of the class structure that continues to organize the political life of Britain in the twentieth century. The book was praised for its attention to detail and its readability but faulted for its insularity and social and socialist focus. That same year Warner edited *Queen Victoria's Sketchbook,* the first edition ever of the queen's private journals and their watercolor illustrations recording her extraordinary life. Culled from more than fifty albums and sketchbooks kept "with infectious enthusiasm" from 1832 until her death in 1901, the words and images counter the image of the queen "in perpetual mourning," and Warner was praised for presenting this resuscitated portrait of the queen.

The late 1970s saw the appearance of Warner's first novels. *In a Dark Wood* (1977), which moves between the worlds of seventeenth-century China and contemporary London, combines Warner's interest in religion, history, sexuality, and mythology. It tells the story of the Namier family, focusing on Gabriel Namier, a Jesuit priest whose life and scholarship intersect with a seventeenth-century Jesuit missionary whose biography Namier is writing. Warner's faithful chronicling of 1970s fads and issues (astrology, early feminism) never translates into clichés; rather, her characters remain complex and the plot compelling. At the time reviewers faulted the novel for ostentatious erudition, which Jane Larkin Crain, in the 11 December 1977 *New York Times Book Review* described as "everywhere on proud display in the pages of her novel." Both Crain and Susan Kennedy, writing in the *Times Literary Supplement* (17 June 1977), called the novel's structure "schematic," and Kennedy faulted Warner's characters, who, she said, "exist in a polished world of their own."

The Skating Party (1982), Warner's second novel, also juxtaposes differing eras and cultures, exploring myths of gender and sexuality. The party of the title, hosted by Michael Lovage, a university don, serves as a device for gathering characters–including Viola, his wife, his son, his mistress, and fellow professors–whose braided histories and tidy relationships, revealed in flashback, ravel in the course of the evening. Renaissance frescoes, newly discovered in the Vatican and being studied by Viola, provide commentary on the complex human relationships linking the characters and on the assumptions of contemporary culture. The novel was compared to those of Iris Murdoch and was praised for its skillful plotting, characterization, and lyrical descriptions.

Between 1981 and 1984 Warner wrote a series of children's books with illustrations by Malcolm Livingstone: *The Impossible Day* and *The Impossible Night* (both 1981), *The Impossible Bath* and *The Impossible Rocket* (both 1982), and *The Wobbly Tooth* (1984). During those same years Warner published several short stories in literary journals. Throughout the 1980s Warner continued her prodigious output of publications on art, history, and contemporary culture in the *Times Literary Supplement,* the *London Review of Books,* the *New York Times Book Review, Lettre Internationale,* and other venues. She also wrote intro-

Dust jacket for Warner's novel about the devastation produced by colonialism

ductions for many exhibition catalogues and performances and interviewed contemporary news makers and artists such as Isabel Allende.

The 1980s also saw the publication of two well-received works of cultural criticism, one a study of the significance of an historical woman and the other an investigation into the femaleness of certain allegories. In *Joan of Arc: The Image of Female Heroism* (1981) Warner took up the historical figure to whom she would return repeatedly (in a 1984 motion-picture screenplay and in 1996 with the introduction to the transcripts of the trial of Joan of Arc). Here, as part of her ongoing project to study female types both in history and in mythology, the author argues persuasively that Joan of Arc inhabits a nearly unique position in Western history as she was not a queen, a courtesan, an exceptional beauty, a mother, an artist, or (until this century) a saint. Further, she is unusual in that her heroism belongs to the arena of action rather than the more traditionally female spheres of contemplation or domesticity. Her fame thus expands the taxonomy of female types. The book was favorably received. Julia Epstein, writing in *The Nation* (30 May 1981), called Warner's portrait "a persuasive iconological inter-

pretation of Joan's meaning in history and of her spiritual and representational authority." In *Monuments and Maidens: The Allegory of the Female Form* (1985), Warner describes the disjunction between the reality of historical women's subordinated lives and the way female images have been given allegorical power. The book ranges impressively over a wide selection of these images, from the Statue of Liberty to Hildegard of Bingen's *Sapientia*, from Margaret Thatcher to the women of Gresham Common, from Judith to the Little Old Lady of Threadneedle Street.

Like all of Warner's works of cultural criticism, this one is extravagantly documented. However, the book received mixed reviews, praised by Sara Maitland in *The New Statesman* (1 November 1995) as a resource valuable for its treasure trove of information and coherent argument but criticized by Maureen Mullarkey, writing in *The Nation* (11 January 1986), as "pseudofeminist umbrage" and "bad feminism" and by Mary Lefkowitz in the 20 December 1985 *Times Literary Supplement* for engaging in "over-interpretation" that misses the significance of "simple and universal values." Fiona McCarthy, in a 24 October 1985 notice in *The Times*

(London), called it "the most ambitious and best of Marina Warner's studies of female symbolism," and Lucy Lippard in the *Washington Post Book World* (19 January 1986) noted that "the importance of *Monuments and Maidens* is the way it encourages us to read symbolically the art and media images with which we are surrounded."

Warner's next novel, *The Lost Father* (1988), written in 1987–1988 while Warner was a Getty Scholar at the Getty Center for the History of Art and the Humanities, is a postmodern tour de force demanding an engaged, equally postmodern reader—a many voiced, hybrid work with a foregrounded narrative structure that flaunts and flouts novelistic conventions. Warner chronicles the attempts of Anna, an English novelist, to reconstruct the life of her Italian grandfather (and, through him, her own identity) through letters, newspaper reports, family stories, and her own memories, all of which prove to be both "true" and profoundly misleading. The novel enjoyed a generally positive reception; though Carole Angier, writing in the 16 September 1988 *New Statesman,* found its foregrounding of form awkward and its characters "too many" and "too literary," Lorna Sage, in the *Times Literary Supplement* (16 September 1988), praised it as a "moving" and "bookish" work, and Ann Cornelisen commended Warner (in the 7 May 1988 *New York Times Book Review*) for "add[ing] new dimensions and perspectives to the role of the domestic myth in our imaginations." *The Lost Father* was short-listed for the Booker Prize and won the Regional Commonwealth Writers' Prize and the PEN/Macmillan Silver Pen Award.

A sojourn in 1991 at Erasmus University, Rotterdam, where Warner was Tinbergen professor, allowed her to begin work on a long-term project exploring the history and significance of fairy tales. *The Absent Mother, or, Women Against Women in the Old Wives' Tale* (1991) is the text of her public lecture delivered at the university and lays out her plan for a larger project that would ultimately be realized in a wide variety of works in the 1990s. Warner's editing of *Wonder Tales: Six Tales of Enchantment* (1994) makes available six French tales by six women writers who lived in the Paris of Louis XIV, as translated by six contemporary scholars (including A. S. Byatt). Warner's introduction delineates common themes and suggests ways in which the tales comment on domestic issues of the era ("men and matrimony") as well as court politics and foreign policy. In *Managing Monsters: Six Myths of Our Time* (1994), Warner turned to an examination of contemporary "fairy tales." The six essays of the volume, each detailing a modern myth, were originally delivered on radio programs as part of the BBC's annual Reith Lectures. The book takes up various cultural myths (for example, "boys will be boys,") and vocabulary productive of myth (for example, "liberal") and examines both how we "manage" the power of such myths and how they provide essential tools for living. The book was well received and praised for its style as well as its insights on contemporary culture. An exploration of fairy tales in the movies, Warner's *L'Atalante* (1993) provides critical commentary on Jean Vigo's 1934 motion picture of the same name and compares Vigo's treatment of mythic themes with those of other French surrealist directors.

Warner's work with fairy tales culminated in 1994 with *From the Beast to the Blonde: On Fairy Tales and Their Tellers,* a study tracing the history of the genre from its classic origins. Most important is the way in which Warner articulates the link between women and fairy tales in their roles as mythic makers and tellers of the tales (for example, Mother Goose) and their roles within the tales as hags and princesses, absent mothers and stepmothers, daughters and fairy godmothers, showing how narratives by (sometimes) and about women have both enabled and undermined female autonomy. The book has been widely and enthusiastically reviewed though often the attention called to its feminist perspective has the effect of diminishing its significance. The reviewer in the summer 1996 *Virginia Quarterly Review* called it "a brilliant scholarly work" and "essential reading for specialists and anyone interested in the genre from a feminist point of view." Nicholas Tucker, in the *New Statesman* (11 November 1994), noted that while "Warner's feminist position may not be the whole answer," it is nonetheless "constantly enlightening" and a "brilliant work." At the same time he calls her critique of a Disney version of a fairy tale (which she condemned for "naturalizing female, and especially maternal, malignancy in the imagination of children") "slightly unhinged."

In the midst of these various and far-reaching cultural studies Warner has continued to publish fiction. Her fourth novel, *Indigo, or Mapping the Waters* (1992) revisits the cultural map first charted in William Shakespeare's *The Tempest* (1623). Like Warner's other novels, this one explores the relationship between past and present: the generations of the Everard family, from their origin on the Caribbean island of Enfant-Beate as European colonists to their lives in present-day London. The novel effects its time-traveling magic through postmodern conventions, exposing the devastation of colonialism through a carnival of voices. The novel received fine reviews. Though Louis B. Jones, in the *New York Times Book Review* (13 September 1992), argued that "Warner succeeds only half the time in the novelist's peculiar witchery of shifting shape to get inside the skin of her characters," he praised the way in which "the intimate cruelty of a modern English family [is] portrayed with the joyful vengeance, the specificity, of art." Harriett Gilbert, in the 28 February 1992 *New Statesman,* called the book "a wonderfully intricate maze of narratives, arguments, [and] themes." David Nokes, writing in the *Times Literary Supplement* of 21 February 1992, compared the work to Jean Rhys's *Wide Sargasso Sea* (1966), calling Warner's novel "an extraordinary imaginative achievement, a work at once mythopoeic and iconoclastic."

Warner continues to publish at a prodigious rate, not only major works but also an astonishing number and range of short stories, reviews, and essays in scholarly and popular journals. *Cinema and the Realms of Enchantment* (1993) includes three essays based on seminars offered by the British Film Institute, where Warner was a visiting fellow. *Mermaids in the Basement* (1993) is a collection of short stories (gathered from individual publication in a variety of journals) about the pressures and possibilities of women's lives. The stories show Warner a confident storyteller in many voices—working class, academic, even biblical—and several contexts: contemporary, historical, and mythic. She also publishes increasingly on contemporary art, in journals, exhibition catalogues, and book introductions, notably "A Sense of Things" in *Richard Wentworth* (1993) and "Through the Narrow Door" in *David Nash: Forms Into Time* (1996). In 1996 Warner and composer John Woolrich collaborated to produce a short opera based on the classical writer Apuleius's *The Golden Ass.* Titled *In the House of Crossed Desires,* the opera toured England, receiving disappointing reviews. Her growing reputation in literary and academic circles won her an honorary D. Litt. from the University of Exeter in 1995. In addition she has served on the National Council for One-Parent Families, the Advisory Council for the British Library, and other civic and cultural boards.

Warner has taken a research fellowship at Trinity College Cambridge for 1998 in order to complete another novel. The year will also see the publication of a new critical study, *No Go the Bogeyman: On Scaring, Lulling and Making Mock.* Thus Warner continues her remarkable pace of production in both fiction and cultural criticism, providing perceptive commentary on phenomena that often go unnoticed while reflecting in another mode, through her novels, on the contemporary human experience.

Interviews:

Lisa Appignanesi, "Marina Warner, with Lisa Appignanesi," *Guardian Writers in Conversation,* 54 (Northbrook, Ill.: ICA Video, 1989);

David Dabydeen, "Marina Warner," *Kunapipi,* 14 (1992): 115–23;

Dabydeen, "Spinning a Yarn with Marina Warner," *Kunapipi,* 16 (1994): 519–529.

References:

Todd Richard, "The Retrieval of Unheard Voices in British Postmodernist Fiction: A. S. Byatt and Marina Warner," in *Liminal Postmodernisms: The Postmodern, the (Post-)Colonial, and the (Post-)Feminist,* edited by Theo D'haen and Hans Bertens (Amsterdam: Rodopi, 1994), pp. 99–114;

Chantal Zubus, "What Next Miranda?: Marina Warner's *Indigo,*" *Kunapipi,* 16 (1994): 81–92.

Auberon Waugh
(17 November 1939 –)

Merritt Moseley
University of North Carolina at Asheville

See also the Waugh entry in *DLB 14: British Novelists Since 1960.*

BOOKS: *The Foxglove Saga* (London: Chapman & Hall, 1960; New York: Simon & Schuster, 1961);

Path of Dalliance (London: Chapman & Hall, 1963; New York: Simon & Schuster, 1964);

Who Are the Violets Now? (London: Chapman & Hall, 1965; New York: Simon & Schuster, 1966);

Consider the Lilies (London: M. Joseph, 1968; Boston: Little, Brown, 1969);

Biafra: Britain's Shame, by Waugh and Suzanne Cronjé (London: M. Joseph, 1969);

A Bed of Flowers; or As You Like It (London: M. Joseph, 1972);

Country Topics (London: M. Joseph, 1974);

Four Crowded Years: The Diaries of Auberon Waugh, 1972–1976, edited by N. R. Galli (London: Deutsch, 1976);

In the Lion's Den: Fifty Essays (London: M. Joseph, 1978);

The Last Word: An Eye-witness Account of the Trial of Jeremy Thorpe (London: M. Joseph, 1980; Boston: Little, Brown, 1980);

Auberon Waugh's Yearbook: A News Summary and Press Digest of 1980 (London: Pan, 1981);

A Turbulent Decade: The Diaries of Auberon Waugh, 1976–1985, edited by Anna Galli-Pahlavi (London: Deutsch, 1985);

Another Voice: An Alternative Anatomy of Britain (London: Firethorn Press, 1986); republished as *Brideshead Benighted* (Boston: Little, Brown, 1986);

The Entertaining Book, by Waugh and Teresa Waugh (London: Hamish Hamilton, 1986);

Waugh on Wine, edited by Jan Fry (London: Fourth Estate, 1986);

Will This Do? The First Fifty Years of Auberon Waugh: An Autobiography (London: Century, 1991);

Crash the Ash: Some Joy for the Beleaguered Smoker (London: Quiller, 1994);

Way of the World (London: Century, 1994);

Auberon Waugh

Way of the World: The Forgotten Years, 1995–1996 (London: Century, 1997).

OTHER: *The Literary Review Anthology of Real Poetry,* edited by Waugh (Southampton: Ashford, Buchan & Enright, 1990).

Auberon Waugh is an important figure in the world of postwar British letters, the author of five novels that comprise only part of his claim to critical attention. He published his first novel, *The Foxglove Saga* (1960), at the age of twenty-one; a precocious book somewhat in the vein of his father, Evelyn, it was followed by four more in eleven years. Since that time he has published no more novels, turning his attention instead to public affairs, the changes in contemporary culture (usually, in his view, its deterioration), and literary issues addressed from the point of view of a reviewer or editor rather than a novelist. He has a powerful and distinctive voice and stance. Arguably his most lasting achievement will be his invention of the mock diary, which is a form of fiction even if not a conventional novel.

Auberon Alexander Waugh was born on 17 November 1939 in Dulverton, Somerset, England. His father was the famous novelist and journalist Evelyn Waugh; his mother was Evelyn's second wife, Laura Herbert Waugh. Waugh's father was middle-class, though upwardly mobile; his mother was descended from nobility. Auberon, who has been enlisted in the class war all his life on the anti-proletarian side, writes in his 1991 autobiography, *Will This Do? The First Fifty Years of Auberon Waugh:* "Perhaps only professional snobs will be able to derive much enlightenment from my mother's pedigree, and not even they can hope to experience quite the same degree of satisfaction as I do when I contemplate it." There were seven children in the family; Auberon was the second, and the first son. Auberon has written about his father's indifference, amounting to active hostility, to all the Waugh children—an indifference readily evident in Evelyn's published letters and diaries and reciprocated by the children. Auberon writes of his feelings at age five for his father: "I would gladly have swapped him for a bosun's whistle" (although they did grow closer once Auberon was grown up and a writer himself). His mother was more interested in her cows than in her children.

The Waughs were Roman Catholic (Evelyn a celebrated convert), and Auberon's education was in Catholic schools—Old Hallows, a prep school in Somerset, followed by Downside, a public school. There he earned an exhibition (in American terminology, a scholarship) to Christ Church, Oxford, but deferred his matriculation in favor of doing his national service, then required for all British men. He became an officer in the Royal Horse Guards. On service during a civil conflict in Cyprus, he accidentally machine-gunned himself. As he describes it in his autobiography:

> I had noticed an impediment in the elevation of the machine gun on my armoured car, and used the opportunity of our taking up positions to dismount, seize the barrel from in front and give it a good wiggle. A split second later I realized that it had started firing. No sooner had I noticed this, than I observed with dismay that it was firing into my chest. Moving aside pretty sharpish, I walked to the back of the armoured car and lay down, but not before I had received six bullets—four through the chest and shoulder, one through the arm, one through the left hand.

As a result of his wounds, which were expected to be fatal, Waugh lost a lung, his spleen, and a finger and brought down on himself a long hospitalization and recovery and considerable pain in later life.

After nine months in the hospital and some time at the family home, Combe Florey, in Somerset, he went to Bologna, Italy, with a friend and lived there in a bohemian way for some months. During this time he wrote his first novel, using his own experiences in boarding school, the army, and the hospital. In 1959 Waugh went up to Oxford. His college was Christ Church, one of the grander ones, of which Sebastian Flyte was an ornament in Evelyn's *Brideshead Revisited* (1945). He did little work while at Oxford and left after his first year. By this time he had submitted his first novel, *The Foxglove Saga,* to Chapman and Hall, also his father's publisher, and it was accepted. Since the age of twenty Waugh has made his living as a writer.

The Foxglove Saga tells the story of Martin Foxglove, who has all of the advantages of life, and his relations with another boy, Kenneth Stoat, who is ugly, unappealing, and unfortunate. Since Martin is a creature of unconsidered privilege, some readers have thought that the relatively unsympathetic treatment of him might mean that the author sympathized with the unfortunate Kenneth, but this interpretation does not seem to be the case. The novel satirizes all sorts of people and activities. Like Evelyn Waugh's novels, this one abounds in a sort of affectless treatment of shocking events. The story opens with a group of monks discussing the imminent death of one of their number; in a worldly, not very religious way, they are interested only in who will get his typewriter and his special mattress.

Martin and Kenneth move through a Catholic boarding school, the army, and a convalescent facility, permitting readers to assume that the novel is a fantasia on its author's experiences at Downside, in the Guards, and recovering from the wounds received in Cyprus. In *Will This Do?* Waugh has confirmed this assumption, expressing regret that a "more experienced novelist would have made three novels of it, but it is always the way of first novelists to squander their material." The ending hurries through later events in the characters' lives with slightly facetious haste.

The reviews of *The Foxglove Saga* were mixed; some of Evelyn Waugh's friends, including Graham Greene and John Betjeman, contributed glowing blurbs, while other reviewers complained of the supposed advantages its twenty-one-year-old author had derived from his father's celebrity. That it was published by Evelyn's own publisher, and appeared in the same year as a revised edition of *Brideshead Revisited*, invited comparisons. Both novels feature paired protagonists, one of whom is a gilded youth and the other less favored, though the tone is very different. *The Foxglove Saga* is much more like early Evelyn Waugh, the author of *Decline and Fall* (1928). In both, the comedy is accompanied by studied outrageousness.

The Foxglove Saga sold fourteen thousand copies in paperback, a large sale. Waugh had a good income, and on 1 July 1961 he married Teresa Onslow, daughter of the earl of Onslow. They have four children. In the family tradition (besides Evelyn Waugh, Auberon's uncle and sister wrote novels), his wife and children are writers: Teresa, Sophia, and Daisy write novels, while Alexander and Nathaniel wrote a prizewinning musical, *Bon Voyage,* in 1996.

Between 1963 and 1972 Waugh wrote four more novels. His second, *Path of Dalliance* (1963), received bad reviews, in part because it was about Oxford and invited comparisons with *Brideshead Revisited. Paths of Dalliance* moved (as its author had done) from school, army, and recuperation to university. It centers on a young man named Jamey Sligger who (like Waugh) is sent down after a year at Oxford. In a relationship similar to that of Kenneth Stoat and Martin Foxglove, Jamey is the less privileged and somewhat overlooked friend of a boy named Frazer-Robinson, who is always treated well because his family is rich. Both have come from a cranky old Catholic school called Cleeve. Jamey and Frazer-Robinson become involved in university politics and in sponsoring a show by a fraudulent artist from London. A girl with whom they are friendly dies, and Jamey is expelled from Oxford for no good reason. He goes to live with his mother, a comic eccentric; meanwhile his brother, who has been in prison, brings home a fellow inmate with whom Mrs. Sligger falls in love. Waugh has said that Mrs. Sligger, a parody of unthinking liberalism, was based on Shirley Williams, a Liberal member of Parliament. whom he blamed for destroying the state school system. Like his creator, Jamey eventually goes into journalism in London.

In the background is an odd conspiratorial story about a priest at Cleeve named Rapey Rawley but nicknamed "Creepy Crawley" who corresponds with a network of Cleeve boys, all of whom spy on each other and give him information which he uses in unsavory ways. Part of the flavor of the book—its sometimes rather sophomoric humor—may be found in Creepy Crawley's name, the group name "the Rapists" for his acolytes, and the name of one character, Mrs. Droppings.

In 1965 the author's third, and least successful, novel appeared. *Who Are the Violets Now?* is built up out of the conditions of the author's life at the time. As a "special writer" for the Mirror Group, Waugh had been assigned to research and write a special report on "Women at Work" for *Women's Own*. This job made him answerable to the editor of that magazine, whom he describes in *Will This Do?* as his "smirking, blue-haired, violet-scented persecutor." He spent his time at his desk in the Mirror building writing *Who Are the Violets Now?*, which, as he describes it in *Will This Do?*, "is about a poor young hack journalist working for a woman's magazine whose editor sucks violet tablets until his hair goes blue."

The problems with this novel stem from its author's rather reckless satire on political postures, which overwhelms the episodic plot. The protagonist, Arthur Friendship, works for *Woman's Dream* magazine and spends his evenings working for Education

Dust jacket for the U.S. edition of Waugh's first novel, the story of two boys, one fortunate and attractive, the other unlucky and ugly for Peace. He is a foolish idealist mocked—or rather destroyed—by events. The leader of Education for Peace turns out to be a Nazi who is eventually kidnapped and taken to Israel for trial. Arthur loves Elizabeth Pedal, who in turn falls in love with a crudely caricatured American black activist and poet named Thomas Gray (usually referred to as "Toe-mass" and broadly caricatured as a demagogue). Arthur heroically goes into a burning room to save a baby but accidentally saves no more than a bundle of laundry while completely disfiguring himself; and when, on the strength of a promotion to writing the Pet's Corner column, he sets out to propose to Liz Pedal, he is killed in a car wreck. Waugh's satirical targets include black people, attitudes toward black people, women's magazines, heroism, politics, men, and women. Reviewers sometimes complain that Waugh's novels are unsatisfactory because the author despises everyone in them and gives the reader no moral center. This judgment comes closest to being true of *Where Are the Violets Now?*

Consider the Lilies, which appeared in 1968, is Waugh's best novel. Narrated by a modern Anglican clergyman named Nicholas Trumpeter, it humorously dramatizes the emptiness, as the author presents it, of modern liberal Christianity. Waugh has frequently denounced modern trends in Roman Catholicism; here his focus is on the established Church of England. Trumpeter has become a priest because it is the easiest path to a comfortable living. He spends almost all of his time reading Erle Stanley Gardner in his study, though he complains of his heavy burdens. He preaches sermons on topics such as the dangers of flammable nighties and finally develops a preoccupation with his belief that the world suffers from an anal obsession. The remainder of the clergymen in this book are just as bad: one thinks he is Jesus Christ; another refuses to conduct any services at all, even on Easter; a third is exclusively interested in pets.

Trumpeter is not just a bad minister; he is an evil man, though in the affectless way of Waugh's villains. He conducts an affair with the daughter of his patron, a millionaire named Mr. Boissaens, while fending off Boissaens's randy wife. He considers killing off his own inconvenient wife, but this action turns out not to be necessary.

Waugh's last novel, *A Bed of Flowers; or As You Like It* (1972), has a more thoroughly constructed plot than his others and is more topical, referring quite emphatically to the civil war in Nigeria which pitted the central government against the rebel province of Biafra. Waugh had strong convictions about Biafra, naming his fourth child Nathaniel Thomas Biafra Waugh and collaborating on a book called *Biafra: Britain's*

Dust jacket for the U.S. edition of Waugh's novel tracing the career of a young man from school, through the army, to Oxford

Shame (1969). His critique of the Labour government for its support of the Nigerian regime against the Biafrans is incorporated into the time scheme of *A Bed of Flowers;* it begins on the night of Harold Wilson's election as prime minister in 1966 and ends with the election of Edward Heath in 1970.

The plot is partly derived from William Shakespeare's *As You Like It* (circa 1599–1600), including characters named Oliver, Orlando, Rosalind, and Celia while incorporating some gender confusion—Orlando takes bad acid and becomes unable to tell that Rosalind is a girl. The central characters are a group of hippies who retreat into Somerset. There is a mystical-religious flavor to the book, partly governed by the proximity of the retreat to the legend-filled town of Glastonbury and partly by the fact that the hippies discover the Holy Grail but bury it again. Rather surprising for the generally conservative Waugh, this novel makes the hippies into sympathetic characters, while the representatives of status, power, and wealth are the bad people. This treatment is partly because the hippies all champion the cause of

Auberon Waugh

DLB 194

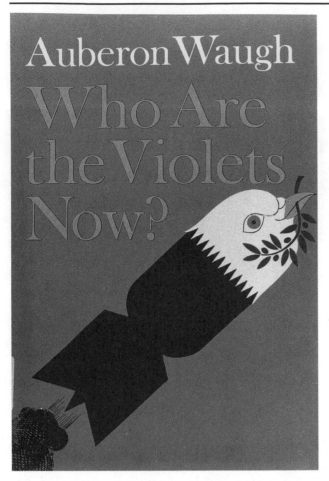

Dust jacket for the U.S. edition of Waugh's satirical novel about a woman's-magazine writer whose foolish idealism destroys him

the Biafrans while the establishment opposes them for selfish and discreditable reasons rather than on any principle.

In 1973 Waugh announced that he would publish no more novels until Parliament had enacted a Public Lending Right provision to enable authors to profit when their novels were circulated by libraries. This provision is now in place, but he has not resumed his fiction and seems unlikely now to write any more novels. The need for Public Lending Right is undoubtedly not the major reason for his fictional silence. He continues to be interested in fiction; he was for a long time one of the most influential reviewers of new novels in Britain, and in his role as editor of *The Literary Review* he not only commissions many fiction reviews but often comments on the state of the contemporary novel in his editor's column, "From the Pulpit."

Waugh's novels were most successful when they were the least didactic, or least openly didactic. His best novel, *Consider the Lilies,* depicts a whole series of deplorable human beings and actions with the lightest

of touches. Nicholas Trumpeter, the narrator, reveals himself as an unworthy man—not to mention an unworthy man of God—in all that he says; but it is hardly a revelation, as he is unashamed of his worldliness, murderous intentions, or manic obsessions. Most important, the novel is thoroughly funny.

In *A Bed of Flowers* one can see the novel going awry because of Waugh's political concerns. He professes to believe that nobody in Britain really cares about politics and to feel contempt for almost all politicians, but the structure of *A Bed of Flowers*—framed by the elections of Wilson and Heath—and even more insistently its misplaced Biafran theme tend to skew it away from Waugh's real strengths as a novelist in the direction of a political tract. His books need lightness, insouciance, and a sort of amoral playfulness, which suffer from the intrusion of serious political themes. The same flaw affects *Where Are the Violets Now?,* particularly in the unamusing depiction of the Black Power figure.

In 1960 he was hired to write for the *Daily Telegraph,* and since that time he has written columns, usually about politics, contemporary fiction, or wine, for the *Catholic Herald, The Spectator, The New Statesman,* the *News of the World,* the *Sun, The Times,* the *Sunday Telegraph,* the *Evening Standard,* the *Daily Mail,* the *Independent, Books and Bookmen,* and *British Medicine.* He has several times been named "Critic of the Year" or "Columnist of the Year"; he currently writes for the *Daily Telegraph* and the *Sunday Telegraph.* As a columnist, Waugh identifies his gift as "making the comment, at any given time, which people least wish to hear"; as a book reviewer, he is characterized by what Peter Hebblethwaite called "brusque common sense, a savage irony, and a disregard for the niceties of *lit. crit.*" This disregard for niceties includes his penchant for reviewing the author's picture on the dust jacket, suggesting, for instance, that an author looks as if he is dying of syphilis. Waugh, who has said that "the key quality in reviewing is not judiciousness or erudition or good taste, least of all is it moderation. It is liveliness of response," was identified by J. A. Sutherland as "the most influential reviewer of novels in Britain."

In 1970 he was appointed political columnist for *Private Eye,* a fortnightly magazine of satire and political commentary. Though this was neither the first nor last of Waugh's stints as a political commentator, he professes distaste for politics, calling himself an "antipolitical conservative" in *Who's Who* and writing in *Way of the World: The Forgotten Years, 1995–1996* (1997) that "nobody in Britain outside a tiny circle of misfits and deviants is interested in politics." He shortly became, instead, the diarist, contributing "Auberon Waugh's Diary" to *Private Eye* from 1972 to 1986. In the latter year he was appointed editor of the *Literary*

292

Review, a monthly periodical over which he continues to preside. He lives at Combe Florey, an impressive Georgian manor in Somerset, which his wife bought from his mother in 1971.

In addition to the book on Biafra (co-authored with Suzanne Cronjé), Waugh's nonfiction books include *The Last Word: An Eye-witness Account of the Trial of Jeremy Thorpe* (1980), an account of the murder-conspiracy trial of the leader of Britain's Liberal Party, against whom Waugh once facetiously ran for Parliament on the Dog Lovers' Party ticket; *Auberon Waugh's Yearbook: A News Summary and Press Digest of 1980* (1981); *The Entertaining Book* (1986), written with his wife, Teresa; and *Crash the Ash: Some Joy for the Beleaguered Smoker* (1994), part of his campaign against the antismoking campaign. He also edited *The Literary Review Anthology of Real Poetry* (1990), part of another campaign, this one in defense of poetry that rhymes, scans, and makes sense, a prize for which is awarded every month in the *Literary Review*. Selections from his columns have appeared in several volumes. *Country Topics* (1974) collects his contributions to the *Evening Standard* under that title, in which he wrote about "lush places." *In the Lion's Den* (1978) includes fifty essays written for *The New Statesman*. The title may allude to the odd fact of a man of Waugh's opinions finding a home at that journal, which was then the most forceful left-wing weekly in Britain. In these essays he attacks the working classes (a frequent topic in all his journalism), the ugliness of modern England, and other features of contemporary life. In one essay, "The Ghastly Truth," he writes about himself, particularly about the invitation to submit information for *Who's Who* and his decision to list his recreation then as "gossip" (it is still listed thus in the 1997 edition).

Waugh's column having moved across the political spectrum to the more conservative *Spectator,* he published a collection of these pieces in 1986 called *Another Voice: An Alternative Anatomy of Britain.* Presumably to take advantage of the popularity on American television of *Brideshead Revisited,* the book was published in the United States as *Brideshead Benighted.* There is a strong flavor of the jeremiad in these pieces, though they are never without wit. Readers will find interesting material on such subjects as "Wetness of the Middle Classes," "Smaller Genitals," and so on. One whole section is called "The Sad State of Britain" and includes such essays as "The Laziest People on Earth." He rails against prostitutes; against working-class idleness; against various aspects of the "dependency culture"; and against several other predictable, though not necessarily customary, targets. He frequently compares England unfavorably

with France, a country in which he and his family have had a second home since 1963.

Waugh has been wine correspondent for several publications, and a collection of wine columns was published in 1986 as *Waugh on Wine.* In 1990 he became a regular columnist for the *Daily Telegraph,* with "The Way of the World" appearing three times a week. Selections from these columns have been published as *Way of the World* (1994) and *Way of the World: The Forgotten Years, 1995–1996.* In the introduction to the first of these he explains how he understands his function:

> It is my contention that gloom, if genially presented, and without rancour, is an enjoyable emotion, as well as being quite plainly the best approach to our national predicament. I see my role as that of a comic, raising morale by making merry jokes as the country goes to the dogs.

Among the features of modern Britain that persuade Waugh that it is in decline are most modern fads—computers, television shows, dieting, any sort of jargon—and the proletarianizing and Americanizing of English life. In a typical column he writes about dieting:

> It destroys the brain cells and permanently impairs mental performance. It distorts moral perceptions and tends toward unsafe driving, removing all libido while making the dieter more prone to HIV and its concomitant scourge, AIDS. It adversely affects foetuses and is linked with an increase in cot deaths. It makes those who fall victim stupid, mad, ugly and boring. Death is seldom long delayed.

As part of his resistance to the spread of American popular culture Waugh has inveighed against "hamburger gases," which he blames for many modern ills, including the murders of John Lennon and President John Fitzgerald Kennedy. He elsewhere describes Chelsea Clinton as "a resplendent example of what young America is all about"—"her father is rumoured to have been eating a hamburger and watching TV when he begat her." From time to time he suggests that Vince Foster was murdered by Hillary Clinton for smoking in the White House.

Waugh's gloomy views on several contemporary English phenomena are gathered together in a column from 14 June 1996:

> Many have remarked on the sinister effect that cartoons can have on a national character. There are many wonderful things about the New World culture, but most of the things that are less wonderful can be ascribed to a mixture of Mickey Mouse and hamburgers—to which some might add mobile phones.

Mrs Quoran's dining room was not a place where the men were encouraged to hold general discussion groups after breakfast. ["It looks like war", said Mr Dent. He paid six pound ten weekly for the first floor front room, and his opinions were generally treated with some respect. The prospect of war evidently pleased him, as he blew down his pipe until it made a bubbled noise. ["Chaos has come", said Jacques. At the age of 22, he spoke as if he had just finished fighting two world wars. [Nobody wanted to know what he thought, anyway. For three guineas a week for the top floor back room, Mrs Quoran felt he should be seen but not heard. ["It's ten to nine", she said significantly. "I suppose we shall all be blown up", said Jacques moodily. [Mr Dent grunted. He obviously thought it would do the flower of a nation's youth a bit of good to be blown up. [They both looked at the third lodger, who was racing through his fried eggs. Martin Stanton was a captain in the Army Intelligence Corps. If anybody could shed some light on the morning's news, it was he. [" I must dash", he said. Capt Stanton, the only lodger at "Albany Chambers" Ebury Street, who went to work in a bowler hat, had to be at Whitehall by nine. [What do you think about this Berlin business?" said Mr Dent. ["Berlin isn't really my province", said Captain Stanton "I'm in S.E. Asia. But if you want to know what I think." He suddenly looked serious, mature and very reasonable. ' I think the Russians are just a bit peeved with us for refusing to sell them those aeroplanes. We've had six Berlin crises in the bad old days, when the Russkis were just trying it on. Nowadays, they're not such bad chaps, when you get to know them. They're hurt that we're not prepared to go as far as some in this peaceful coexistence lark, And they're showing that they can be difficult, too. Can't say I blame them." [Mrs Quoran decided that conversation...

First page of the manuscript for Who Are the Violets Now? *(Collection of Auberon Waugh)*

There has been an unexpected development in the case of an English girl said to have contracted CJD [a deadly brain disease derived from eating beef made from cows with mad cow disease] from eating hamburgers. Her friends say she has never eaten hamburgers, or any red meat, and would go to a hamburger restaurant to eat chicken burgers.

She may prove to be the first authenticated case of the baleful effects of passive hamburger eating. It seems unlikely that she has CJD, which has nothing to do with cows or meat, but she has shown many of the classic symptoms of ordinary hamburger poisoning–irrational, inarticulate violence, kicking desks in the middle of class, short temper and depression.

Mobile phones are now known to cause cancer as well as uncontrolled garrulousness. . . . scientists in Los Angeles are now embarking on a research programme to establish the consequences of passive mobile telephoning.

This is caused by sitting next to someone who is using his machine. The symptoms include irrational rage. It is thought that people can become infected even if they only shake hands with someone who has been using a mobile telephone.

Waugh's more-imaginative flights, such as his analysis of hamburger gases, and his almost quixotic stands in favor of that which everyone else is against (for instance, his suggestion that, rather than becoming more democratic, the United Kingdom should become less so by the elimination of the elected House of Commons and the expulsion from the House of Lords of everyone except hereditary peers), found even freer scope in the major accomplishment of his journalistic career, "Auberon Waugh's Diary" in *Private Eye*. The diary also freed him to enjoy his interest in untrue gossip and his gift for fantasy. He said in an unpublished interview that he believes that the diary is his greatest achievement, the one most likely to outlast his lifetime. It began in 1972 and ran until he left to edit the *Literary Review* in 1986. The diary entries were collected in two volumes: *Four Crowded Years: The Diaries of Auberon Waugh, 1972–1976* (1976), and *A Turbulent Decade: The Diaries of Auberon Waugh, 1976–1985* (1985). Though it is certainly not a novel, it may be helpful to think of the diary as an extended fiction. As he explains in *Will This Do?*:

> The essence of the "Diary," as it emerged, was that it was a work of pure fantasy, except that the characters in it were real. If ever some president or head of state paid an official visit, I was there to greet him. If ever the Queen gave a ball or luncheon party, I was there to dance with her or help her survive the terrible bores who had in fact been invited. . . . The technique, whenever possible, was to find someone who had been present and could give an amusing account of what had happened, and then stretch

Dust jacket for the U.S. edition of Waugh's novel about a corrupt Anglican priest

> and distort it, inserting myself in whichever role seemed appropriate–the sexual opportunist, the millionaire patron of the arts and learning, the M.I.5 or CIA agent, the drunk, the Thomist theologian, the confidential adviser to princes and presidents.

An entry typical in its mixture of fact with fiction is one for 11 December 1981 (included in *A Turbulent Decade*) that reads in its entirety:

> On a train journey to Durham, I sit opposite someone pretending to read the *New Statesman* and take it away from him. The man is obviously ill. He puts up no resistance.
> It is the first time I have seen this magazine for years, though I was a subscriber for 18 years before that and wrote a regular column in it for nearly three years. Today's issue has a huge photograph of Peter Tatchell: "The Purge is on. If Tatchell goes, what will be left of Labour?"
> If you have any answers to these questions, you will have to keep them to yourselves as I see the Editor no longer prints readers' letters. Probably his readers are too illiterate to write, in any case.
> Or perhaps there aren't readers left. Looking closely at the young man sitting opposite me in the train, I see he is

dead. Poor fellow, he doesn't look as if he had a very enjoyable life. I put the magazine back between his lifeless fingers and wander down to the Buffet for a thoughtful pork pie.

His tone is an odd mixture of urbanity and savagery, and he uses language that is often outrageous, calling a famous newspaper proprietor an "Elephant Man lookalike," for example, or a woman writer "the moustachioed hell-cat." In one piece (collected in *A Turbulent Decade*), writing of an election for an office in the National Union of Journalists, Waugh comments only on the "hideous faces" of the candidates: "One looks more like a pig than a human being, one like a drunken stoat; one tries hard to look like Jesus blowing bubbles, another is an obvious murderer of small children."

There is something schoolboyish about the Waugh presented here. He advises on how to use stink bombs to disrupt political meetings. He makes up nicknames for public figures (a common practice in *Private Eye*): for instance, he began calling Harold Evans, then editor of the *Sunday Times,* "Dame"—presumably because it reminded him of Dame Edith Evans—and before being forced by a lawsuit to stop referring to Evans at all, he had progressed to "Dame Twankypoo Fancyshanks, 53." He enjoys inventing rumors: that Prince Andrew has never learned to speak; that Princess Anne's son has four legs; that Lord Mountbatten was a homosexual Communist spy; that Lord Snowdon was a half-Jewish Welsh dwarf; that Marshal Tito was a woman ("My late Father claimed to have seen her once during the war breast-feeding a seal pup on the Island of Vis. 'There's nowt so queer as folks,' he remarked in his broad Lancashire accent"). Despite the occasional disclaimer—for instance, "My whole life, as this Diary shows, is a lie. All the characters in it are invented, none bears any resemblance to anyone living or dead"—he did use living people's names and was sued more than once. On one occasion he wrote about another journalist, Norah Beloff, describing her as

> delicious 78-year-old Nora Balsoff who sometimes wrote under the nom-de-plume Nora Bailiff . . . Miss Bailiff, a sister of the late Sir Alec Douglas-Home was frequently to be seen in bed with Mr Harold Wilson and senior members of the previous administration, although it is thought that nothing improper occurred.

The nickname, the ascription of a comically false age, and the reference to the "late" Douglas-Home were inadequate to prevent a legal judgment against Waugh.

Waugh may be correct in believing that he has invented a new form of fiction, the "spoof diary." In

any event it gave his imagination its greatest scope for expansion and experimentation, and the results are his best work since *Consider the Lilies.*

Waugh's autobiography, *Will This Do?,* sheds ample and useful light on his early years, the background to his novels, and his journalistic career, as well as his own ample love for his family, rather different from his childhood experience. The story is worth telling in its own right, but the tone, as usual with Waugh, provides the primary source of enjoyment. There is the usual deadpan narration of the outrageous, as when he recalls some proletarian refugees billeted in his grandmother's house during the war: "I have a memory—although it might be no more than the memory of a dream—that my self-appointed enemy among the evacuees, called Jackie, ended up being sawn in half at the Pixton sawmills. I often wondered whether I had any part in it." Despite the occasional settling of scores and the outbursts of distaste—for the "kindergarten assemblies," the "new Mickey Mouse church of Cardinal Hume and Archbishop Worlock," which is what remains of Roman Catholicism in England, for instance—this is a humane and admirable autobiography.

Waugh's output has been enormous and varied. In everything that he writes he rejects timidity and conventional thinking, saying things that are unpopular, in bad taste, or even obnoxious with an irony and a fastidiousness of style that make them enjoyable even to many readers who cannot share his convictions. He is essentially a comic writer, and his voice is distinctive in contemporary British writing.

References:

Neal Ascherson, "Beyond Discussion," *London Review of Books,* 3 April 1980;

Peter Hebblethwaite, "Son of Waugh," *America,* 126 (20 May 1972): 534–536;

Rhoda Koenig, "A Handful of Mud: Auberon Waugh's War on Manners," *Harper's,* 261 (December 1980): 86–92;

Patrick Marnham, *The Private Eye Story: The First 21 Years* (London: Deutsch, 1982);

Geoffrey Moorehouse, "At Home with the Fogey of Combe Florey," *Guardian,* 16 February 1980, p. 17;

Merritt Moseley, "Auberon Alexander Waugh," in *Encyclopedia of British Humorists,* edited by Steven H. Gale (New York: Garland, 1996), pp. 1183–1189;

J. A. Sutherland, *Fiction and the Fiction Industry* (London: Athlone Press, 1978), pp. 98–102;

A. N. Wilson, *Penfriends from Porlock* (London: Hamish Hamilton, 1988), pp. 254–266.

Fay Weldon

(22 September 1931 –   )

Ann Hancock
University of the West of England, Bristol

and

Harriet Blodgett
California State University, Stanislaus

See also the Weldon entry in *DLB 14: British Novelists Since 1960.*

BOOKS: *The Fat Woman's Joke* (London: MacGibbon & Kee, 1967); republished as . . . *And the Wife Ran Away* (New York: McKay, 1968);

Down among the Women (London: Heinemann, 1971; New York: St. Martin's Press, 1972);

Words of Advice [play] (London & New York: S. French, 1974);

Female Friends (London: Heinemann, 1975; New York: St. Martin's Press, 1975);

Remember Me (London: Hodder & Stoughton, 1976; New York: Random House, 1976);

Words of Advice [novel] (New York: Random House, 1977); republished as *Little Sisters* (London: Hodder & Stoughton, 1978);

Praxis (London: Hodder & Stoughton, 1978; New York: Summit, 1978);

Puffball (London: Hodder & Stoughton, 1980; New York: Summit, 1980);

Watching Me, Watching You (London: Hodder & Stoughton, 1981; New York: Summit, 1981);

The President's Child (London: Hodder & Stoughton, 1982; Garden City, N.Y.: Doubleday, 1983);

The Life and Loves of a She-Devil (London: Hodder & Stoughton, 1983; New York: Pantheon, 1984);

Letters to Alice: On First Reading Jane Austen (London: M. Joseph/Rainbird, 1984; New York: Taplinger, 1985);

I Love My Love: A Play (London & New York: S. French, 1984);

Polaris and Other Stories (London: Hodder & Stoughton, 1985; New York: Penguin, 1989);

Rebecca West (London & New York: Viking, 1985);

The Shrapnel Academy (London: Hodder & Stoughton, 1986; New York: Viking, 1987);

Fay Weldon (photograph by Isolde Ohlbaum)

The Hearts and Lives of Men (London: Heinemann, 1987; New York: Viking, 1988);

The Rules of Life (London: Hutchinson, 1987; New York: Harper & Row, 1987);

The Heart of the Country (London: Hutchinson, 1987; New York: Viking, 1988);

Wolf the Mechanical Dog (London: Collins, 1988);

Leader of the Band (London: Hodder & Stoughton, 1988; New York: Viking, 1989);

Party Puddle (London: Collins, 1989);

Sacred Cows, Chatto Counterblasts, no. 4 (London: Chatto & Windus, 1989);

The Cloning of Joanna May (London: Collins, 1989; New York: Viking, 1990);

Darcy's Utopia (London: Collins, 1990; New York: Viking, 1991);

Moon over Minneapolis, or, Why She Couldn't Stay (London: Collins, 1991; New York: Penguin, 1992);

Growing Rich (London & New York: HarperCollins, 1992);

Life Force (London: HarperCollins, 1992; New York: Viking, 1992);

A Question of Timing (London: Colophon, 1992);

Affliction (London: HarperCollins, 1993); published as *Trouble* (New York: Viking, 1993);

Angel, All Innocence, and Other Stories (London: Bloomsbury, 1995);

Wicked Women: A Collection of Short Stories (London: Flamingo, 1995; New York: Atlantic Monthly Press, 1997);

Splitting (London: Flamingo, 1995; New York: Atlantic Monthly Press, 1995);

Worst Fears (London: Flamingo, 1996; New York: Atlantic Monthly Press, 1996);

Big Women (London: Flamingo, 1997; New York: Atlantic Monthly Press, 1997).

PLAY PRODUCTIONS: *Permanence* (in *Mixed Doubles: An Entertainment on Marriage*), London, Comedy Theatre, 9 April 1969;

Words of Advice, Richmond (England), Orange Tree Theatre, 1 March 1974;

Friends, Richmond, Orange Tree Theatre, April 1975;

Moving House, Farnham, Redgrave Theatre, 9 June 1976;

Mr. Director, Richmond, Orange Tree Theatre, 24 March 1978, revised, 1994;

Action Replay, Birmingham Repertory Studio Theatre, 22 February 1979;

I Love My Love, Exeter, Northcott Theatre, February 1981;

After the Prize, New York, Phoenix Theatre, November 1981; produced as *Woodworm,* Melbourne, Australia, Playbox Theatre, March 1983;

Jane Eyre, adapted by Weldon, Birmingham Repertory Studio Theatre, 1986;

The Hole in the Top of the World, Richmond, Orange Tree Theatre, 1987;

Someone Like You, Cambridge Theatre Workshop Tour, 1989; London, Strand Theatre, March 1990;

Tess of the d'Urbervilles, adapted by Weldon, West Yorkshire Playhouse, 1992.

TELEVISION SCRIPTS: *The Fat Woman's Tale,* Granada, 1966;

Wife in a Blond Wig, BBC, 1966;

Office Party, Thames, 1970;

"On Trial" (episode of *Upstairs Downstairs*), London Weekend Television, 1971;

Hands, BBC, 1972;

Poor Baby, Anglia TV, 1975;

The Terrible Tale of Timothy Bagshott, BBC, 1975;

Aunt Tatty, adaptation of the Elizabeth Bowen short story, BBC, 1975;

Married Love, BBC, 1977;

Pride and Prejudice, adaptation of the Jane Austen novel, BBC, 1979;

"Watching Me, Watching You" (episode of *Leap in the Dark*), BBC, 1980;

Life for Christine, Granada, 1980;

Little Miss Perkins, London Weekend Television, 1982;

Loving Women, Granada, 1983;

Redundant, or, The Wife's Revenge, BBC, 1983;

On First Reading Jane Austen, BBC, 1985;

The Heart of the Country, BBC, 1986;

Growing Rich, Anglia TV, 1992;

Blood Relations, BBC, 1996.

RADIO SCRIPTS: *Spider,* BBC 3, 1972;

Housebreaker, BBC 3, 1973;

Mr. Fox and Mr. First, BBC 3, 1974;

The Doctor's Wife, BBC 4, 1975;

Polaris, ABC, 1977;

"Weekend" (episode of *Just Before Midnight*), BBC 4, 1979;

All the Bells of Paradise, BBC 4, 1979;

I Love My Love, BBC 4, 1981; ABC, 1983;

The Hole in the Top of the World, BBC 4, 1993;

A Hard Time to Be a Father, BBC 4, 1995;

Everyone Needs an Ancestor, BBC 4, 1995;

Heat Haze, BBC 4, 1995;

Web Central, BBC 4, 1995.

SELECTED PERIODICAL PUBLICATIONS—UNCOLLECTED: "Towards a Humorous View of the Universe," *Women's Studies: An Interdisciplinary Journal,* 15 (1988): 309–311;

"Will No One Rid Us of These Turbulent Priests?," *Times Saturday Review* (London), 20 February 1993, pp. 4–6;

"Mind at the End of its Tether," *Guardian,* 11 January 1997, p. 21.

Fay Weldon's skill at satire, wry humor, and witty prose have helped to establish her reputation as a novelist whose primary subjects are the lives and natures of women. She is also an accomplished stage, radio, and television playwright. Weldon has the feminist urge to improve women's attitudes toward themselves and their sisters and an imagination fertile in finding unusual embodiments for her independent attitudes and unsentimental values. After writing more than twenty novels and many short stories, she has achieved both critical and popular success, and her work has been translated into fifteen languages. She has acquired in her later years a considerable public persona, her image drawn no doubt from some of her more-recent fictional heroines. A gift for mythologizing is apparent in her work and no less so in her representations of herself.

Weldon was born on 22 September 1931 in the village of Alvechurch in Worcestershire as Franklin Birkinshaw though she has been known to conceal this "rather silly" first name. Her father, Frank Thornton Birkinshaw, was a physician; her mother, Margaret Jepson Birkinshaw, published two light novels in the 1930s under the pseudonym Pearl Bellair. There were better-known authors in the family as well: Weldon's grandfather, Edgar Jepson, a turn-of-the-century editor of *Vanity Fair,* was a prolific writer of best-selling romance adventures until the 1930s; her uncle, Selwyn Jepson, wrote mystery-thriller novels and movies, radio, and television plays until the 1970s. During early childhood Weldon immigrated to New Zealand with her parents, where she later attended Girls' High School in Christchurch. From the time she was six, when her parents were divorced, she lived with her mother and sister, seeing her father only during summer holidays—a circumstance reflected in her books in the preponderance of daughters reared by mothers alone. It was a difficult time for the family, as she indicated in a 6 September 1987 *Sunday Times* interview: "in deeply conventional New Zealand, we were a unit outside society; decent women were simply not divorced. . . . Outcasts!" When Weldon was fourteen, her mother received a small legacy, just sufficient for their fare home, and Weldon returned to England to live in one room in Belsize Park, London. By her account it was a period of "hardship and deprivation" in her life. It was also an intensification of living in a household of women, now with her grandmother as well as her mother and sister, besides attending a convent school, Hampstead High School in London—all of which made her feel that "the world was composed of women." She later theorized that experiencing so female a milieu since childhood had made her forever independent of the need for male approbation and therefore able to write more openly and honestly. Her environment no doubt also contributed to the diminished role

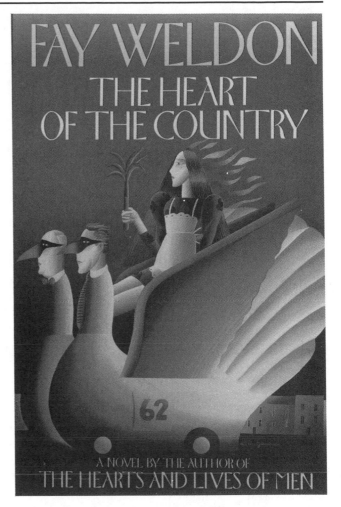

Dust jacket for the U.S. edition of Weldon's novel about a rural woman's rebellion against male domination

men play in her books. In 1949, on a scholarship, she entered St. Andrew's University in Scotland, where she earned her M.A. in economics and psychology.

By 1955 she had married a Cambridgeshire schoolteacher many years older than she and had borne her first son, Nicholas. Interviewer Hunter Davies alleges that Weldon "affects to have forgotten" her first husband's name and likewise the marriage, which was brief. Weldon tends to cast herself in the unmarried mother role that recurs in her novels. She has said, "I am all of them [my characters] to some degree," because she has known the frustrations, helplessness, feelings of compromise, and desperation she has depicted in them. By the 1950s she had already tried writing novels, but in desultory fashion, and had only accumulated rejection slips for them. With no particular professional ambitions as yet, in another period of "odd jobs and hard times," she drifted first into writing propaganda for the Foreign Office, then into doing market research and answering problem letters for the London *Daily Mirror,* and finally into composing advertising copy. She worked her way up to more prestigious firms and continued in advertising until the 1970s. Meanwhile, she remained close to her family. When her sister died of cancer in 1969, leaving three children, Weldon assisted her mother in caring for them.

In 1960 she married Ronald Weldon, a London antique dealer, with whom she had three sons "at distant intervals" (Daniel in 1963, Thomas in 1970, and Samuel in 1977). The Weldons settled in Primrose Hill, a conventional North London suburb, where they lived for some fifteen years. Weldon combined domesticity successfully with her ever-expanding writing career, which really began only in the mid 1960s. Her marriage, she felt, had finally given a focus to a life "messed up hopelessly until I met my husband." She refused to wear a wedding ring, regarding such banding as a symbolic insult to women, but she delighted in the title "Mrs.," declaring herself in many ways conventionally female and refusing to subscribe to the notion that it would be a better world for women without men. Without them, she would much later insist, "one misses the richness of life. . . . the vibes that men radiate . . . make them essential." So conventional did she seem as devoted wife and mother, despite her career, that she was invited to participate in a David Frost debate in 1971, on the assumption that she would mock the radical agitators who were currently in the British news for denouncing the Miss World contest as a flesh market. Instead she disrupted the program by hailing their efforts. Even had the Frost researchers troubled to read her first—and feminist—novel, already published by then, before inviting her to speak, they could not have predicted her stand.

Already one of the most successful advertising copywriters in England—she was responsible for the famous slogan "Go to work on an egg"—by the late 1960s Weldon was also well advanced in her career as scriptwriter (and later scenario writer) and playwright. Her one-act *Permanence* was part of a multiact play on the theme of married life, *Mixed Doubles,* which included other distinguished contributors such as Harold Pinter and was produced in London at the Comedy Theatre in 1969. And there were radio plays, such as *Spider* (1972), which won the Writer's Guild Award for best radio play in 1973; and *Polaris* (1977), which won the Giles Cooper Award for best radio play in 1978. For the BBC and English commercial networks she has written many television plays (plus movies) on a wide range of subjects. In 1971 she wrote an episode for the *Upstairs, Downstairs* series, "On Trial," which won the SFTA Award for best series. Her five-part dramatization of *Pride and Prejudice* (1979) has been praised for its fidelity to Jane Austen's manner and perceptions.

Television writing became Weldon's entry into fiction. Her first novel, the seriocomic *The Fat Woman's Joke* (1967), was originally written as a television play (*The Fat Woman's Tale,* 1966) and then overextended into a novel. But it is a skillful, if minor, work that introduces some of Weldon's typical themes and methods, and critics admired its humor. Middle-aged, tubby Esther (who will triumph without losing a pound) has left her paunchy husband Alan in the aftermath of the ill-advised crash diet they undertook to regain something of their youthful selves. While he continues to philander with his slim young secretary, Susan, Esther retreats to a dingy basement apartment where she gorges herself and testily parades her marital woes before her younger friend, Phyllis, who has sought her out. Although Esther's mother, her eighteen-year-old son, and Susan also visit this ironic Job to urge her back to her husband, Esther assents only after he enters his plea too. Meanwhile she has had somewhat of a rebirth of personality while vegetating underground, represented by the sprouting of a potted plant—Weldon often reinforces themes with symbolic objects and names, traditional analogies, and myths. Esther's too-omniscient reminiscence of the past month is told for her by a narrator, and dialogue preponderates as always in Weldon's novels. The narrator rather awkwardly interleaves in Esther's tale a separate account of the love lives of Susan's roommate and Susan, who finally prefers the son to his father.

Stout and aging in a world where youthful looks count, Esther conveys Weldon's fervent resentment of the devaluation of woman to a brainless, sexual object, a pretty and docile doll. Esther, whose sexuality has waned and in whom a more valid basis for self-respect is struggling to emerge, has seen (like Weldon) that it is a "fearful thing to be a woman in a man's world accepting masculine values" when "their opinion of womankind is . . . conditioned by fear, resentment and natural feelings of inferiority." But acknowledging women's woes while denying the right to self-indulgence over them is the distinguishing trait of a Weldon novel. Weldon will have no basking in self-pity, as Esther tries to do, or putting all the blame on men; women share in ruining lives, including their own. Whether Esther, like the reader, recognizes all the ways in which she has denied Alan's needs, trammeled her energies, and reduced her marriage to gourmet meals is not entirely clear; later Weldon heroines will be more explicit about their blameworthiness. What Esther does recognize clearly is that she needs her marriage—it is one of "those human organizations that stand between us and chaos." The marriages Weldon depicts are usually, if not invariably, failures in communion of spirit even when they occasionally succeed as sexual outlets; yet Weldon does not scorn marriage in her novels.

When she wrote *The Fat Woman's Joke,* Weldon claimed to have no knowledge of a women's movement. By the time of her more elaborately structured second novel, the satiric yet compassionate *Down among the Women* (1971), she evidently did. This book is a meditation on contemporary womanhood and an illustration of it through glimpses into the lives of the semiautobiographical Scarlet, her family, and her four girlfriends. It is told at the beginning, end, and occasionally in between by a first-person, reminiscent narrator who elsewhere lapses into third person. The "I" is Scarlet's friend Jocelyn, who serves as a persona for Weldon (and has been given her Foreign Office experience). *Down among the Women* takes its title from the refrain starting most of the chapters, which is the theme song of devastating introductory passages of commentary on the female condition. Enlivened by pointed jokes, anecdotes, and cross-patter as well—Weldon is always uninhibited about the form of the novel—these illusion-breaking but clever chapter introductions convey her feminist themes more effectively than her narrative, where the main story of Scarlet and her family is encumbered by Scarlet's sketchily portrayed friends. They, and Scarlet's stepmother, Susan, are still "down among the girls," rather than the women; they have yet to learn that the great enemy is not just men, but existence, which tends to chaos and cancer. They are "down" because they are the preliberation females of the 1950s, still subjugated to subordinate roles and general inconsequence. But "down" is also both a lament for women, who have only a "brief dance in the sun" before going "down into the darkness" of domestic stupor, and a tart reprimand to them for living "at floor level" and looking upward only "to dust the tops of the windows." However, the narrator optimistically (if ironically) envisions a brave new woman evolving, and Weldon shows such evolution working its way through generations of Scarlet's family.

Scarlet and her friends constitute the youth of the 1950s discovering rebellion against the strictures of the past, if not against their need of men. Not so Byzantia, Scarlett's illegitimate daughter, who becomes the nihilistic young woman developed by the 1960s, a self-assured radical intent on tearing

Dust jacket for the U.S. edition of Weldon's novel about Starlady Sandra, who deserts her family to follow her musician lover's band

down "the old order" of women by the 1970s. Byzantia cannot fancy seeing success in terms of men, the "symptom . . . of a fearful disease from which you all suffered," not that she can name the disease. Weldon finds glib Byzantia frightening in her single-mindedness, and the idea that freedom is not so simple as Byzantia assumes provided inspiration for Weldon's next book. Critics admired this novel for its witty lines, its richly varied comic effects, and its discerning and clever version of the female condition.

In 1974 Weldon saw the one-act *Words of Advice,* her second play on marital life, performed; the next year she published her substantial, better-focused third novel, *Female Friends,* the story of fortyish Chloe and her longtime friends, Marjorie and Grace. This novel is told sometimes from Chloe's first-person point of view but more often by a third-person narrator or in the form of terse, play-script dialogue. The narrator and Chloe often merge, but whereas the narrator always conveys Weldon's attitudes, Chloe only develops assent to them. Covering only two days in the present as Chloe resolves her marital crisis, *Female Friends* simultaneously recaptures a more eventful past (individual and joint) which began for the three women in Ulden in 1940. The three friends may have exasperated and backbitten each other since then, but they have also "clung together for comfort." Although they feel "our loyalties are to men, not to each other," these three friends attest to the possibility of the female community that forms out of distress and to which men are inconsequential. That all three have slept with artist Patrick Bates, and that Grace and Chloe have even borne his children, scarcely ripples their friendship. Having gravitated together because they sensed each other's emotional needs as children, they remain each other's mutual support as adults; and Weldon urges even more such alliances. Her friends quite rightly press Chloe to leave her contemptuous, bullying husband, Oliver, a hack movie writer, but she reassures herself that she is better off than the childless spinster Marjorie and hedonistic divorcée Grace and clings to her demeaning marriage.

Actually, Chloe is worse off. Weldon flatters neither her egotistical male figures here, nor their friendships: temporary camaraderie for bouts of drinking and sex or alliances for profit. At the heyday of their marriage, Oliver loves Chloe "as much as he loves himself—and what more than this can any woman ask of any man?" Yet Weldon remains careful about allotting blame. Chloe's friends have explicitly been responsible for men's deaths; Chloe herself pushed the au pair, Françoise, into Oliver's bed; and, most important, Chloe knows that she lets Oliver exploit and domineer over her.

The central thematic issue of women's control over their lives Chloe resolves to change—"women live by necessity, not choice." Weldon grants the powerful reality that women are shackled by fears and dependencies forged by maternal indoctrination. The powerless, Weldon also sees, lose their nerve; after a deprived childhood and a submissive adulthood Chloe dares not challenge fate: to her, that is asking for trouble. It also remains true that women are at the mercy of physical nature: their active hormones, their cancer-prone reproductive systems. And incalculable chance, or fate beyond individual control, creates its own level of necessity. The train on which Chloe and Marjorie first met stopped in Ulden by mistake; its cargo of evacuee children (such as Marjorie) was intended for elsewhere. However, Weldon insists that women must avoid the spineless habit of giving fate the credit or (as is Chloe's habit) the blame for their lives since

fate merely creates opportunities, not the directions they will take. Women are responsible for what happens to them, not in blame now but in obligation to self-respect; they must assert choice over necessity.

Chloe finally leaves Oliver. With five children to care for, she is not free, but she is freed of her husband's and her mother's negative influence; she has attained freedom of choice, a state that Weldon wisely counts as victory enough. With good reason *Female Friends* was favorably reviewed, earning particular praise for its terse prose, controlled tone, and avoidance of feminist tendentiousness in favor of believable, sharply realized characters and situations. As one reviewer said, the "real triumph of *Female Friends* is the gritty replication of the gross texture of everyday life, placed in perspective and made universal."

In the summer of 1976 the Weldon family moved to a substantial country house near Shepton Mallet, Somerset. The relocation proved more agreeable to Ronald Weldon, whose business flourished in Somerset, than to Fay Weldon, who would discover that she sorely missed her own friends and the London ambience. In 1976 Weldon's play *Moving House* was produced, and she started what turned into three years of work on her adaptation of *Pride and Prejudice*. She also published another novel, the moral values of which perhaps reflect Austen's influence. In any case, the strength of the mother-child bond, prominent in *Female Friends,* recurs as a motivation for the uncanny events of this fourth novel, *Remember Me* (1976), which is about human identity and the roles that shape it.

The unhappy ghost of Jarvis's first wife, middle-aged Madeleine, killed in an auto crash early in the book, refuses to rest until her teenage daughter, Hilary, is out of the clutches of her unloving stepmother, Lily. (Madeleine haunts the more kindly Margot, the doctor's wife, until she undertakes to mother Hilary.) Lily herself finally decides that "To have a husband is nothing. To be a wife is nothing. Sex is an idle pastime. To be a mother is all that counts"—sentiments not necessarily Weldon's, but a fair rendition of many women's sense of identity, and not without Weldon's approval. If Madeleine's ghostly presence precipitates an identity crisis for mean-spirited Lily, proud to be an architect's wife when she was once just a New Zealand butcher's daughter, more centrally that presence shatters and restores middle-aged Margot, whose ego is quivering for appreciation outside her roles as devoted wife and mother. Weldon sensibly has no quarrel with such feminine roles; her quarrel is only with letting roles become absolutes. Her narrator (now clearly distanced from the characters and prone to evaluating them) deliberately presents the characters and repeatedly lets them see themselves in terms of their roles in relation to others, even young Hilary, who identifies herself as "daughter of a dead mother, child of a lost father . . . [and] Lily's obligation." Although Madeline so resents being "stripped of my identity" as Jarvis's lawful wife that her life is corroded, she will recognize (too late) that she must change and be just "myself. Neither daughter nor wife, but myself." Weldon insists that women have, moreover, their moral identities to consider.

The incredible return of a ghost is rendered highly probable through a novel filled with mundane domestic details rather than sensational incidents. (The precise observation of daily life includes a new fictional device: line-by-numbered-line analyses of the obfuscations with which family conversations disguise actual motives.) Furthermore, the pervasive theme, "we are all part of one another," does much to explain Madeleine's continued presence. A psychic link with the dead, forged by guilt, might well let them prey on the minds of the living. Margot knows that sixteen years ago she slept once with Jarvis, even if he, most insultingly, has forgotten the incident. During the course of the action Margot acknowledges her long-suppressed awareness that her son, Laurence, is the fruit of that brief encounter and therefore should be brought up beside Hilary as her brother. More important, in a further development of oneness, she also acknowledges her guilt before Madeleine, whom she once "wronged": Madeleine was part of her in being "my sister, after all."

As a satirist Weldon does not spare her characters exposure of their pretensions, hypocrisies, and self-indulgences, but she is less willing to turn an epigram at their expense here, and this novel lacks anyone approaching a villain. Even Renée (a minor character) is portrayed more sympathetically than is Weldon's wont with lesbians. Greater charity is not just a plea in this novel, but a practice. The responses of reviewers, who were of mixed minds about this book, were captured by the *Times Literary Supplement* reviewer, Victoria Glendinning, who concluded her list of objections with the admission that she found herself reading it "with an avidity way beyond the call of duty." The most frequent criticisms were of authorial intrusions, primer-style question-and-answer dialogue, and role typing. But the negative comments were balanced by praise for solid construction, shrewdness, and authenticity.

Weldon discarded mellowing of attitude and domestication of fantasy for her next novel, *Little Sisters,* published in England in 1978. (It appeared in America in 1977 as *Words of Advice,* a title reused

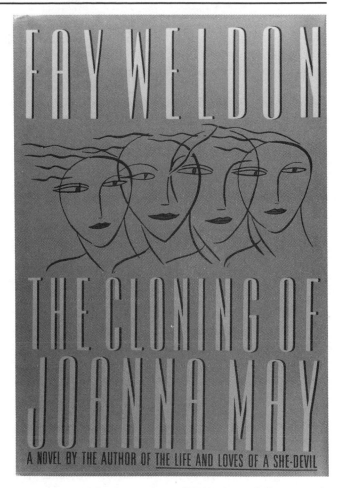

Dust jacket for the U.S. edition of Weldon's novel about genetic experimentation and obsessive love

from her earlier, but unconnected, play.) This book, with its thinly developed characters, improbably exaggerated situations, and abrupt reversals, is a satiric modern fairy tale, not a realistic novel. It mocks the shoddy parvenus and aspirants to wealth and glamour of the 1970s and the illusion-ridden, sensation-seeking folk of the 1960s, when the enemy was "forced back by peace and love and a little help from hallucinogens." Cautioning against the glittering promises of wealth and luck in fairy tales, Weldon subverts them with wicked wit, but she uses the psychological wisdom and moral certainty they embody to develop her maturation theme, coupled here with a characteristically Weldon plea for greater sisterhood.

In 1978 Weldon's play on scientism in the welfare state, *Mr. Director,* was produced, and she published her ambitious sixth novel, *Praxis,* nominated for the Booker Prize. A grimmer book than her preceding ones, *Praxis* was written under more-trying circumstances. While living in Somerset and writing it, Weldon feared she might die of a current pregnancy complicated by placenta praevia (misattached placenta). Although intellectually certain that she would give birth safely, she was emotionally far less secure and thought of *Praxis* as her last testament.

The narrator quickly explains the strange name of the title character as meaning "turning point, culmination, action; orgasm; some said the Goddess herself"; whereas her sister Hypatia's name comes from "a learned woman; stoned to death by an irate crowd for teaching mathematics when she should have stayed modestly at home." The outlandish names their Jewish father, Ben, gave them "out of a culture so far gone as to be meaningless" are changed by their Christian mother, Lucy, into a more prosaic Patricia and Hilda. Yet the spirit of the goddess persists. Pat-Praxis Duveen (divine), an entirely individualized character, is also an ironic, great goddess declined into modern woman, but with her cult resurgent in the Eleusinian mysteries of the women's movement. Hilda-Hypatia, the thinker, is her own woman, an ambitious and half-mad intellectual who uses her mind to protect herself from reality and becomes a successful, antifeminist career woman. But she is also implicitly a distorting aspect of Praxis's nature. She has stood Praxis, the doer, on her head "metaphorically, often enough, until I doubted the truth of my own perceptions."

The symbolic suggestiveness enriches the themes of women's need to regain a sense of female importance and cohesiveness ("It does not take a man to make a woman cry") and the courage to act by conviction instead of sheltering behind men, respectability, and nature; the women's movement convinces Praxis of the importance of these truths. Blind Nature remains the great enemy, decayer of female flesh and perverter of values; "Nature our Friend is an argument used, quite understandably, by men," with Nature as "no more than our disposition, as laid down by evolutionary forces, in order to best procreate the species."

Praxis's story, told in retrospect, begins in Brighton with her traumatic childhood in the 1920s and ends in London in the present, spanning a period of change in some women's, if not men's, attitudes toward womanhood. Ben beats Lucy and abandons her to madness and institutionalization. Praxis's unwashed college boyfriend, Willie, exploits her to gain his degree at the expense of hers (as in *Female Friends*), but then Praxis doubts her self-worth and still assumes that catching a man is the goal of life. Yet she outgrows being a servant to Willie and then a suburban doll-wife to Philip, abandoning him and her prim children to steal her girlfriend's man; and when finally betrayed in turn, she

becomes a zealous convert to, even a heroine of, the women's movement. Nonetheless, like narrator Jocelyn of *Down among the Women,* she retains reservations about the New Young Woman: "Heartless, soulless, mindless—free!" The women's movement educates her but proves no panacea for Praxis, who has yet to come to personal terms with her sense of a meaningless life.

The novel alternates between Praxis's first- and third-person accounts, the latter being the voice of her writing personality, on whose veracity she sometimes comments. Like most Weldon narrators, Praxis inclines toward Weldon's recurrent sentiments and characteristic voice: deft, ironic understatement and wry appraisals. She also shares Weldon's copywriting experience. Writing her story while confined to her room with injuries, imprisoned in despair and self-doubt, Praxis has been recently released from two years in jail for smothering the Down's syndrome infant of her foster daughter (an opportunity for Weldon to explore right-to-life attitudes). Playing Oedipus, the swollen-footed Praxis (who once slept with her own father) is searching out the truth of her past, looking for "the root of my pain and yours" to see if it is inherent in existence or something foisted on women. (It is both and more.) Recollection proves to be a cathartic act of vision that finally frees her from isolation and returns her to faith "in some kind of force which turns the wheels of action and reaction, and gives meaning and purpose to our lives." But reaffirmation comes only after Praxis (a true Weldon heroine) has fully accepted responsibility for the course of her life and can say, "I did it all myself" when asked "what have they done to you?" at the hospital. If people cannot change circumstances, they can modify their attitudes and consequent behavior, and Praxis, who courted pain throughout her life, by now sees her share in exacerbating her ordeals.

Praxis is one of Weldon's best novels, with the most fully realized female character, who succeeds in unifying a crowded plot and cast. The control of tone and, in Praxis's past, of atmosphere, is impressive. Social comedy is subdued, largely embedded in minor characters; earnestness prevails. Although there was some objection to occasional obscurities and simplifications and needless extension of Praxis into Everywoman, reviewers admired this book. They praised its energetic narration, polished style, and "personal and idiosyncratic" version of woman's plight, happy that Praxis had "all the exasperating contradictions of a real woman."

In 1979 *Action Replay,* Weldon's drama on sexual incompatibility and warfare, was produced, and in 1980 her seventh novel, *Puffball,* was published.

The novel reflects her dangerous pregnancy in Somerset (as does her 1978 short story "Angel, All Innocence"). But it was completed when she had already removed herself and her children to a terraced house in Kentish Town, North London, in summer 1979. Now living not far from the neighborhood where she had grown up, she would henceforth commute on weekends to Somerset. That country life had palled on her is evident enough in her novel though there the pregnant wife remains the country mouse whom the husband visits on weekends. *Puffball* shares with *Remember Me* Weldon's fascination with the weird. As she had done, her characters live in the shadow of numinous Glastonbury Tor, a region steeped in the occult tradition and, to Weldon, imbued with an elemental power whose energy people may try to harness to their own ends as her villain Mabs does with manipulative malice. The novel takes its title from a recurrent image: the swelling mushroom that usually resembles a pregnant abdomen, but sometimes the human brain, and therefore is an apt symbol for the central conflict of the book between mind and biological mechanism. Satire is muted, and the story entirely positive.

Twenty-eight-year-old Liffey persuades her husband, Richard, who works for an advertising agency, to move to an isolated Somerset cottage by agreeing to the pregnancy she has always feared. There she becomes, at first, the unsuspecting prey of their witchlike neighbor Mabs, whose powerful concoctions give Mabs's husband, Tucker, entry into Liffey's bed, then threaten her pregnancy and life—occasions for much suspense. But the baby (it is Richard's) is safely born, despite placenta praevia, and Richard, who has philandered away his weekdays in London and deserted his wife for infidelity, returns and is accepted back for the child's sake. Not only has a healthy baby been born, but as a result of pregnancy, marital disillusionments, financial problems, and local ordeals, a more mature and expansive Liffey has been reborn. Even Richard, who rejected the adult responsibilities of fatherhood and fidelity, shows signs of growth, accepting what he assumes is Tucker's child rather than lose Liffey. (Before allowing publication of this book, Weldon rewrote her male characters so that they would not be ciphers.)

The simple story proceeds chronologically through fifteen months of present time, told by an omniscient narrator clearly distanced from characters who are no more complex than the formal structure. Complexity belongs to the thematic structure instead. Although Nature here is no longer the decayer of female bodies but the creator of new life, biological and spiritual, a major theme is still the tyr-

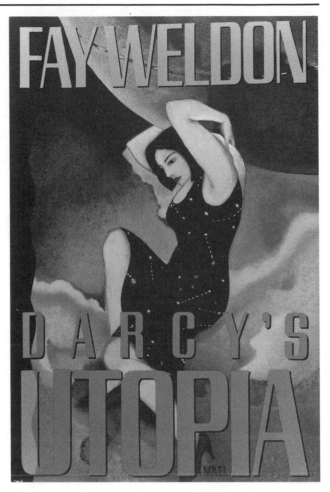

Dust jacket for the U.S. edition of Weldon's polemical novel about a confidence trickster who founds a new religion based on bizarre economics

anny of the biological functions that control our bodies, of the chemistry that dictates so much of our behavior.

However, capable of fulfilling her nature as the human being Nature chanced to evolve, Liffey discovers the desire to feel herself "part of nature's process: to subdue the individual to some greater whole." Nor does Weldon mock her; like Praxis, Liffey has found a meaningful "force." That life is more than body chemistry is amply evident from Weldon's ironic use of extended, clinically precise descriptions of physiological processes, from menarche through ejaculation and conception to parturition: the "inside" story accompanying outer events.

Puzzled by this book, missing the comic writer, and sensing a softening of attitude, reviewers objected above all to such an "intrusion" of physiological data. But they failed to see the integral role and narrative value of the factual passages, which give *Puffball* a resonance its slim story otherwise lacks. If the impersonal functioning of a Nature beyond our control is manifest in Weldon's biology lectures, so too is Nature's orderliness and purposefulness, in contrast to the confusions and dishonesties in the outer events of the narrative. Nor can Weldon resist some explicit praise for Nature's works in the form of highly specialized cells "enabling their owner to read, and write, and reason in a way entirely surplus to its survival." Nature proves something to marvel at too, an attitude that may be irrelevant to Nature's mechanical processes but is pertinent to human existence and Weldon's fiction. She consistently says that by their attitudes people control the quality of their lives; the mind has its way of mastering matter as well as fate—let women take heed.

Watching Me, Watching You (1981), a collection of all Weldon's short stories to that time, was followed in 1982 by *The President's Child*. A novel that has been described as a "feminist thriller," it presents a woman who advances from the Australian outback, to Washington high life (of the less reputable sort), to a home and career in London only to have political intrigue and murderous conspiracy suddenly intrude on her private life.

In 1983 Weldon's play *Redundant, or, The Wife's Revenge* was shown on the BBC, to be followed by a novel for which the subtitle of the play could also serve: *The Life and Loves of a She-Devil*. As a novel and later as a television serial (1986) and a movie (titled *She-Devil,* 1989), it has attracted much controversy, particularly among feminist readers and viewers who find some startling ambivalence in this account of female revenge. Having lost her philandering husband (diminished from the start by his name, Bobbo) to the pretty, rich Mary Fisher, who embodies the romantic fictions she writes, Ruth, six feet two inches tall with a hooked nose and hairy moles on her chin, embarks on the life of a "she-devil," taking on an identity ascribed to her in a moment of fury by her husband. From clumsy, inept, victimized housewife Ruth remakes herself as desirable multimillionairess in her determination to achieve revenge, power, money, and the ability "to be loved and not love in return." Once she abandons home (which she causes to burn down), children (dumped on husband and mistress), and wifely role, she becomes dynamic—sustained and driven by hatred of her rival. With little apparent effort she moves through a succession of sexual relationships (with men and women) and a series of identities—Vesta Rose, Polly Patch, Molly Wishant, Marlene Hunter—bringing financial ruin and imprisonment for fraud upon her husband, condemning Mary Fisher to a life of domestic chaos as caretaker for both Ruth's children and her own incontinent

mother, and achieving spectacular material and social success for herself. But her final, and for readers perhaps most ambiguous, accomplishment is the total remodeling of her large, ungainly body, through excruciatingly painful, expensive, prolonged surgery, into a replica of Mary Fisher. The novel concludes with Mary's death from cancer and Ruth's takeover of Mary's "High Tower" which she shares with a broken Bobbo, who has to endure her lovers and her indifference: "it is not a matter of male or female, after all; it never was, merely of power. I have all, and he has none. As I was, so he is now."

Thematically *She-Devil* draws clearly on *Praxis* though the wild excesses of the plot move beyond the condensed social realism of the earlier novel. Nature is again the archenemy, especially of women; as she-devil, Ruth is defiantly "unnatural" and allows no limits, natural or social, on her behavior. In a shift of perspective Weldon shows that identities may be assumed temporarily and then cast aside; the essential self, which previous heroines seek, is a fiction, "all inessential, and all liable to change and flux, and usually the better for it." Maternal feeling is both significant in women's lives and subject to changing circumstances. Both Praxis and Ruth leave their children and conclude that everybody's lives will be improved as a consequence. Ruth encourages Vickie, a young single mother, to sell her two children to obtain her freedom. In the alternating chapters of third-person past and first-person present narration that have become a mark of Weldon's writing, the novel combines the picaresque, with its crowd of characters and events, with the sage and sonorous pronouncements of the she-devil, the would-be wise woman who is a Praxis grown more desperate in a man-made world.

The moral of the tale is an uncomfortable one. In allusion to fairy tales, the ugly duckling becomes a swan; the self-mutilating ugly sister actually gets the prince, even if, like the little mermaid, her legs are racked with pain. Ruth becomes both empowered and empowering to other women; in re-creating herself, she brings opportunities for others to achieve independence and happiness. Indeed she proves that women can be powerful, at the same time repeatedly exposing the weaknesses of men, and the body she reviles as abnormal receives approbation from various sexual partners and a resident of the separatist commune she joins for a time (interestingly, an episode cut for the American edition of the book). She becomes evangelical in her vision of an improved female lot: "Out there in the world . . . everything is possible and exciting. We can be different women: we can tap our own energies and the energies of women like us." However, this vision of vibrant female power is not enough for her. Ruth's paramount desire is for idealized feminine beauty and to be able to "look up to men," physically if not intellectually, so it may be that, as Patricia Juliana Smith has suggested, she "embarks on an inevitably self-defeating and self-erasing strategy, that of becoming the very object of her own wrath." Although Ruth professes to scorn the delusions of romantic love (Mary Fisher "is a writer of romantic fiction. She tells lies to herself, and to the world"), and certainly love emerges here as elsewhere in Weldon's work as a kind of disease–it is not a coincidence that Mary succumbs to cancer after falling in love–her participation in the world appears to require the context of romance. She might be said to use her hard-won freedom merely to renew her oppression. Ultimately power remains in men's hands. Through the very excesses of Ruth's campaign for self-renewal Weldon disrupts romantic mythology, patriarchal values, and notions of fixed identity; but Ruth's fate is reminiscent of Charlotte Brontë's *Jane Eyre* (1847), in which the heroine achieves a perfect marriage only in social isolation and with a husband broken physically and mentally. She has paid a high price for her desire, but the question remains as to whether she does it in self-awareness or is the victim of self-delusion. Though faulted for some minor lapses into melodrama and for tones of stridency rather than the anticipated sharpness, this "fierce" novel was seen as a bold and welcome advance in Weldon's writing, "more audacious and striking in design than anything that's gone before" (*Times Literary Supplement,* 20 January 1984).

She-Devil was adapted by Ted Whitehead for the BBC in 1986 after Weldon's own adaptation of her work was, curiously, rejected as not "true to the spirit of the book . . . rather cruel and hard and harsh," according to Weldon. Attracting large audiences when it was shown in four episodes on BBC 2, it was repeated the following year and broadcast in the United States. Although it won a BAFTA award for best drama series, it received some criticism in Britain for its "surreptitious cravings for old female values." The film version, starring Meryl Streep and Roseanne Barr, was generally seen as an unsatisfactory dilution of the original novel.

In a somewhat different style is *Letters to Alice: On First Reading Jane Austen* (1984). Composed as a series of letters from "Aunt Fay" to a punk niece, this book is described in its dedication as an epistolary novel, but it is more accurately a mixture of earnest treatise on the creation and reading of fiction and a lively study of Jane Austen, whose writing features sporadically throughout Weldon's career. The

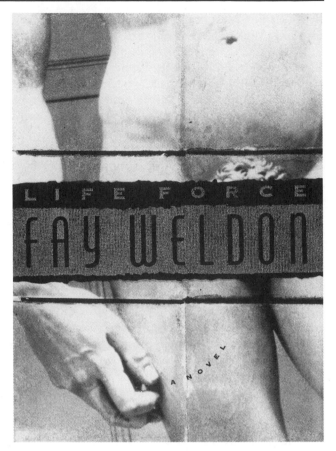

Dust jacket for the U.S. edition of Weldon's humorous novel about a group of middle-aged female friends and the lover they have shared

point of departure for the book is Alice's failure to appreciate Austen, whose work is compulsory reading in her English literature course but which she finds "boring, petty and irrelevant." Her traditionalist humanist aunt attempts to persuade her of the enduring significance of literature and, in particular, of Austen's novels: "only persist and thou shalt see. Jane Austen's all in all to thee." It is a colorful, if currently unfashionable, appeal for the classics and for the value of reading. Alongside engaging accounts of Austen's life and context are chatty discussions of the writing process and the literary world, with some pointed remarks about Weldon's own critics, and an idiosyncratic reading list for the "easily distracted."

A second volume of short stories, *Polaris and Other Stories,* appeared in 1985 along with a book about Rebecca West, continuing Weldon's investigation of other female novelists. *Rebecca West,* like *Letters to Alice,* is no conventional biography but rather an imaginative and irreverent response to a fellow novelist in epistolary form. Four letters, in which Weldon encourages and advises a twenty-two-year-old West at the time of the birth of her son by H. G. Wells in 1914, re-create the writer's likely difficulties as the mistress of an older, famous man. Like *Letters to Alice,* the book perhaps tells more about Weldon than its subject; acknowledging women's longing for love while representing the object of love with a degree of cynicism, Weldon urges the young West to seek "self-determination."

In the mid 1980s Weldon began to incorporate into her fiction, in tandem with her prime interest in relationships and marriage, wider social issues ranging from war to genetic engineering, plastic surgery to environmental pollution, economics to technological development. This shift brought the charges from a few of her critics that she risked becoming a polemicist rather than a novelist, that style is sometimes sacrificed to content, and that her writing, for one unimpressed critic, Laura Cumming in *The Observer* (10 December 1995), is "the stuff of newspaper features." Others, more appreciative of her ambitious and experimental approach, saw her managing the balance between didacticism and entertainment and emerging as an influential and innovative twentieth-century writer. Probably most would agree that her forte remains her sharp analyses of the sex war; but her various exhortations can add urgency and surprise to her work.

The Shrapnel Academy (1986) provides an example of the broadening of theme. Slighter than previous novels, it seems better suited to the short-story form or even a radio play. A miscellaneous group of people—military heroes, a weapons salesman, a journalist for the *Women's Times* invited in error—congregate at a country-house center for military studies during a blizzard to attend a celebratory dinner and the annual Wellington lecture. An *Upstairs, Downstairs* conflict reminiscent of Evelyn Waugh's *Black Mischief* (1932) develops between the guests, headed by the colonial Joan Lumb, and the servants, led by the virtually psychotic Acorn. The servants no longer number about thirty as Joan believes but include several hundred men, women, and children "of every race except Caucasian." In the tradition of black comedy the dog of one of the visitors is turned into paté and fed to the assembled guests as a prelude to violent but unjustified revenge for the death in childbirth of a servant, Miriam. In an unfortunate coincidence the phone lines are dead and the power cut off; believing themselves to be under siege, and stirred by their fears of native revolt, the military men devise a campaign, the only response of which they are capable. They succeed in blowing up the entire house and its many inhabitants with some sample miniaturized weapons; but ironically by that time the servants had seen sense and were peace-

fully sleeping below. The narration is interspersed with often quite lengthy passages of factual detail of battles, developments in weaponry and famous military leaders—"[a] quick description of the Battle of Borodino, on the way to Moscow? You can bear it?"—which, though lively and intimate in style, are overused and seem to serve only to prolong the story. As a satire on the human folly of warmongering, *The Shrapnel Academy* makes its point about our increasing destructiveness with some energy, but the characters are ciphers and the authorial intrusions a little sanctimonious.

Three new works of fiction were published in 1987: *The Hearts and Lives of Men,* originally written in installments for *Woman* magazine; *The Rules of Life,* a futuristic black-comic novella; and *The Heart of the Country,* first a four-part serial on the BBC. *The Hearts and Lives of Men* has been dubbed by Weldon a "cheerful novel" which self-consciously draws on a Dickensian model of serialization in plot structure and alludes to Charles Dickens's writing with Weldon's naming of the pivotal character, the loving and lovable, ever-hopeful little Nell. The novel is framed as fairy tale, its positive message qualified as usual by the buoyant narrator's generous application of cynical, knowing commentary but maintaining to the end a wry adherence to the enduring power of love. It opens with "love at first sight" between successful art dealer Clifford and an artist's beautiful young daughter, Helen, and escorts the reader briskly through the 1960s and 1970s, combining adept social chronicle with an account of the couple's on-and-off relationship. Helen and Clifford marry and remarry (twice), with a succession of substitute partners between times, including the rich but unloved and totally unscrupulous Angie; but at the heart of the tale is their first child, Nell, product of romantic passion. Having been kidnapped during her parents' bitter custody battle and miraculously saved from death in a plane crash, Nell spends a trying childhood in several improbable homes, including a French château inhabited by two ancient senile aristocrats, a nightmarish children's home, and a farm community of stoned hippies, before eventual reunion with her parents.

Personality and fate triumph over circumstance in this largely optimistic novel. The lovable, who have, as Nell has, "a profound sense of [their] own worth," seem to have charmed lives while those who lack confidence and self-esteem, such as Angie and Evelyn, Helen's mother, are unappreciated and doomed. Evelyn endures an unhappy life with her irascible artist husband, John Lally, who denies her material goods and the chance to have more children. However, after her death from a cerebral hemorrhage, the second wife, Marjorie, cheerful, self-assured, and firm, has a child and a new kitchen in no time at all: "[it] was Marjorie's habit to smile, as it had been Evelyn's to weep." There is plenty of wickedness as well as weakness in the story, but the narrator exercises a benign compassion over all her fallible creations. As a wise woman who is sensible, responsible, moral, but indulgent, the narrator, in cosy collusion with the reader, forgives all and hopes for the best: "The best we can do is wish that they all live happily ever after, and I think they have as good a chance as any of actually getting away with it." The effects of the novel rely largely on the twists and turns of plot and anticipation of the inevitable happy ending. Calculated to please the magazine readers for whom it was originally written, it is Weldon's most fairy-tale novel, in which female beauty equals goodness; lovely women are thwarted by jealous witches; and virtue and love triumph.

The Rules of Life offers a mildly dystopian comic vision of a Great Britain in 2004, ordered and guided by paternalistic government, in which the too fat and the too thin, all those outside their "optimum weight band," are heavily taxed, as is anyone who fails to do "exercise of a regulation kind." The unpredictability of the weather has been overcome, and HIV sufferers are neatly dispatched to live together in Scotland. Control and order are all. Yet death remains the great taboo—the saying of the word "now has the ring of obscenity"—and the search for the secrets of life has escalated. "Pulp priests" of the new religion of the GSWITs (the Great Screen Writer in the Sky, feared by the narrator to be a B-movie writer) transcribe, by means of technological advance, the words recorded from "rewinds" (ghosts) in the hope of learning something of the meaning of life and death. The voice of the charming and seductive Gabriella Sumpter, now three months dead, introduces disorder, desire, and fantasy into the world of the elderly narrator-recorder with her highly colored reminiscences and many "rules of life," which range from a host of esoteric laundry tips to worldly advice and observations: "monogamy, amongst interesting and lively people, is rare"; "no one becomes rich by doing good." As evidence of a divine message, Gabriella's life story adds little to the sum of knowledge, but it anarchically disrupts the narrator's existence by inspiring love. Normality is restored only by the more prosaic account of Gabriella given by her (living) former lover and by the narrator's return to his wife, Honor, and "a plate of high-fibre beans on unbuttered wholemeal toast." A reviewer for the *Times Literary Supplement* (11 September 1987) saw the

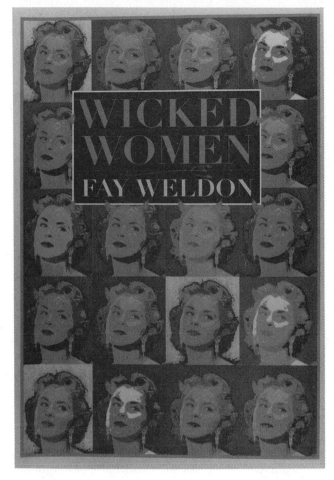

Dust jacket for the U.S. edition of Weldon's 1995 short-story collection

book as offering "some menacingly plausible predictions of a not-too-distant future" and suggested the greatest threat might be the appalling restrained blandness of the envisioned future. Gabriella is a true Weldon heroine: willful, selfish, and disruptive, the antidote to dull homogeneity. The novella shares with *The Shrapnel Academy* and *The Hearts and Lives of Men* an unfailing comic inventiveness, but none of these works really carries forward the development of Weldon's most powerful themes.

Closer critical attention has been paid to *The Heart of the Country,* which Ann-Marie Herbert has called "Weldon's most overtly feminist novel." Again writing in alternating first and third person, Weldon invents a new justification for her method in this novel: Sonia, the outspoken narrator, writes from the "loony-bin" as a therapeutic exercise in creative writing and seeks to "objectivise myself as others see me—that is to say in the third person," as "instructed" by her psychiatrist. Sonia finds this process difficult, and *she* erupts into *I* regularly despite good intentions: "I'll try and keep out of it, I promise you, except in the third person." The objectification, or commodification, of women is perhaps the most compelling theme of the novel: when one character becomes a man's kept mistress, she is said to exchange "her body for his flat"; the climactic scene involves the women posing on a carnival float, "dressed as traditional housewives, in bright waisted dresses and with frilly aprons and waving feather dusters at the passing crowd" in a spectacle aimed at the town's two most powerful businessmen, who "run everything." Weldon is always acutely aware of the economic basis of male/female relationships.

The Heart of the Country begins, "Oh the wages of sin!" Beautiful but stupid Natalie is about to lose husband, home, and possessions, and she at first assumes, in the guilty female way that Weldon believes endemic, that her loss is a consequence of her lukewarm infidelity with the local antique dealer, Arthur. However, as turns out to be the case for Sonia, recently left by her husband, a wife's adultery is merely an excuse, not a reason, for desertion. Husbands are almost always congenitally unfaithful in Weldon's writing. But Natalie suffers as those women do "who live by the good will of men" and therefore "have no control over their lives"; she joins the ranks, alongside Sonia and her friend Ros, of the "underprivileged," the unsupported mothers whose battles with the Department of Health and Social Security are a full-time job in themselves. At times the reader assumes that Natalie's plight is the fault of men, but women, out of envy of her sexual attractiveness, or merely malice, let her down as often as men do, failing to inform her of her rights as a deserted wife and mother. Weldon's male characters are rarely appealing and usually blameworthy, but her searching moral vision does not deny women responsibility. Condemned in particular are the complacent acceptance of the status quo and the refusal to claim independence, which allows for the continuance of unsatisfactory structures: "if you want things to change you have to make them change." By living only in the present, her characters fail to see the possible consequences of their action or inaction. Yet this is a novel that takes a harder line against male power and privilege than some of Weldon's other writing. Through Sonia's radical feminist outbursts, the reader's attention is focused on power inequalities in a direct way.

Increasingly incensed by the unscrupulous dealings of Arthur and Angus (the town's real estate agent and Natalie's lover after she is passed on to him by Arthur), whose acquisition of wealth, sex, and power is often at the expense of the women around them, Sonia finally displays her hatred of these men, and men in general: "while women adapt and adapt and adapt, men will continue to get away with everything." Having rebuked her friends, who are bemoaning their lot, with "you can stop colluding," she draws together, at least temporarily, the women of the novel in the "ancient spirit of carnival, when the images of the hated were paraded through the streets." Grotesque and ridiculous effigies of Arthur and Angus adorn the ends of a float which is drawn through the town to the accompaniment of the song "Little Boxes" and Sonia's vociferous protests: "I told them about the wickedness of men, and the wretchedness of women. I told them they were being had, cheated, conned. . . . I blame the guilty men . . . Seducers, fornicators, robbers, cheats!" Her last defiant act is to set alight the float, killing Flora, Natalie's eighteen-year-old former cleaning lady, who acts out unwittingly the ancient role of virgin sacrifice.

Order returns to the town—Sonia is locked up, Natalie finds a new man and is happy—but some instability remains to the end. The arsonist Sonia, deemed mad, is offered marriage by her psychiatrist, but she refuses. "Happy endings are not so easy," she says. Perhaps as a means of assuring reader satisfaction, Weldon generally provides calm endings, with a restoration, if incomplete, of the status quo; so Sonia's resistance is noteworthy. Reviewers found the novel intelligent and challenging, the current of feminism running "strong and swift." There was a sense that she had taken on too many satirical targets—there is a subplot involving rural environmental concerns—and that her wicked men were cardboard targets, but *The Heart of the Country* was well received.

A spontaneous act of rebellion forms the starting point of Weldon's next novel, *Leader of the Band* (1988). A more reflective and less plot-driven novel than usual, it features as first-person narrator Starlady Sandra, age forty-two, a well-known astronomer and host of a popular television program, "Sandra's Sky," whose sudden desertion of husband and job to follow mad Jack the trumpeter and his band to France for the summer prompts much contemplation on her life, her friends, and family as she plays her role as camp follower. In part the novel is a celebration of Sandra's erotic abandonment to the sexual pleasures she shares with Jack; its more serious element involves her musing on her Nazi warcriminal father and his genetic experimentation, through which Sandra was born to a young gypsy mother who has declined into madness. She is haunted by the ghosts of her bizarre family, including a suicidal half brother, to the extent that she has remained deliberately childless, feeling she should "keep her genes to herself." Sandra is a woman in flight "from my own life, my own past, and the revenge of my friends," trying to convince herself that through love or lust she is "Sandra Born Again," the weight and the boredom of the past forgotten. However, Weldon is ever the realist, and Sandra decides quite soon that Jack may not be her savior after all. Having discovered that she is pregnant, she contemplates her return home, back to her post as "next in line to being Astronomer Royal."

One of the female problems Weldon confronts in *Leader of the Band* is the problem of the successful woman, a type not much in evidence in her earlier work. Sandra makes great efforts to hide from Jack that she is clever and famous, anticipating what he later confirms—that "men are more comfortable with women who are lesser than they." Even when Jack discovers who she really is, Sandra continues to play down her status and enhance his. She freely acknowledges, just as she-devil Ruth does, her desire to "look up to a man," and in most unsisterly fashion she despises the miserable dowdy wife of her lover: "I wanted a better rival." Weldon seems to confirm that happy relationships may depend on women's willing subjugation of themselves. In her next novel, *The Cloning of Joanna May* (1989), the stable, happy marriage of Angela and Gerald is sustained by Angela's pretense that she is "less than Gerald in all things because thus she preserves the domestic and marital peace." Weldon has indicated the pressures imposed on her own marriage by her success. The *Times Literary Supplement* reviewer (15 July 1988) found little to offer in the way of story in *Leader of the Band* but plenty of robust fun and the maintenance of Weldon's capable blending of the "endearing and the didactic."

Leader of the Band marked a change of publisher after Weldon became dissatisfied with the sums offered by Hutchinson; widely reported in the British press was a contract from Collins for £450,000 for her next three novels. She had already voiced publicly her views on parsimonious publishers (to the surprise of the publishers who were present) at the Booker Prize dinner in 1983 when she chaired the panel of judges. Weldon has often stated her belief in the moral duty of the writer, but money is for her an important motive for writing, and at this point in her career she could command high rewards. Some reviewers and critics saw her as a victim of her own success, turning out work that is variable in quality to maintain output. At the same time, her novels were beginning to receive serious critical attention in literary journals and books.

The interest in genetics and the possibility of cloning that permeates *Leader of the Band* becomes central in *The Cloning of Joanna May*. Against the backdrop

Dust jacket for Weldon's novel about a woman who discovers that her recently deceased husband was unfaithful

of the Chernobyl nuclear disaster the aging Joanna May tries to come to terms with her status as a divorcée after nearly thirty years of marriage. Her former husband, Carl, is a monster, rich and powerful, a potent mix of Frankenstein and Dracula; as an abused child who "started life in a kennel," he has refused Joanna children, fearful like Sandra of his genetic inheritance, the "bestial blood" he carries. However, to maintain a supply of "perfect" wives, he has, without Joanna's knowledge, produced from one of her eggs four clones, born to and brought up by different mothers. During the course of the novel the clones become aware of one another and their sister/mother Joanna, and, as in *The Heart of the Country*, the getting together of women proves explosive.

The horrifying experiment conducted by Carl, whose desire to control Joanna is so extreme that he arranges the murders of her two lovers, enables Weldon not only to make real the consequences of genetic experimentation but to continue her interrogation of personal identity. Joanna, who has all her adult life allowed herself to be defined by her husband, begins to reflect on her own identity—"who is there when I say 'I'?"—and redefines herself and the boundaries between self and other. Acknowledging her dependence on Carl, who "was intertwined in my mind and body," she nevertheless acquires a new strength and independence from her knowledge of the clones. When Carl informs Joanna of their existence, he tells her "you are nothing," but in fact she is quite the contrary, gaining a voice and a stature she did not have before.

In a tarot reading done for Joanna by one of her lovers, she picks for herself the Empress card, which is surrounded by the four Queens, clearly representing her clones. In a typical bit of Weldon magic, fate unites the clones, who are then prompted to reevaluate their unsatisfactory lives and join in a common quest for the truth about their origins. Their effect as a combined force is apparent when they visit Dr. Holly, their creator; he is so overwhelmed that he has an epileptic fit. They form a cohesive unit: "They had rapidly acquired the habit, now they were together, of dividing a sentence up between them and handing it out, with fourfold emphasis." They overstep the limits prescribed by Carl May and are, to a degree, reinforced through sharing: "The soul was multiplied, the guilt divided." Joanna finds her life opening out: "I was no longer just a wife; I was a human being, part of a larger universe beyond her husband."

The monster Carl meets a fitting end, dying of radiation sickness after jumping into a nuclear cooling pond in a publicity stunt to prove its safety, but not before he is himself cloned. Little Carl, born to one of the clones, is brought up by Joanna, the child she never had and almost the husband she has regained. There remains some sadness at the end of the novel. Weldon, however cynical her world-view, never quite denies love, and Joanna is still haunted by Carl: "I do love him. Never stopped."

Some critics have observed a failure of feminism in conclusions such as this one because her heroines remain committed to a constraining ideology of love: "the disruptive potential of [her] female characters' growing self-awareness is finally . . . only potential." But her refusal to present idealistic solutions to difficult problems is, as others have noted, a mark of her seriousness and realism, and she never has been a textbook feminist. Life is improved in her novels but not transformed. In reviews of *The Cloning of Joanna May* there was some concern over sloppiness of style as Weldon's concerns grow larger, but the novel was seen as intelligent and provocative.

By the end of the 1980s it was quite likely that critical works on contemporary English women's fiction would include a section on Weldon, and critical articles began to appear, among them a reading of *The Cloning of Joanna May* as a revision of T. S. Eliot's *The Waste Land* (1922). Weldon has managed to engage successfully with both the academic world, in particular the ever-growing sector of feminist criticism and theory, and the general readers who keep her work in print and on the shelves in bookshops.

By the time of the publication of her eighteenth novel, *Darcy's Utopia,* in 1990, Weldon had earned a reputation as a novelist "in the business of making pronouncements." In the previous year she had published a Chatto and Windus "Chatto Counterblasts" pamphlet, *Sacred Cows,* prompted by the furor brought about by Salman Rushdie's *The Satanic Verses* (1988). Adopting the "fictional" *I,* here described as "leftish, humanist feminist," which she has claimed to be "much harder, sharper and disagreeable" than her everyday self, Weldon launches into various British "sacred cows"—freedom of speech, the National Health Service, the state education system, multiculturalism, and contemporary, overintellectualized feminism. Though the pamphlet has caused accusations that Weldon is shallow, elitist, and puritanical in her views, it does reinforce her increasing engagement with political debate in its broadest sense. Thus it was no surprise when in *Darcy's Utopia* she turned her fertile imagination to economics. This novel is the tale of Eleanor Darcy (no doubt an ironic allusion to two of Austen's most upright and self-controlled creations, Elinor Dashwood from *Sense and Sensibility,* 1811, and Mr. Darcy from *Pride and Prejudice,* 1813), cofounder, with her now imprisoned husband, once a university vice chancellor, of Darcian Monetarism, an extravagant and wayward Utopian vision of a transformed Britain. A generous portion of the novel consists of interviews between Eleanor and one of two journalists, Hugo, writer for the *Independent,* or Valerie, composing for serialization in a woman's magazine (and included in the novel) a "Fiction Biography" of the woman of many identities and enormous confidence (perhaps rather like the older Weldon herself). Eleanor was previously known as Apricot and Ellen, and by the end of the novel it is uncertain whether she has become Alison and run off with a BMW salesman or alternatively the creator of a new religion. Apparently affected by the ambiguous, charismatic Eleanor, Hugo and Valerie, who are little more than puppets there to listen and report, leave their families to carry on a passionate affair in a Holiday Inn, from which they emerge, faintly puzzled, when Eleanor's influence has passed. During the interviews Eleanor reveals her theories: history will be ignored; people will change their names at the various life stages; money will be dispensed with through hyperinflation; school is to be optional; fetuses will be aborted unless the pregnancy is approved by a committee of neighbors; and so on. Eleanor is a particularly slippery character, and it is difficult to determine whether the novel is an exaggerated expression of Weldon's more radical and outlandish views or a portrayal of a consummate trick-

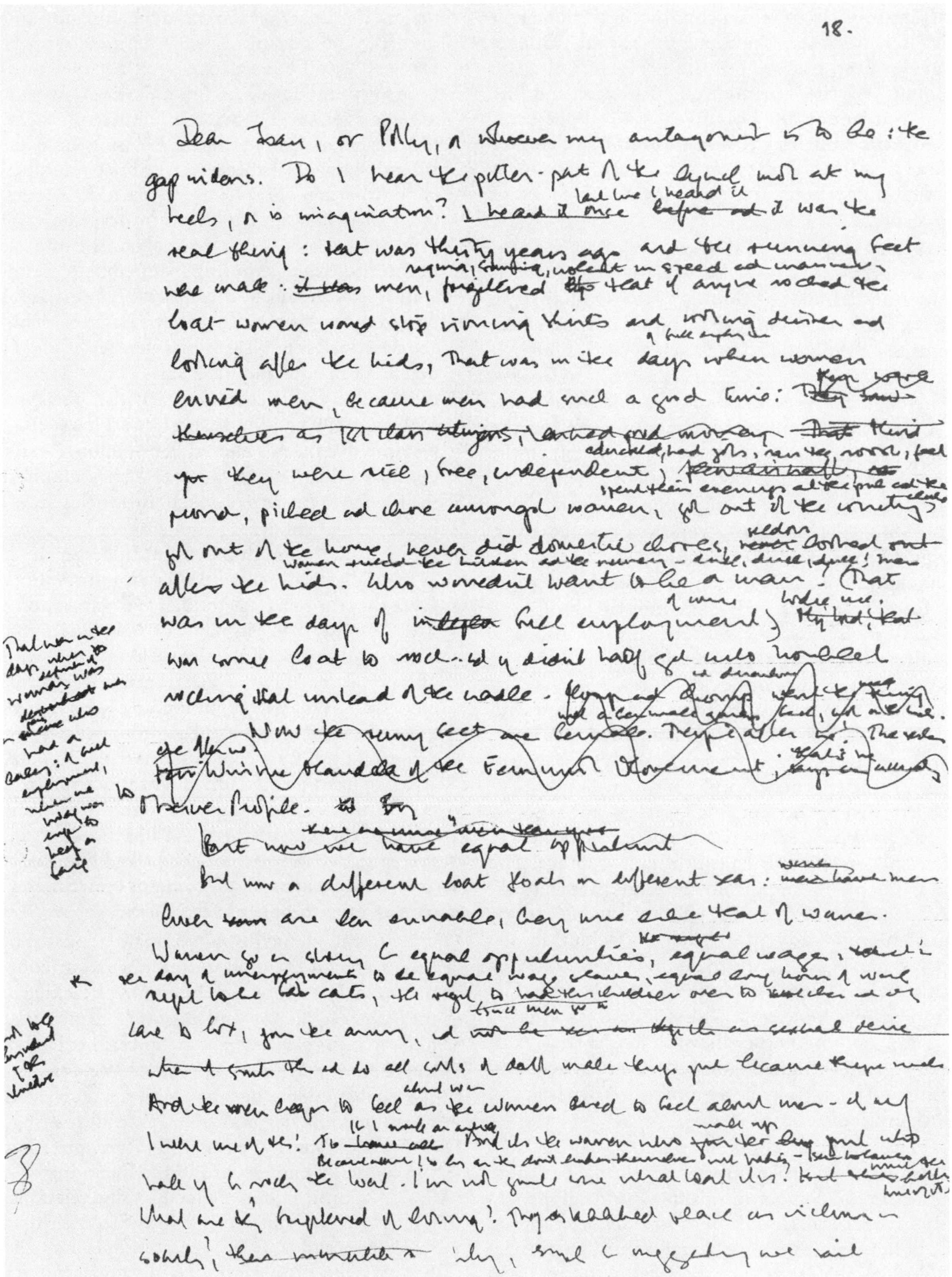
18.

Dear Joan, or Polly, or whoever my antagonist is to be: the gap widens. Do I hear the pitter-pat of the [illegible] at my heels, or is it imagination? I heard it once before and it was the real thing: that was thirty years ago and the running feet were male: it was men, frightened that if anyone [illegible] that women would stop ironing shirts and cooking dinner and looking after the kids. That was in the days when women envied men, because men had such a good time: [illegible] for they were rich, free, independent, [illegible] picked and chose amongst women, got out of the country, got out of the home, never did domestic chores, seldom looked after the kids. Who wouldn't want to be a man? That was in the days of full employment [illegible]

[illegible]

But now a different [illegible] Women go [illegible] equal opportunities, equal wages, [illegible]

Page from the manuscript for Weldon's work-in-progress, a novel with the working title "Mind the Gap" (Collection of Fay Weldon) ster. Certainly Hugo seems convinced; the last sight of him is as he enters the Sixteenth Darcian Chapel as a gray-suited pastor about to perform. Criticism was made of the fragmented structure and the author's presence as "polemicist and puppeteer," both of which meant the book did not "altogether work as a novel," but it was praised for tackling a difficult subject and for "some neat depictions of self-deception."

A third collection of short stories, *Moon over Minneapolis, or, Why She Couldn't Stay* (1991) preceded a return to more-familiar Weldon territory with two minor novels. *Growing Rich* (1992) started out as a television serial on Anglia TV and then appeared in book form, closely followed by *Life Force* (1992). In *Growing Rich* a wheelchair-bound narrator, aided by observation and a large helping of imagination, follows the fortunes of three young girls living miserably in the dreary, flat East Anglian town of Fenedge. Their vicissitudes and triumphs are many—this is a novel with a fast-moving plot—and are reflected in the ever-changing fortunes of the town and its inhabitants. Throughout readers are offered two possible explanations for events: luck or the work of the devil, here embodied in Driver, a chauffeur in a black BMW (though as Driver reminds readers, "the Prince of Darkness is the Prince of Luck"). It is a witty and vigorous tale of temptation, merging social realism with black fairy tale. *Life Force* is dominated by Leslie Beck, or rather his penis, which "was one seventh exactly of his height," or ten inches, and which has been experienced by most of the female characters in the novel. Like *Female Friends,* the book is a retrospective view of the lives of a group of friends now in middle age. The novel is filled with humorous nostalgia; Leslie Beck, though seedy and foolish, brought the kind of energy, excitement, and adventure that is lacking in the women's marriages. *Life Force* shares with *Growing Rich* an emphasis on the discontent of both sexes. The Devil picks up "the scent of discontent" and makes things happen, for good or ill, while Leslie Beck, "this rampaging smelly naked monster with curly red hair, this muscled goat," may be a more pedestrian image of devilish enticements.

Personally 1992 was not a good year for Weldon: her marriage broke up after her husband of more than thirty years left her for his therapist, and she was finally divorced in 1994. There was intense press interest in her domestic arrangements during this time; she told Valerie Grove that she evaded the attention by saying she was in fact Fay Weldon's sister Frances, to whom she has since become "quite devoted." In interviews she exhibits the engaging mix of self-mockery, humor, and stoical cheerfulness alongside sadness and genuine anger that is the trademark of her

fiction. It is clear that she was quite unhappy about the divorce; she said in a 1993 interview with Hunter Davies, "I still have a lot of getting over to do. It's been very emotional. . . . I don't know how women of my age ever survive when it happens to them." She held responsible in part her increasing fame and considerable financial success, but her strongest feelings and attribution of blame are revealed in a series of attacks on what she has come to describe as "therapism." A course of Kleinian analysis she undertook in her thirties when suffering from anxiety and depression was, she said in the *Times* (20 February 1993), helpful to her—"what changed me, I used to think"—and she described it in a 1985 interview with John Haffenden as "a painful and necessary thing." However, in two scathing articles in major British newspapers in 1993 and 1997 and in several interviews, she shows just how far she has altered her opinion. Read in tandem with Weldon's 1993 novel *Affliction* (published in the United States as *Trouble*), these articles attest to her belief in the fatal damage done to marriages by counselors of the more dubious kind. She even "jested" (Weldon's word) on the BBC radio program *Start the Week* that the marriage guidance organization Relate was about to change its name to Separate (to the indignation and horror of Relate workers), and she claims, "I have never known a relationship to survive therapy." Her argument about therapy in its many different guises is that it has become the new religion, a "controlling and ravening monster" which puts excessive emphasis on the individual at the expense of society. While she has sympathy with the tolerant assistance of those in distress, she implies that too many therapists are in search of power and financial reward and could be accused of trying to "rewrite the narratives of other people's lives."

In this context *Affliction* might almost stand as a case study in the devastating misuse of counseling therapies. It is a short and bitter novel, lacking any but the blackest humor and narrated in a brisk third-person with relentless gusto. Spicer, husband of central character Annette, is probably Weldon's most unreasonable, monstrous man, and his cruel, selfish, intolerable behavior makes for painful reading. After ten years of marriage (though it transpires later that the couple did not get around to marrying or putting Spicer's house in joint ownership), the relationship between Annette, finally pregnant with their first child, and Spicer suddenly deteriorates. Spicer's beliefs and habits, even his preferences in food, change almost overnight, to Annette's consternation and bewilderment. It emerges quite soon that he has been visiting a therapist who fills his head with astrological nonsense and psychobabble. More sinister is the suggestion at the end of the novel that, as a hypnotherapist, Dr.

Rhea Marks has been erasing, or at least distorting, his memories; certainly he denies much of what Annette tries to remind him about their experiences together. The novel is uncharacteristically partisan. Annette does everything a sane, loving person might do to save her relationship, while being accused not only by Spicer but by her best friend and her mother of behaving irrationally and needing therapy herself. She is constantly thwarted, even abused, by her husband and the therapists from hell (Dr. Rhea's husband, Herman, also a therapist of sorts, is equally despicable). The Markses' motives become obvious as their hold on Spicer becomes stronger—they want his house—and, having been convinced that he is "destined for spiritual greatness" and is beyond materialism, Spicer turns the house over to them, giving Annette, who has by this point lost the baby and been gravely ill, nothing.

As an act of vengeance, *Affliction* is powerful, but it is not Weldon at her best. Although it is steeped in social realism and has none of the wilder fantasy or supernatural elements of earlier fiction, it is strangely less plausible than many of the other novels. In the absence of the distance and balance her comedy and narrative methods usually contribute, the reader may doubt the credibility of the characters and their actions. Weldon's gender bias becomes apparent with her representation of Spicer. In *She-Devil* and *Darcy's Utopia* the reader is encouraged to applaud the heroines' changes of identity and to condone manipulative behavior; Weldon has a "preoccupation with metamorphosis" and sees it as empowering for women. In men, on the other hand, it constitutes treachery and hypocrisy and is to be despised.

The press was alerted to *Affliction* before it even reached the bookshops. Letters and articles appeared in British newspapers, evidence of an extraordinary interest in the issue, condemning or supporting Weldon's point of view. Therapists became, briefly, the subject of heated public debate. Critical reception of the novel was mixed, with the reviewer for *The Guardian* (8 February 1994) finding it overplayed—"[Weldon's] appetite for the grotesque overwhelms the subtle horror of her message"—and the dénouement inappropriately farcical while the reviewer for *The Observer* (13 February 1994) deemed it "the finest novel Weldon has written in years." There was disagreement as to whether Annette was a blameless victim or a fool. Nevertheless all agreed that the book had something important to say, and no one missed its autobiographical anger.

There was a return to form in Weldon's exhilarating 1995 novel, *Splitting,* in which the consequences of an unwanted separation are again the keynote and are dealt with inventively and with comic mischief.

The central character of *Splitting,* whose name, Angelica, conveniently takes a variety of short forms, finds herself, when ejected from her marital home, "cracking and splitting" into Angel, Jelly, and Angelica as well as her wifely persona of Lady Rice, to be joined later by Ajax (AJA+X), a male "narrator," and Angela. Lady Rice, who "stays at home" in the Claremont Hotel to agonize over the causes of the marital breakdown, uses her "alter egos as strategies for survival." Each is generally aware of the thoughts and activities of the others as Jelly seeks her financial due by tampering with letters from her husband's lawyer; Angel finds solace in sex with the chauffeur, aptly named Ram; and Angelica wastes money on clothes and shoes. The other selves help Lady Rice deal with the pain of separation but are also an extension of what Weldon stresses in much of her writing: "to be thus divided in three is what many women report." The commonplace "perforation" of personality is merely enhanced when Lady Rice finds herself on "shifting sand," having lost what she believed to be permanent. The answer to suffering, for Lady Rice's personae, is immersion in creative distraction in many forms; the narrative constantly changes direction, from the story of Lady Rice's marriage, told by Ajax; to Jelly's experiences as an employee of the lawyer Brian Moss; to the saga of Lodestar House, once the home of the bohemian Violet, adored by the literati of her time and now subject to legal wrangles over inheritance. Eventually Angelica suffers temporary amnesia and is freed from her past to become Angela Maize, would-be prostitute in a revamped Lodestar House that fulfills the fantasies of its guests. In an extravagant get-together characters from the novel, dead and alive (ghosts, or are they just holograms?), live out their dreams with the help of Una's Happy Boys and Girls in a place "where they could be themselves, where what you wanted to see, you saw," where gender (defined by Una as "nature's error") is fluid and Angela is able to give birth to a new self. It is a triumphant recovery for Angelica, implausible but satisfying: "The past is the problem," Angela would say airily. "The secret of happiness is to forget it altogether." *Splitting* was seen as a return to laughter and invention, "gloriously preposterous" with some "invigorating wishful thinking" in the giving back of control to a character who, in the wake of a failed marriage, "does more than survive."

Whether or not Weldon herself chose this route to happiness is unknown, but she married her business manager, Nick Fox, in 1995 and continued her prolific output. A fourth book of short stories previously published in a range of magazines in Britain and the United States, *Wicked Women,* also appeared in 1995; and her twenty-first novel, *Worst Fears,* was published in 1996, dealing with a woman whose husband has recently died. Her mourning speedily turns to hatred when she discovers from the women around her that her husband was in fact a philanderer, and she sets out to achieve a cathartic revenge. Still courting controversy, Weldon received contradictory reviews for this novel. An antagonistic reader thought it "thinner and more slapdash than many in her oeuvre," conceived depressingly from paranoia (*The Guardian*, 7 November 1996); but for a fan it had "all the familiar, enjoyable hallmarks" (*The Observer*, 10 November 1996). The latter reviewer believed that with *Worst Fears* "[Weldon's] place as one of the sharpest satirists writing in English on contemporary sexual manners is still assured."

Interviews:

Melvin Maddocks, "Mothers and Masochists," *Time*, 101 (26 February 1973): 91;

John Heilpern, "Facts of Female Life," *London Observer Magazine*, 18 February 1979, pp. 36–37;

Angela Neustatter, "Earth Mother Truths," *Guardian*, 20 February 1979, p. 24;

Elisabeth Dunn, "Among the Women," *London Telegraph Sunday Magazine*, 16 December 1979, pp. 55, 58, 61, 64;

Pauline Peters, "The Fay behind *Puffball*," *Sunday Times* (London), 17 February 1980, p. 36;

Michelene Wandor, ed., *On Gender and Writing* (London: Pandora Press, 1983), pp. 160–165;

John Haffenden, *Novelists in Interview* (London: Methuen, 1985), pp. 305–320;

Brenda Polan, "Reading between the Power Lines," *Guardian*, 14 August 1985, p. 18;

Libby Purves, "Weldon Takes the High Wire," *Times* (London), 2 September 1987, p. 15;

"Gentle Rebel Who She-Devils the Hardback Heavies," *Sunday Times* (London), 6 September 1987, p. 10;

Joanna Briscoe, "Sweet Anarchy, Poisoned Utopia," *Guardian*, 19 September 1990, p. 17;

Angela Lambert, "Not Such a She-Devil," *Independent on Sunday* (London), 5 May 1991, pp. 13–14;

Valerie Grove, "Ups and Downs among the Women," *Times Saturday Review* (London), 25 January 1992, pp. 10–11;

Hunter Davies, "Fay Weldon, a Sexy Rich Granny Having Fun," *Independent* (London), 2 February 1993, p. 13.

References:

Flora Alexander, *Contemporary Women Novelists* (London: Edward Arnold, 1989), pp. 51–55;

Martin Amis, "Prose Is the Leading Lady," *New York Times Book Review*, 2 October 1977, pp. 13, 52;

Regina Barreca, ed., *Fay Weldon's Wicked Fictions* (Hanover, N.H. & London: University Press of New England, 1994);

Liz Bird and Joe Eliot, "The Life and Loves of a She Devil (Fay Weldon–Ted Whitehead)," in *British Television Drama in the 1980s*, edited by George W. Brandt (Cambridge: Cambridge University Press, 1993), pp. 214–233;

Anita Brookner, "The Return of the Earth Mother," *Times Literary Supplement* (London), 22 February 1980, p. 202;

Liz Fekete, "Fay Weldon: Radical Heretic or Social Puritan?," *Race and Class*, 31, no. 2 (1989): 73–78;

Betsy Ford, "Belladonna Speaks: Fay Weldon's *Waste Land* Revision in *The Cloning of Joanna May*," *West Virginia University Philological Papers*, 38 (1992): 322–333;

Ann-Marie Herbert, "Rewriting the Feminine Script: Fay Weldon's Wicked Laughter," *Critical Matrix: The Princeton Journal of Women, Gender and Culture*, 7, no. 1 (1993): 21–40;

Olga Kenyon, "Fay Weldon and the Radicalizing of Language," in her *Women Novelists Today: A Survey of English Writing in the Seventies and Eighties* (New York: St. Martin's Press, 1988), pp. 104–128;

Agate Nesaule Krouse, "Feminism and Art in Fay Weldon's Novels," *Critique*, 22, no. 2 (1978): 5–20;

Lorna Sage, *Women in the House of Fiction: Post-War Women Novelists* (London: Macmillan, 1992), pp. 153–160;

Patricia Juliana Smith, "Weldon's *The Life and Loves of a She-Devil*," *Explicator*, 51 (Summer 1993): 255–257;

Patricia Waugh, "Contemporary Women Writers: Challenging Postmodernist Aesthetics," in her *Feminine Fictions: Revisiting the Postmodern* (London: Routledge, 1989), pp. 168–217;

Pauline Young, "Selling the Emperor's New Clothes: Fay Weldon as Contemporary Folklorist," *Folklore in Use*, 2 (1994): 103–113;

Anthea Zeman, *Presumptuous Girls: Women and Their World in the Serious Woman's Novel* (London: Weidenfeld & Nicolson, 1977), pp. 64–65.

A. N. Wilson

(27 October 1950 –   )

Russell Greer
Texas Woman's University

See also the Wilson entries in *DLB 14: British Novelists Since 1960* and *DLB 155: Twentieth-Century British Literary Biographers.*

BOOKS: *The Sweets of Pimlico* (London: Secker & Warburg, 1977);

Unguarded Hours (London: Secker & Warburg, 1978);

Kindly Light (London: Secker & Warburg, 1979);

The Healing Art (London: Secker & Warburg, 1980);

The Laird of Abbotsford: A View of Sir Walter Scott (Oxford & New York: Oxford University Press, 1980);

Who Was Oswald Fish? (London: Secker & Warburg, 1981);

Wise Virgin (London: Secker & Warburg, 1982; New York: Viking, 1983);

The Life of John Milton (Oxford & New York: Oxford University Press, 1983);

Scandal; or, Priscilla's Kindness (London: Hamish Hamilton, 1983; New York: Viking, 1984);

Hilaire Belloc (London: Hamish Hamilton, 1984; New York: Atheneum, 1984);

Lilibet: An Account in Verse of the Early Years of the Queen until the Time of her Accession (London: Blond & Briggs, 1984);

How Can We Know? An Essay on the Christian Religion (London: Hamish Hamilton, 1985; New York: Atheneum, 1985);

Gentlemen in England: A Vision (London: Hamish Hamilton, 1985; New York: Viking, 1986);

The Church in Crisis, by Wilson, Charles Moore, and Gavin Stamp (London: Hodder & Stoughton, 1986);

Love Unknown (London: Hamish Hamilton, 1986; New York: Viking, 1987);

Landscape in France, text by Wilson, photographs by Charlie Waite (London: Elm Tree, 1987; New York: St. Martin's Press, 1988);

Stray (London: Walker, 1987; New York: Orchard, 1989);

A. N. Wilson (photograph © Tara Heinemann)

Penfriends from Porlock: Essays and Reviews 1977–1986 (London: Hamish Hamilton/New York: Viking, 1988);

Tolstoy: A Biography (London: Hamish Hamilton, 1988; New York: Norton, 1988);

Incline Our Hearts (London: Hamish Hamilton, 1988; New York: Viking, 1989);

The Tabitha Stories (London: Walker, 1988); republished as *Tabitha* (New York: Orchard, 1989);

Eminent Victorians (London: BBC Books, 1989; New York: Norton, 1990);

Hazel the Guinea-Pig (London: Walker, 1989; Cambridge, Mass.: Candlewick Press, 1992);

A Bottle in the Smoke (London: Sinclair-Stevenson, 1990; New York: Viking, 1990);

C. S. Lewis: A Biography (London: Collins, 1990; New York: Norton, 1990);

Against Religion, Chatto Counterblasts, no. 19 (London: Chatto & Windus, 1991);

Daughters of Albion (London: Sinclair-Stevenson, 1991; New York: Viking, 1992);

Jesus (London: Sinclair-Stevenson, 1992; New York: Norton, 1992);

The Rise and Fall of the House of Windsor (London: Sinclair-Stevenson, 1993; New York: Norton, 1993);

The Vicar of Sorrows (London: Sinclair Stevenson, 1993; New York: Norton, 1994);

Hearing Voices (London: Sinclair-Stevenson, 1995; New York: Norton, 1996);

A Watch in the Night (London: Sinclair-Stevenson, 1996; New York: Norton, 1996);

Paul: The Mind of the Apostle (London: Sinclair Stevenson, 1997; New York: Norton, 1997).

OTHER: Sir Walter Scott, *Ivanhoe,* edited by Wilson (Harmondsworth: Penguin, 1982);

Bram Stoker, *Dracula,* edited by Wilson (Oxford & New York: Oxford University Press, 1983);

Leo Tolstoy, *The Lion and the Honeycomb: The Religious Writings of Tolstoy,* edited by Wilson, translated by Robert Chandler (London: Collins, 1987; San Francisco: Harper & Row, 1987);

John Henry Newman, *Prayers, Poems and Meditations,* edited by Wilson (London: SPCK, 1989; New York: Crossroad, 1990);

The Faber Book of Church and Clergy, edited by Wilson (London: Faber & Faber, 1992);

The Faber Book of London, edited by Wilson (London: Faber & Faber, 1993).

As a novelist, editor, critic, biographer, and journalist, A. N. Wilson has created a significant body of work since the late 1970s. Frequently compared to the work of Barbara Pym, Kingsley Amis, and Evelyn Waugh, his novels are popular comedies of manners or farces, celebrated for their wit and for their perceptive criticism of contemporary British society. His narrow preoccupation with the Anglican church, English politics, sex, and middle-class sensibilities, however, has drawn as much criticism as praise.

Andrew Norman Wilson was born on 27 October 1950 in Stone, Staffordshire, into a family with ties to the pottery industry—his father once served as a managing director of Wedgwoods. After initial schooling with Dominican nuns, Wilson attended preparatory school in Great Malvern. He was at Rugby School from 1964 to 1969 and New College, Oxford, from 1969 to 1972, where he studied Old and Middle English and linguistics under John Bayley and Christopher Tolkien. In 1971 he won the Chancellor's Essay Prize and married his tutor, Katherine Duncan-Jones, a fellow in English of Somerville College, Oxford. The couple have two daughters.

After graduation Wilson taught at New College, Oxford, and for Edward Greene's tutorial agency. In 1973 he read theology and studied briefly at St. Stephen's House, Oxford, for the Anglican priesthood, which he did not pursue. In 1975 he won the Ellerton Theological Prize and worked for five terms as an assistant master at Merchant Taylors' School, London, and then as a junior lecturer at St. Hugh's College, Oxford, from 1976 to 1982 and New College, Oxford, from 1977 to 1980. From 1981 to 1983 he was the literary editor of *The Spectator* in London, and in 1989 he served as a presenter of the *Eminent Victorians* television series, which he turned into a book. In 1990 he was divorced from his first wife and married the art historian Ruth Guilding. He is currently the literary editor of the *Evening Standard.* Wilson has frequently been a party to journalistic and literary controversy, not the least of which has been his public on-again and off-again relationship with Christianity as he has moved from outspoken support of religion in *How Can We Know? An Essay on the Christian Religion* (1985) to an attack on it in *Against Religion* (1991), followed by biographies of Jesus (1992), and the apostle Paul (1997) that have elicited strong public reaction.

As a novelist Wilson's primary strength is his ability to portray convincingly the desires and beliefs of upper-middle-class English professionals: clergymen, actors, politicians, students, and teachers. These portraits are convincing because Wilson faithfully and sympathetically documents the pettiness and irrationality of their desires, usually sexual, and the narrowness of their ideologies. This strength, however, is also Wilson's most profound weakness since he seems unable to create any characters who do not belong to this class or who are not circumscribed by a narrow field of interests. As a result his novels have a certain predictable quality—they all typically feature some kind of religious or sexual angst, which becomes exposed or aggravated by farce, resulting in disillusionment by the character and often by the reader. His novels consistently dwell on themes of faith, sex, and the hypocrisy of English society, but in recent years his fiction has presented a progressively darker and less redemptive vision, particularly in his novel sequence, "The Lampitt Papers" (*Incline Our Hearts,* 1988; *A Bottle in the Smoke,* 1990; *Daughters of Albion,* 1991; *Hearing Voices,* 1995; and *A Watch in the Night,* 1996).

Wilson's first novel, *The Sweets of Pimlico* (1977), was written while he was teaching at Merchant Taylors' School, and it won the John Llewelyn Rhys Memorial Prize. It is the story of a shy, quiet young woman, Evelyn Tradescant, recovering from a failed love affair, who meets and befriends a mysterious old man named Theo Gormann. Evelyn becomes part of his circle and part of an emotional triangle with another of Gormann's disciples, the sweets manufacturer "Pimlico" Price, a homosexual former lover of Evelyn's brother. Even here, in his earliest novel, Wilson displays interest in themes that he continues to pursue later—interrelated, hypocritical English social relationships; farce; sexuality; and the clergy. Evelyn's incestuous sexual relationship with her brother, Jeremy, becomes a metaphor for an inbred English society warped by repressed sexuality. Evelyn and Jeremy's indiscretion is revealed farcically when Jeremy accidently sends a letter meant for Evelyn to his parents, confessing to incest, homosexuality, and failure at college. Their shocked parents call upon a clergyman for support, who comically diagnoses schizophrenia: "You see, as I see it, two Jeremys wrote that letter: the Jeremy who is Evelyn's brother—with all the frustrations and desires of the perfectly normal, healthy, highly-sexed young man . . . and the other Jeremy, the little boy who has made a mess of things, and wants to run home to Mummy and Daddy."

Another important metaphor in this novel, appearing almost two decades before A. S. Byatt used the device in *Angels and Insects* (1992), is that of insects used to describe the meaningless actions of the main characters in the novel. Evelyn has an enthusiasm for water beetles and compares her friends and family to the great silver beetle, the screech beetle, and the whirligig beetle: "She wondered if human relations would be any easier if the only indication of gender which we possessed was the shape of our feet," like the great silver beetle. The point of this figurative language somewhat obscurely relates to a speech given by Gormann to Evelyn at the end of the novel as she reads to him a selection from Charles Darwin's *On the Origin of Species* (1859). He explains, "this reads too much like life . . . this savage process of selection is what dogs our lives. We cannot be all to all. And I find myself only able to be all to one," a vague reference to the emotional triangle connecting Gormann, Price, and Evelyn. That selection, however, fails to happen because of an explosion at an art gallery that leads to Gormann's death and Evelyn's rather passive agreement to marry Price. Although the critic Susannah Clapp, writing in *The New Statesman* (27 May 1977), believed that the novel was about "the disconnected-

Dust jacket for the U.S. edition of Wilson's novel about the friendship of three young women

ness of people's lives and the heady attractions provided by enormous wealth and purposeful mysteriousness," clearly *The Sweets of Pimlico* is also an early attempt by Wilson to make a statement about the naturalistic forces—particularly sex—that blindly shape and drive the lives of contemporary middle-class society.

Wilson's next two novels, *Unguarded Hours* (1978) and *Kindly Light* (1979), share a common protagonist, Norman Shotover, and many of the same characters. Norman's innocence and passive nature lead him from failure in love into a theological college for the lack of anything else to do. Once there Norman becomes ordained by a drunken, eccentric, wandering bishop of the Eastern Church and becomes a figure through whom Wilson can criticize the church and modern social problems. Norman's inert but normal personality is a foil to a series of bizarre sexual revelations and characters such as Norman's friend Mungo, the Dundee of Caik, who farcically despises the Lake District. In a review in *The*

Dust jacket for the U.S. edition of the third novel in Wilson's Lampitt Papers series

Listener (11 May 1978), John Mellors criticized the novel for its simplicity:

> Unfortunately, too many of Wilson's selected targets are only sitting-ducks. It is easy enough to make fun of a radical dean who writes books called *Chuck It, God* and *I Can't Get No Satisfaction*. Effeminate male homosexuals, and girls who run health food shops but deep down inside want to be chained to a kitchen sink, are equally easily mocked.

Norman reappears in *Kindly Light* as a member of the outlandish Catholic Institute of Alfonso (the C.I.A.), a crude representation of the Society of Jesuits. It is three years after events in *Unguarded Hours,* and Norman, who no longer believes in God, wants to leave the church but does not know how to tell his superiors. In farcical prose reminiscent of Waugh, his supervisor watches Norman closely for signs of being a spy and a traitor and misinterprets actions that comically bring Norman success and celebrity. With his bizarre friend Lubbock, Norman escapes the church, and they meet again years later

as teachers. This overcomplicated plot is illuminated with flashes of wit, but as a whole it collapses under its debt to earlier English writers of farce. Paul Ableman wrote in *The Spectator* (2 June 1979): "A. N. Wilson undoubtedly has a huge talent. It would be splendid if he could now demonstrate that it extends beyond mastering the craft and technique and—most depressingly—outlook of an obsolete mode of fiction." Patricia Craig, writing in *The New Statesman* (25 May 1979), believed that in this novel Wilson's reach exceeded his grasp: "Even the hero fails to provide a fixed central point, since he's characterized by little more than his successive occupations: priest, schoolmaster, grapefruit picker, film extra, research assistant to a mystic. Though much of the scenario is very funny, the book appears seriously strained by its excess of material."

Wilson's next novel, *The Healing Art* (1980), is a black comedy that explores the consequences of a careless error that profoundly affects the lives of two women: Pamela Cowper, an Oxford lecturer in her late thirties, and Dorothy Higgs, an unattractive, middle-aged, lower-class housewife. Their physician accidentally switches their X-rays, telling Pamela, who is healthy, that she is dying of cancer, and telling Dorothy—who really has the disease—that she is well. As a result Pamela travels to America to spend her last days with the man she loves and becomes bisexually involved in a love triangle with her friend's lover. Dorothy, who is dying of bone cancer, undergoes a sickening deterioration, beginning with bones that start to break mysteriously. The meeting between Pamela and an emaciated Dorothy is dramatic, as Pamela discovers the error and its consequences and realizes that a mistake and not a miracle has given her a reprieve from death. The brutality and shocking dark comedy of this novel make it a leap forward in Wilson's art. Simon Blow in *The New Statesman* (6 June 1980) attributed its success to Wilson's ability to "make us laugh just when we should cry." For *The Healing Art* Wilson won the Somerset Maugham Award and the Southern Arts Literature Prize for 1980 and the Arts Council National Book Award for 1981.

In *Who Was Oswald Fish?* (1981) Wilson presents a tangled web of meaningless lives given significance by their biological ties to Victorian philanderer and architect Oswald Fish. As the characters in the novel discover their relationship to Fish and to one another, the reader experiences the purposeless, sexually driven existence that characterized Fish's own life—an existence that has been passed on to his descendants and to the reader. Wilson signals this central theme in several conversations between two main characters, both of whom do not know at the time of their first sexual encounter (in Kensal Green cemetery) that they are related. Fred Jobling asks, "Is this what we are hurtling towards. . . . Is this where it all leads—just to damp and mould?" His partner, the sensual Fanny Williams, replies, "Now you know what I mean about emptiness at the heart of the universe." Set against the background of the 1979 campaign for prime minister, this novel presents a collection of unsympathetic protagonists, described by Angela Huth in *The Listener* (12 November 1981) as the kind found in "a very high-class strip cartoon which induces sudden laughter and painful sympathy." Fanny, a former model who owns a chain of fashionable boutiques, purchases a ruined Gothic church (St. Aidan's, Purgstall Heath) that had been designed by Fish. When she seeks to restore the church, however, the reader encounters Fish himself through his sexually explicit diaries discovered by Fanny's grandmother, as well as through Charles Bullowewo, a black Old Etonian barrister who is Fish's illegitimate offspring. The novel substitutes wit for genuine character development but succeeds in delighting with farce and ingenuity.

Wise Virgin (1982) traces the moral growth of a self-involved scholar and librarian named Giles Fox who has devoted his life to editing a medieval text, the "Tretis of Love Hevenliche," that praises the wisdom of virginity for nuns. A series of tragedies has robbed him of his sight and two wives, leaving him a pitiful figure in his library, surrounded by two maidens—his teenage daughter, Tibba, and his assistant, Miss Agar. More tragedy follows, however, as his edition is rejected by his press; he rejects the advances and possibility of happiness with Miss Agar; and his daughter leaves him for attachment with the homosexual Captain de Courcy. Critical reception of the novel has been mixed; the relentlessness of its tragedy prompted John Sutherland to write in *The London Review of Books* (18 November–December 1982): "It would be unbearable if Wilson's narrative were to let us feel. But response is unaesthetically frozen by the Arctic objectivity of it all." Others, however, have praised Wilson for an apparent growth in his ability to present fully developed characterizations; for example, in *Punch* (13 October 1982) Stanley Reynolds said: "In a time when feminist writers produce grotesque stereotyped male characters and when male novelists create wooden ladies, it is amazing to read a young English novelist who has the old-fashioned ability to breathe life into all his characters." *Wise Virgin* was named one of the *Observer* Books of the Year, and it won the W. H. Smith Annual Literary Award for 1983.

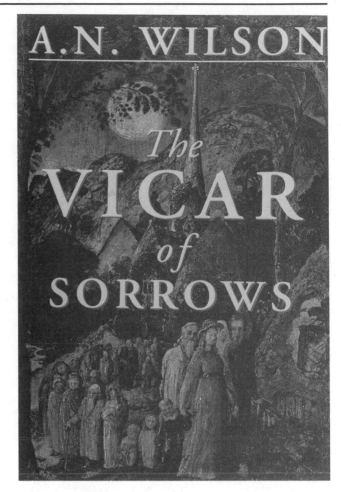

Dust jacket for Wilson's novel about a clergyman who loses his faith and whose life is subsequently destroyed

Wilson continues his social criticism in his next novel, mixing it with political satire. *Scandal; or, Priscilla's Kindness* (1983) criticizes British political society by displaying the cultural and psychological forces that lead to "scandal." Wilson shows the word itself to be inadequate to describe the falsity and weakness common to a British society where a vast gap exists between public morality and private sexuality. Caught in this gap is Derek Blore, a prominent, self-made British politician and cabinet member with a taste for kinky sex. Catering to his sadomasochistic desires is a dim-witted prostitute named Bernadette, controlled by the Russians, who subjects Blore (dressed as a schoolboy) to pleasurable punishment in her Hackney flat, obtaining incriminating tapes and photographs in the process. Also on center stage is Priscilla, Blore's beautiful wife, who began the marriage patronizing her red-faced husband but to her chagrin finds herself forced to admire him as he rises to higher and higher office. A kind of equilibrium in their marriage finally establishes itself, however, with the de-

Dust jacket for the U.S. edition of the penultimate novel in Wilson's Lampitt Papers series, a novel about history and memory

struction of Blore's career when his involvement with the prostitute, the Russians, and a botched murder attempt is exposed by Priscilla's own lover, a Fleet Street journalist named Feathers.

This is a novel primarily about betrayal: Blore betrays his country and his family; Feathers betrays Priscilla; Priscilla betrays Blore; Bernadette betrays Blore; and so on. While Wilson skillfully captures the pain of such betrayal, only the anguish of Blore's son, tormented by his schoolmates because of his father's disgrace, is completely successful. Pat Rogers, in *The London Review of Books* (15 September–5 October 1983), identified a central problem: "the novel lacks the underlying metaphor (the profession of healing, Victorian architecture, Medieval legend) which has sustained its three predecessors." Equally significant is a confusion of sympathy because the reader has no one with whom to identify. As a result Blore's final descent is a farce: he is arrested in church while dressed absurdly as a Viking—a scene that becomes a supreme moment of disaffection instead of enlightenment.

In *Gentlemen in England: A Vision* (1985) Wilson re-creates the ideological clashes of late-Victorian England by presenting them in the minds of the Nettleship family and its associates. Geologist and atheist Horace Nettleship clashes with his son, Lionel, who develops a passionate hunger for Christianity in its most enthusiastic forms. Poor Horace receives no comfort at home from his estranged wife, Charlotte, who has not spoken to him in years and who suddenly develops a passion for a young painter. Hovering around this domestic and cultural drama is Marvo Chatterway, a social gadfly who knows everyone. As these people clash and emerge wiser, Wilson produces what may be his most profound criticism of society, both Victorian and modern. That criticism takes its sharpest focus in scenes of a restored monastery in Malvern Hills to which Lionel retreats while following his spiritual leader, Father Cuthbert. Instead of a glorious medieval cloister, however, Lionel discovers something much more squalid: the new Llangendedd is unimpressive and small, peopled with monks who hide the cigarettes they crush beneath their sandals and who engage in flagellation and secret homosexual trysts in the woodshed. The crowning moment of disillusionment for Lionel and the reader occurs when the brothers of Llangendedd witness an "apparition"—a dubious vision of the Virgin Mary:

> "Oi told yer Oi'd 'it it wiv me bat."
> "It was like a great bird."
> "It were more like a flash of light."
> "Or like a lady."
> "Yeah, it were. It were like a lady. It was like as if Our Blessed Lady herself flew over our 'eds as we prayed and prayed, like."
> "It was Our Lady!" Brother Angelus's effusive tones now rose above the starling-twitter of the boys. "Who can doubt it?"

In *Love Unknown* (1986) three young women—Monica, Belinda, and Richeldis—share a flat and become close friends, but a misadventure leads to tangled relationships twenty years later as Monica has an affair with Simon Longworth, Richeldis's husband. Richeldis meanwhile struggles to care for her dotty mother, a previously acclaimed publisher who is lost in fantasy. Once again Wilson skillfully uses farce to uncover the twisted lies and hypocrisy binding together families and society, but typically that criticism is the point of the novel, and the novel does not rise above it to create an important vicarious experience.

Incline Our Hearts is the first of five novels in the "Lampitt Papers" series, narrated by Julian Ramsey and chronicling his involvement with the Lampitt family. In this first novel, written in the style of a memoir, Julian remembers his younger days, criticizing the entire process of autobiography and describing the horrors of English boarding school. After Julian's parents are killed during World War II, he comes to live with his uncle Roy, a country rector infatuated with an important local family—the Lampitts. At his boarding school Julian becomes infatuated with his art teacher but learns to his horror of her involvement with the mysterious Raphael Hunter, whose path is to cross Julian's throughout his life. Eventually Hunter becomes entangled with the Lampitts also, as he schemes to obtain the private documents of a famous author who is a member of the family, producing, as a result, a scandalous book that destroys the relationship between Uncle Roy and the Lampitts. Michiko Kakutani, writing in *The New York Times* (10 January 1989) called the novel a "sentimental education," one that makes readers aware that "memoirs and biographies, like fiction, are attempts to make sense of experience—illusionary efforts to impose a narrative order on the multifarious and contradictory stuff of life."

The story continues in *A Bottle in the Smoke* when Julian Ramsey gives up a safe career in the factory that employed his father to embrace a career as an actor and writer in 1950s London. A twist of fate involves him with another Lampitt, this time Anne, whom he marries. Once again, however, Raphael Hunter enters Julian's life after scandalously damaging several key relationships. Again Hunter hurts Julian. While Julian becomes involved in trying to recover the papers of Jimbo Lampitt, his marriage to Anne crumbles, and she begins an affair with Hunter. Simultaneously Julian takes on the successful role of Jason Grainger on the popular radio series *The Mulberrys,* introduced in the previous novel as a model of family life for young Julian's aunt. The climax of the novel is the death of Dan Muckley, the alcoholic, defeated writer of *The Calderdale Saga* and hanger-on at the Black Bottle pub. Muckley's death is an attempt by Wilson to give this novel some form, but the result is uneven: readers understand Julian better but do not necessarily sympathize with him.

In *Daughters of Albion* Julian tells the story of Albion Pugh, who was the chosen favorite of James Petworth Lampitt. It is the 1960s, and Miles Darnley, editor of the magazine *The Spark,* sets into motion renewed interest in Pugh, who is involved with Julian's first schoolboy crush.

In *The Vicar of Sorrows* (1993) Wilson detours from the Lampitts and picks up on a familiar theme—a clergyman who has lost his faith in God and whose life begins to fall apart. With the death

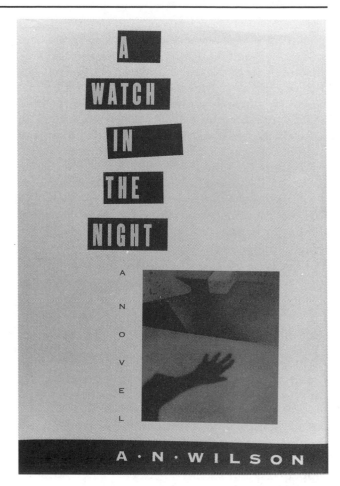

Dust jacket for the U.S. edition of the novel in which Wilson reveals the secret of Jimbo Lampitt's murder and concludes the Lampitt Papers series

of Francis Kreer's mother, Francis painfully discovers that she had a lover and that he must split his inheritance with this man, whom he detests. He goes into a deep depression. Complicating his situation, he suddenly falls in love with a beautiful young woman who plays the violin and travels with a band of free spirits. His family, church, and community are shocked when he leaves his wife for her. Particularly poignant is a battle royal fought between Francis and Alison Bill, his daughter's teacher, over access to the child. Francis's descent is hellish, as he finds himself cast adrift in society without any of the usual supports. Without true religious belief his depression reveals to those around him his lack of sympathy. His parish attacks him; his church abandons him; and his family shuns him. At the end of the novel he is alone and hallucinating in a climactic church scene after discovering that his daughter Jessica, who had been looking for him, has been kidnapped and raped. This is Wilson's darkest novel to date, with echoes of *King Lear* in it.

His most recent novels, *Hearing Voices* and *A Watch in the Night,* are a continuation and completion of the Lampitt Papers, weakly bringing the story into the current day and beyond. In *Hearing Voices* Julian appears in the year 2000 in a one-man show depicting Jimbo Lampitt—whose homosexuality remains forever in question because the proof (the Lampitt papers themselves) disappears after the unsolved murder of their American owner. In a series of flashbacks to the 1960s, Julian remembers taking LSD at a party, periods of insanity, and failed love affairs. The novel drowns in "hearing voices," failing (as the others have done) to stand on its own terms as a complete novel. The array of detail referring to the previous three works is bewildering despite a glossary called "A List of Characters Mentioned in the Story," which includes more than fifty people.

A Watch in the Night, which concludes the Lampitt chronicles, shares the fate of *Hearing Voices* in its debt to the previous works. In this concluding volume Hunter finally confesses his role in Jimbo Lampitt's death, a mystery that has held together the entire series. The strength of this novel, though, is not Julian's story, set as it is late in his life; instead, admirers of Wilson will enjoy the many digressions on current events and issues, including the ubiquitous nature of homosexuality in the British upper class and attacks on "Booker Prize" mentality among literary circles. His most profound contribution throughout the series undoubtedly will be seen as his observations on the creative process itself.

Wilson has also written biographies, with considerable success and controversy. Some supporters of Lewis responded harshly to *C. S. Lewis: A Biography* (1990) and its allegations that Lewis was an adulterer, a drinker, and a bully. While praising Wilson's wit, prose style, and introduction of new sources—many of them oral testimony—critics accused him of sloppy research and psychological misrepresentation. Yet John Fitzpatrick argued in the June–July 1990 issue of *CSL: The Bulletin of the New York C. S. Lewis Society* that "The portrait of Lewis is, on the whole, a sympathetic one, and future students of Lewis will neglect Wilson's insights at their peril."

Wilson has sparked similar interest with *Paul: The Mind of the Apostle* (1997), though its *Times Literary Supplement* reviewer (28 March 1997) called Wilson's book readable but superficial, filled with "meagerly substantiated suggestions." Wilson himself believes that he is arguing that Paul founded a sect within a sect of Judaism, never intending to establish Christianity. He proposes that Paul, unlike Christ, preached to the gentiles an apocalyptic vision. Christ himself, Wilson believes, had an "absolute contempt for the gentiles."

Wilson's prolific output in biography, fiction, and journalism should probably be read as part of one project connected with his attempt to reconcile the chaotic, immoral impulses of society and human nature with a moral, orderly, sometimes Christian worldview. In his effort to assert these issues as primary in the late twentieth century, when many others have asserted that they are not, Wilson joins writers such as Graham Greene, Muriel Spark, and Iris Murdoch in intent if not accomplishment. As a novelist he shows flashes of biting humor and warm insight into the minds of a narrow social class, but his thematic concerns appeal primarily to a small audience and will probably continue to do so.

Interview:
Rosemary Hartill, "Sermons on the Mount," in her *Writers Revealed: Eight Contemporary Novelists Talk about Faith, Religion, and God* (New York: Peter Bedrick Books, 1989), pp. 93–111.

References:
John Beversluis, "Surprised by Freud: A Critical Appraisal of A. N. Wilson's Biography of C. S. Lewis," *Lamp-Post of the Southern California C. S. Lewis Society,* 16 (December 1992): 4–19;
John Fitzpatrick, "Further In or Farther Out? Whither The 'Cultists'?," *CSL: The Bulletin of the New York C. S. Lewis Society,* 21 (June–July 1990): 13–16;
Fitzpatrick, "Who Is This A. N. Wilson and Why Is He Saying Those Terrible Things about C. S. Lewis?," *CSL: The Bulletin of the New York C. S. Lewis Society,* 21 (June–July 1990): 2–4;
Ortwin de Graef, "Sad, but True—and Funny: Notes on A. N. Wilson's Fiction," *Restant: Tijdschrift voor Recente Semiotische Teorievorming en de Analyse van Teksten,* 17 (1989): 389–408;
Eugene McGovern, "Wilson's 'New' Lewis," *CSL: The Bulletin of the New York C. S. Lewis Society,* 21 (June–July 1990): 4–7;
Gerald Weales, "Jesus Who?," *Gettysburg Review,* 6 (Autumn 1993): 688–696;
Gregory Woolf, "Off Center, on Target," *Chronicles: A Magazine of American Culture,* 10 (October 1986): 35–36.

Colin Wilson
(26 June 1931 –   )

Nicolas Tredell
Sussex University

See also the Colin Wilson entry in *DLB 14: British Novelists Since 1960.*

BOOKS: *The Outsider* (London: Gollancz, 1956; Boston: Houghton Mifflin, 1956);

Religion and the Rebel (London: Gollancz, 1957; Boston: Houghton Mifflin, 1957);

The Age of Defeat (London: Gollancz, 1959); republished as *The Stature of Man* (Boston: Houghton Mifflin, 1959);

Ritual in the Dark (London: Gollancz, 1960; Boston: Houghton Mifflin, 1960);

Adrift in Soho (London: Gollancz, 1961; Boston: Houghton Mifflin, 1961);

Encyclopaedia of Murder, by Wilson and Pat Pitman (London: Barker, 1961; New York: Putnam, 1962);

The Strength to Dream: Literature and the Imagination (London: Gollancz, 1962; Boston: Houghton Mifflin, 1962);

Man without a Shadow: The Diary of an Existentialist (London: Barker, 1963); republished as *The Sex Diary of Gerard Sorme* (New York: Dial, 1963); republished as *The Sex Diary of a Metaphysician* (Berkeley: Ronin, 1988);

Origins of the Sexual Impulse (London: Barker, 1963; New York: Putnam, 1963);

The World of Violence (London: Gollancz, 1963); republished as *The Violent World of Hugh Greene* (Boston: Houghton Mifflin, 1963);

Brandy of the Damned: Discoveries of a Musical Eclectic (London: Baker, 1964); republished as *Chords and Discords: Purely Personal Opinions on Music* (New York: Crown, 1966); republished as *Colin Wilson on Music* (London: Pan, 1967);

Necessary Doubt (London: Barker, 1964; New York: Trident, 1964);

Rasputin and the Fall of the Romanovs (London: Barker, 1964; New York: Farrar Straus, 1964);

Beyond the Outsider: The Philosophy of the Future (London: Barker, 1965; Boston: Houghton Mifflin, 1965);

Eagle and Earwig (London: Baker, 1965);

The Glass Cage (London: Barker, 1966); republished as *The Glass Cage: An Unconventional Detective Story* (New York: Random House, 1967);

Introduction to the New Existentialism (London: Hutchinson, 1966; Boston: Houghton Mifflin, 1967); republished as *The New Existentialism* (London: Wildwood House, 1980);

Sex and the Intelligent Teenager (London: Arrow, 1966; New York: Pyramid, 1968);

The Mind Parasites (London: Barker, 1967; Sauk City, Wis.: Arkham House, 1967);

Bernard Shaw: A Reassessment (London: Hutchinson, 1969; New York: Atheneum, 1969);

A Casebook of Murder (London: Frewin, 1969; New York: Cowles, 1970);

The Philosopher's Stone (London: Barker, 1969; New York: Crown, 1971);

Poetry and Mysticism (San Francisco: City Lights Books, 1969); enlarged edition (London: Hutchinson, 1970; San Francisco: City Lights Books, 1986);

Voyage to a Beginning: A Preliminary Autobiography (London: Woolf, 1969); revised and enlarged as *Voyage to a Beginning: An Intellectual History* (New York: Crown, 1969);

The God of the Labyrinth (London: Hart-Davis, 1970); republished as *The Hedonists* (New York: New American Library, 1971);

The Killer (London: New English Library, 1970); republished as *Lingard* (New York: Crown, 1970);

The Strange Genius of David Lindsay, by Wilson, J.B. Pick, and E. H. Visiak (London: Baker, 1970); republished as *The Haunted Man: The Strange Genius of David Lindsay* (San Bernardino, Cal., Cal.: Borgo Press, 1979);

Strindberg (London: Calder & Boyars, 1970); republished as *Strindberg: A Play in Two Scenes* (New York: Random House, 1972);

The Black Room (London: Weidenfeld & Nicolson, 1971; New York: Pyramid, 1975);

The Occult, A History (London: Hodder & Stoughton, 1971; New York: Random House, 1971);

Colin Wilson (photograph © Jerry Bauer)

L'Amour: The Ways of Love, text by Wilson photographs by Piero Rimaldi (New York: Crown, 1972);

New Pathways in Psychology: Maslow and the Post-Freudian Revolution (London: Gollancz, 1972; New York: Taplinger, 1972);

Order of Assassins: The Psychology of Murder (London: Hart-Davis, 1972);

Strange Powers (London: Latimer New Dimensions, 1973; New York: Random House, 1975);

Tree by Tolkien (London: Covent Garden Press/INCA Books, 1973; Santa Barbara: Capra Press, 1974);

A Book of Booze (London: Gollancz, 1974);

Jorge Luis Borges (London: Village Press, 1974);

Heinrich Hesse (London: Village Press, 1974);

Wilhelm Reich (London: Village Press, 1974);

Hesse-Reich-Borges: Three Essays (Philadelphia: Leaves of Grass Press, 1974);

Ken Russell: A Director in Search of a Hero (London: Intergroup, 1974);

The Return of the Lloigor (London: Village Press, 1974);

The Schoolgirl Murder Case (London: Hart-Davis, MacGibbon, 1974; New York: Crown, 1974);

The Craft of the Novel (London: Gollancz, 1975; Salem, N.H.: Salem House, 1986);

Mysterious Powers (London: Aldus Books/Jupiter, 1975); republished with *Spirit and Spirit Worlds* by Roy Stemman as *They Had Strange Powers* (Garden City, N.Y.: Doubleday, 1975); republished with *Minds without Boundaries* by Stuart Holroy as *Mysteries of the Mind* (London: Aldus Books, 1978);

The Unexplained (Lake Oswego, Oreg.: Lost Pleiade Press, 1975);

Enigmas and Mysteries (London: Aldus Books, 1976; Garden City, N.Y.: Doubleday, 1976);

The Geller Phenomenon (London: Aldus Books, 1976);

The Space Vampires (London: Hart-Davis, MacGibbon, 1976; New York: Random House, 1976);

Science Fiction as Existentialism (Hayes: Bran's Head Books, 1978);

Mysteries: An Investigation into the Occult, the Paranormal, and the Supernatural (London: Hodder & Stoughton, 1978; New York: Putnam, 1978);

Frankenstein's Castle—The Double Brain, Door to Wisdom (Sevenoaks, U.K.: Ashgrove Press, 1980);

Starseekers (London: Hodder & Stoughton, 1980; Garden City, N.Y.: Doubleday, 1980);

The War against Sleep: The Philosophy of Gurdjieff (Wellingborough: Aquarian, 1980); enlarged as *G. I. Gurdjieff: The War against Sleep* (Wellingborough: Aquarian, 1986; San Bernardino, Cal.: Borgo Press, 1986);

Anti-Sartre, with an Essay on Camus (San Bernardino, Cal.: Borgo Press, 1981);

Below the Iceberg: Anti-Sartre and Other Essays (San Bernardino: Borgo Press, 1981; St. Austell: Abraxas, 1994; revised and enlarged edition (San Bernardino, Cal.: Borgo Press, 1996);

Poltergeist! A Study in Destructive Haunting (London: New English Library, 1981; New York: Putnam, 1982);

The Quest for Wilhelm Reich (London & New York: Granada, 1981; Garden City, N.Y.; Anchor Press/Doubleday, 1981);

Witches, as Una Woodruff (Limpsfield: Dragon's World/Paper Tiger, 1981; New York: A & W Visuals, 1982);

Access to Inner Worlds: The Story of Brad Absetz (London: Rider, 1983);

Encyclopaedia of Modern Murder, 1962-82, by Wilson and Donald Seaman (London: Barker, 1983; New York: Putnam, 1984);

A Criminal History of Mankind (London & New York: Granada, 1984; New York: Putnam, 1984);

The Janus Murder Case (London & New York: Granada, 1984);

Lord of the Underworld: Jung and the Twentieth Century (Wellingborough.: Aquarian, 1984); republished as *C. G. Jung: Lord of the Underworld* (Wellingborough: Aquarian, 1988; San Bernardino, Cal.: Borgo Press, 1988);

The Psychic Detectives: The Story of Psychometry and Paranormal Crime Detection (London: Pan, 1984; San Francisco: Mercury House, 1985);

Rogue Trooper, Book One, by Wilson, Gerry Finley-Day, and Dave Gibbons (London: Titan, 1984);

Afterlife: An Investigation of the Evidence for Life after Death (London: Harrap, 1985; Garden City, N.Y.: Doubleday, 1987);

The Bicameral Critic, edited by Howard F. Dossor (Bath: Ashgrove, 1985; Salem, N.H.: Salem House, 1985);

The Essential Colin Wilson (London: Harrap, 1985; Berkeley: Robert Briggs/Celestial Arts, 1986);

The Personality Surgeon (London: New English Library, 1985; San Francisco: Mercury House, 1986);

Rudolf Steiner: The Man and His Vision: An Introduction to the Life and Ideas of the Founder of Anthroposophy (Wellingborough: Aquarian, 1985);

An Essay on the "New" Existentialism (Nottingham: Paupers' Press, 1986; San Bernardino, Cal.: Borgo Press, 1988);

The Laurel and Hardy Theory of Consciousness (Mill Valley, Cal.: Briggs, 1986);

Aleister Crowley: The Nature of the Beast (Wellingborough: Aquarian, 1987; San Bernardino, Cal.: Borgo Press, 1989);

The Encyclopedia of Unsolved Mysteries, by Wilson and Damon Wilson (London: Harrap, 1987; Chicago: Contemporary Books, 1988);

Jack the Ripper: Summing Up and Verdict, by Wilson and Robin Odell, edited by J. H. H. Gaute (London & New York: Bantam, 1987);

The Musician as "Outsider" (Nottingham.: Paupers' Press, 1987; San Bernardino, Cal.: Borgo Press, 1989);

Spider World: The Tower (London: Grafton, 1987); republished in three volumes as *Spider World: The Desert* (New York: Ace, 1988), *Spider World, Book Two: The Tower* (New York: Ace, 1989), *Spider World, Book Three: The Fortress* (New York: Ace, 1989);

Spider World: The Delta (London: Grafton, 1987; New York: Ace, 1990);

Autobiographical Reflections (Nottingham: Paupers' Press, 1988);

Beyond the Occult (London & New York: Bantam, 1988; New York: Carrol & Graf, 1989);

The Magician from Siberia (London: Hale, 1988);

The Mammoth Book of True Crime, edited by Howard F. Dossor (London: Robinson, 1988; New York: Carroll & Graf, 1988);

The Misfits: A Study of Sexual Outsiders (London: Grafton, 1988; New York: Carroll & Graf, 1989);

The Decline and Fall of Leftism (Nottingham: Paupers' Press, 1989; San Bernardino, Cal.: Borgo Press, 1990);

Existentially Speaking: Essays on the Philosophy of Literature (San Bernardino, Cal.: Borgo Press, 1989);

Written in Blood: A History of Forensic Detection (London: Equation, 1989);

The Mammoth Book of True Crime 2, edited by Damon Wilson (London: Robinson, 1990; New York: Carroll & Graf, 1990);

Music, Nature and the Romantic Outsider (Nottingham: Paupers' Press, 1990; San Bernardino, Cal.: Borgo Press, 1990);

The Serial Killers: A Study in the Psychology of Violence, by Wilson and Donald Seaman (London: Allen, 1990);

Marriage and London with: Paris, Leicester, London Again: Being Chapters 7 and 8 of the Author's Autobiography: "Voyage to a Beginning" (Nottingham: Paupers' Press, 1991; San Bernardino, Cal.: Borgo Press, 1991);

Mozart's Journey to Prague: A Playscript (Nottingham: Paupers' Press, 1992; San Bernardino, Cal.: Borgo Press, 1992);

Sex, America and Other Insights: Being Chapters 13, 14 and 15 of the Author's Autobiography Voyage to a Beginning (Nottingham: Paupers' Press, 1992; San Bernardino, Cal.: Borgo Press, 1992);

Spider World: The Magician (London: HarperCollins, 1992);

Unsolved Mysteries: Past and Present, by Wilson and Damon Wilson (Chicago: Contemporary Books, 1992; London: Headline, 1993);

World Famous Crimes of Passion (London: Magpie, 1992);

World Famous Cults and Fanatics, by Wilson, Damon Wilson, and Rowan Wilson (London: Magpie, 1992);

World Famous Gaslight Murders (London: Magpie, 1992);

World Famous Serial Killers (London: Magpie, 1992);

World Famous Strange Tales and Weird Mysteries, by Wilson, Damon Wilson, and Rowan Wilson (London: Magpie, 1992);

The Metal Flower Blossom and Other Plays (San Bernardino, Cal.: Borgo Press, 1993);

The Strange Life of P. D. Ouspensky (London: Aquarian Press/Thorsons, 1993);

World Famous Murders, by Wilson, Damon Wilson, and Rowan Wilson (London: Robinson, 1993); republished as *Giant Book of World Famous Murders* (London: Magpie, 1994); republished as *World Famous True Crimes* (Bristol: Paragon, 1995);

Outline of the Female Outsider (St. Austell: Abraxas, 1994);

World Famous News Stories: Weird, Funny and Peculiar,, by Wilson, Damon Wilson, and Rowan Wilson (London: Magpie, 1994);

World Famous Strange but True, by Wilson, Damon Wilson, and Rowan Wilson (London: Magpie, 1994);

World Famous True Ghost Stories, by Wilson, Damon Wilson, and Rowan Wilson (London: Magpie, 1994);

Introduction to the New Existentialism: The Author's Emendations, edited by Maurice Bassett (Burke, Va: Maurice Bassett, 1995);

A Plague of Murder: The Rise and Rise of Serial Killing in the Modern Age, by Wilson and Damon Wilson (London: Robinson, 1995); enlarged as *A Plague of Murder: The Rise and Rise of Serial Killing in the Modern Age* (London: Robinson, 1995); republished as *The Killers among Us: Sex, Madness and Mass Murder* (New York: Warner, 1997);

The Atlas of Holy Places and Sacred Sites (London: Dorling Kindersley, 1996; New York: DK, 1996);

An Extraordinary Man in an Age of Pigmies: Colin Wilson on Henry Miller (Ann Arbor, Mich.: Roger Jackson, 1996);

From Atlantis to the Sphinx (London: Virgin, 1996; New York: Fromm International, 1997);

Tree of Life: The Inaugural Exhibition of the American Visionary Art Museum, by Wilson, Rebecca Hoffberger, and Roger Maley (Baltimore: American Visionary Art Museum, 1996);

Ghost Sightings (New York: Sterling, 1997);

Mysteries of the Universe (London: Dorling Kindersley, 1997; New York: DK, 1997);

UFOs and Aliens (London: Dorling Kinderlsey, 1997; New York: DK, 1997);

Strange Vanishings (New York: Sterling, 1997);

The Books in My Life (Charlottesville, Va.: Hampton Roads, 1998);

Ghosts and the Supernatural (New York: DK, 1998);

Psychic Powers (New York: DK, 1998).

PLAY PRODUCTIONS: *The Metal Flower Blossom,* Southend-on-Sea, Essex, 1958;

Viennese Interlude, Scarborough, Yorkshire & London, 1960;

Pictures in a Bath of Acid, Leeds & Yorkshire, Leeds Playhouse, 15 September 1971;

Mysteries, Cardiff, 1979;

Mozart's Journey to Prague, U.K. Tour, October–December 1991.

OTHER: "Where Do We Go from Here: A Discourse," in *Zero Anthology of Literature and Art,* volume 8, edited by Themistocles Hoetis (New York: Zero, 1956), pp. 41–53;

"Beyond the Outsider," in *Declaration,* edited by Tom Maschler (London: MacGibbon & Kee, 1957; New York: Dutton, 1958), pp. 13–41;

Robert H. V. Ollendorf, *Juvenile Homosexual Experience and Its Effect on Adult Sexuality,* introduction by Wilson (London: Luxor, 1966);

Brocard Sewell, *My Dear Times Waste,* introduction by Wilson (Faversham, Kent: St. Albert's, 1966);

"Existential Psychology: A Novelist's Approach," in *Challenges of Humanistic Psychology,* edited by James F. T. Bugental (New York: McGraw-Hill, 1967), pp. 69–78;

"Vietnam War," in *Authors Take Sides on Vietnam,* edited by Cecil Woolf and J. Bagguley (London: Owen, 1967; New York: Simon & Schuster, 1967), pp. 76–77;

E. H. Visiak, *Life's Morning Hour,* introduction by Wilson (London: Baker, 1968);

"The Dominant Five Per Cent," in *Papers from "The Criminologist,"* edited by Nigel Morland (London: Woolf, 1971); republished as *The Criminologist* (New York: Library Press, 1972) pp. 231–241;

Nevill Drury and Steven Skinner, *The Search for Abraxas,* introduction by Wilson (Sudbury: Spearman, 1972);

Peter Haining, ed., *The Magicians: Occult Stories,* introduction by Wilson (London: Owen, 1972);

Michael Harrison, *The Roots of Witchcraft,* foreword by Wilson (London: Muller, 1973; Secaucus, N.J.: Citadel, 1974);

Alexander G. Kelly, *Jack the Ripper: A Bibliography and Review of the Literature,* introduction by Wilson (London: Association of Assistant Librarians, 1973);

"*A Man's Man,*" in *E. M. Forster: The Critical Heritage,* edited by Philip Gardner (London & Boston: Routledge, 1973) pp. 453–456;

William Arkle, *Geography of Consciousness,* introduction by Wilson (Sudbury: Spearman, 1974);

"Dominance and Sex," in *Sexual Behavior—Current Issues: An Interdisciplinary Perspective,* edited by Leonard Gross (Flushing, N.Y.: Spectrum, 1974) pp. 453–456;

Henri de Monfreid, *Adventures of a Red Sea Smuggler,* translated by Helen Buchanan Bell, introduction by Wilson (New York: Hillstone, 1974);

Arthur Rosenblum, *Unpopular Science,* introduction by Wilson (Philadelphia: Running Press, 1974);

David Foster, *The Intelligent Universe,* preface by Wilson (New York: Putnam, 1975);

W. A. Harbinson, *Knock,* introduction by Wilson (London: Intergroup, 1975);

Willy Reichel, *An Occultist's Travels,* introduction by Wilson (Philadelphia: Running Press, 1975);

Donald Rumbelow, *The Complete Jack the Ripper,* introduction by Wilson (London: Allen, 1975; New York: Graphic Society, 1975);

"The Flawed Superman," in *Beyond Baker Street: A Sherlockian Anthology,* edited by Michael Harrison (Indianapolis & New York: Bobbs-Merrill, 1976) pp. 311–333;

T. C. Lethbridge, *The Power of the Pendulum,* foreword by Wilson (London: Routledge, 1976);

David Lindsay, *The Violet Apple and the Witch,* introduction by Wilson (Chicago: Chicago Review Press, 1976);

Emanuel Swedenborg, *Heaven and Hell,* translated by George F. Dole, introduction by Wilson (New York: Pillar, 1976);

Colin Wilson's Men of Mystery, edited by Wilson (London: Allen, 1977); republished as *Dark Dimensions: A Celebration of the Occult* (New York: Everest House, 1977);

John Dunning, *Truly Murderous,* introduction by Wilson (Blandford: Harwood-Smart, 1977);

Stuart Holroyd, *Briefing for the Landing on Planet Earth,* introduction by Wilson (London: Allen, 1977);

Marc Alexander, *To Anger the Devil,* introduction by Wilson (London: Spearman, 1978);

David Conway, *Ritual Magic: An Occult Primer,* foreword by Wilson (New York: Dutton, 1978);

George Hay, ed., *The Necronomicon,* introduction by Wilson (Sudbury: Spearman, 1978);

Anthony Roberts, ed., *Glastonbury: Ancient Avalon, New Jerusalem,* afterword by Wilson (London: Rider, 1978);

"Royalty and the Ripper," in *Royal Murder,* edited by Marc Alexander (London: Muller, 1978);

Joseph Campbell and Richard Roberts, *Tarot Revelations,* introduction by Wilson (San Francisco: Alchemy, 1979);

J. H. H. Gaute and Robin Odell, *Murderer's Who's Who,* foreword by Wilson (London: Harrap, 1979);

"Man Is Born Free, and He Is Everywhere in Chains" and "The Right to Work," in *Lying Truths: A Critical Scrutiny of Current Beliefs and Conventions,* edited by Ronald Duncan and Miranda Weston-Smith (Oxford & New York: Pergamon, 1979), pp. 3–7;

"A New Look at the Paranormal," in *Bedside Book,* edited by Julian Schuckburgh (London: Windward, 1979);

"The Occult Detectives," in *Genette Is Missing,* edited by John W. Tate (Newton Abbot, Devon: David & Charles, 1979);

"The Search for the Real Arthur," in *King Arthur Country in Cornwall,* edited by Brenda Duxbury and Michael Williams (St. Teath: Bossiney, 1979);

"Timeslip," in *Aries I,* edited by John Grant (Newton Abbot, Devon: David & Charles, 1979);

The Book of Time, edited by Wilson (as consultant editor) and John Grant (Newton Abbot: Westbridge, 1980; North Pomfret, Vt.: David & Charles, 1980);

The Essential T. C. Lethbridge, edited by Tom Graves and Janet Hoult, foreword by Wilson (London: Routledge, 1980);

Christopher McIntosh, *The Rosy Cross Unveiled: The History, Mythology, and Rituals of an Occult Order,* foreword by Wilson (Wellingborough: Aquarian, 1980);

Frank Smyth, *Cause of Death: The Story of Forensic Science,* foreword by Wilson (London: Orbis, 1980);

Robert Cracknell, *Clues to the Unknown,* introduction and postscript by Wilson (London: Hamlyn, 1981);

The Directory of Possibilities, edited by Wilson and John Grant (Exeter: Webb & Bower, 1981; New York: Rutledge, 1981); republished as *Mysteries: A Guide to the Unknown: Past, Present and Future* (London: Chancellor, 1994);

Alfred Reynolds, *The Hidden Years,* introduction by Wilson (London: Cambridge International, 1981);

Bernard Sellin, *The Life and Work of David Lindsay,* foreword by Wilson (Cambridge: Cambridge University Press, 1981);

Marion Weinstein, *Positive Magic,* foreword by Wilson (Custer, Wash.: Phoenix, 1981);

"H. P. Lovecraft, 1890–1937," and "A. E. van Vogt, 1912–   ," in *Science Fiction Writers: Critical Studies of the Major Authors from the Early Nineteenth Century to the Present Day,* edited by E. F. Bleiler (New York: Scribners, 1982), pp. 131–137, 209–217;

"Literature and Pornography," in *The Sexual Dimension in Literature,* edited by Alan Bold (London: Vision, 1982; Totowa, N.Y.: Barnes & Noble, 1983), pp. 202–219;

"The Realm of Experience," in *The Nature of Religious Man,* edited by D. B. Fry (London: Octagon, 1982);

Brocard Sewell, *Like Black Swans: Some People and Themes,* introduction by Wilson (Padstow, Cornwall: Tabb House, 1982);

Negley Farson, *Behind God's Back,* foreword by Wilson (Fellham: Zenith, 1983);

"A Novelization of Events in the Life and Death of Grigori Efimovich Rasputin," in *Tales of the Uncanny* (New York: Reader's Digest, 1983);

Ernest Scott, *The People of the Secret,* introduction by Wilson (London: Octagon, 1983);

"Why Is Shiel Neglected?," in *Shiel in Diverse Hands* (Cleveland, Ohio: Reynolds Morse Foundation, 1983);

Bill Hopkins, *The Leap,* foreword by Wilson (London: Deverell & Birdsey, 1984);

Dale Salwak, *Interviews with Britain's Angry Young Men,* introduction by Wilson (San Bernardino, Cal.: Borgo Press, 1984);

"Belief and Action," in *The Courage of Conviction,* edited by Phillip L. Berman (New York: Dodd, Mead, 1985);

Westcountry Mysteries, introduction by Wilson (St. Teath: Bossiney, 1985);

Lois Bourne, *Witch amongst Us,* foreword by Wilson (London: Hale, 1985);

Adam Crabtree, *Multiple Man,* introduction by Wilson (Toronto: Collins, 1985);

Sir William Barrett, *Death-Bed Visions,* introduction by Wilson (Wellingborough: Aquarian, 1986);

The Book of Great Mysteries, edited by Wilson and Christopher Evans (London: Robinson, 1986);

Catherine Crowe, *The Night Side of Nature,* introduction by Wilson (Wellingborough, U.K.: Aquarian, 1986; New York: Sterling, 1986);

Ted Holiday, *The Goblin Universe,* introduction by Wilson (St. Paul: Llewellyn, 1986);

Simon Marsden, *The Haunted Realm,* introduction by Wilson (Exeter: Webb & Bower, 1986);

Scandal! An Encyclopaedia, edited by Wilson and Donald Seaman (London: Weidenfeld, 1986; New York: Stein & Day, 1986); republished as *An Encyclopedia of Scandal* (London: Grafton, 1987);

"Fantasy and Faculty X," in *How to Write Tales of Horror, Fantasy, and Science Fiction,* edited by J. N. Williamson (Cincinnati: Writer's Digest, 1987);

Marx Refuted: The Verdict of History, edited by Wilson and Ronald Duncan (Bath: Ashgrove, 1987);

William Denton, *The Soul of Things,* introduction by Wilson (Wellingborough.: Aquarian, 1988);

Sir Arthur Conan Doyle, *The Wanderings of a Spiritualist,* introduction by Wilson (Berkeley: Ronin, 1988);

Hubert Lampo, *Arthur and the Grail,* introduction by Wilson (London: Sidgwick & Jackson, 1988);

David Lindsay, *Sphinx,* introduction by Wilson (London: Xanadu, 1988; New York: Carroll & Graf, 1988);

Cesare Lombroso, *After Death–What?*, introduction by Wilson (Wellingborough: Aquarian, 1988);

Raymond Moody, *The Light Beyond*, introduction by Wilson (London: Macmillan, 1988);

Sandy Robertson, *The Aleister Crowley Scrapbook*, foreword by Wilson (Berkeley: Foulsham, 1988);

Bernard Taylor and Stephen Knight, *Perfect Murder; A Century of Unsolved Homicides*, foreword by Wilson (London: Grafton, 1988);

Philippa Burrell, *The Dance of the Opposites*, introduction by Wilson (Haddington: Skilton, 1989);

Charles Lindley, Viscount Halifax, *Lord Halifax's Ghost Book: A Collection of Stories of Haunted Houses, Apparitions and Supernatural Occurrences*, introduction by Wilson (London: Bellew, 1989);

Bernie Neville, *Educating Psyche*, introduction by Wilson (Melbourne: Collins Dove, 1989);

Joyce Robins, *The World's Greatest Mysteries*, introduction by Wilson (London: Hamlyn, 1989);

Robert Turner, *Elizabethan Magic*, introduction by Wilson (Shaftesbury, Dorset: Element, 1989);

"Dear Mrs. Thatcher," in *Dear (Next) Prime Minister: Open Letters to Margaret Thatcher and Neil Kinnock*, edited by Neil Astley (Newcastle-upon-Tyne: Bloodaxe, 1990);

The Mammoth Book of the Supernatural, edited by Wilson and Damon Wilson (London: Robinson, 1991; New York: Carroll & Graf, 1991);

Georg Feurstein, *Wholeness or Transcendence?: Ancient Lessons for the Emerging Global Civilization*, foreword by Wilson (Burdett, N.Y.: Paul Brutton Philosophical Foundation/Larsa, 1992);

Lethal Depression: Murder in the 1930s, edited by Wilson (London: Robinson, 1992; New York: Carroll & Graf, 1992);

Murder in the 1940s, edited by Wilson and Damon Wilson (London: Robinson, 1993; New York: Carroll & Graf, 1993);

The Giant Book of Villains, edited by Wilson, Ian Schott, Damon Wilson, and Rowan Wilson (London: Magpie, 1994); republished as *World Famous Villains* (Bristol: Paragon, 1995);

Colin Wilson's World Famous Crimes, edited by Wilson, Ian Schott, Ed Shedd, Damon Wilson, and Rowan Wilson (London: Robinson, 1995);

Shula Gehrman, *The Silent Circles of Truth*, introduction by Wilson (London: Deutsch, 1995).

SELECTED PERIODICAL PUBLICATIONS–UNCOLLECTED:

NONFICTION

"A Writer's Prospect," *London Magazine*, 3 (August 1956): 48–55;

"The Writer in His Age," *London Magazine*, 4 (May 1957): 53–55;

"Cause without a Rebel," *Encore*, 9 (June/July 1957): 13–35;

"In Touch with Reality," *Encore*, 9 (June/July 1957): 7–9, 46;

"The Month," *Twentieth Century*, 166 (December 1959): 492–498;

"Alexis Kivi," *Aylesford Review*, 4 (Winter 1960–1961): 15–20;

"Can Art Help?," *Studio*, 162 (September 1961): 86–89;

"Henry Williamson," *Aylesford Review*, 4 (Autumn 1961): 131–143;

"Some Comments on the Beats and the Angries," *Outsider Magazine*, 1 (Fall 1961): 57–60;

"Priestley Revalued," *John O'London's*, 7 (1962): 395–396;

"The Paintings of D. H. Lawrence," *Studio*, 164 (October 1962): 133–134;

"Homage to E. H. Visiak," *Aylesford Review*, 8 (Winter 1966–1967): 221–236;

"Bertrand Russell: Philosophical Partygoer," *Books and Bookmen*, 17 (November 1971): 26–29;

"To Be or Not to Be: Sartre's Dilemma," *Humanist*, 86 (December 1971): 363–365;

"The Real Charlotte," *Encounter*, 59 (September–October 1982): 9–18.

Colin Wilson shot to fame in 1956 with his first book, *The Outsider*, a lively and wide-ranging survey of social and spiritual alienation. The book quickly became a best-seller in Britain and the United States and made its hitherto unknown author, a self-educated twenty-four-year-old from the English Midlands, into an international celebrity. But Wilson soon fell from grace, and critics savaged his second book, *Religion and the Rebel* (1957). Since then, however, he has produced more than one hundred books on topics such as philosophy, psychology, literature, murder, sexuality, and the occult. A single idea drives all Wilson's work: that human beings are capable, by means of willpower and intelligent effort, of achieving a state of heightened consciousness which would raise them to the next level of human evolution. He believes that his task as a writer is to develop the conceptual and imaginative frameworks that will foster this "evolutionary leap." The novel, he feels, has a vital role to play in this task since it can grasp the complexity of experience more fully than abstract philosophy. As he says in his "preliminary autobiography," *Voyage to a Beginning* (1969): "Philosophy may be only a shadow of the reality it tries to grasp, but the novel is altogether more satisfactory."

Colin Henry Wilson, the first child of Arthur Wilson and Annetta Jones Wilson, was born on 26 June 1931 in the East Midlands city of Leicester in the United Kingdom. His father, a boot and shoe operative, stayed employed during the economic depression of the 1930s, but his low wage meant that money was tight, especially as the family grew by two more sons and a daughter. Despite financial and cultural constraints, Wilson's imagination and his interest in classical music were awakened by the cinema, which he began to attend from the age of about six. He learned to read relatively late, when he was seven, and read only a weekly comic until he was ten, but from that age he started to read more widely—thrillers, science fiction, true crime and true romance magazines, nonfiction books of science, and in his early teens the classics of English literature. In 1942, aged eleven, he won a place at the Gateway Secondary Technical School in Leicester, and while he was not an outstanding pupil he did develop his interest in science and, in his spare time, in writing. In the school summer holiday of 1944, he began to write a book that aimed to summarize all the scientific knowledge of mankind, producing about ninety thousand words before abandoning the project.

Leaving school at sixteen, Wilson decided to become a writer and spent the next eight years struggling to fulfill that ambition. Between 1947 and 1949 he worked in a wool factory, as a laboratory assistant at his old school, and as a clerk in income tax offices. In 1949 he began writing a story called "Symphonic Variations" about a man who murders a prostitute, which formed the basis of his first novel, *Ritual in the Dark* (1960). In the same year he was called up for two years of compulsory national service in the Royal Air Force, but to his delight he was discharged six months later after claiming, falsely, to be homosexual.

Back in Leicester, he worked on a fairground, on building sites, and on a farm and then went to Paris for three months and, more briefly, to Strasbourg. Returning to Leicester once more, he took an office job in a factory, where he met Betty Dorothy Troop, the works nurse, whom he married in June 1951. They moved from Leicester to London, where their son Roderick was born. Wilson continued to work on his novel, for which he now had ambitious plans: as he says in *Voyage to a Beginning*, "[i]t was to possess the power of *Crime and Punishment,* and the length and technical complexity of *Ulysses.*" He would use the Egyptian *Book of the Dead* for a design, as James Joyce had used the *Odyssey*. But life in London was often difficult; Wilson went through eighteen months of factory jobs and periods on unemployment benefits, moving frequently; finally, his wife moved back to Leicester, and the marriage effectively came to an end. Wilson worked as a hospital porter, spent a few weeks in Paris, and then returned to Leicester again and worked through Christmas 1953 in a department store, where he met Joy Stewart, who was to become his second wife. In 1954 he returned to London, and after four short-lived, unsatisfactory jobs he decided on the way of life for which he was to become famous: sleeping by night on Hampstead Heath and working on his novel by day in the British Museum Reading Room. Having finished the first part of his novel, he decided to "dash off" an account of his own ideas; this account became *The Outsider* and changed his life.

Published by Gollancz on 28 May 1956, *The Outsider* was immediately acclaimed in the Sunday newspapers by the two most influential English reviewers of the day, Cyril Connolly and Philip Toynbee, and became a best-seller, first in England and then in the United States. Wilson briefly became a celebrity intellectual, but his provocative remarks—his assertions of his own genius, his attack upon Shakespeare as second-rate, his praise of the former British Fascist leader Sir Oswald Mosley—combined with growing reservations among critics about the quality of *The Outsider* to provoke his downfall. This downfall was hastened by adverse publicity about his personal life that culminated in scandal when Joy Stewart's father, having received a garbled report of the contents of one of Wilson's journals, tried to horsewhip him. Wilson and Stewart then retreated from London to Cornwall in the West of England. Wilson's second book, *Religion and the Rebel,* which developed the themes of *The Outsider* in relation to religious experience, met a largely hostile response. The collapse of Wilson's reputation was summed up by a caption in *Time* (18 November 1957): "Egghead, scrambled."

Such abuse might have broken some writers. But as Hilary Corke was to observe in *The Listener* (16 February 1967), "Wilson turned out to be a much tougher egg." He settled down in Cornwall, and he has lived and worked there ever since, apart from lecture tours of the United States in 1961 and of Japan and Australia in 1986 and periods as a visiting professor at Hollins College, Virginia, in 1966-1967, the University of Washington at Seattle in 1967, Dowling College, Majorca, in 1969, and Rutgers University, New Jersey, in 1974. In 1959 he produced a third book, *The Age of Defeat* (published as *The Stature of Man* in the United States), which dealt with the "vanishing hero" in modern literature, and went on to complete the novel on which he had been engaged for eleven years. He felt that he no longer needed to put all his ideas into a novel because he had expressed them in his nonfiction books; he also dropped the elaborate structural scheme based on the *Egyptian Book of the Dead* and produced a more straightforward story. *Ritual in the Dark* was finally published in 1960, the same year his daughter, Sally, was born. He and Joy would also have two sons, Damon, born in 1965, and Rowan, born in 1971; they were married in 1973.

Ritual in the Dark, set in 1950s London, evokes a dramatic week in the life of its twenty-six-year-old protagonist, Gerard Sorme. For five years Sorme, who has a small private income, has lived a solitary and celibate life in boardinghouses, trying with little success to develop a vision of purpose. A chance meeting at a Diaghilev exhibition with Austin Nunne, a rich writer, homosexual, and sadist, acts as a catalyst to his existential development and plunges him into a complex whirl of social and sexual activity that leaves him, at the end of the novel, with a rueful "acceptance of complexity." Through Nunne, Sorme, himself a heterosexual, meets two women—Nunne's aunt and her young niece—and begins affairs with both; he also befriends Oliver Glasp, a self-torturing painter involved with a twelve-year-old girl. Sorme feels affinities with both Glasp and Nunne—all three are "outsiders"—but he has reservations about them, finding Glasp too emotional and Nunne too dependent on physical sensation. Nunne still fascinates him, however, even when—or especially when—it seems that Nunne may be a modern Jack the Ripper. It is only after a considerable inner struggle that Sorme finally rejects Nunne and affirms his own positive vision. *Ritual in the Dark* is a compelling and complex narrative that retains its relevance today, and in certain passages, such as Sorme's vision of Nunne as Nijinsky, Wilson's prose is remarkably effective:

> When he closed his own eyes he saw the dancer, the big body, moving without effort through the air, slowly, unresisted, then coming to earth as silent as a shadow. It was very clear. The face, slim and muscular, bending over him, a chaplet of rose leaves woven into the hair, a faun's face, the brown animal eyes smiling at him, beyond good and evil.

The initial reception of *Ritual in the Dark* ran from dismissal to qualified praise. *The Times* (London) reviewer (3 March 1960) condemned the book's "nugatory thinking, clumsy progress and unkempt style," and Paul West in *The New Statesman* of 5 March 1960 summed up the novel as a "farrago of vision and vastation, chips and psychopathology, self-regarding sexuality and Victorian earnestness."

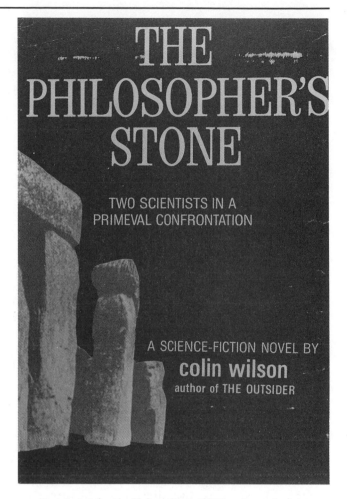

Dust jacket for the U.S. edition of Wilson's novel about evolution and time travel

Both Anthony Quinton in *The London Magazine* (May 1960) and Frank Kermode in the June 1960 *Encounter* acknowledged that the novel was "readable," but Quinton found it "written without distinction" and Kermode felt it was held together by "an immature arrogance." A more sympathetic response, however, came from P. N. Furbank in *The Listener* (3 March 1960); he found the book "[c]lumsy" but commended its "well thought out and original plot" and its "excellent and subtle dramatic surprises" and observed that Wilson "could one day be a novelist to reckon with."

Wilson's second novel, *Adrift in Soho* (1961), is a shorter and more light-hearted work giving greater rein to Wilson's comic gift. The narrator, Harry Preston, tells how as a nineteen-year-old aspiring writer he left his native town in the English Midlands in the winter of 1955 and came to London, where, in the space of a fortnight he met a wide range of bohemians, drifters, and would-be artists who had rejected conventional middle-class life. But *Adrift in Soho* is more than a picaresque tale; it is also a bildungsroman, a voyage of self-discovery in which Harry, at first an innocent abroad, enjoys a rapid initiation into the ways of the world and learns the limits of bohemian freedom, concluding that "For better or worse, I am a bourgeois." He rejects the "philosophy of freedom" represented by the charming rogue Charles Street, who befriends him when he first arrives in London, and finds a more profound and enduring embodiment of freedom in the artistic dedication of the painter Ricky Prelati. At the end of the novel, however, Prelati's freedom is both confirmed and compromised when in some hilarious scenes he becomes suddenly famous through the power of television in a way that echoes Wilson's own sudden rise to celebrity with *The Outsider*. *Adrift in Soho* remains one of the most accessible and accomplished of Wilson's novels.

Adrift in Soho received fewer hostile reviews than had *Ritual in the Dark* though some critics were still dismissive. John Fuller, writing in *The Listener* (7 September 1961), found the novel lacking in substance and judged it "a large step backwards," and Richard Mayne in *The New Statesman* (8 September 1961), found that it read "like disguised and heightened reminiscences." Malcolm Bradbury, however, commended the book in *Punch* (27 September 1961) both "for its social history and its liveliness," and the reviewer in the 8 September 1961 *Times Literary Supplement* found the novel "startlingly alive" and called it a "signpost to a distinguished career as a novelist."

In *The Craft of the Novel* (1975) Wilson writes that in the 1960s he "found it natural to write a novel and a 'philosophical book' at about the same time," and in 1963 Wilson's nonfiction study *Origins of the Sexual Impulse* was immediately followed by a novel that aimed to dramatize questions of human sexuality. First published in the United Kingdom as *Man without a Shadow: The Diary of an Existentialist* (1963), it came out in the United States under the more lurid title of *The Sex Diary of Gerard Sorme* (1963). As this latter title indicates, the novel is in diary form, stars Gerard Sorme, and deals frankly with sexuality, although, as always, Wilson sees sex as important not in itself but as a means to heightened consciousness. Some of the characters from *Ritual in the Dark* reappear, but two new figures enter who are to be important to Sorme's self-development. One is Caradoc Cunningham, a self-styled magician (based to some extent on Aleister Crowley); the other is Diana, the wife of an unworldly composer who eventually decides to leave her husband for Sorme. The Sorme of *Man without a Shadow*, like the Sorme of *Ritual in the Dark*, is obsessed with the idea of developing and sustaining an intensity of consciousness; he recognizes that Cunningham has to some extent a similar desire and possesses a certain dynamism, but he also sees him as radically flawed, lacking in discipline, and too preoccupied with defying social conventions. Sorme is interested in the idea of magic as a possible means—like sex—of releasing hidden forces, but he is skeptical of Cunningham's occult practices, and the matter-of-fact way in which he recounts them contributes to the humor of the novel. *Man without a Shadow* culminates in a ceremony involving "sex magic" that goes wrong and results in police inquiries, newspaper publicity, and scandal. As in *Adrift in Soho* there is a strong, wry awareness of the power of modern publicity. In an ending that echoes the events of Wilson's own life at the time of the "horsewhipping" scandal, parts of Sorme's diaries are published in a popular newspaper without his permission, and he has to flee London with his girlfriend.

The sensational aspects of *Man without a Shadow* inevitably provoked some strong review reaction, ranging from the disgusted to the doubtful. Stanley Kauffmann in *The New Republic* (4 May 1963), dismissed it as "a kind of instinctual, semi-mystical exploration of sex as life illuminator and aggrandizer" and suggested that if the novel was not a spoof perhaps Colin Wilson himself was. In the United Kingdom the 1 November 1963 *Times Literary Supplement* found the novel "an extremely distasteful mixture." But in *Punch* (6 November 1963) R. G. G. Price, though dismissing the book as "tosh," found that "somehow Mr. Wilson's vitality comes through." A more thoughtful review came from Bernard Bergonzi in *The New Statesman* (1 November 1963): Bergonzi found *Man without a Shadow* "drab but compelling in a faintly Gissingesque fashion" and "the character of Cunningham interesting enough to be credible"; he felt, however, that the novel suffered "by being made the vehicle for charlatanish ideas and emotions."

Man without a Shadow is comparable in some respects with Wilson's other novel of 1963, *The World of Violence* (published in the United States as *The Violent World of Hugh Greene,* 1963), in which the central character, Hugh Greene, looks back on his life from childhood to late adolescence. From an early age Hugh, a brilliant mathematician, is aware of two worlds: the ordered world of mathematics and the apparently chaotic and arbitrary world of violence. As he grows up he encounters a range of figures who embody different attitudes to living, from hermitlike withdrawal to vigorous involvement in sex and violence, and he learns something from each of them in the course of his own self-development. Rejecting the road of withdrawal, he loses his virginity and plunges into violence when he shoots at a gang of youths who try to attack him. He finally, however, leaves the world of violence for a life in London as a writer and thinker, subsidized by a legacy from a rich, reclusive uncle who saw his nephew as someone who can continue his own attempt to develop a new control over the human mind. The novel is written in a thoughtful, analytic style, keeping a certain distance from the events it describes, and in this respect it contrasts with the immediacy of *Man without a Shadow*. Nonetheless *World of Violence* is exciting at moments and always absorbing.

While *The World of Violence* was dismissed by a reviewer for the 13 June 1963 *Times* (London) because of its "crazy" and "eccentric" protagonist, the *Times Literary Supplement* (14 June 1963) reviewer had a more qualified response, seeing the novel as "very bizarre" but also as "intriguing and irritating by turns." D. A. N. Jones in *The New Statesman* (14 June 1963) judged that the novel drew "too crudely from newspapers and case histories," was "very pretentious," and "tail[ed] off feebly," but he acknowledged it was "often stimulating." *The World of Violence* has remained an underrated novel, although Wilson himself, in *The Craft of the Novel*, acknowledges it as one of his personal favorites.

Wilson's next novel, *Necessary Doubt* (1964), is a "metaphysical thriller" about the pursuit of a suspected murderer. In the use of a thriller-cum-detective story form to explore metaphysical issues, it resembles, as Wilson himself has acknowledged, the novels of Friedrich Durrenmatt, such as *Der Versprechen* (The Pledge, 1958). For the first time in Wilson's fiction, the central protagonist is not based on the young Wilson himself; instead, he is an elderly Austrian, an existentialist theologian, and a celebrity intellectual now living in England. On a snowy Christmas Eve in London, Zweig catches a glimpse, from a taxi, of Gustav Neumann, one of his former students whom he has not seen for many years—and who once told him that he intended to be "a great criminal." Zweig begins to suspect that Neumann may have murdered a number of elderly men for their money, and he pursues him with the help of a retired high-ranking policeman and a writer of occult books and his wife. Zweig's chief concern, however, is not to bring a killer to book but to find out what has really happened to Neumann—and in contrast to Sorme's final rejection of Nunne in *Ritual of Darkness*, *Necessary Doubt* ends with Zweig's decision to throw in his lot with Neumann. He is not wholly sure that Neumann is innocent, but he believes that Neumann is genuinely engaged in a quest to promote human evolution—and that it is therefore necessary to give him the benefit of the doubt. *Necessary Doubt* remains one of Wilson's compelling and intriguing novels. With its Christmas setting it is in a sense a rewriting of Charles Dickens's *A Christmas Carol* (1843), showing its protagonist's conversion not to Christian charity but from Christianity to evolutionary existentialism.

John Fuller in *The New Statesman* (20 March 1964) found that the novel's "philosophical dabblings" could not "disguise its basically antique apparatus," but the reviewer in the 27 February 1964 *Times Literary Supplement* called *Necessary Doubt* "quite a good thriller" and felt that "the whole odd mixture of miscellaneous erudition and casual flim-flam does somehow add up." The review went on to contend that Wilson's "persistence in search of significance," his continuing attempt "to find out about what is really important in life," was deserving of respect. It was a sign that the tide of hostility against Wilson was starting to turn.

In 1965 Wilson published *Beyond the Outsider: The Philosophy of the Future,* which he saw, perhaps with a certain degree of retrospective rationalization, as the concluding work of an "Outsider cycle" whose previous volumes included *The Outsider* itself, *Religion and the Rebel, The Age of Defeat* (1959; published in the United States as *The Stature of Man*), *The Strength to Dream: Literature and the Imagination* (1962), and *Origins of the Sexual Impulse.* As the writing of *The Outsider* had been closely bound up with the writing of *Ritual in the Dark,* so, according to Wilson's own account in *The Craft of the Novel,* the writing of *Beyond the Outsider* led to an attempt to rework in fiction "the basic themes of *Ritual,* in an attempt to create a clearer contrast between the psychology of the criminal and the mystic." The result was Wilson's novel *The Glass Cage,* which appeared in 1966.

Like Gerard Sorme in *Ritual in the Dark,* Damon Reade, the protagonist of *The Glass Cage,* is a recluse, living on a small private income, who comes out of his shell when he becomes involved with a murderer. But Reade, a Blake scholar, lives not in London but in an isolated cottage in the Lake District. Two events shake him out of his seclusion: a visit from a policeman who tells him of a serial killer who leaves Blake quotations scrawled near the bodies of his victims and his decision to marry the young ward of a friend. The friend suggests that because the girl is so young he should delay the marriage for a while and also accuses Reade of not having "the first idea of what the modern world's all about." Reade therefore decides to go to London to try to solve the murders—and with some practical help from a London friend, Kit Butler, he succeeds, through a series of intuitive inferences and apparent coincidences, in tracking the murderer down. He thus demonstrates that his detachment from the modern world does not prevent him from acting effectively in it—indeed the novel suggests that such detachment enables Reade to act more effectively because it brings him closer to the underlying reality of existence. *The Glass Cage* perhaps makes its points too easily. It is less immediately exciting as a thriller than *Necessary Doubt;* and it lacks the ambiguity of the previous novel. Moreover if one contrasts *The Glass Cage* to *Ritual in the Dark,* as the plot parallels and Wilson's own comments prompt the reader to do, the later novel is thinner, partly because Reade does not meet the murderer until a good way into the book and is less intensely involved with him as an individual and partly because London is less strongly evoked. It is not wholly surprising that *The Glass Cage* did not receive an enthusiastic response from reviewers; for example, the *Times Literary Supplement* (3 November 1966) found its prose "lumpy," its characterization "of almost comic-strip simplicity," and its conclusion "dully predictable."

Wilson's next novel, *The Mind Parasites* (1967), was his first venture into science fiction, a genre that had fascinated him since the age of eleven when his grandfather had given him an old science-fiction magazine. It develops an image that Wilson used in his *Introduction to the New Existentialism,* published in the same year: "It is as if man contained an invisible parasite, whose job it is to keep man unaware of his freedom." Wilson also draws on the mythology of H. P. Lovecraft, taking up a challenge from the science-fiction writer August Derleth, who had disagreed with Wilson's statement in *The Strength to Dream* that Lovecraft was "a very bad writer" and had suggested that Wilson should try to do better himself. *The Mind Parasites* purports to be volume three of *The Cambridge History of the Nuclear Age* and takes the form of a story, supposedly compiled from papers, recordings, and reports of conversations, of the struggle of Gilbert Austin, originally an archaeologist, against internal parasites that are draining the human mind of energy and thus preventing the evolutionary development of humankind. With the help of a few select others, Austin eventually defeats the parasites and develops his powers of telepathy and psychokinesis before disappearing in space, perhaps deliberately. The idea of the parasites provides a useful metaphor for Wilson's belief that the human mind usually operates at a level that is well below its potential power, but his vision of the evolutionary future is vitiated by the fact that Austin and his fellow supermen seem to become less than human rather than more than human, displaying an intellectual and ethical obtuseness that hardly seems to justify their sense of superiority over ordinary mortals—as when, returning to earth from space, they feel that, in Austin's words, "the human beings who greeted us seemed alien and repulsive, little better than apes. It was suddenly incredible that these morons could inhabit this infinitely beautiful world and yet remain so blind and stupid." *The Mind Parasites,* especially in its later parts when the evolutionary breakthrough has supposedly been achieved, reads too much like an unbridled power fantasy, working with rather crude categories and unchecked by any sustained irony or self-criticism.

Edwin Morgan made a similar point in *The New Statesman* (3 February 1967) when he spoke of "a rather sinister Nietzchean élitism" in *The Mind Parasites;* he nonetheless concluded that the novel, despite "many absurdities," had "a compulsive interest and readability." In *The Listener* (16 February 1967) Hilary Corke also felt that Wilson's "conviction that a few constitute the intellectually elect, and the rest are irredeemable, has a dangerous whiff of potential or incipient 'fascism.'" But Corke praised *The Mind Parasites* for its optimism and the effectiveness of its central image and made a more general plea for a new attitude toward Wilson: "it's time we forgot and forgave and began to do both him and ourselves justice again."

The Philosopher's Stone (1969), the novel that followed *The Mind Parasites,* is another science-fiction account of a man who takes the "evolutionary leap." Howard Lester, the narrator, tells the story of how he became obsessed with the problem of mortality and eventually found the solution in the cultivation of the heightened consciousness produced by the insertion of a special alloy into the prefrontal cortex. In a fictional enactment of Wilson's most-fundamental beliefs, the ability to sustain heightened consciousness constitutes a move to a higher evolutionary level and offers the key to a much longer life. It also enables Lester and his friend and fellow superman Henry Littleway to "travel in time," not physically but by cultivating the power of "time-vision" in which the mind, using artifacts or images of artifacts from past eras as its starting point, can journey back through the ages. In doing this they learn the true origins of the human race: human beings were originally created as servants of the Great Old Ones—as in *The Mind Parasites* Wilson draws on the mythology of Lovecraft. But the Great Old Ones, evolving too fast, found that their subconscious energies began to destroy them. To avoid total annihilation they deliberately made themselves unconscious, and the human race was left to evolve on its own. But it is always possible that the Old Ones, who have now slept for millions of years, will reawaken, and the human race must continue to evolve if it is to hope to meet them on equal terms when they stir into consciousness once more. *The Philosopher's Stone* is a richer and more substantial work than *The Mind Parasites,* but like the earlier novel it does not convince the reader that Lester and Littleway really have the evolutionary superiority that Lester claims they have achieved.

Peter Buckman's review in *The Times* (London) of 28 June 1969 was enthusiastic about the novel, not only praising Wilson's skill in writing "consciously, in the tradition of a Gothic fantasy by H. P. Lovecraft" but also affirming that *The Philosopher's Stone* "succeeds in making [the reader] think—about his limitations, his laziness and apathy, his lack of an enquiring interest in ideas and knowledge." A later endorsement came from the American novelist Joyce Carol Oates. In her introduction to the Warner Books edition of *The Philosopher's Stone* (1974), she grouped Wilson with John Fowles, Doris Lessing, and Margaret Drabble as novelists who were "consciously attempting to imagine a new image for man, a new Self-Image freed from ambiguity, irony, and the self-conscious narrowness of the imagination we have inherited from nineteenth-century Romanticism." She described *The Philosopher's Stone* as "a peculiar, quirky, exasperating and ingenious variation on a theme by Lovecraft, one of the rare works of science fiction that uses horror not as an emotion so much as an *idea,* the stimulus for forcing the reader to think."

Wilson's next novel, *The Killer* (1970); published in the United States as *Lingard* is a kind of "nonfiction novel" that aims to build a composite portrait of a murderer from details of a range of real-life cases. The story is told by Samuel Kahn, a prison psychiatrist who becomes fascinated by one of his patients, Arthur Lingard, and explores his life and the reasons that led him to crime. Kahn discovers that Lingard, as a boy, had a power of imaginative vision that might have made him an artist; instead he decided to become a criminal. While graphically detailing the deprivations of Lingard's background, Kahn is concerned to emphasize that Lingard's pursuit of crime was ultimately a matter of choice—and that Lingard made the wrong choice. At first Kahn feels that Lingard can reform and live a purposive life, but when he discovers that Lingard is a multiple sex killer Kahn decides he is irredeemable. Shortly afterward Lingard is murdered by a fellow prisoner. As he did with Sorme in *Ritual in the Dark* Wilson traces in *The Killer* Kahn's development from fascination and partial identification with a killer to final rejection. But in contrast to *Ritual in the Dark* the novel has a claustrophobically narrow focus, and its style sometimes comes too close to the clichés of sensational fiction.

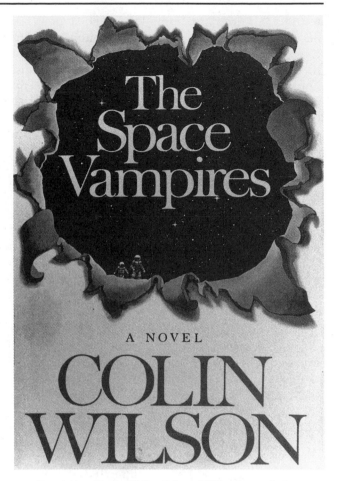

Dust jacket for the U.S. edition of Wilson's novel about alien invaders

The Killer had a mixed reception. Henry Tube in *The Spectator* (30 May 1970) found it "readable" but "unpleasantly so" and "closer to pornography than to a novel." To some extent this response was echoed in *The Times* in a 6 June 1970 review by a leading British crime writer, H. R. F. Keating, who found that the sexual scenes in the novel possessed "the built-in readability" of almost all sexual scenes in fiction but "achieve[d] a remarkable level of repulsiveness." In *The Listener* (21 May 1970), however, Derek Mahon found in *The Killer* a "totally convincing portrait of a certain type of criminal personality."

Wilson's second novel of 1970, *The God of the Labyrinth* (published in the United States as *The Hedonists,* 1971) came as a relief after *The Killer*. It is also well supplied with sexual scenes but has a much broader scope than the story of Lingard. The protagonist of *Ritual in the Dark* and *Man without a Shadow,* Gerard Sorme, returns in *The God of the Labyrinth,* and Wilson has sometimes spoken of these three novels as comprising the "Sorme trilogy." Sorme is now married and has a young daughter, but this does not cramp his sexual style. While he is on an American lecture tour a publisher offers him a large sum to write an introduction to the "sex diary" of an eighteenth-century Irish rake, Esmond Donelly, and to research Donelly's life. Sorme's initial reluctance gives way to fascination as he finds out that Donelly was not merely a lecher but a man of high intelligence whose concerns, despite the years separating the two, are close to Sorme's own. The novel becomes the story of the quest for Donelly, a quest that takes on an occult dimension when Sorme achieves a kind of "double consciousness" in which it seems that his mind and Donelly's are in contact. He thus finds, like Howard Lester in *The Philosopher's Stone,* that "time is an illusion" and also decides that life after death is a reality. His quest for Donelly reaches its climax when, helped by Donelly, he achieves a superhuman extension of sexual energy.

The God of the Labyrinth, like *Man without a Shadow,* aroused strong responses from the reviewers. In a return to the kind of abuse that Wilson had suffered in the aftermath of *The Outsider,* Maurice Capitanchik in *The Spectator* (27 June 1970) dismissed Wilson as "a pretentious bore" and said that Sorme "purports to be a prophet of consciousness-enhancing sex, but really he represents the rationalisation of a neurosis." Clive Jordan in *The New Statesman* (27 June 1970) acknowledged that the novel "starts well as a kind of literary detective story" but felt it then "degenerates rapidly into esoteric sexological hokum." Clifford Bendau, in his *Colin Wilson: The Outsider and Beyond* (1979), is similarly unenthusiastic, despite his general sympathy for Wilson; he calls the novel "an unquestionably redundant survey of Sorme's sexual adventures" which is "no more than a minor part of Wilson's canon." But in some respects *The God of the Labyrinth* may be one of Wilson's most effective novels. The passages of eighteenth-century pastiche that it incorporates make special demands on Wilson's prose, to which he rises quite well; the conventions of the pornographic novel are employed and parodied with some skill and much comedy; and the expository and didactic elements rarely absent from Wilson's fiction are woven into a larger whole. Today, however, one would have to challenge the strong sexist bias of the novel, in which women appear to exist mainly to bear children and to give men pleasure.

In an interesting postscript to *The God of the Labyrinth,* Wilson attempts to disarm charges that he is a pornographer, and in doing so he offers a more general outline of the approach to writing novels that he feels he has developed. This involves "bring[ing] the Brechtian alienation effect to the novel" by using a range of genres, often of a popular kind, but "aiming at an effect approximating to parody" which will undermine the fictional illusion and stimulate readers to think about the philosophical issues Wilson wishes to explore. In this perspective he offers a classification of his novels in terms of the genres they parody. While *Ritual in the Dark* was "still basically a realistic novel" subsequent novels more consciously used "conventional forms": *Adrift in Soho,* the picaresque novel; *The World of Violence,* "the German *Bildungsroman* with comic overtones"; *Necessary Doubt* and *The Glass Cage,* the *roman policier;* *The Mind Parasites* and *The Philosopher's Stone,* science fiction; *The Black Room* (still unpublished in 1970), the spy novel; and *The God of the Labyrinth,* the pornographic novel. To some extent, as John A. Weigel suggests in *Colin Wilson* (1975), Wilson's approach may be a rationalization of technical failures in his fiction, and it is true that Wilson often fails to maintain the kind of detachment from the genre forms he employs that would be necessary for successful parody.

As Wilson indicated in his postscript to *The God of the Labyrinth, The Black Room* (1971), his next published novel, uses the form of the spy story. Like *The Mind Parasites* the germ of *The Black Room* can be found in *Introduction to the New Existentialism,* which has a chapter on the real-life sensory deprivation experiments at Princeton University. The protagonist of *The Black Room* is the composer Kit Butler, who appeared, with a somewhat different personality, as Damon Reade's friend in *The Glass Cage.* Butler is inveigled into joining a select group of people who are being tested by British and American intelligence agencies to see how long they can resist the acute sensory deprivation experienced in the lightproof, soundproof "black room." Butler soon finds he can resist the room far better than anyone else in his group; he suggests that the secret is to learn to summon "energy of emergency"—the sense of power, meaning, and purpose that sudden crisis provokes—even when an actual emergency is absent. Butler believes in the evolutionary importance of his discovery; but the intelligence agencies of the United Kingdom, the United States, and the Soviet Union want to use that discovery for their own short-term purposes, and a conflict between the values of evolution and espionage emerges. The abrupt ending of the novel, which leaves its thriller action unresolved, is a cue to see the novel as a parable of evolutionary existentialism rather than a tale of spying. Novelist Auberon Waugh, however, in *The Spectator* of 27 March 1971 remarked that the novel had "everything one could reasonably expect of a spy thriller" and was "thoroughly enjoyable" but mocked its philosophical ambitions. Wilson himself, speaking to Diana Cooper-Clarke in *Interviews with Contemporary Novelists* (1986), called *The Black Room* "my central novel" because it dealt with "the whole question of what we should do if we were placed in a non-stimulus situation." This novel represents perhaps Wilson's most successful use of a popular form for serious purposes.

The year *The Black Room* was published, 1971, also saw the appearance of Wilson's *The Occult,* a massive survey of paranormal phenomena in the context of Wilson's vision of the evolutionary potential of human consciousness. *The Occult* was quite favorably reviewed and brought about something of a Wilson revival; its sales eased the financial pressure under which Wilson had worked in the 1960s. But the book's success seemed to divert his energies from fiction. While his general productivity remained prodigious his output of novels slowed down in the 1970s and 1980s. He produced two competent police procedural stories, *The Schoolgirl Murder Case* (1974) and *The Janus Murder Case* (1984), which drew on his encyclopedic knowledge of crime and occasionally hinted at his philosophical concerns; Marcel Berlins in *The Times* (20 September 1984) called the latter novel a "multilayered who-and-whydunit of the mind." *The Space Vampires* (1976) was another excursion into science fiction, concerning the battle against menacing aliens who, brought back to earth from a derelict spaceship, start to feed off the life energy of human beings. Tom Hutchinson, in a brief review in *The Times* (11 November 1976), defined the novel as "gothic SF" that "nails you back in your seat with terrific force" but dismissed its philosophical concerns as "Mr. Wilson's usual outsider-sexual hobby-horses."

The Personality Surgeon (1985) tells the story of Charles Peruzzi, a doctor whose desire to help humankind leads him out of conventional medicine into a "devil's pact" with tycoon Ben McKeown, who provides him with the money to develop his "personality surgery." This involves using computer and video technology to help people (including McKeown's wayward son) to fulfill their hidden potential—if they choose to do so. In *The Work of Colin Wilson: An Annotated Bibliography and Guide* (1989) Colin Stanley identifies Peruzzi as "a new kind of Wilson hero," but he does not seem very impressed with him, summing him up as "amiable, rounded, middle class, altogether lacking 'edge,' and rather too bland, a far cry from Gerard Sorme." John Nicholson in a 20 March 1986 review in *The Times* (London) was impressed neither with Peruzzi nor with the novel as a whole, which

he dismissed as "pretty dotty." It is notable, in fact, that from the early 1970s Wilson's excursions into fiction no longer received much review attention, even of a hostile kind, in national British newspapers or journals. On the other hand, starting with John A. Weigel's *Colin Wilson* in 1975, a number of monographs and books on Wilson began to appear.

In 1988 Wilson published *The Magician from Siberia,* a novelization of Rasputin's life originally written for *Reader's Digest,* which is quite successful in evoking Rasputin's boyhood and youth but devotes too much of its later narrative to external events. Wilson's major fictional effort in the 1980s and 1990s has been the *Spider World* series of science-fantasy novels (1987–1992) that tell the story of Niall's struggle, first against giant spiders who occupy the earth and then against the malevolent Magician. These works have received high praise from Wilson's admirers—for example, Howard F. Dossor calls the first two volumes "the product of a master craftsman and a mature philosopher whose intellect is balanced with a profound wisdom." But it has to be said that in the 1990s these novels look somewhat old-fashioned, and it is significant that the publishers of the trilogy have not commissioned a planned sequel. As Wilson approaches his seventies he continues to edit and write works on true crime and the supernatural, but it remains to be seen whether he will produce any further fiction of substance.

Wilson has continued, unrepentantly, to make the kinds of claims for his own abilities that helped to arouse such hostility at the time of *The Outsider.* In his 1986 interview with Diana Cooper-Clarke, while claiming he no longer cared about his literary reputation he nonetheless said: "I suspect that I probably am the greatest writer of the twentieth century." This judgment will never be widely shared, but Wilson's novels are a stimulating contribution to postwar fiction, and some of them, especially *Ritual in the Dark,* are likely to endure.

Interviews:

Daniel Farson, "Colin Wilson Explains: 'My Genius,'" *Books and Art* (October 1957): 24–25;

"Interview with Colin Wilson," *Torque,* 2 (Autumn 1970): 5–12;

Daniel Grotta, "Conversation with Colin Wilson," *Oui,* 2 (December 1973): 71, 74, 92, 129–130;

Joyce Carol Oates, "Conversation with Colin Wilson," *Ontario Review,* 4 (Spring/Summer 1976): 7–15;

Chris Simons, "Chris Simons Talks to Colin Wilson," *Writer's Review* (February/March 1979): 10–16;

Jeffrey M. Elliot, "Colin Wilson: The Outsider," *Fantasy Newsletter,* 3 (November 1980): 4–7, 31;

Lisa Tuttle, "Interview: Colin Wilson," *Twilight Zone,* 3 (March/April 1983): 24–28;

Dale Salwak, "Colin Wilson: The Man behind *The Outsider,*" *Interviews with Britain's Angry Young Men* (San Bernardino, Cal.: Borgo Press, 1984);

Robert Anton Wilson, "The New Age Interview: Colin Wilson," *New Age Journal* (April 1985): 59–66;

Diana Cooper-Clarke, "Colin Wilson," in her *Interviews with Contemporary Novelists* (London: Macmillan, 1986; New York: St. Martin's Press, 1986).

Bibliography:

Colin Stanley, *The Work of Colin Wilson: An Annotated Bibliography and Guide* (San Bernardino, Cal.: Borgo Press, 1989).

Biography:

Sidney Campion, *The World of Colin Wilson: A Biographical Study* (London: Muller, 1962).

References:

Kenneth Allsop, *The Angry Decade: A Survey of the Cultural Revolt of the Nineteen-Fifties,* revised edition (Wendover, Bucks: Goodchild, 1985);

Clifford P. Bendau, *The Outsider and Beyond* (San Bernardino, Cal.: Borgo Press, 1979);

K. Gunnar Bergstrom, *An Odyssey to Freedom: Four Themes in Colin Wilson's Novels* (Uppsala, Sweden: University of Uppsala, 1983);

Howard F. Dossor, *Colin Wilson: The Man and His Mind* (Shaftesbury: Element, 1990);

Harry Ritchie, *Success Stories: Literature and the Media in England, 1950–59* (London: Faber & Faber, 1988);

Colin Stanley, ed., *Colin Wilson, a Celebration: Essays and Recollections* (London: Woolf, 1988);

Nicolas Tredell, *The Novels of Colin Wilson* (London: Vision, 1982; Totowa, N.J.: Barnes & Noble, 1982);

John A. Weigel, *Colin Wilson* (Boston: Twayne, 1975).

Papers:

Collections of Colin Wilson manuscripts, letters and other materials are held at University of California, Riverside: Center for Bibliographical Studies; University of Texas, Austin: Harry Ransom Humanities Research Center; Cornwall County Library Services: Local Studies Library; Redruth Public Library, Cornwall; Leicestershire Libraries and Information Service: Humanities Library, Local Studies Section, Bishop Street, Leicester.

Books for Further Reading

Acheson, James, ed. *The British and Irish Novel since 1960.* New York: St. Martin's Press, 1991.

Adelman, Irving. *The Contemporary Novel: A Checklist of Critical Literature on the British and Novel Since 1945.* Metuchen, N.J.: Scarecrow Press, 1972.

Allen, Walter. *The Modern Novel in Britain and the United States.* New York: Dutton, 1964.

Astbury, Raymond, ed. *The Writer in the Market Place.* London: Bingley, 1969.

Bergonzi, Bernard. *The Situation of the Novel.* London: Macmillan, 1970.

Bergonzi, ed. *The Twentieth Century.* Volume 7 of *History of Literature in the English Language.* London: Barrie & Jenkins, 1970.

Blair, John G. *The Confidence Man in Modern Fiction: A Rogue's Gallery with Six Portraits.* London: Vision, 1979; New York: Barnes & Noble, 1979.

Bradbury, Malcolm. *Dangerous Pilgrimages: Transatlantic Mythologies and the Novel.* London: Secker & Warburg, 1995; New York: Viking Penguin, 1996.

Bradbury. *The Modern British Novel.* London: Penguin, 1993.

Bradbury. *No, Not Bloomsbury.* New York: Columbia University Press, 1988.

Bradbury, ed. *The Novel Today: Contemporary Writers on Modern Fiction.* Manchester: Manchester University Press/Totowa, N.J.: Rowman & Littlefield, 1977.

Bradbury, ed. *Possibilities: Essays in the State of the Novel.* London & New York: Oxford University Press, 1973.

Bradbury and Judy Cooke, eds. *New Writing.* London: Minerva, 1992.

Bradbury and David Palmer, eds. *The Contemporary English Novel.* London: Arnold, 1979; New York: Holmes & Meier, 1980.

British Council. *The Novel in Britain and Ireland Since 1970: a Select Bibliography.* London: British Council, 1994.

Burgess, Anthony. *Ninety-nine Novels: The Best in English Since 1939. A Personal Choice.* London: Allison & Busby, 1984; New York: Summit, 1984.

Burgess. *The Novel Now: A Guide to Contemporary Fiction.* London: Faber & Faber, 1967; New York: Norton, 1967.

Burns, Alan, and Charles Sugnet, eds. *The Imagination on Trial: British and American Writers Discuss Their Working Methods.* London & New York: Allison & Busby, 1981.

Cassis, A. F. *The Twentieth-Century English Novel: An Annotated Bibliography of General Criticism.* New York: Garland, 1977.

Cope, Jackson I., and Geoffrey Green, eds. *Novel vs. Fiction: The Contemporary Reformation*. Norman, Okla.: Pilgrim, 1981.

Crosland, Margaret. *Beyond the Lighthouse: English Women Novelists in the Twentieth Century*. London: Constable, 1981; New York: Taplinger, 1981.

Federman, Raymond, ed. *Surfiction: Fiction Now . . . and Tomorrow*. Chicago: Swallow Press, 1975.

Firchow, Peter, ed. *The Writer's Place: Interviews on the Literary Situation in Contemporary Britain*. Minneapolis: University of Minnesota Press, 1974.

Fletcher, John. *Novel and Reader*. London & Boston: Boyars, 1980.

Gindin, James. *Post-War British Fiction: New Accents and Attitudes*. Berkeley & Los Angeles: University of California Press, 1962.

Glicksberg, Charles I. *The Sexual Revolution in Modern English Literature*. The Hague: Martinus Nijhoff, 1973.

Gray, Nigel. *The Silent Majority: A Study of the Working Class in Post-War British Fiction*. London: Vision, 1973.

Gunn, James. *Alternate Worlds: The Illustrated History of Science Fiction*. Englewood Cliffs, N.J.: Prentice-Hall, 1975.

Hall, James. *The Lunatic Giant in the Drawing Room: The British and American Novel Since 1930*. Bloomington: Indiana University Press, 1968.

Hazell, Stephen, ed. *The English Novel: Developments in Criticism since Henry James*. London: Macmillan, 1978.

Jameson, Storm. *Parthian Words*. London: Collins & Havrill, 1970.

Kaplan, Sydney Janet. *Feminine Consciousness in the Modern British Novel*. Urbana: University of Illinois Press, 1975.

Klaus, H. Gustav, ed. *The Socialist Novel in Britain: Towards the Recovery of a Tradition*. Brighton: Harvester, 1982; New York: St. Martin's Press, 1982.

Lee, Alison. *Realism and Power: Postmodern British Fiction*. London & New York: Routledge, 1990.

Lewald, H. Ernest, ed. *The Cry of Home: Cultural Nationalism and the Modern Writer*. Knoxville: University of Tennessee Press, 1972.

Lodge, David. *After Bakhtin: Essays on Fiction and Criticism*. London & New York: Routledge, 1990.

Lodge. *The Art of Fiction: Illustrated from Classic and Modern Texts*. London: Secker & Warburg, 1992; New York: Viking, 1993.

Lodge. *Language of Fiction: Essays in Criticism and Verbal Analysis of the English Novel*. London: Routledge & Kegan Paul/New York: Columbia University Press, 1966; revised edition, London & Boston: Routledge & Kegan Paul, 1984.

Lodge. *The Modes of Modern Writing: Metaphor, Metonymy, and the Typology of Modern Literature*. London: Arnold, 1977; Ithaca, N.Y.: Cornell University Press, 1977.

Lodge. *The Novelist at the Crossroads and Other Essays on Fiction and Criticism.* London: Routledge & Kegan Paul, 1971; Ithaca, N.Y.: Cornell University Press, 1971.

Lodge. *The Practice of Writing: Essays, Lectures, Reviews and a Diary.* London: Secker & Warburg/New York: Viking, 1996.

Lodge. *Working with Structuralism: Essays and Reviews on Nineteenth- and Twentieth-Century Literature.* London & Boston: Routledge & Kegan Paul, 1986.

Madden, David. *A Primer of the Novel: For Readers and Writers.* Metuchen, N.J. & London: Scarecrow Press, 1980.

Massie, Allan. *The Novel Today: A Critical Guide to the British Novel 1970–1989.* London & New York: Longman, 1990.

McEwan, Neil. *The Survival of the Novel: British Fiction in the Later Twentieth Century.* London: Macmillan, 1981.

Miles, Rosaline. *The Fiction of Sex.* London: Vision Press, 1974; New York: Barnes & Noble, 1976.

Morris, Robert K. *Old Lines, New Forces: Essays on the Contemporary English Novel, 1960–1970.* Rutherford, N.J.: Fairleigh Dickinson University Press, 1976.

O'Connor, William Van. *The New University Wits and the Ends of Modernism.* Carbondale: Southern Illinois University Press, 1963.

Palmer, Helen H., and Anne Jane Dyson. *English Novel Explication: Criticism to 1972.* Hamden, Conn.: Shoe String Press, 1973.

Parker, Peter. *The Reader's Companion to the Twentieth Century Novel.* Oxford: Fourth Estate, Helicon, 1994.

Ross, Stephen D. *Literature and Philosophy: An Analysis of the Philosophical Novel.* New York: Appleton-Century-Crofts, 1969.

Schlueter, Paul, and Jane Schlueter. *The English Novel: Twentieth Century Criticism,* volume 2: *Twentieth Century Novelists.* Chicago, Athens, Ohio & London: Swallow Press/Ohio University Press, 1982.

Shapiro, C. *Contemporary British Novelists.* Carbondale: Southern Illinois University Press, 1965.

Smith, David J. *Socialist Propaganda in the 20th-Century British Novel.* Totowa, N.J.: Rowman & Littlefield, 1978.

Spilka, Mark, ed. *Towards a Poetics of Fiction.* Bloomington & London: University of Indiana Press, 1977.

Staley, Thomas F., ed. *Twentieth-Century Women Novelists.* London: Macmillan, 1982.

Stevenson, Randall. *The British Novel since the Thirties: An Introduction.* Athens: University of Georgia Press, 1986.

Sutherland, John. *Fiction and the Fiction Industry.* London: Athlone Press, 1978.

Swinden, Patrick. *The English Novel of History and Society, 1940–80.* New York: St. Martin's Press, 1984.

Swinden. *Unofficial Selves: Character in the Novel from Dickens to the Present Day.* London & New York: Barnes & Noble, 1973.

D. J. Taylor. *A Vain Conceit: British Fiction in the 1980s.* London: Bloomsbury, 1989.

Todd, Richard. *Consuming Fictions: The Booker Prize and Fiction in Britain Today.* London: Bloomsbury, 1996.

West, Paul. *The Modern Novel.* London: Hutchinson, 1963.

Wicker, Brian. *The Story-Shaped World: Fiction and Metaphysics.* London: Athlone Press, 1975.

Wilson, Colin. *The Craft of the Novel.* London: Gollancz, 1975; Salem, N.H.: Salem House, 1986.

Ziegler, Heide, and Christopher Bigsby, eds. *The Radical Imagination and the Liberal Tradition: Interviews with English and American Novelists.* London: Junction, 1982.

Contributors

Marco Abel ....*Pennsylvania State University–University Park*
Geoffrey Aggeler ....*University of Utah*
Harriet Blodgett ....*California State University, Stanislaus*
Cheryl Bove ....*Ball State University*
Catherine Burgass ....*Staffordshire University*
Peter Childs ....*John Moores University*
Philip Harlan Christensen ....*SUNY at Suffolk County Community College*
Cairns Craig ....*University of Edinburgh*
Anne Margaret Daniel ....*Princeton University*
Dan Friedman ....*Yale University*
Kate Fullbrook ....*University of the West of England, Bristol*
Russell Greer ....*Texas Woman's University*
Ann Hancock ....*University of the West of England, Bristol*
William M. Harrison ....*State University of New York, College at Geneseo*
Cynthia Ho ....*University of North Carolina at Asheville*
Dennis Jackson ....*California State University, Sacramento*
Kari Boyd McBride ....*University of Delaware*
David W. Madden ....*University of Arizona*
D. Mesher ....*San José State University*
Tim Middleton...*University College of Ripon & York, St. John*
Merritt Moseley ....*University of North Carolina at Asheville*
Caryn McTighe Musil...*University of Maryland at College Park*
William F. Naufftus ....*Winthrop University*
Malcolm Page...*Simon Fraser University*
P. B. Parris ....*University of North Carolina at Asheville*
Rob Spence ....*Edge Hill University College*
John J. Su...*University of Michigan*
David Thomson ....*University of British Columbia*
Nicolas Tredell ....*University of Sussex, Brighton, UK*
Jackie Turton ....*University College Chester*
Aiping Zhang ....*California State University, Chico*

Cumulative Index

Dictionary of Literary Biography, Volumes 1-194
Dictionary of Literary Biography Yearbook, 1980-1997
Dictionary of Literary Biography Documentary Series, Volumes 1-16

Cumulative Index

DLB before number: *Dictionary of Literary Biography*, Volumes 1-194
Y before number: *Dictionary of Literary Biography Yearbook*, 1980-1997
DS before number: *Dictionary of Literary Biography Documentary Series*, Volumes 1-16

B

C

F

L

Cumulative Index

Moxon, Edward
[publishing house] DLB-106

Moxon, Joseph
[publishing house] DLB-170

Mphahlele, Es'kia (Ezekiel)
1919- DLB-125

Mtshali, Oswald Mbuyiseni
1940- DLB-125

Mucedorus DLB-62

Mudford, William 1782-1848 . . . . . . DLB-159

Mueller, Lisel 1924- DLB-105

Muhajir, El (see Marvin X)

Muhajir, Nazzam Al Fitnah (see Marvin X)

Mühlbach, Luise 1814-1873 . . . . . . DLB-133

Muir, Edwin 1887-1959 . . . . DLB-20, 100, 191

Muir, Helen 1937- DLB-14

Muir, John 1838-1914 . . . . DLB-186

Mukherjee, Bharati 1940- DLB-60

Mulcaster, Richard
1531 or 1532-1611 . . . . DLB-167

Muldoon, Paul 1951- DLB-40

Müller, Friedrich (see Müller, Maler)

Müller, Heiner 1929- DLB-124

Müller, Maler 1749-1825 . . . . DLB-94

Müller, Wilhelm 1794-1827 . . . . . . DLB-90

Mumford, Lewis 1895-1990 . . . . . DLB-63

Munby, Arthur Joseph 1828-1910 . . . . DLB-35

Munday, Anthony 1560-1633 . . . . DLB-62, 172

Mundt, Clara (see Mühlbach, Luise)

Mundt, Theodore 1808-1861 . . . . . . DLB-133

Munford, Robert circa 1737-1783 . . . . DLB-31

Mungoshi, Charles 1947- DLB-157

Munonye, John 1929- DLB-117

Munro, Alice 1931- DLB-53

Munro, H. H. 1870-1916 . . . . . DLB-34, 162

Munro, Neil 1864-1930 . . . . DLB-156

Munro, George
[publishing house] DLB-49

Munro, Norman L.
[publishing house] DLB-49

Munroe, James, and Company DLB-49

Munroe, Kirk 1850-1930 . . . . DLB-42

Munroe and Francis DLB-49

Munsell, Joel [publishing house] DLB-49

Munsey, Frank A. 1854-1925 . . . . DLB-25, 91

Munsey, Frank A., and
Company DLB-49

Murav'ev, Mikhail Nikitich
1757-1807 . . . . DLB-150

Murdoch, Iris 1919- DLB-14, 194

Murdoch, Rupert 1931- DLB-127

Murfree, Mary N. 1850-1922 . . . . DLB-12, 74

Murger, Henry 1822-1861 . . . . DLB-119

Murger, Louis-Henri (see Murger, Henry)

Murner, Thomas 1475-1537 . . . . . . DLB-179

Muro, Amado 1915-1971 . . . . DLB-82

Murphy, Arthur 1727-1805 . . . . . DLB-89, 142

Murphy, Beatrice M. 1908- DLB-76

Murphy, Emily 1868-1933 . . . . . . DLB-99

Murphy, John H., III 1916- DLB-127

Murphy, John, and Company DLB-49

Murphy, Richard 1927-1993 . . . . . DLB-40

Murray, Albert L. 1916- DLB-38

Murray, Gilbert 1866-1957 . . . . . . DLB-10

Murray, Judith Sargent 1751-1820 . . . . DLB-37

Murray, Pauli 1910-1985 . . . . . . DLB-41

Murray, John [publishing house] DLB-154

Murry, John Middleton
1889-1957 . . . . DLB-149

Musäus, Johann Karl August
1735-1787 . . . . DLB-97

Muschg, Adolf 1934- DLB-75

The Music of *Minnesang* DLB-138

Musil, Robert 1880-1942 . . . . . DLB-81, 124

Muspilli circa 790-circa 850 . . . . . . DLB-148

Musset, Alfred de 1810-1857 . . . . . DLB-192

Mussey, Benjamin B., and
Company DLB-49

Mutafchieva, Vera 1929- DLB-181

Mwangi, Meja 1948- DLB-125

Myers, Frederic W. H. 1843-1901 . . . DLB-190

Myers, Gustavus 1872-1942 . . . . . . DLB-47

Myers, L. H. 1881-1944 . . . . DLB-15

Myers, Walter Dean 1937- DLB-33

Myles, Eileen 1949- DLB-193

N

Nabl, Franz 1883-1974 . . . . DLB-81

Nabokov, Vladimir
1899-1977 . . . . . DLB-2; Y-80, Y-91; DS-3

Nabokov Festival at Cornell Y-83

The Vladimir Nabokov Archive
in the Berg Collection Y-91

Nafis and Cornish DLB-49

Nagai, Kafū 1879-1959 . . . . DLB-180

Naipaul, Shiva 1945-1985 . . . . . DLB-157; Y-85

Naipaul, V. S. 1932- DLB-125; Y-85

Nakagami, Kenji 1946-1992 . . . . . . DLB-182

Nancrede, Joseph
[publishing house] DLB-49

Naranjo, Carmen 1930- DLB-145

Narrache, Jean 1893-1970 . . . . DLB-92

Nasby, Petroleum Vesuvius (see Locke, David
Ross)

Nash, Ogden 1902-1971 . . . . DLB-11

Nash, Eveleigh
[publishing house] DLB-112

Nashe, Thomas 1567-1601? DLB-167

Nast, Condé 1873-1942 . . . . DLB-91

Nast, Thomas 1840-1902 . . . . DLB-188

Nastasijević, Momčilo 1894-1938 . . . . DLB-147

Nathan, George Jean 1882-1958 . . . . DLB-137

Nathan, Robert 1894-1985 . . . . DLB-9

The National Jewish Book Awards Y-85

The National Theatre and the Royal
Shakespeare Company: The
National Companies DLB-13

Natsume, Sōseki 1867-1916 . . . . . . DLB-180

Naughton, Bill 1910- DLB-13

Naylor, Gloria 1950- DLB-173

Nazor, Vladimir 1876-1949 . . . . . . DLB-147

Ndebele, Njabulo 1948- DLB-157

Neagoe, Peter 1881-1960 . . . . DLB-4

Neal, John 1793-1876 . . . . DLB-1, 59

Neal, Joseph C. 1807-1847 . . . . . . DLB-11

Neal, Larry 1937-1981 . . . . DLB-38

The Neale Publishing Company DLB-49

Neely, F. Tennyson
[publishing house] DLB-49

Negri, Ada 1870-1945 . . . . DLB-114

"The Negro as a Writer," by
G. M. McClellan DLB-50

"Negro Poets and Their Poetry," by
Wallace Thurman DLB-50

Neidhart von Reuental
circa 1185-circa 1240 . . . . DLB-138

Neihardt, John G. 1881-1973 . . . . DLB-9, 54

Neledinsky-Meletsky, Iurii Aleksandrovich
1752-1828 . . . . DLB-150

Nelligan, Emile 1879-1941 . . . . . . DLB-92

Nelson, Alice Moore Dunbar
1875-1935 . . . . DLB-50

Nelson, Thomas, and Sons [U.S.] DLB-49

Nelson, Thomas, and Sons [U.K.] . . . DLB-106

Nelson, William 1908-1978 . . . . . . DLB-103

Nelson, William Rockhill
1841-1915 . . . . DLB-23

Nemerov, Howard 1920-1991 . . . DLB-5, 6; Y-83

Nesbit, E. 1858-1924 . . . . DLB-141, 153, 178

Ness, Evaline 1911-1986 . . . . DLB-61

Nestroy, Johann 1801-1862 . . . . . . DLB-133

Neukirch, Benjamin 1655-1729 . . . . DLB-168

Neugeboren, Jay 1938- DLB-28

Neumann, Alfred 1895-1952 . . . . . DLB-56

Neumark, Georg 1621-1681 . . . . . . DLB-164

Neumeister, Erdmann 1671-1756 . . . . DLB-168

P

Cumulative Index

W

ISBN 0-7876-1849-7

90000

9 780787 618490

ISBN 0-7876-1849-7

90000

9 780787 618490